D1522483

GRAMMATICAL THEORY IN WESTERN EUROPE

1500–1700

Trends in Vernacular Grammar I

GRAMMATICAL THEORY IN WESTERN EUROPE

1500–1700

Trends in Vernacular Grammar I

G. A. PADLEY

Department of French
University College Dublin

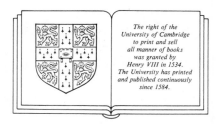

The right of the
University of Cambridge
to print and sell
all manner of books
was granted by
Henry VIII in 1534.
The University has printed
and published continuously
since 1584.

CAMBRIDGE UNIVERSITY PRESS

CAMBRIDGE

LONDON   NEW YORK   NEW ROCHELLE

MELBOURNE   SYDNEY

Published by the Press Syndicate of the University of Cambridge
The Pitt Building, Trumpington Street, Cambridge CB2 1RP
32 East 57th Street, New York, NY 10022, USA
10 Stamford Road, Oakleigh, Melbourne 3166, Australia

First published 1985

Printed in Great Britain by the University Press, Cambridge

Library of Congress catalogue card number: 84–12104

British Library Cataloguing in Publication Data
Padley, G. A.
Grammatical theory in Western Europe 1500–1700:
trends in vernacular grammar I.
1. Linguistics—Europe—History   2. Grammar,
Comparative and general—History
415'.094   P81.E9

ISBN 0 521 22307 5

TO MARGUERITE GIRARD

To build a house without a foundation is labour
in vain, and to learn without grammar is as empty
as the winds. – Old Carmarthen inscription

CONTENTS

ix

ACKNOWLEDGMENTS

I am grateful to Deutscher Akademischer Austauschdienst for a generous grant which enabled me to spend several months in Germany collecting material for the German section of this work. My thanks also go to the staffs of the Bodleian and the British Library; the Bibliothèque Nationale, the Bibliothèque Mazarine and the Bibliothèque de l'Arsenal in Paris; the Göttingen and Heidelberg University Libraries, the Heidelberg Germanistisches Seminar, the Herzog August Bibliothek in Wolfenbüttel; and last but far from least Archbishop Marsh's Library in Dublin. I am also much indebted to Professor Hugh Ridley for expending time and energy on locating German grammars for me, and to Dr Vera Čapková for translating articles from Czech. Lastly, I am grateful to the Niedersächsische Staats- und Universitätsbibliothek, Göttingen, and to the Herzog August Bibliothek, Wolfenbüttel, for permission to reproduce the illustrations.

PREFACE

This study was originally intended to present a history of the whole field of grammatical theory in the five major West European languages. Such a project proved however to be impracticable, if only because the cost of a book that size would have been prohibitive. Instead I have brought together in a single volume those West European grammarians whose work follows some kind of overt theory, whether philosophical or pedagogical, leaving for a later study those authors, including the Vaugelas school in France, the early Latinizing grammarians and the rhetorically orientated Italian ones, who follow the dictates of usage. The treatment has also had to be limited to those vernaculars – English, French, German, Spanish and Italian – of which the present author has a sufficient reading knowledge. The overriding aim is to bring together grammarians from these five major language areas and relate their work to antecedent and contemporary trends in the underlying Latin tradition. Works on the grammar of a single vernacular have already appeared prefaced by an introductory survey of that tradition, but the grammars treated in those works have rarely if at all been subjected to detailed comparison with their Latin counterparts, even in the case where the same author produces both a Latin and a vernacular grammar. Further, in the present volume it is not simply a question of demonstrating that vernacular grammar has been influenced by the inherited framework of Latin grammar, but of indicating the extent and the success or otherwise of the transfer of a linguistic theory or metalanguage from Latin grammatical practice to vernacular work. A second, no less important aim has been to give some idea of the complex interaction of pedagogical and theoretical influences. Grammars cannot be considered *in vacuo*, divorced from the educational practice or the general cultural background of their times. Much work on vernacular grammars has consisted solely of a description, however painstaking and in however minute detail, of the external structure of the various works, without setting them in

xiii

their cultural background, relating them to existing grammars of Latin, or bringing out the underlying philosophical and pedagogical theories on which they depend. The author of even so excellent a study as I. Michael's *English Grammatical Categories and the Tradition to 1800* (1970) admits that, as a busy Vice-Chancellor, he had to resist the temptation to 'place the grammars in the intellectual history of the country, especially among the ideas about language by which they were (or, more often were not) influenced'. M. H. Jellinek, in his much earlier and minutely detailed *Geschichte der neuhochdeutschen Grammatik von den Anfängen bis auf Adelung* (1913–14), regrets the absence at his date of both a history of linguistic theory and a treatment of the development of general grammar. Since that time much effort has gone into work in both these areas, but in the case of specifically German grammatical theory, especially that of the seventeenth century, the complaint is still valid. In the present work the aim has been, however imperfectly, to link grammars to contemporary theory, both linguistic and pedagogical, and to ideas prevalent in the general culture of the times. Those who are familiar with research in these fields will recognize that I have inevitably had to depend to no small extent for this background material on the findings of other scholars. But if my treatment of these matters is necessarily in part a summary of existing scholarship, I hope I have left no debt unrecorded.

The Latin and the vernacular traditions in sixteenth- and seventeenth-century grammatical theory are an indivisible whole. This means that unavoidably some of the authors dealt with in my *Grammatical Theory in Western Europe 1500–1700: The Latin Tradition* must also be treated here, though I have tried to give a different emphasis. Also though some grammarians, particularly English ones, have already been covered by others, I hope my own discussion will shed additional light on the interaction both with the Latin tradition and with contemporary notions of language theory and pedagogy. Some authors are however presented here for the first time, at any rate in English. It must be stressed that this study is not intended to be a treatment of the separate history of each vernacular grammar. Rather it is an attempt to consider West European grammar as a cultural whole. In the English-speaking world in particular, writers on the history of grammar have tended to stay within the confines of one vernacular tradition. Just as European culture in general has

xiv

Preface

for centuries been a single whole, European *linguistic* culture too, and that in spite of language barriers, is a single entity. It is my hope that this book will underline afresh this obvious but sometimes neglected fact.

The writing of a history of this kind is a strenuous task, and E. F. K. Koerner's 'Four Types of History Writing in Linguistics'[1] sets daunting standards for whoever is intrepid enough to undertake it. They are indeed counsels of perfection, with considerable dissuasive power. One can only read them, bear them in mind, and launch out into the deep, trusting that one will not too blatantly fail to meet their requirements.

Dublin, December 1983   G. A. PADLEY

[1] In E. F. K. Koerner, *Towards a Historiography of Linguistics*, Amsterdam, 1978, pp. 55–62.

INTRODUCTION

A first category of humanist vernacular grammarians consists of those who, to a large extent basing themselves on already existing Latin grammars, provide for each West European vernacular a Latin-based description ultimately, as are their immediate sources, indebted to Donatus (*c.* 350) and Priscian (*c.* 500), the standard authors who provided both the Middle Ages and the Renaissance with the foundations of their theory and description.[1] These Latinizing vernacular grammarians are in general not orientated towards theory, contenting themselves with repeating the word-class definitions of their Latin models,[2] but not otherwise presenting a theoretical interest apart from that of the often ingenious subterfuges by which they constrain vernacular structures into the Latin mould. They have already been treated by other writers on the history of grammar.[3]

[1] On the Latin grammatical framework inherited by the early humanist grammarians see H. Keil, *Grammatici Latini*, Leipzig, 1857–74, I–IV; H. Steinthal, *Geschichte der Sprachwissenschaft bei den Griechen und Römern* (2nd ed.), Berlin, 1891; L. Kukenheim, *Contributions à l'histoire de la grammaire grecque, latine et hébraïque à l'époque de la Renaissance*, Leyden, 1951; R. H. Robins, *Ancient and Mediaeval Grammatical Theory in Europe*, London, 1951, and *A Short History of Linguistics* (2nd ed.), London, 1979; G. A. Padley *Grammatical Theory in Western Europe 1500–1700: The Latin Tradition*, Cambridge, 1976, pp. 29–57.

[2] The important humanist models available to them were Lorenzo Valla's *De linguae Latinae elegantia* (*c.* 1440, first printed 1471), Perotti's *Rudimenta grammatices* (*c.* 1464, first printed 1473), Sulpizio's *Grammatica* (1475), Antonio de Nebrija's *Introductiones Latinae* (1481); Johannes van Pauteren (Despauterius), whose grammatical output was published by Robert Estienne in 1537 under the title *Commentarii grammatici*; Melanchthon's *Grammatica Latina* (1525) and *Syntaxis* (1526), Linacre's *De emendata structura Latini sermonis* (1524); and the various editions of Lily's *Shorte Introduction of Grammar* (1549).

[3] For general accounts of the Latinizing vernacular grammars of the period see the following works, several of which are now somewhat dated: C.-L. Livet, *La Grammaire française et les grammairiens du XVIe siècle*, Paris, 1859; A. Loiseau, *Etude historique et philologique sur Jean Pillot et sur les doctrines grammaticales du XVIe siècle*, Paris, 1866; J. Tell, *Les Grammairiens français depuis l'origine de la grammaire en France jusqu'aux dernières oeuvres connues*, Paris, 1874; A. Benoist, *De la Syntaxe française entre Palsgrave et Vaugelas*, Paris, 1877; G. Huth, 'Jacques Dubois Verfasser der ersten latein-französischen Grammatik (1531)', *Programm des Königl. Marienstifts-Gymnasiums zu Stettin*, 1899, pp. 3–21; M. H. Jellinek, *Geschichte der neuhochdeutschen Grammatik von den Anfängen bis auf Adelung*, Heidelberg, 1913–14; L. Kukenheim, *Contributions à l'histoire de la grammaire italienne, espagnole et française à l'époque de la Renaissance*, Amsterdam, 1932 (reprinted Utrecht, 1974); O. Funke, 'William Bullokars *Bref Grammar for English* (1586). Ein Beitrag zur Geschichte der frühneuenglischen Grammatik', *Anglia*, LXII (1938), pp. 116–37, and 'Die Frühzeit der englischen Grammatik. Die humanistisch-antike Sprachlehre und der national-

Introduction

By and large, they belong to a northern grammatical tradition standing in contrast to the more rhetorically orientated grammars of the south, whose authors may be placed in a second category of sixteenth- and seventeenth-century grammarians. The honour of having produced the first vernacular grammars goes to Italy and Spain. As W. K. Percival points out in his important article 'The Grammatical Tradition and the Rise of the Vernaculars',[4] grammars of the vulgar tongues in the fifteenth and sixteenth centuries were confined almost exclusively to Italy, Spain and France. Percival's article is required reading for anyone who ventures into the tangled domain of vernacular grammar, for it makes a number of pertinent observations that need to be borne in mind from the outset. First, he regards the question of whether there ever *was* a 'characteristically Renaissance approach' to language and grammar, with more or less ascertainable chronological boundaries, as 'very much a debatable issue'. He considers that fifteenth-century humanist grammar has its theoretical foundation in 'certain trends' in the grammatical tradition of Provence and northern Italy. If one discounts the two novel departures provided by J. C. Scaliger's *De causis linguae Latinae* (1540), which really belongs with the philosophical grammar movement of the following century, and by Antonio de Nebrija's epoch-making venture into Castilian vernacular grammar (1492), Renaissance linguistics becomes 'nothing more than a further step in the development of medieval grammatical theory, a mere offshoot of one local variety of the medieval grammatical tradition'. If Percival can prove his thesis, it is of capital importance for a study of the origins of vernacular grammar. Two things, he concedes, have so far prevented the verification of his theory: the lack of knowledge of the primary source material between 1350 and 1600, and the lack of mutual awareness among scholars working respectively in the

sprachliche Gedanke im Spiegel der frühneuenglischen Grammatiker von *Bullokar* (1586) bis *Wallis* (1653). Die grammatische Systematik und die Klassifikation der Redeteile', *Schriften der literarischen Gesellschaft Bern*, IV (1941), pp. 1–91; I. Poldauf, 'On the History of some Problems of English Grammar before 1800', *Prague Studies in English*, LV (1948), pp. 1–322; J.-C. Chevalier, *Histoire de la syntaxe: naissance de la notion de complément dans la grammaire française (1530–1750)*, Geneva, 1968; I. Michael, *English Grammatical Categories and the Tradition to 1800*, Cambridge, 1970; E. Vorlat, *English Grammatical Theory 1586–1737*, Louvain, 1975. On the English and French grammars of the period see further Padley, unpublished section (pp. 252–458) of Oxford doctoral thesis (1970): 'Grammatical Theory in Western Europe 1500–1700. A consideration of the theories of the Latin grammarians, and of their application by the vernacular grammarians of English and French'.

[4] *Current Trends in Linguistics*, ed. T. A. Sebeok, The Hague and Paris, XIII, 1975, pp. 231–75.

Latin and the vernacular grammatical traditions. The trends of which he speaks make their appearance quite early:

> Renaissance linguistic theory had its origins in a tradition of lexicographic and grammatical writing which emerged in northern Italy and Provence in about the eleventh century and developed to some degree independently of the...northern tradition...The peculiarity of this southern tradition was that it was oriented towards rhetoric rather than dialectic, rhetoric in this instance being not the art of forensic eloquence but the technique of written composition, or the *ars dictandi*, as it was called in those days.[5]

The distinction Percival draws here between a logic-chopping North and a rhetorically orientated South is indeed a valid one, borne out by the eclipse of the early rhetorical schools such as Orleans by the Aristotelian logicians of the University of Paris. Percival suggests, as a source for much in humanist grammar, the *Regulae grammaticales* of Guarino Veronese, composed some time before 1418, and constituting the 'first humanistic grammatical treatise', the 'prototype on which all subsequent humanist grammars of Latin were based'.[6] This grammar undertakes a reform of medieval syntax, and unmistakably influenced early Italian humanist grammars of Latin such as that of Perotti. Though for Percival humanist grammatical practice has its roots in medieval theory, what makes it specifically humanist is its treatment of syntax, a part of grammar which had 'undergone a purge' at the hands of Guarino. To investigate the matter in detail would require, as Percival notes, a close knowledge both of medieval theory and of Guarino's syntactic practice and its parallels in humanist grammars. Such an enquiry would be more specifically relevant to the Latinizing grammarians of our first category, which are not the object of the present study. More relevant at this point is the fact that the North–South cleavage posited by Percival is illustrated in the respective regions by two very different types of grammatical production. In the South, Valla's *De linguae Latinae elegantia* is only the first in a series of rhetorically conceived grammars.

[5] *Ibid.*, p. 233.
[6] *Ibid.*, p. 238. The British Library volume (I. A. 30276) beginning '[P]artes grammatice sunt quattuor. videlicet littera, syllaba, dictio et oratio' is ascribed in the catalogue to Guarino Veronese and tentatively dated 1480. It deals mostly with verbs and verb government, using the medieval terms 'persona agentis' and 'persona patientis' to indicate subject and object functions, and setting up semantic classes of 'verba acquisitiva' (requiring a following dative), 'effectiva' (taking an ablative) and 'possessiva' (taking a genitive), etc. The British Library editions of Perotti's *Rudimenta grammatices* (Venice, 1473; composed *c.* 1464) are described on their title-pages as published 'cum additionibus regularum...Guarini Veronensis'.

In this regard the early Italian vernacular grammars simply insert themselves into an existing tradition. A preoccupation with correct usage was always a hallmark of Renaissance grammar, but in Italy, thanks to the length and intensity of the 'questione della lingua' debates as to which dialect should be the standard literary one, questions of usage and rhetorical matters tend to usurp the whole field of grammar. A similar process, at a much later stage, takes place in seventeenth-century France when, the language having been codified and the various veins of grammatical theory temporarily exhausted, grammarians imitating Vaugelas concentrate solely on the prescription of good usage. The Italian 'questione della lingua' and the seventeenth-century French movement towards the purification, and some would say the accompanying impoverishment, of the language are matters of absorbing interest. Their importance for a history of grammatical theory is however only incidental. The present study accordingly proposes to concern itself with yet a third category of grammarians.

Here, a distinction can be made between on the one hand those early vernacular grammarians who content themselves with describing their native tongue in terms of a grammatical framework designed for Latin, forcing the vernacular into a Latin straitjacket, and on the other hand those who, though often enough equally guilty in this respect, also adopt the metalanguage, the overt linguistic theory of their Latin models. In this way the vernacular is made to conform to a double norm, to that of Latin grammar as such, and to the exigences of a theory. All grammars of course have a pedagogical purpose, and one may add to this group those grammarians who are self-consciously pursuing a pedagogical theory. Often enough, of course, these two subcategories cross-cut each other, the particular linguistic theory being pressed into service to serve pedagogical ends. To treat the whole of West European vernacular grammar in one volume would be a vast, and economically unviable, undertaking. In the present work I therefore propose to examine some of the causes, both theoretical and pedagogical, that lie behind certain strands in the tangled skein of the grammatical output of the period, leaving aside the more or less purely descriptive grammarians, be they simply adaptors of vernaculars to the Latin framework, or writers of prescriptive and rhetorically orientated grammars designed to inculcate correct usage. The touchstone is whether the authors treated follow an overt theory, linguistic or pedagogical. In limiting the study to those authors, it is possible to give a not too unwieldy account of some of the major currents in the grammatical theory of the period: the rise of Ramism, the drive to produce a more manageable pedagogy and one more appropriate to the vernaculars, the shifting relationships between logic, rhetoric and grammar, the influence of seventeenth-century rationalism and of empiricism as exemplified by the English Royal Society, and the spread in the vernaculars of various theories of general or universal grammar. Further, this study aims to show the extent to which grammatical theory remains dependent on the great Latin sources of the sixteenth and seventeenth centuries. Overall, it is a study of norms, and their working out in the development of vernacular grammar. On a theoretical level, these norms are provided by a small number of seminal Latin works: Linacre's *De emendata structura Latini sermonis* (1524); Ramus' *Dialecticae institutiones* (1543) and *Grammatica* (1559); J. C. Scaliger's *De causis linguae Latinae* (1540); Sanctius' *Minerva* (1587); Campanella's *Grammatica* (1638); and the *Grammatica audax* (1654) of the Spanish bishop Caramuel. These major Latin works, together with developments in the relative standing of logic and rhetoric and the great pedagogical impetus associated with (among others) Comenius, provide the intellectual framework within which the *theoretical* basis of much of vernacular grammar between 1500 and 1700 has to make an accommodation. It is against this backcloth that a shift of emphasis running from the extremes of Ramism to those of universal grammar can be examined.

Part I
Grammar and pedagogy

1. THE IMPACT OF RAMISM:
HISTORY OF A WITHDRAWAL

Much of sixteenth- and seventeenth-century grammatical theory is a reflection of the changing status and relationships of the three Renaissance 'arts' of logic, grammar and rhetoric. The Renaissance is the period in which logic, though it retains its place in the university curriculum, is 'dethroned' by grammar and gradually disappears from the schools.[1] Of cardinal importance here is the question whether rhetoric also is to be deemed an integral part of grammar, or treated as a separate and distinct branch of learning. The history of linguistics shows a regular swing of the pendulum between periods of 'observational adequacy' (to use the term popularized by Chomsky) in which the province of grammarians is 'the practical knowledge of the general usages of speakers and writers',[2] and periods of 'explanatory adequacy' in which their aim is to demonstrate the underlying 'causes' of a language by applying to it a logical or philosophical metalanguage. Medieval Modistic linguistics had followed the latter of these two aims, while early humanist grammarians had by and large followed the former. The divorce of rhetoric from grammar holds the danger of course that it will increasingly be seen as an optional extra, an additional beautification of language, and that grammatical studies will take on an aridity like that which, for some, characterizes the Bloomfieldian descriptive linguistic school of the thirties and forties of the present century. Further, the adoption of an 'observational' or an 'explanatory' approach determines the status of logic, which will be seen either as an extra-linguistic device ensuring economy of description, or as providing the underlying bases of language itself. The importance of Ramus in the history of linguistics lies in his having, with far-reaching

[1] See F. Watson, *The English Grammar Schools to 1660: their Curriculum and Practice*, Cambridge, 1908, p. 3.
[2] Thus Dionysius Thrax (see R. H. Robins, *A Short History of Linguistics* (2nd ed.), London, 1979, p. 31).

effects, achieved the divorce between logic, grammar and rhetoric. His actual contribution to grammatical theory forms part of a much wider movement, in which his ideas were applied to wide areas of pedagogy and thought in the Europe of the sixteenth and seventeenth centuries. At the most general level, the theories of Pierre de la Ramée or Petrus Ramus (1515–72) have important implications for the increasing interest in method, an interest which finds its culmination in Descartes' *Discours de la méthode*. It has been traditional to see him as some kind of intellectual revolutionary, as the declared opponent of all things Aristotelian. Certainly, he began his career with a flamboyant enough gesture, defending in the University of Paris – par excellence the Aristotelian stronghold – a thesis whose title is commonly translated as 'Whatever Aristotle said was false'.[3] Modern scholarship however rejects the popular idea of Ramus as an 'intellectual knight-errant sent in from outside to dispatch scholasticism'[4] and win a crushing victory over the forces of Aristotelian obscurantism. He is in fact typical of a good deal of sixteenth- and seventeenth-century thought in that while attacking the more glaring weaknesses of Scholasticism he also preserves its basic suppositions. But that his attitudes were seen as revolutionary by his followers seems clear. It is therefore legitimate to enquire into the nature of this supposed revolution, of which Ramus' ideas on grammatical theory form only a part. In certain respects his career is an epitome of the struggle between eloquence and philosophy, between the humanist and the Scholastic approach, which was taking place in the Paris of his day. Two of the phases which W. J. Ong distinguishes in the development of Ramus' thought, the dialectical or methodical phase and the period in which his interest turned to mathematics, are of premier importance for the intellectual history of the sixteenth and seventeenth centuries. They illustrate two central facets of Ramism, its obsession with method and a dialectical approach and, above all, what amounts to its mania for quantification.[5]

[3] 'Quaecumque ab Aristotele dicta essent, commentitia esse.' See for example P. A. Duhamel, 'The Logic and Rhetoric of Peter Ramus', *Modern Philology*, XLVI (1949), p. 163; W. and M. Kneale, *The Development of Logic*, Oxford, 1962, p. 301; J. E. Sandys, *A History of Classical Scholarship*, Cambridge, 1908, II, 133. W. J. Ong (*Ramus: Method, and the Decay of Dialogue*, Cambridge, Mass., 1958, p. 46) rejects the translation of 'commentitia' by the English word 'false', suggesting instead the paraphrase 'inconsistent because they are poorly systematized and can be called to mind only by the use of arbitrary mnemonic'.

[4] Ong, *Ramus*, pp. 37–8. [5] See *ibid.*, p. 32.

The impact of Ramism

Much has been made of Ramus' anti-Aristotelianism, but his supposed rebellion[6] is but the latest in several attempts to escape from the Aristotelian straitjacket, including those of Valla and Vives. The points at issue in Ramus' own particular quarrel with Aristotle are set out in his *Aristotelicae animadversiones* (1545). His chief complaints turn around Aristotle's corruption of the ancient world's supposedly simple approach to the arts curriculum[7] and his not having imitated nature, and it is indeed chiefly for this latter reason that he declares Aristotle's art of logic to be worthless.[8] Aristotle's great sin is to have initiated the corruption of logic, to have marred the simplicity and above all the practicability of Plato's dialectic.[9] This he has done – and the criticism is pregnant with results for linguistic theory – by ignoring the boundaries between the 'arts' and allowing logic to contaminate other subjects. The impact of these strictures on the Aristotelian stronghold of the University of Paris was such that a royal decree was obtained forbidding Ramus to teach philosophy, on the grounds that he was himself corrupting youth in a 'rash, arrogant and impudent' fashion. He was however soon reinstated, and his position from 1547 onwards was that of a court favourite, rather than the persecuted rebel a succession of critics have made him out to be. In 1546 he published, in the *Oratio de studiis philosophiae et eloquentiae conjungendis*, his proposals for combining philosophy and literary eloquence, and this and his new title of Professor of Eloquence[10] and Philosophy are indicative of the direction his scholarly endeavours are henceforward to take. The treatment of eloquence together with philosophy was ancient practice,[11] and this is one example among many of Ramus' tendency to innovate by reintroducing forgotten approaches from Classical times, rather than by iconoclastic rejection

---

[6] Ong notes (*Ramus and Talon Inventory*, Cambridge, Mass., 1958, p. 56) that Ramus was 'at a loss to find what was really wrong' with Aristotle.

[7] *Aristotelicae animadversiones*, Paris, 1543, f. 3^r: 'Aristoteles simplicem antiquorum veritatem, et exercitationem depravavit.'

[8] *Ibid.*, f. 4^v: 'in commentariis autem Aristotelis nihil est ad naturae monitionem propositum ...ars igitur dialectica in commentariis Aristotelis nulla est.'

[9] See Duhamel, 'The Logic and Rhetoric of Peter Ramus', p. 167.

[10] The purpose of François I's 'lisans du Roy en l'Université de Paris', inaugurated in 1530, was to encourage the new humanism in opposition to the University's Scholastic and dialectical bias. They formed the nucleus of what was later to become the Collège de France.

[11] Quintilian (*Institutio oratoria*, ed. C. E. Little, Nashville, 1951, I, 20) notes that 'eloquence and philosophy were formerly [i.e. in the time of Cicero] not divided: but since orators and philosophers pulled apart, the philosophers have been getting worse steadily and are now very unworthy.'

of what had gone before. In his actual practice, far from rejecting Aristotle out of hand he revised and adapted him. In this regard, it may be noted that the humanists by no means operated such a complete break with the medieval past as has been supposed. They were still to some extent marked by Scholasticism, in a situation in which humanism was 'in great part the product of the scholastic mind',[12] and in this respect Ramus can be seen as one of those scholars who act as a bridge between medieval and modern times.

One of Ramus' major contributions is in the area of logic, and here it is important to bear in mind that for the Renaissance 'logic and rhetoric are the two great arts of communication, and the complete theory of communication is largely identified with both'.[13] It follows that the history of linguistic theory is in turn closely bound up with these two arts. In Renaissance times, writers of books on logic and rhetoric also tended to produce grammars as well, and as in the similar case of the seventeenth-century Port-Royal authors, whose grammar and logic are inextricably intertwined, one cannot understand Ramus' contribution to grammatical theory without first examining his approach to logic.[14] But his dialectic, and indeed his whole intellectual output, have to be viewed against the background of contemporary trends. His importance lies in his fortuitous presence in Paris at precisely the time when a number of trends are converging. It is just at the time when the humanist movement has spent its first impetus and is in danger of degenerating into a sterile Ciceronianism, while the University itself stagnates in the old Scholasticism, that a new movement originating in the Rhineland comes, as Ong graphically puts it, into collision with the Parisian dialectal engine.[15] At the origin of this movement is Rudolph Agricola, whom Ong singles out as a 'prime inspiration for much of Northern European humanism', and as the 'logician of the new age', standing behind almost all subsequent attempts to move away from Aristotle's *Organon*.[16] Agricola's *De inventione dialectica* (*c*.1479) was widely known in manuscript versions decades before it first appeared in print.[17]

[12] Ong, *Ramus*, p. 93.

[13] W. S. Howell, *Logic and Rhetoric in England, 1500–1700*, Princeton, 1956, p. 4.

[14] In my treatment of Ramus' dialectic it will be obvious, even where no explicit reference is made, that I am deeply indebted to Ong's *Ramus* and to the work by Howell mentioned in the preceding note.   [15] Ong, *Ramus*, p. 97.

[16] *Ibid.*, pp. 94, 123. Ong notes however (p. 125) that the Agricolan development was 'not an anti-Aristotelian phenomenon in any sense except perhaps in spirit'.

[17] Ong (*Ramus and Talon Inventory*, p. 538) gives the first dated edition as Louvain, 1515.

Thomas Elyot's *Boke named the Governour* (1531) prescribes that once a pupil has attained the age of twelve years his master ought to 'rede to hym some what of that parte of logicke that is called *Topica*, eyther of Cicero, or els of that noble clerke of Almaine, which late floured, called Agricola'.[18] By the time Ramus' own dialectic appeared, Agricola's had already gone through over forty printed editions. It was brought to Paris by Johann Sturm in 1529 at a time when Scholastic logic had exhausted its possibilities,[19] and humanists were deserting the practical medieval rhetoric in search of a more elegant and stylized Latin. It is against this background that one must set Ramus' reaction against Scholastic logic – more particularly as represented by Peter of Spain's *Summulae logicales*, whose three-hundred-year reign in the Schools was about to come to a close – and his quest for a new dialectic. The hub of the matter lies in a shift in the always uneasy relationship between logic and rhetoric – a shift which was to have profound consequences for European thought in the following centuries. Traditionally, these two 'arts' had covered more or less separate provinces though there had been a certain amount of overlapping. The Ramist–Agricolan revolution consists in extending the province of logic or dialectic to cover all discourse. As Agricola puts it in the technical language of the dialectician, 'there are no places of invention proper to rhetoric'. The places or *loci* must be treated by logic alone – hence the name 'topical logic'[20] for the Ramist type of dialectic.

Central to Ramist theory is this insistence on strict observation of the boundaries between logic and rhetoric. Since, under the rules governing what each 'art' can take as its province, nothing of logic must be taught under rhetoric, it follows that the only role left to rhetoric is a stylistic one, that of providing ornamentation. Dialectic in its turn inherits much of the role of rhetoric, and becomes *the* art of discourse. The result is that enthronement of 'method' which, as the title of Ong's book[21] underlines, leads inevitably to a 'decay of dialogue'. The technical procedure of the dialectician is this: 'the Agricolan-Ramist operation...substitutes for the more usual three-part dialectic...a two-part dialectic rhetorical in orientation in that

---

[18] f. 35ᵛ.

[19] As Ong puts it (*Ramus*, p. 57), Scholastic logic was 'dying of the frustration attendant upon its failure to develop a symbolic system adequate to its ambition'.

[20] The *loci* or 'places' were called τόποι in Greek.

[21] *Ramus: Method, and the Decay of Dialogue*.

its two parts were the *inventio* and *dispositio* of ancient rhetoric and in that it was shaped radically around the rhetorically oriented topical heritage'.[22] Ramus' *Dialecticae partitiones* and *Dialecticae institutiones*, both published in 1543,[23] are in fact in some measure rhetorics as much as logics, and the history of Ramist thought turns to a great extent around the tensions between the two traditions. In the *Aristotelicae animadversiones* (f.78) Ramus had already rejected the ruling Aristotelian logic in favour of a single dialectic governing all discourse and all branches of knowledge, and it is this insight that he now develops. As he puts it in the French version of his *Dialectica* of 1555, 'Dialectique ou Logique est une et mesme doctrine pour apercevoir toutes choses.'[24] Aristotle's system of two logics, one for science and one for opinion, thus stands condemned. Ramus' censure of Aristotle for not sufficiently following nature is also of relevance here, and it is worthy of note that Ramus preferred Plato's logic to that of Aristotle. It is basic for him that the 'arts' should imitate nature, and he accordingly lays down that logic should be an *imago naturalis dialecticae*,[25] reflecting a 'natural dialectic' in the mind of man: 'the art of dialectic should proceed from the imitation and observation of the dialectic of nature'.[26] Ong too interprets the synonymous terms *natura dialecticae* and *naturalis dialectica* as signifying an innate dialectic which all human beings possess,[27] a notion which is already present in some medieval Scholastic logicians. Hence for Ramus the three parts of logic, in these two early works, are *natura*, *doctrina* and *exercitatio*:[28] nature (i.e. reason), art or teaching, and use or habit. Ramus is thus allied on the one hand to the rationalist search for underlying causes (*ratio*) found in Scaliger and Sanctius, and on the other to the seventeenth-century empiricists' insistence on use and observation. Ramus sees 'use' as a major criterion in his reforms, and

[22] Ong, *Ramus*, p. 115.
[23] They are virtually the same work, though the latter is the better known, and represent the source for the later *Dialectica* (1555), and indeed for Ramus' whole system of thought.
[24] *Dialectique de Pierre de la Ramee a Charles de Lorraine cardinal, son Mecene*, Paris, 1555, p. 4.
[25] *Aristotelicae animadversiones*, f. 4ᵛ.
[26] *Ibid.*, f. 3ᵛ: 'ars enim dialectica debet ab imitatione, et observatione naturalis dialecticae proficisci'.
[27] Ong notes (*Ramus*, p. 177) that *natura* 'in this context, does not mean specifically essence or principle of operation...but basically it retains its older, more elemental sense of origin or birth'.
[28] These are obviously borrowed from Quintilian: 'Skill in speaking is advanced by nature, by art, by practice' (*Institutio oratoria*, ed. Little, I, 117). In Ramus' later editions they become *inventio, dispositio* and *exercitatio*.

we may extend to him that 'odor of empirical science which clings not only to Peter of Spain, but to many other scholastic logicians',[29] including Ramón Lull. Ramus' definition of dialectic as an *ars bene disserendi*,[30] a training in the ability to discourse, has often been thought to be his own invention, but it has in fact a long tradition behind it, going back to Cicero's *De oratore*.[31] The term *disserendi* is of central importance, since according to Ong it 'controls the whole field of mental activity from classical times through the Middle Ages and into the Renaissance'. Here again, as in so many respects, Ramus is not an innovator. The other Ramist–Agricolan innovation, the division of logic into the two parts invention and judgment, similarly goes back to Aristotle's Topics, and was according to W. S. Howell[32] a recurrent feature of Scholastic logic. As the 1574 English translation of the *Dialectica* puts it, 'invention teacheth to invente [i.e. discover] argumentes', while judgment or disposition 'teachethe to dispone and place orderly the argumentes invented, to the ende we may judge well and rightly'.[33] Gone however, in the reaction against Aristotle, is any treatment of the time-honoured ten categories or predicaments.[34] Above all, perhaps, one may retain in Ramus' reform of logic the balance between reason and experience, between principles and observation. There is no room in his system for an 'art de raison sans usage'.[35] Finally, the vast influence of the *Dialectica* must be noted. W. J. Ong's *Ramus and Talon Inventory* (1958) lists some three hundred editions, all but a dozen or so appearing before the end of the seventeenth century. Its importance for the development of linguistic theory lies essentially in its provision of a single system of logic for both science and opinion – the *unica methodus* so much praised by his followers – and a single theory of invention and arrangement for both logic and rhetoric.[36]

The first Ramist work on rhetoric, the *Institutiones oratoriae*,

[29] Ong, *Ramus*, p. 56.
[30] 'Ars bene disserendi et vera et falsa dijudicandi.' Cf. Ramus' *Dialectique*: 'Dialectique est art de bien disputer'.
[31] Cf. Ong, *Ramus*, p. 178.   [32] *Logic and Rhetoric*, p. 149.
[33] *The Logike of the Moste Excellent Philosopher P. Ramus Martyr, Newly Translated...per M. Roll. Makylmenaeum Scotum*, London, 1574, pp. 17, 71. There is a Scolar Press reprint (Leeds, 1966) of this work.
[34] For an explanation of these terms see Padley, *Grammatical Theory* (1976), pp. 59–60. As the 1574 *Logike* puts it, 'heare hast thou nothing to learne...but onlye ten places of invention, with disposition of the proposition, syllogisme, and methode'.
[35] *Dialectique*, p. 139.
[36] Cf. W. S. Howell, *Logic and Rhetoric*, p. 155.

appeared in 1545, ascribed to Ramus' co-worker Omer Talon,[37] though it seems likely that Ramus had a hand in it, and even more likely that he contributed to its successor, the *Rhetorica* of 1548.[38] The work is obviously meant to be a companion volume to Ramus' *Dialectica*, and it too became well known, Ong's *Ramus and Talon Inventory* listing over one hundred and fifty editions.[39] In close parallel to the definition of logic as an *ars bene disserendi*, rhetoric is defined as an *ars bene dicendi*, or art of expressing oneself well.[40] Ramus' proclamation of a divorce between logic and rhetoric was to have profound repercussions, but judgment between the two parties to the divorce was far from even, for of its five traditional parts – elocution, pronunciation, invention, disposition and memory – rhetoric retained only the first two, while invention and disposition (or judgment, including memory) became the province solely of logic. In his anxiety that each 'art' should stay strictly within its own boundaries, Ramus regarded invention as having been contaminated by the rhetoricians. There was no point, he held, in having invention and disposition taught by both 'arts', any more than the 'tropes' should be matter for both rhetoric and grammar. His reforms meant in practice that rhetoric was left to concern itself with such matters as style, delivery and ornamentation. It seems in fact to have been treated with a certain disdain, as a necessary condescension to the perverse stubbornness of the groundlings, a kind of sugar on the pill of learning: 'In short, all the tropes and figures of elocution...which together make up true Rhetoric...separate from Dialectic, serve no other purpose than to guide the tiresome and stubborn hearer...and are only brought into use because of his contumaciousness and perversity, as Aristotle truly teaches in the third book of his Rhetoric.'[41] Rhetoric is thus pared down to a matter of 'tropes and

[37] *Audomari Talaei Veromandui Institutiones oratoriae*, Paris, 1545.

[38] See Ong, *Ramus*, pp. 270–1. Ong holds that Ramus certainly rewrote the text of the 1567 and 1569 editions, and (p. 82), basing himself on evidence from Nicolas de Nancel, Ramus' secretary (*Petri Rami vita*, Paris, 1599, p. 41), that 'there is strong reason to believe that the *Rhetorica* was largely Ramus' from the beginning, and that the work out of which it grew, the *Institutiones oratoriae*, was also largely his'. The later editions bear such titles as *Audomari Talaei Rhetoricae libri duo Petri Rami praelectionibus illustrati*, or *Rhetorica e Petri Rami praelectionibus observata*, etc.

[39] Ong, *Ramus*, p. 3, notes that though 1567 is usually given as the date of publication of the Talon *Rhetorica*, there were in fact already more than twenty editions by that date.

[40] Rendering the term *dicendi* as 'expressing', Ong (*ibid.*, p. 271) notes that it does not exclude written expression.

[41] *Dialectique*, p. 134.

16

figures', restricted to *elocutio* and *ornamentum*,[42] a view which inevitably leads to the notion that the plain truth, presented by logic, can be expressed with or without ornamentation, that thought can be clothed in a variety of garments.[43] This is not to say that the traditional Ciceronian rhetoric did not continue to hold sway, with a strong influence right to the end of the period 1500–1700,[44] and ultimately some kind of compromise between the two systems was inevitable, with Ramism in the pure state becoming increasingly rarer than the various mixed approaches. Important for our present purposes however is Ramus' decisive rejection of the Southern rhetorical culture in favour of the logically orientated Northern one: 'despite all the humanist fine talk in favor of eloquence, dialectic, not rhetoric, tends to remain the dominant factor in Renaissance linguistic'.[45]

It is interesting to note the convergence of several currents in the further development of the Ramist movement. In the first place Ramus' humanism was of the Northern variety, whose goal was the moral improvement of society, in a context in which Renaissance and Reformation were facets of a single movement.[46] Ramus was a Protestant, and Ramist thought has distinct Huguenot overtones, providing according to Perry Miller[47] a connecting link between Scholasticism and puritanism, and establishing in the puritan mind its obsession for logic. In the second place, the divorce of rhetoric and logic, allied to puritan Protestantism, induces a suspicion of words, which are suspected of veiling the plain truth, and a preference for an unadorned style.[48] Thirdly, Ramism's reliance on 'method' and diagrams reflected or induced a simplistic view of learning in which everything comes down to a matter of 'arts' – an *ars disserendi* for logic, an *ars dicendi* for rhetoric, an *ars loquendi* for grammar, etc. – which can be mastered by following Ramus' dichotomies and

---

[42] For the various meanings *ornamentum* held for Ramus and his contemporaries, see Ong, *Ramus*, pp. 277–8. Ong considers that Ramist rhetoric 'relies more on ornamentation theory than perhaps any other rhetoric ever has'.

[43] It should be added that this view of the relative functions of logic and rhetoric is not confined to Ramus, but can also be found for example in Melanchthon's *De rhetorica libri tres*.

[44] See W. S. Howell, *Logic and Rhetoric*, p. 318.

[45] Ong, *Ramus and Talon Inventory*, p. 53.

[46] See F. P. Graves, *Petrus Ramus and the Educational Reformation of the Sixteenth Century*, New York, 1912, p. 5.

[47] *The New England Mind: The Seventeenth Century*, New York, 1939.

[48] Ong (*Ramus*, p. 285) holds however that the plain style 'was not prescribed by Ramus' rhetoric...[but] made inevitable by the whole mental setting which constitutes Ramism'.

his prescriptions. The notion that there is a method, a key, the use of which guarantees success in any endeavour, so potent in the New England and indeed the puritan Anglo-Saxon mind in general, is very much present in Ramism. It is precisely out of what Ong calls the 'collision' between Sturm and Agricola's Rhenish rhetoric and Parisian dialectics that the mid-sixteenth-century interest in 'method' is born – and that long before Descartes.[49] This interest has a pedagogical as well as a scientific dimension, and is closely bound up with the university curriculum, with the attempt – already suggested by the Spaniard J. L. Vives[50] – to reform the 'corruption' of the arts and bring some order into their boundaries. 'Method' touches every academic sphere, and a discussion of it is highly relevant to a study of Ramus' application of his theories to grammar.

It is in the 1546 edition of the *Dialecticae institutiones*[51] that we find the first treatment of method, based – and here Ramus goes beyond his model Agricola – on three general laws from Aristotle's *Posterior Analytics*, laws which more than anything else are basic to the Ramist reforms.[52] Ramus uses the laws as a standard by which to judge whether a proposition is scientifically sound, and they take the place in his system of the five predicables (of genus, species, difference, property and accident), by means of which Scholastic logic attempted to 'define and delimit the boundaries of scientific statements'.[53] Once again, as Ramus rejects one set of Aristotelian criteria only to replace them by others, he shows himself to be a conservative reformer who reorganizes the old order rather than make a completely new start. The three laws as they appear in the *Posterior Analytics* (I.iv,736) are Latinized by the Ramists as *lex de omni*, *lex per se*, and *lex de universali*,[54] which may be Englished as the laws of universality, homogeneity, and

[49] See Ong, *ibid.*, p. 230. He regards as utterly inadequate any view of method as stemming from Bacon and Descartes. On the growth of the modern concept of method see his ninth chapter.

[50] Vives, whose *De tradendis disciplinis* (1531) contains a section 'De causis corruptarum artium', thought bad logic had corrupted every branch of knowledge. He saw logic not as an end in itself but as an 'organum' or instrument.

[51] *Dialecticae commentarii tres authore Audomaro Talaeo editi*, Paris, 1546. Although ascribed to Omer Talon it was, according to Ong (*Ramus and Talon Inventory*, p. 85), certainly by Ramus alone.

[52] See W. S. Howell, *Logic and Rhetoric*, p. 158. Before Howell, the laws were customarily treated as Ramus' own invention.

[53] *Ibid.*, p. 19.

[54] In the original Greek the three laws concern τὸ κατὰ παντὸς, τὸ καθ' αὐτὸ and τὸ καθ' ὅλον.

primacy of the general. As Ramus puts it in his *Scholae in liberales artes*: 'Nothing should be included in an art unless it is universally and necessarily true, unless it is homogeneous with all of the art, unless it is proper to that art only.'[55] He sees the laws in practice as touchstones for determining the organization of knowledge, and in particular of the Paris arts curriculum. They later became known among Ramists as the *lex veritatis*, the *lex justitiae* and the *lex sapientiae*. The 'law of truth' restricted the arts to that which is universally true; the 'law of justice' defined the province of each art, and above all implied careful marking of the boundaries between them; the 'law of wisdom' prescribed lines of organization within an individual art. This last law is also expressed by Ramus in the terse formula *generalia non speciatim specialia non generatim*: that which is of general application in an art should be stated first, and only afterwards that which is of particular application. As the English translation of the *Dialectica* quaintly puts it: 'Doe not entreate therefore generall matters particulerly, nor particuler matters generally, for in so doing thou playest the Sophistes parte, as Aristotle teacheth in the first booke of his posteriors.'[56] In 1546 Ramus had distinguished two methods, a method of teaching and a method of prudence. By 1569 we have a single method with two uses: one for the arts, and one for poets and orators, and it is this *unica methodus*, applicable to both science and opinion, to both logic and rhetoric, on which Ramus' followers lay great stress, the translator into English of the *Dialectica* describing it as a 'perfecte methode' which 'maye be accommodate to all artes and sciences'.[57] Though Bacon opposed this theory of a single method, regarding it as a 'kind of cloud that overshadowed knowledge for a while and blew over' and 'very injurious to the sciences',[58] his opinion should be set against that of a modern critic, W. S. Howell,[59] in whose view Ramus' remarks on method are the most important

---

[55] Basle, 1589, p. 827: 'in arte nihil esto nisi κατὰ παντὸς omnino necessarioque verum, nisi καθ' αὐτὸ homogeneum, totiusque artis naturale et essentiale documentum: nisi καθ' ὅλον πρῶτον proprium et reciprocum'. W. S. Howell (*Logic and Rhetoric*, pp. 41–2) interprets Aristotle's 'obscure clues' as meaning that the predicate of a strictly logical proposition must (1) be true of every case of the subject (*de omni*); (2) be harmonious within itself and with its subject (*per se*); (3) belong to its subject in a proximate as opposed to a remote relation (*universale*).
[56] *Logike* (1574), p. 10.   [57] *Ibid.*, p. 12.
[58] *De augmentis scientiarum*, in *The Works of Francis Bacon*, ed. R. L. Ellis, J. Spedding and D. D. Heath, London, 1887–92, I, 663.
[59] *Logic and Rhetoric*, p. 160.

part of his contribution to communication theory, initiating the century-long debate on method that culminated in Descartes' *Discours*. One should also however not neglect W. J. Ong's view that Ramus was attempting the impossible: the amalgamation of the Agricolan topical approach to classification (which Ong sees as dealing only in terms of a 'crude spatial imagery') with an 'abstruse and highly technical discussion concerning the internal structure and economy of a strict science with which he proves quite incapable of dealing'.[60] The key term here is 'spatial imagery', and here again we encounter the central importance of the divorce between Ramus' logic and what Ong calls his 'soundless' rhetoric, involving 'a shift toward the visual throughout the whole cognitive field'.[61] Ramus' separation of logic and rhetoric and his development of his 'single method' are in fact part of a much wider revolution, tied up with the invention of printing and the new Copernican cosmology. There is a reorientation of thought towards emphasis on the visual and the quantifiable,[62] in which the interaction of topical logic, humanism and printing provide a fertile matrix in the long-maturing change in the balance between space and discourse. It produced the Ramist tendency to consider both the real world and the world of thought in terms of spatial models, of diagrams, of easily illustrated dichotomies. There is a resulting 'corpuscular' outlook in which the mental world, just as much as the physical, is regarded as a series of units, of *species* which in turn make up *genera*.[63] The Ramist physico-mental universe is a fragmented one. Further, though it would be a mistake to regard Ramus as a champion of Baconian inductive procedures, he certainly, by what Ong calls his 'carto-graphy of the mind', encourages the increasing primacy given to observation. The resulting desiccation of his system has been the subject of sharp criticism, not least by Bacon himself, who declares roundly that 'while these men press matters by the laws of their method, and when a thing does not aptly fall into these dichotomies, either pass it by or force it out of its natural shape, the effects of their

---

[60] *Ramus*, p. 249.   [61] *Ibid.*, p. 281.

[62] For Ong the roots of this lie far back in the quantified logic of Peter of Spain's *Summulae logicales* (*ibid.*, p. 308). Ong's thesis of the importance, for the new direction of Western thought, of the substitution of Agricola's 'places' for medieval suppositional theory, a substitution 'as logically unacceptable as it was diagrammatically satisfying', is attractive. For a fascinating discussion of the parallels between Ramist topical logic and contemporary printing methods, see *ibid.*, pp. 310–14.

[63] See Ong, *ibid.*, pp. 171, 203, 205.

proceeding is this, the kernels and grains of sciences leap out, and they are left with nothing in their grasps but the dry and barren husks'.[64] Ong too is not unaware of the dehumanizing aspect of Ramus' thought, holding the elimination of the oral dimension from rhetoric and the diagrammatic drives of Ramist logic jointly responsible for producing 'within the human spirit itself the silences of a spatialized universe'.[65]

These spatial analogies hold also for Ramus' approach to pedagogy, with order in the curriculum and within each subject being a matter of the shuffling and reshuffling of simple units.[66] His didactic springs from his dialectic, and is deeply rooted in the Scholastic and humanist tradition within which the dialectic itself originates. It cannot be too strongly emphasized that this tradition is a Latin tradition, that Ramism acquires a kind of 'protective anonymity' (Ong's term) precisely through forming part of the daily routine of Latin instruction that was the lot of the sixteenth- and seventeenth-century schoolboy. Ramism is very much a pedagogical movement and here again it is largely to Ong that we must turn for information.[67] It is above all the university milieu that Ong sees as the explanation of Ramus' pedagogy: the youthfulness of the clientele – the great mass of the students were young boys – the mechanistic mentality formed by quantified logics of the type of Peter of Spain's *Summulae logicales*, the nominalism it encouraged, producing minds 'satisfied that a diagram or its equivalent is adequate to any situation', the stresses set up by the collision between humanism and the university's 'dialectical engine' – all these form the environment in which Ramist pedagogy has its source. For Ramus, each 'art' has a practical end, such as speaking well, which has to be taught in the light of experience, for 'experience begets art'.[68] The defining of these ends, and the business of making sure that each art is taught in its proper place in the curriculum without contamination by other subjects, is

---

[64] *De augmentis scientiarum*, in *Works*, ed. Ellis, Spedding and Heath, I, 663.

[65] *Ramus*, p. 318.   [66] See *ibid.*, p. 247.

[67] C. Waddington's *Ramus: sa vie, ses écrits, et ses opinions* (Paris, 1855) and P. Lobstein's *Petrus Ramus als Theologe* (Strasbourg, 1878) are outdated and have little to offer our present purposes. The next major study, Graves' *Petrus Ramus* gives a good general survey of Ramus' works, though Ong bluntly categorizes it as 'sophomorically conceived, without any real sense of the movement of intellectual history'. Ong equally condemns Waddington's view of Ramus as a 'sixteenth-century Victor Cousin', and Graves' treatment of him as a 'sixteenth-century John Dewey'.

[68] *Scholae in liberales artes*, p. 830: 'Experientia quidem artem genuit'.

the province of method and dialectic, which divide and redivide what is to be taught into parts and sub-parts until the indivisible unit particles of learning are reached. The inculcation of these particles is a matter of *usus* and *exercitatio*, of good old-fashioned classroom drill. 'Few precepts and much practice' is Ramus' watchword: 'I want art and the exercise of art always joined intimately to nature. Since the whole life of man should be nothing other than the use of reason, that is, nothing other than the exercise of natural dialectic...an art is known not so much by precepts as by exercise.'[69] In Ramist pedagogy much is made, as in seventeenth-century theory of the Comenian type, of the virtue of contact with *things*, and theory is justified not by reasoned explanation but by practice. Ong's researches make it clear that it is practical pedagogy rather than new philosophical insights, however important, that determines the new orientations of Ramism. Method itself is seen, in this view, as 'the product of rule-of-thumb pedagogical adjustments rather than of abstract reason'.[70] It is the day-to-day demands of the classroom that determine much of the Ramist output, its ideas evolving *within* an educational tradition, rather than in opposition to it.

Given the fact that theory and pedagogical considerations are inextricably interwoven in Ramus' system, we may expect to see his 'method' closely applied to the arts subjects, and indeed to the teaching and codification of grammar. The implications of the 'method' for classroom teaching are in fact laid down, for the first time, at the end of book II of the rare 1546 edition of the *Dialecticae institutiones*. Having established that method has two varieties, the method of teaching and the method of prudence, the latter having 'almost no training or art in it', Ramus goes on to define the first of these two:

The method...of teaching is the arrangement of various things brought down from universal and general principles to the underlying singular parts...in teaching the general and universal explanations precede...after which follows the special explanation by distribution of the parts; last of all comes the definition of the singular parts and clarification by means of suitable examples.[71]

It is precisely the 'art' of *grammar* that Ramus takes as an exemplification of his procedures. Supposing the definitions and

---

[69] *Dialecticae institutiones*, f. 54 (Ong's translation).
[70] Ong, *Ramus*, p. 307.
[71] *Dialecticae commentarii tres authore Audomaro Talaeo editi*, p. 83 (Ong's translation).

divisions of grammar to be jumbled together in an urn, he has an imagined logician pick out first, 'by the light of the method', the most general statement that can be made about grammar, namely that it is 'the art of speaking and writing well'. Proceeding from the more general to the less general, and on to the particular, the logician picks out in turn the divisions of grammar (orthography, etymology, syntax and prosody), its definitions, and finally individual words and syllables. The catch is that the various definitions and divisions are already in the urn before the logician begins his task. How they are arrived at is a mystery Ramus leaves decently hidden. As illustration of his method he produced two Latin grammars, the *Rudimenta* and the fuller *Grammatica*, both published in 1559.[72] They contain no theoretical discussion, but this is provided in the twenty books of Ramus' lectures on grammar, the *Scholae grammaticae* (1559), which stand in relation to the grammars in a way similar to that in which the Port-Royal *Grammaire et raisonnée* of 1660 stands to the Port-Royal Latin grammar – as a theoretical justification of an essay in practical pedagogy. It is to these *Scholae* that we must look for the theory behind Ramist grammars, but always with the proviso that it was intended for grammars of *Latin*, and will meet with serious obstacles when applied to the various European vernaculars.

At this date the Renaissance cult of good usage, of elegance in expression (though Valla's rhetorically orientated *De linguae Latinae elegantia* is as yet hardly known in Paris) is in the making, and Ramus insists that the aim of grammar is not to teach just any way of speaking ('quomodolibet artem loquendi'), but pure and correct usage ('recte et pure, id est bene loquendi'). The definition of grammar as an 'ars bene loquendi'[73] is a Renaissance commonplace, but once having made it, Ramus is unique in subjecting the art to Aristotle's three laws considered above, bringing out the implications of each in turn for grammatical theory. The first law (*de omni*, the 'law of truth') ensures that only those grammatical precepts are given which are universally and necessarily true.[74] The infinite number of

---

[72] Ramus' secretary Nicolas de Nancel seems to have had a hand in them, filling out the outlines provided by Ramus himself. Ong (*Ramus and Talon Inventory*) lists some fifteen further editions of the *Rudimenta* between 1565 and 1607, and twenty-five editions of the *Grammatica*, variously in France, Germany and Holland, between 1559 and 1694.

[73] *P. Rami Scholarum grammaticarum libri XX* (in *Scholae in liberales artes*, 1578 ed., Basle), col. 4. J. C. Scaliger's *De causis linguae Latinae* (Lyons, 1540) defines grammar as a 'scientia loquendi ex usu'. He and Ramus are exceptional in not adding 'et scribendi'.

[74] *Scholae grammaticae*, col. 4.

contradictions produced by Ramus' predecessors can hardly all be true simultaneously. The second law (*per se*, the 'law of justice') ensures that grammatical rules are homogeneous within the 'art' and internally related to one another.[75] This means that grammar cannot concern itself with what is the province of dictionaries and manuals of rhetoric, heaping together a mass of unrelated lexical meanings ('significationes') such as the traditional apparatus of possessive, derivative and patronymical nouns, or the inchoative, frequentative and meditative verbs, commonly found in the Latin grammars of the day. The explanation of lexical meanings is not a matter for grammarians, who must base their description 'not on what is signified, but on what is consignified, e.g. in number, gender, comparison, case, person, tense, and by the endings of words themselves...all these matters of [lexical] meaning are foreign to Aristotle's law'.[76] It is in the name of this same 'law of justice' that Ramus forbids grammar to teach the 'tropes and figures' of rhetoric. It would no doubt be foolhardy to project Ramus' ideas forward to the twentieth century and, on the evidence of the foregoing quotation, treat him as a precursor of the modern structuralists.[77] The temptation to see the intellectual movements of one's own day as somehow foreordained, and present in embryo in earlier work, is a difficult one to resist. Certainly, Ramus shows an overwhelming preference for formal criteria in describing linguistic structure, and if O. Funke[78] can include him with such philosophically orientated grammarians as Sanctius and Scaliger, it is because of his methodological application of Aristotle's three laws rather than on the strength of his actual linguistic practice, whose dry bones present the letter rather than the spirit of language. It is however important to note that this tendency towards the use of formal criteria is initiated by no less an authority than J. C. Scaliger himself who apportions separate and distinct roles to logician and grammarian, the former concerning himself with the truth of propositions, the latter with their formal structure.[79] Having made this point however, Scaliger goes on to write a 'philosophical' grammar based on meaning. No doubt

---

[75] *Ibid.*, col. 5.   [76] *Ibid.*, col. 5.

[77] Thus e.g. L. Kukenheim, *Esquisse historique de la linguistique française*, Leyden, 1962, p. 18. Similarly Padley, *Grammatical Theory* (1976), but such a view is questioned by P. A. Verburg, *Taal en Functionaliteit*, Wageningen, 1952, pp. 172–84.

[78] 'William Bullokars *Bref Grammar for English* (1586)', p. 117.

[79] *De causis linguae Latinae*, cap. i.

The impact of Ramism

Ramus was aware of the often quoted tag 'The better you are as a grammarian, the worse you will be as a logician.'[80] His use of logic is methodological, employing it as a tool in the establishment of his hierarchy of general and particular statements and in his decisions on what to include and what not to include under the heading 'grammar'. He does not, as the Port-Royal grammarians will do in the following century, press logic into service as a metalanguage positing underlying linguistic structures. His actual linguistic analysis, in theory at least, takes place according to rigidly formal criteria, the setting up of verbal moods, for example, on purely notional criteria being dismissed as a barbarity.[81] The three laws merely provide the methodological framework within which his more strictly linguistic theory can operate. The third law (*universaliter primum*, the 'law of wisdom') for instance ensures that those precepts which apply to several grammatical categories will be discussed once and for all at the outset, and not repeated in the treatment of each separate category. The traditional *species* (derivation) and *figura* (composition) fall under this rule, and must not be described afresh each time a word-class exhibiting them is discussed. More important, the application of this law sounds the death-knell of the traditional division of grammar into the four parts etymology (i.e. morphology), syntax, prosody and orthography. Since the latter two are diffused throughout the whole of grammar like blood in its veins,[82] they cannot be extracted and made subject to Ramus' 'lex catholica'. The parts of grammar are two: *etymologia* and *syntaxis*.

The *etymologia* deals with the properties of single words which are distributed, on the analogy of Aristotle's *kategoremata* and *sundesmoi*, into two major classes: those with a formal ending indicating number, and those without. This results in a four-class system in which formally variable nouns and verbs, on the one hand, are contrasted with formally invariable adverbs and conjunctions on the other. But if Ramus follows Aristotle in regarding the latter as functioning like 'adverbs or adjectives' of the two major word-classes, it is perhaps not wholly on semantic grounds.[83] It is amusing to see

[80] Ascribed to Johannes Dullardus: 'Quanto eris melior grammaticus, tanto peior dialecticus.'

[81] *Scholae grammaticae*, preface.   [82] *Ibid.*, col. 12.

[83] *Ibid.*, col. 6. Aristotle's system contrasts semantically self-sufficient κατηγορήματα (noun and verb) and semantically dependent σύνδεσμοι (the present-day prepositions, adverbs and conjunctions).

25

Ramus, for so long regarded as the arch-enemy of Aristotle, basing his whole grammatical fabric on Aristotle's 'three laws' and his division of word-classes into *categoremata* and *syncategoremata*. To these three laws all grammatical rules are to be submitted for validation, and even the most recalcitrant of anomalies can be made 'catholica' by being subjected to analogical treatment. There is here an obvious echo of the Roman grammarian Varro, to whom, in the potted history of grammatical theory from Plato to Donatus and Priscian provided by Ramus in his *Scholae*, there is an evident debt. In discussing the importance of analogy, Ramus draws a parallel with external reality: 'Is there any part of the world that does not contain innumerable analogies?...he who denies that analogy is founded on reason, fails to see the nature not only of discourse, but of the world itself.'[84] He then quotes Varro's opinion that analogy must be followed, but only in so far as it is not repugnant to common usage. The grammarian is not the sovereign lord of usage but is subject to the custom of the people, who in turn are subject to reason.[85] Quintilian too is cited to the effect that analogy 'rests not on reason but example: speech is governed not by law, but by observation'.[86] Nature, use, and practice based on observation – *natura, usus, exercitatio* – these are Ramus' cardinal tenets. Nature has the primacy: grammar and rhetoric must be based on the purity of natural speech, for the truth of all arts thrives best in nature,[87] and it is for this reason that use is held to be 'the truest judge and master of all who study speech'.[88] There remains however the question of *which* particular usage to adopt, and here again Quintilian is followed. Just as rules for the good life rest on the agreed prescriptions of all good men (the 'consensus bonorum'), so must the art of 'speaking well' seek the sanction of the learned (the 'consensus eruditorum'). Though Ramus dismisses the *grammatica exegetica*, dealing with poetic usage and rhetoric and practised by Dionysius Thrax and the great Latin grammarians of the later classical period,[89] as a 'pars nulla' with no place in that *grammatica methodica* whose sole purpose is the description of linguistic structure, and expressly excludes poets as unreliable guides, he none the less holds that since Latin is a book language –

[84] *Ibid.*, col. 9.
[85] *Ibid.*, col. 10.
[86] *Ibid.*, col. 10.
[87] *Aristotelicae animadversiones*, f. 4^r.
[88] *Scholae grammaticae*, preface.
[89] Cf. the breadth of knowledge of matters outside grammar in the restricted sense which Quintilian (*Institutio oratoria*, ed. Little, I, 34) requires of the grammarian.

'Hodie populus latinus in libris tantum est' – the model for discourse must be the best Latin authors.[90] Above all Priscian's Latin grammar is recommended, as a 'nobilissima bibliotheca' well stored with examples from great writers. For the vernacular languages it is however the observed usage of native speakers that is recommended.

ii THE APPLICATION OF RAMUS' THEORIES
TO THE FRENCH VERNACULAR

A close consideration of Ramus' two Latin grammars cannot be undertaken here – the reader is referred to the section dealing with them in my volume on the Latin grammatical tradition.[91] Since however in Ramus we have an example of an author of both Latin and vernacular grammars, reference will be made where appropriate to the Latin works when considering his grammar of French and in determining the extent to which a formally based grammar conceived for Latin is suitable for the description of a vernacular. But before turning to an examination of Ramus' French grammar, we may note the importance of Ramism in the growing movement to give the 'vulgar' languages parity with Latin. The Ramist Dialectic and Rhetoric were in fact often the first works of their kind to appear in a particular vernacular,[92] and it is significant in this regard that the Dialectic was, until the mid-seventeenth century, printed three times as frequently as the Rhetoric. As Ong remarks,[93] there was no point in having a vernacular rhetoric unless vernacular literature was taught in the schools. Once again we are brought up against the fact that education took place in Latin, the vernaculars being sometimes used in the explanation of material, but not themselves constituting an object of study. Doubts as to the capability of the vernacular as a vehicle for learned discourse, joined to the vested interests of scholars, tended to confirm the languages of everyday intercourse in this minor role. The appearance of the Dialectic in English in 1574 is obviously seen as an innovation, for the author thinks it necessary to refer to 'the envious, that thinke it not decent to wryte any liberall arte in the vulgar tongue, but woulde have all things kept close eyther in the Hebrewe, Greke, or Latyn tongues'.[94] The major Ramist work

[90] *Scholae grammaticae*, col. 10.
[91] Padley, *Grammatical Theory* (1976), pp. 84–91.
[92] See Ong, *Ramus*, p. 305.   [93] *Ibid.*, pp. 305–6.
[94] *Logike*, p. 15.

to appear in French is the *Dialectique* of 1555, which is by Ramus' own hand.[95] It has been highly praised, C. Waddington[96] calling it the most important philosophical work to be written in French before Descartes' *Discours de la méthode*, and W. S. Howell singling it out as 'the best short statement of Ramus' theory of logic, and thus of his major contribution to learning'.[97] The influence of the Dialectic in France cannot however be compared to the way in which Ramism swept all before it in the German universities, and Ramism quickly disappears from the French scene after Ramus' death in 1572. Its influence is more diffuse, showing itself in the various developments of 'method' such as that illustrated by the various Port-Royal language manuals and the work of Descartes. The Rhetoric too has its part to play in the rise of the vernacular, the translation–adaptation by Antoine Fouquelin or Foclin, *La Rhetorique francoise* (1555), being the earliest Ramist rhetoric in French, or indeed in any vernacular.[98] It went however through only one further edition (1557), yet another indication of the dominance of Latin over the rhetorical tradition, though it was intended to be the companion volume to the *Dialectique* in the same way as Bernard Lamy's Rhetoric was later conceived as the fellow to the Port-Royal Logic. The Ramist educational reform itself did not bear much fruit in France, being completely eclipsed in the following century by the Jesuit ascendancy, and leaving behind as virtually its only trace an obsession with 'method'.

Of more interest for our present purposes is the grammar of French in which Ramus applied to a vernacular language the system of linguistic analysis he had laboriously worked out for Latin. The anonymous first edition appeared in 1562, simply entitled *Gramere*,[99] and a version was, almost inevitably, translated into Latin in 1583. It was printed in a reformed spelling, adapted from Louis Meigret's

---

[95] *Dialectique de Pierre de la Ramee a Charles de Lorraine cardinal, son Mecene*, Paris, 1555. A Latin translation appeared in the following year.

[96] *Ramus: sa vie, ses écrits, et ses opinions*, p. 106.

[97] *Logic and Rhetoric*, p. 153.

[98] *La Rhetorique francoise d'Antoine Foclin de Chauny en Vermandois*, Paris, 1555, based according to Ong (*Ramus and Talon Inventory*, p. 95) on the 1548 edition of the Talon *Rhetorica*.

[99] Ong (*Ramus and Talon Inventory*, pp. 348–9) lists the following editions: *Gramere*, Paris, 1562 (very rare, not listed by Livet, *La Grammaire française et les grammairiens du XVIe siècle*), *Grammaire de P. de la Ramee...a la royne, mere du roy*, Paris, 1572; *Grammaire de Pierre de la Ramée...revue et enrichie en plusieurs endroits*, Paris, 1587; and the Latin edition, *Grammatica Latino-Francica, a Petro Ramo Francice scripta, Latina vero facta...per Pantaleontem Thevenium*, Frankfurt-am-Main, 1583 (also 1590). Orthography apart, there is little significant difference between the various French language editions, despite the additions and modifications in that of 1572.

system, but this was an innovation which Ramus did not repeat in the later editions.[100] As with the Rhetoric, given the pedagogical ascendancy of Latin the production of a vernacular grammar may seem to have been a foolhardy enterprise, but no doubt Ramus wished to add his own contribution to the endeavours of such early vernacular grammarians as Dubois and Meigret. F. Brunot, who has little good to say of the work, holds that Ramus brought it out in undue haste as a mere pendant to his other grammars, taking much of his illustrative material from Meigret and from Henri Estienne's *Conformité du language françois avec le grec*.[101] Brunot admits however, with obvious regret, that the grammar is of less interest for the history of the French language than for the history of grammar, and his strictures do not apply to Ramus' linguistic theory, which is of no concern to him.

Since the 1562 edition of Ramus' French grammar is very rare, reference is made in this study to that of 1572. Though André Wéchel, printer of this as of so many other of Ramus' books, remarks[102] that his works – as was commonly believed of bear-cubs at the time – needed long licking before assuming their definitive shape, the difference between the two editions does not significantly affect the grammatical theory. Ramus is at pains to show that the French language, or 'langaige Gaulloys' as he calls it, is not descended structurally from either Frankish ('Francoys') or Latin. He is in tune with the growing nationalistic pride in the vernacular when he brashly states that 'grammar and all other liberal disciplines were in ancient times in *langaige Gaulloys* in the schools of our Druids, without anything from Greek or Latin'.[103] His lack of historical linguistic knowledge is shown by his belief that although the vocabulary of the vernacular is Latin and Frankish, its grammatical structure is 'Gaulloyse', foreign elements in the language being 'habillees a la Gaulloyse' and accommodated to a structure that owes nothing to either language. Matters of formal structure – the number and case of nouns, person and conjugation in the verb, the whole 'bastiment et structure' of the language – have remained obstinately

---

[100] Ong notes (*Ramus and Talon Inventory*, p. 347) that the various spelling reforms were doomed when Ronsard rejected them.

[101] *Histoire de la langue française*, Paris, 1966–, II, 155.

[102] In the preface to *A. Talaei Rhetorica, P. Rami praelectionibus illustrata*, Paris, 1567.

[103] *Grammaire de P. de la Ramee...a la royne, mere du roy* (hereafter referred to as *Grammaire*), introduction.

'Gaulloys'.[104] Once he leaves the mythical territory of language origins and turns to linguistic description, it goes without saying that Ramus will apply to French grammar the principles of 'method' elaborated in his Dialectic, rigorously confining grammar to its own prescribed terrain uncontaminated by encroachments from the other 'arts'. As the 1574 *Logike* (p. 9) puts it, 'Is he not worthie to be mocked of all men, that purposethe to wryte of Grammer, and in every other chapiter, mynglethe somthing of Logick, and some thing of Rhetoricke?' The French grammar also closely follows the theoretical lines laid down in the *Grammatica Latina* and the *Scholae grammaticae*, and in the treatment below the significant parallelisms are pointed out in the notes. Once again, grammar is defined in terms of the inculcation of correct speech and usage,[105] though here again there is the problem of *which* usage to prescribe. Significantly, Ramus now departs from the doctrine contained in the *Scholae*, which recommends for Latin the imitation of the best authors:

> According to Plato, Aristotle, Varro, Cicero, the people are sovereign lord of their own language, holding it as a freehold, without allegiance to any other lord. It is not taught in the lecture halls of professors of Hebrew, Greek and Latin at the University of Paris, as those fine etymologizers think, but at the Louvre, the Palais, the markets, the quaysides, and the Place Maubert.[106]

The seeds of Ramus' word-class system are to be found in his remarks on Varro in the *Scholae grammaticae*.[107] Varro had set up a fourfold arrangement of the word-classes, which would seem to rest on a formal basis: (1) those classes which consignify tense but are not marked for case; (2) those that while possessing case do not show tense; (3) those which have both these distinguishing marks; and (4) those which have neither – giving a four-part system of verb, noun, participle and adverb. The parallel with Ramus' own four-class system[108] of words marked for number (noun and verb) and words not so marked (adverb and conjunction) is obvious if we bear in mind that in Ramus' scheme it is tense and person on the one hand, and

---

[104] *Ibid.*, pp. 2–3. 'Parquoy je confesse', says the docile *disciple* of Ramus' catechetical master/pupil dialogue, 'que la Grammaire Francoyse cest la Grammaire Gaulloyse.'

[105] *Ibid.*, p. 3: 'Ung art de bien parler, qui est de bien et correctement user du langaige.' Cf. *Grammatica* (1576 ed. Frankfurt-am-Main, p. 5): 'Grammatica est ars bene loquendi.'

[106] *Grammaire*, p. 30. Cf. *Scholae grammaticae*, col. 5: 'Materies grammaticae est sermo popularis et patrius.' [107] Col. 61.

[108] On the word-class system Ramus devised for Latin see Padley, *Grammatical Theory* (1976), pp. 86–8.

gender and case on the other, that keep verb and noun apart. After a long disquisition on the matter in the *Scholae grammaticae*,[109] Ramus comes to the conclusion that it is *number* that must be regarded as the 'essential difference' separating noun, pronoun, verb and participle from the remaining classes. His overriding dichotomy is that which contrasts 'words with number' and 'words without number', a division which may at least in part be attributable to certain remarks in Priscian.[110]

It is this word-class system, designed for Latin with its abundance of formal markers, that constitutes the grammatical corset into which the wayward body of the French vernacular must be squeezed. The *Grammaire* has accordingly for instance the same division of the 'mots de nombre' (the *voces numeri* of the Latin grammar) into 'finits' consignifying number by means of a formal ending, and 'infinits' which, though demonstrably nouns, pronouns, verbs or participles, make difficulties for Ramus' system by being devoid of formal markers. There is the same insistence on *generalia* (those features common to more than one word-class) being treated once and for all at the beginning, instead of being allowed to sprawl through the entire grammar. Thus 'espèce' (derivation, as in *vin/vineux*) and 'figure' (the formation of compounds, as in *dit/contredit*) are treated at the outset. The definitions of the parts of speech are those of the Latin grammar translated into French, with whatever adjustment the vernacular demands. The Latin definition of the noun as a word of number with gender and case is repeated with the omission of the reference to case,[111] Ramus here standing in sharp contrast to his contemporaries who more or less unanimously posit for French the six cases of Latin. With his division of the words with number into 'finits' and 'infinits' (the *finita* and *infinita* of the Latin grammar), Ramus is on safe ground as long as he can make a straight contrast, as in *courons/courir*, between words of the same class one of which shows an overt marker of number while the other does not. Where he is at a loss is for instance with the numerals (included in his

[109] Col. 62.
[110] Priscian notes that certain grammatical distinctions are made 'in finalibus literis': in the noun 'casuum differentia *et numeri*', in the verb 'temporis et personarum differentia *et numeri*', where number is clearly the common element (H. Keil, *Grammatici Latini*, II, 405, my italics).
[111] *Grammatica*, p. 14: 'Nomen est vox numeri cum genere et casu.' Cf. *Grammaire*: 'Nom cest ung nom de nombre avec genre.'

31

noun-class) which are semantically plural but formally invariable. He concludes somewhat lamely that 'a few plural nouns do not end in *s*', just as in the Latin grammar he had been forced to make an exception for the *monoptota*, or invariable nouns with only a single case form.

In his treatment of Latin it would seem that for Ramus it was gender that was the chief 'special difference' distinguishing nouns.[112] The definition of gender in the Latin grammar as a 'difference of the noun according to sex' is on the face of it a purely semantic, non-grammatical one, as is the French grammar's 'If the noun is appropriate to the male, it is masculine; if to the female, feminine.' Gender not always being formally marked in the Latin noun, he follows the common Renaissance practice of recognizing gender by means of the 'articles' *hic/haec/hoc* placed before nouns in paradigms. The printing of declensions in this way was a pedagogically useful device, and it provided Ramus, at a loss how to proceed, with a convenient formal marker. It required no great ingenuity to transfer this procedure to French, and to declare that 'gender is commonly shown by the article in the singular'.[113] Some rules can of course be based on noun endings, but – his gender-marking articles apart – Ramus is obliged also to introduce semantic criteria (names of trees are masculine, of fruits feminine, etc.) of the type that had long been familiar in traditional Latin grammar, but were quite alien to his formally based system. But at least, unlike so many of his contemporaries, he jettisons the cumbersome system of five genders set up for Latin,[114] and is to be congratulated on having followed Meigret in not positing a neuter gender (the *genus fictum* of his Latin grammar) for French. In the *Scholae* he had already noted that certain languages, such as Chaldean, Hebrew and Syriac, got on very well without a neuter gender, and he obviously intends in his French grammar to get away from the Latin model, for he has the pupil in his catechetical dialogue exclaim that 'Certainly this grammar of gender is very different from Latin grammar, and it would seem that our *Francois*, though they have a few words from Latin, have none

[112] *Scholae grammaticae*, col. 64: 'Differentiam nominum et verborum in adsignificatione temporis Aristoteles instituit, ego propriam nominis in genere video.'

[113] *Grammaire*, p. 66.

[114] In his Latin grammar Ramus had set up the traditional genders masculine, feminine, neuter (called by him *fictum*), 'commune' and 'omne'.

32

the less clothed them *a la Francoyse*...in order to naturalize them.'[115]
As in the Latin grammar, gender is the basis of the distinction
between substantive and adjective, the former having only one, while
the latter has a choice of three in Latin and two in French. Even in
Latin however Ramus had not been able to demonstrate this entirely
on formal principles, for whereas adjectives in *-us/-a/-um* exhibit
formal differences for three genders, those such as *fortis* and *felix* have
respectively two and three genders under one formal ending. The
silence, pronouns apart, concerning case in the *etymologie* (i.e. the
morphology), and the omission of any reference to it in the definition
of the noun, indicate that Ramus was well aware of the inapplicability
of the category to French. Though he mentions case in treating
prepositional syntax, nowhere does he set up declensions. His
criterion being a purely formal one, the only equivalent he can find
to the 'special terminations of the noun' indicating case in Latin is
the use of the articles in such expressions as *L'hôte, venez ça* and *Ecoutez,
la belle fille*, where they are curiously regarded as markers of the
vocative. No distinction is made between common and proper nouns,
these categories being for Ramus purely semantic and therefore
superfluous.

Given the small number of formal criteria invoked by Ramus, in
his Latin grammar each major word-class has to be a hold-all for
sub-classes which in traditional grammar are treated as separate
parts of speech, giving the following dichotomies:

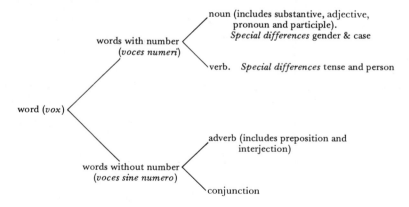

words with number
(*voces numeri*)
  noun (includes substantive, adjective,
  pronoun and participle).
  Special differences gender & case

  verb.   *Special differences* tense and person

word (*vox*)

words without number
(*voces sine numero*)
  adverb (includes preposition and
  interjection)

  conjunction

---

[115] *Grammaire*, p. 66. One is not quite sure whom Ramus means by *Francois* – Franks, or
latter-day French?

33

Cutting across this scheme is a further division into *voces numeri finitae*, in which a formal number distinction in their endings corresponds to a semantic distinction, and *voces numeri infinitae* such as *nequam*, *amare*, which obstinately run counter to Ramus' system by exhibiting semantic and syntactic behaviour stamping them as words of number, but with no accompanying formal mark. Conjunctions enjoy a class to themselves because of their syntactic, linking function. Thus does Ramus take Aristotle's semantically based dichotomy of *categoremata* and *syncategoremata*[116] and turn it, possibly with some help from Varro, into a formally based one.

Early grammarians of French had always been in some doubt as to whether to give the article full word-class status, or treat it as an appendage of the noun, and in an attempt to preserve the integrity of his four-class system, Ramus treats it, very summarily, as a noun with gender-marking function. Unlike so many other grammarians of the period, who saw them as case-markers, he does not make the mistake of treating the forms *du*, *des*, *au* and *aux* as articles, but falls into the opposite error of treating them as a sub-class of prepositions whose peculiar property is to 'reject' articles. Since the Latin model provided no precedent for the treatment of articles, the field was open to speculation, but Ramus contents himself with allowing them the function of markers of a morphological category, while – inevitably in view of his prejudices – ignoring any wider semantic implications such as a deictic function or the indication of definiteness. As in the Latin grammar, the pronoun too is regarded as a noun, a peculiarity Ramus shares with the important Spanish grammarian of Latin, Sanctius.[117] Since pronouns show variation for gender and 'case' they must according to Ramus' formal criteria be nouns, and since person is the 'special difference' distinguishing verbs, they cannot be separately defined as markers of person. He is however obliged to violate his formal principles by declaring invariable pronouns to be of all numbers, cases and persons, and to recognize the syncretism of e.g. *me* and *te* (one form for two cases) and *soi* (one form for four cases). The treatment is somewhat disorganized, and is further

---

[116] Aristotle himself uses the terms κατηγορήματα and σύνδεσμοι. It would seem to have been Priscian who first used the term *syncategoremata* for the semantically dependent classes.

[117] Ramus, *Scholae grammaticae*, col. 104: 'Grammatici...pronomen speciem vocis a nomine diversam faciunt, quem errorem ante refutavi.' Cf. Sanctius, *Minerva* (1587), I, cap. 2: 'Pronomina non dubiis rationibus a partibus orationis reiicimus...si pronomen differret a nomine, eius natura per definitionem posset attingi; at vero nulla est definitio pronominis.'

complicated by the retention of a feature traditional in Latin grammar and repeated by Renaissance vernacular grammarians by which *je* and *tu* are treated as demonstratives, and *il* and *soi* as relatives. The system gives ten types of 'noun' in all, duly declined in six cases, though only *tu* is vocative, and the inclusion of *que* among the nominatives is curious. The analysis is continued in the syntactic section of the grammar, the whole treatment representing yet another attempt to force the French pronominal series willy-nilly into the straitjacket of the Latin case system. To attain this result while preserving his four-word-class system, Ramus flagrantly contradicts his definition of the French noun by introducing case as a criterion.

The verb is distinguished from the other 'words with number' by the special differences tense and person,[118] the latter being understood not in the traditional semantic terms of speaker, hearer and person referred to, but as a formal morphological category, a 'special termination' of the verb. The stumbling-block here of course is that Latin is richer in such endings than French. Ramus' distance from the customary theory of his day may be measured by comparing his terse, purely formal definition ('a word of number with [markers of] tense and person') with that of Priscian, almost universally copied by Renaissance grammarians: 'a part of speech with tenses and moods, not marked for case, signifying action or being acted upon'.[119] In his *Scholae* Ramus had already condemned Priscian's mentalist description of mood as a 'diverse inclination of the mind showing its various states',[120] and dismissed mood altogether as an 'absurda et explodenda confusio'. It is tense that is for Ramus the primary feature of the verb, and it is in terms of the morphological endings of tense that his scheme is set out. The usual tense scheme of both ancient and humanist grammar can conveniently be expressed in a diagram:

```
                              imperfect
     present
     past            perfect
     future
                              pluperfect
```

[118] *Grammaire*, p. 75: 'ung mot de nombre avec temps et personne'. Cf. *Grammatica*, p. 49: 'Verbum est vox numeri cum tempore et persona.' Sanctius (*Minerva*, I, cap. 13) expresses approval of this definition: 'Verbum est vox particeps numeri, personalis, cum tempore...Haec definitio vera est et perfecta; reliquae omnes grammaticorum ineptae.'

[119] Keil, *Grammatici Latini*, II, 369.

[120] In the *Scholae grammaticae* (cols. 131–4) Ramus demonstrates the considerable confusion that reigned among grammarians in the treatment of mood.

Ramus adds to this a further dimension from Varro, that of aspect, justifying in the *Scholae* a distinction between completive and incompletive tenses ('tempora perfecta et infecta').[121] Varro's system is usefully set out in R. H. Robins' *Short History of Linguistics* (second ed., p. 51):

	incomplete aspect	complete aspect
past	*discebam* I was learning	*didiceram* I had learned
present	*disco* I learn	*didici* I have learned
future	*discam* I shall learn	*didicero* I shall have learned

Robins notes that in putting *didici* in the present completive slot only, as in Greek, Varro did not allow for the fact that in the Latin 'perfect' there is syncretism of two meanings: simple past ('I learned', corresponding to the Greek aorist), and perfect ('I have learned'). Strictly speaking then, *didici* should appear in both aspectual series.

This mixed temporal/aspectual system that he has devised for Latin, Ramus now attempts to graft onto the French verb in terms of *temps imparfaicts* and *temps parfaicts*. As in the Latin grammar, mood is not separately distinguished on either formal or semantic grounds, but the modal tenses are simply included in numbered series along with the other tenses. The present incompletive series, together with its Latin equivalents, is as follows:

1. aime (*amo*) 2. aime (*amem*) 3. aimerais (*amarem*) 4. aimasse (*amarem*)[122]

Following common practice, what is now known as the French conditional is equated with the Latin imperfect subjunctive (though Ramus does not so name it) in *-arem*. The past incompletive series consists in turn of two tenses:

1. aimais (*amabam*) 2. aimais (*amarem*)

Since Ramus refuses to name the subjunctive as such, he is in the anomalous position of ascribing two present tenses to the one form *aime*, in contradiction of his doctrine that changes in grammatical category must be consignified by corresponding changes in form. Similarly, in the past tenses, *aimais* figures in two separate slots for

---

[121] *Ibid.*, col. 135. Ramus explicitly states that he has followed 'Varronem huius analogiae principem et authorem'.

[122] The spelling of the French verbal forms has here been modernized.

no better reason than that it translates both Latin *amabam* and Latin *amarem* – a good example of the way in which the primacy of Latin continues to distort the description of vernacular structure. Since the imperative is a mood, it too must be consigned to the anonymity of a numbered tense series. The future incompletive accordingly has two tenses, the second of which translates the Latin imperative:

  1. aimerai (*amabo*) 2. aime (*ama; amato*)

The last three tenses of the present incompletive series (*aime, aimerais, aimasse*) are also considered to have a future meaning. The single past completive tense given in the morphology, *ayme* (a spelling which presumably corresponds to the modern *aimai*), corresponding to Latin *amavi*, is referred to as a perfect, though Ramus notes that it is sometimes 'aorist' and sometimes not.

It was customary in the sixteenth century to claim that French, unlike Greek and Latin, had no 'art de syntaxe', a claim grammarians gladly accepted as an excuse not to enter the tangled domain of vernacular construction. Ramus sees the refutation of this in the variety of compound tenses in French, supplying the vernacular's lack of unitary perfect and passive forms by means of a 'syntaxe de plusieurs mots'. It is accordingly not in the morphological section (*etymologie*) of his work but in the syntax, by definition for him that part of grammar which deals with circumlocutions,[123] that Ramus, as later in English his follower Ben Jonson, reveals the full complexity of the verbal system. Here again, mood is ignored and the various temporal series are indicated by number only. The complexity of the system of four past tenses, the varied forms of which are in each tense equivalent to one Latin form, can be gauged from the following table:[124]

I *amavisti* (Latin 2nd pers. perfect indicative)
  1. aimas 2. eus aimé 3. as aimé 4. as eu aimé
II *amaveris* (Latin perfect subjunctive) preceded by *vu que, combien que,* or *O que volontiers*:
  1. as aimé 2. aies aimé 3. aurais aimé 4. avais aimé 5. as eu aimé 6. aies eu aimé 7. aurais eu aimé 8. avais eu aimé

[123] See the statement in the *Scholae grammaticae*, col. 141.
[124] The spelling has again been modernized. Ramus does not of course attach names to any of the tenses.

III *amavisses* (Latin pluperfect subjunctive) preceded by *quand, si,* or *vu que*

1. aurais aimé   2. eusses aimé   3. avais aimé   4. aurais eu aimé   5. eusses eu aimé   6. avais eu aimé

IV *amaveras* (Latin pluperfect indicative)

1. avais aimé   2. aurais eu aimé.[125]

To these are added a future perfect: *amavero* 1. aurai aimé   2. aurai eu aimé. It will be noted that certain forms appear in as many as three different series, thus invalidating any claim Ramus may make as to the determination of separate tenses by purely formal criteria. All he has done is to demonstrate that the Latin tense distinctions are translatable into French, producing a gloss to the Latin verb rather than a scheme arising from vernacular structure. These twenty past tense forms are further classified according as they have definite (*oriste*) or indefinite (*aoriste*) meaning. This distinction, unknown to Latin grammar, is taken from Greek grammatical theory,[126] where it has a basis in the Greek verb. Here may be seen the influence of Henri Estienne's *Conformité du language françois avec le grec* (1565), Ramus' being one attempt among many to attribute to the vernacular features in common with Greek. Thus does he vindicate the French language in the face of charges that it is deficient in tenses, though his provision of twelve periphrastic equivalents of the Latin past infinitive *amavisse* may be thought to pass the bounds of modesty. The suppression of mood enormously increases, in both the Latin and the French grammar, the complication of his verbal system. His determination to make Latin and French correspond at all possible points involves him, no less than his semasiologically defining contemporaries, in considerable confusion.

A problem for Ramist grammar is posed by those forms which, though belonging grammatically in the four major classes of 'words without number', show no formal variation and have to be catered for by a special sub-class of *voces numeri infinitae*. This category includes the infinitives, and the treatment of infinitives and participles in the *Grammaire* can only be understood in the light of the long discussion in the *Scholae*[127] of what grammarians called perpetual infinitives (e.g.

---

[125] *Grammaire*, pp. 173–5. A series of periphrastic passives is also given.
[126] It also appears in the French vernacular grammars of Dubois and Pillot.
[127] Cols. 137–44.

amare) and participial infinitives (gerunds and supines). The traditional view saw the former as 'infinita' in person only,[128] the latter as 'infinita' in person, voice and tense. The debate in the *Scholae* turns on whether the various infinitive forms do in fact lack person and/or tense, and whether the 'participial infinitives', though they are marked for case, can really be classed as nouns.[129] Ramus holds that infinitives do not so much lack person, as contain all persons latently or *confusae*,[130] and that if this is true – as Priscian concedes – there is no reason why gerunds and supines (*legendum, lectum,* etc.) should not similarly contain tenses 'infinita et confusa'.[131] This somewhat arid discussion is mentioned here in order to give an example of the careful disquisitions in Ramus' *Scholae* that lie behind the brash assertions in his *Grammaire*. The tradition of vernacular grammar cannot be well understood without reference to the Latin one that underlies it, and more especially is this true of an author such as Ramus who produces both Latin and vernacular works. After reading the theoretical treatment in the *Scholae*, it is not surprising to find that the *Grammaire* in its turn divides infinitive forms into 'perpetuel' and 'gerondif'. It then further divides the 'perpetual infinitive' into present (*aimer*) and preterite (*aimé*),[132] the latter being the formally invariable past participle, in modern terminology, used in compound conjugations with *avoir*. The term 'gerondif' is used for the similarly invariable forms in *-ant*, as in *aimant*. The term 'participe' is reserved, as in Meigret's grammar,[133] for those forms which show number and gender agreement with their subjects. Ramus' definition of participles as nouns[134] depends on their possession of the 'special difference' of gender, and since the invariable forms do not show agreement, he is obliged to put them

[128] It was traditional in Latin grammar to view infinitives as devoid of person, and on these grounds some grammarians excluded them from the verb class, Priscian e.g. regarding them as having the grammatical 'force' of nouns.

[129] Priscian, as Ramus notes in the *Scholae grammaticae* (col. 142), sees gerunds and supines as nouns 'quia casus habeant'.

[130] E.g. first person in *cupio amare* and second in *cupis amare* (*ibid.*, col. 142).

[131] The embarrassing presence of case in gerunds and supines can be got round by declaring them to have the 'species' or semblance of case rather than its reality: (*Scholae grammaticae*, col. 142) 'Participialia nominalis casus speciem potius habent, quam veritatem.' Cf. Ramus' *Grammatica*, p. 50, where the *infinitivum participiale* is described as 'quod flectitur *specie* nominalis casus' (my italics).

[132] Here again the modern spelling is given.

[133] *Le Tretté de la grammere françoeze*, 1550. Cf. also Nebrija's *Gramatica de la lengua castellana*, 1492.

[134] *Scholae grammaticae*, col. 145.

into his cross-cutting sub-class of 'mots de nombre infinits'. Since he is the first French grammarian prior to the Port-Royal grammar to require that the form in *-ant* used with verbal signification is invariable, he is presumably also reserving the term 'gerondif' to this strictly participial use, keeping the term 'participe' for the variable form used adjectivally.[135] Ramus' 'verbe infini perpetuel preterit' or invariable past participle conjugated with *avoir* is identical with Meigret's 'infinitif parfait ou preterit' and the Spaniard Nebrîja's 'nombre participial infinito'. The same Latin tradition must be assumed to underlie them all, the interest of Ramus' version consisting in the fact that it can be directly compared with his own theoretical discussion in the *Scholae*. Of especial interest is the fact that a problem of Latin grammar – how to cater for unmarked forms which none the less must be held to signify person and tense – has been utilized to make a clear distinction between the function of variable and invariable participles in the vernacular.

In treating his 'words without number' Ramus has really no criterion other than the 'principal signification' of each word-class and whatever syntactic considerations apply.[136] To the syntactic definition of the adverb given in the Latin grammar,[137] he adds in the *Grammaire* a semantic requirement: they signify quantity or quality.[138] The way is then open to a listing of precisely those 'significations' of time, place, manner, etc., common to semantically based grammars from ancient classical times to the present century, that are so conspicuously absent from Ramus' Latin grammar. They constitute a flagrant contradiction of his declared intention (*Scholae*, book VI) of defining with no mention of the lexical signification of a word-class[139] as opposed to its formal consignification of grammatical meanings, and his condemnation of Theodore Gaza – the first author of a humanist Greek grammar in the West – for classifying

[135] Usage in this respect fluctuated until late in the seventeenth century. Cf. Loiseau, *Etude historique et philologique sur Jean Pillot et sur les doctrines grammaticales du XVIe siècle*, p. 103: 'le 3 juin 1669 l'Académie put dire avec juste raison: "La règle est faite. On ne déclinera plus les participes présents".'

[136] *Grammaire*, p. 116. The word without number is 'celuy, qui *outre sa principalle signification* ne denote aucun nombre' (my italics).

[137] *Grammatica*, p. 74: 'Adverbium est vox sine numero, quae voci alii adiungitur.'

[138] *Grammaire*, p. 116: 'Ladverbe cest ung mot sans nombre, qui est adjoinct a ung aultre: et est de quantite ou qualite.'

[139] 'nulla significationis facta mentione'. It is amusing to note Brunot's satisfaction (*Histoire*, II, 154) at finding that though Ramus' theories in general result in confusion, 'du moins les adverbes sont classés...dans les anciens cadres'.

adverbs under Aristotle's ten 'inept and derisory' categories.[140] Since Ramus finds no valid reason for giving them independent status, interjections (following a time-honoured Greek tradition) and prepositions are classed as types of adverb. The conjunction is however kept distinct, on the syntactic grounds of its linking function, but here again the only criteria that can be found to satisfy Ramus' urge to dichotomous classification are semantic ones:

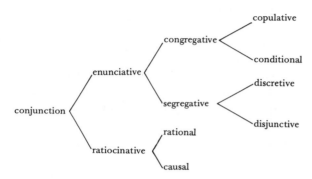

These categories could be paralleled in any Latin grammar of the period, and are illustrative of Ramus' dilemma: how to define in purely formal terms a word-class system already predetermined on a partially avowed semantic basis. This dilemma becomes acute in the categorization of classes which have no overt formal markers and – always assuming that this section of the grammar is his – it would seem that Ramus is almost obliged, given the lack of a fully worked-out contemporary syntactic theory, to fall back on semantic criteria. The inappropriateness of a morphological approach to the 'words without number' is confirmed by the extreme shortness of the section devoted to them in the *Scholae*.

This last defect is in some measure compensated for in the French grammar by the unusual amount of space Ramus gives to syntax. Renaissance authors – apart from the notable exception in England of Thomas Linacre[141] – had tended to neglect this part of grammar, and Ramus is the first French vernacular grammarian to give it extended and methodical treatment. Though on a theoretical level his interest is eloquently mirrored by the two paltry columns in the *Scholae*, which no more than briefly mention a few figures such as

[140] *Scholae grammaticae*, col. 178.
[141] *De emendata structura Latini sermonis*, 1524.

41

syllepsis and *enallage*, the Latin grammar also deals with syntax at considerable length. Its treatment is however the customary one in terms of word agreement (*convenientia*) and government (*rectio*). Renaissance grammar is word-based, and the syntax in the French grammar is similarly a syntax of individual word-classes treated in turn rather than a thorough examination of linguistic structure. Only in treating those classes – the 'words without number' – for which he is obliged to set up syntactic criteria as opposed to morphological ones, does Ramus really interest himself in construction. Syntax consisting 'almost solely in agreement and mutual communion of the properties',[142] the plan is almost identical with that followed in the Latin grammar. Ramus castigates however those grammarians who 'without cause and reason assert that we have no art of syntax',[143] showing the beginnings of a recognition of the analytical character of French in the emphasis he gives to word order. French has a 'certain order in discourse which cannot be in any way altered', in contrast to the classical language, whose word order is frequently 'corrupted' by stylistic transpositions.[144] The constant pedagogical concern surfaces once more in the insistence that the teaching of syntax is only profitable in so far as it takes its examples from approved usage. The instructor must, that is, not invent examples to illustrate his rules, but apply the rules to an authentic linguistic corpus.[145] He must not, in a misplaced zeal for supposed correctness, 'alone unsheathe his sword in opposition to the whole of France'.[146] A knowledge of actual usage is, Ramus concludes – and here he puts into practice the insistence on empirical observation and the imitation of nature that is an important feature of his theoretical works – of more effect for good speaking and writing than all the rules of grammar ever invented.[147]

An important shift of emphasis in the French grammar is occasioned by Ramus' realization, contrary to the general opinion of his times, that French nouns are not marked for case. This means that though the term *gouverner* does sometimes appear in other contexts (e.g. p. 169, 'Le verbe deliberatif gouverne linfiny'), the use of the concept is largely confined to the syntax of prepositions. Case

---

[142] *Grammaire*, p. 125. [143] *Ibid.*, p. 171.
[144] *Ibid.*, pp. 182, 129. [145] *Ibid.*, pp. 124–5.
[146] The obvious target of these remarks is Meigret, whom Ramus had in his first edition (1562) joined in condemning certain widespread usages.
[147] *Grammaire*, p. 209.

having been rejected, Ramus is left in his treatment of the nominal system with the morphological markers of number and gender, which means, since government was at that time seen in terms of the relationships between case-marked words, that his syntax will inevitably consist 'almost solely in agreement'.[148] The broad dichotomy of *convenientia* and *rectio*, so prominent a feature of the Latin grammar, is thus missing in the French one. Ramus' approach is however not exempt from the contemporary obsession with drawing parallels between French structures and Greek or Latin ones. The possession of an article is of course vaunted as proof of equality with Greek,[149] and the fact that pronouns are sometimes not expressed is similarly seized on as a demonstration of the vernacular's claim to be taken seriously. Behind the modernity of Ramus' approach to word order there still lurk remnants of Scholasticism. He does not, any more than do his contemporaries, define the subject/predicate relationship, but simply designates the noun as 'suppost' and the verb as 'appost'. Interestingly, disjunctive pronouns such as *moi* and *toi* uttered alone in reply to questions are also regarded as 'supposts'. Ramus may be applauded for noting that French infinitives can function as nouns (*le boire*), but he feels obliged to point to the supposed Greek origin of this usage, and describes it as an example of an 'appost pour le nom'. The continued presence of the medieval terms *suppositum* and *appositum* in both Ramus and Sanctius is noteworthy.[150]

Only in the section on prepositions is there a vestige of the treatment of word government, Ramus declaring that the 'whole government of nouns and verbs' is covered by the six 'prepositions' *à, au, aux* and *de, du, des*. These are seen, as in contemporary Italian grammatical theory, as signs of cases. Having refused to regard nouns as *formally marked* for case, Ramus finds himself obliged, if he is at some point to retain the notion of 'gouvernance', to set up genitives and ablatives, etc., by means of prepositions, thus following common Renaissance vernacular usage. 'This is a singular syntax of our

---

[148] *Ibid.*, p. 125: 'presque seulement en convenance et mutuelle communion des propriétés. Cf. *Grammatica*, p. 78: 'Convenientia est, quando voces communibus proprietatibus conveniunt.'

[149] Brunot (*Histoire*, II, 155, n. 1) sees here a debt to Henri Estienne's *Conformité*.

[150] For a discussion of the terms *suppositum* and *appositum* see Padley, *Grammatical Theory* (1976), p. 52. See also V. Salmon, 'James Shirley and Some Problems of Seventeenth-Century Grammar', *Archiv für das Studium der neueren Sprachen* CXCVII: 4 (1961), pp. 287–96, *passim*.

prepositions, differing greatly from that of the Greek and Latin prepositions,' declares the loyal yes-man pupil in the dialogue, seeing in it yet one more proof that the vernacular 'takes its essence from itself'.[151] Ramus is not however, any more than his contemporaries, able to resolve the puzzle presented by the amalgams *au* and *du*, etc. Since they function as case markers, he has to regard them as purely prepositions, which leads him to the absurdity of stating that although normally names of rivers take an article they can also, as in 'il coule au rhône', appear without it. The importance of Ramus' treatment however lies in the fact that, since he refuses case to nouns, it is more plainly evident in his system than in those of others that prepositions, often grammatically redundant in Latin, are in the vernacular (together with word order) the sole markers of pertinent syntactic relationships.[152] What masks this grammatical insight is the customary imposition on the vernacular structural system of the Latin grid of cases.

Ramus' somewhat breathless treatment, giving the dry bones of French grammar without any of the theoretical material that constitutes the interest of his *Scholae grammaticae*, is reminiscent of the relationship between the rather fragmentary *Grammaire générale et raisonnée* of 1660, and the same Port-Royal school's *Nouvelle Méthode latine* – with this capital difference, that in the Port-Royal case the theoretical justification is in the vernacular work, not the Latin one. Both vernacular grammars are the fruit of many years' hard thought about grammatical theory, and it is worth noting that in the hundred years that separate them no grammars of comparable importance are published in France. Elsewhere, important grammars of Latin appear, but in France at any rate the production of grammatical works is limited to practical teaching manuals, produced by schoolmasters for austerely pedagogical purposes, and, in the seventeenth century, to the empirically based *Observations* and *Remarques* of the prescribers of correct usage of whom Vaugelas is the best known. Against this background, and if no account is taken of the progress of Latin grammatical theory in the interim, the Port-Royal *Grammaire générale* appears as the harbinger of a new dawn, as the means of escape from that 'vicious circle which Ramus was the last magician

---

[151] *Grammaire*, pp. 202–3.
[152] The syntax of gender agreement is of course itself grammatically redundant in French.

to draw'.[153] Certainly Ramus can be held to have tried to enclose the grammar of French within an immanent formal system whose inadequacies are those that can be imputed to any 'structuralist' approach: the atomistic treatment of linguistic phenomena in isolation without any all-embracing coherence, the recognition of isolated *faits de parole* rather than of *faits de langue* in an interrelated system, the taking for a 'model' of what is only a description of a particular surface realization[154] — though these criticisms smack of course of hindsight. J.-C. Chevalier has well noted that the stumbling-block of the Ramist approach to grammar is the exceptions, as with that sub-class of 'words of number' which remain obstinately invariable and must be classified according to mentalistic or syntactic criteria which remain unconfessed. The contrast between Ramus' grammar and that of Port-Royal lies in the lack in the former of what Chevalier calls 'schémas d'organisation', a contrast which he further characterizes as the difference between a 'static' and a 'dynamic' grammar.[155] One hardly needs reminding that these are precisely the terms in which many would oppose a present-day structuralist approach to a transformational-generative one. It is interesting that Chevalier resists any temptation to put the 'philosophical' grammars of Scaliger (*De causis linguae Latinae*, 1540) and Sanctius (*Minerva*, 1587) on one side of the fence and Ramus' formally based grammars on the other. Such a procedure would, he says, be an 'abusive simplification', for the two types of approach are interdependent. It remains true however that in Ramus logician and empirical linguist constantly get in each other's way. Under the smooth surface of a rigorous order imposed by logic, with its deceptively convincing dichotomies, there is a certain confusion in which, in an attempt to keep the system together, semantic and formal criteria are mingled. More particularly his formal approach, unaided by any concept of, as in Port-Royal, the logical relationships underlying surface realizations, is unable to create a valid syntax. One cannot found a syntax on morphological markers alone. The profound difference between the Ramist and the Port-Royal approach lies, in the last analysis, on a different employment of logic. Whereas Ramus uses

---

[153] Chevalier, *Histoire de la syntaxe*, p. 284.

[154] Cf. Loiseau's early criticism (*Etude historique et philologique sur Jean Pillot*, p. 112): 'son esprit philosophique lui fait chercher sans cesse des principes, et il ne voit que des faits avec toute leur brutalité'.

[155] *Histoire de la syntaxe*, pp. 305, 357.

it as a tool in pedagogical and methodological demarcation, as providing the framework within which a grammar must be written, the Port-Royal authors see it both as a metalanguage and as one of the component levels of linguistic structure.

iii RAMISM IN GERMANY AND BRITAIN

Ratke and his followers

Perhaps in part because of Ramus' status as Protestant martyr, but also no doubt because of features peculiar to the direction humanism was taking in the countries of northern Europe, the success of Ramism in Britain and Germany, particularly the latter, was immeasurably greater than that it enjoyed in Latin Europe. In Spain, thanks to the efforts of Francisco Sanchez (Sanctius) to reform the teaching of the arts curriculum at Salamanca University on Ramist principles, it might have had a brilliant future, but thanks possibly to Ramus' own brushes with the Inquisition, the only important Spanish witness to his doctrines is to be found in Sanctius' great Latin grammar, the *Minerva* of 1587.[156] In Italy the situation was similar, Ramism being opposed in all universities except Bologna. It was in Germany that Ramus' teachings enjoyed a vogue that for a time swept all before it. From the period when, after Ramus' death, his publisher Wéchel moved to Frankfurt-am-Main, Germany was for a century the chief centre of Ramism, whose influence came to a peak between 1580 and 1620. In a situation in which 'the didactic drive, indigenous to the university movement, appears in Germany unmasked and bare',[157] almost all Protestant chairs of philosophy came to be occupied by Ramists, and the higher reaches of pedagogy rapidly became a Ramist preserve. J. T. Freige's version of Ramus' Dialectic, the *Paedagogus* (1582), ensured the spread of Ramus' ideas into the whole field of university teaching in the arts, and indeed into wider cultural areas. German translations of the Dialectic appeared from 1587[158] onward, and the headway made by Ramist logic inevitably brought it into conflict with Scholastic logic and the established dialectic of the influential Philip Melanchthon. Here an intellectual difference is doubled by a religious one, for Melanchthon's Lutheran followers

---

[156] For details see Padley, *Grammatical Theory* (1976), pp. 98–102.
[157] Ong, *Ramus*, p. 164.
[158] F. Beurhaus, *P. Rami Dialectica verdeutscht*, Erfurt, 1587.

suspected Ramists of Calvinist leanings. Furthermore the Melanchthonian logic, in general use at German universities, was based on
Aristotle and thus acceptable to traditionalists. Conflict eventually
led to Ramism being proscribed at several universities, more particularly in Catholic areas, and an uneasy compromise was established
in which elements of the Melanchthonian and Ramist dialectics were
combined with features of the older Scholastic logic to form a mixed
'Philippo-Ramist' approach more acceptable to the university than
undiluted Ramism.[159] The doctrines of Ramus are rarely found in
Germany in their pure form.

Equally in the area of vernacular grammar, there are no pure
Ramist works. It is Ramus' general method rather than every last
detail of his grammatical theory that is followed, and that, particularly
in the group of grammarians who collaborate with the educational
reformer Wolfgang Ratke or Ratichius, for pedagogical reasons.
Ratke himself had been exposed to Ramist doctrines at the University
of Rostock, though he was later to deny having been influenced by
Ramus. Among those who at different times collaborated with him
and also underwent Ramist influence were Christopher Helwig and
Christian Gueintz, the latter being one of the scholars called to
Köthen in 1619 by Fürst Ludwig of Anhalt to prepare a series of
manuals for use in schools. It is indeed not as Ramist grammarians
that Ratke and his circle are important, but rather as animators of
an important pedagogical reform based on the use of the German
Muttersprache, and as advocates for pedagogical reasons of theories of
universal grammar. Both these aspects of their work will be treated
in later chapters. Their importance in the spread of Ramism lies in
the fact that as Protestants they were influenced by Ramus' principles
of organization, if not to any notable extent by his linguistic theory,
and that they used those principles in organizing the grammatical
teaching of the vernacular. It is important to bear in mind that the
vernacular enjoyed in Protestant Germany a status superior to that
which it had in Catholic countries. God was as elsewhere held to have
communicated with man through the scriptures, but more specifically
in Germany through the *vernacular* Bible, in the composition of which

[159] Examples of Latin grammars are the *Grammatica Latina Philippo-Ramea* (Herborn, 1591)
with Melanchthon's eight parts of speech in preference to Ramus' four; and the *Compendium
grammaticae Latinae Mauritio-Philippo-Ramea* (Herborn, 1613 – 'Mauritio' refers to Maurice,
Landgrave of Hesse).

Luther acted as His chosen instrument.[160] It is essential to remember that German, not Latin, was the language of the Protestant Church.

Already in 1612–13 Ratke had sketched out a vernacular grammar, the 'Sprachkunst', the final version of which was ready at the end of 1615.[161] This date coincides with that of the publication of the second edition of Caspar Finck and Christopher Helwig's *Grammatica Latina*,[162] which follows the 'philosophical', Scaligeran trend but with distinct Ramist formal features. The two works resemble each other closely, particularly in the definitions of the parts of speech, and the question remains open whether Ratke copied Finck–Helwig's first edition (of which Jellinek's *Geschichte* gives no record), or whether the latter two authors used Ratke's manuscript in preparing their second one.[163] The Ramist elements in the 'Sprachkunst'[164] are at all events few. They include the definition of grammar (by no means peculiar to Ramus) as the art of speaking well ('ein kunst wol zusprechen'), and give its two parts as *etymologia* and *syntaxis* ('Erklerung' and 'Ordenung'), though treatment of the latter is in fact absent. The word is defined in Ramus' curiously non-Ramist terms as 'that by which something is named'.[165] The definitions of noun and verb stem from a Greek tradition with little in common with Ramus' approach,[166] and the retention of mood as a verbal category, together with the mixed formal and semasiological criteria used, are equally incompatible with his theory. As time goes by Ratke's grammatical works become however progressively more Ramist in tone, particularly in their increasing passion for dichotomies. The *Allgemeine*

[160] Cf. the dedicatory foreword to J. Clajus' *Grammatica Germanicae linguae* (1578).

[161] It must at any rate have been completed some time between 1613 and 1617. See E. Ising, *Wolfgang Ratkes Schriften zur deutschen Grammatik (1612–1630)*, Berlin, 1959, I, 24 (and n. 1), who gives the date of composition as between 1612 and 1615.

[162] Giessen, 1615. M. H. Jellinek, *Geschichte der neuhochdeutschen Grammatik*, II, 3, mentions only this second edition. For a discussion of the work see Padley, *Grammatical Theory* (1976), pp. 162, 164–6.

[163] The Ratichian *Compendium grammaticae Latinae* (1620) also owes something to Finck–Helwig, at any rate in its framework, which shows an obsessive use of dichotomies grafted onto a Melanchthonian base.

[164] The work is printed for the first time in Ising, *Wolfgang Ratkes Schriften*, II, 9–22.

[165] Ramus' 'nota qua unumquodque vocatur'. A similar direct translation from Ramus occurs in the rendering of his definition of 'etymologia' (*Grammatica*, p. 5: 'quae vocum singularum proprietates interpretatur') as 'welches lehret, wie man eines iglichen Worts eigenschafft erkennen müge'.

[166] 'Sprachkunst' (Ising, *Wolfgang Ratkes Schriften*, II, 11): the noun is declinable for case and signifies a thing without time; the verb is formally variable for mood and signifies a thing with time.

Sprachlehr or universal grammar of 1619,[167] commonly known as the
Köthener Sprachlehr, already differs to a notable extent from the
'Sprachkunst' in layout and terminology. In accordance with the
Ramist requirement that the general be treated before the particular,
number and person are described at the outset as 'properties' of all
declinable words.[168] The emphasis is more on formal criteria than
in the 'Sprachkunst', noun, pronoun and participle having the
'properties' gender and declension, while verb and participle share
the 'property' tense. Similarly based on formal criteria, in direct
translation from Ramus or a Ramist source, are the definitions of case
as a 'variation in the word by means of a special mark',[169] and of
tense as 'a variation in the word according to the difference of
tense'.[170] This grammar is however an excellent example of the
German tendency to follow a mixed, 'Philippo-Ramist' tradition.
The word-class definitions are from the mainstream of grammatical
practice, largely couched in semantic terms, and mood is both
retained and defined in mentalistic terms[171] that would have been
anathema to Ramus. The short exposition of syntax gives no
examples from German. The main Ramist feature of the *Sprachlehr*
is its adherence to Ramus' methodological principle 'generalia
generatim et semel' – the treatment of the general at the outset and
once only.

The later grammatical works show a rearrangement of the Ramist
ground-plan. In a series of *Lehren* or classroom manuals dealing with
the separate parts of grammar, Ratke removed word derivation and
composition from the *etymologia*, and treated it in a distinct
'Wortbedeutungslehr' or manual of word meanings, leaving
morphology and syntax to be treated as the central problems of
grammar in his 'Wortschickungslehr' (*c.* 1630),[172] a work in which
the use of dichotomies attains almost manic proportions. Apart from

[167] *Allgemeine Sprachlehr nach der Lehrart Ratichii/Grammatica universalis pro didactica Ratichii*,
Köthen, 1619. This was the only one of the Ratichian vernacular grammars to be printed,
the others surviving only in manuscript form. The German version is reproduced in Ising,
Wolfgang Ratkes Schriften, II, 23–37.
[168] The immediate source for this may well be Finck–Helwig.
[169] Cf. Ramus' 'specialis terminatio nominis'.
[170] Cf. Ramus' 'differentia verbi secundum praesens, praeteritum et futurum'.
[171] *Allgemeine Sprachlehr*, p. 13 (Ising, *Wolfgang Ratkes Schriften*, II, 33): 'Die Weise ist eine
verwandlung des Sprechworts, nach des Gemüts fürhaben.' The 'intention of the mind' is
the criterion, not any change in form.
[172] Reproduced in Ising, *Wolfgang Ratkes Schriften*, II, 97–268.

this however the Ramist elements are again few, and the remarks on syntax apply to Latin rather than to the vernacular.[173] Where Ratke is seen to follow Ramus is in the methodical procedure that characterizes all his different 'Lehren': a tightly organized framework, and a practical approach that aims to be 'naturgemäss' (in conformity with nature, a cardinal Ramist requirement) and universally applicable to every subject of the curriculum. On the other hand, the works were meant to be easily assimilable by young pupils. In both these respects Ramus' system offered an obvious model, though such is the rigid austerity of Ratke's manuals, with everything aridly dichotomized, that they must have represented a torment for the pupils exposed to them. It is the organizational aspect of Ramus' teachings that is attractive to Ratke as a pedagogical reformer, so it is not surprising that the Ramist element in his grammar is by and large confined to the ordering of the material, while his definitions are taken from or modelled on the Latin grammars of Finck–Helwig, Frischlin and Melanchthon, with some influence from J. C. Scaliger.

Ratke's fellow-workers Helwig and Gueintz wrote grammars plainly showing his influence, particularly in terminology. As already mentioned, Helwig had collaborated with Caspar Finck in the production of a Latin grammar which owes much to J. C. Scaliger, but is also clearly Ramist in its insistence that it is not lexical meaning that is the province of the grammarian, but (with acknowledgments to Ramus' *Scholae*) grammatical meanings formally consignified.[174] 1619, the year of the appearance of the *Köthener Sprachlehr*, saw the posthumous publication of a grammar by Helwig as sole author, the *Libri didactici*,[175] presenting a universal grammar plus individual grammars of the three classical languages and Chaldean. Its interest for a study of vernacular grammar lies in the fact that it was accompanied by a German version, virtually identical with the Latin one, under the title *Sprachkünste*,[176] which shares with the *Sprachlehr* the distinction of being one of the earlier universal grammars written

---

[173] Only in the 'Rhematica ad Germanicam linguam applicata' (*c.* 1630), a preliminary version of the 'Wortschickungslehr', is there a short sketch of vernacular syntax.

[174] *Grammatica Latina* (2nd ed.), Giessen, 1615: 'ita, ut non versetur in ipsis significationibus, verum in proprietatibus signficationum'.

[175] *Libri didactici grammaticae universalis, Latinae, Graecae, Hebraicae, Chaldicae*, Giessen, 1619.

[176] *Sprachkünste: I. Allgemaine welche das jenige so allen Sprachen gemein ist in sich begreifft. II. Lateinische. III. Hebraische*, Giessen, 1619.

in the vernacular. It in fact precedes the *Sprachlehr* in actual date of composition, and is pedagogically more satisfactory in that it largely omits the definitions contained in its Latin companion, and avoids the Ratichian profusion of dichotomies. It deals with the general before the particular in proper Ramist fashion, and distinguishes the parts of speech by the morphological criteria of *variatio, originatio* and *resolutio*.[177] The first of these has to do with the consignification of grammatical meanings (Helwig reemploys the medieval term *modi significandi*) by means of word endings. *Originatio* and *resolutio* are respectively the *species* and *figura* of traditional grammar, and concern derivation and compounds. After this promising beginning, however, noun and verb are defined in purely semantic terms, the former as 'that by which something is named', the latter as signifying *actio* or *passio*. It is almost as if Ramist features are grafted onto an otherwise semantically orientated grammar, in a curious mixture of the two traditions in which for example substantive and adjective are defined in terms of the signification of essence, but definitions of grammatical accidents are repeated word for word from Ramus. The description of gender as 'a difference of the noun according to sex' and of tense as 'a difference of the verb according to present, preterite and future', translations from Ramus' Latin, are perhaps little more than a gesture towards a reigning fashion. Helwig is patently not using the term 'difference' solely in Ramus' formal sense, for he goes on to define mood (for which Ramus provides no model) in mentalist fashion as a 'difference of the verb' showing the state of mind of the speaker. Much of his grammar must be traced to other sources. His three-part word-class system owes more to Hebrew grammar – among Ratke's collaborators it was Helwig who was responsible for oriental languages – and possibly to Sanctius, than to Ramus. The third part of speech, the *advocabulum*, rendered in German as *Beiwort*, is so called on grounds of semantic dependence ('weil es der Red keinen Grund kan setzen'), and groups together syncategoremata defined in terms of the signification of a 'circumstance or disposition of the mind'.[178] This last phrase constitutes a summary of everything that pure Ramist theory rigorously excluded from grammar. Helwig's work is firmly in the 'mixed' tradition, mingling irreconcilable elements of

[177] I have retained the Latin terms. In what follows, the Latin and German versions of the grammar have been consulted conjointly.
[178] *Libri didactici*, p. 2. These *advocabula* express 'aliquam circumstantiam vel animi affectum'/'einen Umbstand oder Bewegung des Gemüts'.

two main approaches, the traditional semantically based one, and the Ramist formal one.

The same remarks may be made concerning Christian Gueintz, called to Köthen in 1618 to work on the Ratichian pedagogical reforms, and author of a *Deutscher Sprachlehre Entwurf* (1641).[179] This 'sketch' of German grammar seems to be an enlarged edition of the *Köthener Sprachlehr* of 1619, whose terminology Gueintz borrows wholesale, and whose definitions, mingled with those of Finck–Helwig, he takes over virtually unaltered. The confused treatment adds nothing of moment to the question of Ramist influence, which appears chiefly in the plan of the grammar and in the obsessive use of dichotomies. Ramist method simply forms a framework within which Gueintz repeats the work of his predecessors. The proliferation of dichotomies begins right at the start: a theory of grammar must bear in mind both *Endbetrachtung* and *Mittehandlung*, the former dealing with both the *wesendlich* and the *zufaellig*. That which is *wesendlich* is again either *innerlich* or *eusserlich*, the former concerning itself with either *Woerter* or *Dinge*. Those *Dinge* which are *zufaellig* are in turn either *gemein* or *sonderbar*. And so Gueintz continues throughout the whole grammar, producing a branchy forest of endless binary concepts through which it is difficult to pick one's way. It is hard to believe that this interlocking system of dichotomies, often dealing with very minor and pedantic distinctions, is really necessary to the exposition. It represents the harmful side of Ramism, its confining of knowledge within obligatory dichotomies, its arid enumerations. Ramus' influence on German vernacular grammar is in fact in general less on the grammatical theory espoused than on the methodology. Gueintz' actual grammatical material follows various non-Ramist forerunners such as Clajus and Ritter. Only the skeleton of his grammar, including the organization of the syntax,[180] is Ramist.

Similar evidence of the extent to which Ramist methodology had become a vogue is provided by Johannes Girbert's *Deutsche Grammatica*,[181] which gives the dry bones of grammar in closely ordered tables. Perhaps no other grammar so completely illustrates the diagrammatic tendencies of Ramist thought. Each page of

[179] Published in Köthen.
[180] In his syntax Gueintz follows Finck–Helwig's Latin grammar of 1615.
[181] *Die Deutsche Grammatica oder Sprachkunst.* Muelhausen in Dueringen, 1653.

Girbert's grammar is in effect a close-packed diagram, whose multiple dichotomies, bracketed and sub-bracketed, show the indubitable impress of Ramus' method. Word accidents are classified as *general*, affecting all words (covering derivation and composition); *special* (covering analogy, anomaly, number and person); and *'specialissimae'* (affecting one or two word-classes only). This methodology is specifically Ramist, and Ramist too is the treatment at the outset of the categories gender, declension, case, mood, tense and conjugation. The term used for case – *Zahl-Endung* or number-ending, is perhaps an echo of Ramus' 'words with number' or *voces numeri*. First Girbert discusses a word-class in general terms, under the headings *definitio*, *divisio* (e.g. the substantive/adjective division of the noun class) and *affectiones* or accidents. Only afterwards are the individual *canones* or rules given. The system of parts of speech and their definitions are however the traditional semantically based ones, and there is little trace of Ramus' purely formal criteria. Nowhere perhaps are the effects of the Philippo-Ramist compromise more evident than in grammar. Rather than a linguistic theory to be applied to the vernacular in all its detail, Ramism to these German 'mixed' grammarians is a methodological procedure.

The British manifestations of Ramism

Ramism penetrated into Britain under similar auspices to those which, in part at least, had ensured its spectacular success in Germany, namely the status of Ramus as a Protestant martyr, which perhaps initially inflated his reputation.[182] Certainly it is in puritan strongholds, in St Andrews and in Cambridge, that Ramism makes its chief impact. The important name at St Andrews is that of Roland Mac Ilmaine, who published Ramus' Dialectic for the first time in London in 1574 and enthusiastically propagated Ramist doctrine. The names of Andrew Melville and George Buchanan (translator into Latin of Linacre's *Rudimenta grammatices*) have also been put forward. Melville began at Glasgow a Ramist curricular reform which he later continued at Aberdeen and St Andrews, but he can hardly have influenced Mac Ilmaine, for he was on the continent between 1564 and 1573, and only became an active propagator of

[182] W. and M. Kneale, *The Development of Logic*, p. 302, regard the undue success of Ramism as 'unfortunate' for Britain and for northern Europe in general.

Ramism on becoming principal of Glasgow University in 1574.[183] As for Buchanan, it seems unlikely that he was a Ramist.[184] None the less, it is clear that St Andrews cam claim precedence in introducing Ramism into Britain, though Cambridge followed close behind. At the latter university however the movement was much more widely based, with international connections. The earliest expounder of Ramist logic was Lawrence Chaderton (or Chatterton), but the movement also numbered some better-known names, among others Abraham Fraunce, Gabriel Harvey, William Temple, Dudley Fenner and Everard Digby. The University Press was still printing Ramus' Dialectic as late as 1672. As for Oxford, it has been customary to regard that venerable stronghold of Aristotelianism as comparatively untouched by the Ramist tides that ran so strongly in Cambridge.[185] W. S. Howell however rejects the view that Oxford held completely aloof, pointing to Charles Butler of Magdalen, who particularly in rhetoric prepared 'the books that carried Ramism into the public schools of England throughout the seventeenth century'.[186]

Ramist studies in Britain received their impetus from two initial impulses – the publication of Ramus' Dialectic, and the influence of immigrants from or in contact with the Huguenot colony at Frankfurt-am-Main. The printer of the first British editions of the Dialectic, Thomas Vautrouillier, was himself a Huguenot. The English language version of 1574, the *Logike*,[187] was translated from the Latin by Mac Ilmaine. According to W. J. Ong there were more translations of the Dialectic into English than into any other vernacular, a total of nineteen editions or issues having appeared by 1700.[188] Free adaptations also appeared, probably the best known being Abraham

---

[183] See W. S. Howell, *Logic and Rhetoric*, p. 189.

[184] He has been suggested by Graves, *Petrus Ramus*, p. 213, as the person responsible for introducing Ramist philosophy into St Andrews.

[185] V. H. H. Green for instance (*A History of Oxford University*, London, 1974, p. 54), while noting that Ramist views were spread by John Rainalds, President of Corpus Christi College, sees Oxford opinion as generally hostile.

[186] *Logic and Rhetoric*, p. 193. For an account of the spread of Ramism at Oxford and Cambridge in the late sixteenth and early seventeenth centuries, see pp. 354–63.

[187] *The Logike of the Moste Excellent Philosopher P. Ramus Martyr, newly translated and in divers places corrected after the mynde of the author*. The author is given as 'Roll. Makylmenaeum', variously rendered by Howell as 'Mac Ilmaine' and by Ong as 'M' Kilwein'. Listing the work as No. 253 in his *Ramus and Talon Inventory*, Ong notes that it follows Ramus' text at the stage of the Basle edition of 1569.

[188] Among the earliest, in addition to Mac Ilmaine's, Ong's *Ramus and Talon Inventory* lists translations by Dudley Fenner (1584 and 1588) and Abraham Fraunce (1588).

Fraunce's *The Lawiers Logike*,[189] an attempt to apply Ramist analyses to legal cases. The extent to which Ramism penetrated into a wide area of culture is illustrated by titles claiming to make Ramus' precepts 'plaine to the meanest capacity'[190] – Ramism without tears – and by the fact that Edward Phillips' *The Art of Reason in the Art of Logicke*[191] appeared in a more comprehensive work entitled *Mysteries of Love and Eloquence* (1658), and also in *The Beau's Academy* (1699). Until about 1570 Aristotelian logic still reigned supreme, but from then on the position changed radically, so much so that in discussing the period 1570–1700 W. S. Howell can claim that there was 'almost a complete monopoly for Ramus' logical and rhetorical theory in the early part of that epoch and...a position of considerable weight throughout'.[192]

The Ramist Rhetoric was published somewhat more rarely in Britain than the Dialectic, but again there are more translations into English than into any other vernacular.[193] But though it appeared in fewer editions than its counterpart, W. J. Ong reminds us that 'it has not been sufficiently noted that Ramism makes its first appearance in England under specifically rhetorical auspices', and that British Ramism was centred on 'rhetoric and rhetorically oriented logic'.[194] The logic and the rhetoric were sometimes printed together,[195] and Ong describes as probably incalculable the number of works bearing traces of the Talon–Ramist Rhetoric. The traditional Ciceronian rhetoric with its five divisions, invention, arrangement, style, memory and delivery, continued of course to be taught. But the arrival of Ramus' rhetoric on English soil coincided with a cultural and social

[189] *The Lawiers Logike, exemplifying the Praecepts of Logike by the Practice the Common Lawe*, London, 1588. This adaptation of Ramus' Dialectic was intended for students of the Inns of Court.

[190] Thomas Spencer, *Logicke Unfolded: or, The Body of Logicke in Englishe Made Plaine to the Meanest Capacity*, London, 1656.

[191] Ong (*Ramus and Talon Inventory*, p. 272) describes Phillips' work as an only slightly changed reproduction of 'the catechetical adaptation of Ramus by Robert Fage which first appeared in 1632'. The poet Milton also published in 1672 the Ramist logic he had composed forty years earlier: *Artis logicae plenior institutio ad P. Rami methodum concinnata*, London. He introduced however considerable changes.

[192] On the reception given to Ramus' logic in England see W. S. Howell, *Logic and Rhetoric*, pp. 173–246.

[193] Ong (*Ramus and Talon Inventory*, pp. 85, 89) mentions translations by Dudley Fenner (1584, 1588, 1651, 1681, erroneously ascribed in the past to Hobbes), Abraham Fraunce (1588) and John Barton (1634). [194] *Ramus*, p. 303.

[195] An example is Robert Fage's *Compendium of the Art of Logick and Rhetorick in the English Tongue, Containing all that P. Ramus, Aristotle and Others have Writ Thereon*, London, 1651. The rhetoric in this work is Fenner's 1584 translation, while the logic is Fage's of 1632.

situation that was highly favourable to its acceptance and growth: 'the rapid substitution of a new class of men of law for the old aristocracy...[the need for] a practical form of logic answering religious and public requirements...a method of persuasion... essential to religious propaganda',[196] all meant that in the seventeenth century rhetoric became a major subject in the schools. A specifically Ramist rhetoric appealed both to the practical needs of the new bourgeoisie and to the requirements of the puritan divines who were beginning to pullulate. Mac Ilmaine's version of the Dialectic indicates how Ramus' method can be accommodated to preaching, recommending the use of the rule of wisdom in avoiding 'tautologies and vaine repetitions', and of the rule of truth in detecting 'trickes of poysonable sophistrie'. He trusts that God will 'plante this our rule of veritie [Ramus' second law] in the hartes of all men, but most chieflie in the breasts of the Pastors of the Churche, who have the charge and dispensation of his holye worde'.[197] Particularly in the education of the puritan clergy, Ramus' Dialectic and Rhetoric played an important part in the inculcation of a plain style of writing and pulpit oratory calculated not to draw a veil between the faithful and the straightforward Word of God. An example of a manual is Thomas Granger's adaptation of Ramus, *Syntagma logicum, or The Divine Logike, Serving Especially for the Use of Divines in the Practice of Preaching*.[198] Ramus' rhetoric and logic did not however penetrate into Britain without generating a certain amount of controversy, centred chiefly in Cambridge and engaging in particular the considerable polemic energies of Sir William Temple the elder and Everard Digby. Though the quarrel had an international dimension, drawing in Rhineland Ramists, in England it was around these two men that the controversy on method centred. In the decade immediately preceding this debate, there were already signs that the supremacy of Aristotle and Cicero in logic and rhetoric was weakening, and advocacy of Ramus' 'single method' was on the increase. In 1580 Temple published his *Admonition that the Single Method of Peter Ramus be Retained and the Rest Rejected*,[199] to which Digby replied in the same year in a work arguing in favour of Aristotle's double method against Ramus' single one.[200] The breadth of the controversy, which continued

[196] P. Rossi, *Francis Bacon: From Magic to Science* (translated from the Italian, Bari, 1957, by S. Rabinovitch), London, 1968, pp. 142–3.
[197] *Logike*, p. 10.   [198] London, 1620.
[199] Published in London under the pseudonym Francis Mildapet of Navarre.
[200] *De duplici methodo libri duo, unicam P. Rami methodum refutantes*, London, 1580.

in further works, may be gauged by the impressive collection of Ramist works in Trinity College, Dublin, of which Temple became fourth provost.

Greaves, Jonson, Hume, Gill, Butler

These controversies may seem to have little to do with grammatical theory, but in the 'art' of grammar too, practitioners were eager to apply Ramus' single method. As in Germany however, Ramist linguistic theory in the pure state found few adherents. The only two grammars which attempt to apply it unalloyed to the structure of English, widely separated in date, are Paul Greaves' *Grammatica Anglicana* of 1594 and the dramatist Ben Jonson's *English Grammar* of 1640, which is however prior to 1623 in date of composition. It is fascinating to speculate on whether V. Salmon[201] is right in suggesting that if the example of these two authors had been followed, a structuralist approach to the description of the vernacular would have arisen centuries earlier than it did. Speculation is however futile, for after Greaves and Jonson there were no more attempts to apply unadulterated Ramist theory to the grammar of English. Those works showing Ramist influence resemble their German counterparts in effecting a compromise in which elements of Ramus' system are incorporated into a more traditional, semantic approach. Such works are Alexander Hume's *Of the Orthographie and Congruitie of the Britan Tongue* (c. 1617), Alexander Gill's *Logonomia Anglica* (1619), and Charles Butler's *English Grammar* (1633). All five of the grammars listed above take of course as their basis Ramus' Latin grammar, an English translation of which appeared in London and Cambridge in 1585.[202]

Greaves' *Grammatica Anglicana* (1594) claims in its title[203] to be based on Ramus' single method, and to present a description of English chiefly in so far as it differs from Latin. The two claims are

[201] 'James Shirley and Some Problems of Seventeenth-Century Grammar', p. 269.
[202] *The Latine Grammar of P. Ramus, translated into English*, London, 1585. The Cambridge edition of the same year, with the same title, is more or less identical.
[203] *Grammatica Anglicana, praecipue quatenus a Latina differt, ad unicam P. Rami methodum concinnata... Authore P.G.*, Cambridge, 1594. The only extant copy is in the British Library. There is some dispute as to what the initials *P.G.* stand for. Joseph Ames' *Typographical Antiquities* (1790) gives the author's name as 'Paul Graves', and in this he is followed by O. Funke, *Grammatica Anglicana von P. Gr. (1594)* (= *Wiener Beiträge zur englischen Philologie*, LX), 1938. R. C. Alston, *A Bibliography of the English Language*, I, 2, item 2, opts for 'Greaves'. See also G. Scheurweghs, 'Problems of English Grammar: The Grammatica Anglicana of Paul Greaves (1594)', *English Studies*, LX (1959), pp. 135–6.

mutually exclusive, for a system based on purely morphological criteria cannot well be applied to a language such as English, in which grammatical relationships that in Latin are indicated by formal congruence are expressed syntactically. As for Ben Jonson's *English Grammar*, though published in 1640 it was probably completed by 1623 or earlier.[204] Its chief source is Ramus' *Grammatica Latina*, in the Paris edition of 1572, and he probably also used the *Scholae grammaticae*.[205] It in turn, as in the case of Greaves, represents an attempt to accommodate English structure to a formally based theory designed for Latin, an attempt accompanied by Ramus-inspired protestations as to the sovereignty of usage, but also by a curious and deliberate archaism in the examples chosen as illustrations. He succeeds no more than Greaves in resolving the problem of the application of Ramist theory to an analytical language, and his grammar still labours, like those of his non-Ramist predecessors, under a too close identification of English structures with those of Latin. Since he and Greaves are both very closely dependent on Ramus' *Grammatica Latina* they will be treated together here, as jointly representing English vernacular grammatical theory's only excursion into pure Ramism.[206] A major difference between them is that whereas Greaves' grammar exudes a bare formalism, with few definitions, Jonson mingles his Ramist preoccupations with an emphasis on usage and the spoken word. His preface is at once a claim that English is a fit tongue to be learnt by foreigners, a plea that it be considered the equal of other languages in copiousness and

[204] The original MS was destroyed by fire in 1623. The 1692 revision of the 1640 edition, long unknown to or ignored by Jonson's editors, is first referred to in C. H. Herford and P. Simpson's *Ben Jonson*, Oxford, 1925, which gives the 1640 edition in vol. II (pp. 416–35), with accompanying notes in vol. XI (pp. 165–210). The Lanston Monotype Corporation's facsimile (1928), ed. S. Gibson, gives the text of the 1640 edition together with variants from that of 1692, omitting however the Latin notes accompanying Jonson's first four chapters. A detailed comparison having shown that these variants do not affect essentials, I have used the version of the grammar as it stands in the 1640 folio edition of Jonson's works (*The Workes of Ben Jonson*, London, 1640–1), in which it occupies pp. 31–84 of a separately paginated section in vol. II. There is an edition by A. V. Waite (New York, 1909) and a Scholar Press facsimile (Menston, 1972).

[205] In the Basle edition of 1578. Herford and Simpson note that Jonson's library contained an edition of Lily's *De octo orationis partium constructione libellus* (London, 1540) and a Leipzig edition (1556) of Linacre's *De emendata structura Latini sermonis* of 1524. He must also have known J. C. Scaliger's *De causis linguae Latinae* (1540), which he mentions in the Latin notes to his grammar. The Latin grammarians he cites all seem to be taken from the pages of Ramus and Scaliger. (See Herford and Simpson, *Ben Jonson*, I, 271, and XI, 165.)

[206] Inevitably, certain of the conclusions arrived at here will be similar to some of those in O. Funke's study, 'Ben Jonsons *English Grammar* (1640)', *Anglia*, LXIV (1940), pp. 117–34.

elegance, and a short statement of Ramist and Baconian principles:
'Experience breedeth Art: Lacke of Experience Chance. Experience,
Observation, Sense, Induction, are the fower Tryers of Arts...In
Grammer, not so much the Invention, as the Disposition is to be
commended.' It is easy to recognize here Ramus' 'experientia artem
genuit', which is reflected in Jonson's professed intention to base his
description on 'observation of the English language now spoken, and
in use'.[207] In Jonson's discussion, the parallels with Ramus are close,
showing that he must have read carefully both Ramus' *Grammatica*
and his *Scholae*. His treatment of orthography and prosody as 'diffus'd
like the blood, and spirits through the whole' is directly inspired by
the *Scholae*,[208] and the banning of prosody in particular from
grammar means the amputation from it of an important rhetorical
element. Equally taken from Ramus, and perpetuating a long
tradition of word-based grammar, is the statement that single words
must by their very nature be treated prior to any syntactic
discussion.[209] Both Jonson and Greaves follow Ramus in making the
formal indication of grammatical accidents the sole criterion in
classifying the parts of speech. They accordingly repeat Ramus'
distinction of *voces numeri* and *voces sine numero*, rendered by Jonson as
'words of number' and 'words without number'. In this they differ
sharply from the rest of the English vernacular tradition, which
follows ancient and humanist practice in giving first a largely
semasiological definition of a particular word-class, and then a
separate treatment of its accidents. The prior treatment, in Ramist
fashion, of 'common affections' of word-classes, means in turn that
Jonson discusses derivation and composition at the outset.[210]

The interest of Greaves' and Jonson's grammars lies in the extent
to which, while accommodating vernacular structure to a method of

[207] *English Grammar*, title page.
[208] Ramus, *Scholae grammaticae*, col. 12: 'Prosodia autem et orthographia per totam grammaticam, ut sanguis et spiritus per universum corpus, fusae sunt.' This dictum is traceable to J. C. Scaliger. In contradiction of it, Jonson does in fact preface his grammar with a section on 'letters and their powers' and syllables.
[209] Jonson gives no acknowledgment, but his marginal note in Latin (*English Grammar*, p. 34: 'dictionis natura prior est, posterior orationis') is taken from Ramus' *Scholae grammaticae* (col. 7).
[210] Though Jonson repeats Ramus' four-part system of noun, verb, adverb and conjunction, his grammar contains a curious insertion, with no organic connection with the rest of the material, ascribing to English the traditional eight parts of speech of 'the Latines' plus the article as a ninth. It is perhaps part of an earlier version of the grammar included by Jonson's posthumous editor. Later in the work the article is included among the pronouns.

analysis devised for a different type of language, they are none the less able to cater for idiosyncrasies of English usage. Here, their omissions are sometimes more significant than what they actually say. Greaves for instance, while defining nouns as 'words of number' (*voces numeri*), refrains from adding Ramus' 'with gender and case', simply noting that English nouns usually form their plural in -*s*. Formally unmarked plurals such as *sheep* and *swine* can be conveniently accounted for by labelling them 'infinita numero', pressing into service the term reserved by Ramus for Latin invariable nouns such as *nequam* ('an injury'). Some words (*bowels*, *scissors*) must be treated as only occurring in the plural, others (*goodness*, *agility*) as being always singular. Greaves' list of uncountable nouns such as *cider* and *wheat* is however, in a departure from Ramist requirements, justified in semantic terms. Jonson, in contrast, ascribes both case and gender to English nouns. By 'declension' however he means formal derivation, though not all derived forms are covered by the term, diminution for instance being treated as a 'common affection' expressed in substantives by the endings -*ell*, -*et*, -*ock* and -*ing*, and in adjectives by the termination -*ish*. Where he particularly diverges from Ramus is in setting up a semantically based division of nouns into common, proper and personal, a procedure doubly foreign to Ramus' system, for it introduces a non-formal criterion based on the ancient distinction of *qualitas* in the noun,[211] and at the same time makes 'person' a nominal distinction (intended to apply to pronouns as a noun sub-class), whereas for Ramus it is one of the 'special differences' of verbs distinguishing them from nouns. Jonson appears in fact to have taken over this section from Gill,[212] with no thought as to how it squares with the Ramist system.

Another stumbling-block presented by English syntax lies in the fact that English adjectives do not show agreement in number or gender with their substantives. Greaves pointedly leaves out Ramus' reference to gender marking as a means of distinguishing substantive from adjective, but he can only get round the number problem by stating that adjectives have number 'by virtue of their substantives'.[213] This view implies either treating number as a solely semantic concept

---

[211] On this distinction see Padley, *Grammatical Theory* (1976), p. 37.
[212] *Logonomia Anglica*, London, 1619 and 1621.
[213] 'Distinctio numeri nulla est [in adjectivis], nisi gratia substantivi.'

that can inhere in a part of speech without corresponding formal marks to consignify it, or holding that a word possesses certain grammatical features simply because it is constructed with another word that *is* formally marked for them. It is a non-Ramist procedure which the citing of *many* and *all* as plurals of *much* and *every* does little to alleviate. Jonson adroitly side-steps the issue by introducing a *word of number infinite* 'that varieth not'[214] (Ramus' class of *infinita*) and applying it to adjectives and present participles. The effect is however spoilt by his retention of Ramus' distinction between substantives 'of one only Gender, or (at the most) of two', and adjectives 'of three genders'. Since the adjective is however 'always infinite', i.e. invariable, Jonson is obviously, in a treatment similar to Greaves' treatment of number, regarding gender as a semantic category attributable to a word simply because it is in (formally unmarked) construction with another word. Were it not for the influence of the formally congruent Latin model, no doubt it would never have occurred to grammarians to attribute gender to the invariable English adjective.[215]

The non-existence of gender as a category of the English noun is by no means obvious to grammarians at this date. In Latin and French the various semantic criteria that are applied are cross-cut by formal ones, but in English the only possible classification is on the lexical basis of the indication of sex. Though Jonson often repeats Gill verbatim, following for instance his definition of the masculine gender as that which 'comprehendeth all Males, or what is understood under a Masculine Species',[216] he further complicates matters by applying to English the full six-gender system of Latin.[217] The semantically determined examples, also taken from Gill, presuppose that the genders of Latin nouns will be faithfully repeated in English, names of islands, countries and cities being feminine, and names of stars masculine. Ramus' formal criterion of syntactic congruence with *hoc* being inapplicable to English, the neuter is defined as indicating inanimate things and named, in an obvious translation of Ramus' *fictum genus*, the 'feined gender'. Jonson's 'promiscuous or

---

[214] Ramus' '[vox] quae non adsignificat' (*Grammatica*, p. 14).

[215] Some humanist grammarians (e.g. Sanctius) were aware that if the formal syntactic agreement did not exist in Latin, the question of adjectival gender would not arise there either.

[216] Cf. Gill, *Logonomia Anglica*, 1621, p. 40

[217] Masculine, feminine, neuter, common, promiscuous or epicene, doubtful.

epicene' gender, 'which understands both kindes...as, when we call them *Horses*, and *Dogges*, in the masculine, though there be *Bitches*, and *Mares* amongst them', is inspired by Latin practice, as is his 'common or doubtful' gender, described as occurring 'with some elegance' in the words *friend* and *enemy*. If Jonson is here obliged to fall back on the traditional Latin scheme, it is no doubt because English lacks formal gender-markers on which to base a Ramist classification. In contrast, the treatment of case is more in accordance with Ramist principles, being based on strictly formal criteria. Only two cases are prescribed for English, an 'absolute' catering for unmarked forms and a 'genitive' in -s,[218] a treatment recalling the *rect* and *oblique* cases of Charles Butler's *English Grammar* of 1633.

Having no Ramist model to follow in treating the articles, Jonson again looks to Gill for a lead, defining the 'finite' article *the* on syntactic criteria as appearing before common nouns but not proper ones, and the 'infinite' article *a/an* in semantic fashion as having 'a power of declaring, and designing uncertaine, or infinite things'. Though he defines them as 'in gender, and number infinite' (an echo of Ramus' *voces numeri infinitae*), he counts them as pronouns. Greaves similarly, in an attempt to stay within Ramus' four-word-class system, treats the articles as adjectives together with the numerals, called by Ramus *adjectiva infinita numeri*. He also follows Ramus in classifying pronouns as types of nouns, though since English pronouns show 'case' distinctions he is obliged to treat them as anomalous. Here, in attributing case to the pronoun but denying it to the noun, he is in striking contrast to the overwhelming majority of English vernacular grammarians. Even in the pronoun he recognizes only two cases, 'rectus' (nominative) and 'obliquus' (accusative), and hence he is at a loss to find an appropriate slot for the form *whose*, which is not the genitive of *who* in his system, any more than *his* is the genitive of *he*. With Jonson too it is the accusative, not as in nouns the genitive, that constitutes the second term of his two-case system, and he similarly treats the pronoun as an 'irregular Noune, varying from the generall precepts'. The description of the interrogative pronoun *who* (only *which* is given as a relative) as 'taken for a

---

[218] Jonson's first declension contains those nouns with plural in -*s* and no separate formally marked genitive plural. His second contains nouns with plural in -*en* which do have a separate genitive plural. The forms *houses/housen*, *eyes/eyen* and *shooes/shooen* figure in both declensions. Nouns with a mutated vowel or diphthong in the plural are treated as irregular members of the first declension.

Substantive' rests perhaps on the fact that it possesses a genitive case, though it coincides (fortuitously?) with Priscian's treatment of *quis* as signifying substance. The interrogatives *what* and *whether* are described as 'infinite [i.e. invariable] and adjectively used'.

The English noun, according to Jonson 'in easinesse, and short-nesse, much to be preferred before the Latines, and the Grecians', offers for that very reason little to facilitate a grammatical treatment according to Ramist morphological criteria. With the verb too, Ramist terminology has to be strained if it is to be accommodated to English. Both Greaves and Jonson faithfully repeat Ramus' definition of the verb as a word of number varied for tense and person, but Greaves at once qualifies this by noting that the plural of the English verb is identical with the first person singular. He also omits the whole question of mood, setting up no subjunctive or optative forms, and treating the imperative (*hate thou*) as a first future. The ablaut and zero past forms are catered for by a division into 'simple forms' (*writed*), 'contracted forms' (*writ*), 'anomalous forms' (*wrote*) and 'simply anomalous forms' (*cast*). Ramus had treated the present tenses as *infecta* or incompletive and classified the past into both incompletive and completive (*perfecta*). There are traces of this Varronian treatment in Greaves, but the distinction seems to mean little to him, for he uses the term *perfectum* to refer not only to 'I have been hated', but also to 'I was hated'. Jonson, who similarly omits all reference to mood and follows Ramus in relegating compound tenses to the syntax, makes a more serious attempt to set up an aspectual division. His 'three only tymes' of the verb, all of 'imperfect' aspect and confined to those Latin forms in Ramus' system that are not represented in English by compound tenses, is as follows:

present	past	future
amo	*amabam*	*ama, amato*
I love	I loved[219]	love[220]

Since Ramus' first future (*amabo*) is represented in English by a compound tense, it is accordingly missing from this table, his second future (the traditional imperative) being alone retained. All other

---

[219] Jonson gives *loved* as the counterpart of *amabam*, without realizing that it equally translates *amavi* in non-perfective use. No more than Varro and Ramus has he understood that *amavi* should occupy a slot in both the completive and the incompletive series.

[220] Cf. the comparative tables of Ramus' and Jonson's verb paradigms in O. Funke, 'Ben Jonsons *English Grammar* (*1640*)', p. 131.

tenses are 'expressed by a Syntaxe' and therefore treated under verbal construction later in the grammar. The absence of formal symmetry in the English verbal system is a source of regret to Jonson, minimizing as it does the application of the Ramist formal criterion of person. The disappearance of earlier plural forms (e.g. *we loven*) is 'a great blemish', marring the symmetry of time and person as 'the right and left hand of a Verbe', and bringing 'a lamenesse to the whole body' of English structure.[221] Jonson's definition of person as 'the speciall difference of a verball number' (Ramus' *specialis terminatio verbi*) finds little scope when applied to English verbs. They require indeed 'the stampe of some good Logick, to beat them into proportion', and it took 'much painful churning' on Jonson's part before he finally arrived at a system of conjugations.[222]

Having followed Ramus' example in excluding mood from the verbal system, Jonson has the problem of explaining away certain forms, such as the subjunctive in *It is preposterous to execute a man before he have beene condemned*, in which *have* is treated as a plural exceptionally following a singular subject. The compound tenses are treated as phenomena of government, the second element in e.g. *I have loved* being governed by the first. With *I may love* ('amem'), *I might love* ('amarem'), *I shall have loved* ('amavero', correctly described as an amalgam of future and past, a fact few earlier grammarians apart from Linacre had perceived), and *I might have loved* ('amaverim' and 'amavissem'), Jonson produces a system of English tenses corresponding to all points to Ramus' Latin one. His close dependence on this classification, though to some extent masked by the relegation of compound tenses to the syntax, is evident.

In the treatment of the formally unmarked word-classes or 'words without number' Greaves and Jonson follow Ramus closely, Jonson's definition of the adverb – 'as it were an Adjective of Nounes, Verbes; yea, and Adverbs also themselves'[223] – contrasting with the com-

---

[221] *English Grammar*, p. 62.

[222] Jonson's first conjugation groups verbs whose past tense ends in *-ed* or *-t*; his second contains those that form their past by a change of 'letters', whether vowels or consonants; the verbs of the third class (e.g. *found*) have a 'change of Dipthongs'; and those of the fourth (e.g. *can, sell*) show both vowel change and the addition of a dental suffix. This represents a distinct advance on Gill's system. It should be borne in mind that some verbs in Jonson's third conjugation which do not now show diphthongs (e.g. *fall* and *hold*) did in fact have them in early-seventeenth-century English. The absence of a clear distinction between letter and sound is however confusing.

[223] Cf. Ramus, *Grammatica*, p. 74: 'tanquam adiectivum nominum, verborum, adverbiorum etiam ipsorum'.

monly held view of it as modifying verbs only. With the conjunction, too, his elaborately set out semantic dichotomies are precisely those of Ramus. In the syntactic section it is significant, in view of the fact that the vernacular languages were held to have no true syntax, that Greaves' discussion is, compared with the extensive treatment in Ramus' Latin grammar, very thin. Having rightly banned case from nouns, he can have no government or *rectio* based on it, and the lack of formal marks of syntactic agreement in English means that he can only with difficulty demonstrate concord or *convenientia*. He makes one or two attempts to indicate the importance of word order (the adjective precedes the noun – *a yoked swine is a terrible beast*), but on the whole he is reduced to presenting snippets of usage arranged according to word-classes. More important is his recognition of English prepositional structures as the equivalent of Latin case distinctions ('quasi casuum discrimina'), and there is a present-day structuralist air to his substitution procedures, in which for example the syntactic slots in which the word *a* can appear are not identical with those in which the word *one* can appear. *Then straight one fet* [*fetched*] *the prisoner* is a possible English construction, **Then straight a fet the prisoner* is not. Jonson, determined to demonstrate gender agreement in nouns, manages to do it (since pronouns are types of noun) by pointing to the collocation of *Esau* with a following *he*, of *Jesabel* with *she*, and of *an idol* with *it*, though the argument loses some of its force when *it* is also allowed to substitute for *he* and *she*. Semasiological features quite foreign to a formalist approach survive however from the traditional Latin syntaxes, though Jonson does draw attention to analytical features of English such as the use of *than* in the comparative, in contrast to the synthetic Latin and Greek, which have no 'signe going betweene' the two terms of comparative and superlative constructions. Double comparatives and superlatives (*the more readier, the most basest*) are praised as 'a certaine kind of English Atticisme...imitating the manner of the ancientest, and finest Grecians'.[224] His syntax is less dependent on Ramus than his morphology, perhaps inevitably, given the analytical character of English. Like Greaves, in the absence of a model to follow, he can often only confine himself to retailing titbits of usage and pointing out items of word order. Important however is his remark that the whole 'rection' or government of Latin grammar is 'neere-hand

[224] *English Grammar*, p. 77.

declared' by the English prepositions.[225] The Ramist base-lines, as indeed in Ramus' own *Grammatica Latina*, are less readily perceptible in the syntactic sections of Jonson's grammar than in the 'etymology' or accidence. His dilemma lies in the fact that though inflection was generally regarded as the appropriate method of indicating grammatical relationships, it is precisely to the analytical vernaculars, and more especially to English, that Ramus' formal system designed for an inflected language is least applicable. Jonson and Greaves' dependence on Ramus is too close, and their attempt to apply to English a system which has to be strained (as by the introduction of a category of invariable *voces infinitae*) even to fit the facts of a highly synthetic language such as Latin, does not produce a linguistic description appropriate to the vernacular.[226]

Grammarians of English did not, apart from Jonson, follow the lead given by Greaves.[227] The only other English grammar of the period conceived wholly in formal terms is not based on Ramist principles, but owes its inspiration to two sources: Lily's Latin grammar,[228] and a thoroughly contemporary pedagogical impetus. This work, John Hewes' *Perfect Survey of the English Tongue* (1624) is not so much a survey of English as an exposition of Lily's rules designed to facilitate the translation of English into Latin. It is a study

---

[225] *Ibid.*, p. 81.

[226] Of Thomas Tomkis' 'De analogia Anglicani sermonis liber grammaticus' of 1612 (British Library MS 12 Reg. F. xviii, ff. 1–15), Michael (*English Grammatical Categories*, p. 549) says: 'The relation between Tomkis's grammar and Ben Jonson's needs investigation. In many places Tomkis's Latin exactly corresponds to Jonson's English. This cannot arise from a common source, such as Ramus, because the correspondence is particularly close in the section on the articles...No common English source suggests itself, and the question is roused [*sic*, for "raised"?] whether Tomkis saw the first, and full, form of Jonson's grammar, or whether Jonson saw Tomkis's.' It may be noted that, since Ramus' Latin grammar does not provide a model for the treatment of articles, it is precisely here that either author might be tempted to plagiarize another English one. John Evelyn's manuscript 'English Grammer' of *c.* 1650 (British Library Add. MS 15950, ff. 94–8) expressly claims to have 'wholly followed B. Jonson, who hath taken singular paynes to Methodize our Language'. Where these grammars do in fact coincide with Jonson's is in the examples used. The Ramist content of both these slight works is nil.

[227] The only author who shows even traces of having been influenced by Greaves is Henry Hexham, whose grammar of English appears as an appendix to his *English and Netherduytch Dictionarie* (Rotterdam, 1648). It is difficult to see why Poldauf ('On the History of Some Problems of English Grammar before 1800', p. 61) includes him among Ramist grammarians as a 'slavish follower' of Greaves. He follows Greaves here and there, as in the ordering of the pronouns, but his grammar is emphatically not a Ramist one. If there *is* a direct influence on Hexham's somewhat clumsy and amateurish grammar, it is that of Lily, and possibly beyond him Linacre.

[228] On this work, of cardinal importance for several centuries of English grammatical endeavours, see Padley, *Grammatical Theory* (1976), pp. 24–7.

of the vernacular as it may 'best conduce or accord with the Latines', whose reliance on 'the termination of their wordes' is stressed. Hewes shares the growing contemporary belief, expressed in Ascham's *Scholemaster*, that a sound training in the vernacular is a necessary preliminary to classical studies. His aim is accordingly not an independent examination of English structure, but the easing of the path to Latin. The absence of semasiological definition in his grammar is striking, but there is an equal absence of Ramist features. If Hewes too is to be regarded as an early 'structuralist', it is not by design. He has stumbled upon his formal approach while in search of a pedagogical method. Composed about the same time as Jonson's grammar, the *Perfect Survey* derives its formal approach from Lily's theory of signs rather than from Ramus. Lily's signs themselves were as much a pedagogical device as a means of linguistic description. He teaches for instance that the genitive case may be known 'by this token *Of*', but such indications are intended as aids to the student in deciding what particular Latin case to use in translations, rather than as analyses of English structure. They constitute no proof that Lily was to any notable extent aware of the analytical character of English as opposed to Latin. Similar aids are the recognition of an English infinitive by means of its preceding sign *to*, and of a potential mood in the verb by the preceding 'tokens' *may* and *can*, etc.[229] Following Lily's example, Hewes treats such words, 'which the Latine Dialect doth not expresse at all', as *signs* a knowledge of which is indispensable to the translator. The description of the vernacular that emerges from his procedures is a kind of mirror image of the language as applied to the translation of Latin. His purely formal approach is well illustrated by his treatment of substantive and adjective, avoiding both the customary semantic definitions, and the pitfalls of Ramus' description in terms of gender marking. The substantive is that word which may be preceded by *a* or *the*, and the adjective is defined solely in syntactic terms as collocable with the words *man* or *thing*.[230] Prepositional phrases are treated as case equivalents, in precisely the same way as in the early Italian vernacular grammars, which see prepositions as *segni de' casi*. Verbal mood is retained, but defined in terms of each individual mood's preceding 'signs'. Thus the potential mood, as in Lily's Latin

[229] W. Lily, *A Short Introduction of Grammar*, London, 1557, pp. 17–18.
[230] These definitions are present in Melanchthon.

grammar, is known by its signs *may*, *might*, *would* or *should*. Lists are established of English conjunctions similar in meaning to those introducing subjunctive clauses in Latin, and then the verbs accompanying them in English utterances are in turn assumed to be in the subjunctive. The indicative, having no preceding sign, must however be defined semantically in terms of the indication of an affirmation or a denial.[231] Similarly, while the present tense is 'best known by the time', all other tenses are described solely in terms of their signs. Curiously the signs, as in Bullokar's *Bref Grammar for English* (1586), seem not to form an integral part of the tenses they indicate. The existence of unitary tense forms in Latin creates a strong presupposition that English will have them too, the first element of a compound tense having merely a marking function. It is also evident, since *did* and *was* are signs of both perfect and imperfect, that Hewes has primarily in mind the second element and the Latin tense that is its equivalent. Noteworthy is his treatment of the traditional three concords of Latin grammar[232] in terms of word order rather than formal congruence, the nominative subject for example being that substantive which precedes the verb.[233]

The authors of the other three grammars considered in this section – Alexander Hume's *Of the Orthographie and Congruitie of the Britan Tongue* (*c.* 1617), Alexander Gill's *Logonomia Anglica* (1619) and Charles Butler's *English Grammar* (1633) – are much less willing than Greaves, Jonson and Hewes to dispense with the semantic criteria of the long-established Latin grammatical tradition.[234] Already the author of two Latin grammars and a grammatical commentary,[235] Hume shows in his grammar of English a marked avoidance of technical terms. It is not his work but that of Gill, Mulcaster's successor as High

---

[231] J. Hewes, *A Perfect Survey of the English Tongue, Taken According to the Use and Analogie of the Latine*, London [1624], p. 16.

[232] The agreement of adjective with substantive, of relative pronoun with antecedent, and of nominative subject with verb.

[233] *A Perfect Survey*, pp. 20–31.

[234] Hume's grammar did not appear in printed form until H. B. Wheatley's edition, *Of the Orthographie and Congruitie of the Britan Tongue; A Treates, noe shorter then necessarie, for the Schooles*, Early English Text Society, v, London, 1865. It is thought to have been written shortly after the visit of James I (James VI of Scotland) to Edinburgh in 1617, and is thus contemporary in composition with Ben Jonson's grammar. Of its thirty-four pages, only 27–34 contain strictly grammatical material.

[235] The grammars are Hume's *Prima elementa grammaticae* and his *Grammatica nova...ad methodum revocata*, both published in 1612. The commentary, *Schola grammatica*, is bound in the same volume with the *Grammatica nova*.

Master of St Paul's School, that constitutes the first really thorough grammar of the vernacular.[236] The fact that it is written in Latin may seem curious, but it should be remembered that the native tongue was not taught in the grammar schools, which existed to teach the Latin language. Further, any foreigner wishing to familiarize himself with English – and Gill's grammar is addressed in part to the foreign learner – would naturally approach it via his own tongue or via Latin. The language of learning was Latin, works written in the vernacular tending either to remain unprinted, or to stay out of print for a long time.[237] Gill was a Cambridge man, and his work forms part of the puritan stream that ran so strongly at Cambridge and was open to Ramist influence. The interest of his grammar is cultural rather than theoretical, his somewhat confused mixture of acknowledged sources giving an indication of the reading of a cultivated man of his time. Grammatically his sources are unusually varied, mingling philosophical elements with the Latin tradition both ancient and humanist, and traces of Greek and Hebrew theory with Ramist trends. His work is much more important than Hume's – which being unprinted remained without influence – its wide cultural basis linking it with the main intellectual currents of the period. It far exceeds the narrow bounds of Ramist formalism, being provided with a historical introduction (complete with specimen of Old English), a prosody, and a syntax of much greater length than those of previous grammars of the vernacular. Taken all together, these various elements constitute the most comprehensive early grammar of English. Declaring the English language to be no less elegant and ornate, no less suited to set forth the thoughts of the mind, than any other tongue, he takes pains to compare it with Latin, Greek, Hebrew, and other vernaculars, stressing those features that are peculiar to it.[238] The title of the work, *Logonomia*, is revealing, indicating what Gill calls a 'comprehensio regularum', a set of rules applicable to any

[236] Gill, *Logonomia Anglica*, 1619. As the Bodleian Library copy of this rare edition, containing Gill's MS corrections, was unavailable at the time the notes for this study were compiled, I have used the second edition of 1621. The two editions do not greatly differ, the changes having to do with phonology and Gill's proposed system of orthography. The Scolar Press edition (Menston, 1968) reproduces the Folger Shakespeare Library's copy of the edition of 1621.

[237] Hume's *Orthographie and Congruitie* was not printed until centuries after his death, Mulcaster's *Elementarie* (1582) did not again appear before 1925, and Ben Jonson's grammar never saw schoolroom use.

[238] *Logonomia*, dedicatory foreword: '[Lingua] Anglica suos habet idiotismos, qui Latine vix aut omnino reddi non possunt.'

language. In this sense his work constitutes an incipient universal grammar. Its structure however, particularly in the syntax – whose division into 'simple' and 'schematistic' (i.e. covering the figures of speech) doubtless owes something both to Linacre and to Sir Thomas Wilson's *Art of Rhetorique* (1533) – has little to differentiate it from early humanist grammars of Latin. Gill's interest in historical linguistics and orthographical reform, together with his cultural background, add breadth to his work, but his compromise between Ramist formalism and the humanist tradition, with a veneer of Aristotelianism, is not really appropriate to the description of the vernacular.

The third grammarian to show a mixed semasiological–formal approach, Charles Butler, was Oxford's leading Ramist and the author of rhetoric textbooks for schools.[239] It should not be forgotten that Ramism in Britain was above all a rhetorical movement, even the Ramist logics published there having a rhetorical bias. As Joseph Webbe remarks in his *Appeale to Truth* (1622) 'Grammar hindreth the elegancie of speech,' and the strict maintenance of rhetoric in its own compartment seems not to have been to English taste. Butler's grammar[240] is of the same orthoepic kind as Hume's, the actual grammatical material being similarly meagre, and being treated under the heading 'Of Words'. Also as with Hume there is no syntax, Ramist influence occurring chiefly in the classification of the parts of speech, mingled with the traditional humanist semantic approach and a use of Lily's system of 'signs'. Though Butler has the unusual merit, for his date, of realizing that English is 'a dialect of the Teutonick', he gives Hebrew the customary pride of place as 'the language of our great Grandfather Adam, which, untill the Confusion, all people of the earth did speake'. Apart however from 'divers dialects, which time hath caused', the 'Teutonick' language is assumed to have continued virtually unaltered since Babel. As in other grammars of the period, the patriotic motive is well to the fore: 'The Excellencie of a Language…doeth consist chiefly in three

[239] Butler edited the Ramus–Talon rhetoric, *Rameae rhetoricae libri duo*, for school use in 1597. It went through six editions by 1629.

[240] *The English Grammar, or the Institution of Letters, Syllables, and Words, in the English Tongue*, Oxford, 1633. On some points more specifically connected with the internal history of the development of English vernacular grammar, see V. Salmon, 'Wh- and Yes/No Questions: Charles Butler's *Grammar* (1633) and the History of a Linguistic Concept', *Language Form and Linguistic Variation. Papers dedicated to Angus McIntosh*, ed. J. Anderson (*Current Issues in Linguistic Theory*, xv), Amsterdam, 1982, pp. 401–26.

things, Antiquitie, Copious Elegancie, and Generalitie: for the first
the Hebrew, for the second the Greeke, for the third the Latine, for
all the English is worthily honoured.'[241]

The 'mixed' grammarians are much closer than either Greaves or
Jonson to the traditional approach of ancient and humanist Latin
grammar, in spite of Hume's claim in his *Schola grammatica* to have
reduced grammar to its Ramist dimensions, dismissing prosody to
rhetoric.[242] Of the two parts *etymologia* and *syntaxis* of his Latin
grammars however, only the former is repeated in his vernacular one,
which consists only of an orthographical section followed by a
morphological treatment of the 'congruitie of our Britan tongue'.
Gill retains the four humanist divisions of orthography (called
'grammatica', thus restoring to grammar its earlier meaning of
written characters), *etymologia*, syntax and prosody while Butler, like
Hume providing no syntax, divides grammar into letters,[243] syllables,
words and 'words' adjuncts' (i.e. accent and punctuation).

Ramist theory requires that what is common to two or more
word-classes be treated at the outset. Both Gill and Butler accordingly
begin their grammar with a discussion of derivation as a feature of
words in general. Though Gill has some notion of historical
derivation – he thinks *fish* may be derived from Latin *piscis* – he uses
the term 'derivative' in its synchronic sense as applying to suffixal
variation. Having however made the customary synchronic division
of words into primary and derived, he imposes on the latter a further
diachronic one of native words ('nostratia') and loanwords
('peregrina'). There is accordingly a curious confusion of synchronic
elements defined formally in terms of suffixes, and a muddled
diachronic theory. Comparison and diminution are treated here, the
former expressible both by the 'signs' *more* and *most*, and by formal
variation (*-er*, *-est*). Diminution is similarly expressed either by the
'particle' *tiny*, or by such endings as *-kin*. Also treated in this section
are affective devices such as emphasis by syllable stress or by
repetition (*an old old man*). Again, the pedagogically orientated 'sign'
theory contained in the Colet–Lily Latin grammar is pressed into
service to provide the analytical components of English with a formal
description assimilable to the Ramist one covering morphological

---

[241] *The English Grammar*, foreword.

[242] *Schola grammatica*, p. 1: 'Grammatica ex Ramo definio...Quartem partem ad Rhetoricam
rejicio.' In his Latin grammars Hume treats syllables under 'etymologia'.

[243] I have made no attempt to follow Butler's orthographical system closely.

endings. With Ramus this use of 'signs' did not extend beyond an application to gender, of which *hic*, *haec* and *hoc* can be treated as markers. Given this modification of the Ramist approach, Gill can hold that in English word variation is effected either by signs or by endings.[244] Butler's similar initial treatment of derivation has Varronian features. To 'original' words (which may be primitive, simple or 'rect') he opposes 'deduced' ones (which may be derivative, compound or 'oblique'). Here, as with Varro, suffixal derivation and formal variation for case are on the same footing. This fact, together with the extension of the term 'case' ('rect' and 'oblique') to verb forms, *estranged* for example being an 'oblique' form of the 'rect' *estrange*, suggests that 'case' has for Butler a value similar to that of *ptōsis* in early Greek grammatical theory. He defines it as 'the different termination of the same word, in the same Number and Person; as *man mans*, *love loved*'. English accordingly has two cases, 'rect' and 'oblique', in both noun and verb. This analysis, which works very well when applied to agglutinative structures, is less successful, as in twentieth-century Bloomfieldian morphemic theory, when applied to amalgams such as are contained in the past tense *took*. Butler's system is meant to function only within the same number and person. *Men* is thus not a case variation but a plural, and *lovest* and *loveth* are not separate cases, but 'divers persons of the cases'.[245] This limitation as opposed to Latin, in which 'every variation in...Person is with them counted a Case', is presumably occasioned by his determiniation to restrict the 'cases' of the English verb to two, in order to retain symmetry with the noun. Case, applicable to both noun and verb, occupies in Butler's system a position similar to that occupied by number in Ramus' grammars. Both terms indicate formal variation, but Butler's term is more limited in scope.

Not far removed from Butler's view of 'case' is Hume's use of the term 'person', defined in his English grammar as 'the face of a word, quhilk [which] in diverse forms of speache it diverselie puts on'.[246] Seen in this way 'person' is simply another name for formal

---

[244] *Logomia Anglica*, p. 52. Vorlat, *English Grammatical Theory*, is mistaken in stating that Hume and Gill 'invent the sign-theory'. Its origins are of course in Latin grammars, in Colet and Lily or even, much earlier, Nebrija.

[245] *English Grammar*, p. 32.

[246] *Of the Orthographie and Congruitie of the Britan Tongue*, Wheatley, p. 27. Cf. the definition of person in Hume's *Grammatica nova*, p. 6, as a 'subsistentia rei voce notata'. In Ramus' system, person has the status of a 'special difference' of the verb, and is refused to noun and pronoun. For a treatment of Hume's Latin grammars see Padley, *Grammatical Theory* (1976), pp. 111–17.

variation, identical with Ramus' category of 'number'. Hume's employment of the word 'face' recalls Sanctius' and J. C. Scaliger's similar use of the Latin term 'facies' (no doubt translating Greek *prosopon*), and Linacre's use of 'prosopice' for that part of syntax he treats in medieval fashion in terms of transitive and intransitive 'personae'.[247] Hume's description of the indeclinable parts of speech as 'impersonal' (i.e. formally invariable) is an echo of Linacre's treatment, and in both authors it runs parallel to an Aristotelian treatment of these word-classes as semantically subordinate to the major classes. Linacre is indeed named by Hume in his *Grammatica nova* as 'first among grammarians' and his chief model.[248] In spite of this praise however, all previous grammarians, Linacre included, are found wanting in some respect or other. Ramus himself, 'whose method had penetrated into the schools', is censured, after Hume's perusal of both his Latin grammar and his *Scholae*, for having produced not so much a grammar as a logic. The result of ten years' reading and reflection was finally an eclectic grammar, bringing together elements from Linacre, Ramus and other sources. As for Gill's division of the word-classes, it is at first sight the Aristotelian grouping into on the one hand noun and verb, and on the other semantically dependent classes which cannot function separately from them. Since noun and verb are distinguished from each other by the Ramist formal criterion of number, he ends up with a three-part system determined partially by meaning and partially by form, two criteria which in the pure Ramist theory are irreconcilable. That Gill ignores the aspect of grammatical consignification presented by the syntactic functions of his *voces consignificativae* or indeclinables is shown by his view that the only problem offered by them being their lexical meanings, they are the province of dictionary-makers rather than of grammarians. Particularly in English, with its relative paucity of formal endings, a slide away from grammar in the direction of lexicography is noticeable in the period under consideration.[249]

[247] Vorlat, *English Grammatical Theory*, while noting that person is for Hume 'not merely a pronominal accident, but underlies his division of the various parts of speech', does not recognize the sources of this in Linacre and Sanctius, leaving the impression that it originates with Hume himself.

[248] *Grammatica nova*, foreword: 'Linacrum grammaticorum...principem sedulo verso; illius praecepta in ordenim pro meo captu redigo.' Hume says he consulted Sulpizio, Melanchthon, Manuzio and Valla, but 'above all Linacre'.

[249] *Logonomia Anglica*, p. 67. Gill refers the indeclinable, consignifying word-classes to the 'lexicographos harum rerum'.

Vernacular grammarians were always at a loss to know whether to give the article (for which Latin offered no model) full word-class status, or to treat it as some kind of appendage of the noun. Hume's treatment ties in with his borrowing from Linacre of the ultimately medieval notion of syntactic 'person', which underlies medieval modistic grammar's treatment of government. Following this model, Hume's syntax[250] regards a noun's 'person' as determined by another substantive noun (*the king of Britan*, cf. Thomas of Erfurt's treatment[251] of *filius Socratis* – 'the son of Socrates' – as a transitive personal construction), an adjective (*the best king*) or a relative (*the king whom*). This repeats of course notions contained in Hume's *Prima elementa* (1612), which sees in *filius Socratis* a subject governed by an 'adjunct'.[252] It follows that when Hume describes the 'person' of a noun as determined or undetermined, he is not referring to any function exercised by the articles. *A* and *the* are merely 'notes' accompanying respectively already undetermined or already determined nouns, and it is in this sense that they are described as 'particles of determination'.[253] Gill is similarly unwilling to grant them full word-class status. Devoting some space to their usage[254] without developing a consistent theory, he includes them for both semantic and formal reasons with his *voces consignificativae* as 'prepositive' articles distinct from his pronominal 'relative or subjunctive' articles.

The grammarians under consideration in this section are remarkable for their readiness to combine semasiological criteria with Ramus' formal ones, particularly when peculiarities of English structure render his methods difficult to apply. There is also a reluctance to abandon well-established categories, as when Gill divides nouns into common, proper and personal (this last in order to distinguish the sub-class of pronouns) on semantic grounds quite alien to Ramus' system. With Ramus, the principal word-classes are

[250] Though Hume gives no separate syntax section, his morphology does of course, in the manner of the day, raise syntactic issues.
[251] *Grammatica speculativa* (*c.* 1310), capita xlviii,li. (Consulted in G. L. Bursill-Hall's edition, London, 1972). See the discussion in G. A. Padley, 'L'importance de Thomas Linacre (env. 1460–1524) comme source dans l'évolution des théories grammaticales en Europe au XVIe et au XVIIe siècles', *Langues et Linguistique*, Université Laval, Quebec, VIII: 2, pp. 36–9.
[252] Pp. 28–31.
[253] *Of the Orthographie and Congruitie of the Britan Tongue*, pp. 27, 32.
[254] For details see Gill's syntax (*Logonomia Anglica*, pp. 72–4) and Poldauf, 'On the History of Some Problems of English Grammar', pp. 187–8.

kept apart by distinct formal marks: in the noun those of case and gender, in the verb those of tense and person. Any modification of his scheme, whether or not in the interests of a truer account of English structure, tends to produce difficulties for its authors. Since gender is not a category of English nouns and he has extended the term 'case' to verbal endings as well as nominal ones, Butler for instance is left with only tense as the feature distinguishing verbs from nouns. Verbs and nouns are both 'words of number and case', but respectively with and without 'difference of time'.[255] Since however he regards mood and tense in English as 'not distinguished, as in Greek and Latin, by terminations', but as indicated by 'signs and supplements' added to an unmarked 'verb absolute', he cannot treat tense in quite Ramus' manner as formally marked. This semantic time-difference stems from Aristotle's view of nouns as signifying 'without time', and verbs as signifying time in addition to their lexical signification. This tradition is not uncommon in Greek grammars, and is also found in Linacre, but it is only exceptionally followed in works on the vernacular.[256] Butler then goes on to define the noun further, following Colet's definition in his section of Lily's Latin grammar, as the 'name of a thing', a description solely in terms of nomenclature which, often repeated, is an important element in the drift away from a strictly grammatical approach to a lexico-graphical one. The noun is also, on a formal level, capable of receiving an article. The adjective again is defined partly in the formal terms of preceding articles, partly in the customary seventeenth-century semantic ones of the signification of quality. It 'implyeth a quality belonging to a Substantive, without which [substantive] he cannot have *a* or *the* before him', a definition which includes the syntactic criterion that adjectives are only preceded by articles when forming part of the structure article + adjective + substantive. Thus, in the absence of Ramus' gender-marking criterion, is the Latin grammarians' formal definition of the sub-stantive as that which can receive one of the 'articles' *hic, haec* or *hoc*

---

[255] Aristotle (*De interpretatione*, 2 and 3) defines the verb as that which προσσημαίνει χρόνον, i.e. that which consignifies time or signifies it in addition. Linacre's definition of the noun as signifying 'sine ulla temporis *adsignificantia*' exactly renders the sense of προσσημαίνει. Lily perpetuates this (*A Short Introduction of Grammar*, p. 9), without however realizing that it is grammatical consignification that is at issue, not lexical signification: 'Nomen est pars orationis quae rem significat sine ulla temporis...differentia.'

[256] It is found e.g. in Theodore Gaza's Greek grammar of 1496.

somewhat tortuously applied to the facts of English structure, where an article often immediately precedes an adjective but relates syntactically to its following substantive.

Having defined the noun (which at this date and for long afterwards includes the adjective as a sub-class) as a 'word of number and case' Butler is, like others who attempt to apply Ramist formal criteria to English, again in difficulties with the formally unmarked adjective. He tries to solve the problem by comparing it to the invariable nouns of Latin (e.g. *nequam*) which can be held to cumulate 'all both numbers and cases, under one voice'. Gill similarly, having defined nouns as 'words of number', has to take refuge in the solution already suggested by Greaves: adjectives have number by virtue of their accompanying substantives. The root of the problem lies in grammarians' inability, fostered by a long tradition, to split adjectives and substantives into two separate classes. In Latin there is some excuse for treating them as members of the same class, since they share a common set of endings. Had grammarians seized on the invariability of the English adjective (formally it belongs with Ramus' 'words without number'), at least one major stumbling-block in the way of their application of Ramist principles to English would have disappeared.

The continued force of the semasiological tradition is illustrated by Butler's comparative or 'respective', described in the not uncommon terms of the indication of an increase or diminution of signification. His 'respectives' include a diminutive (*sweetish*) which 'decreaseth the signification of his Positive in part', and a privative (*unsweet*) which 'decreaseth it altogether'.[257] Again, the approach is mixed, for on the formal level comparison is marked by 'certain peculiar Notes', namely the 'subjunctive particles' *-er*, *-est*, and the 'integral signs' *more, most*. Diminutives similarly can be formed either by the addition of the particle *-ish* or by the sign *somewhat*, and privatives by the 'prepositive particle' *un-* or the sign *not*. What this owes to Lily's theory of signs is obvious. It represents a marriage of that theory, which caters for free function words, with Ramus' theory which concerns morphological endings, or what would now be called bound morphemes. Ramus however would not, at any rate in theory,

[257] *English Grammar*, p. 37.

76

have included diminution, which he regarded as a 'prolixa institutio' of no concern to the grammarian.[258]

Gill's six 'cases' are distinguished, necessarily in view of the lack of endings, by word position or by 'signs'. The nominative and accusative are known by their pre- or post-verbal position, the genitive by the sign *of*, the vocative by the sign *O*, etc., in the manner commonly adopted by grammarians of the vernacular. The accident 'declension' refers to the singular/plural variation, and the inflected genitive in -*s* is not mentioned at this stage. Butler, in contrast, avoids setting up several cases in terms of Lily's sign system, his single 'oblique' case being the inflected genitive; but his 'rect' case (defined as the nominative preceding the verb) can be used with prepositions to render Latin oblique cases 'as the sense shall require'. Hume is more obviously in the Lily tradition, with case indicated in English not by terminations, but by 'noates, after the manner of the hebrues'. The mark of the nominative is the 'particle of determination' (i.e. the article), that of the genitive *of* or -*s*, of the dative *to* or *for*, etc., the accusative being identical with the nominative. The authors recognize the analytical character of English, but in their determination to demonstrate that it has a case system, they compensate for the lack of endings amenable to Ramist analysis, by substituting for them a system of signs.

The mixed character of these grammars is again illustrated by the fact that though Butler and Gill attempt to follow Ramus in counting noun and pronoun as a single word-class,[259] they still attempt to give the pronoun special status by applying to it traditional criteria such as substitutability for other nouns, and person. Gill calls it a *nomen personale* divisible into substantive and adjective. No English grammarian prior to him uses the term 'personal' to describe pronouns, and it no doubt stems from Greek tradition, being present in a Latin translation of Theodore Gaza's Greek grammar of 1496.[260] Since the term is used by both Gill and Butler, and later in Bishop Wilkins'

---

[258] In the theoretical *Scholae grammaticae*. He does in fact mention diminution in his Latin grammar.

[259] Colet, in his section of Lily's Latin grammar, had already conceded that 'a pronowne is moche lyke a noune'.

[260] See O. Funke, 'Die Frühzeit der englischen Grammatik', pp. 65, 85. A much earlier precedent than Gaza exists however in Probus (Keil, *Grammatici Latini*, IV, 232), who is the first Latin grammarian to use the term 'pronomina personalia', reserving it to *ego, tu, ille* and their plurals.

Essay, it may well have come to form part of English pedagogical practice.[261] Gill's use of person as the primary criterion leads him to justify including *alone, any, either* and various other terms among the pronouns on the grounds that they denote neither quantity nor quality, but solely 'personalitas'. Ramus had treated the pronoun as an anomalous noun for purely structural reasons, and Butler seeks to imitate this by calling it an 'imperfect' noun because it cannot receive a preceding article. It has the traditional function of a substitute for 'nouns absolute', and in contrast to them its oblique case is the accusative, for which it has distinct forms, not the genitive.

In the treatment of the verb, traditional semasiological features are again inextricably mixed with Ramist formal ones. Hume's definition of it as a 'word of all persons declyned with mood and tyme'[262] is Ramist in so far as with him the term 'person' indicates formal variability, and is equivalent in his system to Ramus' number criterion. But Ramus' 'special difference' of person distinguishing the verb from all other word-classes has been extended to all declinable classes, which will land Hume in difficulties when he comes to discuss the agreement of noun subject and verb; and further, the semantically unstable category of mood, rejected by Ramus, has been included. In treating agreement Hume holds that the person of the verb (no doubt because of the fewness of its endings in English) is determined or 'noted' by its noun or pronoun subject. His classification of noun and pronoun as a single word-class, his transference of definitions unchanged from his Latin grammar to his English one, and his ambiguous use of the term 'person', in which it is not always clear whether he intends it in its traditional sense or as the formal equivalent of Ramus' category of number, all conspire to make his treatment of the verb confused and inappropriate to English structure. Butler, who similarly substitutes case for Ramus' number criterion as the accident common to both noun and verb, finds parallel difficulties in straining his system to fit the linguistic facts. He has to cater for the morphological 'cases' added to the unmarked 'verb absolute' or basic form (as in *love/loved*), and for the indication of tense by free-standing 'signs and supplements'. It is these latter, including zero, that appear solely to constitute the marks of tense,

[261] Michael (*English Grammatical Categories*) notes that the term was in regular use among reforming grammarians using a vernacular terminology after 1700.
[262] Hume's definition of the verb is identical with that in his *Prima elementa*.

for tense and mood in English are 'not distinguished, as in Greek and Latin, by terminations'.[263] The 'first person of the first tense of the first mood' is regarded as the basic form or 'rect case',[264] the 'oblique case' being that which ends in -ed or -en. These 'oblique' endings correspond in Butler's system to the formal marks of 'number' in that of Ramus, all else being a matter of 'signs'. Thus the simple past *loved* can be regarded as an oblique case plus zero sign, or (in its form *did love*) as a 'rect' case preceded by the sign *did*. Since the past participle functioning alone has no sign before it, it is 'all one with the oblique case'. Irregular verb forms are treated as 'anomalies of obliques' or, in invariable forms such as *cast*, as being always in the 'rect' case. Such analyses remind one forcibly of certain Bloomfieldian structuralist ones of the present day, in which e.g. *took* is treated as an allomorph (Butler's 'anomalous' form) plus a zero morpheme of past tense. Butler's 'signs and supplements' are clearly not the equivalent of Gill's 'mere signs', but integral parts of the verb, which consists of sign + 'verb absolute' + case ending.[265] Gill's treatment differs from Butler's in being wholly in terms of signs, by which in English 'we sufficiently express all the dispositions of the mind'.[266] He resembles Bullokar (1586) in seeing the auxiliaries *have* and *had* as purely signs ('mere signa'), not forming part of the verb itself, perhaps in an attempt to attribute unitary verb forms to English on the analogy of Latin, with *have* and *had* restricted to the role of indicators of tense that they have for the pedagogy of the period in teaching translation into Latin.[267]

The emphasis on the 'dispositions of the mind' is a commonplace of the semantically orientated grammars of both ancient and humanist times, and is more particularly a feature of the traditional treatment of mood. For this very reason mood was rejected by Ramus, a rejection in which he is not however followed by the three

[263] *English Grammar*, p. 43.

[264] This procedure recalls Priscian's treatment of the first person indicative as the *prima positio verbi* corresponding to the nominative or *prima positio nominis*.

[265] A discussion of Butler's contribution to the history of specific features of the vernacular would have to include many other points. Poldauf for instance ('On the History of Some Problems', p. 271) draws attention to Butler's treatment for the first time of the distinction between *I have gone* and the 'emphatically resultative' *I am gone*, and Salmon (see note 240 above) has discussed his treatment of wh- and yes/no questions.

[266] *Logonomia Anglica*, p. 53.

[267] Michael, *English Grammatical Categories*, p. 440, notes however that Gill's division of conjugations into those verbs taking -ed in the past, those varying in one position (*run*) and those varying in two (*speak*), provides the basis for future classifications.

authors considered here. Hume's definition of mood as an 'affection of the verb serving the varietie of utterance', as concerning those parts of discourse that depend solely on 'our own will', simply continues a long tradition. It contains an echo of Linacre's description of mood as the expression of a 'voluntas, vel affectio animi' – presumably, in view of Hume's high praise of Linacre, a conscious one. But of Linacre's further requirement that a mood be grammatically consignified by a change in the form of a verb ('per vocem consignificata') there is no trace in Hume's treatment.[268] Once again there is apparent the readiness of grammarians, even those following (if only partially) the Ramist model, to abandon formal criteria in favour of lexicographical or vague mentalistic ones.

Butler's three pages, Hume's two, and Gill's thirteen-and-a-half lines are symptomatic of their lack of interest in the 'words without number' (Butler), 'words impersonal' (Hume) or 'voces consignificativae' (Gill). Or perhaps, given the absence of formal markers in these words, they can find little to say about them? Hume defines them as words which 'in all forms of speach keepe one face', and in accordance with his view of adverbs as 'syncategoremata' tallying in a kind of sequence of tenses with their verbs,[269] he describes adverbs as 'adhering most commonlie with a verb with one face in al moodes, tymes, numberes and persons'.[270] More remarkable however than this cavalier treatment of the formally invariable word-classes is the complete absence in both Hume and Butler of a syntax. This lack in Hume's grammar is much to be regretted, for his syntax would no doubt have followed the idiosyncratic model of his *Grammatica nova* (1612), with its division of construction into 'personal' and 'impersonal' and its close dependence on Linacre.[271] The only member of the trio to provide a syntax, Gill, is also the only vernacular grammarian before Jonson to treat the matter in any detail. He closely bases himself on the rules of concord (*convenientia*) and government (*rectio*) given in grammars of Latin. English adjectives are accordingly made to agree with their substantives, and

---

[268] The influence of Linacre is also seen in Gill and Butler's repetition of his potential mood, with the signs *may, might, would, could*, etc. Michael *ibid.*, p. 429, finds the tone of Hume's discussion of mood 'strikingly modern', and its resemblance to parts of Wittgenstein's *Tractatus* 'not only stylistic'.

[269] Cf. Hume's *Prima elementa*: 'Tempore verba conveniunt cum syncategorematis.'

[270] *Of the Orthographie and Congruitie of the Britan Tongue*, p. 32.

[271] For details see Padley, 'L'importance de Thomas Linacre', pp. 21–2, 36–8; and *Grammatical Theory* (1976), pp. 116–17.

all verbs with their preceding nominatives. In *The good examples of parents ought to be a rule of life to children*, the words *good, ought* and *rule* are all held to be in congruence with *examples*. Gill recognizes however that English adjectives are 'formally variable [*mobilia*] for neither case nor number', and draws the conclusion that they only 'cohere' with their substantives. Even so, there are difficulties in reconciling his description with actual examples of English structure. Forms such as *three foot high* have to be regarded as idiomatic expressions of space and time in which 'coherence' does not take place, and the element *sea-* in *sea-water* (as also *Oxford* in *Oxford glove*) is treated as a 'barren substantive'[272] which substitutes for an adjective instead of giving birth to one by a derivational procedure. Since such elements are capable of standing alone in other structures, they cannot by definition be adjectives, but 'supply the force of the adjective itself'.[273]

Gill's *rectio* or treatment of word government is based on the theory of signs, for 'all our cases are in their endings one case, distinguished only by signs, or by position'. Prepositions are accordingly signs of cases. The forcing of English into the Latin grammatical mould is particularly evident in this section, with the explanation, long familiar in Latin works, of case government in semantic terms, as when *a man of wisdom* is treated as an example of a 'genitive of the possessor'. Gill in fact simply writes the customary Latin syntax, applying its categories – verbs taking accusative, dative or ablative; the use of accusative or ablative in the expression of instrument, material or cause, etc. – to English. His final injunction to the reader is: 'Where no rules are given for the government of a word, follow the syntax of Latin.' Such is the continued prestige of Latin that even when an author concludes, as Gill does, that its formal markers of congruence have no counterpart in' English, he still expects the structures of the two languages to coincide, even if the supposed concords of English can only be expressed in the purely semantic terms of 'coherence'.

To enter the intellectual realm of Ramism is to enter a vast world of thought, with profound repercussions for the development of European linguistic culture. Few movements can however have been so exposed to excessive praise and blame. For R. R. Bolgar for

---

[272] 'Substantivum sterile'.   [273] *Logonomia Anglica*, p. 69.

instance Ramus is a towering figure whose identification of major 'weaknesses in the existing structure' of European thought was 'as essential to Bacon's logic of discovery and to Galileo's method of analysis and construction as manure is to a growing plant', making him 'an essential tributary in the stream that takes us to Locke and Newton'.[274] In this respect it is interesting to note that Bacon himself had little good to say of 'that most dangerous of all literary corroders who constricts and distorts reality with his narrow method and his summaries'.[275] Nor were some of Ramus' contemporaries more complimentary, for according to W. J. Ong[276] he was dismissed by them as the *usurarius*, 'the usufructuary, the man living off the increment of intellectual capital belonging to others' and amassed over the centuries. Certainly, as we have seen, Ramus was no revolutionary. Though he made a great show of attacking Aristotle, in practice he made him the final court of appeal in the delimitation of the subjects of the arts curriculum. His interest for a present-day history of linguistics rests on two things: his separation of grammar, logic and rhetoric, and his application to language analysis of purely formal criteria. In the latter contribution it is noteworthy that, though popularization of his methods in other fields can be held to have 'filled the world with logic-choppers',[277] in linguistic description he uses – in accordance with his theory that each 'art' should remain uncontaminated by the others – logic only in delimiting his subject-matter and in prescribing its framework. Logic never has with him the status of a metalanguage or an underlying content level. A major consequence of this is that while on the one hand Ramus has been seen by some modern critics, in his refusal to use meaning as a criterion, as a forerunner of structuralism, on the other hand his 'obsession with the formal and the morphological' undoubtedly encloses him within the circularity of his own system.[278] It is of course precisely this obsession with formal markers that makes his method

---

[274] *The Classical Heritage and its Beneficiaries*, Cambridge, 1954, p. 289.

[275] In the *Temporis partus masculus*, cited by Rossi, *Francis Bacon*, p. 66. See Bacon's criticism of Ramus' dichotomous procedures in *The Works of Francis Bacon*, ed. Spedding, Ellis and Heath, I, 63, and III, 530.

[276] *Ramus*, p. 7.

[277] Duhamel, 'The Logic and Rhetoric of Peter Ramus', p. 171.

[278] Chevalier, *Histoire de la syntaxe*, p. 269. Particularly interesting is Chevalier's remark (p. 278) that since the categories of Aristotelian logic have their basis in categories of the language, it follows that Ramus is in the uncomfortable position of rejecting categories of thought in the name of a formal system founded on those same categories. As a result he creates (p. 284) 'une grammaire fictive dont la rigueur est purement immanente au système créé'.

of linguistic description appropriate to Latin, though even there some ingenious mental acrobatics are required to make the language facts square with the theory. On the other hand, it is also this predominantly morphological approach that renders Ramus' system inappropriate to the description of the European vernaculars, which rely more on prepositions and word order than on formal endings in the indication of grammatical relationships. The application of his system to these vernaculars may perhaps be seen as a curiosity of the times, resulting from the temporary vogue of other aspects of Ramus' thought, and from his status as a Protestant martyr. Much more important for later developments is his strict separation of logic, grammar and rhetoric. The whole vast panorama of sixteenth- and seventeenth-century grammatical theory unrolls in large part against the background of the coming together again of these three. And the process is predominantly a pedagogical one.

2. THE PEDAGOGICAL MOTIVE: VERNACULAR GRAMMAR AS INSTRUMENT

i GERMAN MYSTICISM AND PATRIOTISM

As with other European vernaculars, the desire to enrich and improve the German language springs from feelings of inferiority, more particularly vis-à-vis the early and brilliant example provided by Italian. A powerful incentive to improvement must indeed have been the scorn in which German was held by early humanists, who regarded it as a barbarous language little amenable to civilizing influences. If a rich vernacular linguistic tradition was quick in developing in Italy, it was above all because of the prior existence of prestigious writers – Dante, Petrarch, Boccaccio – worthy, in an age devoted to the imitation of classical models, to be set beside the great authors of Greece and Rome. Outside Italy there was no such early established tradition of vernacular authorship, or of grammatical and rhetorical writing. Further, in Germany medieval practice was firmly entrenched, and the clash between it and the new humanism was sharper than elsewhere.[1] When grammars of German do finally begin to appear (the first complete one is Albertus' *Teutsch Grammatick* of 1573) the impulse is as elsewhere given not by any wish to introduce the vernacular into the schools, but by the desire to make the much-scorned German language more accessible to foreigners. Accordingly, as in the case of French and English and in marked contrast to Italian, the first grammars of the vernacular are in Latin, and present only the academic interest of the way in which they adapt or do not adapt Latin grammatical practice to the structures of German. Only later, in a second wave of vernacular grammars, is the impetus provided by a conscious attempt to infiltrate the mother

---

[1] See Percival, 'The Grammatical Tradition and the Rise of the Vernaculars', p. 256. Percival notes that the historical process of the adoption of humanist grammar north of the Alps is 'an extremely complex one', in which little is known of the German pre-humanist grammatical tradition.

tongue into the schools, or to initiate students into vernacular-based rhetorical studies. It goes without saying that in these later works practical, pedagogical interests are well to the fore, with little in the way of overt grammatical theory. For a theoretical approach worthy to be compared to that of the great Latin theorists (J. C. Scaliger's *De causis* of 1540, Sanctius' *Minerva* of 1587) we have to await J. G. Schottel's *Teutsche Sprachkunst* (1641), and above all his *Ausführliche Arbeit* (1663), in which a specifically German contribution to universal grammar is developed.

A characteristic which Italian and German linguistic endeavours of the period have in common is a preoccupation, far exceeding that in England or in France, with the question of which dialect to take as the basis for literary and grammatical writing. The centralized systems of government in France and England gave the language of the Court an inevitable social preeminence, and in Italy the Tuscan or Florentine dialect of the three great 'trecentisti' Dante, Petrarch and Boccaccio had valid claims to preference, though even so debates occasioned by the 'questione della lingua' raged throughout the sixteenth and seventeenth centuries. In Germany no dialect could claim precedence on either political or literary grounds. The underlying folk unity of the German peoples results however in a peculiar status, in which religious considerations play a large part, being accorded to the German language as a whole. It is not uncommon for European vernaculars to be credited with Adamic origins,[2] and German is no exception. In claiming that German was spoken by all men (hence the term *alman* used in some languages to designate the Germans), early patriots are doing no more than was being done elsewhere,[3] and attempts to provide the vernacular with very early, even divine, origins are not lacking in the first grammars. Johannes Clajus (1578),[4] though he supposes Hebrew to have been spoken by all men before the confusion of tongues, believes that the German language took its beginnings from that event, giving the often repeated derivation of *Deutsch* from *de + Askenas*, the nephew of

[2] For theories concerning the language of Adam, and their influence on linguistic thought, see D. S. Katz, 'The Language of Adam in Seventeenth-Century England', *History and Imagination. Essays in Honour of H. R. Trevor-Roper*, ed. H. Lloyd-Jones, V. Pearl and B. Worden, London, 1981, pp. 132–45. See also Padley, *Grammatical Theory* (1976), pp. 139–40.
[3] See the opinion of an early German revolutionary, cited by A. Daube, 'Die Anfänge einer deutschen Sprachlehre im Zusammenhang deutscher Geitesgeschichte', *Zeitschrift für deutsche Bildung*, XVIII (1942), p. 21, that 'Adam ist ein tuscher [i.e. deutscher] man gewesen'.
[4] *Grammatica Germanicae linguae*, s. l., 1578.

Noah's son Japhet and the mythological father of the Germanic peoples.[5] Important here is Stephan Ritter's argument (*Grammatica Germanica nova*, 1616) that Hebrew must be held to be preeminent because it 'contains within itself the mysteries of the Holy Trinity', an argument that will in turn be applied to Luther's translation of the Bible. Though Greek is second in dignity to Hebrew, and Latin third, Ritter puts German first among the vernaculars because of its 'antiquity, purity, gravity and amplitude'. Whereas the Romance languages are nothing but corruptions of Latin,[6] resulting from the necessity for peoples under the Roman yoke to 'fracture, mangle and cut up' Latin words, distorting them to suit their own speech organs, German is *sui generis*,[7] an 'inviolated virgin' using loanwords by choice, not by necessity. Several strands meet here that will be of primary importance in the development of attitudes towards the German vernacular and hence, particularly in the case of Schottel, in determining the direction taken by German linguistic theory. The venerable antiquity of the German language, its exceptional purity and unique origins, are features which constantly reappear as justifications of choice of dialect and of theoretical analysis. Closely linked with the belief that German is the 'Ursprache der Menschheit', the original language of mankind, is the corollary that it has some kind of divine origin. The belief in a divine quality immanent in the German language is widespread among the learned, and is central to much thought about the vernacular from the sixteenth century, down through Schottel's mid-seventeenth-century theories, right on to the time of Leibniz. It already finds expression in the very early *Teütsche Grammatica* (*c.* 1534) of Valentin Ickelsamer, whose definition of *etymologia* as 'the true right understanding, or the explanation and demonstration of the origin of words' owes much, as he himself acknowledges, to the Jewish practice of 'philosophizing' on the basis of the Hebrew letters, in which lie hidden 'deep secrets'. The lore of the Kabbalah (the word has something of the sense of Latin *traditio*, indicating wisdom handed down from previous generations) spread throughout Europe after the expulsion of the Jews from Spain in 1492. It had a particular fascination for the seventeenth century

[5] S. Ritter, *Germanica nova* (1616) similarly holds that, 'with some permutation of letters', *tu + Ascanes* gives *Tuiscan*, and hence *Tutschen*. Girbert's *Deutsche Grammatica* (1653), following Gueintz' *Deutscher Sprachlehre Entwurf* (1641), imputes this derivation to 'Aventinus' (i.e. Johann Turmair).
[6] 'ex lingua Latina eaque depravata'. [7] Ritter uses the Greek term *autarchēs*.

which hoped, in the words of John Webster's *Academiarum examen*,[8] that a knowledge of its mysteries might assist in overcoming the disadvantages caused by the 'ruines of Babell'. These mysteries are based, for a recent interpreter of kabbalistic doctrines, on the belief that 'The secret world of the godhead is a world of language, a world of divine names that unfold in accordance with a law of their own. The elements of the divine language appear as the letters of the Holy Scriptures,' each of which 'represents a concentration of energy and expresses a wealth of meaning which cannot be translated, or not fully at least, into human language'.[9] The motivation behind the Renaissance revival of the study of Hebrew was thus not entirely linguistic, and it is a Hebrew scholar, Reuchlin, who quite early popularizes the Kabbalah in his *De verbo mirifico* (1494)[10] and *De arte cabalistica* (1517),[11] each of which devotes a section to letters and their hidden meanings. Taking for instance the scriptural reference to the stone which the builders rejected, he demonstrates that in the Hebrew word for stone (*aben*) there lie concealed the words for father (*ab*) and son (*ben*).[12] The demonstration is meant to show that Hebrew, with its hidden meanings, is a divine language on a completely different footing from other tongues. The interest of Ickelsamer lies in his having extended kabbalistic analyses to the vernacular, thus sowing the seeds of traits which will reappear in the work of the reforming grammarian Wolfgang Ratke. A study of kabbalistic lore offers insight on two levels: into the power of divine Revelation and (compare Paracelsus)[13] into the secrets of Nature. Since these secrets were held to be contained in the original Adamic language, it is not

[8] London, 1654, p. 25.

[9] G. Scholem, *On the Kabbalah and its Symbolism*, New York, 1969, p. 36. See also concerning the Kabbalah D. Katz, *Philo-Semitism and the Readmission of the Jews to England 1603–1655*, Oxford, 1982, pp. 71–6. On the Kabbalah in Germany see A. Daube, *Der Aufstieg der Muttersprache im deutschen Denken des 15. und 16. Jahrhunderts*, Frankfurt-am-Main, 1940, pp. 40–2, and her already cited 'Die Anfänge einer deutschen Sprachlehre', p. 25.

[10] *Johannis Reuchlin Phorcensis Cnapnion vel de verbo mirifico*, Basle, 1494.

[11] *Joannis Reuchlin LL. Doc. De arte cabalistica libri tres*, Hagenau, 1517.

[12] *De verbo mirifico*, f. 4ᵛ. In Hebrew, vowels were not an integral part of the orthographical system. The words involved here are '*eben* ('stone') '*ab* ('father') and *ben* ('son'). In the case of '*eben* Reuchlin would seem to have changed the presumed *e* to *a*, though he was not to know that modern research posits in fact a reconstructed *a*. He is no doubt concerned however with the consonant *letters* (including that representing an initial glottal stop), and here it can plainly be demonstrated that the same consonants appear, in the same order, in on the one hand '*ab* and *ben*, and on the other '*aben* or '*eben*. Vowel points had been perfected in the ninth to tenth centuries, with the precise object of preventing misinterpretations.

[13] See C. Webster, *The Great Instauration: Science, Medicine and Reform 1626–1660*, London, 1975, p. 330 and *passim*.

surprising that on the one hand this language was traditionally held to be Hebrew, and that on the other there was an increasing desire to prove that German itself was in fact the language of Adam. Ratke's pedagogy, as we shall see, saw the vernacular as a tool for increased insight both into Revelation and into the workings of Nature. This notion of an almost mystical power in the vernacular is a constant thread in German linguistic theory, underlying many of Schottel's analyses, and perhaps finally reappearing in Wilhelm von Humboldt's idea of an inner form ('innere Sprachform') underlying the surface realizations of language.[14] Its beginnings are plain to seek in Ickelsamer's claim that 'such art [as that of the Kabbalah] is also present to no small extent in our German words', and only gross neglect of the vernacular prevents men capitalizing on it. A contributory factor here however is doubtless also the strong tradition of German mysticism, for Ickelsamer was himself a devotee of the mystical ideas of Schwenckenfeld. Of particular relevance among German mystics is Jacob Boehme, whose idea of a 'Natursprache' used in the Garden of Eden ties in with widespread notions of an Adamic language which enabled man before the Fall to 'see into the heart of things'. In this 'Natursprache', the individual letters – in a scheme that recalls the assignment by the seventeenth-century language planners of certain facets of the universe to certain letter combinations – are direct indications of the essence of things. All naming of things involves for Boehme the unveiling of mysteries, more particularly in five divinely inspired languages, including Hebrew, Greek and Latin, which have their remote origin in the 'Natursprache', and whose perfection is guaranteed by their participation in the purely 'mental' language of the Holy Spirit. The words of these languages still stand in a direct correspondence to the essential nature of things in the universe, but Boehme also believes that the German vernacular too, were men but able to see it, has the same qualities. All phenomena of the outer world are 'Signaturae' or symbols of the inner one, and by reading them aright it is possible to participate in the 'mental' language of God. The symbolism hidden in the letters of the German language, no less than in Hebrew, Latin and Greek, thus provides a route to communion with the Divine. The importance of Boehme, along with the Kabbalah, in seventeenth-century

[14] In his *Über die Verschiedenheit des menschlichen Sprachbaues*, Berlin, 1836. For discussion see Robins, *A Short History of Linguistics* (2nd ed.), p. 175.

speculation is shown by the fact that John Webster gives an account of his doctrines in his *Academiarum examen* (1654), and by Joachim Polemann's assertion (1662) that 'the botomlesse mercy of God hath set up this Jacob Boehme and also this our Philosopher Helmont, as two bright torches for this present age'.[15] Ickelsamer's approach is however also linked to the aims of the Protestant Reform. To learn to read – and the teacher of spelling is above all 'ein Werkzeug Gottes', a tool in the hands of God – is ipso facto to be placed in contact with God's Word in the Scriptures. The conviction that the German language contains the hidden expression of the divine essence finds support from a further major influence on attitudes to the vernacular, that of Luther, whose translation of the Bible is of primary importance for the development and cultivation of the mother tongue. For Luther not only are Greek and Hebrew to be cherished as the sacred languages of the Scriptures. They also constitute the guarantee of the divine character of the German translation, which is itself sanctified by them 'as from a spring'. In Protestant Germany, it becomes an established point of doctrine that inspiration passes from the Greek and Hebrew originals, via the divinely appointed work of Luther, into the vernacular Bible. The special position of Luther as the mediator of this pure and inspired German is well brought out by Johannes Clajus in the foreword to his *Grammatica* (written in Latin) of 1578:

the Bibles and other writings of Luther...I acknowledge to be not so much the work of a man, as of the Holy Spirit speaking through a man, and I am fully of the opinion that the Holy Spirit, who spoke pure Hebrew through Moses and the rest of the Prophets and Greek through the Apostles, has also spoken good German through his chosen instrument Luther.[16]

In view of this, it is not surprising that Luther sees languages in a way that will become a constant theme of both Ratke and Schottel – as nothing less than sheaths for the sword of the spirit, 'die scheyden, darynn dis messer des geysts stickt'.[17]

If it is impossible to consider the development of grammatical theory in isolation, apart from the general cultural history of the

[15] J. Polemann, *Novum lumen medicum*, London, 1662, p. 116. A translation of Boehme's *De signatura rerum* appeared in London in 1651.

[16] Foreword. This testimony to Luther's standing as an arbiter of good German is repeated, this time in the vernacular, in Johannes Girbert's *Deutsche Grammatica* of 1653.

[17] *An die Radherrn aller stedte deutsches lands: das sie Christliche Schulen aufrichten und hallten sollen*, Wittenberg, 1524, f. Ci'.

times, it is equally impossible to treat it separately from the pedagogical situation in which grammarians found themselves. In
Germany in particular the study of grammatical theory cannot be
divorced from that of pedagogy, which in turn is closely bound up
with the history and development of the German standard language
or *Schriftsprache*. German school grammars have indeed been held to
constitute the written witness to the reciprocal influence of the living
language and vernacular pedagogy.[18] This vernacular grammatical
pedagogy is in turn bound up, at any rate in its origins, with the
practice of the Latin schools. At the beginning of the humanist period,
teachers of Latin were far from offering any conscious encouragement
to the study of the vernacular for its own sake. Manuals were however
in use in which Latin phrases were occasionally accompanied by a
German translation, texts of Donatus with interlinear German
glosses being not uncommon.[19] These glosses apart, the first steps in
the practice of including German phrases in a Latin grammar are
commonly ascribed to Aventinus (Johann Turmair), whose *Grammatica nova fundamentalis* appeared in 1512, and who justified the
procedure by noting its prevalence in Italy. This no doubt grudging
concession was designed to make the first steps in Latin easier, the
aim being to abandon it as soon as possible and give instruction solely
via the Latin medium. Only gradually did the notion arise that the
mother tongue could itself be learnt from grammars at a stage prior
to the pupil's arrival in the Latin school. Of great importance here,
once again, is Valentin Ickelsamer's *Ein Teütsche Grammatica* of
c. 1534,[20] which though but fragmentary is written in German, and
may be considered the first grammar of the vernacular. It gives an
interesting insight into the genesis of such grammars. In Turmair
(1512) the Latin text is simply accompanied by German exemplifi-

[18] See R. von Raumer's contribution (pp. 130–296, 'Der Unterricht im Deutschen') to
K. von Raumer's *Geschichte der Pädagogik vom Wiederaufblühen klassischer Studien bis auf unsere Zeit*
(3rd ed.), Stuttgart, 1857, part III. I am indebted to R. von Raumer's account in some of what
follows.
[19] See Percival, 'The Grammatical Tradition and the Rise of the Vernaculars', p. 250.
Examples of such translated grammars, printed or unprinted, do not however appear to be
extant.
[20] I have consulted this work (published in Augsburg?) in H. Fechner's Neudruck: *Vier
seltene Schriften des sechzehnten Jahrhunderts...mit einer bisher ungedruckten Abhandlung über Valentinus
Ickelsamer von Dr. F. L. Karl Weigand*, Berlin, 1882. The editor notes that there exists only one
copy of this work of Ickelsamer, which is in his own possession. For the probable date of
publication see Weigand's foreword, p. [29]. He follows R. von Raumer ('Der Unterricht im
Deutschen') in thinking a date prior to 1531 unlikely.

cation: 'Dictio, *ain wort*. Illa dictio est nomen, cui in nostra lingua potest addi *ain*, ut homo *ein mensch*, equus *ein pferdt*.' This is of course a purely pedagogical device, whose aim is not the teaching of the vernacular. Its use constitutes however the first faltering, if unconscious, steps towards a vernacular grammar. Ickelsamer's importance lies in his having taken the next step. His aim being the humble one of teaching Germans to read their own language, he sees that it is insufficient simply to take elements of Latin grammar and translate them word for word. He stresses that it is not enough merely, as in the 'gemeinen kinder Donaeten' or glosses of Donatus for school use, to render Latin *nomen* by 'der nam', *verbum* by 'das wort', etc. The grammarian must translate each term in such a fashion that he gives 'not only the name, but its whole office and essence', together with details of use and appropriate examples. Ickelsamer constantly underlines that it is necessary to do more than badly translate ('schlecht teütschen') the Latin model. The treatment must however have a theoretical basis, and this basis is provided by the principles and source ('grund und ursprung') of the eight parts of speech. This means that at its very beginnings German vernacular grammar is firmly word-based: 'That in which the eight parts of speech are properly put into German and explained...to give a proper, well-founded understanding of German words and speech, together with a good German Syntax or Construction...that could properly be called a true German grammar, and perhaps one day someone will produce it.'[21] Ickelsamer sees his business as to ground his pupils in the eight parts of speech, but constantly bearing in mind that he is schooling them in their mother tongue (his aim is 'die teütschen zu schul fueren') and teaching them how to use each part in truly German fashion. Even in much later times however, when authors are pursuing the teaching and enrichment of the vernacular for its own sake, they still feel obliged to justify their labours by claiming to be easing the way to Latin.

Side by side with their origins in the translation of sections of Latin manuals, early German grammars grow also from another strand in pedagogical practice, namely the various early orthographies aiming to teach reading and writing to those with no knowledge of Latin and no intention of ever obtaining any. One purpose of such works

[21] *Teütsche Grammatica* (Fechner's Neudruck), ff. Ai^v–Aii^r.

was to make the German Bible accessible to the unlearned, and it is here that the role of Luther, and of the collaboration between Luther and Melanchthon, is of importance. It is impossible fully to understand German vernacular linguistics and pedagogy without bearing in mind that the impetus to them came above all from the need, following on the violent upheavals of the Reformation, for the religious education of the laity. It is religious and nationalistic, rather than intellectual motives, that lie behind the movement to produce a vernacular grammar. Above all, in Protestant Germany, account must be taken of the all-pervading influence of Luther, whose exhortation of 1524 to the German municipalities concerning the establishment of Christian schools[22] contains in germ a number of what were to become common attitudes to the mother tongue. Luther was far from being an opponent of Latin, yet he expresses himself in terms not dissimilar to those of later pedagogical reformers: 'what does it profit us to teach the Latin, Greek and Hebrew tongues and other liberal arts, when we could just as well teach in German the Bible and God's Word, which are sufficient for salvation.' Elsewhere in the same work however he is less sweeping, holding that 'if we make the mistake of abandoning languages [i.e. the classical ones], we shall not only lose the Gospel, but finally reach the point where we cannot speak or write either Latin or German correctly'.[23] The widespread dissolution of monasteries and cathedral chapters had in fact left education in a sorry state, what remained being narrow and Latin-centred, and essentially based on learning by rote. By the mid-sixteenth century the crisis in education was such that it threatened the stability of the hard-won Reform itself, and in redressing this situation Luther and Melanchthon, seen as the twin instruments of the Divine purpose,[24] act as complementary forces. In the second half of the century Melanchthon's *Grammatica Latina* reigned supreme in the schools. His views on the role of grammar and the teaching thereof appear in a letter of 1540 to the Frankfurt bookseller Egenolph, in which he expresses the Church's primary need of good language teaching. Without a grounding in grammar, preachers are condemned either to mute silence or to shameless ranting.[25] Melanchthon's sympathies were however very much

---

[22] *An die Radherrn.*   [23] *Ibid.*, ff. Biv^r–Ci^v.

[24] As Winshemius put it in his funeral oration for Melanchthon, 'Gott hat diese seine zwei Werkzeuge verbunden.'

[25] Cited by R. von Raumer, 'Der Unterricht im Deutschen', p. 198.

bound up with the old *Klosterschulen*, and it is doubtless Latin grammar that he has in mind. But thanks to the widespread use of Luther's Bible, catechism and hymns, the need for some kind of instruction in German was becoming daily more pressing, and Melanchthon too began to realize the necessity for a vernacular element in pedagogy. For him however the Reform and the humanist movement were intimately united, and under his leadership and that of Johannes Sturm the Protestant school system continued to be dominated by the classical language. Luther too was very much a man of the Renaissance, and one may note in this respect his praise of Hebrew, whose lack of compound words he regarded as constituting one of its superiorities over German. But whereas Melanchthon confined himself to the written word, to the fixed prescriptions of Latin, Luther was of the opinion that the vernacular languages are better learnt by oral practice – 'aus der mündlichen Rede' – at home, in the market-place or in church. For him even Latin and Greek, with their fixed and certain rules, are better acquired by actual practice than by book learning. Allied to this preference for oral models is one, linking Luther with Comenius' pedagogical methods and central also to the English Protestant mind, for things over words. Grammar teaches the meaning of words, but a prior and overriding requirement is a knowledge of what the things signified by words actually are. Knowledge is of two kinds, that of words and that of things, and the former without the latter is of little avail. Here then are two strands in Luther's teaching that will eventually lead to a demand for primary schools whose curriculum emphasizes *realia* and the use of the vernacular, lead in fact to the theories of Wolfgang Ratke.[26] Beyond all this however, as we have seen, Luther regarded languages as divine instruments, the 'Werkzeuge' of God, made holy by their use as the vehicle of the Scriptures. For the humanists language was very much concerned with their ideals of *copia*[27] and *elegantia*. For Luther it was the instrument by which God's Revelation was made known to men, a vehicle of the spiritual ('die scheyde darynn dis messer des geysts stickt'), a doctrine which as P. Hankamer remarks is of incalculable importance for the development of theories concerning the vernacular in Germany. But Hankamer stresses that

[26] Cf. K. von Raumer, *Geschicte der Pädagogik*, I, 170–2. For a discussion of Ratke's theories see below.

[27] See on this aspect of humanist linguistic endeavours the chapter 'Copia' in T. Cave's *The Cornucopian Text. Problems of Writing in the French Renaissance*, Oxford, Clarendon Press, 1979.

in the final analysis the humanist approach to language and that of Luther have much in common and remain bound together by the 'geschichtlichen Augenblick' of Reformation history.[28] Given the coincidence at many points of humanist's and reformer's aims, it is altogether appropriate that in 1528 Luther and Melanchthon should combine forces in drawing up an 'Unterricht der Visitatoren' on the state of the schools, in which they conclude that the ignorance and superstition of the lowest classes must be combated by some form of instruction in the mother tongue. In his directive to the German municipalities in 1524, Luther had already noted the extent to which the schools had been allowed to decay, 'like dry grass where no flowers bloom'.[29] Not only, as a result, was the Gospel not known, but proficiency in German had also deteriorated, and it is clear that for Luther these phenomena are closely connected.[30] His remedy is not however the setting up of schools 'as they have hitherto existed, in which a pupil spent twenty or thirty years learning Donatus and Alexander, but yet learnt nothing'. The aim is not to teach a boy sufficient bad Latin to become a 'Pfaff' or parson, but to let him attend school one or two hours a day, and spend the rest of the time at home learning things of practical use.[31] It goes without saying that at home he will be exposed to the vernacular, and the entire balance of education will be tipped in its favour.

The altogether exceptional preeminence of Luther, together with the special position enjoyed by the mother tongue as the 'Kirchensprache' of German Protestantism, must constantly be borne in mind in considering the development of the earliest vernacular grammars, more particularly in so far as the choice of a standard dialect is concerned. Luther's belief that the German language is the most perfect because it has many features in common with Greek[32] is beside the point. What is of overwhelming importance is the widespread propagation of Lutheran German: in the Bible, in catechisms and hymns, and in daily use in the vast movement to bring the Protestant faith to the laity via the mother tongue. The only influence in any way comparable in the spread of a model of elevated vernacular prose is that of the King James Version of the Bible in England. In Italy,

[28] P. Hankamer, *Die Sprache, ihr Begriff und ihre Deutung im sechzehnten und siebzehnten Jahrhundert*, Bonn, 1927, pp. 38–9.
[29] *An die Radherrn*, f. ii[v].
[30] *Ibid.*, f. Ci[v]. [31] *Ibid.*, ff. Diii[r], Eii[r].
[32] *Tischreden oder Colloquia Doct. Martin Luthers*, ed. J. Aurifaber, Eisleben, 1566.

thanks to the early preeminence of Tuscan as the literary dialect of Dante, Petrarch and Boccaccio, the problem of which dialect to choose as standard, though it occasioned protracted debate, had presented itself in less acute form. In Germany by contrast, the progress of the vernacular and the emergence of a strong claimant to the position of standard dialect proceeded at a much slower rate. In 1573 Albertus had already noted that German showed a dialectal variety paralleled by scarcely any other tongue,[33] and it is hardly surprising that the seventeenth century was well advanced before anything like a standardized *Schriftsprache* was on the way to being solidly established. Here again, if in 1578 Clajus describes the speech of Erfurt as not the least among German dialects, it is as he explains because of that town's connection with Luther.[34] Clajus' illustrative examples are taken from Luther's Bible and other works by him, and it would be difficult to overestimate the importance of Luther's German as a unifying factor in the development of a standard dialect. In the seventeenth century this religious impulse is still a motivating force in Ratke's efforts to produce a High German koinē calculated to deliver men from mutual enmity and religious doubt. Gradually however, it is the usage of the imperial chanceries that comes to furnish the preferred model. Johannes Girbert's *Deutsche Grammatica* of 1653, a compendium of grammatical practice and attitudes to the vernacular from Clajus (1578) to Schottel (1641) gives important testimony in this regard, recommending 'only the so-called *Communis Germanicae Mercurius*, which has up to now been used by the German Empire itself in its decrees, chanceries, consistorial courts and printing presses'.[35] The chanceries, Girbert concludes, are the 'true teachers of the pure German language'. In practice there were departures from the models provided by Luther and the chanceries, in two main directions. For the grammarians of the Low German area, the *Niederdeutsche*, who gradually eclipsed in importance the native speakers of High German in the south, High German was above all an artificial language learnt from books. The grammars produced by them are no longer simple classroom manuals or aids for foreigners, but guides to correct High German usage for Low-German-speaking adults. For this school, the preferred model coincides with no single dialect. It is the task of the grammarian,

---

[33] *Teutsch Grammatick oder Sprachkunst*, Augsburg, 1573, dedicatory foreword.
[34] *Grammatica Germanicae linguae*, dedicatory foreword.   [35] F. A2^v.

employing principles such as analogy, to deduce this ideal German from the actual material of speech. Seen in this light it is the grammarian himself, applying his analogical principles, who is in a major sense the constructor and arbiter of the language. Diametrically opposed to this approach is that of the East Midland grammarians, the *Ostmitteldeutsche*, who base themselves, convinced as they are that theirs is the best German, on the living usage of the best speakers, a usage which does not necessarily coincide at all points with the rules prescribed by the *Niederdeutsche*. The latter produce a *Schriftsprache* based on purely written usage. The East Midlanders are much more inclined to follow oral models and the intuitions of the *Sprachgefühl*. It is however the first stream that produces the important grammarians, the *Ostmitteldeutsche* tending to cultivate more rhetorical studies.[36]

A corollary of the widespread belief that the vernacular is by its very nature refractory to rules is found in the notion that grammatical rules are not needed by native speakers. In 1641 Christian Gueintz is still complaining that up to that date it has not been thought necessary to devote serious study to the mother tongue, which is supposed to be 'taken directly from Nature: not learnt from teachers; but from nannies: not in schools; but in the cradle, after the example of the brave Gracchi in Rome'.[37] These last-named are not infrequently cited in early works on the European vernaculars as proof that native speakers need do no more than, in the words of Kaspar Stieler (1691), 'suck in the language with their mothers' milk' – a belief which for Stieler explains why the cultivation of the vernacular is accounted 'one of the lowliest arts'.[38] Gueintz claims that if the Latin and Greek tongues, at first graceless and worthy of small praise, have acquired great prestige, it is because of the care bestowed on them and the heroic deeds recounted in them. The German language is now ripe to undergo a similar elevation in status: 'But where is the model to be followed? Where is the rule? Others have sought it out for their languages and found it. Who can suppose that the same cannot be done for our German mother tongue?'[39] References to the growing importance of the vernacular and the need, in imitation of other peoples, to provide it with rules and refine it,

---

[36] On these two opposing schools see Jellinek, *Geschichte der neuhochdeutschen Grammatik*, I, 112–15.   [37] *Deutscher Sprachlehre Entwurf*, foreword.

[38] Foreword to his *Der Teutschen Sprache Stammbaum und Fortwachs*, Nuremberg, 1691.

[39] *Deutscher Sprachlehre Entwurf*, foreword.

are a commonplace in writings of the period. Already, at the date of the publication of the first vernacular grammars, important works composed in German had appeared. Paracelsus (1495–1541) taught medicine in the language. In 1518 appeared Lorenz Friez's medical treatise, *Der Spiegel der Arznei*, while Albert Dürer published the first German mathematical work in 1525, followed by a book on architecture in 1527. Already in 1573, in the first real grammar of German, Albertus sees no reason why, when the Romance languages born of the corruption of Latin are being 'comprised in rules', Germans should lag behind in 'enquiring into the principles of their language'. But even as late as 1653, eighty years later, Girbert can still complain that foreign languages are preferred to the vernacular, and 'we have never yet correctly learned or understood our mother tongue'.[40]

Divided though the earlier German vernacular grammarians may be in the matter of the particular dialect they seek to impose, they are united in the grammatical framework they prescribe: it is that of traditional Latin grammar. And here a prestigious model was to hand, that of Philip Melanchthon,[41] who occupied in grammatical matters, at any rate in Protestant Germany, a position analogous to that of Nebrija in Spain, Despauterius in France, and Lily in England. He has been called the 'most complete type of the reconciliation of humanism with Protestant and Germanic consciousness',[42] realizing the considerable feat of reconciling in one system Renaissance humanism, medieval Aristotelianism, and the brash energies of the Protestant Reform. He thus softens the intransigent position occupied by Luther, making it more amenable to humanist influences. But in spite of this the predominantly linguistic culture of the humanists remains very much subject to religious orthodoxy, caught up in the drive towards purity of expression in the service of God's Word. Since Melanchthon's Latin grammars of 1525 and 1526[43] were the most widely used in Protestant

---

[40] *Die Deutsche Grammatica oder Sprachkunst*. Many of Girbert's remarks on the qualities and status of the vernacular are taken from Schottel's *Teutsche Sprachkunst* of 1641.

[41] *Melan chthon* is the German name *Schwarzerd* put literally into Greek.

[42] W. H. Woodward, *Studies in Education during the Age of the Renaissance 1400–1600* (*Contributions to the History of Education*, ii), Cambridge, 1906, 214–15. See also Bolgar, *The Classical Age and its Beneficiaries*. Bolgar holds that Melanchthon 'narrows the field of classical knowledge prescribed by Erasmus'.

[43] For Melanchthon's Latin grammars see Padley, *Grammatical Theory* (1976), pp. 20–1, 38, 45–6, 50–1. I have consulted them in Robert Estienne's Paris editions: *Grammatica Latina* (1527), and *Syntaxis* (1528).

Germany, they inevitably provided the model for vernacular grammarians in need of a framework on which to base their description of the mother tongue. Quite apart from his influence on the early Latinizing grammarians of German not treated in this volume,[44] he also inevitably affects those authors whose interests are pedagogical rather than primarily linguistic, or who are cultivating the vernacular for its own sake rather than as a gateway to Latin. An interesting early work offering a kind of half-way house between grammars treating the vernacular purely as an aid to the learning of Latin (or at any rate forcing the vernacular into a Latin mould) and those which treat inculcation of the mother tongue as an end in itself, is Johann Becherer's *Synopsis grammaticae* of 1596,[45] of which I have unfortunately been unable to locate a copy in Germany or elsewhere. According to M. H. Jellinek's description[46] of this work, which offers a synopsis not only of Latin and Greek but also of German grammar, it contains features which in the next century are typical of the more enterprising teachers of the vernacular. Though Becherer is himself a reformer of Latin teaching rather than a proponent of a vernacular pedagogy, he is the first grammarian to exclude the optative from the paradigms of German, and to remove indicative forms which previous to him had been incorporated in the subjunctive. His vernacular section is clearly intended as a prolegomenon to Latin studies, but points of interest are his application of the same methodology and terminology to all three languages, and his refusal, in Ramist fashion, to repeat separately in each section matter that is common to all three . Though these are devices that later form an important element in the Ratichian reforms, Becherer seems however to have had little or no influence on succeeding grammarians.[47] His real interest is in the reform of Latin grammatical teaching, as is

[44] After Ickelsamer's fragmentary volume (*c.*1534), the first complete vernacular grammars are those of Laurentius Albertus (1573), Albert Ölinger (1574) and Johannes Clajus (1578), three works closely related by their common dependence on Melanchthon. In the same Latinizing tradition are Stephan Ritter (1616) and Heinrich Schöpf (1625). The Latinizing tendency is summarized by Johannes Girbert (1653). Other Latinizing grammarians – Kromayer (1618), Olearius (1630), Gueintz (1641), Bellin (1660), Pölmann (1678) and Prasch (1687) – either owe much to the authors listed above or, since they show Ramist influences and/or form part of the pedagogical reform initiated by Wolfgang Ratke, are treated in the appropriate sections of this study.

[45] *Synopsis grammaticae tam Germanicae quam Latinae et Graecae*, Mülhausen, 1596.

[46] *Geschichte*, I, 85–7.

[47] Jellinek finds that Becherer's work has several points in common with Johann Kromayer's *Deutsche Grammatica* of 1618.

shown by his *Theses pro synopsi grammatica* of 1609[48] (which I have been able to see), consisting of notes on selected points in Melanchthon's Latin grammar and, as the subtitle puts it, 'containing the causes why in the school at Mülhausen the commonly used method and rules of grammar have been abandoned'. Becherer's work is proof of an early interest, in some quarters at any rate, in the reform of language teaching.

The Ratichian reforms

Any consideration of grammatical theory in the seventeenth century must be set against the background of the vast movement for the reform of linguistic pedagogy of which Comenius is the best-known representative. The inordinate amount of time spent in bringing pupils to a point at which they could profit from Latin authors, and the uniformly poor quality of the results obtained, led many throughout Europe to question the value of grammar teaching in general and call for its abolition. In early seventeenth-century Germany however, a group of reformers gathered around Wolfgang Ratke developed methods which not only had far-reaching implications for teaching in general, but also called for grammatical works themselves to be adapted to the requirements of new grammatical norms. The grammars produced by this group are first and foremost attempts to put into practice a particular educational theory. Their obsession with organization means, at this date in Germany, that these manuals will be markedly Ramist in framework, while the desire to inculcate a basic grammar that can later be applied to any language results in an early type of universal grammar whose sources are pedagogical rather than philosophical. The Ramist aspect of the Ratichian grammars has already been treated above, and their contribution to theories of universal grammar will be considered in a later chapter. The aim at this point in the present study is to discuss Ratke's pedagogical theories in so far as they affect his attitude to grammar, and to the position of the vernacular in education.

Ratke is at first sight one of life's born failures, an archetypal wandering scholar–teacher whose peregrinations led him, between 1612 and 1635, from one to another of the princedoms that then made up the German Reich, following a pattern in which preliminary

[48] Published in Erfurt.

enthusiastic acceptance of his ideas inevitably gave way to rejection. Though jealous princelings rivalled with one another to obtain his services, Ludwig of Anhalt even putting him in prison to prevent his ideas spreading to other courts, his difficult temperament, his reputation as a 'homo heterodoxus' and perhaps above all his religious ecumenism made him enemies. He usually succeeded in antagonizing even his collaborators and benefactors, and despite his immense industry his ideas made little headway. Partly to blame no doubt were the debilitating effects of the Thirty Years War, which meant that an exhausted Germany had little energy to spare for pedagogical causes. Equally to blame however is the fact that most of Ratke's prolific output remained unprinted, hidden away in unconsulted manuscripts.[49] Perhaps because of a failure to take these works into account, earlier opinion of Ratke's achievements was almost universally hostile.[50] In more recent years the pendulum has swung in Ratke's favour, particularly thanks to K. Seiler's *Das pädagogische System Wolfgang Ratkes* (1931),[51] an important work which goes far to redress the injustices done by previous writers. Seiler has not only gone to the original manuscript sources for his assessment, but he has also attempted to estimate Ratke's importance against the background of the cultural ideas of the time. Dismissed as a mere practical pedagogue when he was in fact a great theoretician, scorned as a charlatan when he was in reality a martyr to his convictions, Ratke is in Seiler's opinion one of the most original thinkers of his time. A reconsideration of Ratke's pedagogical work in the light of hitherto unpublished sources is similarly undertaken in E. Ising's *Wolfgang Ratkes Schriften* (1959),[52] which prints grammars that have not previously been easily accessible to scholars.

Already in 1612, Ratke had taken advantage of the fact that the Electors of the Holy Roman Empire were assembled at Frankfurt,

[49] They finally found their way to the Gothaer Landesbibliothek, but there too they lay long unheeded.

[50] R. von Raumer's 'Der Unterricht im Deutschen' treats Ratke harshly, but the unbalanced view of him that has circulated is due in particular to two books: G. Krause's *Wolfgang Ratichius, oder Ratke im Lichte seiner und der Zeitgenossen Briefe*, Leipzig, 1872, and J. Lattmann's *Ratichius und die Ratichianer*, Göttingen, 1898.

[51] K. Seiler, *Das pädagogische System Wolfgang Ratkes nach den handschriftlichen Quellen im Zusammenhang der europäischen Geistesgeschichte dargestellt*, Erlangen, 1931.

[52] As Ising remarks, 'In allen Arbeiten über Ratkes pädogogische Ansichten fehlt bisher eine gründliche Untersuchung der von ihm benutzten Quellen.'

in order to present to them a 'Memorial'[53] outlining his proposed pedagogical reforms. This document sees it as 'the right use and course of Nature, that young people should first learn to read, write and speak their native tongue correctly and fluently', to the end that they may 'in future better understand their teachers in other languages'. By other languages Ratke means of course Latin, Greek and Hebrew, which constitute together with German the four 'Haubtsprachen' or major literary languages from which all others originate.[54] This reference to the classical tongues may represent a sop to the Electors, as the only basis on which they were likely to accept the introduction of a more consolidated instruction in German. Ratke was a Lutheran, and already in this preliminary document there is evidence of the influence of ideas stemming from the Protestant Reform. The overriding aim of language teaching is universal access to the Word of God, for only by this means, according to Ratke, can polemics over scriptural interpretation cease, allowing the 'ancient Catholic and Apostolic doctrine' to enjoy a peaceful and unadulterated existence throughout the German Reich.[55] This universalism, setting up norms intended to be valid for the whole of Germany, is a constant preoccupation with Ratke. Before dismissing it as naïve one should bear in mind that his youth had been marked by the spectacle of a Germany torn asunder by wars of religion. In view of this it is not surprising that he calls for a consideration of ways in which 'in the whole Reich, a united[56] language, a united government, and finally a united religion, may be conveniently introduced and peacefully maintained'.[57] The Electors, either alarmed at his suggestions for religious unity or dismissing them as the work of a crank, took no action on his plans. The principal features of the 'Memorial' however, the introduction of practical subjects into the curriculum, and the use of the vernacular in instruction, remained central to the Ratichian reform.

Ratke's plans began to take serious shape when he was called to Anhalt-Köthen together with the linguistic scholars Joachim Jung

---

[53] Printed in Ising, *Wolfgang Ratkes Schriften*, 1, 101–4. It is also reproduced in P. Stötzner, *Ratichianische Schriften*, 1, Leipzig, 1892.

[54] 'Memorial', f. 63ᵛ (Ising, *Wolfgang Ratkes Schriften*, 1, 102).

[55] *Ibid.*, f. 63ᵛ (Ising, *Wolfgang Ratkes Schriften*, 1, 103).

[56] Ratke uses the term 'einträchtig'.

[57] 'Memorial', f. 63ʳ (Ising, *Wolfgang Ratkes Schriften*, 1, 101).

and Christoph Helwig. Their association however repeated the common pattern, being marked by strife and dissolved after only two years. In Köthen itself, where the three reformers bent themselves to the task of drawing up a complete system of knowledge with logically based divisions and subdivisions reminiscent of Ramus, the movement met with ridicule. Ratke had become acquainted with Ramus' work while a student, and it is no doubt to him that he owes the encyclopedic, universal knowledge aspect of his endeavours. The trio's grandiose plans foresaw in fact the production of an 'Allunterweisung' or encyclopedia, and many of their proposed titles include the word 'allgemein' or universal. The ambitious programme included both a universal rhetoric ('Allgemeine Rednerlehr') and a universal natural science ('Allgemeine Naturkündigung'), to which were to be added a metaphysics and a logic. Among pedagogical works proposed were a general introduction to didactics,[58] together with an organizational 'constitution' and a teaching manual intended for 'the Christian school'.[59] A summary of Ratke's pedagogical aims, more particularly as they concern the use of the mother tongue in education, is contained in the Report on his methods furnished by Helwig and Jung.[60] The authors, condemning the 'tyranny' hitherto exercised by Latin, and the widespread use of rote learning[61] and of translation into an imperfectly known foreign tongue, claim that by Ratke's methods students can be brought to an excellent knowledge of any language within the space of one year. More importantly, they stress the necessity of pedagogical use of the vernacular. The essential features of Ratke's language pedagogy are contained in three treatises reprinted by P. Stötzner.[62] The 'Artickel auff welchen

---

[58] This was printed as the *Allgemeine Anleitung in die Didacticam*, Köthen, 1617, which is the second appearance of the work, for Evenius had brought out a pirate edition (Halle, 1615) under the title *Desiderata methodus nova Ratichiana, linguas compendiose et artificiose discendi*.

[59] Respectively the 'Allgemeine Verfassung der christlichen Schule' (1626–8) and the 'Lehrartlehr der christlichen Schule' (1630). Mention may also be made of 'Etliche Punkte auf welchen die Didactica oder Lehrart Wolfgangi Ratichii gründlich beruhet' (1618), the 'Lehrordnungen zu der neuen Lehrart Ratichii' (1619–20), and the 'Schuldieneramtslehr' (1631–2).

[60] C. Helwig and J. Jung, *Kurtzer Bericht von der Didactica, oder Lehrkunst Wolfgangi Ratichii*, Frankfurt-am-Main, 1613. A shorter 'Nachbericht' is given by these authors as an appendix to the 1614 (Frankfurt) edition of Luther's *An die Radherrn*. A further report, equally favourable, was made by the Jena professors Grawer, Brendel, Walter and Wolf: *Didactica oder Lehrkunst Wolfgangi Ratichii...durch etliche Professoren der Universitet Jena* (1613), the Magdeburg 1614 edition of which is reproduced in Stötzner, *Ratichianische Schriften*, i.

[61] *Kurtzer Bericht*, p. 11: 'ubung an sich selbst gibt kein wissenschaft'.

[62] 'Artickel' (1614/15), 'In methodum linguarum' (1615) and 'Anlaitung' (1614/15), respectively pp. 11–25, 26–45 and 46–60 of P. Stötzner, *Ratichianische Schriften*, ii, Leipzig, 1893.

fürnehmlich die Ratichianische Lehrkunst beruhet' (1614/15)[63] gives the general outlines of Ratke's system: 'Everything [is to be done] according to the order or course of Nature. For Nature uses a special order proper to herself, by which man's understanding apprehends something that must be taken into account...for all teaching and learning that is contrary to Nature is harmful.'[64] It follows that a language must be acquired according to its own 'gründliche Eygenschafft' or fundamental nature, not 'constrained by grammar'. The pupil's manual must not be the grammar book, but 'a single dependable author': 'When the language is taught out of a suitable author, the natural characteristics of the language are imparted.'[65] Already in this pamphlet stress is laid on Ratke's guiding principle of uniformity or harmony ('Gleichförmigkeit') in all things. 'In all languages, arts and sciences there must be a uniformity, both as concerns teaching methods and textbooks'. Above all, everything must be taught first in the mother tongue. The 'In methodum linguarum generalis introductio'[66] is clear that before the grammar book is even placed in the pupil's hands, its broad lines should be explained 'in lingua vernacula'. He must first be introduced to the author, and only secondarily to grammatical rules.[67] Again, too, there is the emphasis on proceeding in harmony with Nature. The pupil should spend more time on what is accessible to his understanding than on what he has merely committed to memory by rote learning. 'This same order is that followed by Nature in imprinting on the mind the "species" of things. For first of all is given the real Being which actually exists outside the mind...which is directly presented to the sense of seeing, and thence finally to the mind, whence it is subsequently placed in the memory.' To place emphasis on the learning by heart of things not yet understood is to 'invert the very order of Nature'.[68]

The Ramist provenance of all this insistence on following Nature's law is obvious. More original is the emphasis, in the 'Anlaitung in

---

[63] Published in Johannes Rhenius' *Methodus institutionis quadruplex*, Leipzig, 1617. Rhenius' foreword states that he received it from Ratke's own hand, and that Ratke ascribed its authorship to Jung and Helwig. [64] Stötzner, *Ratichianische Schriften*, II, p. 11.

[65] *Ibid.*, pp. 16–17.

[66] This work was written by Ratke himself. Stötzner (*Ratichianische Schriften*, II, 26–45) takes it from Johannes Rhenius, who included it in his *Methodus* (1617). It had already appeared in Halle in 1615 in the pirated *Desiderata methodus nova Ratichiana*.

[67] Stötzner, *Ratichianische Schriften*, II, 38.

[68] *Ibid.*, p. 38.

der Lehrkunst W. Ratichii' (1614/15), on the role of the mother tongue in the service of universality, and it is not without significance that this treatise has been ascribed to Helwig.[69] Though he (as the orientalist of Ratke's group) insists that 'no art must be bound to one language alone, as if they were not to be further carried out and practised in other tongues', the *gateway* to this universality is the vernacular, the 'foundation and ground' of all studies. The conclusion he draws is that of the entire Ratichian reform: 'Wer einen rechten grund legen will an der Jugend, der muss es thuen in der Mutter Sprach.'[70] It is this very requirement of pedagogical universality that lies behind the Ratichian theories of general grammar, treated later in this study. It cannot be too much emphasized that for Ratke, as for so much of seventeenth-century thought, the movement towards universal grammar is didactically motivated.

Ratke had already produced, while in Amsterdam, an 'Universa grammatica Latina' (1608), whose concise and somewhat arid form was to be repeated in his vernacular grammars. Of these only the *Allgemeine Sprachlehr* or general grammar (1619), accompanied by a Latin version, appeared in print.[71] It had been preceded by a purely vernacular grammar, the 'Sprachkunst',[72] elaborated between 1612 and 1615, and was followed after Ratke had left Köthen by a vernacular syntax ('Wortschickungslehr') and semantics ('Wortbedeutungslehr'),[73] none of which achieved printed form. While K. Seiler holds that it is precisely on these various unprinted works that Ratke's final reputation must rest, it has been maintained that he cannot with certainty be shown to have contributed to any of the works actually *printed* at Köthen during his stay there.[74] E. Ising thinks it likely that the *Sprachlehr* is from Ratke's own hand,[75] whereas

[69] Stötzner (*Ratichianische Schriften*, II, 46–60) takes this work from a miscellaneous volume of MSS labelled 'Ratichiana et similia' in the Weimar Library. On pp. 6–7 he gives reasons why it could well be ascribed to Helwig, and suggests the date 1614/15.

[70] *Ibid.*, p. 47.

[71] *Grammatica universalis pro didactica Ratichii/Allgemeine Sprachlehr nach der Lehrart Ratichii*, Köthen, 1619. Both versions are reprinted in G. Vogt, *Wolfgang Ratichius*, Langensalza, 1894. The German version is reproduced in Ising, *Wolfgang Ratkes Schriften*, II, 23–37. The work is commonly referred to as the 'Köthener Sprachlehr'.

[72] Printed for the first time in Ising, *Wolfgang Ratkes Schriften*, II, 9–22.

[73] Both printed for the first time in *ibid.*, II, 97–268 and 271–318.

[74] See Jellinek, *Geschichte*, I, 89.

[75] *Wolfgang Ratkes Schriften*, I, 25, and II, 5. H. E. Brekle ('The Seventeenth Century', *Current Trends in Linguistics*, XIII, ed. T. A. Sebeok, The Hague and Paris, 1975, p. 314) takes a similar view. Ising notes however the absence of details as to the origin and development of the *Sprachlehr*.

M. H. Jellinek[76] thinks it may be modelled on Christoph Helwig's *Sprachkünste* published in the same year. Though Ising takes the view that Helwig simply took his terminology from Ratke's unprinted 'Sprachkunst', opinion remains divided as to which of the two, Ratke or Helwig, was the sole or principal author.[77] At issue here is the grammatical terminology employed, that of Ratke's *Sprachlehr* differing in important respects from that used in the 'Sprachkunst' and the question as to which of the two authors precedes the other in the use of certain vernacular terms.

As we have seen, the vernacular was already to some extent in use as an aid to the teaching of Latin in the first half of the sixteenth century. Where Ratke differs from previous practice is in insisting that a thorough grounding in the mother tongue should precede instruction in Latin, and in proposing to extend the vernacular to the teaching of more practical subjects. In the first of these aims he can be held to have provided the model for Comenius.[78] His approach has, of course, its down-to-earth, practical side, with pedagogical requirements prescribed down to the least detail. His pamphlet 'Wie man die grammatica treiben soll in der teutschen sprachen' lays down again that language teaching should be based on a 'particular author', from whose pages the 'characteristic qualities' of each language may be learnt. For the vernacular, the work specifically prescribed is Luther's New Testament,[79] which alone contains a German pure enough to serve as a model. But as already mentioned Ratke, long seen as only a practical, down-to-earth pedagogue, has been treated by recent research as above all a theoretician. There is a hint of this in the titles of the various works produced at Köthen, which require their subject-matter to be 'maintained in the true harmony of Faith, Nature and Language'.[80] Ratke's pedagogy can in fact only be understood in the light of his theory of harmony, of which it is the practical application. The twin

[76] 'Zur Geschichte der Verdeutschung der grammatischen Kunstwörter', *Zeitschrift für deutsche Wortforschung*, XIII (1911–12), p. 83.

[77] On this question see B. Kaltz, 'Christoph Helwig, ein vergessener Vertreter der allgemeinen Grammatik in Deutschland', *Historiographia Linguistica*, V:3 (1978), p. 231. Kaltz holds that Jellinek's thesis has not been convincingly disproved.

[78] H. Geissler, *Comenius und die Sprache*, Heidelberg, 1959, thinks Comenius' early *Grammaticae familiaris praecepta* (no longer extant) was influenced by Ratke's suggestion that instruction in the vernacular should precede Latin studies.

[79] See 'Anlaitung' (Stötzner, *Ratichianische Schriften*, II, 57).

[80] This is true e.g. of the 'Wortschickungslehr'.

poles of his system are Revelation and Nature, each in its particular way providing a basis for knowledge. But though the Bible alone is the source of supernatural knowledge ('lumen gratiae'), divine Revelation also has its part to play in the obtaining of knowledge by virtue of man's own nature ('lumen naturale'), for 'since God the Creator is all in all, so also in Him are the prototype and order of all created things'.[81] The distinction between *lumen naturale* and *lumen supernaturale* is a commonplace of medieval thought, being found in Thomas Aquinas and seemingly originating with Albertus Magnus.[82] Among the 'various points'[83] on which Ratke bases his pedagogy is the requirement that everything should be done according to Nature, with the teacher, imitating this order, starting with simple matters before moving on to more complex ones. Since Nature abhors disorder, its imitation offers – and here the influence of Ramus is evident – a ready-to-hand method.[84] The interplay between natural and supernatural knowledge[85] is of central importance for Ratke, the former being inconceivable without the latter. Since Nature is created by God, it follows that the truth is to be found in it, but original sin prevents man from attaining to knowledge solely by its aid, without the added help of supernatural Revelation. It is the light of the divine Word that enables the human intellect to grasp the universe 'by the light of Nature'. The eternally true laws the human mind is able to attain to – there is here a rationalist bias typical of one aspect of seventeenth-century thought – are as it were guaranteed by the interplay of Nature and Revelation. This faith in an intellectual order with both a natural and a divine basis has also its implications for linguistic theory. Here too Ratke posits an underlying harmony, an immanent system, reposing in the last analysis on the divine will, and offering an explanation for those features in which languages agree. This 'language harmony' forms the basis, as will be seen in a later chapter, for Ratke's theories of universal grammar.

---

[81] 'Ordnungslehrart', II, 1, 1.

[82] See Seiler, *Das pädagogische System Wolfgang Ratkes*, p. 10, n. 1.

[83] 'Etliche Punkte auf welchen die Didactica oder Lehrart...beruhet' (1618).

[84] Ratke discusses these points in ch. 1 of his 'Lehrartlehr der christlichen Schule'.

[85] For a discussion of the Stoic and neo-Platonic versions of this type of theory, and their status in Renaissance and Reformation thought, see Seiler, *Das pädagogische System Wolfgang Ratkes*, pp. 48–52. Seiler notes (p. 49) that neo-platonism offered a form of thought 'in der sich die Kirchen, besonders der protestantischen Seite, mit der neuen Hochwertung der Menschennatur aussöhnen konnten'. Ratke and his contemporaries could not of course accept the Stoic pantheist view.

In elaborating his theory of harmony Ratke was as not infrequently happens in the seventeenth century returning to Scholastic models. Medieval thought had also attempted to integrate *lumen naturale* and *lumen supernaturale* in one system, embracing both revealed and natural knowledge. The problem in such a system was how to bring in new knowledge, and how to keep some sort of balance and order between the various 'arts'. Ramus had tried in his particular way to bring order into the system he inherited, and Melanchthon had once more made the attempt to link faith and knowledge in a single all-embracing scheme. The narrow orthodoxy of the early seventeenth-century reformers put paid however to this attempt. Faith and knowledge were henceforth to be in some degree antagonists. Ratke's theory of knowledge was intended to reconcile them. If his system were to be adopted, contradiction and error would be possible only in so far as they arose from men's faulty judgments. And Ratke was confident that, if the lost harmony between faith and nature were restored, disputes due to different religions, languages and modes of government would disappear, for men would *of themselves*, once the obstacles caused by the loss of harmony were removed, exercise their judgment and choose the good.

The once flourishing schools of Germany were at their lowest ebb around 1600, and it was this trend that Ratke's pedagogical theories, based on his notion of harmony, were calculated to reverse. Harmony was to reign not only between revealed truth and the epistemology of the various branches of learning, but between the branches themselves, the whole forming a pedagogical system illuminated by and tending towards its divine source.[86] Every teaching manual was to be drawn up in accordance with the ideal harmony of Faith, Nature and Languages, the last-named being subordinated to the overriding unity of Faith and Nature. Since harmony is the essential characteristic of Nature, any pedagogical system founded on Nature must itself necessarily possess harmony between its parts.[87] But though harmony furnishes the central notion on which Ratke founds his didactic, his work contains little elaboration of the concept. Indeed, though it provides the basis for his epistemology, elsewhere Ratke is typical of his age in following Aristotelian models and

[86] Cf. G. Rioux, *L'Oeuvre pédagogique de Wolfgangus Ratichius (1571–1635)*, Paris, 1963, p. 240.
[87] Ratke makes this clear in the 'Lehrartlehr der christlichen Schule'.

Scholastic logic. In his requirement that all education must be in conformity with Nature, that it must consider 'first a thing in itself, then the manner of a thing',[88] and that conclusions must be tested by experiment, he is in turn reminiscent of Bacon, though as K. Seiler points out,[89] the basing of knowledge on induction and experiment is a notion he could equally well have obtained from Ramus.[90] In any case one should beware of assuming that Ratke would give either term the meaning it has for Bacon or for modern science. There is however undeniably a distinct Ramist element in his theories. Teaching each branch of learning as a 'peritia' or practical skill founded on experience, he insists that it must not be divorced from 'experientia', without which it has no real basis.[91] As Ramus had put it, 'experience begets art'.[92] Similarly Ramist is the requirement that the teacher should proceed from the general to the particular, in line with Ramus' treatment of 'generalia generatim'. According to the 'Allgemeine Verfassung der christlichen Schule' (1626–8) this is the order followed by Nature herself. Of particular importance for our purposes here is the dictum, again founded on Nature, that all education should proceed from the known to the unknown.[93] It provides the theoretical basis for Ratke's argument that a grounding in the mother tongue must precede instruction in Latin, and for his claim – constituting a theory of general grammar – that it will provide a preliminary grammatical framework applicable to all other languages. Parallels with Comenius are obvious, the systems of the two scholars being based on a similar belief in divinely inspired natural laws which are the same everywhere. In Ratke's doctrines however the *lumen supernaturale* has a special role to play, for without

---

[88] See Ratke's 'Artickel auf welchen fürnehmlich die Ratichianische Lehrkunst beruhet' (1614/15), ed. P. Stötzner, *Ratichianische Schriften*, II, 16.

[89] *Das pädagogische System Wolfgang Ratkes*, p. 62.

[90] No direct Baconian influence on Ratke can be demonstrated. Seiler 'Das pädagogische System Wolfgang Ratkes', pp. 61–2) argues that his supposed journey to England, if indeed he ever went there, must have taken place in May 1603, whereas Bacon's *De dignitate et augmentis scientiarum* did not appear until 1605. Seiler rules out any direct contact with Bacon or his writings, finds no indication of Ratke having read Bacon while in Holland, and concludes that there was no great influence. Cf. however Rioux, *L'Oeuvre pédagogique*, who thinks there can be no doubt of Bacon's influence, since certain formulae in Ratke's works agree 'word for word' with certain aphorisims in the *Novum organum*.

[91] 'Schuldieneramtslehr' (1631–2), II, chs. 20 and 21.

[92] *Scholae in liberales artes*, p. 830: 'experientia quidem artem genuit'.

[93] 'Omnia docenda per notiora'. An account of this method is given in 'Methodum linguarum generalis introductio', ed. P. Stötzner, *Neudrucke pädagogischer Schriften*, XII, Leipzig, 1892, p. 38.

it human knowledge can never be true knowledge.[94] Further, over and above any Baconian or Comenian insistence on the primacy of *things*, in the last resort Ratke's classifications – and here he resembles Bishop Wilkins and the English language-planners later in the century – rest on the categories of Aristotelian and medieval Scholastic philosophy.[95] Relevant here is Ratke's penchant for encyclopedism, for the drawing up of systematic tables embracing the whole of learning, in which the most immediate influence was no doubt the theologian Johann Lipsius of Strasbourg, but which again has medieval antecedents, for example in the work of Ramón Lull. What is peculiar to Ratke is that this systematization was to take place in the vernacular, as well as in the classical languages.

All of the features mentioned above – the insistence on the primacy of the vernacular, the theory of harmony, the imitation of Nature, the Ramist elements and the drive to encyclopedic systematization – are discernible in the Ratichian grammars. The desire for universalism, in the name of harmony, finds expression in the fact that the various manuals were to be produced in the classical languages and in various European vernaculars, and in the publication of the *Sprachlehr* in both German and Latin. The major feature of the reforms was however the teaching of all subjects in the mother tongue, with the high moral purpose of improving the German people – 'die teutsch Sprache und Nation zu bessern und zu erheben'. Here of course Luther's Bible has a primary role to play. The improvement of the status of the vernacular was in part, though unintentionally, brought about by the humanists themselves. Their insistence on the use of correct models had led to the disappearance of the lingua franca for the learned world provided by medieval spoken Latin, leaving a gap to be filled by the vernacular. As K. Seiler remarks, this workaday Latin lingua franca and medieval pedagogical methods fell into disuse together.[96] This means among other things that the vernacular could not become an object of instruction in its own right. As for the practical application of the notion of harmony, the principle of 'Gleichförmigkeit' or uniformity that runs all though Ratke's peda-

---

[94] See Seiler, *Das pädagogische System Wolfgang Ratkes*, p. 59.

[95] Seiler, *ibid.*, pp. 62–3, notes that whereas Bacon knew only the Scholastic form of syllogistic logic and rejected it, Ratke could find support for his own system in the Aristotelian variety.

[96] See *ibid.*, pp. 32–5, for an interesting discussion of these matters.

gogical endeavours requires a general concordance between the Köthen group's grammars of German, and their manuals for other languages. Since according to the 'Allgemeine Verfassung' it is from the principle of harmony that there 'flows the clarity and truth of all learning and languages', it follows that the grammar of German will be in its broad lines applicable to any other language. The grammars must accordingly all follow the same plan. The principle of 'Gleichförmigkeit' has rationalist implications, and it is not without interest that all the volumes printed in Köthen bear the pronouncement 'Ratio vicit, vetustas cessit' – in the name of reason, the old must give place to the new. Yet in spite of this brash pronouncement, and in contrast to the modernity of his pedagogical approach, Ratke's grammars do not innovate in matters of linguistic theory. His interests are pedagogical: 'No greater harm can befall the arts, than when the young are not well drilled in grammar.'[97] He is by and large content to repeat the mixed formal/semasiological approach inherited from the Latin tradition. If there is now and then a marked Scaligeran flavour to his definitions, it is because he has simply translated them word for word from Nicodemus Frischlin's *Quaestiones grammaticae* of 1584, itself based directly on J. C. Scaliger.

Much more interesting than either the 'Sprachkunst' or the *Sprachlehr* – apart from the latter's universalist implications, which will be considered elsewhere in this study – is the 'Wortschickungslehr' (*c.* 1630) which offers a theoretical discussion that is markedly absent from the other two grammars. This work, whose title-page bears the typically Ratichian pronouncement that 'custom disappears, reason prevails, truth finds its place', provides in its third book the first detailed treatment of German syntax. The term 'Wortschickung' implies the fit use of words in agreement, and the 'schickend Wort' or word aptly used in construction is exemplified in both of Ratke's twin sources: in the divine Revelation and in Nature. The Bible is the supreme example of the use of the 'schickend Wort', for the Holy Spirit employs in it words that are both fitting ('geschickt') and rational ('verstendig'). It is present in Nature, because of man's natural aptitude for expressing his thoughts in a rational and concordant way. Further, as with the language-planners later in the century, there is a natural agreement between phenomena

---

[97] 'Sprachkunst', p. 2 (Ising, *Wolfgang Ratkes Schriften*, ii, 9).

and their linguistic expression, for men's words 'without contradiction tally with the things' of Nature.[98] An indication that Ratke sees language and Nature as isomorphic is provided by his treatment of primary words as 'taken from Nature'.[99] Again, the function of the word aptly used in linguistic construction ('das schickend Wort') is that of a sign or 'Zeichen' which must 'clearly indicate the meaning of the thing'.[100] All this does not mean however that a knowledge of the 'Gleichförmigkeit' or harmony of language is innate in mankind. It is an art which must be learnt,[101] hence the importance of pedagogical method in Ratke's theory of language acquisition.

Similarly more interesting than either the 'Sprachkunst' or the *Sprachlehr* is Ratke's semantics or 'Wortbedeutungslehr' (*c.* 1630), which represents an attempt to elaborate a theory of word derivation on a synchronic basis. The treatment rests on the Scaligeran matter/form dichotomy, in which the 'Materi' (sounds[102] and syllables) of language attain a 'Form' or meaning by which 'each thing is indicated singularly and without confusion'.[103] In this way a relationship is established between form and content, in terms of which derived words can be accounted for, and which can be invoked to distinguish between derivation and composition. The influence of Scaliger or his imitators is seen in the definition of the word as a 'sign put together from linguistically apt syllables in order to indicate things as they are in reality to the intellect.[104] This definition applies only to the 'bedeutend Wort' or lexical term considered under its semantic aspect, and is in contrast to the 'schickend Wort' used in grammatical construction. As with the other works, so with the 'Wortbedeutungslehr', its theoretical justification is based, as its title-page proclaims, on the 'true harmony of Faith, Nature and Languages'. The 'bedeutend Wort' or item of lexis is equally with the 'schickend Wort' to be demonstrated from Scripture, the Holy Spirit having inspired 'meaningful words, in order that man might the sooner be brought to a knowledge of God and of himself'. Again,

[98] 'Wortschickungslehr', pp. 13, 15–16 (Ising, *Wolfgang Ratkes Schriften*, II, 99, 101–2).
[99] 'Sprachkunst', p. 10 (Ising, *Wolfgang Ratkes Schriften*, II, 101).
[100] 'Wortschickungslehr', p. 15 (Ising, *Wolfgang Ratkes Schriften*, II, 101).
[101] *Ibid.*, pp. 14–15 (Ising, *Wolfgang Ratkes Schriften*, II, 100–1).
[102] Ratke's employment of the term 'Lautbuchstaben' would seem to indicate that he was aware of sounds as well as letters.
[103] 'Wortbedeutungslehr', p. 6 (Ising, *Wolfgang Ratkes Schriften*, II, 276).
[104] *Ibid.*, p. 5 (Ising, *Wolfgang Ratkes Schriften*, II, 275).

therefore, the 'bedeutend Wort' is above all to be found in Luther's Bible. But here too, the system demands the dual operation of Revelation and Nature, for it is in the latter that the names of things are contained, and it so happens that they coincide exactly with the 'bedeutende Worte'. Given this isomorphism, the purpose of the 'Wortbedeutungslehr' is, in accordance with puritan Protestant thinking on such matters in England, to present things as they are in reality, thus enabling men to distinguish clearly between what is true and what is false.[105] It is Nature which, seemingly in two stages, first discovered letters and set them together, and then gave the resultant words individual meanings as 'the signs of things'. It is however God who implants in man the 'natural inclination' to meditate on these meanings and increase their number by his own efforts,[106] and it is this provision that allows for the development of new forms in derivation and composition. The 'bedeutend Wort' accordingly stems either 'immediately' from whoever first gave names to 'the beasts and birds under the heavens, and the cattle in the field', or 'mediately' from the further deliberate propagation of meaningful terms.[107] Apart from these theoretical considerations, the grammatical model followed is patently Latin grammar's division of words according to 'species' (primary and derived forms) and 'figura' (simple and compound ones). But though clearly based on a common procedure in Latin grammars, Ratke's 'Wortbedeutungslehr' represents the first attempt to provide a semantically based theory of word derivation applied to the vernacular. It contains perhaps the germs of Schottel's attempt, later in the century, to base a whole theory of linguistic description on German's exceptional capacity for word-building.

A close account of Ratke's largely derivative grammatical theory would be tedious. The *etymologia* (the vernacular terms are 'Wortforschung' or 'Worterklerung') of his grammars, giving the traditional definitions and accidents of the parts of speech, does not offer any great interest, based as it is on the Latin models provided by Finck–Helwig[108] and Frischlin,[109] and beyond them by Melanchthon

---

[105] *Ibid.*, pp. 3–4 (Ising, *Wolfgang Ratkes Schriften*, ii, 274).
[106] *Ibid.*, p. 5 (Ising, *Wolfgang Ratkes Schriften*, ii, 276).
[107] *Ibid.*, p. 6 (Ising, *Wolfgang Ratkes Schriften*, ii, 276).
[108] Finck and Helwig, *Grammatica Latina*, second (and only extant) edition, Giessen, 1615. These authors themselves no doubt take some of their definitions from Frischlin and/or Scaliger.
[109] N. Frischlin, *Quaestionum grammaticarum libri IIX* (? = VIII), Venice, 1584.

and Scaliger.[110] The undoubted Ramist element (treated earlier in this study) is present more in the methodology and in an extensive use of dichotomies than in any attempt to apply Ramus' formally based grammatical theory. The very eclecticism of Ratke's borrowings[111] would seem to suggest that, though he had determined views on pedagogy, he had no very strong preferences in grammatical theory. Here only a few examples from the various grammars will be given, where they seem more particularly to illustrate Ratke's methods. The 'Wortschickungslehr' for instance gives a much fuller treatment of the adjective than the 'Sprachkunst' and the *Sprachlehr*, a treatment in which Ratke's predilection for Ramist dichotomies is exercised to the full. A preliminary dichotomy divides adjectives into indicators ('anzeigende') and numerals, the former being divided in turn into those expressing a circumstance and those expressing an enquiry. A circumstance is indicated either 'bedeutlich' or 'mitbe-deutlich', that is to say as a full lexical signification or a consignifier. The former type groups adjectives into various semantic classes, such as those of place and time. Consignified circumstances are indicated in two ways: by 'Sammlung' (*all, ganz,* etc.) or by 'Verentzelung' (*ein jeder, welcher,* etc.). Those adjectives expressing enquiry are classified into questioning (*der wie vielste?*) and responding (*der erste*). The numeral adjectives, after a primary division into 'zusammen-setzende' and 'ordnende', are similarly teased out into a series of lumbering dichotomies, presented in catechetical fashion. The whole must have been a considerable chore for the wretched pupil. The monotonously pat question-and-answer sequence on numerals is typical of the method throughout:

Q. Worinne bestehet das zusamensetzende?
A. In der zusamenfügung und ausdrückung.
Q. Wie in der zusamenfügung?
A. Entweder der entzlen oder sorten.
Q. Was füget die entzlen zusamen?
A. Das schlechtzehlende.
Q. Was ist die schlechtzehlende?
A. Welcher die zahl schlechter dinge bedeütet...

[110] Scaliger, *De causis linguae Latinae.*
[111] The rules for the article in the German version of the 'Wortschickungslehr', for instance, largely coincide with those in Clajus' *Grammatica Germanicae linguae* (1578), though Ratke provides his own examples.

Q. Wie in der ausdrückung?
A. Entweder der vermehrung oder mass.[112]

One wonders what it must have been like to be at the receiving end of Ratke's reforms, and can only guess at the monotonous antiphonal chanting that must have gone on in practice, whatever the good intentions.

One consequence of the reform was the replacing of Latin technical terms by vernacular ones, sometimes with amusing results, as when the Latin *accusativum*, itself a mistranslation,[113] is rendered as 'anklagiger'.[114] Apart from such details however, Ratke's various morphologies offer nothing that cannot be found in Melanchthon, Frischlin, Finck–Helwig and Scaliger. Often enough his definitions are a mixture taken from two or more of these authors. As for syntax, his predecessors had paid but slight attention to vernacular construction, and indeed Ratke's own 'Sprachkunst' gives no syntax at all, while the treatment in the *Sprachlehr* extends to a mere four pages – admittedly out of a total of only twenty-two. It is patently Latin-based, treating syntax under the headings concord and government, and defining relationships between words in terms of semantic 'qualities'. The rules coincide precisely with those long familiar in Latin: two or more substantives referring to the same thing must be in the same case; adjectives agree with their substantives in case and number; of two substantives referring to different things, one governs the other in the genitive case. These rules do none the less have a validity for German, which is a case language, that they do not have for the more analytical French and English. They are however enunciated *in vacuo*, for no examples of their application are given. As in other matters it is to the 'Wortschickungslehr' that we must turn for a fuller treatment. This work devotes a full forty pages to syntax, of which nine deal with figurative

[112] 'Wortschickungslehr', pp. 68–9 (Ising, *Wolfgang Ratkes Schriften*, II, 163–4).
[113] The Greek term, *aitiatikē*, in fact meant 'causative'. The misunderstanding was apparently initiated by Varro (see Robins, *A Short History of Linguistics*, p. 35).
[114] The full set of case-terms is:

Latin grammar	'Sprachkunst'	'Wortschickungslehr'
nominativum	nenniger	Nennbug
vocativum	ruffiger	Ruffbug
accusativum	anklagiger	Werckbug
genitivum	gebäriger	Besitzbug
dativum	dagebiger	Kriegbug
ablativum	abtragiger	Lassbug

constructions, a subject to which he gives more attention than any of his vernacular predecessors.[115] Since the 'Wortschickungslehr' is expressly 'auff die teütsche Sprache gerichtet' (title-page) and its examples are taken from Luther's Bible, it might be expected to give a specifically vernacular syntax. The treatment here again however, though it is overlaid by a network of dichotomies, does not differ markedly from Latin practice. The overriding principle is that of word government, and the discussion of the syntax of each part of speech in turn perpetuates the word-centred character of Renaissance grammar. An important feature of vernacular structure is however recognized in the division of verbal construction into 'behülflich' (concerning the auxiliaries) and 'zufällig'. The auxiliary verbs govern no cases, but only the verb with which they are constructed, either in proximity or at a distance. When not functioning as auxiliaries, they do of course govern cases. The 'wesentliche' auxiliaries (*ich bin, ich werde*) have a nominative case before and after them – a Latin rule which has more sense in German than when transferred unthinkingly to English and French. Rules such as that requiring *ich bin* to take a genitive of possession (*Die Stimme ist Jacobs Stimme*), or a dative (*Dem Thoren ist die thorheit eine freüde*), seem however to have little point. Much of the discussion consists of an enumeration, based on semantic criteria, of the cases governed by different verbs. The verbs of remembrance or forgetting, hardy annuals of the Latin grammars, take for instance either genitive or accusative. Each case is treated in turn, with illustrative examples from Luther's Bible. Direct imports from Latin grammar, also, are the adjectives signifying 'advantage, equivalence, favour or their contraries', all of which take a dative case. The figurative syntax, by far the fullest treatment of the figures of speech yet to appear in a vernacular grammar, offers ample scope for dichotomies. The syntax of figures is not however, as in the seminal discussion of ellipse in Sanctius' *Minerva* (1587), elevated to the status of a necessary component of linguistic theory. The bias is rhetorical rather than grammatical.

In comparison with the importance of his pedagogical endeavours, Ratke's influence on the development of grammatical theory must

---

[115] Ising (*Wolfgang Ratkes Schriften*, 1, 65), noting that Ratke divides syntax into 'richtig' and 'figürlich', describes this as his 'eigenes Einteilungsprinzip'. He had however predecessors in the Latin grammars of the period.

be admitted to be slight. Though he seeks to renew the methods of grammar teaching, attempting to integrate it into his universalist theory of harmony, his manuals do not depart significantly from established Latin theory, repeating well-worn definitions from Donatus, Melanchthon and Frischlin. Even his adoption, in the 'Sprachkunst' (1612–15) of Scaligeran definitions from Frischlin's *Quaestiones* may be at third-hand via Finck–Helwig's Latin grammar.[116] Plagiarism was however a way of life for the grammarians of the period, and such questions are of little importance, given that the main thrust of Ratke's endeavours, and his abiding influence, are in the realm of pedagogy. E. Ising sees in his work the beginnings of German school grammar and there can be no doubt that, via the penetration of his methods into the schools he not only gave a powerful impetus to the developing drive for purity in the mother tongue, but also determined to a large extent the nature of vernacular grammatical terminology. Certainly it is from Ratke's time on that the production of grammars for schools shows a marked increase. To him above all must be attributed the real beginnings of a willingness to treat the vernacular as an object of study in its own right. With him too begin (via Ramus) the encyclopedic approach and the drive towards universal education. It is no doubt exaggerated to credit his work, as does K. Seiler,[117] with a pan-European dimension and an influence on the entire cultural life of his time. His efforts were effectively impeded by the religious wars, and much of his theory consists of a curious blend of recognizably modern ideas and Scholastic epistemology. He remains however a great initiator, a stimulus to new approaches to pedagogy, and it is in large part due to his efforts that the vernacular became not only the tool of a pedagogical method, but the gateway to learning in general. Certainly, as the arrogant 'Ratio vicit: vetustas cessit' of his title-pages indicates, he saw himself as the harbinger of a new age.

[116] Since a first edition of this work is not extant, there is no possibility of knowing whether the definitions concerned were already contained in it, and therefore available to Ratke, or the authors themselves used Ratke's definitions (from Frischlin?) in their own revision.

[117] *Das pädagogische System Wolfgang Ratkes*, pp. 4,7.

Other authors

A self-confessed follower of Ratke's pedagogical reforms, Johann Kromayer, whose *Deutsche Grammatica zum neuen Methodo* appeared in Weimar in 1618,[118] notes however in his foreword that the 'neue Lehrart' promised by Ratke has not as yet been brought to fruition, either because of the scorn with which the reforms were greeted, or because the various collaborators have gone their separate ways. His own grammar is intended as a further contribution to the Ratichian 'didactica', to the reforms of which the decaying school system stands so urgently in need. If a grammar appropriate to the task has been slow in appearing it is, he says, because its would-be authors were striving for perfection. Kromayer himself had already in 1614 sketched out a pedagogical reform on Ratichian lines and tried it out in a school, and his *Deutsche Grammatica* was intended for classroom use in the duchy of Weimar. It in fact preceded by a year both Ratke's *Sprachlehr* and Helwig's *Sprachkünste*, and may be regarded as the first complete grammar of German to be written in the vernacular.[119] Its purpose is still however, as its author admits, to inculcate the elements of the mother tongue as a preparation for Latin studies, and it is accordingly not intended for a higher level than the *Volksschule* or primary school. The technical terms are left in Latin, no doubt because the student will meet them later in the Latin school, but the grammar is a very simple one giving a minimum of information, with an avoidance of complicated classification in sharp contrast to for example the tortuous dichotomies of Gueintz' *Deutscher Sprachlehre Entwurf* (1641). Kromayer has obviously been at some pains to produce a grammar that could actually be used in schools. Far from attempting to inculcate a complete knowledge of German grammar, he contents himself with familiarizing pupils with the 'notiones secundae' – number, case, declension and the parts of speech – in order that these notions may later be applied to the learning of Latin. In this respect, and for the same pedagogical reasons, his work is to some extent a general grammar in the same tradition as Ratke's *Sprachlehr* and Helwig's *Sprachkünste*. Kromayer is not aiming at the

---

[118] I have consulted the Göttingen University Library's xerox copy (Ling. VII 1372) of the Weimar edition of 1625.

[119] Jellinek (*Geschichte*, I, 95) does not rate this work very highly, though he admits that pedagogically it represents an advance on the *Köthener Sprachlehr*. He thinks its importance for the development of vernacular grammar has been overestimated.

perfection he condemns Ratichians for seeking, but contents himself, in accordance with their principle of 'Gleichförmigkeit', with following the plan of their grammars of Latin, Greek and Hebrew. This involves him in treating at the outset those accidents that are common to more than one word-class, and in treating the indeclinable parts of speech (in extremely concise fashion) before the declinable ones. The treatment is in general slight, consonant with his aim of presenting the barest elements of grammar in the vernacular before proceeding to the serious business of teaching Latin. His cavalier treatment of the indeclinables probably results from the fact that little need be said about them in preparing pupils for the later confrontation with the classical language. A different aim might have produced different results, as in Jacob Brücker's *Teutsche Grammatic* (1620),[120] in which unusual attention is given to the indeclinable word-classes. Jellinek[121] treats it in his chapter on German grammar as an introduction to rhetoric, and it is no doubt his rhetorical bias that causes Brücker to devote so much space to adverbs, prepositions and conjunctions. This work is also unusual in providing in its syntactic section a separate chapter dealing, again in accordance with Brücker's rhetorical interests, with the analysis of complex sentences. The grammar is intended to be at least in part a manual of composition, catering for practical needs and in particular for those of the *Kanzleien* or imperial chanceries. Himself a teacher, first in Heidelberg and later in Frankfurt-am-Main, Brücker is convinced that vernacular schools should be established, following the pattern of the Latin ones, in which in addition to other basic knowledge children would learn to write and understand their mother tongue. He belongs, it is true, to the 'mother's milk' school which holds that the rules of grammar are better learnt in the home than out of a book, but this means that for him written *Schriftsprache* and colloquial *Umgangssprache* coincide.[122]

More directly intended for classroom use is Tilmann Olearius' *Deutsche Sprachkunst* (1630),[123] which, though no longer under the direct influence of the Ratichian school, has points in common with it. It is a rather delightful little handbook, even slighter than that of Kromayer, with charming explicatory woodcuts accompanying

[120] Published in Frankfurt-am-Main.   [121] *Geschichte*, I, 104–7.
[122] Though Brücker predates Pudor's *Grundrichtigkeit* (1672) in treating complex sentences, his treatment is but slight.
[123] Published in Halle.

simple information kept to the minimum, in refreshing contrast to the usual overloaded school grammars. Similarly appropriate to the practical schoolroom situation is Olearius' method of teaching to read by means of cards, each with a letter and an illustration. A Ratichian feature is his claim that his illustrations of points of grammar can be used later by the pupil in studying other tongues: 'for this little book is not merely a compendium of German grammar, but it also contains *generalissima praecepta* which can be used with many other languages'. Though for Olearius instruction in the vernacular is intended to precede that in other tongues, for him too it represents a gateway to Latin, and indeed his German *Sprachkunst* is followed in the same volume by an application of the 'new method' to the learning of Latin 'speedily and with pleasure'. Though in the foreword stress is laid on the importance of a thorough knowledge of the mother tongue for officials, the clergy, scholars and men of affairs, the book is in fact no more than a very elementary primer. Perhaps it is intended at least in part as a manual for the teacher, for its chief interest, apart from the novelty of the illustrations, lies in the short statement of pedagogical principles contained in the foreword. Olearius stresses that his method is aimed at children, whose 'fivefold *potentiae animae*' should be appealed to in teaching. These 'mental faculties' are the senses; the 'phantasia' or 'sensus communis'; the memory; the intellect; and the judgment. A trait which links his approach to that of English 'sensualist' grammarians of a slightly later period such as Mark Lewis is his insistence that children learn more easily through the eye than through the ear.[124] Hence his own use of visual aids, which appeal both to 'phantasia' and to memory. His pictures also facilitate comprehension, for they present in immediately assimilable form such notions as case and tense, which would otherwise have to be learnt slowly and painfully from written definitions that children seldom really understand. The comparison with Comenius' illustrations to his *Orbis pictus* is irresistible. And how modern-sounding is Olearius' 'nothing is more difficult for children, in the customary method of learning to read, than to have to sit still, stay silent, and keep their eyes fixed on the book'. In his system the pupil plays an active role, not the passive one prescribed by Ratichians. He even uses the term 'lusus grammaticus', the grammatical game, surely one

[124] Cf. Lewis' *An Essay to Facilitate the Education of Youth, by Bringing Down the Rudiments of Grammar to the Sense of Seeing*, London?, 1671?

The imperfect, indicating an incomplete action still in process, is represented by a man looking over his shoulder, 'as one who, while running away, yet looks back as if he would prefer to remain'.

The perfect tense, signifying a completed action, is represented by a picture of a thief with his hands tied behind his back: 'der hat gestolen'. (T. Olearius, *Deutsche Sprachkunst*, Herzog August Bibliothek, Wolfenbüttel.)

of the earliest instances of the 'play way' in education. By the use of pictures even the rules of syntax can be turned into a *lusus grammaticus* and 'played with pleasure'. Olearius himself must have felt in need of diversion, for in an accompanying fly-leaf advertising his grammar he claims to have spent more than a decade 'striving in the dust of private teaching'.

The work of Christian Gueintz – *Deutscher Sprachlehre Entwurf*, Köthen, 1641 – stands in close relationship on the one hand to the Ratichian reform, and on the other to the endeavours of the academy known as the Fruchtbringende Gesellschaft. In the setting up of such academies Germany had lagged far behind Italy. Such topics as the relationship of a standard dialect to the other speech communities, the role of court usage, and the respective importance of written and oral norms, which were already in the first half of the sixteenth century the subject of lively debate in Italy, were not to any great extent treated in Germany before the seventeenth. Already in the sixteenth century Florence had its Accademia della Crusca, which under Salviati's leadership imposed the written norm of the 'sommi trecentisti' Dante, Petrarch and Boccaccio. It was not until the following century that, at a time when the cultivation of the French language by the upper classes threatened to relegate German to the status of a lower-class dialect, a few leading figures began to take palliative measures. Of the resultant German academies the Fruchtbringende Gesellschaft, founded in Weimar in 1617 by Fürst Ludwig of Anhalt-Köthen, was the oldest and most prestigious. Consciously modelled on the Italian academies, it reached its highest point between 1630 and 1650. Once Weimar had taken the lead, other academies followed: the Aufrichtige Tannengesellschaft in Strasbourg, the Hirten-und Blumenorden an der Pegnitz, the Deutschgesinnte Genossenschaft, and others. In the forties of the seventeenth century these societies stimulated interest in the mother tongue, and numbered among their members well-known grammarians. J. G. Schottel (known in the academy under the pseudonym 'der Suchende'), Kaspar Stieler ('der Spate') and Christian Gueintz ('der Ordnende') were all members of the Fruchtbringende Gesellschaft. The importance of German grammar as such in their deliberations was however slight, though they played a role in the drive towards linguistic purity. Only the Fruchtbringende Gesellschaft invites comparison with the Accademia della Crusca, though M. H. Jellinek compares them to the former's disadvantage, noting that the only work of importance produced by the academy (Gueintz' Orthography) is far from equalling Salviati's *Vocabolario*.[125] A feature of Gueintz' grammar that is consonant with his membership of the academy is his preference for the *Schriftsprache*, for the usage of the 'Scribenten' whether pre-Lutheran or more recent. He classifies them into users of a straightforward everyday style, and more ornate

[125] *Geschichte*, I, 120. Jellinek stresses that the Gesellschaft cannot claim any credit for Schottel's work.

writers. It is from the former, and above all from Luther, that the genius of the language is to be learned.

In 1618 Fürst Ludwig had called Gueintz to Köthen to collaborate in the Ratichian reforms, and though he left four years later it was under Ratichian auspices that he produced his grammar. Though it owes something to Clajus and Ritter, it is clearly influenced by the *Köthener Sprachlehr*. Not only does Gueintz take technical terms wholesale from the *Sprachlehr*, merely putting them into German, but he also repeats its definitions with little alteration. What above all marks his grammar as being in the Ratichian tradition is the methodology, in particular the abundant use of Ramist dichotomies. Within this methodological framework his material is unoriginal. He too believes that 'when young people are properly instructed in this language, they will the more easily attain to others'. His claim that German is superior to the other vernaculars because it 'originates for the most part from Hebrew' is now easily dismissed. The influence of the Fruchtbringende Gesellschaft is to be seen however in his choice of features contributing to this preeminence:

> The completeness of the German language is such that there is almost nothing that cannot be named by it: for it is the richest in words...in that from three root-words over four hundred good, pure and serviceable German words, each with a different meaning, can be formed. This being so it has no need of foreign words, and remains unentangled with other languages.[126]

The features justifying the serious study of the German vernacular are its purity, its almost unlimited capacity for word-formation, and its provision of a gateway to other tongues.

This preoccupation with the riches of the German language and its fecundity in the formation of compounds finds its highest theoretical expression in the work of Schottel, who founds on it a general linguistic theory.[127] Vernacular grammarians had always pointed to the abundance of prepositions in German, and it is no doubt a sign of increasing awareness of vernacular structure when Johann Bellin publishes in 1660 his *Syntaxis praepositionum Teutonicarum*.[128] This solid work (the main body of which consists of close on three hundred

---

[126] *Deutscher Sprachlehre Entwurf*, p. 11.

[127] Schottel's contribution to grammatical theory is treated below, in the chapter on universal grammar.

[128] Both this and the identical 1661 edition were published in Lübeck. Despite the partially Latin title, the work is written in German.

pages) is of particular interest for its very long foreword setting out Bellin's pedagogical principles and his view of the mother tongue. He begins with the customary lamentations over contemporary neglect of the vernacular, which is scorned by foreigners and held in low esteem by native Germans. In rebuttal of this attitude Bellin devotes a long section to those great men throughout history – beginning with the 'primal originator' Ascenas – who sought to maintain and improve the language. Once again the importance of vernacular study is assessed in terms of its use in the learning of Latin, more especially in translation exercises. It is however – and it is a complaint voiced elsewhere at this period – precisely the supremacy of Latin, allied to the *laissez-faire* attitude of schoolmasters, that is to blame for the encouragement of bad habits in the vernacular. Continually confronted with *ad* plus accusative and *sine* plus ablative, it is all too easy for the pupil, at any rate in the Lower Saxon schools cited by Bellin, to write *zu mich, *ohne mir, etc. All too often such errors are heard from the master himself: 'solche undeudsche verdeudschung von einem undeudschen Deutschen Lermeister'. These 'Verdeutschungen' were of course virtually the only German the pupils heard in school, since instruction was given in Latin. It is no doubt to counter such errors that Bellin published his syntax of the preposition, but he additionally recommends, as does Ratke, prior exposition in the vernacular, with the advantage (and here he cites Ratke's fifth rule of pedagogy) that the pupil is free to pay attention to the matter he is being taught, undistracted by the intricacies of a foreign language. As to the dialect in which instruction is to be given, Bellin proposes the use of the 'Hochdeudsche sprache' as practised by those 'true teachers of pure language' the chanceries of the Holy Roman Empire. In learning this dialect it will help if one frequents the citizens of Meissen, though he admits that nowhere is it spoken with complete purity. It can only be acquired in its wholly correct form from Luther's Bible, and Bellin does not fail to quote Clajus to the effect that having spoken correct Hebrew and Greek through the prophets and apostles, the Holy Spirit has now spoken good German through Luther's version of the Scriptures. The correctness of Luther's Bible thus has a divine guarantor. Besides being the vehicle of Revelation, it is also par excellence the source of pure German, and for Bellin, continuing the by now well-rooted tradition of the inspired character of German, these two facets are inseparable. So important is the role of Luther's Bible that a distinction is made between the pre-Lutheran and the post-Lutheran usage of the chanceries, the latter being both more elegant and more correct than the former. To these models may be added the Psalter of Opitz, who held among German writers, if Bellin's lavish praise is to be believed, a position comparable to that of Vergil and Cicero among Latin ones. But what is learnt from authors must be consolidated by industrious perusal of grammar books, the best being that of Schottel, though it is precisely in the syntax of prepositions that his exposition lacks clarity, a defect Bellin's own work proposes to remedy. In summing up the position of the vernacular in the schools of his day he can find no better words than those of Schottel's first 'Lobrede' or eulogy:

Nowhere art thou, O German language, poorer than in that place where thou shouldst be rich, nowhere more mute and silent than where thy lovely voice should sound forth...In the schools thou art swept under the benches in the dust, where no teacher or pupil can seek, let alone find thee.[129]

Bellin's attempts to redress the balance were however in large measure frustrated by the hostility encountered by his eccentric system of orthography.

Similar eccentricities prevented Isaac Pölmann's *Neuer hoochdeutscher Donat* (1671)[130] from receiving its due appreciation from his contemporaries. Though the work, intended to be superseded by a fuller one, is no more than a manual of declensions and conjugations, its methodology is so unusual that it is hardly surprising that the author had difficulty in getting it into print, and finally had it published at his own expense. Pölmann was a cleric by profession and tells us he took two years over his task, working at it as and when his pastoral duties allowed. He appears to be quite uninfluenced by previous work, basing his systems of declension and conjugation on his own observations, and justifying them by the fact that though the vernacular has now reached the peak of perfection, there still exists no 'perpetua Germanismi analogia', no grammar based on a consistent principle. Pölmann's undeniable eccentricity lies in his having taken as his consistent principle the phases of the moon, in reference to which paradigms are classified as *plenus*, *medius*, *bicornis* or *novilunius*, with at the side of each an illustration of the moon in the appropriate phase. This gives a very distinctive appearance to

---

[129] *Syntaxis praepositionum Teutonicarum*, foreword, p. [xxxviii].
[130] Published in Berlin.

Gleich wie der Mond itzt voll sich an dem Himmel zeiget:
Bald bald ☾ : bald hörnig ☾: bald der Sonnen zu sich neiget/
   Und gleichsam gar nicht ist / weil niemand sehen kann/
   Drey gantzer Tage lang/ den schwartzen ● Himmel-Mann:
So ists beschaffen mit der DECLJNATJON
Hochdeutscher Sprache: Die/ ob sie sich zeiget schon
   Als voller Mond O zu erst: Doch wird sie bald geringe/ ☾/ ☾:
   Bald schwartz ●: So daß man sie kaum merket aller Dinge.

Luna velut plenO mox eſt ſpeĉtabilis Orbe:
   Mox media ☾, & rara ☾ eſt : nigraque ● ; at *una* tamen.
Sic Germanorum quoque D E C L I N A T I O plena eſt, O,
   Et media ☾. & rara ☾ eſt: nigraque ●, at *una* tamen.

A 2   II. Nu-

V. Modus declinandi eſt triplex: *Plenus* O: *MEDIUS* ☾,
quò pertinet *bicornis* ☾: & *novilunius* ●.

   1. Zum vollen Mond / O / gehören lauter ADJECTIVA. Et
hic Modus declinandi rapit & capit omnes quinque termina-
tiones declinantes, *e, es, em, en, er*, hinc reĉtè vocatur *Plenus*.

   2. Zum Mittelmond ☾/ und zum Zweyhörnigen ☾/ gehören
lauter SUBSTANTIVA. Et quia hunc modum deficiunt
quædam ſyllabæ declinantes, præſertim *em*, & pro re natâ, *e, er*,
& *en* : hinc reĉtè vocatur *MEDIUS & Bicornis*.

   3. Zum schwartzen Mond ● gehören ſo wol ADJECTIVA,
als SUBSTANTIVA, Et hic in univerſum abſolvitur unicâ illâ
terminatione euphonicâ **en**/ id quod docebunt, Paradigmata.

   4. Pronomen demonſtrativum & Relativum

   Der/ die/ das/ declinatur *abundanter*, per omnes re-
ſpeĉtivè declinandi MODOS, O, ☾, ●, h. m.

Maſcul.		*fœmin.*		*neutr.*	
S. O		O		O	
1. der	●	1. die ●		1. das	●
2. déß	☾ deſſen	2. der/	deren	2. déß	☾ deſſen.
3. dem/ deme		3. der		3. dem/ deme	
4. den		4. die		4. das	

Plur. O

1. 4. die	O	☾		●
2. der/	derer/	dere/		deren
3. den	----	----		denen.

Die Stimm' und deren Hall/ ſonat Germanicè, & analogicè.
Die Stimm und dero Hall/ ſonat Sileſiacè, præter analogiam.

Three passages from I. Pölmann's *Neuer hoochdeutscher Donat*, illustrating his use of the phases
of the moon as a teaching device. (Niedersächsische Staats- und Universitätsbibliothek,
Göttingen.)

his pages, but his 'lunacy' is really no more than a striking pedagogical device for emphasizing linguistic features based on very sound observation. As the title *Donat* indicates, his grammar is not intended to give more than the rudiments, but in view of their gift for straightforward observation of linguistic structure it is a pity that both his work and that of Bellin lapsed into obscurity. More conventional is Christian Pudor's *Grundrichtigkeit* (1672),[131] a work in which the more strictly grammatical section is slight, but which is noteworthy in being the first German grammar to give more than a minimal treatment of sentence structure.[132] While rejoicing that thanks to the efforts of the Fruchtbringende Gesellschaft and of a few individuals the German language has finally been 'raised up from the dust [an obvious echo of Schottel's first 'Lobrede'] in which it lay for so long, and brought into the light of day cleansed and pure', Pudor still finds much to deplore in the situation of the vernacular, comparing it unfavourably with that in other European countries. Germans, particularly scholars, are still all too inclined to devote their energies to languages other than their own, and Pudor's tabulation of 'the best of what is useful and necessary for the *Grundrichtigkeit* and elegance of the German language' is yet one more attempt to redress the situation. In this attempt, what he has provided is as much a rhetoric as a grammar – his touchstone is *Zierlichkeit*, 'elegance' – and is indicative of the widespread contemporary feeling that as compared with other vernaculars the German language lacks polish. Another school grammar whose concern with the improvement of German extends beyond the bounds of the classroom is Johann Ludewig Prasch's *Neue, kurtz-und-deutliche Sprachkunst* (1687),[133] which is intended not only to provide a grounding in the vernacular as a preparation for Latin studies, but also for the use of 'Kanzleyen', 'Druckereyen' and 'Schreibstuben'. Again, as with Bellin a quarter of a century previously, the pretext for bringing out the work is the impracticability of Schottel's grammar for school

[131] Published in Cölln an der Spree. I have used the reprint in *Documenta Linguistica, Quellen zur Geschichte der deutschen Sprache des 15. bis 20. Jahrhunderts*, ed. M. Rössing-Hager, Hildesheim and New York, 1975.
[132] In this regard the full title is significant: *Der Teutschen Sprache Grundrichtigkeit und Zierlichkeit...darinnen gewiesen wird...wie man eine einfältige Teutsche Rede, durch zierliche Versetzung, Verwechselung, Erweiterung, Zusammenziehung...ausschmücken könne: aus vielen Teutschen Rednern, und Poeten zusammengetragen.* [133] Published in Regensburg.

use. While the monumental *Ausführliche Arbeit* is a 'golden book' of reference for the teacher, Prasch fears it will be beyond the comprehension of even those pupils who can afford to buy a copy. He therefore offers in its stead his own grammar, in order that the young may obtain sufficient elements of the 'Teutsche Mutter-Haubt-und Heldensprache' with less 'ungewachsene Füsse' than they are accustomed to.

The grammatical theories

The grammatical theory of the above authors will now be treated as a single whole, with attention being drawn to individual contributions which emphasize a trend or seem important in their own right. Whether for Ramist pedagogical reasons, through the influence of the academies and in particular of the Fruchtbringende Gesellschaft, or as Gueintz suggests because they are thought to fall within the province of universal grammar, these authors pay unusual attention to derivation and composition, which are treated at the outset as categories affecting all word-classes. Pudor in particular has an exceptionally long and important preliminary section on these matters, obviously owing much to Schottel. He takes a positive pleasure in adducing examples of up to four elements (*Oberberghauptmann*), of adjective plus adjective (*armseelig*), of noun plus verb (*Rahtgeber*), and of 'Vorwort' plus adjective (*unwiederaufbringlich*). This part of grammar is increasingly treated as the century goes on, being singled out with pride as a special characteristic of the German language, and a feature in which it is thought to be manifestly superior to Latin. Such is its fecundity that some authors see German as giving birth not only to its own ever-ramifying and rich vocabulary, but to other languages as well. It is this generative power, this possession of a store of fertile root-words, that Prasch invokes as proof of his claim that Latin is derived from German. In the absence of a properly based diachronic theory all things are possible, but no doubt this claim is the earlier belief that German was the original language, in a new form. At all events it shows a new confidence in the vernacular vis-à-vis Latin, an upsurge in national pride which leads Gueintz to institute comparisons with Rome, which subjugated other peoples by imposing its language on them. For Gueintz, political and linguistic supremacy go together to an extent that recalls Nebrija's much earlier claims for Castilian.[134]

Again probably for pedagogical reasons, some authors produce modifications of the traditional Latin system of eight (or nine if the article is included) parts of speech. The most revolutionary of the modifications is Olearius' three-part system of noun, verb, and 'Flickwoerter' embracing the traditional indeclinables. The most prestigious and best-known example of this tripartite system applied to Latin occurs in the *Minerva* (1587) of the great Spanish grammarian Sanctius, who concludes on philosophical grounds that in all languages the parts of speech cannot be more than three – the noun, verb and particle found in 'all oriental languages' and more particularly in Hebrew. Aristotle too had posited a three-part system of *onoma*, *rhema*, and a class of words (the *sundesmoi*) consignifying with these two, and Olearius similarly gives his 'Flickwoerter' the subordinate function of 'tying and patching together' the two main word-classes.[135] The classification was well known to logicians, who as Frischlin mentions in his *Quaestiones* of 1584 commonly treated the indeclinables as 'syncategoremata' or consignifying particles.[136] Frischlin does not however transfer this from logic to grammar. The closest parallel to Olearius' approach in a vernacular grammar is provided by Christoph Helwig's *Sprachkünste* (1619), which has the three main classes noun, verb and 'Beiwort' (called in the Latin version 'advocabulum'), within which framework pronoun, participle and the indeclinables are treated as sub-classes. It may be supposed that Olearius' immediate source is in fact Helwig, though since the latter's work was published in both German and Latin and intended as a demonstration of universal grammar rather than of the structure of German as such, Olearius himself may be considered the first actual grammarian of the vernacular to use the system. Though not used again by a German grammarian before Bödiker in 1690, this tripartite classification later became common and was much in vogue, again for philosophical reasons connected with universal grammar, in the eighteenth century. Gueintz has a four-part scheme in which noun and pronoun form a single class signifying 'without time', and verb and participle make

---

[134] *Gramatica de la lengua castellana*, 1492.

[135] *Deutsche Sprachkunst*, Halle, 1630, p. 40: the *Flickwoerter* 'dieselbe [i.e. noun and verb] ineinander knuepfen und flicken'.

[136] *Quaestionum grammaticarum libri IIX* (? = VIII) p. 72: the particles 'nullum animi sensum exprimunt, nisi addantur Nomini, aut Verbo'.

up a contrasting one signifying 'with time'. The indeclinable parts are in turn grouped as 'Haubtwoerter' (adverb and preposition) and 'Nebenwoerter' (conjunction and interjection). The immediate source of the second dichotomy is the *Compendium grammaticae Latinae* produced by the Ratke circle in Köthen. The source of the first one is again Frischlin and J. C. Scaliger, who treat noun and pronoun as identical, except that nouns signify things directly, whereas pronouns do so secondarily, at one remove from reality.[137] The result is what is virtually a four-class system, in which the article is counted with the pronoun, and the distinguishing mark separating the two overall divisions is the presence or absence of number and person. The only other author to set up what is quite openly and unashamedly a four-part system is Prasch, with 'Nennwort' (noun, pronoun and participle), 'Wirck-oder-Zeit-Wort' (verb), 'Vorsetzwort' (preposition) and 'Nebenwort' (adverb, conjunction and interjection). The preposition figures separately because, unlike the 'Nebenwoerter', it governs cases. Typically, the main reason for Prasch's classification is a pedagogical one: the fewer categories there are in a subject, the easier it is to grasp. Whatever the reason given, there is a general tendency everywhere as the eighteenth century approaches to simplify the classification of the parts of speech, whether on pedagogical or philosophical grounds.

In defining the parts of speech the tendency is to abandon definitions by formal criteria, to give a bare minimum of information, and to use as pedagogical devices the 'Kennzeichen' or signs that precede the parts in discourse. The noun for instance is defined either in purely semantic terms as signifying a thing, or in those terms plus the requirement that it can be preceded by an article. Popular since Melanchthon's use of it in his Latin grammar is the stipulation of substantives as nouns which cannot be followed by *Mann*, *Weib*, or *Ding*. Another widespread approach is the treatment of the substantive as that which can stand alone in discourse and can receive only one article, and the adjective as that which cannot stand alone but has the choice among all three of *der*, *die* and *das*.[138] The most interesting

[137] Frischlin's noun (*ibid.*, p. 73) signifies 'rem primo', as does that of his model Scaliger (*De causis linguae Latinae*, p. 135).
[138] The stipulation as to syntactic dependence or independence is an inheritance from medieval modistic grammar. Prasch's term 'Wesenswort' for the substantive is obviously based on Scaliger's contention that it signifies essence rather than substance. The first German grammarian to give the adjective separate status as a part of speech is Pudor.

treatment, in line with later developments in grammatical theory, is that of Olearius, who reserves the definition 'the name of a thing' to the substantive, defining adjectives by contrast as 'names of qualities'. The exigences of his three-word-class system however cause him to group together as adjectives both those traditionally so called and pronouns, which differ from other adjectives only in the indication of person.[139]

In the subclassifications of the noun a good deal of the semantic framework inherited from the grammarians of Latin still persists, as in Gueintz' treatment of *koeniglich* as a 'Besitz nennwort' (Latin grammar's 'nomen possessivum'), or of *Boehmisch* as a 'Landartige nennwort' ('nomen gentilium'). Such traits illustrate the continuation of the Latin grammarians' over-multiplication of semantic criteria not necessarily coinciding with changes in form. The confusion of semantic and formal criteria meant that the ordering of declensions, which is a complicated matter in German because of the existence of separate weak and strong forms in the adjective, often ran into difficulties. Even Schottel still follows a gender-determined system of masculine, feminine and neuter declensions with the adjectives lumped together in a fourth one. A distinct improvement on this is made by Prasch in 1687, with five declensions determined according to the ending, including zero, of the genitive singular. It is Pölmann (1671) however, with his seeming eccentricities, who first brings some order into the system with a fresh criterion – that of the larger or smaller number of case-endings displayed by each declension. Using what is obviously a pedagogical device, he treats those paradigms exhibiting the complete set of possible endings (*-e, -es, em, -en, -er*) as 'full moon' declensions, or more properly 'full moon' modes of a single declension. Only the present-day strong adjectives fill this requirement, the weak ones with their few distinct endings being assigned to the opposite extreme, the 'new moon' mode. Substantives, never having the full set of endings, range from 'semi-lunar' with four (*Fuss, Pferd*) or three (*Vater, Himmel*), via the 'horned moon' mode with two (*Ofen, Huendlein*), to 'new moon' forms with a single oblique ending (*Mensch, Liebe*). A distinction is thus made between strong and weak masculine substantives, and a kind of sliding scale is set up

---

[139] A hardy annual in grammars of the period is the difficulty experienced in keeping substantival and adjectival 'pronouns' apart. Pölmann's correct classifications are for his date, save for his inclusion of the articles among the adjectives, an example of rare penetration.

according to the number of endings present. For each paradigm the lunar status of each particular mode of declension is indicated in the text by an illustration of the appropriate phase of the moon.[140] Though this gives the printed page a somewhat exotic aspect, Pölmann is in spite of his eccentricities the first grammarian to bring order into the German declensional system. His single-minded application of his lunar phases no doubt made the whole complicated matter much easier for children to grasp.

The aims of these writers are indeed practical pedagogical ones, but this means that any very advanced grammatical theory, in for instance word-class definition, is precluded. Such theory as there is, is in any case derivative. Gueintz for example usually goes to Ratke's *Sprachlehr* for his definitions, as in his description of the pronoun as denoting a person without time. The eclecticism of these authors is well illustrated by his additional reference (from Scaliger via Finck–Helwig) to secondary signification by pronouns as opposed to primary signification by nouns.[141] Thus do snatches of a more intricate, philosophically based theory come to the surface in pedagogically orientated works, no doubt to the confusion of the pupils. It is as if these ready-made definitions (Prasch for example simply takes over those of Schottel) were merely grafted onto simple teaching grammars with which they have no organic connection. Often a definition is not given at all, or it is a commonplace such as Melanchthon's treatment of the pronoun as a word with deictic and anaphoric function used to avoid needless repetition. Where these authors differ from the received Latin tradition is in their simplifications, in their jettisoning of certain criteria, above all formal ones, and in their use of recognitional devices to aid easy comprehension. This simplification is noticeable above all in the pared-down definitions of the verb, whether they repeat Melanchthon's purely semantic one in terms of the signification of *actio* and *passio* ('Thun oder Leiden'),[142] or see the signification of time as the primary function. Of pedagogical interest are Kromayer's further stipulation

[140] Pölmann's classes of 'adjectiva nativa' (uninflected forms in predicative use), 'formata' and 'serva' (strong and weak forms) are simply Ölinger's (*Underricht der Hoch Teutschen Spraach*, Strasbourg, 1574) classes of *absoluta*, *articulata*, and *inarticulata* by other names, though it should be noted that Ölinger's criterion was syntactic use rather than type of ending.

[141] *Deutscher Sprachlehre Entwurf*, p. 53; the pronoun 'bedeutet ein Ding, nicht vornemlich sondern hernacher'.

[142] Thus e.g. Kromayer, Olearius and Prasch.

that the verb is that word which is preceded by *ich, du,* etc., and the stark simplicity of 'Pölmann's 'formally variable part of speech which is conjugated'. Definitions of voice are simple and transformational in character. Kromayer's active verbs are those from which a passive can be made, and conversely his passives can be transformed into actives. It follows that 'neutral' verbs (*ich stehe*) are those which cannot form a passive. These authors are not of course the inventors of these procedures, which had long been a commonplace of Latin grammars. What is instructive is that they use such pedagogically useful criteria in preference to, or in addition to, more notional ones. Only Gueintz, prompted by his branching dichotomies, attempts something more ambitious, with a division into 'durchgehend' (transitive) and 'selbsthaftend' (intransitive), the former divisible in turn into active and passive, defined semantically in terms of transitivity.[143] The general view of the verb's function, the one that is to be perpetuated in school grammars throughout Europe, is sufficiently indicated by the vernacular term for it: *Wirckwort*, an 'action word'.

Little is said on the matter of tense by most grammarians. The traditional view of the past tenses was that imperfect, perfect and pluperfect differed from each other in the signification of greater or lesser distance from the present. According to this view, the imperfect refers to an action begun but not yet completed, an action nearer to the present than that indicated by the perfect. Kromayer follows this system, as do Gueintz and Prasch, with an imperfect 'recently or not yet completely past', a perfect 'completely past', and a pluperfect 'long since or previously past'.[144] It is Olearius who shows most interest in the matter, since he is at pains to devise a means of teaching tense distinctions by means of his pictures. His imperfect, indicating what has 'partly happened but is not completed', is represented by a man running away but with a backward glance over his shoulder 'as if he would prefer to stay'. His perfect indicates a completed action as in *der hat gestolen*, and is accordingly represented by a thief with his hands tied. Finally, and amusingly, the pluperfect is illustrated by a man climbing out of his open grave and saying *ich*

---

[143] *Deutscher Sprachlehre Entwurf*, p. 63.
[144] See Jellinek, *Geschichte*, II, 412–13. Only Johann Bödiker (*Grund-Sätze der Deutschen Sprachen*, Cölln an der Spree, 1690) dissents from the customary classification of the past tenses, with an imperfect (*Alexander zog in Asien*) indicating actions long past, and a perfect (*Es ist gestern ein fremder Kerl eingezogen*) indicating a recent action.

war gestorben, as one who 'has been long away and is concerning himself afresh with what happened a long time ago'. These graphic means no doubt pushed the point home more quickly than pages of written explanation would have done. An awareness of vernacular structure is indicated by the emphasis that is put on the teaching of the 'Huelffwoerter' *sein*, *werden* and *haben*, whose conjugations are frequently required to be learnt before those of other verbs. A similar awareness is shown by the general abandonment of the optative mood. Gueintz does not even mention the subjunctive, while Olearius has no present subjunctive, and distinguishes *ich hatte* and *ich hette* simply as imperfects 1 and 2. This is either simplification in the interests of pedagogy, or a Ramist refusal to recognize moods other than as members in a numbered sequence of tenses. Pölmann, it is true, redresses the balance with no less than four periphrastic future subjunctives. That the authors are still by and large peddling a Latinized grammar is shown by the persistence of periphrastic vernacular equivalents of gerund and supine. Though their treatment of the indeclinable word-classes calls for no particular comment, the continued force of the Latin model – in this instance Melanchthon – is shown by the almost universal treatment of the adverb as indicating a circumstance of the verb. The semantic subtleties of adverbial subclassification are still rife, and give Gueintz more than ample scope for his dichotomies.

That there is an overall similarity of treatment in the handling of syntax can also be put down to the use of a common Latin model. Differences are largely confined to matters of detail or to methodology. In Gueintz' grammar for example, the only important features differentiating his syntax from others – apart from his virtual ignoring of the article and the absence in his system of a subjunctive (an absence he nowhere comments on) – are his marked predilection for Ramist dichotomies and his obvious links with the Köthen grammarians. Within this Ramist and Ratichian framework he offers little that cannot also be found in the early Latinizing vernacular grammarians Clajus and Ritter. If in following the Ratichian *Compendium grammaticae Latinae*,[145] which in turn imitates Finck–Helwig on this point, he treats syntax under the separate headings of concord ('uebereinstimmung') and government ('annemung'), he is only making explicit a general practice. In all the authors identical

---

[145] Köthen, 1620.

examples from Clajus and the Latin tradition are met with, and all, with the exception of Pudor, continue to treat syntax word-class by word-class. In neither concord nor government do they offer much that cannot be found in their predecessors, whether Latin or vernacular. It is rare that, as in one instance in Kromayer, a whole sentence or 'gantze Rede' is treated as a syntactic unit, and even then the example is the time-honoured *Borgen macht Sorgen* from earlier grammars. Once the authors have noted the agreement of adjective with substantive and of nominative case with its following finite verb, they find little to say on concord. Gueintz draws attention to apposition (*Herr Gott Vater*) and notes that the word order *Vater unser*, current long before Luther's Bible, is sanctioned by Hebrew, Greek and Latin usage. A more ambitious, though very slight, section is that in which Olearius treats the sequence of tenses, as in *Ich tuhe es, dass du es auch thust*/'facio ut facias', and *Ich gab dir Geld, dass du mir Korn gebest*. Throughout his syntax parallel German and Latin examples are given, which would suggest that his chief aim is to indicate similarities of structure. The treatment of the indeclinable word-classes, which offer little basis for a discussion of concord, is necessarily yet thinner. Much more extensive, given the existence of a case system in German, is the space devoted to government, only Prasch maintaining that the proper place for its indication is the dictionary. But here more than ever the rules and examples of earlier grammarians are repeated. Gueintz' treatment in particular stands out for its repetition of the semantically based criteria of the Latin tradition and of such earlier vernacular grammarians as Clajus. All the time-hallowed rules and examples are there: substantives denoting an office or profession are in the genitive (*Er ist seines handwercks ein Schneider*), those denoting praise or blame (the 'laudem vel vituperationem' of the Latin grammarians) have either genitive, or ablative plus *von* or *an* (*ein weib schoener gestalt/geschlanck am leibe*). Here it may be noted that, though Gueintz seemingly thinks first of the Latin rule and then seeks an example of it in the vernacular, he none the less offers alternative, semantically equivalent vernacular prepositional structures. The point is however that these specifically vernacular structures too are deemed to be amenable to Latin rules prescribing genitives or ablatives, etc. Similarly in the treatment of the verb authors repeat semantically based rules from Latin grammar. Verbs denoting possession, use, lack or accusation govern a genitive case:

Er wird eines Diebstals beschuldiget. It is almost as if the authors, after diligent search, are relieved to find the identical structure in German. Vernacular alternatives are however here also frequently given as in the pair *gedencke meiner/gedencke an mich.* It should be borne in mind however that German, unlike French and English, does have case-marked equivalents to the Latin expressions the rules were designed to cater for. The mistake lies in treating idiomatic vernacular prepositional structures as also falling under these rules. The only interesting departures from these procedures are provided by Prasch and Olearius. The former, noting 'elliptical' constructions such as *Wir sind des Herren* for *Wir sind des Herren Knechte,* and *Ich freue mich dess* for *Ich freue mich im Betrachtung dess,* puts forward the doctrine that verbs cannot govern a genitive case, but only appear to do so because of the deletion of an 'understood' substantive.[146] What gives Olearius' treatment its interest, once again, is his use of explicatory illustrations. The rules are given in their original Latin, but the one requiring active verbs to govern an accusative is illustrated by a smith striking an anvil, while verbs denoting a cause or instrument and taking the ablative are accompanied by a picture of a boy taking an apple from a tree. The treatment by the authors of the syntax of the indeclinables is again thin. Even where, exceptionally, J. Bellin devotes an entire work of some three hundred pages to the syntax of prepositions,[147] it consists of no more than an expanded version of the customary detailed treatment of case government. Only occasionally, in slight, hesitant sketches does one feel that the authors are on the verge of saying something interesting about syntax, something beyond the constructions of such word-based structures as *das Haus des Herrn.*

These strictures do not however apply to Christian Pudor's *Grundrichtigkeit* of 1672,[148] which is the only work among those considered in this section to break away from notions of government and concord affecting small groups of words, and provide a full-length treatment of sentence structure. The bulk of this work is concerned with the way in which words make up phrases, these in turn form sentences or clauses which can be combined into periods, and the periods themselves are finally integrated into the *oratio,* or 'volkom-

---

[146] This is Sanctius' doctrine. See G. Clerico, *Franciscus Sanctius, Minerve ou les causes de la langue latine,* Lille, 1982, p. 44.
[147] *Syntaxis praepositionum Teutonicarum.*
[148] *Der Teutschen Sprache Grundrichtigkeit und Zierlichkeit.*

mene Teutsche Rede'. To each of these four syntactic processes a separate section is devoted. The phrase or 'Redensart' is defined as a string of words in grammatically correct construction which does not constitute a complete statement, as in the examples *die Stadt Rohm* or *des Vaters Haus*. Compatibility rules worthy of a modern structuralist grammar are given indicating the type and order of the word-classes used in its formation. The sentence ('Spruchrede' or 'Sentenz') must by contrast contain a word in the nominative case and a finite verb, regardless of the number of subordinate elements that can be added to either part – a specification which shows an awareness of the notions of both the minimal sentence and the existence of a hierarchy in syntax. Sentences may be simple, compound or contracted. Examples of compound ('zusammen-gesetzt') sentences are *Alexander streitet und ueberwindet, Alexander und Darius streiten,* and *Alexander ueberwindet; Darius aber wird geschlagen.* Questions, answers, and narrative statements are all different types of sentence, the last-named being classified according to the nature of the conjunctions joining their parts. Though the discussion of relative clauses cannot rival the celebrated analyses of the Port-Royal grammarians, the existence of such clauses, even in embedded form as in *Ich habe deinen Brief, welchen du geschrieben, empfangen,* is recognized and catalogued. As an example of a contracted sentence Pudor gives *Er hat es lachend geredt,* as opposed to the expanded structure *Er hat gelachet, und geredet.* A period (*Schussrede*) can consist of up to four sentences or clauses. It can also be considered, after the manner of the rhetoricians, as containing the two parts protasis ('Vorsatz') and apodosis ('Nachsatz'), as in *Wer Gott von Herzen liebet: Der befleissiget sich auch seine Gebot zuhalten.* The rules for the pronunciation of periods obviously belong more to rhetoric than to grammar, though Pudor pays quite exceptional attention to matters such as the intonation curves of questions, which are indeed of grammatical relevance. Periods must not be bellowed forth on one note, but speakers should begin softly, gradually increase the loudness of the voice, and let it fall again towards the end. Finally, the *oratio* or complete discourse is made up of a number of well-formed periods and may be in either prose or verse. Pudor's dependence on Latin rhetorics is shown by his use of the terms 'ungebunden' and 'gebunden' (*oratio ligata*) for these two genres. Pronunciation must in either type be suited to the matter, whether solemn or light-hearted, and gestures should not be overdone. It is noteworthy that Pudor feels it necessary to include such information under the heading of the 'Grundrichtigkeit' or basic correctness of the German language. The overriding aim of his grammar is to provide an introduction to rhetoric. The last eighty pages of the work form in fact a rhetoric proper, dealing with the 'Zierlichkeit' or elegance of the language, under the headings of linguistic purity, transposition, variation, amplification and contraction, the four last-named being devices used in literary composition. For purity of language the guides he recommends are Georg Neumarck's *Poetische Tafeln*, the usage of the better courts and chanceries, and the writings of Luther. Transposition of words and phrases to different places in the sentence, and variation (e.g. *Teutschland* for *die Teutschen*) are clearly stylistic matters, though Pudor also treats the separation of verb and prefix (as in *er nahm mich hoefflich an*) under the heading of transposition. But even the purely stylistic procedures doubtless owe something to a long grammatical tradition of word-class interchangeability exemplified by the 'enallage' of parts of speech in Linacre's *De emendata structura* (1524). In contrast with the brief aridity of his treatment of word-class morphology, it is these two long sections, on the 'Grundrichtigkeit' or correct structure of the German language and its 'Zierlichkeit' or elegance, that form the major interest of Pudor's grammar. Its bias, a sign of the times, is overwhelmingly rhetorical.

At this point it will be convenient to consider two authors, one of whom shares Pudor's interest in rhetoric while the other shares his interest in the structure of the sentence as a whole, but both of whom follow in the wake of the renewed attention to word structure stimulated by J. G. Schottel's *Ausführliche Arbeit von der Teutschen Haubt Sprache* (1663).[149] The two works concerned are Johann Bödiker's *Grund-Sätze der Deutschen Sprachen* (1690)[150] and Kaspar Stieler's *Kurze Lehrschrift von der Hochteutschen Sprachkunst*, published as

---

[149] Since Schottel takes the word structure of German as the basis for a theory of general grammar, he is treated in the second part of this study among the other universal grammarians.

[150] *Grund-Sätze der Deutschen Sprachen in Reden und Schreiben, samt einem Bericht vom rechten Gebrauch der Vorwoerter*, Cölln an der Spree, 1690. I have been unable to locate a copy of this first edition, and have used instead that brought out in Berlin in 1746 by J. J. Wippel, with his own and Leonhard Frisch's notes. This edition follows Frisch's earlier revision of 1723, which reappeared in 1729. Bödiker's son Karl had also republished the 1690 edition in 1701 and 1709 as *Neuvermehrte Grund-Sätze*. Since Wippel gives on each point Bödiker's original text followed by Frisch's observations and his own comments, it is not difficult to abstract Bödiker's own grammatical doctrines. Wippel's additions are clearly in an eighteenth-century tradition, characterized by Jellinek (*Geschichte*, 1, 208) as an outmoded 'Sprachscholastik'.

an appendix to his monumental *Der Teutschen Sprache Stammbaum* of 1691.[151] The work of both these authors springs from the increasing late-seventeenth-century interest in lexicography, and from the emphasis placed by Schottel on root-words, derivation and composition. Though Bödiker's grammar is in many respects very dependent on Schottel, it may be regarded as the first authoritative work to appear after the latter's *Ausfürliche Arbeit*, and it is significant that Bödiker himself saw it as an indispensable preliminary to the major German dictionary whose production was his chief interest, and for which he got as far as assembling a vast store of material. A sign of the contemporary evolution of grammar in the direction of lexicography is his division of his work into the two sections 'German Grammar' and 'Prepositions'. The first of these contains a good deal of lexical material on word origins and derivation, material which Schottel had hived off into his preliminary 'Lobreden' or eulogies of the German tongue. Stieler's *Stammbaum*, published under the pseudonym *Der Spate* ('the late-comer') by which he was known in the Fruchtbringende Gesellschaft, is of course the famous German–Latin dictionary of that name, and the fact that his grammar forms an appendix to it is again an indication that it is meant to serve lexicographical aims. The *Stammbaum*, the first comprehensive dictionary of the German language, grew out of the endeavours of leading members of the Gesellschaft such as Gueintz and Schottel. Since the various local dialects were increasingly giving ground, in the usage of the upper and middle classes, to the High German *Schriftsprache* which had gained a firm footing in east midland Germany, the time was ripe for such an undertaking. Given the role played by Schottel in the assembling of material for a High German dictionary, it is not surprising that Stieler's grammar, like that of Bödiker, to some extent bears his imprint. Schottel's own project,[152] consonant with his linguistic theories, called for the inclusion and stressing of derived and compound forms, and it is only in the light of his proposals that Stieler's dictionary can be properly evaluated.

[151] *The Kurze Lehrschrift* occupies pp. 1–243 of volume III of *Der Teutschen Sprache Stammbaum*, Nuremberg, 1691. I have used the facsimile edition in the series *Deutsche Barock-Literatur*, ed. M. Bircher and F. Kemp, Munich, 1968.

[152] On Schottel's project for a dictionary see pp. 16–19 of the tenth 'Lobrede' of his *Ausführliche Arbeit* (Brunswick, 1663), and Stieler's reference in his foreword to 'der weiland hochberühmte Suchende' (i.e. Schottel). There are obvious parallels to be drawn between Stieler's dictionary and that part of Schottel's work entitled 'Die Stammwoerter der Teutschen Sprache nebst ihrer Erklärung'.

Schottel's *Ausführliche Arbeit* (the 'summa philologica' of the baroque period)[153] and Stieler's *Stammbaum* are the complementary peaks of German linguistic achievement in the seventeenth century. Though Stieler is in some ways more informative than Schottel on the general tendencies of the times, he shares Schottel's almost mystic approach to German word-formation, comparing it to that 'very wonderful and unusual' Chinese tree from whose trunk and numerous branches hang tendrils which themselves put out roots, producing a composite tree capable of sheltering three thousand people. It is this prodigious and fecund tree that provides him both with his title – *Der Teutschen Sprache Stammbaum und Fortwachs* – and with a fit illustration of the self-propagating capacities of German roots. His dictionary, as an indication of this extraordinary fecundity of the German language, is intended to combat not only those who see little need further to cultivate a vernacular 'so mit der Muttermilch eingesogen', but also those, more learned, who see foreign tongues as the only ones capable of forming the intellect. If the language is to realize its full possibilities its users must be made aware of its rich vocabulary, and the basis of this necessary word-stock is High German, which seemingly for Stieler excludes all the existing dialects, even that, often praised by grammarians, of Meissen. Stieler goes out of his way to stress that this High German norm, used by the administrative institutions of the *Reich*, by the clergy and scholars and in merchants' letters, is not and cannot be coincident with any actually spoken dialect. On this point Stieler's view is that of Schottel: the dialects are by nature corrupt, and hence cannot contain within themselves any principle of regulation.[154] This principle seems for Schottel and Stieler to be present only in a kind of hypostatized, ideal language existing over and above the dialects. Stieler stresses that he is not dealing with 'teutsche Mundarten', but with a 'universal *Reichs Haubtsprache*' comparable to the Greek *koinē* of earlier times, though his view seemingly differs from that of Bödiker, who sees High German as indeed an artificial creation, but one developed out of the dialects by the industry of scholars. Bödiker would however have agreed that this is the sole German norm to be developed and propagated, the only one worthy of serious study. For the mastery of Stieler's 'lingua

---

[153] The work has been so called by Hankamer, *Die Sprache*.

[154] Stieler makes here (*Stammbaum*, III, 1) an overt reference to Schottel: 'wie der beruehmte Suchende urteilet. *Omnibus dialectis aliquid vitiosi inest, quod locum regulae in lingua ipsa habere nequit.*'

Germanica imperialis' close and careful training is necessary, the fact of having been born German conferring no advantage.

Given their lexicographical bent, the interest of Bödiker's and Stieler's grammars lies in what they have to say about derivation and composition, rather than in their treatment of the remaining features of the parts of speech, which differs little from that of the pedagogically orientated authors already discussed. The importance he ascribes to roots and word-formation, to individual words and their morphology, means however that for Stieler, in theory at any rate, the traditional 'etymologia' or 'Wortforschung' occupies a special position as dealing with the sources and causes of language and the seeking out of what lies hidden behind each word. Bödiker's division of the parts of speech, following Olearius and perhaps philosophically based models such as that of Sanctius, into noun/verb/particle seems to hold promise of some kind of quasi-mystical theory, but it owes less to semantically based tripartite systems such as that of Aristotle, than to formal criteria resembling those used by the early Roman grammarian Varro. In any case, his scheme is no more than a hold-all for the usual eight or nine-part system. Apart from their emphasis on derivation and composition, these two authors offer little that cannot be found in most teaching grammars of the period. Melanchthon is still pressed into service, as in Stieler's definition of the noun as signifying a thing, in contrast to the verb, without action or time, or as in the by now obligatory treatment of the adverb as specifying the 'circumstances' of the verb. Hardly calling for comment too are such items as the definition of substantive and adjective in the medieval terms of semantico-syntactic dependence or independence, or of such 'Kennzeichen' as adjectival endings and the number of possible preceding articles. These observations are the common property of pedagogical grammars at this date.

Such variations as there are from the previously accepted grammatical norm are of small account when compared with the unusual extent of these authors' treatment of composition and derivation. The greatest glory – 'das allervornemste Kunststueck' – of the 'fruchtbarer Sprachbaum' of the German language is according to Stieler its ability to form compounds, to produce by joining existing elements together 'a new sense', one of the elements none the less constituting the 'Hauptsinn' or main sense to which the intellect is chiefly attracted. Such remarks, and the space devoted to a discussion of the various word-classes that can enter into composition, are sufficient indication that Stieler's chief interests are those of a lexicographer. Bödiker's treatment, in line with his conviction that root-words are the 'Grund und Hauptwerk' of every language, is more theoretical, bolstering his claim that a language cannot function properly as an instrument of communication unless its 'foundation stones' or roots are securely in place. German holds a special place among languages by virtue of its possession of more monosyllabic words than any other (with the possible exception of Chinese). Given the high information content of such words as compared with polysyllabic ones he is led to claim, with Schottel, that all German roots are necessarily monosyllabic, a view which contradicted *ostmitteldeutsch* usage[155] and was hotly contested by Gueintz and others. Analogy takes precedence in Bödiker's system over usage, and it is the workings of analogy that are invoked in his perception – worthy, among present-day linguists, of André Martinet's theory of language economy – that a language would be impossibly complicated if each separate case distinction required its own separate word-form.[156] The application of his theory is not without complications for his own grammar, for if as he insists all German prepositions are roots or *Stamm woerter*, it follows that they must all be monosyllabic. But seeming exceptions such as *gegen* and *hinter* can be held to have been monosyllables in earlier German, and since compounds such as *zuwider*, being polysyllabic, automatically exclude themselves from the preposition class, Bödiker can in good conscience count them as adverbs. This time it is not the Latin tradition, but Schottelian theory that leads to a distortion of the facts. In an attempt to forestall other difficulties, caused by the existence of prepositions in both separable and inseparable use, Bödiker's definition of the preposition is twofold: it links a case-marked word to the verb governing it, and it forms compounds with nouns and verbs. The cross-cutting of the case-government criterion by the separable/inseparable dichotomy had already, in much earlier vernacular grammar, caused difficulties for Clajus. Bödiker neatly solves the problem, though only to his own satisfaction, by declaring all forms which govern cases but do not enter into composition to be adverbs, and only those forms which satisfy his double criterion

---

[155] *See Jellinek, Geschichte*, II, 138.
[156] As an example of the resulting complications Bödiker gives an imaginary paradigm of the concept 'table': nom. *mensa*, voc. *O. schilchan*, acc. *stolezam*, gen. *trapeza*, dat. *tabellae*, abl. *a borda*.

of both case government and possible presence in compounds to be prepositions. Since according to him the correct use of the prepositions is responsible for the functioning of half the language, half his grammar is devoted to them, though in practice he does little more than increase the number of semantic categories established by Schottel. Stieler foreseeably and more sensibly argues, while noting that the whole question of case government belongs properly speaking in the syntax, that the semantic side of the study of prepositions, and indeed of adverbs too, is better undertaken with the help of a good dictionary. As a lexicographer, he is conscious of what belongs in the grammar and what in the lexicon, and avoids placing the traditional and endlessly multipliable semantic distinctions in the former. But both his own work and that of Bödiker are indications of the way in which, at this date, grammar is in fact moving towards lexicography and nomenclature.

In keeping, too, with the increasing tendency to regard grammar as an introduction to rhetoric, Bödiker mingles stylistic matters with more properly syntactic ones. His view of syntax as the main part of grammar seems promising, though he may be simply repeating Girbert's remarks in the same sense. His definition of syntactic construction as serving to express concepts, successful communication having taken place when concepts are transferred intact from speaker to hearer, recalls medieval doctrines.[157] Though syntax is a necessary part of grammar, it is quite frankly seen as laying the foundations for rhetoric and oratory, with a division into regular or 'ordinata' and irregular or 'figurata', the latter including such matters as ellipse and unusual word order. Bödiker notes that German agrees in many respects with Latin and Greek, but its age and dignity is such that it may be regarded as *sui generis*, owing nothing to any other tongue. It is more natural than either of the classical languages in two respects: its names approach more closely to nature, and it has a natural word order which coincides with that prescribed by universal grammar. It is worthy of note however that while Bödiker holds the morphological features derivation and composition to be common to all languages, he treats syntax as varying with each individual language. This forms an interesting contrast to the Englishman (or Welshman?) Bassett Jones' dictum that nations differ in 'vocality'

---

[157] Cf. Thomas of Erfurt, *Grammatica speculativa*, cap. xlv: 'expressio mentis conceptus compositi, est finis constructionis'.

but agree in syntax, thus proving 'the product of words to be more from nature, as of Sentences from Reason'.[158] Assuming however that at least some elements of syntax are common to all languages, Bödiker provides a set of general rules, followed by special ones applying to the 'idiotismus' of German itself, to such items for example as the position in the sentence of separable verbal prefixes. A modern note is provided by the classification of these idiosyncrasies under language (covering the whole speech community), historical period, place (i.e. dialectal variations), person (the idiolects) and circumstance (various registers such as formal and colloquial discourse). Regular syntax is divided into that of agreement and government, also called (another curious medieval echo) intransitive and transitive respectively. This regular construction is treated word-class by word-class, differs little from previous ones, and in fact takes its rules in large measure from Schottel. Bödiker's chief interest is obviously that 'syntaxis ornata' whose purpose is to 'delight the mind and the senses'. It is significant – and part of the contemporary campaign to prove the superiority of German over Latin and Greek – that he regards these languages as having inherited from their German mother tongue (*sic*) only their 'Zeug' or linguistic basis, not their 'Zierlichkeit' or elegance. Many of the elegances of German cannot be reduced to rule, but must be learnt from usage. They must all however follow Bödiker's three criteria of purity, clarity and elegance of expression. The first, 'Reinlichkeit', is to be obtained from the usage of 'reasonable speakers' and from the grammar and dictionary. Again, a precondition is a good German lexicon purged of foreign accretions, a project on which Bödiker himself had long laboured, though he finally had to limit himself to giving a few suggestions for such a work in his foreword. The second criterion, 'Deutlichkeit', is fulfilled by choosing such words as appropriately express the concepts to be transmitted, the overriding aim being to make oneself clearly understood. 'Zierlichkeit', finally, the achievement of elegance, is the concern of rhetoric. Care must be taken that no one of these criteria is allowed to encroach on the others. With this end in view, Bödiker sets up three classes of sentence: the 'phrasis grammatica', giving the straightforward literary sense, the 'phrasis metaphorica' with various figurative

[158] B. Jones, *Herm'aelogium: or, an Essay at the Rationality of the Art of Speaking*, London, 1659.

meanings, and the 'phrasis adagiosa' with one rigidly fixed non-literal meaning determined by usage. The last-named (Bödiker's example is *Er haelt hinter dem Berge*, 'he keeps what he is doing to himself') is of particular interest as belonging in the category of fixed idiomatic expressions which André Martinet in our own century characterizes as 'expressions figées', or utterances which must be learnt as a whole and in which no lexical item can be commuted with another. Bödiker recommends the student to keep commonplace books in which such idioms may be noted down.

With Stieler again, a very close dependence on Schottel for the details of his syntax is quite evident.[159] He too regards syntax as the cornerstone of grammar, giving as his reason the fact that it deals with 'die ganze Rede', the whole utterance or sentence. His approach indicates a long-awaited awareness of the true function of syntax, and particularly promising is his statement that he regards the individual word-classes as no more than building blocks to be used in the higher activity of grammatical construction. This does not prevent him from then going on to treat syntax, according to long-hallowed tradition, word-class by word-class. Again, there is the by now customary division of construction into 'gemein' or common, expressing 'bare things' in pure and correct language, and 'zierlich' or ornamental, whose purpose is to delight and persuade. Stieler notes however that the latter belongs more to rhetoric and proposes, in contrast to Bödiker, to deal almost solely with the former type. He divides it into general syntax (dealing with word order) and special (taking account of the function of morphological endings), and taxes previous authors with having treated them together in confused fashion. Of particular interest is his extended treatment of word order, placed first for pedagogical reasons. For the first time in a German vernacular syntax, the order of the elements of the entire sentence is given. The favourite sentence pattern noun (with preceding article) or pronoun + auxiliary verb + preposition + noun + main verb is described, and the adverb is required to stand close to the 'last verb' in order the better to emphasize its 'circumstances'. Attention is drawn to what later grammarians have called the 'verbale Klammer' of German, in which the auxiliary stands early in the sentence and

[159] S. Sonderegger's 'Nachwort' to Bircher and Kemp's facsimile edition of the *Stammbaum* (Munich, 1968) emphasizes this point by giving parallel tables of contents from Stieler's *Kurze Lehrschrift* and Schottel's *Ausführliche Arbeit*.

the main verb form is relegated to the end. Stieler notes that in subordinate subjunctive clauses introduced by *dass* etc. the verb also has final position, and a sentence such as *Die Schönheit des Leibes ergiebt sich der geringsten Krankheit* is closely analysed to establish the correct sequences. Particularly noteworthy is Stieler's realization that the main verb or auxiliary verb constitutes the second element in the normal sentence pattern. His section on word order is long and detailed, and has more to do with the individual intricacies and usage of German than with grammatical theory. But here for virtually the first time one has the impression that the vernacular sentence and its idiosyncrasies are being treated as an object of study in their own right, unconnected with any Latinizing preconceptions. It is the freshness of their separate approaches to syntax – Bödiker's rhetorical bias and Stieler's perception of the importance of word order in the vernacular – together with their preoccupation with lexicography, that mark out the grammars of these authors from those of the pedagogical grammarians previously considered.

What emerges from a consideration of these German grammars is perhaps above all the patriotic motive behind them, powered at first by feelings of inferiority vis-à-vis the other main European vernaculars. Also predominant are dialectal problems (the question of which idiom to adopt as preferred usage, a preoccupation absent from English grammars of the same period), and the notion that the German language is *sui generis*, owing nothing to earlier tongues. Always a prominent feature of German linguistic scholarship in the centuries treated here is the parallel notion of a divine quality immanent in the language, whether it is seen in terms of the Kabbalah and various mystical theories, or in terms of Luther's belief in the special spiritual status of the language of the vernacular Bible. Above all perhaps one is left with a profound impression of a deep-seated pedagogical motive. Here more than ever one is reminded of W. J. Ong's insight that method frequently owes more to 'rule-of-thumb pedagogical adjustments' than to the application of reason. It is not without interest that on the one hand German universal grammar is deeply based in pedagogy, and on the other its quasi-mystical streak is continued in Schottel's work, and indeed has a descendant in certain aspects of that of Wilhelm von Humboldt in the nineteenth century.

ii ENGLISH PRAGMATISM

The background

The mysticism pervading much of German work is entirely absent from the English pedagogically orientated grammars of the period, which are firmly rooted in practical language teaching. The Spanish pedagogical reformer Luis Vives had already in 1531 made the claim that a teacher was better equipped to give instruction in Latin and Greek if he also possessed a thorough knowledge of his mother tongue.[160] Medieval students had picked up Latin to some extent by actually using it, and hearing it spoken around them as an often rough-and-ready lingua franca at the university. The ideal of many Renaissance schoolmasters was indeed to reinstate Latin, but of a more elegant type, as the language of daily oral intercourse among scholars, perhaps with the aid of some kind of direct method. Others again saw the possibility of using the vernacular as a tool in the learning of Latin. In the seventeenth century, in addition to a continuing desire to demonstrate that English is in no way inferior to Latin and Greek, there is then a drive to increase its status yet further by showing its value as a gateway to classical learning. The primary purpose of the English grammar schools was still the inculcation of Latin as the sole medium of learned communication, but their aims were practical rather than literary. Latin literature was indeed studied, but as 'the storehouse of adequate and eloquent expression, the happy hunting-ground of the right thing to discourse about, the right way of saying it',[161] rather than as an end in itself. In this context the vernacular comes to be seen as just one more tool in the service of a Latin-based education, in the production of that 'due succession of fit persons' essential to the service of Church and State. The stultifying way in which Latin grammar was taught, divorced at any rate at the lower levels from any reading of authors, is vividly described in Sir Thomas Elyot's *The Boke named the Governour* (1531)[162] and Roger Ascham's *The Scholemaster* (1570).[163] At this time

[160] *De tradendis disciplinis*, Leyden?, 1531, p. 483. On Vives see F. Watson, *Luis Vives el gran Valenciano (1492–1540)* (*Hispanic Notes and Monographs*, IV), Oxford, 1922.
[161] Watson, *The English Grammar Schools*, p. 5.
[162] Published in London. There is a Scolar Press facsimile, Menston, 1970.
[163] Published in London. Also contained in *Roger Ascham, English Works*, ed. W. A. Wright, Cambridge, 1904 (reprinted 1970).

school grammar had largely become an end in itself, and there is a certain novelty in Elyot's plea that it be reduced to a minimum and treated simply as a short prolegomenon to the study of authors, thus avoiding a long grammatical apprenticeship that 'mortifieth the corage', and whose customary effect is that by the time students finally reach actual Latin literature their 'sparkes of fervent desire of lernynge is extincte'. Nor should it be forgotten that the training he envisages for 'governours' in the higher reaches of the civil administration is set in a wider context than book learning alone, but also embraces morals and manners. The most important and best-known of such 'courtesy books' aiming to produce the all-round man is Castiglione's *Cortegiano* of 1528, of which an English translation appeared in 1561, and a training in manners was later to form an important part of the pedagogical programmes of Mulcaster, Brinsley and Hoole. The Italian influence here is important. Obadiah Walker's *Of Education* (1673)[164] for instance, a kind of English *Cortegiano*, claiming to present the observations of 'some Italian Writers, not ordinary amongst us'.

The average grammar school was however far from reaching the ideal prescribed by Elyot. Its single-minded aim was the inculcation of Latin grammar. An important element in the continuance of the grammatical straitjacket was the peculiar position occupied in the English educational system by Lily's Latin grammar,[165] which along with the Authorized Version of the Bible enjoyed royal protection, and was guaranteed exclusive use in the schools. The continued monopoly of this work contributed perhaps more than any other factor to the belief that Latin consisted of an inviolable set of rules with an existence independent of anything ever actually written in the language. Given the various royal edicts prohibiting the use of any other grammatical works in the schools, contemporary grammarians of Latin were limited to translating, elucidating or supplementing the 'regia grammatica'. The translation of sections of Lily's work into English together with explanatory notes was no doubt in part a subterfuge, allowing publication which would otherwise have been thwarted by its royal privilege. Of importance here however is the opportunity this production of concordances to the royal grammar offered for an enlarged contribution of the vernacular to the teaching

---

[164] Published in Oxford.
[165] For a discussion of this work see Padley, *Grammatical Theory* (1976), pp. 24–6.

of Latin, a contribution which paved the way for an interest in vernacular grammar for its own sake.[166] The fact that by this means pupils were gradually provided with a complete English translation of Lily is indicative both of the failure to inculcate Latin *through* Latin, and of a growing movement to use the vernacular in teaching, if only for the 'weaker sort' of pupil. It is significant that from 1642 on, William Haine's *Lillies Rules Construed* is usually printed in the same volume with the 'regia grammatica' itself. But already in 1640 the increased role of the vernacular in Latin teaching is illustrated by Thomas Hayne's *Grammatices Latinae compendium*, in which 'the most necessary Rules are expressed in English opposite to the Latine, that the one may facilitate and give light to the other'. All this activity does not necessarily indicate an interest in the separate teaching of the vernacular. But these various supplements to Lily were, though no doubt involuntarily, furthering knowledge of the vernacular at the same time as they facilitated the study of Latin.[167] And inevitably, though it took a long time, Lily's monopoly was to be undermined by pedagogical developments.

These developments in pedagogy revolved around two questions: whether to regard grammar as the acquisition of a set of rules and postpone the reading of authors until these rules had been mastered down to the last detail; or on the contrary to begin early with the reading of Latin literature and keep rules to the minimum, deducing them from (admittedly at the outset simple) reading matter. The beginnings of this debate may be followed in the pages of Elyot and Ascham and in Richard Mulcaster's *Elementarie* of 1582.[168] Elyot is of the opinion that rules should be 'fewe and quicke'. He who

---

[166] Among such elucidations of Lily's grammar, all published in London, may be mentioned: J. Stockwood, *A plaine and easie Laying open of the Meaning and Understanding of the Rules of Construction in the English Accidence* [the name commonly given to part of Lily's grammar], 1590, and *The Treatise of the Figures...in the Latin* [i.e. Lily's] *Grammar...for the help of the weaker sort in the Grammar Schools*, 1609; J. Leech, *A Booke of Grammar Questions, for the helpe of yong Scholars, to further them in the understanding of the Accidence, and Lilies verses* (4th ed.), 1650 (but no doubt in existence before 1612); T. Granger, *Syntagma Grammaticum, Or an easie and methodicall explanation of Lillie's Grammar*, 1616; Anon., *Animadversions upon Lillie's Grammar, or Lilly Scanned*, 1625; J. Danes, *A Light to Lilie*, 1637; W. Haine, *Lillies Rules Construed*, 1642; E. Reeve, *The Rules of the Latine Grammar, construed. Which were omitted in the book called Lillies Rules*, 1657; Anon., *Priscianus nascens or A Key to the Grammar School. Serving much to the exposition of the Grammatical Rules of Lilly and the more easie and certain Translating of English into Latine*, 1660; J. Brookbank, *A Breviate of our King's whole Latin Grammar, Vulgarly called, Lillies*, 1660.

[167] They also demonstrate the futility of prescribing a single authoritative text-book.

[168] Published in London. Scolar press facsimile, Menston, 1970. The work is largely an orthography, whose possible influence on the orthographical section of Alexander Gill's *Logonomia Anglica* (1619) falls outside the scope of this study.

confines himself to teaching rules 'whereby a childe shall only lerne to speake congrue latine' is no true grammarian, unless he can in addition speak Latin elegantly and 'expounde good autours'. But Elyot realizes that even with a first-class teacher the learning of Latin is a tiring business – 'a gentyll wytte is therewith sone fatigate' – and accordingly recommends the introduction at an early stage of some 'quicke and mery dialoges' from Lucian.[169] Ascham similarly does not altogether 'contemne Rewles', provided they are presented together with readings from an author. The grammar book however should be no more than a work of reference, a 'Dictionarie for everie present use'. This alone ensures a 'lively and perfite waie of teaching of Rewles: where the common waie...to read the Grammer alone by it selfe, is tedious for the Master, hard for the Scholer, colde and uncumfortable for them bothe'.[170] Mulcaster too stresses that grammar teaching must offer something more than 'the bare Anatomie of a plane rule', citing in support Quintilian, who saw clearly that 'it was one thing to speak like a grammarian, and another thing to speak like a latinist'.[171] Important for contemporary attitudes to grammar is his requirement that the teacher must not only 'waie the rules' but also have an awareness of the genius of the language, of 'that grace, which everie tung hath'. This approach, which has been labelled customary grammar, could not but, given the almost universal opinion that the vernacular was not amenable to rule, reinforce the claims of those who thought the mother tongue none the less worth teaching. The fact remains however that at the date at which Mulcaster is writing 'our own tung remaineth but poor, and is kept verie low through some reasonable superstition, not to have learning in it', and it is still Latin whose claims to be the gateway to knowledge are stressed by him.[172] In view of this central role of Latin in providing entrance to the professions, the debate turns on the question of how it is to be inculcated without undue waste of time, and without leaving the pupil with a permanent distaste for learning. The mass of Latin teachers no doubt, through natural inertia, clung to the time-honoured hammering-in of the rules, and it is here that Lily's grammar had its worst effects. It must have left

---

[169] *The Boke named the Governour*, ff. 30^v, 60^r.
[170] *The Scholemaster*, p. 184.
[171] Quintilian's Latin runs 'aliud est grammatice, aliud Latine loqui'.
[172] *Elementarie*, pp. 50–2.

the child with the impression that a language was simply a collection of nouns and verbs, etc., of rules and paradigms, of word-classes treated in isolation apart from any grammatical function. Here once again the word-based nature of humanist grammar flowed over into pedagogy.

Is Ascham right in supposing that 'all men covet to have their children speake latin'? At any rate he is of the opinion that children should not in the early stages be required actually to speak the language, lest bad linguistic habits become ingrained. Of importance given its early date is his perception that the best way to learn a language is to be constantly exposed to it. Among innovators, the question at issue is whether to teach Latin by some kind of direct method, or to ease matters for the pupil by using his mother tongue as an auxiliary. Throughout the seventeenth century both methods have their exponents. Ascham sees the direct method as an ideal, but in practice recommends an early introduction to authors as the best means of ensuring the acquisition of good Latin. It is interesting however to find Elyot, forty years earlier and closer to medieval practice, advising that the sons of noblemen should in infancy be surrounded only by those capable of speaking pure Latin. An exception is made for the nurse who, though obviously not versed in Latin, should 'speke none englisshe but that, whiche is cleane, polite, perfectly, and articulately pronounced'. But the small amount of time available for the cultivation of the vernacular – which, as with the German 'mother's milk' school of theorists, was thought to be sufficiently acquired at the mother's or the nurse's knee – is shown by the early age at which Elyot's pupil is required to begin serious learning. Beginning Greek at the age of seven, 'he may continually lerne greke autours thre yeres, and in the meane tyme use the latin tonge as a familiar language'. Though Elyot notes (with disapproval?) that French 'nowe is broughte in to as many rules and figures, and as large a grammer, as is latin or greke',[173] he says nothing as to the codification of the English language. The role of 'familiar language' is restricted to Latin.[174] That the debate is still continuing late in the seventeenth century is shown by the anonymous *Examen of the Way*

[173] This is possibly a reference to Palsgrave's recently published *Lesclarcissement de la langue francoyse*, London, 1530.
[174] *The Boke named the Governour*, ff. 18ᵛ, 30ʳ.

of Teaching the Latin Tongue, translated from a French work in 1669.[175] Already in 1582 Mulcaster had expressed his fear lest 'by the lingring about language, we are removed and kept back one degre further from sound knowledge'. The author of the *Examen* adds to this the typically seventeenth-century anxiety that the methods of language teaching in common use will cause pupils 'to preferre the knowledg of Words to that of Things (which is a great Evill)', a Baconian theme which goes hand in hand with seventeenth-century puritan attitudes which reject the 'dross' of the classics in favour of Bible teaching. He advocates a direct method which will, he claims, be 'as commodious for the knowledge of *Things*, as advantagious for the knowledge of *Words*'. The justification of his method lies not only in 'the defectiveness of the Rules' ordinarily used, but in the relative shortness of the time in which Latin can be learnt by it. Crucial here is his claim that the ordinary method takes so long that children forget 'the best part' of their vernacular, and that the great advantage of his own method is that it 'contributes much to the knowledge of our Mother-tongue'. The reading of authors must be introduced early, for otherwise pupils will not, on 'entering into Rhetorick', produce 'any thing but what is very mediocre'.[176]

One way by which mother tongue, though not a subject of instruction in the grammar schools, obtained at least a footing in pedagogical method was via translation. Certainly, if we are to believe Ascham, the efforts of late-sixteenth-century pupils to produce Latin themselves (the 'making of latines', as he calls it) were lamentable in the extreme, resulting in 'an evill choice of wordes, a wrong placing of wordes: and lastlie, an ill framing of the sentence'.[177] To remedy this state of affairs, and the child's 'butcherlie feare in making of latines', Ascham (following hints given in Cicero's *De oratore*) advises the master first to read aloud a passage of Latin, and then 'construe it into English' so that the child may obtain an

[175] The prefatory note to the Scolar Press facsimile edition (Menston, 1969) states that the work is a translation of an (anonymous?) *Examen de la maniere d'enseigner le Latin aux enfans* which had appeared in the preceding year.

[176] *Examen*, pp. 16–17, 22, 59.

[177] The mechanical nature of these exercises was encouraged by the existence of various 'vulgars', or collections of sentences for translation, such as those of Horman (*Vulgaria*, London, 1519) and Whittinton. But whereas the latter gave made-up sentences illustrative of specific points of grammar, Horman already used passages from classical authors. (See L. G. Kelly, *Twenty-five Centuries of Language Teaching*, Rowley, Mass., 1969, p. 51).

understanding of the matter in the vernacular. The pupil then translates the passage into English and, at a later stage, back into Latin.[178] It is accordingly not for its own sake, but because 'making of Lattines marreth children', that the vernacular begins to be heard in the classroom. From these small beginnings it gradually, in the course of the seventeenth century, assumes a more important role as a necessary gateway to Latin. The second way by which the vernacular came to have more standing was via an increasing recognition of what may be termed 'customary' grammar. Here, as we have seen, an important source is Mulcaster's *Elementarie* (1582), which reverses the usual attitude by seeing the primary role of grammar as 'to have the naturall tung of each cuntrie fined to that best, and most certain direction, which the ordinarie custom...can lead hir unto'. Only secondarily is it an aid to the acquisition of Latin or of any other tongue. Though he probably shares some of his ideas with Du Bellay's *Deffence et illustration de la langue francoyse* (1549), he would seem to be among the first to entertain these notions of the 'double use of grammer' and the customary nature of language,[179] and to see the grammar of the vernacular as a separate entity from that of Latin. But in the light of the sixteenth-century view that only in the classical authors can the 'trewe paterne of eloquence' (Ascham) be found, it is inevitable that until quite late in the following century the role of vernacular grammar – in such works as Joshua Poole's *English Accidence* (1646), Jeremiah Wharton's *English-Grammar* (1654) and Joseph Aickin's *English Grammar* (1693) – largely remained the modest one of easing the introduction to Latin studies. It is important however not to lose sight of the pedagogical and cultural background against which this admittedly subordinate employment of English grammar took place. Though some sixteenth-century practice, following Quintilian, had seen grammar as the hand-maid of literature, by the seventeenth century, in spite of the endeavours of Elyot and Ascham, it was if anything even more an end in itself, a collection of rules to whose illustration any pedagogical use of the vernacular must be confined.

Some of the best seventeenth-century minds put their efforts into

---

[178] *The Scholemaster*, pp. 182–3.

[179] *Elementarie*, pp. 49–50. Mulcaster's direct influence seems however to have been small. Watson, *The English Grammar Schools*, pp. 159–60, notes that 'It would be difficult to show that the quality of elementary education was much improved for a hundred years after Mulcaster wrote.'

the artificial language question, which meant that they pinned their faith to an amalgam of categories from the supposedly ideal language Latin, and Aristotelian methods of taxonomic classification, as a basis for a language that would better correspond to *things* in the real world than any of the existing vernaculars. A group centred around Samuel Hartlib were also however interested in the reform of language teaching, and had connections not only with Comenius and his followers on the continent, but also with the German reformers around Ratke.[180] Their emphasis, as befits puritan reformers of the Commonwealth period, is on the obtaining of useful knowledge, but still via Latin rather than the vernacular. Here again however the increasing emphasis on the pedagogical use of the vernacular in attaining a knowledge of Latin meant that by the time of the Restoration it was generally assumed that Latin was in fact best approached via the mother tongue. In this respect the views of Comenius are preceded by those of the reforming Leicestershire schoolmaster John Brinsley. Though his *Ludus literarius*[181] and *The Posing of the Parts*[182] have to do with the teaching of Latin according to 'the continuall use of the bookes of construing of Lillies rules', he is none the less of the opinion that no pupil should be admitted to the grammar school without an adequate reading knowledge of English. He too is to be numbered among those reformers who, by putting Lily's rules into English, gave the vernacular a foothold in the schools. But his *Ludus literarius* goes yet further, giving what I. Michael[183] has called the 'first explicit statement' of the case for the actual teaching of the vernacular. His reforming zeal, as with the Ramists, goes hand in hand with a puritan Protestantism (he was educated at Christ's College Cambridge) which was anxious to provide a counterbalance to the success of the Jesuits in language teaching.[184] Significant is his claim that his methods will enable the

---

[180] For an account of the linguistic and pedagogical interests of the Hartlib circle see V. Salmon, 'Problems of Language-Teaching; A Discussion among Hartlib's Friends', *The Study of Language in Seventeenth-Century England*, Amsterdam, 1979, pp. 3–14. (This article originally appeared in *Modern Language Review*, LIX (1964), pp. 13–24.)

[181] *Ludus literarius: or, The Grammar Schoole*, London, 1612. For a consideration of Brinsley's importance for seventeenth-century pedagogy see V. Salmon, 'John Brinsley, Seventeenth-century Pioneer in Applied Linguistics', *The Study of Language in Seventeenth-Century England*, pp. 33–46. (This article originally appeared in *Historiographia Linguistica*, II:2 (1975), pp. 175–89.)

[182] London, 1612. I have used the second edition of 1615.

[183] *English Grammatical Categories*, p. 154.

[184] See Salmon, 'John Brinsley', p. 36.

pupil to 'proceed as well in our English tonge as in the latine'. Though his vernacular aids to the learning of Latin are not original – his definition of the substantive as that before which 'I may fitly put *a* or *the*' or to which 'I cannot fitly joyne this word *thing*'[185] has a precedent in Melanchthon's Latin grammar nearly a century earlier – they none the less represent a pressing into service of the vernacular in the classroom. The traditional priorities still reign however in Brinsley's proposal that preparatory instruction in English should be the concern of the 'usher' or assistant, leaving the master himself, aided it is true by some use of the vernacular, free to get on with the serious business of teaching Latin.

To Brinsley goes the honour of having produced the first well-planned Latin course in England, worthy to be compared with what the Jesuits had already achieved elsewhere. Much more revolutionary reforms were however proposed a decade later by Joseph Webbe, whose doctrines, contained in his *Appeale to Truth*,[186] his *Petition to Parliament*[187] and various manuscript works of which the chief are 'Methodi in docendo' and 'Propositions concerning Teaching of Languages',[188] represent the most important expression of the reform movement. Yet another in the list of physicians who have interested themselves in language, Webbe aimed to teach Latin without using any grammar at all.[189] His ideas intersect with main currents in seventeenth-century thought at several points. He had for instance written on the Kabbalah, and his proposed reforms are in many ways similar to those of Ratke, of whom it is unlikely however that he had heard. Holding that 'no man can run speedily to the mark of languages that is shackled...with grammer precepts',[190] he deplores the intellectual impoverishment of an educational system in which grammar 'hath well near gotten the whole traffic in learning'. Many of his ideas go back to a much earlier period, to the by then forgotten works of G. H. Cominius, a friend of Erasmus and an early exponent

---

[185] *The Posing of the Parts* (2nd ed.) 1615, f. 2ʳ.

[186] *An Appeale to Truth, in the Controversie betweene Art, and Use; about the best and most expedient Course in Languages*, London, 1622.

[187] *A Petition to the High Court of Parliament, in the behalf of auncient and authentique authors*, London, 1623.

[188] Respectively ff. 331ʳ–41ʳ and 155ᵛ of British Library MS Sloane 1466.

[189] For a discussion of Webbe's pedagogical views see Salmon's already cited 'Problems of Language-Teaching', pp. 4–5, 8–12, and her article 'Some Seventeenth-Century Views on Language-Teaching and the Nature of Meaning', *The Study of Language in Seventeenth-Century England*, pp. 15–31 (first appeared in *Bibliothèque d'Humanisme et Renaissance*, xxiii (1961), pp. 324–40). [190] *An Appeale to Truth*, p. 41.

of methods of teaching Latin without grammar rules.[191] In view of N. Chomsky's assumption that seventeenth-century pedagogy saw language acquisition in terms of innate ideas rather than in terms of pattern-learning, a controversy which took place between Webbe and William Brookes is not without interest for historians of linguistics in our own day.[192] Briefly, it may be said that Brookes defended the traditional method of learning a language through grammar-rules, while Webbe held to the 'pattern-drill' position. John Webster's *Examination of Academies* (1654),[193] a work sharply critical of the educational establishment, praises Webbe's 'brief and easie clausulary method' as being pedagogically superior to the 'tedious, painful, intricate and hard way of Grammar'.[194] With Webbe as with Mulcaster, the approach is based on the customary nature of language. Since 'every Language hath a different Custome. And the difference is either in whole clauses, or in the parts...of clauses', Webbe – exceptionally for his times – thinks it wrong to follow the prevailing method of teaching pupils 'the wordes before the clause'.[195] In his *Lessons and Exercises out of Cicero ad Atticum*,[196] he defines a clause in purely structural terms as a 'perfect member of speech, consisting of one or moe words rightly knit unto other members... Which being broken off in any other part than in his true joynt or knitting, breeds a fracture and disorder', that is to say as a natural speech group or collocation of words. He recognizes indeed, in what is for his date a rare insight, the existence of what we would now call embedded clauses, which main clauses 'carry in their bellies'. A further instance of his modernity is his recognition of the fact that a single word can function as a 'clause', in contradiction of the traditional rule that a sentence must contain a subject and a verb. It was however to be long indeed before these insights bore fruit

[191] The linguistic and pedagogical writings of Georgius Haloinus Cominius, a native of the Low Countries, were formerly thought to be no longer extant. V. Salmon, in a postscript to her 'Some Seventeenth-Century Views', notes however that his *De restauratione linguae Latinae* (1533, but written a quarter of a century earlier) has now been edited by C. Mattheeussen (Leipzig, 1978). See also V. Salmon's 'A Pioneer of the Direct Method in the Erasmian Circle', *Latomus*, xix (1960), pp. 567–77.

[192] Chomsky's assumptions, contained in his *Cartesian Linguistics* (New York, 1966) are queried by V. Salmon in her review of that work (*Journal of Linguistics*, v (1969), pp. 165–87. She buttresses her argument with details from the Webbe–Brookes controversy, which is set out in British Library MS Sloane 1466.

[193] Published in London. Latin title *Academiarum examen.*

[194] P. 23.   [195] British Library MS Sloane 1466, f. 261.

[196] London, 1627, f. A3^r.

in pedagogical practice, though Samuel Hartlib relates[197] that he himself initiated students into Latin without using paradigms, which as a result of the traditional word-by-word approach had become a major tool of language pedagogy. In their place, pupils read a passage from a classical author, duly divided into 'clauses', and in Webbe's method it was these clauses that were repeated by students, not paradigms of a single word. But Webbe's emphasis being on *verba*, in contrast to the seventeenth century's increasing obsession with *res*, his work was in his own day overshadowed by that of the better-known Comenius.[198] V. Salmon observes that the powerful current of thought represented by Comenius and his followers was interested in the labelling of *things* by single words in a one-to-one correspondence, rather than in the cultivation of elegant 'clauses'. It was, as she well remarks, precisely the humanists' failure to recognize the fact that 'a language does not convey meaning by adding one isolated word to another'[199] that lay behind their emphasis on individual words and the rote learning of paradigms. The point at issue here however is that Webbe's 'clausulary method' proceeded without the least appeal to grammatical rules, and once it had been shown that Latin could be learnt without them, the old contention that the vernacular could never be a serious object of study because it could not be 'reduced to rule' fell to the ground.

The grammars

It is against the background of this continuing argument about the place of grammar in the teaching of Latin that we must set the English vernacular grammars of the seventeenth century. The increasing insistence on the role of the vernacular in Latin pedagogy, accompanied by the continued primacy of classical studies, means that several of the more important English grammars of the period – John Hewes' *Perfect Survey of the English Tongue* (1624), Joshua Poole's *English Accidence* (1646), Jeremiah Wharton's *English-Grammar* (1654) – are equally applicable to Latin. Each of these authors claims that his English grammar will facilitate the acquisition of Latin, and

[197] The Progresse in Teaching', British Library MS Sloane 1466, f. 32ᵛ. Cf. Salmon, 'Problems of Language-Teaching, p. 12.
[198] See Kelly, *Twenty-five Centuries of Language Teaching*, p. 38.
[199] ' Some Sevententh-Century Views', p. 131. In what I have had to say about Brinsley, Webbe and the Webbe–Brookes controversy, my debt to Salmon will be obvious.

it is a sign of the times that Edward Burles' *New English Grammar* (1652)[200] is in fact, in spite of its title, a Latin grammar. In view of this ambivalence, I. Michael's *English Grammatical Categories* (1970) treats these works as 'basic' grammars representing a 'brief and partial merging of English and Latin grammars under several influences'. He excludes from this category grammars of Latin in bilingual versions, such as Charles Hoole's *Latine Grammar* (1651) and the dramatist James Shirley's *Grammatica Anglo-Latina* of the same year, which he sees as quite patently intended only for the teaching of Latin. The fact that these 'basic grammars' are meant to be applicable to both languages has of course repercussions for the grammatical theory of English, for since it was 'assumed that children learnt by applying a previously memorized definition', this definition, learnt by heart in English before the child approached Latin, 'often seemed to be the definition of an English category'.[201] It was no doubt at least in part by this means that such rules as those prohibiting split infinitives and the use of an 'accusative' after the verb *to be* were erroneously transferred to the grammar of English. The production of such Latin-orientated 'basic' grammars is however not the only grammatical activity of the seventeenth century. Jeremiah Wharton also sees his *English-Grammar* as 'the most certain guide that ever yet was extant' for foreigners, and as providing the basis for the learning of 'any exotick language'. Quite early in the seventeenth century indeed, it becomes the practice to append short grammars to English textbooks intended for use abroad. These often very rudimentary works show their authors to have little or no acquaintenace with the more important grammatical works of the time, and their ambitions, as for example with the manuals put out to facilitate trade with the Low Countries, remain modest. Among works intended for the Netherlands may be mentioned the *English Grammar* included with Henry Hexham's *Copious English and Nether-duytch Dictionarie* of 1648.[202] Another by-product of this new concern for the propagation of English to foreigners is James Howell's *New English Grammar* of 1662,[203] intended for Spaniards. Yet a third current in seventeenth-century grammatical endeavours is provided by those school grammars that, however naïvely or clumsily, attempt

---

[200] Published in London. [201] *English Grammatical Categories*, p. 492.
[202] Consulted in the Rotterdam edition of 1660.
[203] Published in London.

to make a pedagogical application of Baconian 'sense-realism' theories, the chief works here being those of Mark Lewis, particularly his *Essay to Facilitate the Education of Youth* (*c.* 1670 and 1674). These works are frankly of more interest for their pedagogical approach than for their grammatical theory. Much more important are the well-known grammars of John Wallis and Christopher Cooper, which represent both the English vernacular's final attainment of freedom from the Latin yoke, and an empirical influence stemming from the newly founded Royal Society. Finally, A. Lane's *Key to the Art of Letters*, at the very end of the century, has features which require it to be treated in part as a manifestation of the universal grammar movement. These various strands in seventeenth-century vernacular grammar will now be discussed in turn, beginning with the so-called 'basic' grammars.

John Hewes' *Perfect Survey of the English Tongue* (1624, already mentioned above as a formally based grammar with no debt to Ramus) is a 'survey' of English only in the circumscribed sense that it is 'taken according to the use and analogie of the Latin'.[204] The earlier sections of his work have however the merit of establishing English usage before turning to Latin, rather than simply offering translations of Latin rules. He stresses that the vernacular, though less 'well wrought and polished' in the matter of formal endings, presents a structure distinct from that of the 'dialect of the Latines'. If he has as he puts it 'drawne those Rules of Grammar into short briefes', it is in order to remedy the general lack of awareness of the structural differences between the two languages. His aim remains however to treat the vernacular parts of speech as they may 'best conduce or accord with the Latines', treating English as 'the first ground-worke to the Latine'. The overriding purpose is to provide a service to Latin pedagogy, for without the 'first rudiments' of the vernacular 'many an hard stroke is made at old Priscians head unawares'. Accordingly, if Hewes calls attention to English structural features 'which the Latine Dialect doth not expresse at all', calling them 'signes which demonstrate the use of the following wordes', it is not only because they are peculiar to the vernacular, but also

[204] Published in London. The title states that the work 'Taken According to the Use and Analogie of the Latine...serveth for the plaine exposition of...Lillie, and for the more certaine translation of the English tongue into Latine'.

because without a knowledge of them Latin 'cannot bee translated into our vulgar'. The essential point remains the fact that he regards instruction in English as an indispensable preliminary to Latin studies. Changes in pedagogical method were however slow to come about, though Thomas Grantham's dismissal twenty years after Hewes of the average schoolmaster as a 'braine-breaker, lout, sot and bumbeater' is no doubt exaggerated. He himself sets out to do a little 'breaking' of pedagogues who meet with his disapproval, and his *Brainbreakers-Breaker* (1644)[205] certainly paints a dismal picture of 'the misery that youth groans under, in common Schooles...more like Bridewell than Seminaries of learning'. For all that Ascham had, as he puts it, condemned 'this lip-labour, this learning word for word without book' and Comenius in turn had 'writ sharpely against this dogbolt way', one wonders whether much had really changed in the schools.

Another important work taking the view that a knowledge of the mother tongue is an indispensable prolegomenon to Latin studies is Joshua Poole's *English Accidence* of 1646.[206] The approach envisaged is still the traditional word-by-word one, in which 'before he meddle with Latine' the pupil is required to 'tell distinctly what part of speech every word is'. The further requirement that once he knows this he must also be able to state, for each part, 'what Syntaxis, or ordering it should have in Latine, though in the meane time hee never heard of one Latine word', might be thought to result in a Latinization of English syntax, in which word-classes defined in terms of Latin are arranged, *in English*, in a Latin syntactic order. There is in fact, though Poole condemns the Englishman's preference then as now for remaining silent rather than commit a solecism ('to breake Priscians head, is such a capitall crime with us'), some truth in the criticism[207] that he is ready, in approximating the two languages to each other, to accept both mutilated Latin and mutilated English. In contrast, Jeremiah Wharton's *English Grammar* (1654)[208] is much

---

[205] Published in London.

[206] Published in London. Poldauf ('On the History of Some Problems of English Grammar', p. 77) claims that 'The discovery that familiarity with the grammatical system of one's mother tongue may facilitate learning other languages was first applied to Latin by Joshua Poole...in 1646.' Poole was of course preceded by Hewes in this.

[207] See Poldauf, 'On the History of Some Problems of English Grammar', p. 78.

[208] Published in London. Poldauf ('On the History of Some Problems of English Grammar', p. 75) calls this grammar an admitted compilation of Gill, Jonson and Butler. Wharton does in fact cite Gill, Mulcaster, Jonson and Butler as his sources, and his approach may well owe something to Gill.

more a grammar of the vernacular than those of his two predecessors. The emphasis too has changed. Though English can still serve as an introduction to Latin, it is now the teacher's duty 'as well to accustom them to the exercise of good English, as of good Latine'. Though the method is still a word-by-word one requiring the student to 'distinguish every Part of Speech asunder; the knowledg whereof is of great use...for...the making of Latine', Wharton places an unusual emphasis (common in German vernacular grammars of the period but only at its beginnings in English) on derivation and composition, which not only represent an 'elegancie of the English-tongue', but are invaluable aids in the learning of 'any other exotick language'. Paradoxically, though he holds a knowledge of the vernacular to be a useful preliminary to the acquisition of any 'grammatized language', to which its rules are automatically applicable, he also describes it as itself needing 'little or no Grammar at all'. It is happy in not requiring 'any Declensions of Nouns, any Conjugations of Verbs, any Rules of Concord or Construction, wherein the difficultie of any language doth consist'. These views are mutually exclusive, and it is curious that Wharton should be at such pains to stress the value of the practically grammar-less vernacular in the acquisition of more 'grammatized' languages. His work is illustrative of the growing seventeenth-century tendency to regard grammar as something extrinsic *applied* to a language to make it amenable to study. Since English, with 'little or no variation at all', shows little that Wharton would give the name grammar to, it follows that his approach to it, in contrast to that of Hewes, will be almost entirely semasiological.

Given the analytical character of English, it is however inevitable that as vernacular grammar, from the mid-century on, increasingly frees itself from Latin, emphasis is more and more put on syntactic criteria in defining the word-classes. The most obvious example is provided by Hewes' *Perfect Survey* (1624), which as we have seen represents a departure from the largely semasiological criteria of preceding authors in the direction of an almost Ramist dependence on formal criteria. Where a supposedly formal note appears elsewhere in these authors it is Varronian, doubtless through Vossius[209] or his imitators rather than from Ramus, as in Poole's attribution to noun and participle of case but not tense, and to the verb of tense but not

[209] *De arte grammatica libri septem*, Amsterdam, 1635.

case.[210] Varro's formal system is however, like that of Ramus, largely inapplicable to the structure of English, and Poole in practice treats his word-classes in almost wholly semasiological terms. As to the number of parts of speech, the approach is still somewhat conservative. Though later grammatical theory is to see the development of what I. Michael has called 'vernacular' word-class systems more closely adapted to English, these authors, in the mid-seventeenth century, do not stray far from the traditional eight classes of Latin. They are after all applying Lily's eight-part system to English, in an effort to demonstrate its suitability as a preliminary vehicle for grammar. Hence it is not surprising that the article, as with Bullokar (1586), is a sign of nouns rather than a separate part of speech, a vernacular embarrassment to be treated as an attachment to something else. Of particular interest as illustrations of the way in which the definitions of the parts of speech are evolving during the period are the bilingual Latin/English grammars of the dramatist James Shirley, founder of a school with at any rate initially similar reforming intentions to those of Webbe. Though his *Via ad Latinam linguam complanata* (1649), *Grammatica Anglo-Latina* (1651) and *The Rudiments of Grammar* (1656)[211] do not constitute 'basic' grammars in Michael's sense (as he puts it, they teach Latin *in* rather than *through* English), their successive versions of what is really the same grammar are a convincing demonstration of the evolution away from the formal criteria of the Ramists and Hewes, and in the direction of purely semasiological statements.[212] It is an evolution similar to that to be found in successive editions of Lily's Latin Grammar. Christofer Syms indeed, author of a Latin grammar[213] attaching exceptional importance to formal variation by 'tipes and figures', censures the King's Printer for removing such criteria from Lily's grammar as 'impertinent superfluities'. In a passage worthy of Ramus, Syms asks 'what need so many ambages and winding circuits by mood, tense,

[210] *The English Accidence*, p. 2. These Varronian criteria appear in humanist grammar as early as Nebrija's *Introductiones* (1533 ed., p. [34]).

[211] A much simpler grammar by Shirley is the *Manuductio, or, A Leading of Children by the Hand, through the principles of Grammar* (2nd ed., 1660).

[212] Cf. Salmon, 'James Shirley and Some Problems of Seventeenth-Century Grammar', pp. 87–96. Salmon demonstrates that though Shirley's definitions perpetuate the contemporary confusion of morphological and syntactic, and semasiological criteria, they clearly show an evolution towards exclusive use of the latter that is to be the hall-mark of eighteenth-century theory.

[213] *An Introduction to, or the Art of Teaching, the Latine Speach*, [Dublin, 1634].

number and person', provided the student is 'perfect in variation'. Given this recognition of the primacy of morphological criteria in the actual learning of Latin, it is not surprising that an early-seventeenth-century author such as Hewes, and indeed later authors (paradoxically, in spite of the increasing tendency to semasiological approaches in definition), attach great importance to Lily's system of signs. One set of formal criteria is however being exchanged for another, for these 'signs', intended by Lily as aids in choosing the correct morphological ending when translating into Latin, now acquire, given the relative absence of formal terminations in English, an existence in their own right as indications of vernacular structure. Hewes indeed defines wholly in terms of these signs, in contrast to Shirley, in whose work they are always accompanied by semantically based definitions whose importance increases with each new version of his grammar. The only semantic note Hewes permits himself is the statement that 'all Names are Noune Substantives', inherited from Colet's section of Lily's Latin grammar and itself a parallel indication of the evolution of grammar in the direction of nomenclature. More typical of his whole approach is the description of *a* and *the* as 'signes of Noune Substantives', and of adjectives (in Melanchthonian fashion) as words which may join with *man* or *thing*. This contrasts (to cite a contemporary grammarian of Latin) with Brinsley's use of Colet's full semantic definition of the noun as 'the name of a thing, that may be seene, felt, heard, or understood'. The advantage of Hewes' purely formal method is that it does not involve him in such face-saving mental acrobatics as Brinsley's '*Nihil* is a Name, though it signifie nothing: because it is not meant properly nothing at all, but a thing of no value.'[214]

Among English grammarians after Hewes, what is noteworthy is their continued use of such semasiological definitions – Wharton's 'a Noun is a word that signifies a person or thing', Poole's 'a Noune is a word that signifies a thing, or the nature and property of a thing' – side by side with the structural implications of Lily's system of signs. The most widespread treatment of the noun, as Poole's typical definition suggests, is in terms of concrete substantives signifying *things*, and adjectives and abstract substantives signifying their qualities. In this approach, and in contrast to the inherited

[214] *The Posing of the Parts*, p. 2.

Latin tradition, it is no longer the noun-class as a whole, but the concrete (to use a later term) substantive that signifies a *res* or thing. Not until Mark Lewis' *Essay* of *c.* 1670 do we find an English grammarian ready to separate substantive and adjective as distinct parts of speech, though the treatment of the substantive by Poole, for instance, as signifying 'the thing it selfe', is manifestly bringing that day nearer. That is not however to say that these grammarians are innovating on this point, for a parallel development is also taking place in Latin grammar.[215] Poole and Wharton define the substantive in terms of semantic independence, as signifying 'the thing itself', treating the adjective as the signification of 'a qualitie belonging to som Substantive' (Wharton) or of 'the nature and property of a thing' (Poole), and both define in terms of the presence or absence of a preceding *a* or *the*. Poole provides a semasiological justification of his formal rule – it is precisely *because* a substantive signifies 'the thing it selfe' then it cannot be followed by the word 'thing' – and also adds a syntactic criterion in terms of the ability to stand alone in discourse. We have here then a mixture of semantic and syntactic criteria, together with the pedagogical device of distinction by means of preceding 'signs'.

In treating case, Poole and Wharton similarly give the articles the role of signs, Wharton noting that strictly speaking 'in the English Tongue there is no variation of Nouns by Cases, but only by Number...and signs of the cases'. The authors have no difficulty in adopting the tradition which sees *of* and *to*, with or without articles, as signs of genitive and dative, and *in*, *with*, *by* and *from* as signs of the ablative. Nominative and accusative can then be distinguished by position before or after the verb, and by the fact that their signs are *a* and *the* alone. Wharton however, obstinate in requiring a distinct 'sign' for each case, invents an entirely arbitrary rule requiring *a/an* before nominatives and *the* before accusatives: 'usually it is so, and there is no better way to distinguish them in declining'. True to his principle, he terminates his grammar with the words *An End*.[216] Thus do the rules for the use of signs become, in their turn, a grammatical straitjacket producing unnatural structures. Such is

[215] Seventeenth-century Latin grammarians are in effect replacing the earlier Latin theorists' *the noun signifies a thing together with a quality*, by a new dichotomy in which *the concrete substantive signifies a thing: the adjective and the abstract substantive signify qualities*. On this point the 'basic' grammarians are imitating them.
[216] Poole, *The English Accidence*, p. 4; Wharton, *The English-Grammar*, pp. 34–6.

the pedagogical importance of the signs that they are no longer solely a device for 'resolving' a synthetic Latin structure into an analytical English one, but are also used in the explanation of vernacular morphology. Thus, the *-er* ending of the comparative is 'explained by *more*' and the *-est* of the superlative by *most*. The existence of both types in English facilitates this, but the device is also used with diminutives in *-ish* ('explained by *somewhat* or a *little*') and privatives in *un-* ('explained by *not* or *no whit*'). In treating gender the authors are at a loss for formal marks in English other than indicators of sex such as the termination *-ess*, and are faced, apart from the use of *he*, *she* and *it* in referring to previously mentioned items, with a complete absence of gender-based concord. Wharton sensibly rejects the seven genders of traditional Latin as 'useless' in English, confining himself to the remark that 'som words doe signifie Males; som females; and som neither; and that of the first we must say *hee*; of the second *shee*; of the third *it*.' The treatment of gender in the European vernaculars, as in Latin, is complicated by the confused cross-cutting of what should be two distinct matters: the indication of sex, and the need for some kind of device to indicate syntactic concord. Entirely to the former belongs the 'epicene' or 'promiscuous' gender of Latin in which one sex is evoked (as in *anser* (m) and *vulpes* (f)) to represent individuals of both sexes. In a language such as Latin, where gender is a syntactic device, there is some reason for pointing out these anomalies, if only to secure correct adjectival agreement. Poole starts off with some attempt at a statement of syntactic agreement: 'A word is of the Masculine Gender, when it can only bee joyned with Adjectives of the masculine gender' – a statement which is however devoid of sense when applied to English. He then prescribes the full set of seven Latin genders (including common of two genders, common of three, doubtful and epicene) to the vernacular, holding that an epicene gender is present 'when by the same word you name both the *hee* and the *shee*... as *an Asse, a Beare, an Elephant, a Mouse, a Cat*.' That the word *cat* can be used of both sexes is not a grammatical matter, but such misunderstandings are the inevitable result of a determination to set up for English categories from Latin grammar which have no formal justification in the language.

I. Michael notes that more than 80 per cent of English grammarians before 1800 define the pronoun as a noun substitute, more than half of these also adding the (Melanchthonian) statement that it is used to avoid unnecessary repetition. In the authors considered in this section what may be noted is the extreme simplicity of the definitions – Poole's 'part of speech much like to a Noune', Wharton's 'part of speech much like to a Noun, and always spoken of a Noun' – and the limitation of the definition itself to noun substitution. The Melanchthonian definition occurs later in the text, as in Wharton's remark that demonstratives are used in 'shewing or pointing out a thing'. A new development is an increasing tendency to classify pronouns into adjective and substantive, Hewes even going so far as to treat pronouns as a sub-class of substantives. There are of course precedents for this latter classification in the Latin tradition, in Sanctius and Ramus, and among English grammarians it had been advocated by Gill. When Hewes singles out pronouns for discussion, he refers to them simply as 'persons' or 'relatives'. Poole's pronouns substantive, 'that belong not to another word in speaking', are also termed 'personals', while his pronouns adjective, 'that belong to another word in speaking', group the three classes demonstrative, relative and possessive. The treatment of the pronoun is marked by the same determination to force English into the Latin grammatical mould, that we have seen in Poole's approach to gender. If Wharton sets up accusatives *towards me*, *by her* and *by them*, as opposed to ablatives *from me*, *with her* and *with them*, it is because the determination to find an ablative in English leads him to seek semantic differences in the accompanying prepositions, in a situation in which the grammatical structures are identical. As so often with English grammarians, the lack of formal variation in the language causes them to treat as grammatical distinctions what are in fact lexical ones.

Similarly in defining the verb, the treatment is by now almost wholly semantic, following the contemporary Latin grammarians' parallel tendency to define exclusively in terms of the signification of *actio*, *passio* or *esse*. Wharton's 'A Verb betokeneth the doing and suffering, or beeing of a thing' is typical. What is interesting however is that both he and Poole add a reference to signification of time. The definition of the verb wholly in the semantic terms of the signification of *actio* and *passio* appears probably for the first time in Melanchthon's *Grammatica Latina* of 1525: 'Verbum est vox signifians agere aut pati'. On the same page however, he describes the verb as denoting 'actionem et passionem, cum discriminibus temporum',[217] and it is this tradition that is continued in Wharton and Poole. It may however equally well represent Greek tradition which, via Linacre, lingered longer in England than elsewhere. I. Michael rightly remarks that whereas the distinction of voice in Latin was on formal as well as semantic criteria – 'Active meant primarily ending in -*o*' – the lack of formal marks in English meant that action, passion and existence could be regarded as 'purely semantic categories'.[218] This statement needs however some modification, for a parallel emphasis on the purely semantic is taking place in Latin grammar as early as Melanchthon, and is well established in the most important Latin grammar of the seventeenth century, Vossius' *De arte grammatica* of 1635, which one must suppose would be known to the English grammarians of the time. The likelihood of Vossius' being these authors' model is increased by the fact that he not only defines semantically in terms of *agere, pati* and *esse* (almost precisely Melanchthon's definition of a century earlier), but has an added requirement that the verb consignifies time.[219] Wharton's simple semantic statement that 'a Verb Active betokeneth dooing...a Verb Passive betokeneth suffering...a Verb Neuter betokeneth Beeing' is consonant with this tendency towards wholly semantic definition. Poole, while also furnishing these semantic criteria, has the further requirement – itself rooted in traditional Latin grammatical theory – that a verb active is that which may be transformed into a passive, a verb passive that which may be transformed into an active. This enables him to define 'verbs neuter' (*to wink, to kneel*) as verbs which, though they have active signification, have no corresponding passive form. In contrast to active verbs, they cannot be followed by an accusative case. Since his 'neuter' verbs are in fact the modern intransitives, one wonders why Poole did not make this last criterion his only one, more especially as the search for parallelism with Latin leads him to set up a class of 'neuter' verbs with passive signification (e.g. *to be sick*), but which are incapable of being transformed into actives. The model here, entirely inappropriate to English, is obviously the Latin verb *aegroto* ('I am sick'), which has an active form but a passive meaning.

---

[217] *Grammatica Latina* (1527 ed., Paris), f. 26ʳ.
[218] *English Grammatical Categories*, p. 372.
[219] On Vossius' approach to the verb see Padley, *Grammatical Theory* (1976), pp. 126–9.

It is more particularly in the analysis of tense that sign theory comes to the fore. There are of course semantic definitions of the tenses, as in Poole's characterization of the imperfect (i.e. the simple past) as denoting 'the doing, or being of a thing in time, whilst the thing was in doing or being'; the perfect as indicating 'the time past'; and the pluperfect as referring to 'the time long agoe past'.[220] They are however accompanied by the prescribed signs *do* and *did* for present and past active verbs; *is* and *was* for present and past 'neuter' and passive ones; and *have/had*, *have been/had been* in perfect and pluperfect tenses. *Shall* and *will* are signs of the future. The weakness of the system, apart from the lack of recognition of the progressive tenses (e.g. *I am going* as opposed to *I go*), is that the simple present and past tenses are left without any specific marker. Hewes for instance is reduced to stating that the present 'yee may best know by the time, all others depending on their Signes'. Only the fact that *do* and *did* were in the seventeenth century used in declarative sentences (not, as nowadays, in emphatic ones) allows the authors to produce a complete set of signs for all tenses. This means that *take* and *took* must be tacitly assimilated to *did take* and *did take*. At a loss where no variation in form, apart from the signs, signals tense differences, Wharton has to declare somewhat lamely that in the case of *cast* and *hurt* 'the present tense serveth for all'. Not for the first time, one is reminded of modern structuralist morphemic analyses of the Bloomfieldian type, which work well enough when a one-to-one correspondence between form and meaning (*walked*, *did walk*) can be demonstrated, but are less happy with amalgams such as *took*. And apart from such difficulties, grammarians are still frequently led astray by their Latin model, as when Poole treats *shall have* in *when I shall have loved* as a sign of the subjunctive on the analogy of *cum amavero*, itself mistakenly classified as a future subjunctive by grammarians of Latin.

In spite of its lacunae, the system of signs provided English vernacular grammarians with a fairly clear-cut set of formal markers for recognizing the tenses. In the treatment of mood the difficulty once more is the inability of grammarians to distinguish clearly between formal (including syntactic) criteria and semantic ones. In this they are of course merely continuing a confusion inherited from

---

[220] *The English Accidence*, pp. 10–11.

the Latin tradition, and here it is Linacre who, in spite of his theoretical insistence on the *consignification* of mood by formal marks, paves the way for their approach. His classification of the 'diversae inclinationes' (Priscian's expression) of mood is in the last resort based on meaning, the optative for instance being inevitably, since it is formally identical in Latin with the subjunctive, defined as that which signifies a wish. He brings the traditional number of moods up to six by adding a *potential*, justified on grounds of economy as expressing an 'affectio animi' for which Greek uses two distinct procedures. Since however it is identical in form with the Latin subjunctive and optative, its institution on the grounds that it represents a separate 'affectio animi' leaves the way open to a flood of moods limited only by the number of 'affectiones' that can be invented. Linacre makes these distinctions in the same way as did the Spanish grammarian of Latin Nebrija much earlier: semantically, 'ratione significationis'.[221] Colet's section of Lily's Latin grammar, though it defines mood in semantic terms as 'the maner of spekynge', uses formal sign criteria in addition to semasiological definitions, recognizing the optative by its preceding 'adverbe of wishing' *wold God*, and treating the subjunctive as a syntactically dependent form preceded by a conjunction. The potential mood, inserted in later editions of the grammar in imitation of Linacre, is known by its English signs *may*, *can*, etc. Lily's use of English signs to facilitate learning leads him to put an emphasis on similar signs in Latin, introducing a syntactic, structural criterion that is almost wholly absent in Linacre. The English vernacular grammarians thus have two sources in the indigenous Latin grammatical tradition, though it is likely, given their declared purpose of easing the way to Lily's grammar, that their potential mood stems directly from him. It seems probable that Hewes has first decided how many moods he will have (six, as in Linacre and Lily), and has then cast around for signs to indicate them in English. The only mood without its specific sign is the indicative, known 'by Affirming, Denying, or asking a question'. The subjunctive has its set of preceding conjunctions, and signs

---

[221] See the 1533 edition of the *Introductiones Latinae* (first published in Salamanca in 1481), p. [12]: 'non vocum sed significationum diversitas facit distinctos modos'. Linacre remarks however, *De emendata structura*, I, 15ᵛ, that if form is taken into account the situation is different: 'Modi, si vocum discrimen spectes, quatuor tantum sunt.'

of the remaining moods are *let* (imperative), *to* (infinitive), *may/might/would/should* (potential), and *God grant that*, etc. (expressly given as parallels to *utinam* and *O si*) in the optative. Poole's treatment, apart from his future subjunctive *when I shall or will love*, is similar. Worthy of note is the fact that Wharton's four moods – significantly called 'manner of signifyings' – include (following Butler) a potential but no optative or subjunctive. Though he notes that *be* and *were* (in place of *is* and *was*) are used after the conjunctions *if*, *although* and *unless*, and after 'words of wishing', he does not on this account set up subjunctive and optative moods. His potential signifying a 'power, duty or desire' (cf. Linacre's 'potentiam aut debitum'), has the signs *may, can, might, would, should*. The future infinitive *to love hereafter* is obviously an echo of Bullokar. Wharton's definition of mood as 'that which to the signification of a Verbe addeth the manner of signifying' recalls that given in J. Danes' Latin grammar *A Light to Lilie* (1637).[222] Close correspondences indicate in fact that Wharton's section on mood is largely dependent on him.

The approach to the 'indeclinable' parts of speech is somewhat half-hearted. Again, perhaps the assumption is that they will not differ greatly in use from those in Latin. Hewes' criteria are not particularly helpful: 'If ye doubt of any word in ye beginning of any clause of speech, it is a conjunction.' On the other hand, 'all wordes that yee doubt of in the middle or end of your speech' are likely to be adverbs. Poole notes rather lamely that adverbs are joined to other words 'to declare their signification', while Wharton contents himself with Melanchthon's definition in terms of the expression of 'some circumstance or qualitie'.[223] They have the merit of realizing that adverbs modify other parts of speech besides verbs, but devote most of their discussion to the customary twenty-odd semantic classes. Wharton has the interest of giving whole phrases as adverbs, as in the 'adverb of chance' *as it fell out*. As for prepositions, while Hewes simply advises the student to learn them by heart, Poole gives a thoroughgoing treatment of case government more appropriate to a Latin grammar than an English one. His statement that *of* governs the ablative is obviously made with Latin *de* in mind. The difficulties

[222] Published in London.
[223] Wharton's definition is identical with that in Danes' *A Light to Lilie*, which is traceable to Vossius (*De arte*, III, ii, 15) and beyond him to Melanchthon.

experienced by grammarians in finding valid reasons for separating adverb, preposition and conjunction are no doubt one cause of the following century's tendency to lump them all together as 'particles'.

The common assumption that English had no syntax was due in large part to grammarians' inability to conceive of a syntax other than that provided by relations of concord and case government in inflected languages.[224] At the end of the century Joseph Aickin (1693)[225] holds the three concords of Latin to be 'fundamental rules of all tongues', and Hewes sees no paradox in offering 'the more generall rules of the syntax of the Cases: as they may be conceived in the English tongue'. These sections of the grammars accordingly read like Latin syntaxes, and it is significant that Hewes' very short treatment is followed by long lists of examples in Latin, of which his English examples are simply translations. The three concords of Latin are faithfully repeated, the substantive preceding the verb being in the nominative, except in structures such as *the man I see*, where Hewes (seemingly not recognizing the equivalence with *the man that I see*) holds it to be in the accusative. In government, the theory of signs is a fertile source of confusion. As in the similar Italian theory of 'segni de' casi', there is an interchange of roles in which for example *of* is now a sign of the genitive and now (following verbs) a preposition governing the ablative. Poole's rules of construction, including semasiological criteria for determining which verbs take the dative and which the ablative, do not differ appreciably from those in Latin grammars. Significant in this regard is the fact that his twenty-three-page grammar is followed by fifteen pages of 'rules for the easier turning of English into Latine'. Of the ten chapters of Wharton's grammar only three, treating respectively the parts of speech, derivation and composition, provide strictly grammatical material, the remainder being devoted to orthography, pronunciation and syllables. He sees little point in proposing a syntax of English – 'Here should follow the Rules of Concord, and Construction: but because there is so little, or no variation in the parts of the English tongue:

---

[224] It is curious that references to word order are so few in these early grammars, though V. Kohonen ('On the Development of an Awareness of English Syntax in Early (1550–1660) Descriptions of Word Order by English Grammarians, Logicians, and Rhetoricians', *Neuphilologische Mitteilungen* (1978), p. 45) notes that Brinsley's practice of requiring his pupils to juxtapose an 'English natural order', an 'ordo grammaticus' and an 'ordo Ciceronianus' must have made them aware of peculiarities of word order in the vernacular.

[225] *The English Grammar*, London, 1693.

they are altogether needless' – offering instead rules for derivation and composition. Included here to give some idea of the pedagogical orientation of the minor grammars of the period, these works are both heavily Latinized and highly derivative, depending in varying degrees on the Latin grammarian John Danes, and on Gill and Butler. They are still at this date either trying to hide or brashly vaunting the vernacular's relative lack of formal endings, but they have not, in spite of their preoccupation with 'signs', found a grammar appropriate to its structure. What they have in fact done is to use the system of signs to demonstrate that English has exact analytical counterparts to the Latin morphological system.

Aids for foreigners

To turn from these grammars to the humble, unambitious grammars intended as aids for foreigners is to be confronted with a different kind of approach. James Howell (no doubt a Welshman, if his name and his sometime membership of Jesus College Oxford are anything to go by) claims in the foreword to his *New English Grammar* (1662) to have produced not a basic grammar, 'an English Grammar to learn another Language, as Lillie is for Latin', but 'a meer Grammar of the English it self, for the use of Forreners'. But he is sceptical, possibly in excuse of his own shortcomings, as to the possibility of producing a grammar of the vernacular at all: 'It is a hard task to make a Grammar of a Mother Toung, a harder task to make one of a Dialect, but to make an exact Regular Grammar for all parts of a Subdialect (as the English is) is a task that may be said to be beyond the reach of human understanding.'[226] Even his friend Ben Jonson, a man 'as patient as hee was painfull', had to admit according to Howell that 'the further hee waded herin the more he was still gravelled'. Sceptical from the outset as to the success of his enterprise, Howell himself does not wade far into English grammar, and his work remains slight and unoriginal. Its interest lies in the views expressed as to the impossibility of providing a grammar for the vernacular. Both Howell and Hexham[227] have been held to be

[226] In a letter written in 1630 (*Familiar Letters*, II, London, 1645, sect. VII, letter LV, pp. 203ff.) Howell says of English: 'I cannot call it a regular language, in regard...there could never any grammar or exact syntaxes be made of it.'

[227] *The English Grammar* (1648) included in his *English and Netherduytch Dictionarie*. Consulted here in the Rotterdam edition of 1660.

dependent on Ramist authors, the former on Jonson[228] and the latter on Greaves.[229] In contrast to the Ramist formal approach of Greaves, Hexham's grammatical scheme is however overwhelmingly semasiological, and Howell's grammar too is completely devoid of Jonson's Ramist framework based on number.[230] One can only suppose that in both cases it is their choice (or plagiarism?) of *examples* that has caused them to be seen as indebted to the two Ramist authors. It is true that I. Michael lists only Jonson and Howell as producing traditional eight-word-class 'Latin' systems of the parts of speech to which the article is added as a ninth class. Howell in fact however seems rather half-hearted about it, giving eight parts 'whereunto we adde the prepositive articles *The* and *A*'. On the other hand, he is the first English grammarian to use the terms (though not entirely the present-day concepts) definite and indefinite. The article *the* 'is definit and terminats the understanding', while *a sword* and *a book* are 'indefinit' and 'denote the general Idea of swords and books'.[231] Here, in contrast to Jonson's Ramist formalism, Howell typifies the general flight from formal criteria in the direction of purely semasiological ones. Again, whereas in defining substantive and adjective Jonson tries to transfer the formal gender marks of Latin to English – 'a Substantive is a Noune of only one Gender, or (at the most) of two. And an Adjective is a Noune of three Genders' – Howell prefers the semantic definition in terms of words that 'can stand and be understood by themselfs', and words that 'signifie no real thing, unless they be applied to som Substantif'. It is one of the curiosities of the history of grammatical theory that, in the search for purely semantic criteria suitable to the description of an English vernacular lacking in terminal variation, grammarians once again take refuge in this medieval semantico-syntactic definition. In the matter of gender, with similarly little or nothing in the way of formal marks to go on in English, some grammarians are able to take over the whole complicated gender classification from Latin grammar, and justify its application to English by semantic criteria. Here – and in an

---

[228] See Michael, *English Grammatical Categories*, p. 566: 'The material of the grammar is derived very largely from Jonson.'

[229] According to Poldauf, 'On the History of Some Problems of English Grammar'.

[230] An example of a definition not repeated by Howell is Jonson's 'All Nounes are words of Number.'

[231] Michael notes (*English Grammatical Categories*, p. 361) that Thomas Tomkis' manuscript grammar 'De analogia Anglici sermonis liber grammaticus' (1621) uses the terms 'finitus' and 'infinitus' or 'vagus', while Jonson uses 'finite' and 'infinite'.

approach poles apart from that of Ramus – Howell does indeed follow Jonson closely,[232] sometimes with identical examples, in a cumbersome attempt to provide English with a gender system parallel to that of Latin. Points at which Howell differs from Jonson's Ramist approach could be multiplied. Though Jonson includes the pronoun as a separate item in his list of nine parts of speech he actually treats it, following Ramus, as an irregular noun. Howell in contrast stays within received tradition, seeing pronouns as a separate class 'so called because they stand sometimes for Nouns'. His idiosyncratic vocatives (*O wee! O he! O they!*) are also absent from Jonson's treatment. In the verb too, his woolly 'may be called the Genius and Soul of Speech...no Sentence...can be made without it' is far removed from the dry but precise formalism of Jonson's 'word of number, which hath both Tyme, and Person'. Nor is the setting up of moods (with a present subjunctive *seeing that I am* that has no formal justification other than the preceding conjunction) a Ramist trait. But since he does not depend on Lily's theory of signs either, he gives, in contrast to the authors of 'basic' grammars considered above, separate recognition to both a 'preterimperfect' *I did desire* and an 'aorist or preterperfect' *I desired*, a distinction which I. Poldauf[233] sees as deriving from his knowledge of the Romance languages. Only in the adverb – 'a word without number that is joyn'd to another' – is Howell's definition that of Jonson, but with no indication that he is aware of the Ramist formal implications involved. It is in his illustrative examples ('*st* is an Interjection of silence; *rr* to set dogs together by the eares') that Howell pillages Jonson. He can hardly be held to have imitated his grammatical theory. Above all, as compared with Jonson's, his grammar lacks a syntax. Again the excuse is that even in Jonson's case, 'the further he proceeded, the more he was puzzled'. Though English 'may be said to have the same [structure] that other vulgar Languages and dialects have', it has 'such varieties of incertitudes, changes and Idioms, it cannot be in the compas of human brain to compile an exact regular Syntaxis thereof'.[234]

The tendencies noted in Howell's *New English Grammar* can be matched in Hexham's work. In line with the increasing fashion to define in wholly semantic terms, nouns are 'names of things which

[232] See Jonson's *English Grammar*, p. 57.
[233] 'On the History of Some Problems of English Grammar', p. 272.
[234] *A New English Grammar*, p. 80.

have being and life', but adjectives and substantives are distinguished, in a distant echo of medieval modistic tradition, as syntactically dependent and independent.[235] The verb is also (in contrast to Greaves' 'word of number with time') defined in purely semantic terms as denoting doing or suffering, and has (again in contrast to Ramus' and Greaves' complete exclusion of the category) the six moods, including a potential with the signs *may, can*, etc., of the 'basic' grammarians. This potential mood includes an unlikely pluperfect *I should have had been*, and a passive *I ought to had been loved*, perpetuating such specifically invented monstrosities as Bullokar's (1586) pluperfect infinitive *to had loved*. The only formal definition, that prepositions are words used in apposition or composition, is identical with the one given by Wharton. Unless the 1648 edition of Hexham's grammar, which I have not seen, is very different from that of 1660, his supposed dependence on Greaves must be held to be without foundation.

Baconian 'sense-realism' in the service of pedagogy

Refusing to venture into the uncertain domain of English syntax, Howell can only suggest that his reader should have recourse to 'that great Mistresse of all knowledge *Observation*', a recommendation that is an echo of Jonson's reference (in its turn taken from Quintilian) to 'consuetudo, certissima loquendi Magistra'.[236] One of Jonson's claims for his grammar is that it is empirically based, 'out of his observation of the English language now spoken, and in use'. Increasingly however, there was a desire for knowledge to be based not merely on *verba*, but also on *res*. One result of the widespread dissemination of Baconian doctrines was a dissatisfaction with verbalization, and a search for some kind of sure anchor in things themselves, an attitude acceptable to the seventeenth-century puritans because it stressed the acquisition of knowledge that was of some practical use. This yearning for a closer contact with reality led, particularly in England, to an emphasis on the obtaining of knowledge via the senses, with a new stress on Aristotle's 'Nihil est in intellectu quod non prius in sensu.' Parallel with this, the rationalist current of thought on the Continent was to lead to a reassertion of the role of reason in language, and to the Port-Royal authors' view of the

[235] Hexham uses the Dutch terms 'by-voegelick' and 'self-standige'. I have translated his definition of the noun into English. [236] *The English Grammar*, title-page.

sentence as the expression of an act of judgment. In this respect it is interesting that the kernel of Joseph Webbe's quarrel with William Brookes lies precisely in the latter's insistence on having 'the judgement first satisfied before the sense'. Webbe took the contrary view that in language learning 'nature teacheth to use the sense before the judgment' by 'an action of memory taken from the outer sense'. His position depends on an almost Pavlovian behaviourism, a stimulus-response mechanism 'as in doggs, that once hearinge the bell and presently feeling the lash, will never after heare the bell, but will runne barking or crying, out of a memory of the former punishment'. Though he recognizes that 'the externe senses worke not in Languages without memorie nor eyther of them sincerly without the understandinge' (and there is no doubt that his emphasis on the importance of the 'clause' required the exercise of judgment), in the last resort it is the senses, as 'soe many Gentlemen Ushers to judgment and understanding', that initiate the learning process.[237] Though there is not much evidence of Webbe's own application to pedagogy of these insights, his view that 'wee may and doe goe farre in languages, without judgment or understanding' was bound to find an echo among the more progressive of seventeenth-century schoolmasters. Brookes himself, though he holds that a dependence of judgment on memory is contrary to the course of nature, and seems to have gained from his reading of J. C. Scaliger a belief in some kind of innate ideas or 'praecognita', none the less recommends a 'sensical' method of grammar instruction in which e.g. the concept of number is taught by using the fingers.[238] One should not of course overlook the force of fashion, the fact that in some pedagogical circles Baconian 'sense-realism', mediated by the works of Comenius, was by the mid-seventeenth century becoming something of a cult. Very much in the main stream of progressive thought is Hezekiah Woodward's view (*A Light to Grammar*, 1641) that if grammar can be inculcated 'at the gates of the senses, all sciences will follow by the same light and at the same doors.' In this regard, it would be impossible to overestimate the importance as a textbook of Comenius' *Orbis sensualium pictus* ('the world of sense objects pictured'), which J. E. Sadler[239] has called an attempt to frame a 'true anatomy of the

[237] British Library MS Sloane 1466, ff. 267ʳ, 270ᵛ–271ᵛ.
[238] For Brookes' teaching methods see *ibid.* 8ʳff. ('General Observations Concerning the Art of Teaching') and 88ʳff. ('Mr. Brookes Method of Teaching Grammar'). See also Salmon, 'Problems of Language-Teaching', p. 13, and Brekle, 'The Seventeenth Century', pp. 288–9.
[239] Facsimile edition of the *Orbis pictus*, Oxford, 1968.

universe'. Capital for the application of 'sense-realism' to pedagogy in England is Charles Hoole's translation of this work in 1659.[240] Aristotle's 'Nihil est in intellectu quod non prius in sensu' figures prominently on the title-page, and Hoole's translation of Comenius' preface poses the principle that 'the ground of this business is that sensual objects be rightly presented to the senses'. Comenius' work is however – as indeed he proudly claims – a nomenclature, a tool in the labelling of single concepts by single words as a preliminary to scientific classification.

For an application, if clumsy, of 'sense-realism' to grammar teaching we must turn to Mark Lewis' *Essay to Facilitate the Education of Youth, by bringing down the Rudiments of Grammar to the Sense of Seeing*, first published probably shortly after the appearance of Hoole's translation of the *Orbis pictus*.[241] Lewis' approach is based on two premises, that grammar is best taught via the senses, and that the traditional abstractions proposed to children require an effort of the understanding beyond what they are capable of: 'Doubtless the Doctrine of Grammar is too subtile for children; because it is communicated by Logical Definitions in the Etymologie, and by the signification of words in the Syntax, neither of which Children can reach, who cannot use Abstraction...The Speculative Part of Grammar ought to be left to riper years...' In place of the traditional method, based on prior understanding of grammatical definitions, he proposes one based on sense-realism which is consonant with Nature's own laws:

Whilst we instruct Children, according to the Law of Nature, we must proceed by Sense...The use of the outward Senses is to be mediums to let in Notions to the inward...the progress is natural from the Senses to the

[240] *Joh. Amos Commenius's Visible World. Or, A Picture and Nomenclature of the Chief Things that are in the World; and of Mens Employments therein*, London, 1659 (Scolar Press facsimile, Menston, 1970). On Hoole see J. W. Adamson, *Pioneers of Modern Education 1600–1700*, Cambridge, 1905, p. 157; K. Lambley, *The Teaching and Cultivation of the French Language during Tudor and Stuart Times*, Manchester, 1920, p. 334; Salmon, 'James Shirley and Some Problems of Seventeenth-Century Grammar', pp. 94–6; Watson, *The English Grammar Schools*, pp. 6, 271. See also Hoole's *A New Discovery of The Old Art of Teaching Schoole*, London, 1660. Despite the fact that Hoole brought out an edition of the *Orbis pictus*, Adamson notes that his own pedagogical practice owes nothing to Comenius.

[241] Lewis' *Essay* exists in two versions. The British Library copy of the earlier (London?, c. 1670) version lacks the title-page. It is printed in the same volume with Lewis' [...] *grammaticae puerilis; or the Rudiments of the Latin and Greek Tongues*. The title-page of the latter work has been cut, but Michael (*English Grammatical Categories*, p. 570) suggests the full title *Institutio grammaticae puerilis*, and the date 1671. Lewis' 'English Grammar', in fact a basic grammar, occupies the first fifteen pages. The later version of the *Essay*, published in 1674 in two separately paginated parts, is in the Bodleian and the Wisconsin University Library.

Understanding, and from thence to the Memory: But if you pervert the order of Nature, and represent things otherwise...your Notions, like Monsters, afright Children, and are burthensome to the Memory, as nauseous things are to the Stomach.[242]

By 'sense' however, Lewis means the tangible form of the written word, whose 'permanent marks' are contrasted with the 'transient marks of things' represented by speech. Accordingly – and here the link with Comenius' *Orbis pictus* is plain – he recommends that children should be brought to 'look upon Words as Pictures'. But his actual application of his theory to grammar is not particularly sophisticated, and boils down to the by now familiar doctrine of 'signs'. It is for instance 'obvious to sense' that English nouns are words that can be preceded by *a, an* or *the*. His grammar is a reinterpretation of Lily's signs as sense aids, with a resultant emphasis on formal marks to the exclusion of notional definitions. The customary definitions of the noun as 'the Name of a Thing, seen, felt, heard, or understood', of the substantive as that which 'stands by itself, and requires not another word to shew its signification', or of the verb in terms of 'action' and 'passion' are he insists unintelligible to children.[243] That a substantive takes formal marks of plurality and stands after its adjective, on the contrary, is easily 'distinguished by sense'. Thus, via the different route of sense-realism but with a similar insistence on the 'Law of Nature', Lewis arrives like Ramus at a structuralist position in which logical definitions are abandoned in favour of 'such visible marks, as may be laid down by Particles in the English Tongue, to know the parts of speech by'.[244] His pedagogical aims extend however beyond the narrow confines of grammar, his ultimate purpose being in thoroughly contemporary fashion the inculcation of things rather than words: 'A meer Mechanick with his mother Tongue that understands things, is to be preferred before the greatest Rabby with his millions of words without this knowledge... The knowledge of things is more excellent then words, as much as the end excels the means.'[245] Words are

---

[242] *Essay* (British Library copy, *c.* 1670), pp. 1–2.

[243] Cf. Hoole's foreword to his edition of Comenius' *Orbis pictus*: 'We generally...do teach children, as we do Parrats, to speak they know not what...[and by teaching] Grammar only at the first, we do pusle their imaginations with abstractive terms and secondary intentions, which...they cannot apprehend what they mean.'   [244] *Essay* (1674 ed.).

[245] *An Apologie for a Grammar Printed about Twenty Years Since*, London, 1671, p. 36. This work is printed in the same volume with the British Library copy of the [*Institutio?*] *grammaticae puerilis*, and paginated 31–45. The grammar referred to in the title appears to be no longer extant.

tolerated only in so far as they 'lead to things'. Similarly in his *Rules for Pointing Periods* Lewis maintains, citing Comenius' *Vestibulum, Orbis pictus* and *Janua linguarum* in support, that 'one thus instructed in the knowledge of things...is like to make better progress, when he is advanced to the University...than another, who learns only Appellatives, and a little History'.[246]

Though Lewis gives the eight traditional parts of speech in the Latin section of his grammar, he concludes that six word-classes will suffice 'to express our thoughts by, fully and distinctly' in English. He arrives at his six classes by making pronouns a sub-class of substantives,[247] by treating the article (as a case-sign) with the preposition, and by counting the adjective as a separate part of speech.[248] There is in addition an overall division of the word-classes – recalling the logicians' dichotomy of semantically independent terms and consignifying syncategoremata – into integral words and particles. It is not unlikely that the source for this is Bishop Wilkins' *Essay* (1668).[249] Case signs in this system are treated as 'appendents' of integrals, though the vernacular signs of comparison (*more, most*), mood (*let, may, might, would, could, should, ought, to*) and tense (*do, did, have, had,* etc.) are regarded as 'English particles' corresponding to no distinct and separate word in Latin. Prepositions, in an analysis recalling that made by the Port-Royal *Grammaire générale et raisonnée* (1660) but in fact present in grammatical theory in England at least since Linacre (*c.* 1512),[250] are held to be case equivalents. They have 'the same common Notion as Signs of Cases, and may be looked upon as Latin Particles'. Noun and verb have

[246] *Plain, and short Rules for Pointing Periods, and Reading Sentences Grammatically, with the great Use of them,* London, 1671. A slim pamphlet (eight pages) also printed in the same volume with the British Library copy of the [*Institutio?*] *grammaticae puerilis.*

[247] The pronoun is in practice distributed between substantive and adjective, since 'a Noun Substantive and a Pronoun Substantive have the same common nature in Grammar, and a Noun Adjective, and a Pronoun Adjective, do punctually agree in their Accidents'.

[248] Michael (*English Grammatical Categories,* p. 219) remarks that the *c.* 1670 version of Lewis' *Essay* is 'perhaps the earliest work in which the substantive and adjective are clearly separated as primary parts of speech'. Participle and interjection are excluded as constituting 'contracted sentences'. On this view of the interjection see below in the section on Wilkins' *Essay* in the final chapter.

[249] Michael (*English Grammatical Categories,* p. 278) notes that the use of the 'particle' as a primary category is a feature of the 'vernacular' word-class systems of reforming grammarians of the eighteenth century, who threw off the Latin yoke to a greater extent than their seventeenth-century predecessors.

[250] See Linacre's *Rudimenta grammatices,* p. 39 of the Paris edition of 1533, which treats certain French prepositions as 'articuli sive notae' of case. The early Italian vernacular grammarians similarly treat prepositions as 'segni de' casi'.

a special status, for an indication of the growing importance of logical analysis of the proposition in grammatical studies is provided by the insistence on the presence in every sentence of a substantive 'called the nominative case' and a verb, which together form 'the two Legs upon which a sentence doth stand'.[251] Put another way – Lewis is not above mixing metaphors – the verb is 'the Brain, or nervosum Genus, which gives life and motion to all parts of the Sentence'. Further developing his corporeal analogies (no doubt a pedagogical device) he treats substantives as 'the Sceleton or Bones of the Sentence', and adjectives as providing, as befits 'manners' of substantives, their flesh and muscles. Adverbs are then treated as performing a similar office for verbs – 'Adverbs are to Verbs as Adjectives are to Substantives,[252] namely, the manner of them' – and may be compared to 'membraneous expansions'. Finally, to complete his analogy he treats signs of cases, recognizing their syntactic function, as 'Ligaments to tie these Bones together'.

It is within the limited compass of his pamphlet *Rules for Pointing Periods* that Lewis claims to present 'the foundation of the Syntactical part of Grammar' which will enable the student to 'read sentences grammatically'.[253] In prescribing rules for punctuation, he admits one-word sentences (*Alas* for instance being treated as the semantic equivalent of *It is a sad case*), and clauses without verbs which none the less have 'the import of a sentence wherein a Verb is virtually contained'. Similarly a vocative, as in *Son, come hither*, can be treated as an 'extrasentential phrase'. In view of the contemporary discussion of elliptical constructions by the Port-Royal authors, Lewis' treatment of infinitives, gerunds, participles and interjections as 'contracted sentences' is of great interest. In analyses which recall a long medieval and humanist tradition in Latin grammar,[254] *I desire to learn* for example is resolved into *I desire that I may learn*. Of particular interest is the view of participles as words whose 'ligaments' (the preceding noun in the nominative case, and the signs of mood and tense) are regularly 'ellipted'. In line with this, in the sentence *God created Man, placing him in Paradise* the participial phrase is seen as a

---

[251] *Essay* (British Library copy, *c.* 1670), p. 11.

[252] This notion is found in Jonson, who has it via Ramus. Ultimately it goes back to Priscian (Keil, *Grammatica Latini*, III, 60).

[253] 'The Master builds upon the Sands without a basis; and the Scholar learns by roat without reason, who doth not bottom here.'

[254] For details see Padley, *Grammatical Theory* (1976), pp. 54–5, 102–5, 183, 213–14.

contraction of a logically more complete *whom he did place in Paradise*. The precedents for this go back a very long way, in fact right to Priscian (*c.* 500), who sees present participles as equivalent either to subject plus verb (*hominem loquentem audivi* = *homo loquebatur et eum audivi*), or to *qui* or *quem* + verb,[255] as in Lewis' example. Closer to Lewis' own day, this same equivalence (*amans* = *qui amat*) is found in the *Grammatica audax* (1654) of the Spanish grammarian of Latin Caramuel,[256] and is paralleled in the identical Port-Royal restatement of *canis currens* as *canis qui currit*.[257] The Port-Royal authors explain this by treating the participle as semantically equivalent to a verb minus its primary function of signifying an affirmation.[258] Lewis' own quaintly expressed theoretical justification also has a semantic basis: 'We may resemble these to Nervous Members, that suffer a Corrugation within themselves from their sensibility, being related to the *Nervosum Genus*, or principal Verb in the Sentence.' Quite exceptional for its date is his treatment of subordinate clauses – the 'depending clauses' of the 1674 version of the *Essay* – and the 'compounded' propositions of the *Rules for Pointing Periods*. For a parallel one would have to go to an almost exactly contemporary work, Christian Pudor's *Der Teutschen Sprache Grundrichtigkeit* of 1672. Here again the notion of expansion is important, certain infinitive expressions being recognized as having 'the import of a sentence' or clause. For example, the infinitival structure in *God created man to be lord of the creatures* can be expanded into its semantic equivalent *that he might be lord*. Though the criteria are largely semasiological – a full stop 'terminates Sense that is absolute, full, and perfect' – Lewis recognizes that periods cannot be correctly distinguished 'unless the Natural, and Grammatical order of them be first apprehended'. The verb in the main clause is 'the first Verb in the Natural and Grammatical order', though in elliptic constructions it is 'often suppressed'. Important pedagogically is his view that far from learning syntax from the usual rules, the pupil only arrives at an understanding of it after a frequent application of the system of signs.[259] Basically, he is teaching his pupils to recognize English parts

[255] Keil, *Grammatici Latini*, ii, 565. For Priscian participles exist to compensate for defects in the verb, which lacks case (see *ibid.*, p. 553). His treatment must have been common knowledge among the more erudite of seventeenth-century grammarians.

[256] J. Caramuel y Lobkowitz, *Praecursor logicus, complectens grammaticem audacum*, Frankfurt-am-Main, 1654. For details of his approach see Padley, *Grammatical Theory* (1976), p. 183.

[257] *Grammaire générale et raisonnée*, Paris, 1660, p. 69.   [258] *Ibid.*, p. 96.

[259] *Essay* (British Library copy, *c.*1670), pp. 1–2, 4, 7.

of speech and syntactic procedures by means of formal marks, identical with Lily's system of signs but dressed up in the sensualist theory in vogue at the time. Over and above this there are certain universalist pretensions in his grammar, and a thoroughly late-seventeenth-century application of logical criteria to supposedly elliptical structures. His preoccupations are however constantly those of the practising schoolmaster. By the use of a system of printing in various types that would 'make things plain, and obvious to the Sense of Seeing', he is confident that even for children of 'low parts' grammar learning would become what John Brinsley held it should be: a *ludus literarius* or agreeable pastime. In his somewhat disordered and fragmentary way, he is moving towards the idea that the description of English requires its own distinct set of grammatical categories. He provides a link, as I. Michael remarks,[260] between the constraints of the Latin-based approach and the comparative freedom of the more truly 'vernacular' systems that were to come into vogue in the following century. On the whole however, as with preceding pedagogically orientated grammarians of the vernacular, his 'signs' tend to be used (as indeed he intended them to be) as a kind of visual aid, rather than recognized as specific marks of a syntactic structure very different from that of Latin.[261]

The criterion of 'complete sense'

A forerunner of the eighteenth-century vernacular systems is A. Lane's *Key to the Art of Letters* (1700),[262] whose preface constitutes a plea for 'the Necessity of a Vernacular Grammar'. The work is a close adaptation of the first part of his *Rational and Speedy Method*,[263] published five years previously, the second part of which is a straightforward Latin grammar. Though the first part of the *Method* claims to give 'such Precepts as are common to all Languages', the description is patently based on English, and Lane was able to use

[260] *English Grammatical Categories*, p. 220.

[261] Lewis also published a *Vestibulum technicum: or, An Artificial Vestibulum wherein the sense of [Comenius'] Janua linguarum is contained*, London, 1675. This work is intended as an introduction to the study of Latin and is of interest for its long preface, repeating notions already given in the *Essay* and outlining Lewis' teaching methods, which are patently based on Comenius. Here too 'a sufficient Grammar is brought down to the sense of Seeing', but this time Lewis' earlier suggestion is followed up, in that 'each Part of Speech is distinguished by the Character it is Printed in'. (The British Library copy, the only one extant, is imperfect, ending on the first page of the actual grammar.) [262] Published in London.

[263] *A Rational and Speedy Method of Attaining to the Latin Tongue*, London, 1695.

it virtually unchanged in the first sixty pages of the *Key*. He is firmly in the pedagogical tradition considered above, for though he aims to furnish the 'exactest rules' for English, he too makes the by now customary claim that they will also serve for the easier learning of Latin and other foreign languages. As a teacher in a private school near Stepney he obviously has a pedagogical axe to grind, and though he realizes that the production of a grammar of English may still seem to many 'a very superfluous and ridiculous thing', he is persuaded that not since the fall of the Roman Empire has such an excellent 'expedient to promote all good learning' appeared as his own *Key to the Art of Letters*. But though he is but the latest in a long line of protesters who refuse to accept that young minds should be put to learn a foreign tongue while their own 'lies neglected and uncultivated', his real aim, given that 'it polishes and perfects those noble Faculties of Reason and Speech, by which Men are distinguished from Brutes', is to inculcate grammar as such. If he can claim that beginning with English is the most effectual means of acquiring a foreign language, it is not because of the intrinsic excellences of English (though he is far from disputing them), but because the indispensable 'Art of Grammar', necessary to the acquisition of all languages, is itself best acquired via the mother tongue. Grammar, 'every where misunderstood, and consequently misapply'd, ever since the Latin Tongue ceased to be a living Language', seems almost for Lane to be a separate, reasoned entity, which according to the dictates of practical pedagogy must first be applied to one's native tongue, but which, since 'the unalterable Rules of right Reason...are the same in all Languages how different soever they be', provides the key to the learning of others. Lane's definition of grammar as an Art that teaches the right way of speaking and writing 'according to the particular Form of every Language' would however seem to be at variance with this. In theory he is providing, via English, a universally valid grammar that can be applied to other languages, more especially Latin. In practice, he gives the 'particular Form' of English, and assumes that its description will be appropriate to Latin too. As I. Michael notes,[264] he would have been on safer ground if he had based his argument, not on universal grammar, but on the pedagogically more practical fact that pupils already know their own language and are not therefore in the position of having to acquire

---

[264] *English Grammatical Categories*, p. 499.

both it and its grammatical principles at one and the same time.[265] What is refreshing is that it is the supposedly universal principles of *English* grammar that are held to be valid for *Latin*, not, as was for so long the case, the other way round. This transference is made all the easier however by the fact that Lane's English grammar closely follows the traditional categories of Latin grammar, with no real attempt, as with Wallis, to distance himself from the Latin system. Lane's interest lies in his being the first English grammarian after Wilkins to make universalist claims for his work, and in his being the precursor, in his employment of logic and in his fourfold classification of the parts of speech, of the eighteenth-century movement for the reform of vernacular grammar.[266] It is this fourfold word-class system that constitutes the chief evidence for Lane's claim to be writing a universal grammar, and it will accordingly be discussed later in this study when Lane's position within the universal grammar movement is assessed. Those points which are specifically relevant to the 'particular Form', as he puts it, of English, together with traits which, while typical of the late-seventeenth-century approach, are not of interest for universal grammar, will be considered here. Despite his universalist pretensions, the schoolmaster in him as never far below the surface, for his 'precepts common to all languages' are constantly intermingled with very perceptive comments on English structure. Indeed, his already mentioned definition of grammar as operating 'according to the particular form of every language' is in direct contradiction of the universalist approach. He is however the first practising schoolmaster to seek a philosophical basis for rules of general pedagogical validity, and it must not be forgotten that as with Ratke in Germany it is a pedagogical aim, the desire to teach 'grammar' as a tool in language learning in general, that is behind his espousal of universal grammar.

As will be noted when we come to consider the universal component of Lane's grammars, his theory of the parts of speech rests on the late-seventeenth-century assumption that language is isomorphic with reality. It is however paralleled by an insistence, also typical

---

[265] Michael notes (*ibid.*, p. 498) that the 'curriculum argument' (that Latin is not needed in the education of 'ordinary' children) is not common before the end of the seventeenth century, and is absent from Lane's preface to the *Key*.

[266] Michael refers (*ibid.*, p. 510) to a 'movement of reform' expressed in twenty-five English grammars between 1711 and 1755, all in conscious opposition to the Latin tradition, and all employing what he calls 'vernacular systems' of the parts of speech.

of its age, that the touchstone of correct grammar is the *sense* of an utterance. The words 'in good sense' run through both grammars like a refrain, forming part of virtually every word-class definition, and bear witness to the increasing tendency of English vernacular grammarians to define semasiologically, in terms of the *sense* of grammatical categories, rather than in terms of form and structure. The long-lived definition of the sentence as a group of words making 'complete sense' is a tenacious example of this, though it should be added that it goes back at least to Priscian's 'sententiam perfectam demonstrans', and beyond him to Dionysius Thrax.[267] Further, Lane's own definition of the sentence is that of Aristotelian logic: 'a construction of words wherein something is said of another'.[268] As was noted earlier, grammarians accustomed to the inflection-based grammar of Latin were at something of a loss when confronted with the analytical simplicities of English, and hence tended to drop any attempt at formal definition in favour of an appeal to unsupported lexical meaning. Aware that English word forms can cross class-boundaries, but unable or unwilling to furnish a description of this in terms of structure, Lane falls back on the statement that the different classes (as in *I work a good work*) 'must be distinguished by the sense'. Sense is the last court of appeal in a good many of his analyses. The substantive is not only, in the best seventeenth-century tradition, a 'Word that signifies a Thing', but also a 'Word that can be declined alone in good Sense, in any ones Native Language'.[269] This is of course the medieval substantive/adjective definition in terms of semantic dependence or independence, restated in the seventeenth-century terms of the making of sense. Lane adds that 'Adjectives in English receive no Alteration either as to Number or Case', except in substantival use, as in *secrets* for *secret things*.[270]

The 'precepts common to all languages' enunciated by Lane are based exclusively on the structure of Latin and English. He states baldly that nouns are declined with case: a noun is in the nominative case 'when it is the Subject of a Verb, and then it usually comes in good Sense before the Verb'.[271] Case is thus presented as a universal

[267] Cf. Padley, *Grammatical Theory* (1976), pp. 32, 264.

[268] Cf. Aristotle's identical definition of the verbal predicate as τῶν καθ᾽ ἑτέρου λεγομένων σημεῖον (*De interpretatione*, cap. 3). [269] *Key*, p. 20; *Method*, p. 1.

[270] The adjective is that which 'without a Substantive cannot make good sense'. Lane notes of course the formal changes in *this/these, that/those*.

[271] *Key*, p. 26; *Method*, p. 4.

feature, but in 'good sense' in English it is the product of position in the sentence. If gender is to be recognized as a grammatical category in English, it must also obviously take 'sense' as its basis, and Lane in common with other grammarians shows no awareness of the inappropriateness of the category to the vernacular. Nouns that are chiefly used of females, such as *virgin*, are feminine; those chiefly used of males (e.g. *soldier*) are masculine. Lane notes that in English the neuter gender covers both animate and inanimate, but the preeminence of Latin – and the fact that his universal grammar is intended among other things to ease the path to classical studies – causes him to treat as 'epicenes' (i.e. in his usage common to masculine and feminine) the words *sparrow* (cf. Latin *passer*), *ass* and *child*.[272] Here again a concession is made to English by the statement that epicenes used 'without regard to the Sex' become neuters, as when a small child is referred to as 'it', and in the recognition of 'Sex-distinguishing Words' as in *Male-Child*, *He-Ass* and *Cock-Sparrow*. The influence of Wallis and Cooper on this point is obvious. Here as elsewhere, one has the impression that Lane is writing an introductory universal grammar because it suits his pedagogical theories to do so, but that his schoolmasterly interest in language diversity insists on breaking through, as in the admission invalidating his universalist claims – that some nouns are epicenes in one language, but not in another.[273]

The verb is defined in purely semantic terms as 'a word that signifies the Action, Passion, or Being of a thing, and may be conjugated in good Sense with a Substantive of the Nominative Case before it, and without a Nominative Case cannot make Sense'. The utterance *Me read* is not good sense, for a verb 'must always have a Nominative either express'd or understood: for there can be no Action without an Agent, or Passion without a Patient'.[274] Several strands meet here – the late Latin grammatical tradition's tendency to define in semantic terms only (found however as early as 1525 in Melanchthon) as illustrated in Vossius' (1635) view of the 'essence' of the verb as the signification of acting, the suffering of action, or being; the late-seventeenth-century insistence that the doing, suffering or being is that of a substantive in the nominative case; and the

[272] In Latin grammar however, 'epicene' nouns are those (e.g. *aquila*, masc., and *passer*, fem.) which under a single gender denote both sexes.
[273] *Key*, p. 26; *Method*, pp. 7–8.   [274] *Key*, p. 37; *Method*, p. 11.

underlining of the verb's function as one of the two terms in a logical proposition.[275] As Lane remarks in his Latin grammar, 'Every Sentence may be divided into Subject and Predicate.'[276] The origin in the better-known Latin grammars of a good deal of the material in the *Key to the Art of Letters* and in the universal grammar prefaced to the *Method* for Latin is well illustrated by the treatment of transitive verbs as those which 'in good sense' admit any number of possible accusatives,[277] while intransitive ones are those which 'in good sense' admit only a cognate accusative (*I run a race, I live a life*). Lane's Latin-educated readers would be aware that this was a commonplace of Latin grammar, being found e.g. in Linacre's *De emendata structura* (1524) which gives precisely the two examples *curro cursum* and *vivo vitam*. It goes without saying that 'neuter' verbs denoting existence must be followed by a nominative case, in pursuit of yet another rule of Latin grammar. In the *Key* Lane lists as neuters besides *to be* the verbs *may, must, can* and *ought*. To prove his point he is at pains to demonstrate that (just as the Latin neuter verb *albeo* can be restated as *sum albus*) these verbs can all be 'resolved' by *am* plus an adjective: *can = am able, may = am lawful, must = am necessary*.[278] These verbs have a peculiar status in English. They can neither be transformed into passives, like transitive verbs, nor do they resemble intransitive ones in admitting cognate accusatives, and one suspects that if Lane lumps them in with the verb *to be* it is because he is at a loss to know what to do with them. His analysis rests of course on a long medieval and humanist tradition according to which the verb *to be* is regarded as the root of all others, as in *amo = sum amans*.

Tenses, as in the earlier pedagogical tradition, are known 'by Auxiliary Verbs, commonly called the Signs'. Noting the double aspectual use of the simple past in English, Lane gives it the name 'preterite indefinite', on the grounds that it is often uncertain whether it has a perfect or an imperfect meaning. A 'perfect' is found in *I went to School and said my Lesson*, but an 'imperfect' in *As I went to School I met my Father*. The conjunction *whilst* introduces an 'imperfect' (*whilst I did write = whilst I was writing*) and *after* is followed by a 'perfect' (*after I writ = having written*). Noteworthy here

---

[275] For a discussion of these late-seventeenth-century trends in Latin grammarians see Padley, *Grammatical Theory* (1976), pp. 126–7.

[276] *Method*, p. 69.

[277] *Key*, p. 39. Worthy of note here is Lane's use of the terms 'transitive' and 'intransitive' in line with modern practice.   [278] *Ibid.*, p. 54.

is the typical late-seventeenth-century willingness to transpose
structures into other structures deemed to be semantically equivalent,
and to draw grammatical conclusions from the operation. Since, as
Lane puts it, we cannot know whether the verb is in the perfect or
imperfect 'till the Sense of the Sentence determines it', the grammarian
must demonstrate this sense by 'resolving' the term in question into
an unambiguous semantic equivalent. There are however occasions
when the 'sense of the sentence' entirely escapes him, leading him
to split unnecessary hairs. He realizes that the 'internal action' *I am
loved* is not precisely on the same footing as the 'external or corporeal
action' *the book is read*. He correctly identifies the former as a present
passive but, unaware of the resultative aspect of *the book is read*,
declares it to be 'an immediate Preter Tense' rather than a present.
This leaves a gap in the present passive slot of his verbs expressing
'external or corporeal actions', so he fills it with *the book is a reading*
(where present-day usage has *the book is being read*).[279]

Preposition, adverb and conjunction are treated by Lane as
'particles', a treatment which will be considered in the section on
universal grammar. Here again 'sense' is a major criterion, the
conjunction being defined as the link between one particular sentence
and another, which 'cannot with one Verb compleat the Sense, but
leaves the Hearer in suspence until another Sentence be added'.[280]
This illustrates the way in which grammar is finally moving away
from a word-by-word treatment towards a greater awareness of the
sentence as an overall grammatical unit. Lane makes a point of
refuting the traditional view that conjunctions link cases, insisting on
their sentence-joining function,[281] and in his syntax too he goes
beyond the consideration of simple sentences to embrace complex
ones. Side by side with his constant appeals to sense and his
philosophical disquisitions there goes however, even in that section
of the *Method* supposedly 'peculiar to the Latin tongue', a constant
preoccupation with the specific structure of English. Typical is the
realization that English substantives, as in the first element of the
compound *churchman*, can function as 'possessive adjectives'. The
debt to Wallis and Cooper[282] is obvious. Clearly from this source is

[279] *Key*, p. 52; *Method*, p. 21.
[280] *Method*, p. 23. Cf. *Key*, p. 57.
[281] See also Sanctius' identical view (cf. Clerico, *Franciscus Sanctius*, pp. 41-2).
[282] Wallis' work appeared in 1653, and that of Cooper in 1685. Both are entitled *Grammatica linguae Anglicanae*.

the statement that such elements are 'nothing else but the Genitive of the Possessor under the form of an Adjective'. *The house door* is regarded as *the houses door* shorn of the possessive -*s* 'for the conveniency of pronunciation'. This involves Lane in some clumsiness, for he has to treat *the horses bridles* as a contraction of *the horseses bridles*. He cannot bring himself to admit that since the forms in question have adjectival function they are in fact adjectives, but persists in seeing each as a 'real Substantive of the Genitive Case'. Again, equivalences of sense are pressed into service, a possessive adjective signifying 'the same as the Genitive of the Substantive from which it is derived.'[283] It should not be forgotten that Latin grammarians had for centuries had a category of 'possessive adjectives', and it is possible that Wallis (the term is his) had it in mind when he arrived at his own particular category. However that may be, a passage in Lane's *Method* makes the affiliation clear: 'Adjectives derived of Substantives are called possessive Adjectives; as *regius* from *Rex*.'

Lane's syntax is unusual for both its length and the modernity of its terminology.[284] The use of the terms 'subject' and 'predicate', replacing the traditional 'suppositum' and 'appositum',[285] is explained by his determination to import logical terms into grammar, and it is plain that he sees the grammatical sentence as identical with the logical proposition. His definition is that of Aristotelian logic: 'a construction of words wherein something is said of another'.[286] The Latin *Method* further specifies 'that which is said of any thing is called the Predicate; that of which the Predicate is said, is called the Subject'. It follows that the 'essential parts of a Sentence, without which it cannot be' are the verb and the 'Nominative of the Subject'. Since all other words in a sentence depend 'mediately or immediately' on these two, it is obvious that Lane is here having recourse to Aristotle's system of semantically independent noun and verb and subordinate, consignifying *sundesmoi*. On this basis rests his virtually three-part classification of the parts of speech into substantive and adjective, verb, and semantically dependent 'particle'. By 'nomina-

[283] *Key*, pp. 66–8; *Method*, p. 33.
[284] The syntax occupies some thirty-five pages in the *Method*, and thirty in the *Key*.
[285] For a discussion of the use of these terms see Padley, *Grammatical Theory* (1976), p. 52, and Salmon, 'James Shirley and Some Problems of Seventeenth-Century Grammar', pp. 287–96, *passim*. Lane uses the term 'apposition' in its modern sense of 'the adding of one Substantive to another, to declare and explain it', as in *my father loves me his only child*.
[286] *Key*, p. 74.

tive of the subject' he means that noun which occupies the subject position in the sentence. A curiosity here is the explanation of impersonal structures such as *it rains*. The difficulty here, as in the parallel Latin form *pluit*, is that there is no logical subject, a problem which Latin grammarians solved at any rate to their own satisfaction by providing one in such restatements as *Deus pluit*, or even *pluvia pluit*. Lane ingeniously suggests that the nominative of the subject has been 'suppressed' and replaced by *it*.

If the 'nominative of the subject' is the term preceding the verb, that which follows the verb *to be* and verbs of calling and esteeming is the 'nominative of the predicate' – a transposition into logical terms of the Latin rule that *to be* has the same case after it as before it. In this analysis, *thou art esteemed an honest man* is seen as a contraction of *thou art esteemed TO BE an honest man*, thus retaining the verb *be* as the determining factor in the existence of a 'nominative of the predicate'.[287] The terms on either side of the copula both being nominatives, Lane is left with the problem of justifying the word order of e.g. *London is a city* as opposed to **A city is London*. He accordingly invents the explanation that since *city* is of greater extension than *London*, it must occupy the second place. Subject nominative and predicate nominative are of equal semantic weight only when 'they can be mutually affirmed of one another, and one cannot be said of more things than the other': *Every extended Substance is a Body*, and *Every Body is an Extended Substance* are equally acceptable sentences. Late-seventeenth-century criteria are irremediably lexical and semantic ones. It is difficult for instance to see why, when the grammatical structure involved is precisely the same in each, *the reading of the Bible* and *a boy of a good Countenance* should be distinguished as genitives respectively 'of the object' and 'of the part or property', but these are of course automatically repeated distinctions inherited from Latin grammar.

The chief interest of Lane's syntax lies elsewhere, in his treatment of 'compound' sentences. These consist of two simple sentences joined either by a 'conjunctive particle' (*I read and thou playest*), or by a 'conjunctive adjective' (*This is the boy who broke the Windows*).[288] In contrast with the word-based approach of most of his predecessors, who give accounts of the relations of concord and government

[287] *Ibid.*, p. 79. Similarly *Method*, p. 67.
[288] In Lane's *Method*, the words *who* and *which* are treated as relative adjectives.

obtaining within small word-groups, seldom raising their sights to the clause or sentence as a whole, he gives an analysis of relative, copulative, declarative and final, continuative, interrogative and disjunctive 'compound sentences'. In considering each type he is especially interesting in detailing the structures of which he deems them to be contractions, and demonstrating how these contractions can in turn be 'resolved' into the particular type of sentence under discussion. Some of these contractions, such as the treatment of *He is wiser than I* (nominative) as an abbreviation of *He is wiser than I am*, have long bedevilled grammar teaching, putting *He is wiser than me* officially out of court for over two centuries.[289] Ever with an eye for the peculiarities of English structure, Lane notes however the frequent omission of the relative in English and, to his credit, accepts that in such structures (*this is the Person I spoke of*) the preposition may 'elegantly' stand at the end. One does not know whether to be more astonished by his insight that a whole 'declarative sentence' can function as a nominative (*That thou art idle grieves me much*), or by his parallel provision of the form in common usage (*It grieves me much that thou art idle*), in which the 'nominative' exceptionally follows its verb. His penetrating insights into vernacular structure not infrequently invalidate his claim to be offering 'such Precepts as are common to all Languages', while on the other hand his employment of logic is tipping the scale towards universal grammar. In this respect he constitutes a link between the pedagogically orientated empirical grammarians so far considered, and those who, using logic as a metalanguage, move vernacular grammar into a phase in which theoretical, philosophical considerations outweigh purely observational ones.

iii TOWARDS VERNACULAR FREEDOM: WALLIS AND COOPER

The grammarians so far considered either see the vernacular as the servant of classical studies or, in the case of the Ramists, try to force it to espouse a linguistic theory contrived for a different type of language. Both these groups have a strong pedagogical motivation. The importance of John Wallis and Christopher Cooper lies in their contrast with these authors, not least in the fact that their activities

[289] Lane's actual example is *I am wiser than thou* (*art*), but the interesting point here is the resulting legitimization of the hypercorrect *I* to the detriment of the *me* of everyday usage.

go beyond the merely pedagogical. Wallis in particular was a man of wide-ranging interests, who devised a system for teaching deaf-mutes to speak and also deciphered codes for the Parliamentary side during the Civil War. His political adherence is not without importance, for by about 1640 puritan utilitarianism constituted a major stimulus to the use and development of the vernacular.[290] It was no doubt his scientific training – he was Savilian Professor of Geometry at Oxford and a founder member of the Royal Society – that predisposed him to take an inductive, empirical approach in which data are sought in the vernacular itself, as opposed to a deductive one which involves drawing conclusions about English from a preexistent model – that of Latin. This inductive, empirical bent is more particularly evident in the 'Tractatus de loquela' or treatment of phonetics prefaced to his grammar (1653), a pioneer work constituting the first manual of English speech-sounds that can be called truly scientific.[291] The grammar itself, written in Latin under the title *Grammatica linguae Anglicanae*,[292] represents the first real turning-point towards the treatment of the vernacular as an independent entity susceptible of a grammatical description determined by its own structures. Its influence may be gauged from the appearance of no less than eleven editions by 1765,[293] and in view of its determined effort to throw off the yoke of the Latin model it may seem surprising that it is still written in that language. As a professional scholar of international standing Wallis was however

[290] See R. F. Jones, *The Triumph of the English Language*, London, 1953, p. 288.

[291] Though this treatise has received frequent mention in historical studies of English phonology, the strictly grammatical side of Wallis' achievement has been neglected. M. Lehnert's 'Die Grammatik des englischen Sprachmeisters John Wallis (1616–1703)', *Sprache und Kultur der germanischen und romanischen Völker: Anglistische Reihe*, XXI (1936) deals largely with Wallis' treatment of the sounds of English without touching on grammatical questions. L. Morel's *De Johannis Wallisii Grammatica linguae Anglicanae* (Paris, 1895) simply catalogues the contents of Wallis' 1699 edition. Not until 1941, in O. Funke's 'Frühzeit der englischen Grammatik', do we have a consideration of his grammatical contribution. More recent years have seen the appearance of J. A. Kemp's *John Wallis's Grammar of the English Language…A new edition with translation and commentary*, London, 1972. This is a facsimile of the London edition of 1765, virtually identical with that of 1699, the last supervised by Wallis himself.

[292] *Grammatica linguae Anglicanae. Cui praefigitur, De loquela sive sonorum formatione, tractatus grammatico-physicus.*

[293] Lehnert, 'Grammatik', p. 39, lists ten editions, including 'Pseudo-Ausgaben', (the Hamburg ed. of 1688, identical with the third ed., Hamburg, 1672; and the Leyden eds. of 1727 and 1740). There are in fact eleven editions (Alston's *Bibliography of the English Language from the Invention of Printing to the Year 1800*, I, 7–9, items 14–24), of which three are of the *Tractatus de loquela* only and eight of the *Grammatica*, the eighth being a reissue of the seventh. The additions to eds. two to five, mentioned by Lehnert, are not of importance for the grammatical section of the work.

given to publishing his works in Latin. General culture was still dominated by a Latin-based educational system, and the grammar is manifestly addressed to a learned public capable of reading Latin, and who could be assumed to have a knowledge of Latin grammar. Alexander Gill's earlier attempt – his *Logonomia Anglica* of 1619 – to escape at least partially from the Latin model is similarly written in Latin, and indeed Wallis singles him out in his preface as one of two predecessors (the other is Ben Jonson) whose work is 'not to be scorned'.[294] Wallis himself, in a letter to Thomas Smith,[295] complains of the lack of a 'Grammar, suited to the propriety and true Genius of the Language'. His aim is to provide such a grammar, in which 'not so much the usage of the Latin language, as the individual structure [*peculiaris ratio*] of our own language' is the determining factor.[296] His revolutionary insistence on the individual essence of each separate language[297] possibly has its roots in Bacon's call for a characterology of the sounds and grammatical structure of individual tongues. But given this insistence, it is odd that he should accuse the authors of the Port-Royal *Grammaire générale et raisonnée* (1660) of imitating him,[298] for in his own grammatical work, apart from his phonetic treatise, he makes no claim that his description is universally applicable.

The influence of universalist theories of grammar is more easily traceable in Christopher Cooper's *Grammatica linguae Anglicanae* of 1685[299] (the last grammar of the vernacular to be written in Latin),

[294] It is difficult to see why Wallis also mentions Hexham as having written 'not badly' on grammar. He did not in any case have access to Hexham's work until his own was already at the press.

[295] Printed in vol. III of Thomas Hearne's *Works* (London, 1810). in the foreword to 'Peter Langtoft's Chronicle'.

[296] *Grammatica linguae Anglicanae*, preface to the reader, p. [XIV].

[297] Sixteen years later, John Newton's assertion (*School Pastime for Young Children*, London, 1669) that 'every Speech and Language hath an Idiom proper to itself' already seems less of a novelty. O. Funke, 'Zum Weltsprachenproblem in England im 17. Jahrhundert', *Anglistische Forschungen*, LXIX (1929), pp. i–v, 1–163, claims that Wallis lays the foundations for a language characterology of the type envisaged by Bacon. Brekle, 'The Seventeenth Century', p. 309, repeats Funke's statement.

[298] In the preface to his fifth edition (1699, printed in the *Opera mathematica* of the same date), Wallis holds that 'some Frenchmen' have used a method very similar to his own in their 'Grammaire universelle'. It may well be that, as in his attitude to Descartes, he was over-sensitive to supposed plagiarism. G. W. Raney, 'The Accidence and Syntax in J. Wallis's *Grammatica linguae Anglicanae*: A translation and commentary on its alleged relationship to the 1660 Port-Royal *Grammaire générale et raisonnée*' (unpublished University of Michigan Ph.D. thesis), regards the two works as quite independent and different in orientation.

[299] Published in London. There is a Scolar Press facsimile, Menston, 1968. I have also used J. D. Jones' edition, *Neudrücke frühneuenglischer Grammatiken* (ed. R. Brotanek), v, Halle, 1911. Cooper's *The English Teacher* (London, 1687) is an incomplete translation of the *Grammatica*,

which brings together on the one hand an attempt at a language characterology of the type posited by Bacon, and on the other ideas stemming from the proponents of artificial languages, in particular Bishop Wilkins. Wallis and Wilkins he sees as 'greatly to his purpose', the former as the only grammarian of the vernacular to have accommodated his grammar to its individual structure, and the latter as having in his quest for a philosophical language demonstrated the rational bases ('rationes') of the grammatical art. Significant in view of the parallels between Cooper's *Grammatica* and Wilkins' *Essay Towards a Real Character and a Philosophical Language* (1668) is the fact that Cooper was supported financially while at Cambridge by Bishop Seth Ward, who had important links with Wilkins and the artificial language projectors. If Cooper and Wallis are treated together here, it is not only because of Cooper's similar determination to demonstrate the individual structure, the 'nativa ratio', of the vernacular (he proposes to describe the language as it actually is – 'qualis in se est'), but also because both have a debt to Wilkins.[300] Their work embodies two aspects of the nascent Royal Society, on the one hand its appeal to clarity, empiricism and an inductive approach, on the other its rationalism and its search for universals. In this respect the grammars of Wallis and Cooper, together with George Dalgarno's *Ars signorum* (1661) and Wilkins' *Essay*, constitute a single corpus of puritan-inspired, empirical and rationalist thought about language.

Together with Wallis and Cooper may be bracketed Guy Miège and Joseph Aickin. Though Miège's *English Grammar* (1688)[301] is highly derivative, his work is conceived in very much the same spirit, similarly reflecting a major change in thought about language. Though there is little evidence, apart from his similar treatment of compounds, of the direct influence of Wallis,[302] the aims of the two

with additions, treating speech sounds and omitting the more strictly grammatical material. He is not treated by O. Funke, who terminates his 'Frühzeit der englischen Grammatik' at 1653 with Wallis.

[300] This being so, Wilkins ought perhaps logically to have been treated before these two authors. Since however his work represents an important strand in the universal grammar movement, he is treated with the other universal grammarians below.

[301] I have used the second edition: *The English Grammar, setting forth the Grounds of the English Tongue; and particularly its Genius in making Compounds and Derivatives...A Necessary Work in general for all Persons desirous to understand the Grounds and Genius of the English, and very proper to prepare Young Men for the Latine Tongue* (2nd ed.), London, 1691.

[302] There does not seem to be sufficient evidence to justify Poldauf ('On the History of some Problems of English Grammar', p. 88) in bracketing Miège with Cooper as one of the only two followers of Wallis' methods. Miège's phonetic examples show conclusively however that he did make use of Cooper.

grammarians are identical. Miège too regrets the lack of a truly English grammar, one which will demonstrate the vernacular's freedom from those 'emblems of Babels curse and confusion', inflections. He too seizes on features peculiar to the vernacular such as its ability to form compounds, importing into English grammar the interest in vocabulary and lexicography that is a feature of his grammars of French. In so doing he introduces an approach redolent of the *Académie Française* that is by no means alien to the spirit of the Royal Society that inspires Wallis and Cooper. But whereas in France this approach gives rise to austerely usage-based works such as Vaugelas' *Remarques sur la langue françoise* (1647), grammar in England, thanks to the Royal Society and the artificial language projectors, acquires a more theoretical orientation. Miège has a double interest: on the one hand he takes his native language, French, as the starting-point for empirical observation, and on the other he provides an example of a language teacher exposed to the new spirit of rational enquiry. As for Joseph Aickin's grammar,[303] though in spite of its pretensions it is no more than an abridged version of Cooper, its aim as expressed in its prefatory verses is identical with that of Wallis: to provide 'an English Grammar for the English School'. By its use the learner 'may now obtain the perfection of his mother tongue, without the assistance of Latin'. Once again it is the ease of vernacular grammar that is adduced in its favour, mood being expressed by a mere eight particles, tense by fourteen signs, and syntax by prepositions.

Though Wallis and Cooper have an importance far out-ranking that of Miège and Aickin, these four grammarians may in view of their common aims and approach be treated together as presenting a unified corpus of method and doctrine stemming from the ideals and practice of the Royal Society. For instance, though only Cooper gives an indication of what he understands by grammar – that which 'describes the *ratio* and *analogia* of each individual vernacular... preserving it in all ages from the injuries of time and purging it of errors and barbarism'[304] – it is one to which all four grammarians

[303] *The English Grammar*. The laudatory verses preceding the work give Aickin a somewhat inflated role in the history of vernacular grammar, declaring that though Wallis and Cooper by degrees 'the Tongue did rectifie', it was Aickin himself who, having sifted through their 'confus'd rubbish', worked to such good effect that 'no more on Latine now our Tongue depends'.
[304] *Grammatica*, p. 8.

The pedagogical motive

could subscribe. In this definition the importance of following the *nativa ratio* of the vernacular in its linguistic description is duly underlined, but there is also present a view of grammar, which will be reinforced by the *Académie Française*, as something almost external to a language and applied to it as an insurance against corruption. Latin too, though self-consciously rejected as a model, still looms large by its very absence, no longer dictating the presence of this or that grammatical category in a description of the vernacular, but conditioning what the authors omit as too well known to merit inclusion. Wallis' refusal, for example, to give definitions of the parts of speech, on the grounds that anyone with a knowledge of Latin grammar will already be familiar with them, implies a preliminary assumption that the word-classes of English will function in the same way as those of Latin, requiring no adjustment in definition in order to accommodate them to vernacular structure. In his defence however it may be said that it is precisely his aim to demonstrate the enormous difference ('immanis discrepentia') between the structures of English and those of Latin and Greek. It is this concern with differences in structure, so unusual for its time, that lies behind his treatment of articles and prepositions, as especially relevant to the analytical syntax of English, immediately after the noun. They have the status, made more explicit in Cooper and recalling Wilkins' view of certain particles as 'declarative and some accident', of accidents of nouns substituting for the cases of Greek and Latin.[305] Cooper similarly, in an evident concession to English structure, treats articles and prepositions as grammatical accidents with syntactic function. Declension having been declared 'useless and alien', the syntactic

[305] I. Constantinescu, 'John Wallis (1616–1703): A Reappraisal of his Contribution to the Study of English', *Historiographia Linguistica*, 1:3 (1974), pp. 299–300, rightly sees Wallis' grammar as 'prefiguring linguistic formalism and a structural analysis of language'. The author seems however to regard Wallis as the originator of 'structuralist' positions that are already present in earlier work. To state that Wallis, 'the spokesman of the formalist approach' advocated by Ramus, 'out-structuralized the structuralists by declaring that English had *no* case in nouns' is to ignore the fact that Greaves (who in fact follows the Ramist approach while Wallis does not) had already had this insight in 1594. Nor is the 'essential feature' of Wallis' grammar in recognizing that 'English prepositions serve as a sort of case markers' a new departure. The author of this article appears to think that 'this "theory of signs" that emerged from opposing the characteristics of the vernacular to those of Latin' found its first real application with Wallis. In support the author cites C. R. Troike's article (then at the press) 'Lest the Wheel be too oft Re-invented: Towards a reassessment of the intellectual history of linguistics' (published in M. A. Jazayery, E. C. Polomé and W. Winter, *Linguistic and Literary Studies in Honour of Archibald A. Hill*, Lisse, 1976). There is always a danger that the wheel will be thought to have been invented later than it in fact was.

relationships of nouns are assured by a total of thirty-six 'prepositive articles or prepositions'. Indeed the whole of English construction – 'totum grammaticae Anglicanae fundamentum' – reposes on the use of sixty-four particles and the verb *to be*. Upon this formal structure Cooper superimposes an Aristotelian division of word-classes into the 'principal parts' noun and verb, and others expressing 'circumstances which modify the sense'.[306] The former are in Wilkins' manner 'integrals', and the latter 'particles'. Among English grammarians it is Cooper who follows Wilkins most closely, and it is unquestionably Wilkins (and behind him his model Campanella, who treats adverb and preposition as signifying 'circumstances' of essences) who is the source for this classification.[307] This scheme however, so much at variance with Cooper's earlier treatment of article and preposition as particles indicating purely formal relationships, would seem to be no more than window-dressing, a superimposed theoretical statement with no real relevance to the rest of the discussion. A marked feature of his work is this tendency to clothe the 'nativa ratio' of the vernacular in a semasiological framework borrowed from Wilkins, and ultimately from Campanella's neo-Scholasticism. But it is entirely representative of late seventeenth-century linguistic thought that in reintroducing into grammar (via Wilkins) certain of the semantic niceties of the schoolmen, Cooper takes no account of Campanella's cardinal principle that 'the grammarian considers the *modus significandi* [i.e. the consignification of grammatical categories], not lexical meaning'.[308] Cooper's superimposed semasiological classifications are based on the 'res significatae' (Campanella's term) of the logician, rather than on properly grammatical distinctions. Campanella would no doubt have dismissed this section of his grammar as 'metaphysics'. Wallis provides a sharp contrast, avoiding the traditional intricacies of semantic classification altogether. Any overall grouping of his word-classes must be inferred from the structure of his grammar.[309]

[306] *Grammatica*, p. 96.

[307] Where Cooper differs from Wilkins is in counting both verb and noun as 'integrals', not just the noun, thus bringing his system into line with the Aristotelian one in terms of semantically independent *partes principales* and dependent *partes consignificativae*.

[308] Campanella, in the grammar contained in his *Philosophiae rationalis partes quinque. Videlicet: grammatica, dialectica, rhetorica, poetica, historiographia. Pars prima: grammatica*, Paris, 1638, insists that 'Grammaticus respicit modum significandi, non rem significatam'.

[309] The fact that Wallis treats the preposition at the outset as an accident of the noun, then later groups it with adverb, conjunction and interjection, leads Michael (*English Grammatical*

Cooper's semasiological and philosophical framework requires however some definitions, and his definition of the noun as 'a word which indicates the thing itself or a quality'[310] gives the increasingly usual late-seventeenth-century dichotomy in which concrete substantives indicate tangible realities, while abstract substantives and adjectives denote abstract entities and qualities.[311] Cooper's abstract substantive is distinguished from his adjective in that it denotes not only a quality, but a quality subsisting by itself apart from any thing in which it can inhere. There is here an evolution in which the traditional Latin definition of the noun-class (including both substantive and adjective) as signifying 'substance with quality' is replaced by a new one in which it signifies *either* a thing *or* a quality. Medieval grammarians had already experienced difficulties with nouns such as *nihil* or *caecitas* '(blindness'), which though they behaved grammatically as substantives, could hardly be held to denote a substance. Cooper's definition is an attempt to get grammarians off the hook, but instead of defining such words as subsisting *grammatically* by themselves (i.e. as having syntactic independence as compared with adjectives), he plumps for the philosophical definition and characterizes them as subsisting *semantically* by themselves. This one small point speaks volumes as to the general seventeenth-century evolution away from specifically grammatical definition, in the direction of an approach based on lexical meaning and philosophical abstractions. Cooper's own approach to the grammar of English, laudable in so far as it frequently coincides with that of Wallis, is as we have noted impaired by being overlaid, more especially in the treatment of the noun, by a logical superstructure patently taken from Wilkins. His definition of the noun paves the way for a framework of concrete and abstract substantives, each in turn divided into 'neuter', active and passive sub-classes, with parallel series in the adjectives, that is closely modelled on that used by Wilkins and is illustrated by similar examples. Concrete 'neuter' substantives (i.e. those whose lexical meaning is not that of an agent

Categories, p. 204) to suppose that he is treating all four parts of speech as (Gill's term) 'particles', thus tending towards the reforming four-word-class system that appears at the end of the century.

[310] *Grammatica*, p. 96.

[311] On the substantive/adjective dichotomy see O. Jespersen, *The Philosophy of Grammar*, New York, 1965, pp. 74–5. No doubt it is the absence in their native tongue of formal criteria linking or differentiating the two that causes the English vernacular grammarians in particular to adopt a 'notional' dichotomy.

or of the undergoing of an action) signify, in an exact repetition of Wilkins' terms, 'the *Ens* or thing itself'. The active and passive substantives, in addition to denoting the thing itself, also consignify action or 'passion'. There is a corresponding series of abstract substantives signifying not an *ens*, but an *essentia*. The system gives rise to the following set of distinctions, in which Cooper's Latin equivalents coincide precisely with those of Wilkins:

	Concrete substantives	*Abstract substantives*
neuter	heat ('calor')	hotness ('caloritas')
active	heating ('calefactio')	calefactivity ('calefactivitas')
passive	the being heated ('τὸ calefieri')	calefactibility ('calefactibilitas')

	Concrete adjectives	*Abstract adjectives*
neuter	hot	caloritative
active	heating ('calefaciens')	calefactive
passive	heated ('calefactus')	calefactible

In this system, it is difficult to see why *hotness* is abstract but *heat* is concrete, why *love* is a concrete 'ens' while *amity* is an abstract 'essentia'.[312] The paraphernalia of terms from Scholastic philosophy is taken en bloc from Wilkins, and via him from Campanella. The expressions 'ens' and 'essentia', though equated with concrete and abstract, obviously do not constitute the equivalent of the traditional dichotomy of nouns signifying what is perceptible to the senses, and what is perceptible only to the intellect.[313] Any discrepancy is explained (at any rate to Cooper's satisfaction) by the requirement, following Wilkins and Campanella, that abstract nouns express a 'potentia' or aptitude. 'Ens', 'essentia' and 'potentia' are all primary terms in Scholastic philosophy. The key to the question lies in the fact that the 'neuter concrete substantives' (*heat, love*) are treated as radicals, from which the remaining classes are semantically derived. A thing must first exist, and only later can it have action, 'passion' or essence (i.e. potentiality) ascribed to it. Wilkins however is elaborating, parallel with his grammar, a 'real character' by means

---

312 Cf. Campanella, for whom on the contrary *amor* signifies 'ipsum actum, ut essentia est'.

313 Despauterius for example (*Rudimenta*, f. 17ʳ) makes a distinction between nouns signifying 'quicquid sentitur' and 'quicquid nullo sensu percipitur' which can be traced at least as far back as the Roman grammarian Charisius.

of which his proposed artificial language can be transcribed. To this end his basic semantic categories are treated as radicals each provided with its own specific character, to which may be added 'differences' to cater for the consignification of action, aptitude, etc. This leads him to place *calor* among the concrete, but *caloritas* among the abstract substantives, and it is difficult to escape the conclusion that the real motive behind his system is provided by the derivational forms of Latin, each of which must have its semantic and written counterpart in his new language. These preoccupations are not however appropriate to the composition of a grammar of the vernacular. Cooper's close imitation of Wilkins has caused him to import into English grammar, where they have absolutely no *linguistic* relevance, a set of Scholastic distinctions intended to form the basis of a universal language suitable for scientific enquiry.

Wallis stays firmly on the more practical level of the actual structure of English, to which the 'fictitious and inept collection' of cases, genders and moods inherited from the Latin tradition is quite plainly inappropriate. The 'enormous vexation' of a case system is not a necessary part of English syntax, which uses prepositions in its stead. Cooper too realizes that syntactic relations are indicated in English not by cases, but by 'prepositive particles'. If he makes a concession to traditional terminology in calling English nouns *aptota* (single-case words), it is in order to cater for comparison where the positive degree may be treated as the primary case and the comparative and superlative as secondary ones. It is obvious however that he is here using 'case' in the Varronian sense of 'derived form'. The extreme slowness and reluctance with which grammarians abandon the notion of case in the vernacular is shown by the fact that Wallis is the first English grammarian since Greaves (1594) to do so. Both authors too are clear that while English makes sex distinctions, as in *he-goat* and *female hare*, or in the separate words *boy* and *girl*, it has no category of grammatical gender. Cooper indeed recognizes that even in Latin gender is a syntactic device, a mark of formal congruence, an insight he may owe to Sanctius via Vossius' view of gender as a grammatical category 'solely by reason of structure'.[314] This recognition, as in Wallis' similar dismissal of

---

[314] Vossius, *De arte*, III, ix. 33: 'propter solam structuram'. Cf. Cooper, *Grammatica*, p. 124: 'propter verae concordantiae necessitatem'. Sanctius' view is identical, and he is no doubt Vossius' source.

congruence between adjective and substantive, dispenses both authors from using such devices as the English Ramists' attribution of case and gender to the adjective 'gratia substantivi', by virtue of the substantive it is constructed with. It is finally admitted, with these two authors, that English adjectives carry no formal marks of gender, number and case. This being established however, grammarians are left without any structural criteria other than the fact that the adjective precedes its substantive, which increases the likelihood that they will take refuge in semantic definition. Cooper's definition of the adjective as that which 'demonstrating the nature of the substantive, is predicated of it' is typical of this late-seventeenth-century reliance on purely semantic and logical criteria. On this view the adjective is an 'adjuncta natura' of the substantive. Here the structuralist simplicity of Wallis' grammar is in sharp contrast, for he merely notes that adjectives are joined to substantives, without specifying anything as to their semantic 'nature'. Of particular interest is his recognition of those structures that are peculiar to the vernacular, such as the 'possessive' adjectival use of *man's* in *man's nature*, and his realization that in *the King-of-Spain's Court* the 'whole aggregate' behaves like a single substantive in receiving a possessive -*s* ending. The adjectival function of the first element of such compounds as *sea-fish*[315] is catered for by a category of 'respective adjectives', which are 'nothing other than the substantive word-form ["vox substantiva"], used adjectivally'.[316] They are in fact similar to Gill's 'sterile substantives' as in *sea-water*, so called because they do not give birth to any formal variation to indicate their changed function.[317] Since adjectives usually accompany only substantives, Wallis sees *sun* in *sun-shiny* as having 'degenerated' into an adverb, or alternatively the compound can be treated as a derivative of the prior form *sun-shine*, in which *sun* is without question a 'respective adjective'. Interesting in view of the Port-Royal view of certain words as constituting 'abbreviations' of prepositional phrases, and in view of the general contemporary tendency to resolve unitary grammatical structures into semantically

[315] Michael (*English Grammatical Categories*, p. 311) says the presence of this example in succeeding grammatical works acts like a 'radioactive tracer' in demonstrating Wallis' influence.
[316] *Grammatica*, p. 82.
[317] Cf. Michael, *English Grammatical Categories*, p. 310. Michael notes (p. 312) that *sea* in *sea-water* is already in 1612 given by Thomas Tomkis ('De analogia Anglicani sermonis', ff. 1–15) as an example of a substantive with adjectival function.

equivalent analytical ones, is the statement that these respective adjectives can be 'much more distinctly' expressed by prepositional structures. Given Wallis' insistence on the function of prepositions in English, the analytical *a ring of gold* is plainly seen as superior to the compound *a gold-ring*. Cooper transposes these practices of Wallis into his own semantic terms, the substantive 'assuming the nature' of an adjective and also containing within itself the semantic import ('vis') of a preposition, *a grass plot* and *a plot of grass* being interchangeable structures. He has however no qualms about adjectives qualifying other adjectives, as in *sea-sick*, or in multiple compounds such as *penknife-sheath*. He adds a category of 'material' adjectives such as *wooden*, which show an added formal element but are equally restatable as prepositional phrases.[318]

In their treatment of the noun the highly derivatory works of Miège and Aickin follow Wallis and Cooper, particularly the latter, very closely. Equally indicative of the growing tendency to purely semantic definition are their definitions of the noun as 'the Name of a Thing...Or [of] some Quality' (Miège, following Cooper) or as 'that which expresseth the Name of every thing' (Aickin). The latter indeed repeats more or less verbatim Cooper's classes of concrete and abstract nouns based on Wilkins. More interesting as indicating acceptance of Wallis' and Cooper's doctrines concerning English structure is Miège's declaration that, apart from the 'genitive' in structures such as *God's glory*, case is 'a Thing incident to the Latine Tongue, but not to our Vulgar Speeches'. Miège sets up the genders masculine, feminine, neuter (i.e. inanimate) and common, but notes, 'where it is convenient to remove the Ambiguity', the existence of terms such as *Man-Servant, he-Cat* and *hen-Sparrow*. In common with other grammarians he states that *ship* can be feminine, and that some plants are 'distinguished by Herbalists into male and female'. Unlike Cooper, he seems not to have entirely realized the difference between the lexical indication of sex differences, and the purely structural character of grammatical gender. He does however follow his models in stating that English adjectives are invariable, and has the merit of noting the adjectival function of what are lexically adverbs, as in *the now king*. Miège follows Cooper in treating articles, number and gender as things 'chiefly to be considered' when discussing nouns, that is to say he sees them, as did Cooper, as noun accidents with

[318] *Grammatica*, pp. 132–7.

a syntactic function.[319] Aickin, following Cooper yet more closely, adds to these the prepositions, treating them quite early in the grammar together with the other 'accidents', and thus recognizing their importance in nominal structures. He makes clear that their function is to supply that 'defect in our Tongue' caused by the absence of case, though unlike most of his predecessors he abstains from giving case names to the prepositional structures *of a kingdom, to a kingdom*, etc.

The articles are treated by Wallis as nouns adjective not differing in use from other adjectives. *A* is a 'numeral article' with the same meaning, though 'less emphatic', as *one*. If it appears only before single nouns, it is 'by material, not formal necessity'.[320] The definite article *the*, called by Wallis 'articulus demonstrativus' in recognition of its demonstrative function, similarly has the signification of *that*, but with less emphasis. Here again, meaning is the criterion rather than such formal or syntactic matters as the ability to stand before certain word-classes. The function of *a* being to particularize, that of *the* is to determine. The opposition particularizing/determining, associated with the numeral/demonstrative one, is however not very clear. Cooper's treatment includes features from both Wallis and Wilkins. To the latter he owes his view of *a* as 'enunciative' – as giving 'a full expression of the following thing' – and of *the* as 'demonstrative and emphatic'. He adds that *a* denotes a 'vague individual', *the* a 'determined individual'. Wallis' distinction between *a* as particularizing and *the* as determining is used by him to explain why the uncountables (he does not of course use the term, but refers to them as words which 'signify homogeneous things, which cannot be divided into distinct and different parts', and have no plural), cannot be preceded by the article *a*, whose function is to denote the 'individual and particular'.[321] But it was to be a long time, not earlier than the end of the following century, before the problem of the distinction between countables and uncountables was finally solved by English grammarians. Early attempts to provide lists of *semper pluralia* and *semper singularia* are, as I. Poldauf[322] observes, perhaps

[319] Cf. Cooper, *ibid.*, p. 116. In the matter of gender, this treatment only holds good for *Latin* grammar, and it is curious, in view of Cooper's later statement (p. 132) that English adjectives have no gender, that he should retain it in his list of 'accidents' determining syntactic relations.
[320] Wallis, *Grammatica*, p. 71.   [321] Cooper, *Grammatica*, pp. 116–18.
[322] 'On the History of some Problems of English Grammar', p. 214. For a long and interesting discussion of the problem of number in English see pp. 211–39.

really unconscious attempts to grapple with this problem. In its solution vernacular grammarians could find little to help them in the Latin tradition. Poldauf, remarking that it is 'the peculiar character of English, attaching its grammatical categories to the semantic rather than to formal...classification, that makes it possible that the loss of the marks of plurality need not accompany the loss of semantic plurality', finds not a single term in the list *alms, bellows, commons, compasses, news, victuals* that would be recognized as a singular by the majority of pre-1800 vernacular grammarians. Here no doubt, contrary to the general tendency to semantic categorization, the formal marks evidently prevented the recognition of what had in fact become semantic singulars.[323]

Wallis notes that the pronoun acts as a noun-substitute but considers it, like Ramus, Gill and Jonson, to be a noun, differing from other nouns only in the irregularity of its declension. From Gill he takes the alternative name 'personal noun'.[324] His distinction between 'rect' (*I*) and 'oblique (*me*) recalls Butler, though Wallis of course does not extend it to his noun-class in general. This seems at first sight to contradict his earlier statement that 'Nouns Substantive ...take no distinction of cases,'[325] but *me* is not seen as a 'case' of *I*, but as a separate pronoun in a permanently oblique form. Wallis in fact avoids the term 'case', preferring instead to speak of rect and oblique 'status'.[326] At all events 'noun personal' and 'noun substantive' are not for Wallis overlapping terms. The terms 'pronoun substantive' and 'pronoun adjective' are nowhere found in his grammar, all adjectival forms (the relative *which*, the demonstratives *this* and *that*) being explicitly excluded from the pronoun class as 'plainly nouns adjective' or, when standing alone, nouns substantive.[327] A division of pronouns into substantive and adjective is found with some grammarians, but not with Wallis. His 'noun

[323] Poldauf (*ibid.*, p. 224) suggests the term 'plurality in division' to cover *ashes* and *scissors*, and 'plurality in multiplication' to cover ordinary plurals. 'The plurality in division', he observes, 'is particularly developed in English, perhaps in keeping with the analytical character of English in general.'
[324] Michael (*English Grammatical Categories*, p. 348) remarks that this is the regular term among those post-1700 reforming grammarians who use a vernacular terminology.
[325] *Grammatica*, p. 68.
[326] With Miège and Aickin too, nowhere is case mentioned, Miège for instance describing pronouns as 'changed' or 'varied' into another form after verbs or in the plural.
[327] *Grammatica*, p. 89. Cf. Wilkins' distinction (*Essay*, p. 306) in which the personal pronouns are substantives, the rest being adjectives which are 'by reason of Ellipsis sometimes used Substantively'.

personal' is a separate sub-class of the noun, not amenable to the substantive/adjective dichotomy, its separateness justified by its formal distinctions of rect and oblique and, precisely, by its absence of adjectival forms.[328] True to his method however, Wallis nowhere gives an explicit definition of it. Cooper again follows Wilkins, treating the pronoun as a noun substitute, but also in J. C. Scaliger's terms as a sign of the noun and not a direct signification of reality. His 'just as the noun is a sign of a thing, so is the pronoun a sign of a noun' is taken unaltered from Wilkins.[329] Also stemming from Wilkins are Cooper's 'personalia' (a term also found in Gill, Butler and Wallis), a class of pronouns which do in fact 'directly denote the thing itself' and 'are not referred to the noun'. Scaliger similarly, in contradiction of his general doctrine on the pronoun, had allowed his personal pronouns to signify 'with no noun understood', indicating the thing itself 'directly to the intellect via a concept, not via the noun'.[330] Cooper's second class of pronouns are those which 'accompany the noun at first mention of a thing', namely the demonstratives. Finally the true noun-substitutes, 'supplying the place of the noun', are the 'relatives'.[331] Once again, we need look no further than Wilkins for the source of all this.[332]

In the verb, Wallis recognizes that English has only two tenses[333] – or rather, to be more precise, that the basic verb form used without auxiliaries shows formal variation for only two – the present and the past imperfect, all others being formed periphrastically with 'auxiliary' verbs, a term he appears to be the first to use. Since these auxiliaries occupy in verbal structures a role analagous to that of prepositions in nominal ones, he devotes a separate section to them.

[328] Cf. Funke ('Die Frühzeit der englischen Grammatik', p. 79), who seems not to have understood this.

[329] Wilkins, *Essay*, p. 305: 'As Nouns are notes or signs of things, so Pronouns are of Nouns.' Cooper's Latin rendering is 'sicut...nomen est signum rei, sic pronomen est nota nominis'. Scaliger's view of the pronoun as referring primarily to the noun it replaces, and only secondarily and indirectly to the thing itself (*res ipsa*) is ultimately traceable to Apollonius. Wilkins has the doctrine via Campanella.

[330] *De causis linguae Latinae*, cap. cxxviii: 'statim per speciem intellectui...non per nomen'.

[331] *Grammatica*, p. 119.

[332] Cf. Wilkins' *Essay*, p. 305: pronouns 'represent things either 1. Immediately and in kind, without respect to the names of those things...2. Mediately by their names, which are either 1. Exprest with the Pronoun...Demonstrative. 2. Supplyed by the Pronouns...as *he, it*, etc....Relative'.

[333] In this Wallis does not, as Poldauf ('On the History of Some Problems of English Grammar', p. 272) suggests, resemble Ben Jonson, who postulates 'three only Tymes', counting the imperative as a future and banishing all compound forms to the syntax.

Interesting is his characterization of the various time relationships involved according to the vantage-point of the speaker, the past imperfect indicating an action that at the time spoken of was a present action, or one that was in process. In particular, his distinction between a perfect tense denoting 'what is *now* past' and a pluperfect denoting 'what was *then* past'[334] allows recognition of the present aspectual nature of the perfect. The greater part of Wallis' treatment is however given over to discussion of the auxiliaries, which are distributed among two main classes. The auxiliaries *do, will, shall, may, can* and *must* are termed 'mutila' or defective because they take part only in a limited number of tense formations, have no past participle (except for *do* and *will* when used independently), and cannot be preceded by other auxiliaries.[335] *Have* and *be*, by contrast, having both these possibilities, are complete or perfect ('integra') auxiliaries. Wallis realizes that *do* and *did* sometimes occur in emphatic use, and he is perhaps the first grammarian to claim that the *shall* form of the future in the first person is merely declarative, while the *will* form promises and threatens, the roles being reversed in the other two persons. A similar distinction is made between *would* (indicating inclination) and *should* (indicating simple futurity). It is noted that *may* and *can* signify 'potentia', but Wallis does not attempt, after the manner of earlier grammarians, to establish parallels between English periphrastic structures containing these verbs, and Latin subjunctive or 'potential' moods. His silence on mood indeed is worthy of Ramus. Latin translations of vernacular forms are given, but he resists the temptation both to claim that the English structures are exact counterparts of the Latin ones, and to set up English moods on semantic bases which have no justification in form. His purely structural treatment of the auxiliaries represents a distinct advance on the rather thoughtless repetition of Lily's system of *signs* by previous vernacular grammarians, for whom they represent aids to the recognition of Latin categories, rather than a conscious analysis of vernacular structure.

Possibly because it is not given separate status as a part of speech by Wilkins, Cooper does not give a definition of the verb but proceeds immediately to an examination of its accidents mood, tense, number and person. Tenses are indicated either by signs or by terminations,

---

[334] *Grammatica*, pp. 91, 96–7 (my italics).
[335] The verbs *let, bid, dare* and *help* used without *to* before infinitives are also so treated.

in two parallel series the first of which consists of those structures made up of the copula plus an 'active adjective' (*is . . .-ing*), the second grouping single-word forms which are held to contain within themselves both these elements. A common enough analysis in the late seventeenth century (cf. the Port-Royal treatment of the verb as an affirmation consisting of an attribute linked to the subject by the copula), this procedure is however found much earlier (1540) in Scaliger's view of *est* in *Caesar est clemens* as a 'linking sign by which clemency is predicated [of Caesar]', and in medieval modistic analyses of the type *amat = est amans*.[336] Cooper's immediate source is no doubt yet again Wilkins, who analyses the verb as an adjective containing a copula and is in turn indebted to Campanella's treatment of *am* and *have* as the basis of all verbs.[337] In an analysis parallel to that of active verbs as consisting of copula plus 'active concrete adjectives' in *-ing*, Cooper treats passives as containing copula plus 'passive concrete adjectives' in *-ed*.[338] Of particular interest is the statement that the active forms in -ing (*he is loving*) are used only in signifying 'a present act',[339] while the unitary forms (*he loves*), regarded as a contraction of them, signify habitual actions. Cooper thus has the merit of recognizing the existence and use of the progressive tenses in English. What is fascinating however is the circuitous route by which he has arrived at this recognition. It is a major contention of the present study that the development of vernacular grammatical theory can only be fully understood if its origins in the underlying Latin tradition are taken into account. In Latin analyses such as *amat = est amans* and in the Port-Royal Grammar's identical *Pierre vit = Pierre est vivant*,[340] the right-hand terms exist only at an underlying logical level, at the level of (dare one say it?) deep structure. Cooper's first procedure, following Wilkins, is to note the equation *he loves = he is loving*. In English by contrast the right-hand term exists at the surface level of discourse, and must be catered for in the paradigms. Cooper is however dressing

---

[336] *De causis linguae Latinae*, cap. cx.

[337] Perhaps it is this treatment of both *sum* and *habeo* as copulas latent in verbs that ultimately lies behind Miège's seemingly eccentric definition of the verb as signifying existence, action or *possession*. Michael (*English Grammatical Categories*, p. 365) finds a similar reference to possession in the definition of the verb, only in John Kirkby's *New English Grammar* (1746) and James White's *The English Verb* (1761). There is always the possibility of course that in all three works 'possession' is a printer's error for 'passion'.

[338] *Grammatica*, p. 108. Here again a parallel with Campanella may be noted.

[339] *Ibid.*, pp. 106–7.   [340] *Grammaire générale et raisonnée*, p. 91.

the whole thing up in neo-Scholastic terms, and what clinches the matter is Campanella's description of *amans* as a participial noun signifying 'essentiam *cum actu praesenti*' (cf. Cooper's description of the forms in *-ing*, in precisely the same terminology, as signifying 'a present act'). Cooper is the first English grammarian to recognize the specific function of the progressive forms in English, but incontestably it is via the neo-Scholastic revival in Latin grammar.

Having arrived at this analysis, he is now in a position to provide each of the five English tenses with a progressive form, in which the *-ing* component always indicates a present *act*, while the preceding signs (*is, was, have been*, etc.) denote present, past or future *time*. The unitary verb forms (e.g. *he loves*), either alone or preceded by *do* or *did* for emphasis, signify by contrast an 'absolute' act. Noteworthy is Cooper's refusal to establish the traditional parallel between the signs *did, have, had* and respectively the Latin imperfect, perfect and pluperfect, a parallelism which 'leads to obscurity, error and incongruity in speech'. *Do* and *have* he assigns to present tenses, *did* and *had* to past ones, setting up a binary division in which the perfect with *have* occupies its correct place in present completive position. His system of tenses, set out according to its 'active signs', is as follows:

Praesens	⎰ Indefinitum *do...* ⎱ Finitum *have...*

Futurum	⎰ Declarativum *shall...* ⎱ Promissivum *will...*

Praeteritum	⎰ Absolutum *did...* ⎱ Destinatum *had...*[341]

The progressive forms constitute a parallel and separate series. Not included in the paradigms is the simple 'aorist' form *I love*, which is simply regarded as a less emphatic equivalent of *I do love*. The system is very much dependent on signs, and on an insistence on neat dichotomies leading to the provision of two futures on a not very sound basis. The future perfect, mentioned in the discussion of mood, is omitted without comment, though Cooper notes that *was going to* is equivalent to the Latin future in *-rus*. In the treatment of voice he rejects the cognate accusatives (*I run* = *I run a race*, cf. Linacre's

---

[341] *Grammatica*, p. 150.

curro = curro cursum) inherited from the Latin tradition, and accepts as 'neutra' only those verbs which, being neither active nor passive, consist of the copula plus a 'neuter adjective'.[342] On this view *I am sick* is a neuter verb with a corresponding active *it makes me sick*, though one suspects that in making this distinction Cooper too had Latin *aegroto* at the back of his mind. Latin influence lingers also in the classification of *come* and *go* as 'neutro-passives'. Largely under the influence of Wilkins, the following four-term voice system is arrived at:

Absoluta	Activa	Passiva	Neutra
I sit down	*I set down*	*I am set down*	*I sit still*
	(*sedere facio*)	(*sedere fio*)	(*sedeo*)

E. Vorlat[343] claims that Wilkins and Cooper are the first English grammarians to analyse the 'intentionality [transitive/intransitive] of the action'. She regards Cooper's use of the terms 'transitive' and 'active absolute' as borrowings from Wilkins, but the latter term at least is current in seventeenth-century Latin grammarians, e.g. Vossius,[344] and the *notion* of transitivity is certainly current much earlier than Wilkins.

In both terminology and contents the treatment of tense in Miège's *English Grammar* of 1688 is plainly influenced by Cooper. Miège's work helps to give wider currency to the recognition of the function of the progressive form. His further specification that it is used 'when we speak of a Thing, that was a doing, but interrupted upon some Incident' (*I was speaking of you, when you came in*) may owe something to the similar rule governing the use of the imperfect and perfect or past historic tenses in French. Certainly, he displays the same concern to tease out the time-relationships expressed by the various tenses, as he does in his French grammar.[345] *Can, may, will* and *must* have both present and future reference; *shall* denotes only the future, and *ought* the present. *Could, might* and *would* similarly refer to both past and future, but *should* to the future only, while *must have, ought to have* and *should have* refer to the past.[346]

---

[342] In this he is not followed by Miège, who states (*English Grammar*, p. 4) ''Tis true there are some Verbs Active that are used Neutrally; as... *this Meat eats well*. And so there are Neutral Verbs that are used Actively... *to run a Race*.'

[343] *English Grammatical Theory 1586–1737*.

[344] *De arte*, v, ii, 6–8.   [345] *A New French Grammar*, London, 1678.

[346] *English Grammar*, pp. 70, 73. Aickin's very derivatory treatment of tense does not call for comment.

In the treatment of mood Cooper follows Wilkins in instituting primary and secondary moods. The indicative is expressed as in Wilkins 'by the simple union of subject and predicate', i.e. without a preceding sign, and is therefore, together with the imperative, regarded as a primary mood. All other moods require a 'modal sign' or particle, and for this reason are treated as secondary. The structure *I would have been* is accordingly analysed into person + modal sign + copula *have* + invariable passive adjective.[347] In attributing copulatory character to the verb *have*, Cooper follows Wilkins and Campanella. All that is not indicative, imperative, infinitive or subjunctive (identical, except for its preceding signs, apart from the form *be*, with the indicative) is included under the heading 'potential', with eight possible modal signs. *Can* denotes 'absolute causal ability', *could* and *might* 'conditional ability', *may* 'absolute liberty', etc. *Will* and *shall* are included here as denoting respectively 'absolute inclination' and 'absolute necessity'.[348] Cooper notes however that they are more particularly used in forming the future tense, with *shall have* denoting a future with past reference. He is the first English grammarian to mention the dropping of *will* and *shall* in temporal clauses (*when I have prepared = cum preparavero*). Miège too uses the term 'potential' to cover expressions with *may* and *might*. He divides the future indicative into 'absolute' (a term taken from Cooper) and 'conditional' (*I should, would, might, could have*), the latter identical with the 'first future' tenses of the subjunctive, whose 'second future' consists of the traditional Latin-inspired [*when*] *I shall have loved*. Miège describes this last as little used after conjunctions, where it is replaced by the 'perfect' [*when*] *I have loved*. Of particular interest is the fact that here Miège's description of the structure of English is patently influenced by the situation in French. In his *New French Grammar* he had already distinguished the 'futures' *parlerai* and *parlerais*, noting that his predecessors erroneously counted the latter as an imperfect subjunctive. This is an excellent illustration of the importance of considering national vernacular grammars not in isolation from each other, but within the general European context. In view of Miège's preoccupation with time relationships, his justification of his 'conditional' tense (is he, following on Cooper's

[347] *Grammatica*, p. 139.
[348] Cf. Wilkins, for whom mood is expressed by 'particulae' denoting *potestatem, libertatem, resolutionem* and *necessitatem.*

reference to the signification of 'potestatem conditionalem', the first to use this term?) is worth quoting in full:

This tense I call a Future, contrary to the Genius of other Grammarians, who place it in the Subjunctive Mood, and call it a Preter Tense. An Errour that proceeds from a fond way of modelling right or wrong our Vulgar Speeches to the Latine Tongue...without considering, that *Amarem* is in effect a Mixt Tense, that relates to the Time to come as well as the Time past. Whereas *I Might*, *Would*, or *Should*, have no relation in the least to the Time past, but rather to the Time to come; unless they be followed with *Have*, the Sign of a Preter Tense.[349]

Though both Wallis and Cooper devote but little space to what they discuss under the actual *heading* of syntax, their treatment of the preposition deals very largely with syntactic matters, this part of speech assuming an importance that far outweighs that accorded to the other minor word-classes. As the seventeenth century goes on there is an increasing reluctance to treat adverb and preposition as separate parts of speech, Wallis for example classing *before* and *near* as 'adverbializing prepositions', while Cooper, in an analysis recalling that of the Port-Royal authors, regards certain adverbs as abbreviations of the structure preposition + substantive. Many of the non-derivative adverbs he treats as 'prepositions without a [following] case', and Wallis too repeats the traditional assertion that prepositions not governing a case-marked word 'degenerate into adverbs'. Prepositions are of vital importance to these authors as indicating relationships of English structure, so much so that, aside from listing the customary semantic classes of adverbs and conjunctions, they take little interest in these two latter parts of speech. Wallis indeed would see no 'grave detriment' if they were, together with the interjection, reduced to a single class.[350] Where an attempt is made (as in Miège and Cooper) to keep adverb and preposition apart in definition, it is on the basis that the adverb expresses a 'circumstance' of a verb, while the preposition expresses a 'circumstance' of a noun, a distinction that ultimately has affinities with Melanchthon's definition of the preposition,[351] but whose immediate source is Wilkins and

[349] *English Grammar*, pp. 71–2. Miège's penetrating analysis may be compared with Aickin's unqualified statement (*English Grammar*, part II, p. 11) that *could, might, would, should* and *ought* 'cheifly declare the preteret tense'.

[350] Miège dismisses adverbs and conjunctions, and indeed prepositions, with the words 'I han't much to say of any of them.'

[351] Melanchthon, *Grammatica* Paris ed. of 1527: '[praepositio] est...articulus verbo nomen adjungens, quod aliquam facti circunstantiam significat'. Cf. Cooper's view (*Grammatica*, p. 127) that prepositions 'substantivorum circumstantias limitant'.

Campanella. What this comes to in practice is that both Wallis and Cooper treat the preposition as a noun accident, equivalent to case in the classical languages.[352] It is for this reason, i.e. because of its status as a 'communis affectio' or accident of substantives, that Wallis chooses, contrary as he informs the reader to common practice, to treat it immediately after the article. Above all however it is its function in English analytical structure that is emphasized. As Wallis puts it, 'Once the meaning of these few words is known, almost the whole of the syntax of nouns is understood at one and the same time,' an opinion which is echoed by Cooper's 'on them depends practically the whole of syntax'. Much of the stimulus for this must come from Wilkins and Campanella, as is evidenced by Cooper's mention of the latter's alternative name 'adnomen' for the preposition.

Trivial in appearance, this change in the place occupied by prepositions in the framework of grammar is pregnant with consequences for future developments in grammatical theory. It is indeed in this respect that Wallis' accusations of plagiarism by the Port-Royal authors might have seemed to him to be well founded.[353] His promotion of these function words to an early and prominent place in his grammar is of primary importance for the analysis of English syntax, for it opens the road to a study of the way the relationship of individual linguistic units to the whole sentence is expressed in a vernacular language.[354] It also puts the relationship of governed and governing terms on a new footing, since it no longer has to be expressed in terms of case. At one and the same time the supposed necessity of the Latin framework is removed, and the emphasis is put on the syntactic relationships between the noun and other elements in the sentence. 'The preposition', says Wallis, 'placed before a substantive that is governed, shows what relation that substantive has to the word (be it verb, noun, or another part of speech) by which it is governed.' It is this very importance given to prepositions as function words, giving primacy to the role of syntactic relations, that

[352] Kemp, *John Wallis's Grammar of the English Language*, p. 36, calls Wallis the first English grammarian to stress the similarity between prepositional function in the vernacular and case function in Latin. No doubt he is referring to grammarians *of* English, for the Paris 1533 edition of Linacre's *Rudimenta* already refers to certain French prepositions as 'articuli sive notae' of case.

[353] Michael, *English Grammatical Categories*, p. 455, claims that 'it is probable that Wilkins was more directly influenced by the Port Royal grammar than by Wallis (but the Port Royal grammar itself owed much to Wallis)', without however providing evidence to support either of these assertions.

[354] An interest in the *relationships* between ideas is very much in the air at the time, as witness book II, chapter xxv of Locke's *Essay*, entitled 'Of Relation'.

opens the way, as J. C. Chevalier has argued,[355] to a logically orientated grammar. Wallis himself sees the connection, for he continues: 'prepositions are commonly used to signify the Logical Arguments (as they are called) or the Topical Places'. Elements from logic are pressed into service to provide the semantic content of syntactic relations, recourse being had to terms such as subject and object, and to the material, efficient and final causes. This employment of logic leads in the case of Cooper to the drawing of fine distinctions: 'Subject and object are the same, but with different regards [*respectus*]; for that which is considered by the mind is called the object: but the same thing, with respect to the properties demonstrated of it by causes, is a subject.'[356] Not since J. C. Scaliger's *De causis linguae Latinae* had Aristotle's Four Causes been so determinedly applied to linguistic description, though with Wallis and Cooper their use is limited to the specification of the semantic content of syntactic relations. Thus for Wallis, *of* signifies 'an object about which' or 'a material from which', while *by* indicates an 'efficient cause'. Cooper has the same description of the function of *by*, adding that the preposition *by* with the meaning 'by reason of' indicates a final cause. The single preposition *of* denotes a subject (*a cup of water*), a relationship (*the son of an earl*), a material cause (*a building of marble*), or an object (*a treatise of philosophy*). The fact that these various uses are a purely semantic matter, not a grammatical one, seemingly escapes these authors.[357] Cooper has in any case simply taken his detailed sub-classification from Wilkins, though the latter may well be indebted to Wallis as well as to his evident model Campanella.

Wallis reserves his actual syntactic section, which like that of Cooper is scanty, for other matters such as word order and derivation (as in the series *to beat, a bat, a battel, a beetle, a battle-door*), in which he shows much interest. Here again however there is a semasiological veneer involving such traditional Latin grammatical terms as 'adjectiva copiae' and 'adjectiva plenitudinis'. Miège too pays exceptional attention to derivation and composition, which are 'the

[355] *Histoire de la syntaxe*, pp. 458, 486–7.

[356] The use of the term 'respectus' is not uncommon in Cooper's treatment as e.g. in his definition of prepositional function as limiting 'substantivorum circumstantias…in eorum variis respectibus' (*Grammatica*, p. 128). Cf. Campanella (*Grammatica*, p. 74) who defines prepositions as 'consignificans rerum seu essentiarum…respectus et circumstantias'. Cooper's immediate source is again Wilkins.

[357] Aickin has a similar importation of logic into grammar, with a division of prepositions into 'causals' and 'locals'.

Way to understand the Bottom of a Language'. His compounds are also semantically classified as expressing 'some Quality of the Body or Mind' (*plump-faced*), ailments (*belly-ache*), employment (*cheese-monger*), etc. The presence of Latin lurks in the background, for the initial elements of structures such as *head-ache* and *London Gazette* have to be explained as imitations of preceding genitives.[358] In this section of grammar Wallis's simple structural statements and insights are in refreshing contrast to the logical intricacies thought necessary in describing the syntax of the preposition. Subject and object for instance, though he sees no reason why they should not continue to be referred to as 'nominative word' and 'accusative word', are held to mark their functions by position alone. He also notes the peculiar ability of English words to cross the boundaries between the parts of speech, remarking on the tendency of nouns to 'degenerate' into verbs, as in *a house/to house*. Cooper, though he declares English syntax to be almost entirely dependent on prepositions, adds to this structural statement a logical element similar to that contained in the Port-Royal Grammar: 'The substantive, about which something is affirmed or denied, agrees with the verb or copula...That which is affirmed or denied is called the predicate.' The reference to 'affirmation' has distinctly Port-Royal connotations, as has the statement that in 'improper and elliptical sentences' from which prepositions are omitted in everyday speech the 'correct' syntax can be restored, constituting yet one more witness to the growing belief that there is an underlying logically correct structure to language.[359] Most of Cooper's assertions – an example is his treatment of the interjection as a sentence substitute – could however stem just as well from Wilkins as from Port-Royal. The sources are perhaps irrelevant. What is important is that English vernacular grammar, hitherto

[358] *English Grammar*, pp. 36–7.
[359] *Grammatica*, pp. 171–2. Salmon, 'James Shirley and Some Problems of Seventeenth-Century Grammar', p. 293, remarks that the terms subject and predicate were not actually used as grammatical (as opposed to logical) terms by English grammarians until early in the eighteenth century. The first use of the terms in a Latin grammar (replacing Ramus' and Sanctius' 'suppositum' and 'appositum') noted by Salmon is in Vossius' *De arte* (1635), no doubt consulted by Cooper, which speaks of 'suppositum sive subjectum' and 'appositum sive praedicatum'. I have however found the terms 'subjectum' and 'attributum' in Q. M. Corradus' *De lingua Latina* (Bologna, 1575), an isolated example of their use thus early by a humanist grammarian. For an interesting discussion of the history of the terms 'suppositum' and 'appositum', and of their ultimate displacement by 'subjectum' and 'praedicatum', see pp. 293–5 of Salmon's article. See also Padley, *Grammatical Theory* (1976), p. 52.

obstinately word-based, is now taking the whole sentence as its province.

In view of the novelty of Wallis' attempt to describe the structure of the English language without reference to the traditional Latin model it is easy to overestimate his importance. Beside such central seventeenth-century trends as the drive for pedagogical reform and the quest for an artificial language in which to express the concepts of the new science, his contribution to linguistic theory may seem relatively slight. As J. A. Kemp stresses in his edition of the *Grammatica*,[360] it does Wallis' reputation no good to claim that he was 'head and shoulders above all previous or contemporary grammarians or that he revolutionized the approach to grammar writing'. If O. Funke[361] sees his work as a giant step forward, it is because he threw off the Latin yoke and paid genuine attention to features peculiar to English. Wallis is undoubtedly of importance for the history of English vernacular grammar, and in this respect his work marks a turning-point. It embodies one of two major contemporary trends, that is to say an empiricism, a readiness to present the observed facts without a priori assumptions, that is typical of the endeavours of the Royal Society. The austerity of his empirical approach may be compared to that of the French 'usage' grammarians, whose chief representative is Vaugelas, reigning in France at the same period. Cooper on the other hand is more interesting for a history of grammatical *theory*, indicative as he is of the coming supremacy of rationalism in grammar. Both authors, by their insistence on the expression of syntactic relationships by means of prepositions, prepare the coming reign of logic in linguistic theory. But it is Cooper with his semasiological framework taken from Wilkins and ultimately from Campanella's philosophical grammar, who best illustrates the second, rationalistic trend. Here again, in the attempt to equate logic with grammar, we may note the extent to which the tenets of Scholasticism continue to inform seventeenth-century thought. They too are an important element in the development, which will reach its apogee in the following century, of a theory of universal grammar using the metalanguage of logic.

The interest of the pedagogically orientated English grammars of the seventeenth century lies in the various stages in the struggle to

[360] *John Wallis's Grammar of the English Languge*, p. 37.
[361] 'Die frühzeit der englischen Grammatik', p. 37.

free the vernacular from the Latin yoke. This struggle is carried out, in true English fashion, on empirical bases, and often enough bears the imprint of classroom practice. It is not perhaps surprising that when a type of general grammar emerges in England, it too has its roots in empiricism and – like the work of Lewis – in Baconian sensualism.

Part II

Universal grammar

3. THE BEGINNINGS OF THE UNIVERSALIST APPROACH

Since N. Chomsky's popularization of the terms,[1] it has been a commonplace of linguistic theory to speak of periods of 'observational adequacy', in which linguists content themselves with the description of the 'surface' details of a language, and periods of 'explanatory adequacy' in which they interest themselves in its underlying content. The medieval modistic grammarians such as Thomas of Erfurt, applying to language the tenets of Aristotelian Scholastic philosophy, with a distinction between 'verbum oris' (surface discourse) and 'verbum mentis' (the logical structure underlying it), belong to a period of the second type.[2] The humanist grammarians of the Renaissance, self-consciously rejecting both the medieval linguists' 'barbarous' Latin and their intricate apparatus of 'modes of signifying' and other Scholastic concepts, represent a return to straightforward linguistic description. Their aim is the reinstatement of elegant Latin, and to this end they base their observations on the grammars of Donatus (c. 350) and Priscian (c. 500), unalloyed by Scholastic accretions. The belief in the existence of an underlying (logical) content entails an accompanying belief that the framework of this content will be applicable to any language, and in this respect the late medieval theorists, though they confine themselves to Latin, are universal grammarians. Their basic assumption is Aristotle's dictum that though men differ in speech, 'the mental affections themselves, of which words are primarily signs, are the same for the whole of mankind'.[3] Their premise is the philosophical one that languages differ in 'accident' but are identical in 'substance'.

[1] Cf. *Aspects of the Theory of Syntax*, Cambridge, Mass., p. 36, where Chomsky equates 'the attempt to achieve explanatory adequacy' with 'the attempt to discover linguistic universals'.

[2] On the terms 'verbum oris' and 'verbum mentis' see Salmon's review of Chomsky's *Cartesian Linguistics*, pp. 174–5.

[3] *De interpretatione*, cap. 1, in H. P. Cooke, *Aristotle: the Organon*, London, and Cambridge, Mass., 1938, p. 115.

Central to their endeavours is the search for some kind of *ratio* or underlying 'cause' of language,[4] a search which during the Renaissance period is temporarily in abeyance. Once the first great impetus of Renaissance descriptivism is spent however, linguistic theory finds itself at a cross-roads. It must either continue with the now exhausted method of description in the mixed formal and semasiological terms of the classical grammarians; or launch out into a thoroughgoing formalism in which the content level of language is ignored; or return to the search for some kind of *ratio* or cause. Many grammarians continued of course to produce works resulting from the first of these choices. The second option is represented by Ramism, which spread through northern Europe like a bush fire and then spent its force. The third, in a return to 'explanatory adequacy' and an attempt once more to apply a metalanguage to linguistic description, is exemplified by J. C. Scaliger's celebrated *De causis linguae Latinae* (1540). The title is significant enough, and it is echoed by Sanctius' *Minerva: seu de causis linguae Latinae* of 1587. It would be difficult to overestimate the importance of these two works as sources for the coming universal grammar movement. With them may be bracketed the Englishman Linacre's earlier *De emendata structura Latini sermonis* (1524). The metalanguage used by Scaliger is Aristotelian philosophy, and it is this thought system, in a neo-Scholastic guise, that forms the basis for the grammatical section of Campanella's *Philosophiae rationalis partes quinque* (1638) and the Spanish bishop Juan Caramuel's *Grammatica audax* (1654). The twin roots of the universal grammar movement are deeply embedded in the cultural history of the times. They are the empiricist, 'sense-realist' strand of thought centred more particularly on England and inextricably bound up with early science and the work of Bacon, and the rationalist movement usually associated with the name of Descartes on the Continent. The immediate source of the European vernacular grammarians' ideas on universal grammar lies however in the Latin works just mentioned. Linacre, Scaliger, Sanctius and Campanella each form the starting-point for important developments

---

[4] Cf. Thomas of Erfurt, *Grammatica speculativa*, cap. xlvi: 'res cognoscitur per suas causas... ergo per suas causas habet definiri'. The notion of causes was of considerable importance for medieval grammarians. G. L. Bursill-Hall (*Speculative Grammars of the Middle Ages*, The Hague and Paris, 1971, p. 28) notes that they looked to the *causae* to 'provide them with the most profound knowledge of the parts of speech, i.e. once these were found, it would then be possible... to determine the proper grammatical function of a word'.

in vernacular theory, and their separate approaches will accordingly be discussed at appropriate points in what follows. First however it will be necessary to consider two German authors, Ratke and Schottel, whose approach owes little to any of these sources. Wolfgang Ratke's universalism springs, as might be expected, from pedagogical motives rather than from any body of linguistic theory, and the approach of Justus Georg Schottel has forbears in the already discussed belief in some kind of mystical origin for the German language. Its origins lie deep in esoteric teachings on the Kabbalah, and in Luther's christianizing of these concepts in his view of language as the sheath of the sword of the spirit. These two authors then will be treated first, as representing a kind of intellectual hinge between the earlier, purely pedagogical approach of vernacular grammarians, and the application to the 'vulgar' tongues of universalist principles based on Latin precedents.

Ratke

In the year 1619 Ratke and his collaborators published a bilingual universal grammar with a specifically pedagogical purpose, the *Grammatica universalis* or *Allgemeine Sprachlehr*.[5] The orientation is almost exclusively didactic, and indeed Fürst Ludwig of Anhalt-Köthen ordered the work to be used in the schools in the year of its appearance. Ratke's concept of universality is not confined to grammar, for his team also produced, in similar bilingual format, both a 'Rhetorica universalis' ('Allgemeine Rednerlehr') and a 'Physica universalis' ('Allgemeine Naturkündigung'). The universalist pretensions of Ratke's *Sprachlehr* are but part of a wider tendency towards universalism in his work, whose aim was to comprehend all culture in a close-knit scientific system (hence the attraction of Ramism) in which all natural and social relationships would be brought into a definite order determined by human reason. In this he was a man of his times. Though he cannot simply be categorized as a rationalist – he has a Baconian insistence on the obtaining of knowledge through experience – in practice he attempted like the English artificial-language planners after him to classify all mental phenomena within an Aristotelian–Scholastic framework. It

---

[5] *Grammatica universalis pro didactica Ratichii / Allgemeine Sprachlehr nach der Lehrart Ratichii.*

is this attempt to comprehend all natural manifestations in a universal system that lies behind his idea of an all-embracing harmony of faith, nature and language ('Harmonie des Glaubens, der Natur und Sprachen'), which though the phrase figures prominently on his title-pages and is central to his didactic conceptions, never reached the stage of a fully argued theory. The notion forms the cornerstone of his linguistic and pedagogical teachings, for it is from harmony that there 'flows the clarity and truth of all learning and all languages'.[6] Lutheran Protestant piety has however also its role to play in the application of this theory, for only in so far as God is seen as the reasoning power informing all creation can an indwelling harmony be ascribed to language.[7] The principle running through 'all languages, arts and sciences', in both content and teaching methods, is what Ratke calls 'Gleichförmigkeit' or uniformity. Its pedagogical application calls for the composition for each individual language studied in school of grammars that 'übereinstimmen', or are all constructed according to the same plan. In this way the student can achieve that clarity of perception ('Scharffsinnigkeit') necessary in discerning both the 'Eygenschafften' or individual characteristics of each tongue, and those features in which the different languages coincide or 'übereinkommen'.[8] It is this pedagogical doctrine that is behind the proposal to translate the *Sprachlehr* into various languages in order to serve as a teaching manual for each. Rather than a theoretically based universal grammar as such, Ratke aims to produce a grammar that is generally applicable on a pedagogical level, and can be used via the medium of any of the main European languages in a practical teaching situation. German grammar, with a few necessary changes, can in this way provide the basis for the teaching of other languages, incidentally furnishing yet another cogent reason for the prior inculcation of the mother tongue. Ratke holds the almost Chomskyan position that once the student has mastered the grammar of his native language he ipso facto possesses the underlying framework of grammar *in general*, and in learning another tongue has only to familiarize

---

[6] The 'Allgemeine Verfassung der christlichen Schule' states that 'auss der Harmony fleusst her die Klar-und warheit aller Lehren und Sprachen'. Ising (*Wolfgang Ratkes Schriften*, I, 36) finds this striving after language harmony also in Ratke's contemporaries J. J. Scaliger (the son of J. C. Scaliger), Conrad Gesner and Elias Hutter.

[7] See Ising, *Wolfgang Ratkes Schriften*, I, 37.

[8] 'Artickel', in Stötzner, *Ratichianische Schriften*, II, 15.

himself with the features that are peculiar to it. Hence the emphasis on the principle of 'Sprachvergleichung' or comparison that motivates the preparation of Ratke's team of the various compendia of individual languages, all written according to the same basic plan and complemented by a 'Verstandtlehr' or logic. For Ratke language comparison is a necessary accompaniment to a theory of general grammar.

'Ratio vicit', declares the optimistic subtitle of Ratke's various works. But far from offering in the manner of Scaliger and Sanctius a demonstration of the underlying *ratio* of language, his *Sprachlehr* differs little from the average humanist teaching grammar. Though one of his overriding aims was to produce works easily assimilated by young pupils, the dry catechetical approach, in which the master no doubt intoned the seemingly endless questions beginning with 'Was ist' etc. and the pupils chanted back replies beginning with the inevitable Ramist 'Zweyerlei' ('twofold'), would be little to the taste of modern educational theory:

> How diverse are the characteristics [of the pure language]?
> Twofold: general and special...
> How diverse are those of the general?
> Twofold: similarity and dissimilarity...
> How is language pedagogy divided?
> Into general and special.[9]

This short excerpt gives an idea of the simple but no doubt deadening catechism of the *Sprachlehr*, whose Ramist inspiration is obvious. Proceeding by slow and lumbering dichotomies Ratke divides the 'pure language' that is the object of grammar into general and particular, and the general into analogous and anomalous, the whole reposing on his concept of 'Gleichförmigkeit' or uniformity. General grammar is defined as that which serves for all languages, but the contribution of the actual body of the *Sprachlehr* to this goal is slight. It is yet another mixed Ramist/traditional grammar, taking its definitions from Donatus, Melanchthon and Frischlin, but with a universalist veneer. But though the *Sprachlehr* is in this respect disappointing, the interest of Ratke's approach lies in his elaboration of the *pedagogical* implications of universal grammar, and more

---

[9] *Allgemeine Sprachlehr*, pp. 1–2.

particularly in his view of instruction in the mother tongue as providing a knowledge of general language structure as a basis for learning the other vernaculars and Latin. It is instructive to note that not only Ratke, but almost all the great philosophically orientated universal grammarians, were closely involved in schemes for educational reform.

Schottel

Ratke laboured mightily to introduce the mother tongue into the schools, but it is not he but Schottel who is referred to (on a plaque outside his former residence in Wolfenbüttel) as 'the father of German grammar'. Nor indeed was Schottel a professional teacher, but an administrator employed by the House of Brunswick. His *Teutsche Sprachkunst*[10] appeared in 1641 in an attempt to rival Gueintz and came into use in the schools of Nuremberg, at that time the centre of a movement concerned with the well-being and purification of the German language. His major contribution to grammatical studies is the *Ausführliche Arbeit von der Teutschen Haubt Sprache*[11] of 1663, an encyclopedic volume of close on fifteen hundred pages, which constitutes the first really important linguistic work in the vernacular. The first three books are a repetition of the *Teutsche Sprachkunst*, but additional matter includes a dictionary of German stem-words, a 'poetica Germanica', and a historical treatment of German writers. This lawyer (the title-page of the *Ausführliche Arbeit* describes him as a 'Hof-und Consistorial-Raht und Hofgerichtes Assessor'), a member of both the Fruchbringende Gesellschaft and the Nuremberg Blumenorden, became after the publication of his magnum opus a kind of *praeceptor grammaticae* for Germany, and probably the best-known proponent of linguistic purism.

There are definite connections between Schottel's work and that of Ratke's circle, particularly in the features that link certain of Schottel's concepts with Ratke's somewhat obscure notion of a natural harmony underlying all languages. The sixth of the 'Lobreden' or eulogies into which the *Sprachkunst* is divided contains

---

[10] Published in Brunswick. A second edition, longer by some three hundred pages, came out in 1651. In 1643 Schottel published *Der Teutschen Sprach Einleitung* (Lübeck), a short treatise dealing with the origins and nature of the German language.

[11] Published in Brunswick. (Reprinted Tübingen, ed. W. Hecht, 1967.)

an almost lyrical section which, with its distinctly Ratichian resonance, sets the general tone for Schottel's linguistic theory:

> What is more magnificent, among the mysteries of the divine gifts possessed by the human soul, than the innermost knowledge of language?...everything earthly is no more than a passing storm...But in language...there is concealed something far different, beyond any earthly origin...Language, says Luther, is the sheath in which lies hidden the sword of the spirit...indeed language runs through all the mysteries of Nature: so that he who is properly versed in language can by that very means find a path through Nature...and even converse with God Himself.[12]

Apart from the admitted Lutheran origins of this, it is not difficult to find in it a continuation of earlier theories as to the mysteries hidden away beneath German words. But if for Luther it is the divine message of the Scriptures that is concealed in them, for Schottel the 'hidden spirit' is that of the eternal secrets of Nature, as well as of the Divine[13] – a motif that is very much present in seventeenth-century German poetry. An echo of Ratichian doctrines is Schottel's belief that if, as he holds, the German language is built on the firmest of foundations, it is because they have been established by God and Nature working in concert.[14] Their permanence is assured by features in which German is particularly rich:

> The structure of any tongue is founded on its original, natural stem-words, which like enduringly firm roots spread moisture through the whole tree of language, allowing its shoots and many-veined branches to spread high and spaciously in finest purity, constant certainty and inexhaustible variety. To the extent that a language is well furnished with such stem-words, so will it bring forth rich and abundant fruit.[15]

We have already met the analogue of Schottel's language tree or *Sprachbaum* in Stieler's *Stammbaum* or 'stem-tree' which, after the manner of his 'wonderful and unusual' Chinese tree, puts out self-propagating roots and branches. There is no doubt that Stieler gets his inspiration for this fecund plant from Schottel. The two

---

[12] *Sprachkunst*, pp. 105–6.

[13] *Ibid.*, pp. 105–6: 'Also lest auch Gott der Herr seinen Willen, die grossen Geheimnissen aus der Ewigkeit, wie auch das wundersamste Wesen der natürlichen Dinge...uns Menschen ...verstehen, nur durch Hülfe und Handbietung der Sprachen.'

[14] *Ibid.*, pp. 105–6: 'also erhebet sich sonderlich die deutsche Sprache aus den gewissesten Gründen, welche Gott und die Natur darin ausgewirkt haben, empor'. Hankamer (*Die Sprache*, p. 126) notes that this motif is present in almost all seventeenth-century German poets, in whose work 'Das Ewige, die Wirklichkeit des naturhaften Lebens drückt sich [in der Sprache] leibhaft aus.'   [15] *Ibid.*, pp. 74–5.

quotations from the latter's *Sprachkunst* contain the kernel of his threefold beliefs about language: it is an almost mystical, hypostatized entity bound up with God and Nature in an existence far removed from any actual human use; its unchanging essence is founded in a system of 'original' and 'natural' stem-words; and its pristine roots must be guarded against corruption and contamination from outside. It follows that for Schottel it is morphology, the traditional *etymologia*, that is the most important part of grammar. The root meaning of the vernacular term ('Wortforschung') coincides with his view of its subject matter as 'the origins, attributes, derivation and composition of individual words, correctly investigated ['erforscht'] and enquired into'.[16] On this view, language is subject to generally valid laws of derivation and composition which it is the task of the grammarian to seek out.

Schottel's complaint that the vernacular is widely seen as having no 'right foundations' on which to base its grammar,[17] is a familiar one. The remedy however is not to follow the Latin model, but to 'set the age-old structure of the language not upon a bottomless, sandy foundation, but upon a firm, correct, immovable German basis, not taking foreign and often unserviceable rubble for squared stone'.[18] It is this 'age-old' German – the phrase 'die Uhralte Hauptsprache der Teutschen' runs like a refrain through Schottel's work – purged of foreign accretions, that forms the basis for linguistic description, and it is no doubt for this reason that he devotes immeasurably more space to historical questions than did any of his predecessors. He shares to a heightened degree the contemporary obsession with proving that the vernacular is the 'original' language, noting with approval Johannes Goropius Becanus' view that the first language is the 'old German or Cimbric [i.e. Celtic]', from which even Hebrew is descended.[19] Though he gives the European languages the status of dialects, they are all for him dialects of Celtic. Conversely, if German roots are present in almost all the languages of Europe, it is because those peoples anciently called Celts 'spoke German'.[20] The model to which his theory of linguistic description is to be applied is not however any of the direct descendants of this

---

[16] *Ausführliche Arbeit*, p. 181. This definition also appears in the *Sprachkunst*.
[17] See *Sprachkunst*, foreword. [18] *Ausführliche Arbeit*, p. 7.
[19] As the table of contents to the third eulogy of the *Ausführliche Arbeit* succinctly puts it, 'Celticam linguam esse Teutonicam'.
[20] *Sprachkunst*, p. 152; *Ausfürliche Arbeit*, foreword and p. 34.

'Uhralte Teutsche oder Cimbrische Sprache'. Schottel had a profound distrust of the spoken word, a distrust which M. H. Jellinek attributes to his Low German origins. His preference goes to written literary High German, an artificial product or 'Kunstsprache' to be mastered only after careful study.[21] The increasing claims of the Meissen dialect of the east midlands to be recognized as a standard he rejects out of hand on the grounds that any actually spoken norms are inappropriate.[22] Any kind of lower-class usage is similarly, at this date, out of the question: did Vergil follow the usage of farm-hands?[23] Good German is to be found in Luther and in the 'Kanzleisprachen' of the imperial administration. The opinions on usage scattered throughout Schottel's work indicate plainly however that in any contest between the claims of even an elevated usage and those of the idealized German his theories require, the latter must be allowed to prevail. It is true that he carefully considers both sides of the question, quoting Seneca to the effect that general acceptance finally legitimizes any usage, even the most seemingly inappropriate, and Quintilian's opinion that the written language must follow norms actually in use. He even seems ready to treat usage as the final arbiter: 'der Gebrauch ist ein rechter Lehrmeister der Sprachen'. But in the last analysis he is simply admitting that usage has its province.[24] Behind most pronouncements on usage at this period lurks the fear that if once it is given its head, corruption will set in, and the language will be irreversibly contaminated. Schottel was a lawyer, and it is to customary law that he turns for his final decision: 'The customary usage of a thing which is not good is no usage. Usage must be according to reason, but it cannot be so if it is clearly against the law.'[25] As the lawyers say, 'aliud esse conseutudinem, aliud corruptelam': custom is one thing, corruption another. Further support is found in Scaliger's remark[26] that a usage running counter

[21] The language cannot be – in contrast to the 'mother's milk' theory – 'schlumpweise aus dem gemeinen Winde erschnappen'.

[22] See Jellinek, *Geschichte der neuhochdeutschen Grammatik*, I, 133. See also K. Miles, *The Strong Verb in Schottel's Ausführliche Arbeit*, Philadelphia, 1933, pp. 10–11. Unfortunately the value of Miles' work is reduced by frequent unacknowledged repetition, sometimes in word-for-word translation, of Jellinek.

[23] *Sprachkunst*, p. 4: 'auch wird Virgilius nicht grossgeachtet haben was ein Bauerhaus hinter dem Viehe...für Worte gebrauchet haben möchte'.

[24] *Ibid.*, p. 2.

[25] *Ibid.*, p. 3. Schottel cites this in Latin, perhaps from a contemporary law manual.

[26] *De causis linguae Latinae*, I, cap. ii.

to the laws of language is no usage, but a perverse corruption.[27] Since usage always carries with it the risk of corruption, it cannot be blindly followed. As Schottel's Latin table of contents puts it, 'Corruptela non est norma in lingua Germanica.'[28] In the age-long analogy/anomaly debate, he accordingly plumps squarely for analogy. Where *ratio* and *consuetudo* are in conflict, the prior claims of *ratio* must lead the grammarian to follow the 'analogica linguae fundamenta'.

These 'analogical foundations of language' are provided by the genius of the German language, hypostatized and independent of any users. Others before Schottel had applied analogy to linguistic description, but no one had thus elevated it to the status of a norm generated by the language itself. Since for Schottel, as for Ratke, the foundations of language are in God and in Nature, it follows that the grammarian, far from *imposing* analogical norms and rules, actually *finds* them already implanted in the language. They are already present in what Schottel calls the 'Grundrichtigkeit' of a tongue, and especially is this true of German, whose innate norms are signposts to good usage – 'des guten Gebrauchs Wegzeiger' – ingeniously implanted in the language's structure.[29] In this way good usage and the ideal, hypostatized norm are brought to coincide. If we take into account Schottel's further claim that the root-words of the 'age-old German language' still in the main bear their original meanings,[30] it is not surprising that it is these roots that constitute the 'signposts to usage', and provide the language with its 'Grundrichtigkeit' or essential, unchanging foundation. The term has connotations of regularity, and it is in the consideration of the etymology and morphology of the language that this regularity reveals itself. Relevant here is Goropius' opinion that the 'German or Cimbric language' is the original one because it contains not only the oldest words, but also the truest and most intrinsic representations of reality. Indeed, if the German language is to be taken as a model of 'Grundrichtigkeit' it must be shown, by a thesis which recalls that of the artificial language-planners in England, to be in concordance

[27] As Schottel puts it (*Sprachkunst*, p. 3), 'Derselbiger Gebrauch, dem ein Hauptgesetz oder der Grund der Sprachen entegen laufft, ist kein Gebrauch, sondern eine missbräuchliche Verfälschung.' [28] *Ausführliche Arbeit*, table of contents to the first eulogy.
[29] *Ibid.*, p. 10.
[30] *Ibid.*, p. 42. Schottel none the less recalls, in an aside, Horace's often-quoted 'Multa renascentur, quae jam cecidere, cadentque quae nunc sunt in honore vocabula, si volet usus.'

with the things of which its words are signs. In that other age-old debate initiated by the Greeks,[31] the nature versus convention controversy, Schottel is accordingly a Platonist (he specifically mentions Plato and Ficino), believing words to contain within themselves something of the nature of the things they represent. German words are particularly apt to express what he calls, using a Latin term, 'ipsius rei consistentiam', and he gives many examples to illustrate their 'elegant congruence with Nature itself'.[32] They are not instituted fortuitously but 'by a certain force and reason' of Nature or, as Ficino puts it, by 'a kind of divine virtue'.[33] The link with earlier opinions, of kabbalistic origin, is confirmed by Schottel's quotation of Ickelsamer's view that there is no word in the entire German language that does not 'have its name from its office, by an especial mystery'.[34] Schottel's standpoint on the words of his native tongue is in agreement: 'their concordant sound is so wonderfully rich, their harmony so much exceeding that of any art, that they are indeed entirely formed by the workings of Nature'.[35] It follows that if the root-words of the language are properly to carry out their function of ensuring its structural stability or 'Grundrichtigkeit', they must be 'euphonious, and intrinsically expressive of their thing, whose name they are'.[36]

Schottel's fourth, fifth and sixth 'eulogies' of the German tongue accordingly treat respectively the 'natural origin and excellent attributes of the German letters and root-words', the 'remarkable derivation of words in which our mother tongue is so wonderfully rich', and the 'wonderfully abounding qualities' of compounds. That the overriding excellence of the German language lies for Schottel in its aptitude for word-formation is shown by his devoting, of the three hundred pages which the *Ausführliche Arbeit* reserves to the noun, well over two hundred to derivation and composition. In his analysis the three constitutive elements of the 'Grundrichtigkeit' of a language are its roots, its derivational suffixes, and its inflectional endings.

[31] On the Greek analogy/anomaly and nature/convention debates see Robins, *A Short History of Linguistics*, pp. 17–22.
[32] *Ausführliche Arbeit*, p. 50: 'Verba germanica ipsa rerum exprimendarum natura elegantissime congruere.'
[33] *Ibid.*, p. 58. [34] *Ibid.*, p. 60.
[35] *Ibid.*, p. 59.
[36] *Ibid.*, p. 62; *Sprachkunst*, p. 75. Many of Schottel's examples are onomatopoeic, or at any rate sound-symbolic, e.g. the word *Wasser*, of which he asks, 'Was kan das Geräusch des fliessenden Wassers wesentlicher abbilden?'

These elements form a closed list, whose members and combinatory possibilities must be known if one is fully to penetrate the hidden foundations of the language. 'In these three...consists the whole fitness of the German language to signify, powerfully and sufficiently, almost everything it needs to signify.'[37] To the fact that things inevitably outnumber the roots required to signify them, Schottel opposes the ability of various combinations of the three basic elements to cater for all desired meanings. Thus by finite means are an infinite number of significations produced.[38] To say that Schottel took his notion of roots ('Stammwörter') from Hebrew grammar would be to state a commonplace. His originality lies in his insistence that *every single syllable* of the language, if it is to contribute to the underlying linguistic system or 'Grundrichtigkeit', must be classifiable under one of the headings root, derivational suffix or inflectional ending. This implies for Schottel however that just as every letter of a word is a single sound unit, so must every root be monosyllabic, both in origin and by its nature.[39] Just as with other norms imposed throughout the history of grammatical theory, this strictly applied requirement leads to a distortion of the forms actually existent in the language. Since Schottel has decreed that every root is monosyllabic, it follows that any final -*e* in a dissyllabic word is ipso facto an inflectional ending. In pursuit of uniformity, he removes the -*e* from singular words such as *Sprache*, but adds it to plural words like *Wegzeiger*, thus giving his printed page a somewhat eccentric appearance. Similarly, in this insistence on monosyllabicity, compounds are to be treated as a basic form or 'Grund' plus a subjoined one, in analyses recalling modern ones of compounds into 'headword' and 'modifier'.[40]

Schottel revives an earlier distinction between *grammatica methodica*, the discussion of linguistic structure, and *grammatica enarrativa*, the consideration of the forms used by poets and prose writers. In this he differs from Vossius,[41] the most important Latin grammarian of the time, who rejects the second of these as having nothing to do with a rational approach to language description. He follows Vossius

[37] *Ausführliche Arbeit*, p. 1247.
[38] Any parallel with Chomsky's generative syntax is here illusory. Schottel remains on the morphological level, his syntactic notions being staidly traditional.
[39] *Sprachkunst*, p. 87.
[40] Cf. Brekle, 'The Seventeenth Century', p. 317.
[41] *De arte grammatica* (1635).

however in dividing *grammatica methodica* into 'natural' and 'artificial',
the former concerning what is common to all languages, the latter
describing features that are peculiar to a particular idiom. He
obviously, like so many of his contemporaries and the medieval
modistic grammarians before them, supposes the categories of Latin
and German to be universal, for the parts of speech, gender and
number, and grammatical concord all fall within the province of
natural grammar. To artificial grammar, on the other hand, belong
formal inflections such as case endings. These comments are however
not reflected in the general treatment of the *etymologia*, which is
derivative[42] and differs little from the customary Latin-based type
of vernacular grammar. The definitions of the word-classes are by
and large those of Melanchthon's Latin grammar of 1525. The syntax
too is much indebted to Clajus (1578), and does not go beyond the
usual discussion of government and congruence. To detail all these
matters here would add nothing to the doctrines established by his
predecessors. The first thousand pages of the *Ausführliche Arbeit*,
devoted to the ten 'Lobreden' or eulogies of the German language,
to word-formation and accidence, and to syntax and versification,
by no means however exhaust the work. A further five hundred pages
are taken up by treatises on such themes as the 'old German Celtic
names', proverbs, and a list of root-words. Thus does Schottel fulfil
his promise[43] to provide a work surpassing the bounds of 'grammar'
in the ordinary sense of the word. His combination in one volume
of various elements of general interest, a résumé of what vernacular
grammarians had so far achieved, and his own original contribution
on the 'Grundrichtigkeit' of the German language, produced a
Sprachkompendium that eclipsed all previous work. In a study other
than one devoted to synchronic theory, his contribution to historical
linguistics, predating that of Leibniz, would have to be discussed.[44]
All future developments in German grammatical theory take their
starting-point from him. The claim of his 'barocke summa
philologica'[45] to an important position in the history of linguistics –
his influence lasted well into the eighteenth century[46] – rests on his

[42] A major source is obviously Clajus' *Grammatica Germanicae linguae* (1578), possibly in part
via Ritter's *Grammatica Germanica nova* (1616).
[43] *Ausführliche Arbeit*, p. 178.
[44] See H. Aarsleff, 'Leibniz on Locke on Language', *American Philosophical Quarterly*, 1 (1964),
pp. 169ff.   [45] Thus Hankamer, *Die Sprache*, p. 124.
[46] No doubt it was the sheer size of the work that delayed the appearance of a second edition
of the *Ausführliche Arbeit* until 1737.

elaborate theory of word-structure, and his basing on it of a universalist theory of 'Grundrichtigkeit' or language purity and stability.[47] He gives in fact the curious example of a universal grammar that is word-based rather than sentence-based, and is deemed to be particularly applicable to his own native tongue. In Schottel too is exemplified the all-pervading drive to purism that is such a prominent feature of late-seventeenth-century European attitudes to language. His root-words are to be kept pure and unadulterated, for a structure is only as firm as its foundations.[48] But over and above the uncertainties of actual usage in the various regional and social dialects there lies the unchangeable, 'age-old' German language, the only true linguistic reality, a hypostatized entity whose nature and rules it is the grammarian's task to lay bare. For Schottel universal grammar of his particular type is both the guarantee of the structural stability of the language and its product.

ii THE SEARCH FOR MODELS: LINACRE, SCALIGER AND THE ARISTOTELIANS

Most authors of vernacular grammars between 1500 and 1700 have no higher aim than the simple – and necessary – production of practical manuals for the classroom or for the use of travellers abroad. They are down-to-earth language teachers with a living to make. Their interests are accordingly pedagogical rather than theoretical, and any linguistic theory is implicit in the derivative framework and definitions of their grammars, rather than the result of conscious cerebration. There are however exceptions to this, some of whom, like Schottel, are among the leading grammarians of their time. Schottel's theoretical stance, as we have seen, is rooted in a long-standing traditional belief, with kabbalistic overtones, in the mysteries implicit in the structure of German words – what P. Hankamer calls his 'philological mysticism' – while Ratke's in many ways similar

[47] Thus, no less than the Latinizing grammarians, or those who use the metalanguage of logic or philosophy, Schottel is following a norm. On the notion of norm in sixteenth- and seventeenth-century grammars see G. A. Padley, 'La norme dans la tradition des grammairiens', *La norme linguistique*, ed. E. Bédard and J. Maurais, Quebec and Paris, 1983, pp. 69–104. Specifically on Schottel see pp. 97–9.
[48] *Ausführliche Arbeit*, p. 49: 'Sicut aedificium fundamini, sic lingua radicibus innititur.' A certain amount of explicatory material in Latin is included, as a gesture to non-German-speaking readers. This concession in no way mitigates Schottel's uncompromisingly purist attitude to the vernacular itself.

doctrine of an at once mystical and natural linguistic harmony is of more relevance for his pedagogy than for his grammatical theory. Those vernacular authors who do follow a developed linguistic theory, find their models in certain great Latin works of the period: in Linacre's *De emendata structura* (1524), J. C. Scaliger's *De causis linguae Latinae* (1540), Sanctius' *Minerva* (1587) and Campanella's *Grammatica* (1638). Taking one or more of these authors as their basis, they evolve systems of universal grammar applicable to the various vernaculars. The interest of their work lies in their application to vernacular grammar of models which, though supposedly universal, are very much conceived with Latin in mind.

Linacre

The first of these Latin authors, Linacre, has been somewhat neglected by writers on the origins of the universal grammar movement. He is however of primary importance, above all as a parallel to, or even a source for, those syntactic notions in Sanctius' *Minerva* that are taken up by the Port-Royal authors in 1660 and are basic for the approach in their celebrated *Grammaire générale et raisonnée*.[49] Yet another of those humanist physicians who take an interest in grammar, and a scholar of international standing, he lectured at Oxford and was in part responsible for the education of Erasmus and Thomas More. His *De emendata structura* (1524)[50] is interesting chiefly for two features: the retention of a medieval syntactic theory in terms of transitive and intransitive 'persons of construction',[51] which does not concern us here; and a treatment of elliptical constructions which, sixty years before Sanctius' similar treatment, provides a basis for later linguistic theory. His influence on vernacular grammarians is discernible in Jean Drosée's quadrilingual grammar of 1544,[52] in the work of Alexander Hume, already considered in treating the Ramist authors,[53] and in P. Giambullari's

[49] On Linacre's influence on theories of universal grammar see Padley, 'L'importance de Thomas Linacre (env. 1460–1524) comme source', pp. 17–56.

[50] Published in London. (There is a Scolar Press reprint, Menston, 1968.)

[51] On these medieval syntactic theories see Robins, *A Short History of Linguistics*, pp. 81–4.

[52] *Grammaticae quadrilinguis partitiones*, Paris, 1544. The preface is dated 1542.

[53] Hume's Latin grammars contain an important syntactic element borrowed from Linacre (see Padley, *Grammatical Theory* (1976), pp. 116–17). His vernacular *Of the Orthographie and Congruitie of the Britan Tongue*, though it too shows Linacre's influence, contains no syntax and is not of interest in a discussion of universal grammar.

De la lingua of 1551.[54] Ultimately, via Sanctius, it is felt in the Port-Royal grammar. Several tendencies come together in his work, which produce a climate favourable to the development of universal grammar. It should of course be borne in mind that the medieval modistic grammarians had evolved a system of universal grammar, reposing on the categories of Scholastic philosophy, and that in returning to such a system authors such as Scaliger and Campanella are repeating their concepts or modifying them. Roger Bacon had quite early decreed that in all languages, however much they may vary in surface details or 'accident', the underlying grammatical 'substance' (to use the technical terms of Aristotelian philosophy) is the same.[55] This underlying substance can in language only be of a semantic or logical nature, belonging to the content level as distinct from the expression level of language. Certain medieval theorists accordingly make a distinction between 'verbum oris' or discourse, and 'verbum mentis' or the underlying mental syntax common to all languages. The modistic grammarians go out of their way to stress that it is not the 'vox' or unit of expression[56] (the material component of language) that concerns the grammarian, but the linguistic sign, that is to say the union of form and meaning.[57] But in practice they virtually ignore the formal side of language, in favour of a philosophically based semantic system of 'modes of signifying' in which e.g. nouns are seen as signifying by the mode of permanence, and verbs by the mode of flux and change. In the final analysis however, they insist on the abiding link between language and the real world: 'grammatica est de signis rerum', words have referents. It is precisely this link that will be tacitly ignored by later, seventeenth- and eighteenth-century universal grammarians, whose grammars are primarily grammars of concepts, with both grammatical form and the dual nature of the linguistic sign kept well in the background. The medieval grammarians follow Priscian, who had himself asked what else a part of speech could be but a mental concept. It is this emphasis on concepts that is the hall-mark of late medieval grammar and, taken together with the belief that the same concepts are present

[54] *De la lingua che si parla e scrive in Firenze*, Florence, 1551.
[55] *Greek Grammar*, ed. E. Nolan and S. A. Hirsch, Cambridge, 1902, p. 27: 'Grammatica una et eadem est secundum substantiam in omnibus linguis, licet accidentaliter varietur.'
[56] One hesitates to use the term 'phonetic' in discussing the work of these early theorists.
[57] Thomas of Erfurt, *Grammatica speculativa*, cap. vi: 'vox inquantum vox, non consideratur a Grammatico; sed inquantum signum'.

in all men and in all languages, it leads to a situation in which different linguistic structures, of which one is taken to be the logically basic one, express at least latently the same concepts. Since Aristotle said that language symbolizes concepts, it follows that for modistic grammarians such as Thomas of Erfurt (*c.* 1300) the purpose of syntax is the expression of concepts or 'passiones animae'.[58] Hence syntax must operate on two levels, that of 'sense'[59] and that of the intellect. The first type occurs when all mental *constructibilia* of a syntactic group are expressed in discourse: *ego lego*. The second occurs when one or more are not expressed, but are apprehended by the intellect: *lego*. In other words there is not an exact correspondence between discourse and the underlying 'mentis conceptum', a fact which gives rise to the constant search in late medieval and humanist grammar for expanded structures into which supposedly abbreviated ones can be 'resolved'. In the examples just given the expanded structure is in fact a possible structure of Latin, but this is not the case in the doctrine that the concept of 'being' underlies all verbs,[60] as in *amat = est amans*. The danger of all this is that it may encourage the belief that language is a matter of the stringing together of lexical concepts, rather than at the same time a matter of the indication of grammatical meanings by accompanying changes in form. In justice to the medieval modistic grammarians it must however be stated that they never lose sight of the fact that *grammatical* meanings are consignified, that is to say signified in addition, over and above mere *lexical* meanings, and it is this fact that is catered for by their doctrine of the 'modi significandi' or ways in which grammatical meaning is expressed.

Scholars at Linacre's date still have one foot in the medieval world, and he himself would have received an education still strongly marked by Scholasticism. It is accordingly not surprising that he too puts emphasis on the consignification of grammatical meanings, but

[58] *Ibid.*, cap. xlv: '*Ea quae sunt in voce, sunt notae passionum earum, quae sunt in anima* [Aristotle, *De interpretatione*, cap. 1]...ergo constructio...in Grammatica, est finaliter per exprimendum mentis conceptum.'

[59] 'Secundum sensum' presumably means here according to the elements of expression that are actually perceived in discourse.

[60] Thomas of Erfurt, *Grammatica speculativa*, cap. xxvii: 'hoc verbum, *est*, in omni verbo includitur, tanquam radix omnium'. Cf. J. P. Mullally, *The Summulae Logicales of Peter of Spain*, Notre Dame, Indiana, 1945, p. xci: 'In defining a categorical proposition, Peter of Spain says that every such proposition is composed of...a subject, a predicate, and a copula...But if a categorical proposition always includes a copula, the verb "is" must be included in every verb as its root...The statement "A man thinks" should be resolved into "A man is thinking".'

this time by corresponding changes in the formal shape of words, with a careful distinction between those categories (such as the division into common or proper nouns) which depend solely on semantic criteria derived from extra-linguistic sources, and those which depend on variations in linguistic form.[61] His system is however sometimes breached, particularly in the treatment of mood in the traditional terms of the expression of a state of mind or 'affectio animi'. At first he claims that in mood such states of mind must be signalled by a change in form – 'per vocem significatae'. His invention of a 'potential' mood however reposes on no corresponding change in form, and is an indication that when it suits his purpose he is prepared to base grammar on meaning to the exclusion of formal structure. The inherited classical models, largely Donatus and Priscian, had relied on a mixture of formal and semasiological criteria. But it is interesting to note how, as time goes on, the formal elements are increasingly jettisoned in favour of purely semantic ones. Authors are of course aware of differences in form, and catalogue them in their paradigms, but such differences play a diminishing role in the *theoretical justification* of their grammars. This tendency begins quite early, notably in the works of Melanchthon, whose rigorous exclusion of formal elements from his definitions, in an anticipation of seventeenth- and eighteenth-century procedures, represents a major departure from the traditional humanist use of mixed formal and semasiological criteria. His noun 'signifies a thing, not an action', while his verb signifies 'to act or be acted upon'.[62] The point at issue here is that these definitions are applicable to any language that contains 'nouns' and 'verbs', regardless of any differences in form between one tongue and another. It is approaches such as these that sow the seeds of a reemployment of universal grammar. Further, they illustrate the contention of this study that the origins of what happens for instance in the Port-Royal *Grammaire générale* and in vernacular grammar in general, lie deep in earlier procedures in the Latin tradition itself. Melanchthon and Linacre are already, in the first quarter of the sixteenth century, setting in motion a bias towards purely semantic description that will come to full fruition in the universal grammar movement.

A tenet of seventeenth-century theory is, to quote A. Richardson's

[61] *De emendata structura*, 1, f. 1^r: 'Nominum variae sunt species, aliae a vocibus, aliae a rebus sumptae.'　　　　　　[62] *Grammatica* (Paris ed., 1527), f. 26^r.

The Logicians School-Master (1657), that language is essentially 'a garment to cloath our thought'. This implies that a particular concept or group of concepts can be 'clothed' in various ways, and it is interesting in this respect that Linacre devotes no less than twenty-eight pages to what he calls the 'enallage' (a Greek word meaning *interchange*) of the parts of speech in discourse. According to this an adjective (e.g. *recens*) can be substituted for an adverb, and adverbs in turn (of especial interest in view of the Port-Royal treatment of adverbs as abbreviations of prepositional phrases) are semantically substitutable for structures consisting of preposition plus relative pronoun (*unde = a quo*). The treatment of 'enallage' had been a feature of the Latin tradition since Priscian (*c.* 500), but what is distinctive to Linacre is the exceptional amount of space devoted to it, and the context – a very extended treatment of syntax and elliptical structures – in which it appears. The implications of this treatment of substitution, namely that mental concepts can be variously actualized by items of discourse, become explicit in Linacre's sixth book ('Of the figures of construction'), in which elliptic structures are held to involve the absence of an element which does in fact appear in the semantically parallel expanded or 'legitimate' construction. He accordingly – a feature in which he will be followed by later grammarians – divides syntax into the two varieties 'justa' and 'figurata', the latter covering logically incomplete structures whose full, expanded version is given by the former. W. K. Percival, while noting that the theory of ellipsis was 'propounded first' by Linacre, regards his treatment as 'merely a further elaboration of notions which had been familiar since antiquity', notions which are illustrated in the 'stylistic manual' of Valla's *De linguae Latinae elegantia* composed around 1440. Valla's analyses, he holds, can be rephrased in Linacre's system without any change of content.[63] Similar views are held by M. Breva-Claramonte, who intent as he is on promoting Sanctius' claims to be 'the father of general grammar',[64] regards Linacre as the 'first immediate source' of his

---

[63] 'Deep and Surface Structure Concepts in Renaissance and Medieval Syntactic Theory', *History of Linguistic Thought and Contemporary Linguistics*, ed. H. Parret, Berlin and New York, 1976, pp. 246–7, 252–3.

[64] *Sanctius' Theory of Language*, Amsterdam and Philadelphia, 1983, p. 7. It is true that Breva-Claramonte is quoting Menéndez y Pelayo, *Obras completas*, XXXVIII (1947), p. 416. He is none the less of the opinion that Linacre simply 'followed Quintilian's and Priscian's theoretical tenets and extended their analyses to cover a larger body of data' ('Sanctius's Antecedents, Part 2', *Language Sciences*, XLV (1977), p. 17), whereas Sanctius applied a logical *ratio* to elliptical constructions.

inspiration, but as producing a less powerful description of elliptic constructions than that of Sanctius, and one only covering 'cases where the evidence for the elliptical elements is obvious from usage'.[65] The attribution of paternity in linguistic history is a pleasing game, and one should not perhaps take too seriously the various descriptions of Sanctius as the father of general grammar, of Schottel as the father of German grammar, or of Saussure as the father of modern linguistics. One must however take issue with Breva-Claramonte's statement that 'in a way Scaliger had continued the work of the *modistae*, and Linacre that of Priscian'.[66] It is my contention that it is Linacre's *De emendata structura* that, sixteen years before Scaliger, first brings back into Renaissance grammar certain tenets of the modistic grammarians. Undeniably, his treatment of ellipse continues a long rhetorical tradition dating at least from Priscian and exemplified in the pages of Valla. Where he represents an advance, or rather a return to modistic hypotheses, is in his definition of 'constructio justa' as that which faithfully reproduces the 'sensus animi' or grammar of the mind.[67] In this he is plainly bringing back into grammar the late-medieval distinction between syntactic structures 'secundum sensum' and 'secundum intellectum', between 'verbum oris' and 'verbum mentis'. The approach is no longer merely rhetorical. A 'figurative' structure such as *Cicero erat brevis staturae* is held to be an abbreviation of the 'true' construction *Cicero erat HOMO brevis staturae*, and *Non est humani judicii* is restated as *Non est RES humani judicii*.[68] Linacre is patently not the first to use many of his expansions. Despauterius' *Rudimenta* (1514)[69] treats the neuter adjective *triste* standing without a substantive as the semantic equivalent of *tristis res*,[70] and follows medieval precedent in 'resolving' *amo* into *sum amans*. Linacre's doctrine that intransitive verbs require logical expansion by the addition of a cognate accusative (*vivo = vivo vitam*) is similarly not original to him. More interesting is the expansion of *me authore* into *me enti authore* on the grounds that without a participle

---

[65] *Sanctius' Theory of Language*, pp. 55, 62.

[66] *Ibid.*, p. 4.

[67] Cf. *De emendata structura*, f. xxii[v]: 'ad sensum animi prodendum, justa se habet partium inter se constructio'. On Linacre's treatment of elliptical structures see Padley, *Grammatical Theory* (1976), pp. 53–5.

[68] *De emendata structura*, f. xxvi[v]. Linacre's use of *res* recalls Sanctius' similar use of *negotium*.

[69] I have consulted the Paris edition of 1527.

[70] The time-honoured example is *triste lupus stabulis* ('a wolf is a sad matter for flocks of sheep') in which *triste = tristis res*.

'understood' this structure is not grammatically acceptable ('nisi participio subaudito consistere non potest'). Linacre's importance in the history of linguistics lies in his having incorporated the 'figures of speech' decisively into grammar, preceding Sanctius on this point by some sixty years, and the Port-Royal Latin grammar by over a hundred. Capital for the future development of universal grammar is his positing of 'true' underlying constructions (as in *me enti authore*) into which logically incomplete 'figurative' ones can be expanded.

Drosée and Giambullari

It is precisely Linacre's view of language as consisting of a string of concepts all of which may or may not be expressed in discourse, that is the standpoint of the universal grammarians. Jean Drosée's[71] quadrilingual grammar (1544) repeats this view, defining the sentence ('oratio') as an arrangement of words in syntactic agreement whose purpose is the expression of mental concepts.[72] There is no doubt as to the source of this, for Drosée mentions Linacre in the Latin section of his grammar, and cites his setting up of a potential mood. Further, in treating each declinable part of speech he follows Linacre in listing separately those features ('secundum rem') that depend on extra-linguistic criteria and are purely semantic, and those ('secundum vocem') that are formally marked. There is in his grammar an almost Ramist formalism, with terse dichotomies and close enumeration of word endings,[73] but it is accompanied by a constant willingness to explain elliptical constructions in Linacre's manner, as for instance in the class of 'transitive' verbs which are held to have cognate accusatives (*vivo = vivo vitam*). The four languages Latin, Greek, Hebrew and French are treated, Drosée being particularly at pains to draw parallels between French and Hebrew. He finds a 'great similarity' between the two languages, holding that by reference to Hebrew 'French words can be more clearly explained'. Especially is this true in their respective 'manieres de signifier', and it is no doubt for this reason that he sets up for French a three-word-class system

[71] The Latin title gives the author's name as 'Drosaeus'. Brunot, *Histoire de la langue française*, II, 138–9, has the spelling 'Drosai', while Chevalier, *Histoire de la syntaxe*, has 'Drosée'.

[72] *Grammaticae quadrilinguis partitiones*, p. 156: 'Quid oratio? Congrua dictionum ordinatio ad sensus mentis exprimendos.'

[73] Drosée precedes Sanctius in remarking that if adjectives did not exist there would be no need for a category of gender (*ibid.*, p. 53).

239

consisting of noun ('to name things and people'), verb ('to signify actions or operations'), and consignifiers. The purely semantic definitions used here are significant, and in sharp contrast to his formalism elsewhere. Any parallels established between French and Hebrew, given the completely different structure of the two languages, must inevitably be semantic ones – based on 'manieres de signifier' – and it is instructive that it is precisely this term (reminiscent of the late-medieval grammarians' 'modi significandi')[74] that will be used by the Port-Royal authors in 1660. The vogue for plurilingual grammars cannot but reinforce any latent tendencies toward universal grammar. In contrast to his Latin section, Drosée's short French grammar is devoid of features showing a debt to Linacre.[75] At the end of the whole work however there is a syntax written in Latin, which confines itself to a definition of terms without examples, and is obviously meant to be universally applicable. Here the debt to Linacre is quite patent, with his medieval division of syntax into 'personal' and 'impersonal', the latter covering the construction of the consignifying word-classes, and of 'personal' syntax into transitive and intransitive.[76] The cardinal point however is Drosée's repetition of Linacre's division of syntax into 'justa' and 'figurata', but with a difference of emphasis. The grammatically correct *constructio justa*, from which no element is missing, represents 'rough and common' language, while figurative syntax corresponds to the speech of the elegant. Significant here is Drosée's remark that the types of construction found in Latin are also valid for French, Greek and Hebrew. Syntax is universal, for it serves everywhere for the signification of mental concepts.

Drosée's few Linacre-inspired remarks are merely indicative of a trend. The first vernacular grammar of any importance to undergo Linacre's influence is Pierfrancesco Giambullari's *De la lingua* (1551), which follows the *De emendata structura* very closely. Much of Linacre's treatment is in fact repeated word for word, with whatever adaptations are necessary to accommodate it to the Italian vernacular. We have already noted that, given the paucity of formal marks in the European vernaculars as compared with Latin, there will be an

[74] It also recalls Nebrija's use of the term 'maneras de significar'.
[75] Drosée acknowledged debt is to Jacques Dubois or 'Sylvius', author of a *Grammatica Latino-Gallica*, Paris, 1531.
[76] These terms are not of course used in their modern sense. The intransitive construction of persons deals with matters of congruence, while the transitive one concerns case government.

The beginnings of the universalist approach

inevitable trend, in transferring grammatical procedures from the Latin model, to rely on semantic criteria. Giambullari's imitation of Linacre reinforces this semantic approach. Since passive meanings are not marked by formal variation of endings in the Italian verb but by periphrastic procedures the traditional division of verbs into active, passive and 'neuter' is rejected in favour of Linacre's transitive/intransitive dichotomy resting on the notion of syntactic 'persons'. This too however involves the positing of a semantic force (Giambullari's 'forza' renders Linacre's 'vis') which is transferred from a verb to the term governed by it. Thus, as in Linacre, certain verbs require the tacit existence of a cognate accusative into which their 'forza' can pass, as in *io vivo* (*una vita faticosa*), *tu corri* (*un' lungo corso*), which again represent the transference to the vernacular of Linacre's *vivo vitam* and *curro cursum*. As Giambullari puts it, transitive verbs 'pass over with the force of their [semantic] value into something else'.[77] Since however Linacre's corresponding passive constructions (*cursus curritur*) have no direct equivalent in Italian, they can only be paralleled by reflexive ones (*si corre de te un' lungo corso*). Giambullari is the only sixteenth-century grammarian of Italian to give more than a minimal treatment of syntax – he devotes six books out of eight to it – and it is here, in his application of Linacre's theory of syntax to a European vernacular, that his chief interest lies. Based on Linacre are his division of syntax into 'costruzione intera' and 'costruzione figurata', and his use of the notion of syntactic 'persons' involving semantic transfer from one word to another: 'they pass with their signification into a different one.'[78] The interesting point here is that though Linacre inherits an established tradition of word government, his application to it of medieval theory gives it an even more semantic basis than it has in the rest of humanistic Latin grammar, and it is precisely this thoroughgoing semantic bias that allows the system to be easily adapted to vernacular languages in which government is not marked by case. Giambullari further follows Linacre in introducing into grammatical syntax the 'figures' of speech, which had long been the province of rhetoric. The construction of the 'sentenzia' is still however very much the concern of rhetoricians, as in the entire division of what he calls 'costruzione virtuoso', dealing with means

[77] 'trapassano in altri con la forza del valor loro'.
[78] *De la lingua*, p. 143: 'passano co'l significato a una diversa'.

241

of rendering discourse agreeable to the hearer or reader and enabling him to *picture* the matter rather than simply hear it. Giambullari is the only author of his date to attempt some sort of integration of the figures of rhetoric into vernacular grammar. His own bias remains however rhetorical. Not before Sanctius' Latin grammar in 1587 will a doctrine of elliptical constructions be given the status of a 'necessary' component of linguistic theory.[79]

Scaliger

The full importance of Linacre for European grammatical theory only emerges when the syntactic theory of Sanctius, of the Port-Royal Latin grammar and the *Grammaire générale et raisonnée*, is considered in the light of his prior contribution. Between Linacre and Sanctius there stands however the philosophical grammar of J. C. Scaliger, itself of great importance for the evolution of linguistic thought. He too represents, after the period of humanist 'observational adequacy' separating him from the philosophically based modistic grammarians, a return to medieval approaches, more particularly in the view of syntax, the chief object of linguistic description, as the expression of mental concepts. His *De causis linguae Latinae* (1540)[80] is the first grammar since the Middle Ages to use the metalanguage of Aristotelian philosophy in an attempt to reach the underlying 'causes' of language. The epistemological framework of this attempt is borrowed from Scholastic philosophy of the Thomist variety, according to which language is a reliable reflection of things in the real world: 'grammatica est de signis rerum', as the modistic grammarians put it. This isomorphism of language and reality is to be of prime importance for one particular strand in universal grammar, namely that represented by the British language-planners' quest for an artificial language that, since it faithfully mirrored the universe, would be a reliable tool for scientific research. Scaliger's Thomistic system is however a tripartite one, in which the human intellect first acts as a reflection of *things*,[81] whose concepts or 'species'

[79] For a fuller account of Linacre's influence on Giambullari see Padley, 'L'importance de Thomas Linacre (env. 1460–1524) comme source', pp. 24–35.
[80] For a consideration of some of the elements in the *De causis* see J. Stéfanini, 'Jules César Scaliger et son De causis linguae Latinae', *History of Linguistic Thought and Contemporary Linguistics*, ed. H. Parret, Berlin and New York, 1976, pp. 317–30.
[81] *De causis linguae Latinae*, cap. lxvi: 'Est enim quasi rerum speculum intellectus noster'.

enter the mind via the senses. These concepts (intermediary between things and language) are then at a third level given linguistic status as words or 'marks of a *species* in the mind.'[82] This would seem to result in that 'virtual identification of linguistic and mental processes' seen by Chomsky as the hall-mark of Port-Royal theory.[83] It is however important to bear in mind – a matter we shall return to later – that the Port-Royal system is for all practical purposes a binary one of words and concepts, or indeed of words *as* concepts. Scaliger's system is still overtly linked to referents in the real world. Relevant here too is the question of whether, as Chomsky requires, some at least of the concepts in the mind are innate. For a theory of universal grammar as envisaged by Scaliger the innateness hypothesis seems to be unnecessary, for he assumes that the concepts or *species* received in Aristotelian fashion will be identical in all minds, only the words that are signs of them differing from one language to another. The term 'horse' (*equus*) refers both to an unchanging phenomenon in the real world, and an immutable mental concept. The underlying mental structure of language is the same for all men everywhere. It is isomorphic with the world of things, which means that it can be described in terms of the philosophical categories of substance and accident, and of Aristotle's Four Causes.[84] Like the seventeenth-century artificial-language planners after him, Scaliger bases his method on two assumptions: that the universe is amenable to description within the superimposed grill of Aristotelian philosophy, and that the resultant categories are also appropriate to *linguistic* description. Basing himself on Aristotle's hylomorphic[85] world-view, which sees objects as consisting of matter (*substance*) and whatever it is that gives each object its particular form (*accident*), Scaliger applies these two categories to language as if it in turn were a substance.[86]

[82] *Ibid.*, cap. lxvi: I have left the word *species* untranslated. Elsewhere Scaliger uses the term *notio*, e.g. cap. i: 'est enim vox nota earum notionum, quae in anima sunt'.

[83] Chomsky, *Cartesian Linguistics*, p. 29.

[84] Material, formal, efficient and final causes. For a discussion of Scaliger's application of his metalanguage see Padley, *Grammatical Theory* (1976), pp. 58–76.

[85] The *Shorter Oxford English Dictionary* defines hylomorphism as (*a*) the doctrine that primordial matter is the First Cause of the universe, (*b*) the Scholastic theory of matter and form. It is the second sense that is relevant here.

[86] See R. G. Faithfull's review of P. A. Verburg, *Taal en Functionaliteit* (1952), in *Archivum Linguisticum*, VII: 2 (1955), pp. 6–7. It is interesting here to compare F. de Saussure's view (*Cours de linguistique générale*, Paris, 1964, p. 169): 'la langue est une forme et non une substance...toutes nos façons incorrectes de désigner les choses de la langue proviennent de cette supposition dans le phénomène linguistique.'

In using Aristotle's Four Causes as a metalanguage, he treats the material cause as defining what we would now call phonetics (the expression side of language), and the formal cause as concerning semantics (the content side of language). This is of course a repetition of medieval modistic theory, in which a word can be considered either *materialiter* (as a unit of expression) or *formaliter* (as a semantic unit). In practice this meant that the modistic grammarians concerned themselves wholly with the semantic element of language, as indeed does Scaliger. His definition of discourse as an arrangement of meaning-bearing signs whose purpose is the expression of a preexistent sequence in the mind ('ad interpretandum animum') is sufficiently eloquent of his importance for the development of universal grammar. The bases of his grammar of concepts and mental operations are however in things themselves: noun and verb signify the *nature* of causes, while conjunction, adverb and preposition signify the *modes of operation* of those causes. His search for a *ratio*, an underlying philosophical basis on which to found the very being of grammar itself, is diametrically opposed to the approach of Ramus, who used logic and philosophy to prescribe the boundaries and framework within which grammar must operate, but rejected them out of hand as metalanguages.

Helwig

In spite of the inroads made by Ramism, Scaliger seems to have had a special attraction for German grammarians, the Ratichian reformers for instance using his word-class definitions freely. Already in 1584 Nicodemus Frischlin's Latin grammar, the *Quaestiones grammaticae*,[87] is closely based on him, and thus offers a ready model for vernacular imitation. An example is the work of Christoph Helwig, who had already collaborated with Caspar Finck on the production of a Latin grammar[88] which owes a good deal to Scaliger, whom it frequently cites along with Peter of Spain, Linacre and Frischlin. As we have seen, Helwig also cooperated with Ratke in the Köthen pedagogical reforms, and though the *methodology* of their works derives unquestion-

[87] Venice, 1584. For a discussion of this work see Padley, *Grammatical Theory* (1976), p. 76.
[88] *Grammatica Latina*. Since Jellinek, *Geschichte*, II; 3, mentions only this second edition, a first one is presumably not extant. The work also has a debt to Ramus. See Padley, *Grammatical Theory* (1976), pp. 113, 157, 162, 164–6.

ably from Ramus, and Helwig's universal grammar was conceived before Ratke's,[89] they can be regarded as joint originators of universal grammar in the German vernacular. Helwig's *Libri didactici*[90] (posthumously) and Ratke's *Allgemeine Sprachlehr* both appeared in 1619. Since Helwig was the orientalist in Ratke's team, it is not surprising that in addition to a treatment of universal grammar and of Latin and Greek, his volume also contains grammars of Chaldean and Hebrew. The vernacular version or *Sprachkünste*[91] is virtually identical with it, though no doubt for pedagogical reasons its definitions are frequently simpler than those of the Latin work. If it seems in some ways to be no more than an appendage to the latter, it is because the primary aim of the schools was still to inculcate Latin, and here it is significant that Helwig did not produce an independent vernacular universal grammar, but a simplified German version of one already composed in Latin. Vernacular school grammars were so often meant to be little more than additional teaching aids, a concession to the fact that instruction in the mother tongue made learning more accessible. Anything more ambitious was aimed at foreigners with no knowledge of Latin, who wished to acquire a particular vernacular for purposes of trade or travel. The fact that it is not uncommon for authors first to write their grammar of or in Latin, and only secondarily produce an application of their theories to the vernacular – outstanding examples are Ramus and the Port-Royal authors – means that the grammar in the mother tongue can only be fully understood in the light of the prior, and often fuller, Latin version. Frequently indeed, since it provides the theoretical flesh to clothe the bones of the somewhat concise vernacular grammar, a perusal of the Latin work is essential. This is if anything yet more so in the case of Helwig, whose *Libri didactici* has an appendix[92] not included in the German version, but giving a concise statement of the principles underlying both works. It interestingly renders the term grammar by 'sermocinatrix', a word that in classical Latin meant a babbler, but came to be used as a term of rhetoric.[93] The

[89] See Jellinek, *Geschichte*, I, 91.

[90] *Libri didactici, grammaticae universalis, Latinae, Graecae, Hebraicae, Chaldicae*, Giessen, 1619.

[91] Giessen, 1619.

[92] The appendix is entitled 'Residuum universalis grammaticae, de natura et proprietatibus linguarum, in communi'.

[93] It translates the Platonic προσομιλιτική. See Lewis and Short's Latin dictionary, Oxford, 1969, sub verbo 'sermocinatrix'.

theoretical basis, as in the definition of grammar as the art of 'making known the thoughts of the mind [*sensa animi*] through speech', and of the word as a 'separate sign of a mental concept', is obviously Scaligeran. Since discourse consists of words (or 'voces') arbitrarily imposed by mankind, and is itself a 'mark of mental concepts', it follows that languages, while differing in form, all indicate the same thoughts.[94] Equally stemming from Scaliger is the attribution of two distinct facets to the *vox* or linguistic sign: a 'material' (phonetic)[95] one, and a 'formal' (semantic) one. Helwig would appear however also to have a debt to Ramus, as in the division of *sermocinatrix* into 'lexical' and 'grammatical' sections, the former dealing with the dictionary meanings of words, the latter with formal differences between words and their construction in sentences.[96] The resulting three types of grammar are 'elementaria' (describing orthography and the sound system), 'dignotiva' (distinguishing word-class differences) and 'constructiva' (concerning syntax). It is this last that constitutes the domain of universal grammar.

Helwig resembles Drosée in taking over from Hebrew grammar a tripartite division of the parts of speech into noun, verb and particle, but here again it is implicit in Scaliger's Aristotelian treatment of noun and verb as principal classes (Helwig's 'Heubtwörter') and the rest as consignifiers.[97] A system which is equally applicable to Latin, Hebrew and German has obvious attractions for a universal grammarian, more especially since it can be defined in mentalistic terms. Noun and verb are the principal word-classes because 'discourse[98] subsists in them as in a basis', in contrast to the

94 *Libri didactici*, p. 14.
95 Helwig uses the term 'sonus articulatus' for this facet of the sign.
96 Kaltz, 'Christoph Helwig, ein vergessener Vertreter der allgemeinen Grammatik in Deutschland', p. 230, rightly remarks that since the medieval modistae did not regard 'phonetics' as a proper object of linguistic study, Helwig's conception of grammar is reminiscent of Scholastic theory. Noting however that he consigns the treatment of word meanings to the lexicon, she then makes the statement that he is concerned (only?) with 'der materielle Aspekt der Wörter'. There seems to be some confusion here, caused perhaps by her reading of H. Roos' statement (Sprachdenken im Mittelalter', *Classica et Mediaevalia*, IX (1947), p. 212) that for the modistae the phonetic shape of words had nothing to do with the 'Formalobjekt' of grammar. She attributes to the modistae the Ramist viewpoint that '"meaning", the "content side" of words should be investigated by other scientific disciplines and not by grammar'. The point is that both the modistae and Helwig are interested not in *lexical* meaning, but in the consignification of *grammatical* meaning.
97 This division is of course also that of Sanctius' *Minerva* (1587), and he too compares it to Hebrew grammar's noun, verb and 'dictio consignificans'.
98 Helwig uses the term 'Rede', translating Latin 'sermo'. Perhaps here it could be rendered by 'sentence'.

particle which 'can furnish no ground for discourse, but is added to give full elucidation, limitation and completion to discourse'.[99] Similarly the three constituent classes *Nännwort* ('that by which something is named'),[100] *Sagwort* (that by which 'one says something that one does or suffers') and *Beiwort*[101], are defined in purely semantic terms. As with other users of this system pronoun and participle are types of noun, and the particle groups adverb, preposition, conjunction and interjection. Adverbs and prepositions are catered for in a single sub-class of 'Umbstandwörter' or words of circumstance. Since not all languages have cases, prepositions cannot be defined as governing them, and Helwig accordingly treats them as 'imperfect' members of their sub-class, which need 'the help of another word in order fully to indicate the circumstance'. The general definition of particles other than the conjunction as denoting 'a circumstance or motion of the mind' cannot but reinforce the trend towards such mentalistic criteria, leading ultimately to the Port-Royal expression of grammatical relations in terms of 'les opérations de notre esprit'. Both Helwig's *Sprachkünste* and the *Grammaire générale et raisonnée* are illustrations of the extent to which Scholastic thought, with its emphasis on mental operations, pervades the seventeenth century.

In his approach to syntax Helwig starts from the notion we have already encountered, that a particular meaning can be variously expressed in discourse: 'Es kan oft eine Mainung vilerlei weise ausgeredet, und also ein einige red vilerlei weise abgewechselt werden.'[102] As examples he gives not only the already mentioned substitution of relative plus verb for participle, but precisely those active/passive transformations that present-day Chomskyan theory cites as evidence of the varied surface realization of a single underlying structure. Previous grammarians had long used this transformation in the treatment of voice, with active verbs partially defined as those which have a corresponding passive. Helwig seems to be the first grammarian to treat the two structures as semantic equivalents. He is however aware of differences in syntax between one language and another, of the fact that each has 'its own singular fashion and

[99] *Sprachkünste*, p. 3.
[100] Cf. Ramus' definition of the *word* as 'qua unumquodque vocatur'.
[101] The Latin version uses the term *advocabulum*.
[102] *Sprachkünste*, p. 16.

characteristic quality as far as word order is concerned'. He was after all deeply implicated in the schemes of the Köthen reformers around Ratke, and shares their concern to show not only the similarities but also the differences between languages. Were it not that he adopts the metalanguage of Scaliger's Aristotelianism, his place would be among the pedagogically motivated universal grammarians discussed earlier.

Alsted

A strong pedagogical purpose similarly provides the driving force for the work of Johann Heinrich Alsted, whose *Encyclopaedia* (1630)[103] contains an article on general grammar. He has the distinction of having taught Comenius, and was instrumental in spreading Ramist theories in Germany. W. J. Ong indeed claims[104] that nowhere outside Alsted's works is the influence of Ramus present 'on such a monumental scale'. Several strands of medieval and Renaissance thought converge in him, some of them of importance for grammatical theory. The most obvious one is an encyclopedism in the modern manner whose immediate source is Ramus, but which also has antecedents in the thirteenth-century scholar Ramón Lull, inventor of a system of grouped fundamental concepts known as the *Ars magna*. Comenius' arranging of phenomena under conceptual headings – his *pansophia*, as he called it – may perhaps be seen as a continuance of this. The 'chain of being' idea current in the seventeenth century, according to which (in Scaligeran fashion) there is an ontological correspondence between the order of the universe and the order of the mind, also has roots here. It in turn has connections with the Jewish Kabbalah by whose aid, it was claimed, the secrets of nature could be penetrated. In the realm of practical pedagogy, this further leads to Alsted's interest in mnemonic systems. That Alsted had more than dabbled in these various sources – Ramus, Lull and the Kabbalah – can be amply demonstrated from his works.[105] Methodologically, they are above all indebted to Ramus' *Dialectica*,

[103] *Scientiarum omnium encyclopaedia septem tomis distincta*, Herborn, 1630.
[104] *Ramus*, p. 298.
[105] His publications include for example a *Systema mnemonicum duplex* (Frankfurt-am-Main, 1610), organized around Ramus' *Dialectica*, and an *Artium liberalium ac facultatum omnium systema mnemonicum de modo discendi...cum encyclopaediae, artis Lullianae et Cabbalisticae perfectissima explicatione* (Frankfurt-am-Main, *c.*1610).

which in this respect may be said to be at the origins of modern encyclopedism.[106] Alsted's discussion of grammar forms part of his treatment of the seven arts of lexicology, grammar, rhetoric, logic, oratory, politics and mnemonics,[107] which in turn is contained in books twenty-one to twenty-seven of his vast encyclopedia. The liberal arts themselves are seen as a sub-section of philosophy. The individual grammars of Hebrew, Aramaic, Greek and Latin are treated, but what particularly interest us here are the eighteen pages, in Latin, devoted to general grammar. Though previous commentators have claimed that Alsted was incorporating Helwig's *Libri didactici*,[108] or that his universal grammar shows 'modistic and Ramistic influences',[109] it seems largely to have escaped notice that his work is virtually a repetition, on a greatly reduced scale, of ideas contained in Scaliger's *De causis*.[110] There are several references to Scaliger in his general grammar, though there is also an important Ramist element stemming from Ramus' *Dialectica*. Obviously of Ramist provenance for example is the recommendation that in treating the 'special' grammars of particular languages the 'method of prudence' should be employed, thus ensuring that universally applicable matters already discussed under the heading of general grammar should not be needlessly repeated. Similarly Ramist is the insistence that purity of language takes precedence over ornament and richness ('copia'), the latter being the province of rhetoric, and only the former that of grammar. The actual grammatical theory is however overwhelmingly taken from Scaliger. This means that Alsted, in contrast to the 'mother's milk' theory in vogue among contemporary German grammarians, holds that a knowledge of grammar cannot be obtained by mere usage or by reading the best authors. Scaliger is cited to the effect that uncertain usage must be corrected by sure and certain laws, the aim of which, in a formula recalling Ratke and Comenius, is to introduce the student 'into the

[106] See Ong, *Ramus*, p. 299.

[107] *Septem artes liberales, quae constituunt tertium encyclopaediae philosophicae tomum* (= books xxi–xxvii of the *Encyclopaedia*).

[108] Thus H. Aarsleff, 'The History of Linguistics and Professor Chomsky', *Language*, XLVI (1970), p. 573. It is true that Alsted uses Helwig's work for the section of his *Encyclopaedia* – the 'Delineatio grammaticae Germanicae' – dealing with vernacular grammar.

[109] Brekle, 'The Seventeenth Century', p. 314.

[110] Salmon, (review of Chomsky's *Cartesian Linguistics*, p. 171) notes that in his second edition, *Encyclopaedia universa in quatuor tomis divisa*, Lyons, 1649, Alsted lists his sources, with constant reference to Scaliger.

entrance [*vestibulum*] of any language whatever'. It is no doubt with this universalist end in mind that Alsted claims the chief function of general grammar is to reconcile in one system grammatical and logical concepts.[111] One important result of this is the notion that cases in general grammar are a matter of logical relationships, a claim others in the seventeenth century were making for prepositional structures. There is however a Ramist element in the insistence that the number of cases in a given language can never be more than the number of actual case *endings*, since any classification by semantic criteria alone would result in an infinitude of cases. As with Scaliger, the grammatical theory involved reposes on two bases: Aristotelian philosophy, and isomorphism with the real world. Just as Aristotle's ten predicaments are 'summa rerum genera', that is to say applicable to whatever exists in the world,[112] so the parts of speech, the 'summa vocum genera', are universally applicable to human language. They may in fact be termed the 'grammatical predicaments'.[113] To Aristotle's division of reality into substance and accident there corresponds grammar's division of the word-classes into signifiers and consignifiers. As with Scaliger, the link with the real world is of primary importance. 'Vox est nota rerum' – words are signs of things. To the permanence and flux of phenomena (the universe is divided into 'res permanentes et fluentes') there correspond respectively the noun and verb of grammar, in precisely the medieval modistic terms taken over by Scaliger. While noun and verb signify 'the causes and effects of things', it is the function of prepositions to express the mode of operation of those causes. In a repetition of Scaliger's phrase, the parts of speech must contain within themselves the 'Universus rerum ambitus'. In the century that sees the rebirth of general grammar, Alsted's contribution is to ensure wide dissemination, through his *Encyclopaedia*, of the ideas of Scaliger.

Aristotelianism (*Ruscelli*)

The aims of Ratke and Schottel were above all pedagogical ones, and it is the dissemination of useful knowledge that is the motor of their

[111] *Encyclopaedia*, XXI, col. 224.
[112] W. S. Howell (*Logic and Rhetoric*, p. 19) describes Aristotle's predicaments of substance, action, quantity, quality, etc., as 'those words which name the possible scientific conceptions men may have as to the nature of reality'. For discussion see Padley, *Grammatical Theory* (1976), pp. 59–60.   [113] *Encyclopaedia*, XXI, col. 218.

encyclopedism and their theories of general grammar. In Italy by contrast, given the already established prestige of the Florentine vernacular based on the eminence as models of Petrarch, Dante and Boccaccio, held to equal that of the great writers of Antiquity, early grammars of the 'vulgar' tongue are not motivated to the same extent by pedagogical considerations. Further, they have a rhetorical bias that is largely absent from the vernacular grammars of northern Europe, and a corresponding absence of overt grammatical theory. Rather than by such matters, their energies are largely absorbed by the protracted debate on the 'Questione della lingua', by the argument as to which dialect to take as the standard for linguistic description: a spoken Tuscan, the archaic written usage of the three great authors, or some kind of pan-Italian extracted from their works and supplemented by elements from the more important of the non-Tuscan dialects. Under the influence of the great law schools at Bologna and elsewhere, the teaching of the arts of oratory and persuasion had always had a major role in the Italian Renaissance. C. Trabalza[114] notes however that the year 1536 marks a turning-point. This, the year in which Ramus defended his anti-Aristotelian thesis in Paris and the *Poetica* was published in the original Greek text in Italy, marks a change in Aristotle's influence – the decline of his dictatorial authority in philosophy, and the beginning of a new supremacy in literary criticism. This new influence extends to grammatical theory, for in both Aristotle's *Poetica* and his *Rhetorica* grammatical categories are described, and these works, together with the contemporaneous printing of the *De interpretatione*, brought once again to the notice of grammarians the theory of the logical proposition. These tendencies are reinforced by the publication in 1540 of Scaliger's *De causis*, the standard example of the application of Aristotelian principles to Latin grammar. The great example of an application of these principles to vernacular grammar is provided by Benedetto Buonmattei's *Della Lingua toscana* (1643).[115] As early as 1529 G. G. Trissino's *Dubbii grammaticali*[116] had already repeated Aristotle's 'just as words are indications and representations of men's concepts, so are letters indications and representations of words',

[114] *Storia della grammatica italiana*, Bologna, 1963, citing J. E. Spingarn, *A History of Literary Criticism in the Renaissance*, New York, 1899.
[115] Published in part in 1623 under the title *Delle Cagioni della lingua toscana*.
[116] Published in Vicenza.

adding that those languages are judged best whose words are most apt to express mental concepts. There is also an early statement of Aristotelian principles in Benedetto Varchi's *Ercolano* of 1570.[117] Though he does not differ from several other sixteenth-century grammarians of Italian in regarding speech as 'the manifestation of the concepts of the mind by means of words', he has however an overt reference to those 'images or likenesses of things' (called by philosophers *spezie*) to which he gives the names *concetti, pensieri* or *intendimenti*. This of course very much recalls Scaliger's 'species' or 'imagines rerum' introduced into the mind by the medium of the senses and then signified by words.[118] These *species*, following indications in Aristotle's *De interpretatione*, were thought to be to some extent copies of external phenomena, and came to be known in medieval epistemology as *intentiones*. Varchi, who was largely responsible for the diffusion of the ideas in Aristotle's *Poetica*, had however a knowledge of Aristotle at first hand. Basing himself on Aristotle, he expresses ideas that are consistent with universal grammar, holding that speech is natural to man as an 'animal civile', and that it is only by constraint that men speak one language rather than another.

The most important example before Buonmattei of at least the *intention* to apply Aristotelian principles to linguistic theory is found in G. Ruscelli's *Commentarii* of 1581.[119] Ruscelli's theory is clearly based on the Aristotelian form/matter dichotomy, with grammatical variation taking place on the conceptual level ('la purissima forma della favella') rather than on that of material, phonetic components. Much of the discussion of 'materia' and 'forma' is bound up with notions of Aristotelian physics, according to which all things are made up of the four elements earth, air, fire and water in varying proportions. In considering the production of vocal sounds, Ruscelli finds it necessary to give a disquisition on the blood, which has a central role in human relationships, for if its essential 'spiriti' are corrupt this has unpleasant consequences for the breath. We learn that in cats, whose bad breath 'corrupts the air they touch', the 'spiriti' are perpetually disordered. Even apart from such digressions,

---

[117] I have used P. dal Rio's edition, *L'Ercolano dialogo di Benedetto Varchi dove si ragiona delle lingue*, Florence, 1846.

[118] *De causis linguae Latinae*, cap. lxvi.

[119] *De' Commentarii della lingua italiana*, Venice, 1581.

Ruscelli's description of the production of human speech makes fascinating reading. It depends on the Aristotelian notion that man has a vegetative soul in common with plants, a sensitive one in common with animals, and a rational or intellectual one. Since the driving force of the soul forces the air we breathe through the arteries of the heart to issue as vocal sounds, it follows that the human intellect, motivating this 'virtù motrice', can itself influence the sounds of speech. All this however concerns only, in Aristotelian terms, the *material* side of language. Of more relevance to the grammarian are the causes lying behind the fact – and one may note the rhetorical bias – that a given utterance is pleasing to some but displeasing to others. These rhetorical effects, according to Ruscelli, are caused less by the 'material' of language than by, in the Aristotelian sense, the 'form.' Of central importance here is the reference to doctrines contained in Aristotle's *De anima*: 'the bodily senses receive the form and species of things, stripped of everything material, in just the same way as paper and wax receive a figure and image cut in metal, without receiving any part of the material of the metal'. In language, the 'form' received by the senses is expressed in two ways. Phonetic form (the 'forma della voce'), as distinct from the actual material of speech, and again in an analysis owing much to rhetoric, has to do with harmony and metre and the expression of the speaker's mood, moving the hearer to either delight or boredom. More important for the grammarian are 'voce articolate' or words, which as 'signs of those things, thoughts and passions we have in our minds', touch other minds through the sense of hearing and imprint on them their various *affetti*.[120]

These Aristotelian principles have for Ruscelli universal validity, determining the number and nature of the parts of speech 'in every language'. Though according to Quintilian actual language use precedes the framing of grammatical laws, it is evident to Ruscelli that since language and the human intellect must have been created at one and the same time, it is the perfectly regulated intellect that is the guarantee of the ordered nature of language. This is precisely the assumed congruence of language and mind that is necessary to a theory of universal grammar. But for Scaliger, though words are signs of concepts, it is the *intellect* that is in the final analysis the mirror

---

[120] For these various applications of Aristotelian doctrines see *ibid.*, pp. 41–59.

of *things* – 'est quasi rerum speculum intellectus noster'.[121] Ruscelli, in a change of emphasis that is also that of the Port-Royal authors in 1660, would have agreed with Leibniz that it is *language* that is 'le meilleur miroir de *l'esprit humain*'. The priority given to the notion of the perfection of the human intellect means that the mind cannot long remain satisfied with language that is not regulated by some kind of logic. It follows that the grammarian must apply to language the reason and order of Nature, as did Aristotle and the Hebrews in limiting the number of parts of speech to three. According to Nature's laws everything in the universe is a thing (expressed linguistically by a name), an operation, or neither of these. Without a name, expressed or understood, there can be no operation, and names and operations together form a complete utterance or *parlamento*. In other words, every sentence must contain both a subject and a predicate. Any additional element – and again the rhetorical bias is evident – contributes only to the 'satisfaction and quieting' of the hearer's mind.[122] Having got thus far however, Ruscelli has a failure of nerve. Since Italian is not a 'newly born' language but receives its 'foundation, ornaments and form' from Latin, it ought to content itself with following traditional Latin grammatical practice. This surrender is oddly at variance with his continual insistence that the precepts he enumerates are applicable to all languages. This does not however diminish the importance of what is the first full-length statement of Aristotelian principles in a grammar of Italian. Its rhetorical orientation is an interesting illustration of the direction Aristotle's influence is taking in the second half of the sixteenth century.

Buonmattei

Ruscelli, happy enough to press Aristotle into service on rhetorical matters, had shrunk at the last moment from applying his philosophical system to the grammar of the vernacular. With Buonmattei

---

[121] Cf. Scaliger's (*De causis linguae Latinae*, cap. i) 'est enim vox nota earum notionum, quae in anima sunt'. He stresses however (cap. lxvii) the link with the real world: 'imagines rerum sunt notiones intellectui'. His theory also supposes, in Thomistic fashion, the *active intervention* of the intellect in the process of conceptualization, as distinct from mere passive reception, as witness his description (cap. lxvi) of the genesis of the word *horse*: 'Equi speciem ab equo eductam intellectus agens in intellectum passibilem impressit'. On the question of 'species' in the mind see Padley, *Grammatical Theory* (1976), pp. 64–5, 76, 162, 233n., 234–5.

[122] *Commentarii*, pp. 72–5.

The beginnings of the universalist approach

there is a shift in emphasis. Given the long tradition and prestige of rhetoric in Italy, he no doubt feels bound to repeat the rhetorical definition of discourse or *orazione* as 'an ordered arrangement of rhetorical arguments, suitable for persuasion', if only to contrast it with the 'grammatical' one. It is interesting to compare the two. The grammatical definition refers to 'an appropriate [*convevole*] union of words capable of manifesting the concepts of the mind'. The cardinal point here is that if language is to express mental concepts its words must be appropriately joined together. Put another way, correct syntactic order and congruence are essential to the expression of thought, and we may note that Buonmattei's definition of discourse is precisely that of Scaliger.[123] In contrast to the rhetorical bias of the purely descriptive grammars of his predecessors he deliberately sets out, a century after Ramus, to produce a 'grammatica metodica' with a philosophical basis.[124] His grammatical work consists of two books, the first of which, though it was already complete in 1613, was published in 1623 under the title *Delle Cagioni della lingua toscana*.[125] This title, with its reference to the causes or reasons of the Tuscan language, already recalls Scaliger's *De causis*. In 1643 the work reappeared as the first part of a much wider one, the monumental *Della Lingua toscana*,[126] which occupies in the history of Italian vernacular grammar a position analogous to that of Schottel's *Ausführliche Arbeit* for German. The first section (identical with the earlier *Delle Cagioni* of 1623) constitutes the more theoretical and philosophical part, through the more practically orientated second part is also well provided with philosophically based arguments and theoretical discussion. But Buonmattei's work is remarkable in fulfilling the requirements of both explanatory and observational 'adequacy', exhibiting as it does, in addition to its philosophical

[123] *De causis linguae Latinae*, cap. iii: 'Est enim Sermo dispositio vocum articulatarum ad interpretandum animum.'

[124] In treating linguistic theory in seventeenth-century Italy, Brekle ('The Seventeenth Century') deals only with Buonmattei and the Latin philosophical grammarian Campanella. He justifies this by quoting C. Trabalza's reference (*Storia della grammatica italiana*, p. 300) to Buonmattei as 'il principe de' grammatici'.

[125] Published in Venice. I have consulted it in vol. IV of the anonymous compendium of Italian vernacular grammars, *Degli Autori del ben parlare per secolari, e religiose opere diverse*, Venice, 1643.

[126] Published in Florence. The title page describes this as the third impression, and a pirated edition had in fact already appeared in Venice under the title *Introduzione alla lingua toscana*. This 1643 edition is identical with the fifth edition (Florence and Verona, 1720) used by Trabalza for his *Storia della grammatica italiana*. Brekle ('The Seventeenth Century') used a Venice edition of 1735.

Universal grammar

examination of 'causes', a wholly laudable empirical orientation aimed at close description of actual Italian usage. It is the former of these two aspects that will concern us here. It is difficult however to imagine the grammar ever having been in classroom use. Not only as in Schottel's case its sheer bulk, but also its constant enquiries into the 'causa logica' of every grammatical category and accident, would hardly recommend its use as a teaching manual. It is indeed the first vernacular grammar worthy to be set beside the great Latin achievements of Scaliger, Sanctius and Campanella. The historian of Italian grammar Trabalza notes that it anticipates both the Port-Royal *Grammaire générale et raisonnée* and Scioppius' Latin *Grammatica philosophica* of 1628.[127] The strongly empirical orientation, on the other hand, links it to a long-standing tradition of exposition of the facts of the Italian language associated with the names of Bembo and Salviati. Given this double nature of Buonmattei's work, and the amplitude of his treatment, it is not surprising that it reigned for long as the standard grammar of Italian, with no serious rival before that of Corticelli in 1745. The only task left to his successors was that of abridging his work and accommodating it to the exigences of pedagogy. After him there was little scope for originality. The philosophical bases of his discussion take him into realms not ventured into by Bembo[128] and the other writers of purely observational grammars. But the practical dimensions of his work make of Buonmattei himself (to use Trabalza's terms)[129] a 'new Bembo or Salviati', a purist basing rules and usage on the archaic written language of the Trecento and more particularly of Boccaccio's *Decameron*. In spite however of the merits of his grammar as a work of practical description, it heralds the decline of the empirical approach, whose products were ultimately depressed to the level of simple teaching manuals for the classroom or for foreigners. His refusal, in spite of his choice of archaic models of usage, to treat etymology (in the modern sense) on the grounds that word meanings are rooted 'nell' animo nostro', foreshadows the coming triumph of

[127] Scioppius (or Schoppe) brought out his work in 1628. I have consulted it in the Amsterdam edition of 1659. Though he published an annotated edition of Sanctius' *Minerva* in 1663, he did not himself, in spite of his title *Grammatica philosophica*, produce a 'philosophical' grammar. Trabalza is thus hardly right (*Storia della grammatica italiana*, p. 302) in stating that Scioppius 'primo in Italia applicò la speculazione filosofica con coscienza critica alla grammatica'.
[128] P. Bembo, *Prose nelle quali si ragiona della volgar lingua*, Venice, 1525.
[129] *Storia della grammatica italiana*, p. 315.

logicism. In theory at any rate his grammar is 'not taken from authority, but convinced by reason'. The fact that in treating the 'cagioni' or underlying causes of language he turns to questions treated in Sanctius' *Minerva* of 1587 leads Trabalza seemingly to regard Sanctius as his model.[130] Neither Trabalza, nor H. E. Brekle in his article 'The Seventeenth Century', mention the possibility of a debt to Scaliger. My own close comparison of the grammar with Scaliger's *De causis* establishes however beyond doubt to my mind that it is the latter that has furnished the model, making of Buonmattei's *Della Lingua* the first major vernacular work in the Scaligeran tradition. The theory tallies exactly, and the evidence of frequent word-for-word correspondences can hardly be overlooked. Buonmattei furnishes yet another illustration of the fact that individual European vernacular grammars cannot be considered *in vacuo*, but must be linked both to what is happening in other countries, and to an underlying Latin grammatical tradition.

Buonmattei's aim is the old Scholastic one of the search for causes. As Thomas of Erfurt had put it in *c.* 1300 'a thing is known by its causes, hence it is by its causes that it must be defined.'[131] Just as the Four Causes form the epistemological framework of Scaliger's grammar, so do they run through Buonmattei's as a constant thread of the argument: 'All these causes are present in all things and hence also in all languages, especially our own.'[132] The material cause underlies (the phonetic form of) words, the formal cause sustains their meaning, while the efficient cause is furnished by the speakers of the language, in this case the people of Tuscany. Most interesting in its relevance to universal grammar is the final cause, which has the syntactic function of indicating concepts – 'esplicare i concetti dell' animo'. It is this process that constitutes the *orazione* or sentence. Though Buonmattei claims to have proceeded without taking into account any previous grammatical work, not only would the Aristotelian provenance of his epistemology be evident to at least the more cultivated among his readers, but the closeness of the parallels would seem to establish beyond doubt that he had an intimate knowledge of Scaliger's *De causis linguae Latinae*. The argument invoked for instance to differentiate single words from connected

---

[130] *Ibid.*, p. 306. Interesting is Trabalza's remark that the discussion in Croce's *Estetica* of the principles underlying grammatical categories closely resembles Buonmattei's treatment.
[131] *Grammatica speculativa*, cap. xlvi.   [132] *Della Lingua*, tratt. I, cap. vi.

speech is a direct borrowing from Scaliger. Whereas the word or *parola* is a sign of a 'species' in the mind,[133] the sentence or *orazione* makes manifest the whole chain of thought – 'gl'interi concetti' – conceived beforehand in the mind. The repetition of the Scholastic epistemological notions involved here is also precisely that, even down to the use of the same example of the term *horse*, already given by Scaliger: the actual horse or *cavallo* is the natural phenomenon the *forma* of which is received into the mind. The sign of this *forma* is the *voce* or material word-shape. Thus, for Buonmattei as for Scaliger, the word at a level at which it begins to interest the linguist is a 'segno d'una spezie dell'animo'. This theory differentiating the word, sign of a single concept, from a syntactic sequence designating a whole series of concepts, has to be retouched to accommodate compound words such as *Granduca*, in which the two elements of the compound together express only one concept.[134] The fact that Buonmattei (via Aristotle) is in the same current of thought as Bacon and the sense-realists is shown by his insistence that the intellect only understands or makes itself understood through the senses. Just as a mirror presents to our sight 'the form and image of the face', so the senses present to the intellect 'the *species* and image of the thing'.[135] This is simply a restatement of Scaliger's 'our intellect is as it were the mirror of things'. All this – which comes directly from Scaliger and not from any Baconian source – is an indication of the extent to which Scholastic, and specifically Thomist, categories still dominate seventeenth-century thought.

Buonmattei devotes three chapters to the age-old questions of whether language is innate or acquired 'by art', whether things received their names haphazardly or according to reason, and who was the first 'imposer' of those names. He concludes that the sounds made by animals within a given species are innate, for they 'have had no other master but nature'. The speech of men too is natural in origin, i.e. is an innate propensity, but the 'how' of it (*il come*) depends on artifice. On the issue of the imposing of names by nature

[133] Scaliger's 'nota unius speciei quae est in animo'.

[134] *Della Lingua*, tratt. VII, cap. i. This is reminiscent, in our own day, of A. Martinet's class of 'synthèmes' (e.g. *bonne d'enfant*) expressing a single concept, and forming what is in point of fact, since nothing can be inserted between its various meaningful elements, a 'word'. See *Eléments de linguistique générale*, Paris, 1960, pp. 138–9.

[135] Buonmattei says he uses the term *spezie* in the sense of 'effigie, ritratto, immagine, o forma'. It is of course a direct repetition of Scaliger's *species*.

or by convention, he holds that whereas naming is a natural function, the choice of particular names is artificial and depends on human 'caprice'. To call the Cape of Good Hope the 'Capo del non' because of its dangers is to proceed according to reason. To change the name to 'Capo di buona esperanza' is mere caprice. As for the 'primo imponente' or first imposer of names, he can hardly have been Adam, but whoever in each individual country first gave a thing its name. Had there been one first imposer for all languages this would have meant, since things are the same for all men, that all languages would have had the same names, which is patently not the case.

It is significant that Buonmattei also entitles a chapter 'How the human mind discourses'.[136] Man is an 'animale discorsivo o razionale', that is to say, in contradistinction to angels who have instant comprehension and communication, a being who gives rational expression to his thoughts by means of [linear] discourse. Since discourse can only exist with the aid of the senses, those 'ministri, nunzi, famigliari, o segretari' of the intellect, speech is the mediator between sense knowledge and the hearer. Buonmattei devotes a good deal of space to what would now be called semiotics, to what he calls 'colori' or symbols, which can be either perfect or imperfect. The 'colore imperfetto' can be the raising of an eyebrow, a gesture with the hand, involuntarily expressing some emotion. The 'colore perfetto' is represented by arts such as painting that consciously imitate nature. Cutting across this dichotomy is one into natural and artificial signs, the first (e.g. clouds as signs of rain) not being within human power. It is the 'segno artificiale', depending entirely on the human will, that concerns human sign systems used for communication, be they 'communi' (known to all) or 'particolari' (secret codes such as smoke signals).[137] At some length, the point is established that words are signs, but Buonmattei is curiously modern in his insistence that speech expresses more than writing, adding to the basic signification of concepts 'lo spirito e l'affetto'. In practice however he sees speech and writing as virtually interchangeable, each being as it were the 'ritratto' or image of the other, since 'no one who writes correctly writes differently from the way he speaks'. It is minor points

---

[136] 'Intelletto umano come discorra'.

[137] *Della Lingua*, tratt. ii, cap. iv. By *colore* Buonmattei means 'tutto quel per mezzo della luce si può discerner dall'occhio'. For a discussion within the Latin grammatical tradition of natural and artificial signs see J. Caramuel, *Grammatica audax* (in *Praecursor logicus*), p. 5. Cf. Padley, *Grammatical Theory* (1976), pp. 181–2.

such as this that furnish irrefutable evidence of the close dependence
on Scaliger, for on this matter Buonmattei is simply repeating
Scaliger's 'neque aliter scribere debemus, quam loquamur'.[138]

Equally Scaligeran is the contention that the number and kind of
the parts of speech will be in direct correlation with the types of
concept that exist in the mind. For Scaliger however the concept is
the middle term between external reality and linguistic expression,
and his word-classes correspond to divisions in Nature. In his system
words correspond to the *res* or things in the universe, and parts of
speech to their *species* or classes, and here Buonmattei, as his use of
the phrase makes clear, has understood the term *species* to have the
meaning it has in 'species in animo' or mental concept. Whatever
the explanation, Buonmattei's understanding of word-classes as
being exactly paralleled by mental operations leads inevitably to a
grammar of concepts and 'opérations de notre esprit' of the type
produced by the Port-Royal authors. On this particular point he
represents a kind of half-way house between Scaliger and the
Grammaire générale et raisonnée.[139] In practice however his position is
translated into a binary division of the word-classes based on a
division of phenomena into *things* and *actions*, corresponding to
Scaliger's dichotomy of 'res permanentes' and 'res fluentes'. This
results in a definition of the noun as a 'sign of things' and the verb
as a 'sign of actions', both reflecting a common seventeenth-century
viewpoint that is rather different from Scaliger's modistic one, though
Scaliger does regard both noun and verb as 'signs of things'.[140]
Scaliger however regards tense rather than action as the special
feature of the verb – it is a 'nota rei sub tempore' – and specifically
condemns any definition in terms of action.[141] Buonmattei's change
of emphasis here brings his definition into line with the customary
seventeenth-century one of the signification of action and 'passion'.
To define nouns as signifying things is of course to encounter the
problem, ignored by the traditional definition as the 'name of a place,
person or thing', that not all concepts signified by nouns refer to

[138] *De causis linguae Latinae*, cap. i. Scaliger however saw writing as an inessential 'accident'
of speech, which Buonmattei seems far from doing.
[139] Cf. Scaliger's 'Si igitur dictio *rerum* nota est, pro *rerum* speciebus, partes quoque suas [i.e.
partes orationis] sortietur' (*De causis linguae Latinae*, cap. lxxii, my italics).
[140] For Scaliger, in modistic fashion, the noun signifies static being (*ens*) while the verb
signifies movement and becoming (*esse*). He defines the noun as a 'nota rei sub tempore'.
[141] *De causis linguae Latinae*, cap. cx: 'falsam esse definitionem veterum, qui verbum
praescripsere agendi, vel patiendi significatione'.

actual concrete things. Buonmattei is aware of this, and defines *thing*
as including not only 'everything above and below the heavens', but
also everything, such as chimeras and centaurs, that is 'believed or
imagined or simulated'. The term 'chimera' was a traditional
example in medieval grammars, occurring for instance in Thomas
of Erfurt, who gives a long refutation of the argument that since
privative terms (*blindness*) and figments of the imagination (*chimera*)
do not signify actually existent entities they cannot be nouns. His
solution of the problem, similar to that of Buonmattei, is to treat such
terms as 'entia secundum animam', but not 'extra animam', i.e. as
having a positive existence in the mind.[142] As for actions, Buonmattei
similarly concludes that they embrace everything, whether true or
feigned, that 'calls to mind not a thing, but the operation of that
thing'. From this to Port-Royal's talk of the objects and operations
of *thoughts* there is but a short step.

Given that they together indicate both thing and action, noun and
verb are essential to the formation of a complete sentence. To give
a fuller meaning however they require the support of the other
word-classes to express their 'accidents or circumstances'. The
philosophical justification for this, based on Aristotle's Causes, is
taken directly from Scaliger. Just as for the latter adverb and preposition signify 'the manner of causes', as against noun and verb's signification of 'the nature of causes',[143] so for Buonmattei prepositions
declare 'il modo delle cagioni' (indicating whether a cause is final,
formal, material or instrumental), while adverbs declare 'il modo de
gli effetti', in other words modify verbs.[144] But though Buonmattei
and Scaliger are applying the same Aristotelian criteria to the
sub-division and classification of the universe, the former ends up
with twelve parts of speech as opposed to the latter's eight. Since
Scaliger is doubtful about including the interjection, he succeeds in
practice in covering the whole sum of phenomena, the 'universus
rerum ambitus, modusque', with only seven. Buonmattei brings the
traditional eight parts of Latin grammar up to twelve by the addition
of the article, the gerund, the 'segnacaso' or indicator of case (treated
as a separate part of speech), and what he calls the 'ripieno' or
ornamental word-class, used for stylistic reasons.

---

[142] *Grammatica speculativa*, cap. ii.   [143] *De causis linguae Latinae*, cap. lxxii.
[144] Scaliger however is at pains to point out (*ibid.*, cap. clviii) that adverbs also modify nouns
(i.e. their sub-class adjectives).

One feature that renders Buonmattei's direct use of Scaliger's *De causis* as a model practically certain is the word-for-word repetition of definitions, as in the treatment of the noun as 'declinable by cases and signifying a thing without reference to time'.[145] Apart from the reference to case, this is Aristotle's definition of the noun as a sound to which meaning is attributed by arbitrary convention, and which signifies without time.[146] These definitions are open to the objection that some nouns (*day, year*, etc.) do in fact signify time, but Scaliger is well aware of this, and Aristotle's accompanying definition of the verb as that which 'signifies time in addition'[147] would suggest that he too realizes that the point at issue is one of added grammatical consignification rather than of simple lexical signification. The medieval modistic grammarians' elaborate system of *modi significandi* was designed precisely for the purpose of keeping grammatical and lexical meanings apart, each *modus*, added over and above the lexical meaning of the linguistic sign or *dictio*, indicating the particular feature that gave a word-class or *pars orationis* its grammatical function. The point may seem an arid and technical one, but the jettisoning of this notion of grammatical consignification by most Renaissance grammarians, in their haste to get rid of what they saw as Scholastic verbiage, led to a situation in which the word-classes, defined increasingly in purely lexical terms, could no longer effectively be kept apart. This led inevitably in the late seventeenth century to a decline into a vague nomenclature, and to the *de facto* replacement, in many areas, of grammar by lexicography. Already, as indeed with Scaliger, Buonmattei's emphasis is on semantics rather than on formal morphological structure, derived words for instance being treated in terms of the semantic increments signified by their endings. If *paura* means 'fear' then *pauroso*, with an additional element of signification, means 'one who has fear', thus completing the simple meaning of *paura* and becoming 'a little less than a compound'. The semantic division of nouns into 'absolute' and 'relative' rests, as with Scaliger, on a supposed division of phenomena.[148] Absolute nouns do not depend semantically on others, while relative ones can only be fully understood in reference to some other term. Each of these classes

[145] *Della Lingua* tratt. VIII, cap. i. Cf. Scaliger, *De causis linguae Latinae*, cap. lxvi.
[146] Aristotle's noun (*De interpretatione*) signifies ἄνευ χρόνου.
[147] τὸ προσσημαῖνον χρόνου.
[148] Scaliger, *De causis linguae Latinae*, cap. xciii: 'Omne quod est, aut est absolutum, aut relativum.'

is represented by one term in a correlative pair such as *father/son* or *master/servant*, in which at least one of the pair semantically implies the existence of its correlate.[149] Buonmattei gives the example *maggiore/minore*. The interesting point here is that this classification is perpetuated by the Port-Royal authors.

It is difficult for a treatment of Buonmattei's grammar not to become (on the level of theory that is to say, not on the level of his empirical description of the Italian vernacular) simply a catalogue of Scaliger's doctrines, so closely are they followed. What is of interest is what he chooses to leave out, perhaps as smacking too much of modistic excesses in grammatical elaboration. Medieval notions explicit in Scaliger's treatment are often only implied in Buonmattei's. Some of the problems he deals with are however those that had already exercised medieval intellects. Such a problem is that of those nouns which signify accident (like adjectives) but behave grammatically like substantives. This matter will be treated later in this study, as it also presented a stumbling-block to the Port-Royal grammarians. Buonmattei realizes that some words he would wish to include among the adjectives – *ciascuno, colui, quale*, etc. – are not commutable in all positions with the general run of adjectives (cf. *il campo verde/il campo è verde*). He accordingly sets up a category of 'perfect' adjectives at once indicating an accident of a substantive, undergoing comparison, and capable of being used predicatively. Those that cannot satisfy all of these conditions can be treated either as a sub-class of adjectives, or as semi-pronouns.

The elaborate semantic classification of the various types of substantive is a common feature of sixteenth- and seventeenth-century grammars, and Buonmattei's, with its nouns of 'similitudine' catering for onomatopoeic matters such as the meowing of cats, is no exception. Where he differs from common practice is in his distribution of nouns according to the Four Causes, the *Pitti* [*Palace*] representing an efficient cause (having been built by the Pitti family), [*the statue of*] *Cosimo* a formal one, and *alabastrino* a material one. This obsession with semantic classification is equally a feature of Scaliger's *De causis*, and though Buonmattei attributes various accidents such as person and case to the noun, this does not mean that for him, any more than for Scaliger, they are determined on the grounds of formal endings.

---

[149] Cf. Scaliger, *ibid.*, cap. xcvii.

In this respect their system is at opposite poles to that of Ramus. Buonmattei correctly notes that in the sentence *Cosimo generò Ferdinando* the subject and object functions are not indicated 'per elementi materiali'. He does not however point out that it is position that determines function here, merely remarking that the two 'cases' involved here are, as elsewhere, distinguished 'with regard to *forma*, that is to say meaning'.[150] The priority given to semantic distinctions is explained by the fact that, as with Scaliger, they are deemed to be 'more noble' than mere material ones based on changes in 'letters'.[151] The material, if less noble, returns however as it were by the back door, for the use as markers of the preceding particles *da*, *di* and *a* shows that nouns vary for case not only in 'significato' but also in 'scrittura e pronunzia'. In this use of markers ('segnacasi') to indicate cases Buonmattei does not differ from the general run of contemporary Italian grammarians. His peculiarity here again lies in his attribution to each case of a name taken from the Aristotelian doctrine of causes: *efficiente* (nominative), *forma* (accusative), *fine* (dative) and *materia* (ablative).[152] The function of the 'segnacaso', which is elevated to the status of a separate part of speech, is to act in lieu of certain cases that are not formally distinguished in Italian. This function cannot be assured by prepositions, for they exist not to mark cases but to signify the various 'manners of causes'. The 'segnacaso' differs from the preposition both in *forma* or meaning and, since it is always monosyllabic, in *materia*. The particles *di*, *a* and *da*, respectively signs of genitive, dative and ablative, are in non-casual use (*pieno d'orgoglio*; *va a Bologna*) prepositions. Article and 'segnacaso' cover between them all those grammatical features of nouns that are signalled in the classical languages by variations in formal endings. Buonmattei's detailed discussion of the usage of articles well illustrates the careful empirical observation that accompanies the philosophically based Scaligeran theory of his grammar. As soon as he lifts his head from these competently described minutiae and begins to theorize however, he gives priority to semantically determined categories over formal ones. As he notes when attributing person to nouns, the absence of formal indication by 'distinti caratteri' does not imply the

---

[150] *Della Lingua*, tratt. VIII, cap. xv.

[151] *Ibid.*, tratt. VIII, cap. xv: 'perche la forma è più nobil dello materia: e più si dee considerar la significazione, che i caratteri'.

[152] The genitive, outside this series, is called *composto*.

absence of a particular grammatical 'significazione'.[153] Again, the fact that semantic categories take precedence over mere formal ones cannot but encourage the elaboration of semasiological criteria applicable to any language, regardless of its particularities of form.

Definitions of the pronoun had always tended to be based, not on any formal differences, but on its ability to act as a noun substitute. Given this particular function, it was tempting to treat it as a kind of noun and several Renaissance grammarians, including Ramus, in fact did so. In order to distinguish them as separate parts of speech Scaliger needed some kind of philosophical justification, and he adopted one which goes back to the early Greek grammarian Apollonius, who saw the pronoun as referring first to the noun it substitutes for and only indirectly to external reality. In contrast to the noun, which signifies a thing directly or 'sine medio', it is a 'notarum nota', a sign of a *sign*, just as a pointing finger or a nod of the head will serve as a sign of a *thing* when haste precludes speech.[154] Buonmattei's definition would also seem to be in this tradition,[155] though he has possibly not noticed that Scaliger is using a simile here, and additionally states that in using pronouns we indicate things as with a finger ('quasi col dito').[156] But the very fact that he repeats the expression shows how closely he follows his model.

Given this very close reliance on Scaliger, it is interesting that in his definition of the verb Buonmattei chooses not to follow him. Though he observes that 'some grammarians' (he can only mean Scaliger) define the verb as a 'nota di cosa con tempo' – a sign of a thing with time[157] – he rejects this approach, preferring his own neat quadripartite system in which nouns signify things, pronouns are signs of nouns, the syncategoremata express accidents of the main classes, and verbs signify actions. Buonmattei's division of the universe is not then the Scaligeran one into things static and things in flux (*res permanentes* and *res fluentes*) taken from the Schoolmen, but one into things and actions. The distinction between nouns signifying

---

[153] Cf. Scaliger's contention that in the series *homo curro, homo curris, homo currit* the formally unvaried nouns are of first, second and third person respectively, the phonetic 'facies' remaining unchanged while the semantic 'vis' is modified.

[154] *De causis linguae Latinae*, cap. lxxii. It should be noted however that for Scaliger *ego* and *tu* are not noun substitutes but signify 'nullo nomine subintellecto', indicating the thing itself 'statim per speciem intellectui…non per nomen' (cap. cxxvii), except in apposition, as in *ego Caesar*.　　　　　　　　　　　　　　[155] *Della Lingua*, tratt. VIII, cap. i.

[156] *Ibid.*, tratt. VII, cap. xxi.

[157] Scaliger's 'nota rei sub tempore' (*De causis linguae Latinae*, cap. cx).

things and verbs signifying actions was however by no means new in grammatical theory. Melanchthon, in so many respects the forerunner of the seventeenth-century bias towards semantic definition, as early as 1525 defines the noun as signifying 'a thing, not an action', in contrast to the verb signifying 'to act or be acted upon'.[158] Buonmattei too, though he notes that the verb is formally varied for mood and tense, regards the signification of action as the 'proper function' of verbs. In doing this he follows the almost universal seventeenth-century tendency to treat the verb as an action word, in contrast to Scaliger,[159] who as we have seen had rejected any definition in those terms. Buonmattei's actual rules for recognizing active, passive and 'neuter' verbs are of interest as involving the notion of transformation. The active verb can be 'transmuted' into a passive by changing the case of the agent noun.[160] The 'neuter' or intransitive verb (*correre*, *dormire*) is that which is incapable of such a transformation. Conversely, 'neutri passivi' such as *riposarsi* have a passive meaning but cannot be transformed into actives.

Mood is defined as 'a certain inclination of the mind, revealing the thought behind the action'.[161] In saying *I love*, one 'indicates one's thought concerning that operation'. In treating tense Buonmattei says somewhat defensively that he follows the usage of authors who put reason and truth before any authority, even though it be commonly accepted. All this to justify his setting up of eight indicative tenses in opposition to the usual five, with neatly balancing perfect and imperfect tenses. The compound forms are treated as single semantic units, for a part of speech (as in his earlier example *Granduca*) can consist of more than one word but indicate only one concept or 'spezie dell'animo'. The treatment of the participle provides yet another demonstration of the extraordinary mixture in Buonmattei's grammar of philosophical theorizing, and a careful consideration of the usage of words, and their meaning in context, that perpetuates the tradition of empirical observation initiated by Bembo. Participles indicate 'with one single sign both the thing and the action', expressing 'the thing and the operation of the thing together'.[162] This is simply the traditional definition of the participle,

---

[158] *Grammatica Latina* (Paris ed., 1527), f. 26^r.
[159] *De causis linguae Latinae*, cap. cx.
[160] *Della Lingua*, tratt. xii, cap. vi.
[161] *Ibid.*, tratt. vii, cap. vii. Scaliger too treats mood as expressing an 'inclinatio animi'.
[162] *Della Lingua*, tratt. vii, cap. xxi.

according to which it partakes of the accidents of both noun and verb, raised to a philosophical level in which concepts reflect the things and actions of the real world. Buonmattei then discusses the sentence *La donna rimase dolente* (Bembo's example) as a demonstration of the fact that participles take on the tense of the verb with which they are constructed. Since *rimase* is past, so is *dolente*. Similarly, in *La donna rimarrà dolente* the participle is in the future tense. But also, appearances to the contrary, the supposedly 'past' participle in *La donna amata del marito* is in the present tense, for the phrase is logically identical with the present tense structure *La donna, la quale il marito ama*. Buonmattei concludes that these examples clearly show that tense in participles is not shown by 'distinct endings' with *dolente* as necessarily present and *amata* as necessarily past. The fact that the forms involved are often adjectives escapes him. The gerund is on similar grounds treated as a separate part of speech, because e.g. *Dio amando crea* is restatable as *Dio crea perche ama*, and hence gerunds express the underlying reasons ('cagioni') of actions. Once again we see the willingness to transpose structures into other, semantically identical ones to prove a point.

In line with his doctrine that the functions of the parts of speech have their counterpart in natural phenomena, Scaliger treats prepositions as signs of the *motus* and *quies* observable in the universe.[163] If nouns signify the nature of causes, prepositions indicate the manner in which those same causes operate.[164] Buonmattei's similarly based cosmology, in which everything that exists is either cause or effect, produces a similar view of the preposition as declaring 'the manner of causes' and indicating 'whether the cause is final, formal, material, or instrumental'.[165] Unlike the 'segnacaso' it is not a case marker, but is used to indicate the logical relationships contained in the Four Causes, 'which for the most part have regard to some verb'.[166] When a word is preposition and when 'segnacaso' can only be judged from the context. As an illustration Buonmattei gives the ambiguous sentence *Fu...purgata la città da uficiali*. Does it mean the city was

---

[163] *De causis linguae Latinae*, cap. clii: 'Omne corpus aut movetur, aut quiescit...Hinc eliciemus praepositionis essentialem definitionem.'
[164] *Ibid.*, cap. lxxii.
[165] *Della Lingua*, tratt. VII, cap. xxi. In tratt. xv however Buonmattei gives the traditional definition commonly repeated from Donatus (Keil, *Grammatici Latini*, IV, 389), and rejected by Scaliger in *De causis linguae Latinae*, cap. clii.
[166] *Della Lingua*, tratt. xv, cap. xii.

cleansed *by* officials, or purged *of* officials? If the former, *da uficiali* is an agent in the ablative case and *da* is a 'segnacaso'. If the latter, *da* is a preposition. Though Buonmattei is in practice obliged also to treat the 'prepositions' *dentro*, *circa* and *con* as case markers, the essential function of prepositions none the less remains the indication not of cases, but of underlying reasons or 'cagioni', *per* in *per amore* for example being a preposition of cause.

Buonmattei's twelfth and last part of speech, the 'ripieno' or ornamental particle, represents an innovation. It has considerable importance, for without it 'our language would not have its entire perfection: it would lack that property that renders it, at least in its locutions, different from all others'.[167] It includes not only stylistically optional elements (*ben* in *Vedde ben venti lupi*), but also grammatically optional ones. Many 'ripieni' (the word means 'filling' or 'padding') have merely ornamental use, serving to give 'una certa grazia' to the word they accompany, but interestingly the words *io*, *tu*, *egli*, etc. ('up to now confused by many with the pronouns') are also 'ripieni' when grammatically superfluous. In *quant'io posso*, as contrasted with *quanto posso*, the form *io* is not a pronoun but a 'ripieno'. This part of speech is defined as 'a particle, not necessary to the grammatical weave, but serving as an ornament of the sentence, for linguistic propriety'.[168] It is not necessary to grammar, because it does not indicate things or actions, or their circumstances and accidents. Without it, the sentence would still 'suffice to express the concepts of the mind'.

What Buonmattei and the other authors treated in this section share with Scaliger is a readiness to apply Aristotelian criteria to language, treating it as a 'substance' (the material, 'phonetic' aspect) whose 'form' consists of the mental concepts it expresses. In the last resort, this view also involves an assumed isomorphism between language and the universe (or rather between language and Aristotelian categorization of the universe) that will resurface in the linguistic theories of the English artificial-language planners connected with the Royal Society.

[167] *Ibid.*, tratt. xix, cap. i.
[168] *Ibid.*, tratt. xix, cap. ii: 'non necessaria alla tela grammaticale'.

4. LANGUAGE THE MIRROR OF THOUGHT: FROM SANCTIUS TO PORT-ROYAL

Buonmattei's promotion of the 'ripieno' or ornamental particle to the status of a part of speech is an indication of the important position still occupied by rhetorical matters in the Italian grammatical tradition. Ramus' attempt to keep strictly separate the three arts of grammar, logic and rhetoric, so fraught with consequences for linguistic studies in northern Europe, had had little if any influence in Italy, where the empirically based grammars did not in any case have a logical orientation, but where the links between rhetoric and grammar were of long date. The importance of the next great grammarian of Latin to be used as a model by vernacular authors, the Spanish grammarian Sanctius, lies precisely in his bringing together again in a unified whole of these three arts essential to Renaissance communication theory. Ramus had of course made use of logic in establishing the boundaries of the arts and in prescribing the methods and framework of his grammars, but he had on the one hand rejected any use of logic as a metalanguage (and indeed any employment of semantic criteria), and on the other excluded rhetoric altogether from linguistic theory. Scaliger had, in a return to medieval Scholastic approaches, given philosophy the status of a metalanguage and brought in once again that search for underlying *rationes* or causes that had been a central feature of the modistic approach. Sanctius not only continues this preoccupation with the *ratio* of language, but gives certain formerly rhetorical matters the status of elements essential to a properly conceived linguistic theory. Francisco Sanchez de las Brozas (better known under the Latin form of his name) published his *Minerva: seu de causis linguae Latinae*, whose title has obvious echoes of Scaliger, in 1587.[1] But though the *Minerva*

---

[1] Published in Salamanca. For full treatment of this work see Breva-Claramonte, *Sanctius' Theory of Language*, and Clerico, *Franciscus Sanctius*. In his article 'Sanctius' *Minerva* of 1562 and the Evolution of his Linguistic Theory', *Historiographia Linguistica*, II:1 (1975), pp. 44–66, Breva had already called attention to a 'recently discovered version of the *Minerva*, which antedates

constitutes in some respects a synthesis of the works of Linacre and
Scaliger, the interests of Scaliger and Sanctius diverge considerably
in their conception of the relationships between morphology, syntax
and logical relationships.[2] The work superficially owes a good deal
to Ramus, whose formally based word-class definitions are repeated
verbatim and without acknowledgment. In any case Sanctius, who
attempted to introduce Ramist pedagogical reforms into Spain, had
had several brushes with the Inquisition and would not perhaps have
wished to publish too openly his adherence to the doctrines of the
Protestant Ramus.[3] Outspoken and independent, sometimes even
turbulent, he was an early exponent of the necessity of using the
vernacular in the teaching of Latin, and was reprimanded for using
this method during his tenure of a chair at the Collegium Trilingue
in Salamanca. His contribution to grammatical theory rests on three
main elements. First, a rationalist approach illustrated by his belief
that the underlying causes of all things can be brought out – 'rerum
omnium reddenda sit ratio'.[4] Here, his insistence on underlying
'causes' and on the need to seek out the *ratio* or logical substructure
of language relates his approach to that of Scaliger, though he also
sees language as amenable to tradition and authority. The important
point is that reason is given precedence. It is necessary however to
be quite clear as to precisely what Sanctius means by the word *ratio*,
which he uses in several different senses. M. Breva-Claramonte sees
its most frequent use – the one that mainly concerns us here – as
referring to the logic of sentence structure, or more specifically to the
difference between this underlying logical structure and actual
speech.[5] Thus it may perhaps be permitted to see the application of

what has always been considered the "first" edition by twenty-five years', published in Lyons
and entitled *Minerva seu de Latinae linguae causis et elegantia*. In *Sanctius' Theory of Language* (p. 3,
n. 5) he notes that this 1562 edition contains, minus the philosophical approach, the same 'basic
tenets' of Sanctius' linguistic theory as the later one of 1587.

[2] See Clerico, *Franciscus Sanctius*, p. 61.

[3] In the 1562 edition Sanctius did in fact mention Ramus. No doubt he thought it politic
to remove the reference from the later edition.

[4] *Minerva*, I, I. On p. 65 of his *Sanctius' Theory of Language*, Breva states that 'Contrary to
Scaliger, Sanctius supports the view that language originally emanated from nature.' This
needs qualifying, for Sanctius (*Minerva*, f. 6ʳ) believes that words signify 'rerum naturam' only
in the *original* language spoken by Adam. But since he cannot believe this to be true of later
languages, he concludes that 'in omni idiomate cuiuslibet nomenclaturae reddi posse
rationem'. All later languages, exactly as with Scaliger, have their word-meanings by
convention or 'ex arbitrio'.

[5] *Sanctius' Theory of Language*, p. 205. See also, on Sanctius' employment of an underlying
logical level, Breva's 'Logical Structures in Sanctius' Linguistic Theory', *Progress in Linguistic
Histioriography*, ed. K. Koerner, Amsterdam, 1980, pp. 45–57. In this article he goes so far as
to suppose that Sanctius was trying to reconstruct the 'originally logical language'.

Sanctius' linguistic theory as involving, to use modern terms, a distinction between deep and surface structure. Breva-Claramonte not only sees it in this light, but regards this 'postulation of underlying levels' as present in earlier linguistic theories in the Latin tradition – a fact which he regards as having been overlooked by many scholars, who have investigated the history of linguistics principally from a merely descriptive standpoint.[6] The second salient feature of Sanctius' grammatical theory is the introduction of the tripartite word-class system, which we have already met in other authors, of noun, verb and particle. Noting the presence of this system in 'all oriental languages' and particularly in Hebrew, he assumes it to be universally valid, and to have originally existed in Greek and Latin. The overwhelming interest of Sanctius' grammar lies however in his third main contribution to linguistic theory, namely the particular status he gives to syntax. This part of grammar had, apart from the very lengthy treatment in Linacre's *De emendata structura* (1524) been neglected by Renaissance grammarians. Scaliger devotes only a few pages to it. Syntactic matters were of course treated in the morphological parts of grammars, but the merit of Linacre and Sanctius lies in their having studied it as such, in its own separate section. Sanctius indeed goes further, seeing syntax as the final object of grammatical description: 'cuius finis est congruens oratio'. The corner-stone of his syntactic doctrines is his theory of ellipse,[7] and it is here that a revolution is operated that is of cardinal importance for the development of theories of universal grammar, and in particular for the genesis of the doctrines contained in the Port-Royal *Grammaire générale et raisonnée* of 1660. Two points emerge here. First, Sanctius brings back logic into linguistic theory, regarding 'elliptic' structures in common use as abbreviations of more logically complete expanded structures, as when *longo post tempore* is treated as an abbreviation of *longo tempore, post id tempus*. He is not of course the inventor of this type of analysis. It is a commonplace of medieval modistic grammar (which treated e.g. *lege* as an abbreviation of the logically complete *impero te legere*),[8] and is set out at length by Linacre

---

[6] *Sanctius' Theory of Language*, p. 234.

[7] G. Clerico ('F. Sanctius: histoire d'une réhabilitation', *La Grammaire générale des modistes aux idéologues*, ed. A. Joly and F. Stéfanini, Lille, 1977, p. 125, n. 1) describes M. Sánchez Barrado's *La elipsis según el Brocense*, Segovia, 1919, as of capital importance for the understanding of Sanctius' grammatical system. She also describes this work as 'introuvable', and in fact I have not been able to see a copy.

[8] Thomas of Erfurt, *Grammatica speculativa*, cap. xxvii.

sixty years previously. Grammarians had however drawn attention to elliptic constructions since the very beginnings of the Latin tradition, the positing of the two syntactic levels *oratio naturalis* and *oratio figurata* dating from Quintilian. But the criterion here is a rhetorical rather than a grammatical one, since Quintilian's underlying structure is justified, as Breva-Claramonte notes,[9] not by an appeal to logic, but by usage or *consuetudo*.

Quintilian's *Institutio oratoria* (*c.* 35–95 A.D.),[10] a work of central importance for Renaissance theories of communication, is aimed mainly at the teaching of rhetoric. From a comparison of Sanctius' and Quintilian's notions of *ratio* Breva-Claramonte reaches the following conclusion: whereas for the latter 'figurative speech does not consist in deviation from the natural or logical sense, but depends on the *consuetudo* of the community', for the former '*ratio* is based on the logic of nature'[11] In other words, while for Quintilian some figures of speech are in such general use that they are no longer seen as figures, for Sanctius every figurative usage is an invitation to the linguist to demonstrate the existence of an underlying logical level. Though he incorporates some of Quintilian's ideas, 'more explicitly than Quintilian, Sanctius postulates two "natural" levels: one of semantics... and the other of syntax (the logical sentence)'.[12] An extensive treatment of elliptic constructions is also present in Priscian's vast *Institutiones grammaticae* (*c.* 500 A.D.), the basis for grammatical description throughout the Middle Ages and the Renaissance, though whether this treatment implies, as Breva-Claramonte maintains, an awareness of an 'underlying level' is perhaps arguable. Certainly his expansion of *Filius Pelei* into *qui est filius Pelei*, an example which Sanctius himself quotes, of *evenit* into *eventus evenit*, and of *curro* into *curro cursum*, would seem to prove the point. Or is he simply adducing – as in *pudet me tui = pudor me habet tui* – semantic equivalents which actually have an at least putative existence in surface structure? Where Sanctius differs from these precedents, and

[9] *Sanctius' Theory of Language*, p. 234.
[10] A translation is contained in *The Institutio Oratoria of Marcus Fabius Quintilianus with an English Summary and Concordance* (ed. Little), Nashville, Tennessee, 1951.
[11] 'Sanctius's Antecedents: The Beginnings of Transformational Grammar', *Language Sciences*, XLIV (1977), pp. 13–14.
[12] *Ibid.*, p. 13. V. Kohonen, 'On the Development of an Awareness of English Syntax', *Neuphilologische Mitteilungen* (1978), pp. 44–58, observes that a distinction was made in the thirteenth century between a 'logico-grammatical *ordo naturalis* and the rhetorical *ordo naturalis*.' (See C. Thurot, *Extraits de divers manuscrits latins*, Paris, 1869.)

in contrast to authors such as Buonmattei who treat rhetorical devices as not a necessary part of the 'grammatical weave', is in his second main point concerning ellipse, in which he promotes the doctrine of elliptic suppletion to the status of a necessary component of linguistic theory and description: 'doctrinam supplendi esse valde necessariam'.[13] Those elements to be supplied in an expansion of a given construction are those which are essential to *ratio*, those 'sine quibus Grammaticae ratio constare non potest'.[14] Thus it does indeed seem – and in this he is a forerunner of the Port-Royal *Grammaire générale et raisonnée* – that Sanctius postulates an underlying logical level to language, the demonstration of which is the task of the grammarian. He thus furnishes a contrast to Ramus, who confines himself to the description of the formal morphological relationships of the surface level of language. Whether this justifies Breva-Claramonte in stating that 'in contemporary linguistic jargon, Ramus would deserve the name of "descriptivist", while Sanctius would be called a "transformationalist"'[15] is open to question. It is always dangerous to use concepts of present-day linguistics outside the context of their own times.[16] J.-C. Chevalier, in any case, would not agree with this distinction between Sanctius and Ramus. Intent as he is on attributing to the Port-Royal authors the honour of being the first to move from the analysis of the 'niveau du discours' to that of the 'niveau de la forme du contenu',[17] he sees Sanctius as not making a clear distinction between logical and rhetorical possibilities of explanation, and remaining, no less than Ramus, 'enclosed within the language he is describing'.[18] It is I think, on the contrary, precisely Sanctius' approach[19] that, reversing Ramus' barren prescription that the arts must stay in their own separate compartments, will enable the Port-Royal authors, in a parallel employment of logic, grammar and the rhetorical figure of ellipse, to lay the foundations

[13] This is the title of the section on ellipse in book IV of the *Minerva*.
[14] *Minerva*, IV, 2.
[15] *Sanctius' Theory of Language*, p. 81.
[16] I hasten to add that I was myself to some extent guilty of this in my own first volume, and may indeed inadvertently have offended in this one. The trap is easy to fall into.
[17] *Histoire de la syntaxe*, pp. 490–1, 499.
[18] *Ibid.*, p. 538. Cf. p. 502, where Sanctius is seen as encountering 'des difficultés insurmontables, de ce que le seul code signalétique qu'il utilise est le code de la langue, en sorte que parole et métalangage sont constamment amalgamés, parce que l'on ne distingue pas nettement l'ellipse à valeur logique de représentation et l'ellipse, figure rhétorique'.
[19] On Sanctius' treatment of elliptical constructions see Padley, *Grammatical Theory* (1976), pp. 102–8.

of their theory of universal grammar. It is also the reason why those foundations must be held to be derivative.

This is not however to say that Sanctius should necessarily be seen as *the* originator of universal grammar. G. Clerico, in a view resembling that of M. Breva-Claramonte, holds not only that his generalization of the application of elliptic procedures authenticated the existence of a *debita constructio* or required construction and thus provided the source for later notions of a 'natural' syntactic order,[20] but that he also, as standing behind the analyses of the Port-Royal *Nouvelle Méthode latine*, has a major role to play in 'the stages in the formation of that general grammar that truly has its birth there'.[21] Though she recognizes that both Linacre and Sanctius posit a 'double level' of linguistic construction, she sees Sanctius as having taken the theory a step further by providing a more comprehensive set of rules and a more powerful synthesis. Here it may be noted that a marked difference between Sanctius' treatment and that of Linacre lies in their respective approaches to *enallage* or substitution (sometimes called in Latin *immutatio*), the traditional procedure in which a study is made of the possibilities of substitution of one part of speech for another in discourse. Linacre, as we have seen, devotes the whole of the second book (ff. 35^r–49^r) of his *De emendata structura* to this question, demonstrating not only the interchange of the various parts of speech, but also for instance the semantic identity of active and passive verbal expressions. These procedures could not but encourage the idea, necessary to a contemporary theory of general grammar, that one and the same thought sequence can be variously rendered by a number of different surface constructions. Sanctius, by contrast, totally excludes any application of *enallage* from his system. This refusal to accept e.g. that what are *formally* substantives can none the less be used with adjectival *function*, and vice versa, has two important consequences. In the first place it involves the blocking of linguistic descriptions at a non-functional level.[22] Hence a rigidity of approach in which Sanctius is at pains to ascribe a single, unvarying sense or value to each part of speech and to each grammatical category. What is once a substantive is always a substantive, and each nominal case has a single unchangeable signification. If, as in *magni emi*, a part of speech seems to have strayed from its original and fixed grammatical

[20] *Franciscus Sanctius*, p. 29. [21] *Ibid.*, p. 69.
[22] See Clerico, *ibid.*, p. 21.

employment, it must be brought back to its pristine value by the restoration of those features deleted by ellipse: *emi hoc magni aeris pretio.* Ellipse in Sanctius' hands thus becomes very much a tool for preserving the coincidence of function and morphological form, to the extent that, in Clerico's words, 'instead of morphology being subordinated to the syntactic rules, it often seems to subject them to its laws'.[23] It follows, and this is the second consequence of Sanctius' refusal to allow words to fulfil diverse functions in discourse and of his arbitrary fixing of words and their accidents in a single semantic and grammatical value, that a theory of ellipse becomes – as indeed Sanctius claims it is – a necessary tool in linguistic description.[24] M. Breva-Claramonte sees this as a virtue in Sanctius: had Linacre been a theoretician 'either he would have sought to reconcile the theory of substitutions with the notion of the logical level of language, or he would have tried to eliminate one of them as Sanctius did'.[25] It is my contention that it is precisely Linacre's use of the two procedures side by side that makes his work of primary importance for the succeeding development of general grammar, allowing an elasticity, absent from Sanctius' approach to syntax, which, together with his insistence on an underlying 'sensus animi', prepares the way for later doctrines concerning the varied surface 'clothing' of logical structures previously elaborated in the mind. It should be borne in mind that not only are many if not most of Linacre's examples of ellipse taken over unchanged by Sanctius, but the latter also repeats his four-fold classification of the figures (according as they operate by addition, deletion, position or substitution), defining them in identical terms. They are in turn repeated by the *Nouvelle Méthode latine.*[26] In view of all this perhaps it is not excessive to see Linacre himself, rather than Sanctius or the Port-Royal Latin Grammar, as the originator (after the virtual eclipse of medieval thought on the matter) of theories of general grammar.

[23] *Ibid.*, p. 21.

[24] Cf. Clerico, *ibid.*, p. 82.

[25] *Sanctius' Theory of Language*, p. 57. Clerico however admits (*Franciscus Sanctius*, p. 58) that 'Certes l'importance égale attachée à l'ellipse et à l'énallage par Linacre, là où ce sont pour Sanctius des figures exclusives l'une de l'autre, mérite réflexion.' On the other hand (p. 60) she holds that the two approaches result in widely divergent views of linguistic mechanisms.

[26] Fifth edition, Paris, 1656, p. 575: 'Nous les réduisons toutes à quatre espèces, selon la pensée du docte Sanctius.'

Correas

The large number of editions of Sanctius during the seventeenth and eighteenth centuries are a sufficient indication of the esteem in which he was held by writers of general grammars. After a long eclipse he has in our own day again become a subject of interest, no doubt in large part because of his status as a forerunner of the Port-Royal Grammar, which in turn was brought back into prominence by the publication of Chomsky's *Cartesian Linguistics* in 1966.[27]

In the seventeenth century, if the influence of Scaliger is everywhere evident in Buonmattei's treatment of the underlying 'causes' of the Tuscan language, it is to the Spaniard Gonzalo Correas that we must turn for an example of a major vernacular grammar with a debt to Sanctius. Correas' work is all the more important in view of the fact that though Sanctius' *Minerva* became widely known throughout Europe it had no immediate repercussions in Spain itself. No doubt it is not without significance that Correas was himself a professor at Salamanca, and had probably been one of Sanctius' students. As with Ratke at the same period in Germany, his interest in universal grammar has a strong pedagogical motivation. Though unlike Ratke he espouses an overt linguistic theory, his work too is an illustration of the fact that the history of grammatical theory cannot be considered apart from the pedagogical realities of the times. At the end of the first quarter of the seventeenth century in Spain there is some doubt, in spite of the long reign of Nebrija's *Gramatica castellana* of 1492 (or perhaps even because of it?), as to the usefulness of a vernacular grammar, which is still seen by many as superfluous. In his preface to Correas' *Arte grande de la lengua castellana*, Juan de Jauregui feels obliged to go out of his way to stress that in Italy authors of the importance of Trissino and Tolomei, Bembo and Ruscelli, all thought it worth their while to occupy themselves with their native tongue. The *Arte grande*[28] appeared in manuscript form

---

[27] On the reasons underlying this revival of interest in Sanctius see Clerico's 'F. Sanctius: histoire d'une réhabilitation'.

[28] I have consulted both the Conde de la Viñaza's edition of the *Arte grande* (Madrid, 1903) and that of E. Alarcos García (Madrid, 1954). The pagination followed is that of the latter edition, based on MS 18.969 in the Biblioteca Nacional. García is somewhat scathing on the subject of Viñaza's edition, the first ever published but which, the original MS being untraceable in 1903, was based on B. J. Gallardo's incomplete copy. For our purposes however the differences between Garcia's and Viñaza's editions are of no great moment. García's introduction, while giving excerpts from Correas' views on usage and phonetic questions, is silent on the subject of grammatical theory.

in 1625, to be followed two years later by a *Trilingue de tres artes*.[29]
The title of the latter reflects the fact that for a short time Correas
held a fellowship at the Colegio Trilingue in Salamanca, whose
mission was the teaching of the three classical languages Latin, Greek
and Hebrew. He was well qualified in all three, for after the closure
of the Colegio he was successively appointed to university chairs in
them.[30] The 'three grammars' treated in the *Trilingue de tres artes* are
Latin, Greek and Castilian, all discussed, as the title makes a point
of stating, 'en romanze' or in the vernacular.[31] Though in most
respects the plan and treatment are identical, the *Arte grande* is a much
more profound and substantial work than the Castilian section of the
Trilingue. Correas had an interest in orthographical reform, his
celebrity in his own day resting on his championship of the rigorously
phonetic approach to spelling evidenced in his *Ortografía kastellana* of
1630. Like so many sixteenth- and seventeenth-century grammarians
he is imbued with a sense of the growing importance of the
vernacular. In an almost obsessive insistence on the non-Latin origins
of Castilian, he denies the commonly held view of it as nothing more
than 'corrupt Latin'. Since there can be 'no doubt' that the
language was brought to Spain by Noah's nephew Tubal, whose
descendants also populated Ireland and spoke one of the seventy-two
tongues resulting from the confusion of Babel, any similarities of
vocabulary with Latin must be accidental. The whole of the
historical section of his work is far-fetched and of little value.[32] His
main interest in any case is with the contemporary state of the
language, now given prestige by the increase in Castilian imperial
power. He is motivated by chiefly pedagogical aims, the growing
seventeenth-century interest in methodology being illustrated by his
claim that his experience in teaching the three languages has
equipped him with the necessary 'method and facility' to compose

[29] Published in Salamanca, this is an abridged version of the *Arte grande*, and often a
word-for-word repetition of it. See on both works Conde de la Viñaza's 'Dos libros inéditos
de Maestro Gonzalo Correas: notas bibliográfico-críticas', *Homenaje á Menéndez Pelayo*, Madrid,
1899, pp. 601–14. This article is virtually identical with Viñaza's prologue to his 1903 edition
of the *Arte grande*.

[30] It does not seem that Correas was ever, as Viñaza states, a professor at the Colegio
Trilingue itself.

[31] The number of languages treated would in fact have been four, were it not that the printer
lacked Hebrew characters.

[32] For his ideas on the history of the language Correas consulted Gregorio López Madera's
Discurso de la certidumbre de las reliquias descubiertas en Granada desde el año 1588 hasta el de 1598
(Granada, 1611), and Fernando de Lara's *Diálogos de las cosas notables de Granada y lengua española*
(Seville, 1603), especially the former.

fuller, clearer and more concise grammars than have hitherto appeared. The grammars of Castilian, Latin and Greek have as with Ratke's works a common plan, thus facilitating the transition from the grammar of the mother tongue to that of the other two. If he is professedly writing a general grammar, it is precisely because such a universalist approach validates his claim that the rules of grammar are best acquired first in the vernacular. The reason he gives is that given by Ratke: 'Grammar in general is common to all languages, and the same in every one.'[33] The precepts are universally valid, but the 'gramática vulgar' offers an easier entrance to them. Once this pedagogical priority of the mother tongue has been established, Correas can in practice subordinate theory to the empirical observation of the forms of the language. Grammar, though defined partially in universalist terms, is also described as dealing with those individual features that belong only to the particular language that is the object of description. If general grammar is based on a conformity between languages, this conformity in turn is an abstraction from the 'natural and customary' speech of language users,[34] and it is this natural and customary speech that Correas sets out to describe. His statement that no language is 'natural' to the whole of mankind is meant in refutation of the widely held view of Hebrew as the only truly natural language. What is common to all languages – and here the influence of Sanctius is apparent – is syntactic congruence. In all else, in all customary matters, languages differ from each other. Since Correas is ready to admit that every speaker of a 'natural' language already knows the grammatical usage of that language this leads to a distinction between 'arte gramatica' and 'arte natural'. Surprisingly modern is his contention that the mass of the people speak and understand their language 'solely by use, governed by the simple and natural art, which has greater weight with them than any precepts and rules that issue from it'.[35] The contemporary exclusion of the ancient division of *grammatica historica*, which dealt with the use by poets and orators of a language which native speakers already knew 'more by popular use than by art', represents for him an impoverishment, and here Correas is in sharp contrast to the growing trend to give priority to *grammatica methodica*, that is to say to the elaboration of linguistic theory. Given this standpoint, it is not

[33] *Arte grande* (Alarcos García's edition, Madrid, 1954), pp. 9–10.
[34] *Ibid.*, p. 129.   [35] *Ibid.*, p. 130.

surprising that in the *Arte grande* he concerns himself more particularly with the language of the people, with idiomatic expressions, and dialect differences corresponding to differences in age, sex, social class or profession. Though all these are embraced by 'la lengua universal', each possesses its own dialect: 'á cada uno le está bien su lenguaxe'. In this respect, Correas' mingling of the precepts of general grammar with close observation of actual speech norms recalls the approach of his contemporary Buonmattei in Italy. The *Arte*, so much more interesting as a descriptive document than the *Trilingue*, gives valuable witness to a 'state of language', that of Castilian in the first quarter of the seventeenth century. If Correas occupies himself with usages that most cultivated people of his date would have regarded as lacking in refinement, it is because he believes that it is precisely among the less elevated classes that the language and its customs are best preserved. From this emerges his argument for the acquisition of a grammar over and above that of the *arte natural*: 'when the natural art is subjected to method or good order, languages are better understood and better preserved'. He may well recognize the individual excellences of untutored Castilian, but in the last resort he wishes to enhance it yet further by the application of 'grammar', which thus becomes almost an entity in itself, applicable to a language in order to improve it. But apart from his extension to Castilian of Sanctius' tripartite system of the parts of speech, he is by no means enterprising in the grammatical theory he applies. Many of his definitions and examples are taken from the time-hallowed pages of Nebrija's *Gramatica castellana* (1492), though not without due thought, for he does not hesitate to deviate from established authority where he judges it necessary. If his grammatical doctrines are in many respects traditional ones, his particular type of empirical approach represents for its date a striking innovation. In a history of Spanish grammar this approach would have pride of place, but here we must confine ourselves to a consideration of Correas' contribution to theories of universal grammar.

Much of Correas' grammatical theory is not specifically universalist, showing features that are part of the common trend in seventeenth-century grammars. His definition of grammar allows both for a universal approach and the empirical observation of the facts of individual languages, for 'though their words and phrases may differ... agreement and congruity seem natural to men, while they disagree in customs and individual matters.'[36] This notion seems to be widespread in the seventeenth century, also being found in an English grammarian's claim that 'the Nations...in point of Syntaxe agree as one; therefore also manifesting the product of words to be more from nature, as of Sentences from Reason',[37] which gives a neat parallel to Correas' distinction between 'arte gramatica' and 'arte natural'. It is in this insistence on syntax as the true object of the grammatical art that the influence of Sanctius on Correas is most apparent, the former's 'oratio sive syntaxis est finis grammaticae' and 'cuius finis est congruens oratio'[38] being closely echoed by the *Trilingue*'s 'El fin de la gramatica es la oracion, ô rrazon congrua i bien concertada.' A translation of the statement in the *Arte grande* reads: 'The object of grammar is *oratio* or congruent speech; its foundation and structure is the joining together of the words and parts of speech that make up and complete the *oratio*.'[39] It is here that the full importance of the setting up of the three parts of speech noun, verb and particle in imitation of Sanctius is revealed. With these three word-classes, according to Sanctius, there is nothing that cannot be expressed by an *oratio*, within which noun and verb play the main grammatical role.[40] Since however, in an argumentation recalling Scaliger, these two cannot by themselves express 'the manner by which the underlying reason of causes may be exhibited',[41] this function must be performed by prepositions and adverbs which may, together with conjunctions, be subsumed into a class of particles. It is this analysis that lies behind Correas' definition of the sentence as the expression of a 'complete thought' to which noun and verb are equally indispensable, with the particle as an 'accessory' with frequently no more than decorative function. The definition appears in various guises, of which that on p. 12 of the *Trilingue* gives the essence: 'The *oratio* is the reason and sense made by noun and verb agreeing in number and person, and is embellished by other parts [of speech] and cases.'[42] Significant here is the Sanctian requirement

[36] *Ibid.*, p. 129.

[37] Jones, *Herm'aelogium; or, an Essay at the Rationality of the Art of Speaking*, preface.

[38] *Minerva*, I, cap. ii.

[39] *Arte grande*, p. 132. Cf. *Trilingue*, pp. 12, 109. I have rendered *orazion* by its Latin equivalent, in common use by Latin grammarians of the time.

[40] *Minerva*, I, cap. ii. The closeness of the parallel may be seen by comparing the passage here with that on p. 314 of Correas' *Arte grande*, which repeats all of Sanctius' examples of languages containing, or assumed to have contained, this tripartite system.

[41] *Minerva*, I, cap. ii: 'modus, per quem causarum ratio explicaretur'.

[42] This definition also appears on p. 132 of the *Arte grande*.

that the three word-classes make up the *oratio* 'by virtue of the concord they must maintain'. A cardinal feature is the use of the term *rrazon* ('reason') as an alternative term for sentence, no doubt in translation of the Latin *ratio* that figures so prominently in Sanctius' treatment. It is this *oracion* or *rrazon* that Correas sees as preeminently 'grammatical' and the principal object of study for the grammarian. Since a three-word-class system of noun, verb and particle provides all that is necessary for a reasoned proposition, it follows, as he insists time and time again, that it is necessarily common to all languages.

Sanctius had assumed that in the original language, thought by many to be Hebrew, things had received their names 'from Nature itself', and that hence there was a natural correspondence between thing and name.[43] Correas holds on the contrary that since things receive their names by the general consent of mankind, there can be no 'natural' languages in this sense, brushing aside as incapable of ascertainment the question whether names, including those imposed by Adam before the confusion of tongues, reflect the nature of things. But though such an enquiry is fruitless in the case of primary roots, it has some sense when applied to derivatives and compounds. Whereas primary words are arbitrary 'signs or marks', derived forms ('motivated' in modern parlance) give 'sure and abbreviated definitions' of things. The emphasis is on the rendering, whether motivated or unmotivated, of concepts. The equation of Latin cases with the vernacular construction particle plus noun carries the implication that all languages have the same 'differences in sense and meaning', variously rendered by their individual structures. This attitude, which sees identical thought processes as expressed by different syntactic procedures, is encouraged by the practice of giving vernacular circumlocutions as semantic equivalents for Latin grammatical categories that have no corresponding form in the vernacular. Behind this lies the desire to prove that the vulgar tongues can, by recourse to periphrasis, express everything that Latin can. Since Spanish *amante* cannot govern cases, Latin *amans* is accordingly rendered not by it but by *él que ama*, Correas even going so far as to call such structures 'Castilian participles'. Similarly *amaturus*, with no unitary equivalent in Spanish, is rendered by *él que ha de amar*. There is an interesting parallel here with Caramuel's contention, in his Latin 'philosophical' grammar, that the present

---

[43] On Sanctius' position concerning the nature/convention issue see Padley, *Grammatical Theory* (1976), pp. 97–8.

participle can be logically equated with the structure relative pronoun plus verb: *amans = qui amat*.[44] The restating of structures in terms of other structures deemed to be semantically equivalent has a long history in Latin grammars, giving the impulsion to similar procedures in vernacular grammars (Correas is of course not alone in this), which in turn reinforce the notion, necessary to a theory of universal grammar, that it is the underlying thought that is the true object of investigation, not the various accidental forms in which that thought can be expressed. There is not however an absolute parallelism between the syntactic structures of Castilian and those of Latin, for Correas shares the growing opinion that the vernacular shows a more natural order of construction, one of its virtues being the 'orden i contestura natural de las palavras'. He wants to have it both ways however, for citing Quintilian's remark that almost all speech is figurative, he claims that this is particularly true of Castilian. Since he mentions Linacre along with Sanctius as having made a lengthy treatment of ellipse, his division of syntax into figurative construction and 'la costruzion llana' may owe a debt to Linacre's *constructio justa* and *figurata*. His treatment of *enallage* (the interchangeability of parts of speech in discourse) has of course its counterpart in Linacre's *De emendata structura*. As for elliptical constructions (so prominent a feature of Sanctius' *Minerva*), he holds them to be of such frequent occurrence in all languages that there is scarcely a sentence in which they do not appear. In Castilian this entails e.g. the rewriting of *Juan de Pelayo* as *Juan hijo de Pelayo*, and of *buenos días* as *os dé Dios buenos días*. This figurative syntax, in line with Correas' models Sanctius and Linacre, is of exceptional length in the *Arte grande*. Only part of it, he admits, concerns grammar, the rest being a matter for rhetoric, but his treatment is an indication of the way in which rhetoric, sternly excluded by Ramus, is once again becoming the province of the grammarian. With the Port-Royal authors figurative construction will, following Sanctius, be elevated to the status of a necessary part of linguistic theory. Correas' importance lies partially at least in his being a comparatively early milestone on this road.[45]

[44] J. Caramuel y Lobkowitz, *Grammatica audax*, in *Praecursor logicus*. For details see Padley, *Grammatical Theory* (1976), p. 83.

[45] Undoubtedly Correas' most important contribution to specifically Spanish linguistics is his empirical approach and his awareness of the riches and subtleties of the vernacular as it is used in the various speech communities. It is however precisely these excellences that cannot figure in a general account of grammatical theory, but constitute material for the history of Spanish grammar as such.

ii PORT-ROYAL: THE VIRTUAL IDENTIFICATION OF LINGUISTIC AND MENTAL PROCESSES

The treatment of elliptic constructions had always formed part of the Latin grammatical tradition. Accordingly the Port-Royal Latin grammar, which appeared in various editions from 1644 onwards, is by no means unusual in expanding *homo est juvenis* into *homo est juvenis homo* or, in Linacre's fashion, *vivitur* into *vita vivitur*.[46] This would in itself be unremarkable, were it not that in his third edition of 1654[47] the author specifically mentions his debt to Sanctius, and founds an entire syntactic theory on it. The first edition had modest, pedagogical aims in keeping with the methods of the Port-Royal schools (the celebrated Petites Ecoles),[48] whose teaching was exceptional in having a practical orientation. In accordance with their principle of proceeding from the already known to the unknown, instruction was given in the vernacular,[49] their *Nouvelle Méthode latine* being, exceptionally for its date, written in French. The aim was not merely to teach Latin, but equally to improve the knowledge of the mother tongue.[50] But though the author, Claude Lancelot, claims that speedy results can be obtained by using his method,[51] he retains Despauterius' traditional order of treatment,[52] regarding his own first edition as no more than 'a stream of which he is the source'.[53] Had matters rested there the Port-Royal Latin grammar would have

[46] For a fuller discussion see Padley, *Grammatical Theory* (1976), pp. 213–15.

[47] C. Lancelot, *Nouvelle Méthode pour apprendre facilement et en peu de temps la langue latine* (3rd ed.), Paris, 1654. I have also consulted the eighth edition (Paris) of 1681.

[48] Various dates have been given for the foundation of these schools. Robins (*Short History*, p. 123) and F. Cadet (*Port-Royal Education*, London, 1898) give the date 1637. F. P. Graves (*A History of Education*, New York, 1914) gives 1643. They were probably not functioning to any real extent before 1646, and were closed by royal command in 1660.

[49] *Nouvelle Méthode latine* (henceforth referred to as *NML*), 8th ed., 1681, p. 22: 'ce que nous sçavons desja, nous doit servir comme d'une lumière pour esclaircir ce que nous ne sçavons pas...nous nous devons servir de nostre langue maternelle comme d'un moyen pour entrer dans les langues qui sont estranges et inconnuës.'

[50] *Ibid.*, p. 14.

[51] Cf. C. Lancelot, A. Arnauld and P. Nicole, *Nouvelle Méthode pour apprendre facilement la langue grecque* (2nd ed.), Paris, 1656, preface: 'l'on a vu des enfans fort jeunes, et d'un esprit mesme assez médiocre, sçavoir passablement toute leur grammaire en moins de deux on trois mois par cette Méthode'.

[52] Despauterius' *Rudimenta* (Paris, 1514) and *Commentarii grammatici* (Paris, 1538) were the ruling grammars in the schools, with a position comparable to that of Lily's Latin grammar in England.

[53] *NML* (1644 ed.), p. 12: 'C'est de luy principalement que j'ay pris les principes et fondemens de la langue Latine...ainsi ce petit livre doit passer pour un ruisseau dont il est la source.'

presented only a pedagogical interest. The third edition of 1654 contains however revisions that have far-reaching implications for the theories presented in the Port-Royal authors' celebrated *Grammaire générale et raisonnée* of 1660. The all-important fact is that in the period of time separating the two editions Lancelot had become acquainted with Sanctius' *Minerva*, reading it 'with the greatest possible care, and with a satisfaction to which I cannot give adequate expression'.[54] The attraction lies in Sanctius' approach to syntax, which he treats 'with an insight [*lumière*] incomparably greater than that of any of his predecessors'. Sanctius' great merit, according to Lancelot, consists in his having abstracted from the tangle of linguistic usage syntactic laws of general application. He has proved that the entire aim of the art of grammar is to demonstrate one fact: that the figurative constructions used in everyday language, containing elements that are understood though not expressed ('sous-entenduës sans estre marquées'), are restatable in terms of the 'essential construction' of the underlying linguistic system. Even expressions which seem to have no other explanation than the caprices of usage can by this means be brought within the scope of 'general laws of ordinary construction'. It follows that the primary task of the grammarian is 'to bring this figurative construction into line with the laws governing the simple one, and to demonstrate that such expressions repose upon the ordinary and essential principles of linguistic construction'. In this 'ordinary' and 'essential' construction 'all the terms are so expressed in their natural order, that it can be clearly seen why one governs another'.[55] A trenchant point here is that this 'natural' order is that of the vernacular.

The Port-Royal *Nouvelle Méthode latine* has thus an open and declared debt to Sanctius.[56] Since it in turn provides the theoretical basis for the syntactic doctrines in the *Grammaire générale et raisonnée* of 1660, it provides yet another illustration of the fact that vernacular grammatical theory is only comprehensible in the light of the parallel Latin grammatical tradition. Particularly is this true where, as in the

[54] The difference between the two editions in this respect was seemingly first pointed out by G. Sahlin, *César Chesneau du Marsais et son rôle dans l'évolution de la grammaire générale*, Paris [1928], p. 13.

[55] *NML*, 3rd ed. (preface).

[56] Noting that his 1654 book 'en enferme un second qui est tout nouveau', Lancelot says 'j'ay allié ensemble ces trois Auteurs [Sanctius, Scioppius et Vossius]... tirant de chacun d'eux ce qui m'a paru de plus clair et de plus solide'. Scioppius (*Grammatica philosophica*, 1628) and Vossius (*De arte grammatica*, 1635) are themselves indebted to Sanctius.

case of Ramus and Lancelot, the author of the Latin work is also the author of the vernacular one. The matter of the authorship of the *GGR*[57] is closely intertwined with the question of whether this work represents a completely new departure in grammatical theory, or on the contrary repeats notions long current in the Latin grammatical tradition, together with a little Cartesian window-dressing. Of the two authors of the *GGR*, Claude Lancelot and Antoine Arnauld, it is the former who is the grammarian, and indeed the preface to the Scolar Press facsimile of the *GGR*[58] treats him as 'undoubtedly the leading figure in the movement towards a new theory of grammar'. Against this however must be set Lancelot's own recognition of his debt to the logician Arnauld, whose ideas, though he 'had never applied himself' to grammatical matters, surpassed in 'curiosity' and aptness anything Lancelot had encountered elsewhere.[59] It is probably Ferdinand Brunot's monumental and authoritative *Histoire de la langue française*[60] that has been most responsible for the perpetuation of the view of Arnauld as virtually the sole author of the *GGR*. 'Lancelot l'a écrite, mais Arnauld l'a pensée' declares Brunot, repeating the Abbé Fromant's condemnation of the 'inconceivable obscurity' in which Lancelot supposedly blanketed Arnauld's clarity of thought.[61] If for Brunot the *GGR* marks a decisive date in the history of French grammar, it is because he sees Arnauld as the first to apply to that grammar a 'philosophical method'. Stephen K. Land's *From Signs to Propositions* (1974) is but among the latest in a series of works that regard Arnauld, co-writer of the *Logique* of 1662, as the 'prime moving spirit', who 'may for the sake of verbal convenience be spoken of as sole author'.[62] It is in fact this Port-Royal *Logic* itself that is, in the opinion of R. Donzé, further responsible for the notion of an Arnauld-inspired 'grammatical doctrine of Cartesian inspiration, taken ready made from a new conception of the relationship between language and thought'.[63] It is however

[57] From now on the *Grammaire générale et raisonnée* will be referred to by the letters *GGR*.
[58] Menston, 1967.
[59] *GGR*, preface.
[60] Reprinted Paris, 1966–.
[61] *Histoire de la langue française*, IV, 53, 59n.1.
[62] Published in London. See p. 77. Cf. also R. Ogle, 'Two Port-Royal Theories of Natural Order', *Progress in Linguistic Historiography*, ed. K. Koerner, Amsterdam, 1980, p. 106: 'scholarship has...tended to confirm that it is indeed Arnauld...who is the major author...and the guiding influence throughout'.
[63] *La Grammaire générale et raisonnée de Port-Royal*, Berne, 1967, p. 7.

Lancelot who brings to the collaboration a knowledge of the centuries-old doctrines of the Latin tradition, and it is these doctrines that are repeated in the *GGR*. As Lancelot remarks in his preface, Arnauld had not previously 'applied himself' to grammar, and his contribution in the field of logic adds little to a core of grammatical theory inherited from Sanctius, from writers of 'philosophical' grammars in Latin, and from the Latin tradition in general. The widespread view of the *GGR* as a completely new departure based on Cartesian principles must in my view be judged erroneous.[64] It was however given further currency by the publication in 1966 of N. Chomsky's *Cartesian Linguistics*, which, while it was the welcome signal for a revival of interest in the *GGR*, proposed origins for it that many have found unacceptable, ascribing to its authors the role of proto-transformationalist grammarians, or at any rate that of in some sense precursors of Chomsky's own theories of language.[65] Cartesianism is in any case not the only claimant to an influence on Port-Royal. If certain of its doctrines appealed to them, it is because they were convinced Augustinians at a time when Augustine seemed to be a presence almost equal to that of a contemporary author.[66] Without Augustine, according to A. Robinet, not only might the *Grammaire générale* and the Port-Royal Logic never have been composed, or at any rate enjoyed the success they did, but language itself would not have been seen as 'representing thought' in the particular way the Port-Royal authors attributed to it.[67] The originality of the *GGR* lies for Robinet not in its being a general grammar, but in its use of 'new bases' taken directly from Augustinianism, and only secondarily from Descartes.

In spite of what has been said above on the subject of Arnauld's contribution to the *GGR*, the latter cannot be considered apart from

[64] H. E. Brekle for instance, in the introduction to his edition of the third ed. (1676) of the *GGR* (Stuttgart, 1966) follows the Abbé Fromant (*Supplément à la Grammaire générale*, 1756) in regarding Arnauld's contribution as the more important one. He concedes however (p. xv) that a final judgment must await a detailed comparison of the *GGR* and the *NML*. A useful corrective here is A. Robinet's observation (*Le Langage à l'âge classique*, Paris, 1978, pp. 21, 27) that the *GGR* is a work of 'general' grammar precisely *because* Lancelot had a knowledge of the work of Scaliger and Sanctius.

[65] Among other refutations of Chomsky's position see A. Joly, 'La linguistique cartésienne: une erreur mémorable', *La Grammaire générale des modistes aux idéologues*, ed. A. Joly and J. Stéfanini, Lille, 1977, pp. 165–99.

[66] Thus Robinet, *Le Langage à l'âge classique*, p. 18.

[67] *Ibid.*, pp. 9, 18: 'Sans le *De magistro*, sans le *De Doctrina christiana*, il n'y aurait pas eu cette *Grammaire*-là, ni cette *Logique*, ni ces Petites Ecoles…impossible, la *Logique de Port-Royal* sans cet arrière-texte [d'Augustin]'.

the Port-Royal Logic,[68] of which Arnauld was co-author with P. Nicole. The supreme importance of the Port-Royal authors for linguistic theory lies in fact in their having reversed the Ramist revolution, in their having brought together again in a unified doctrine the three 'arts' of grammar, logic and rhetoric. They are well aware of what they are doing, for the preface to the Logic ridicules Ramus and his followers for having inflicted on themselves the pains of the damned in 'delimiting the jurisdiction of each science with as much care as is taken to define the boundaries of kingdoms'. Subtitled 'l'art de penser' in a neat parallel to the 'art de parler' offered by the *GGR*, it is a companion work to it.[69] The two complement each other much more closely than Ramus' logic and grammar. The Logic is, as opposed (apart from superimposed details) to the *GGR*, a frankly Cartesian document with in addition a debt to Pascal's unpublished 'De l'esprit géométrique', and to the Port-Royal authors' Augustinianism.[70] Large sections of what it says are however directly applicable to the features of the *GGR* that *can* be claimed to be Cartesian, and it has a similar specifically Port-Royalist orientation. In many ways it represents a different type of logic from those that had appeared previously. Descartes condemned the traditional Aristotelian logics, which he saw as presupposing an already existent body of knowledge rather than acting as instruments of discovery. Since he sees the purpose of study as being 'to direct the mind towards the enunciation of sound and correct judgments on all matters that come before it',[71] the Port-Royal Logic, offering in its subtitle 'several new observations suitable for training the judgment', declares that the true function of reason is to indicate the right ordering of things.[72] Do not most human errors, the authors ask,

[68] A. Arnauld and P. Nicole, *La Logique ou l'art de penser: contenant...plusieurs observations propres à former le jugement*, Paris, 1662.

[69] Aarsleff, 'The History of Linguistics and Professor Chomsky', pp. 572–3, treats the Logic as the 'twin' to the *GGR*. Joly ('La linguistique cartésienne', p. 183) remarks that with the Cartesians 'l'art de penser conduit à l'art de parler', language being 'l'habillement même de la pensée'. Cf. also p. 31 of A. Joly's *F. Thurot, Tableau des progrès de la science grammaticale* (*Discours préliminaire à 'Hermes'*), Bordeaux, 1970.

[70] The authors state that 'ces réflexions...[on] en a emprunté quelques unes d'un célèbre Philosophe de ce siècle [i.e. Descartes]...On en a tiré quelques autres d'un petit Escrit non imprimé, qui avoit esté fait par...Paschal...*De l'Esprit Géométrique.*'

[71] *Rules for the Direction of Mind* (translated by E. S. Haldane and G. R. T. Ross), in *Great Books of the Western World*, XXXI, ed. R. M. Hutchins, Chicago, 1952, p. 1.

[72] Cf. *Logique*, p. 6: 'la principale application qu'on devroit avoir seroit de former son jugement...la justesse de l'esprit estant infiniment plus considérable que toutes les connaissances spéculatives'.

stem from wrong conclusions drawn from mistaken judgments? If Aristotle does not enjoy their wholehearted approval it is because his ten predicaments (though retained in their Logic) contribute little to logic's true goal of training the judgment, and lead men to prefer *verbal* formularies to precise knowledge of things. It is a complaint common in the seventeenth century (it is shared by Bacon) to both rationalists and empiricists. But in the last resort neither words nor things enjoy the confidence of the authors of the Logic. In Cartesian fashion the only matters in which they have complete faith are man's conception of himself as 'une chose qui pense', and his consciousness of the workings of his own thoughts. If they censure Aristotle for leading men to put faith in words, their own attitude to him is none the less ambivalent. They refuse 'generally to condemn' him, though insisting that his 'constraint' has endured too long, and put in a claim for 'that natural and reasonable liberty which consists in approving what we judge to be true, and rejecting what we judge to be false'. The championship of the rights of reason against those of authority sets the general tone of the Logic, though like Ramus before them the authors condemn Aristotle without being able completely to discard him. As a contemporary English writer put it, much of the Port-Royal Logic 'must be own'd to be borrowed from Aristotle, only by cloathing old Terms, under new Ideas'.[73] The Aristotelian notion that knowledge is obtained via the senses – *Nihil in intellectu quod non prius in sensu* – is however rejected out of hand: 'we can have no knowledge of what is outside us other than by the mediation of the ideas within us'.[74] The presence of 'ideas' in the mind, the existence of clear concepts, is as paramount to the Port-Royal authors as to Descartes.[75] An 'idea' they define as 'everything that is in our minds, when we can say with truth that we have a conception of a thing',[76] a definition which recalls the Thomists' *adaequatio rei et intellectus*: when the mind is focused clearly on its object, the resulting concept must correspond to reality. This view leads to a hierarchy of 'ideas' for, in Cartesian fashion, the ideas we have of mental operations such as judgment, reasoning and desire are 'très-claires', whereas those

[73] T. Baker, *Reflections upon Learning, wherein is shewn the Insufficiency thereof* (2nd ed.), London, 1700.

[74] *Logique*, p. 31. Cf. p. 41: 'nulle idée qui est dans nostre esprit ne tire son origine des sens'.

[75] *Ibid.*, p. 41: 'il n'y a rien que nous concevions plus distinctement que nostre pensée mesme, ny de proposition qui nous puisse estre plus claire que celle-là: Je pense, Donc je suis.'

[76] *Ibid.*, p. 35.

we have of 'qualitez sensibles' such as colour, sound, heat and cold are 'confuses et obscures'. Everything however ultimately comes back to a matter of mental operations. Seen in this light, logic consists of 'the reflections that men have made concerning the chief operations of their minds', namely concept formation, judgment, reasoning, and arrangement. This last operation may be termed *method*, a reminder of the extent to which contemporary philosophy and pedagogy concern themselves with methodology. The Port-Royal authors interest themselves in the way knowledge is conveyed by mental concepts and by judgments or propositions about them. In this respect their Logic answers to Descartes' requirements, being a theory of enquiry rather than a theory of communication,[77] but it also inaugurates what W. and M. Kneale[78] call the bad fashion of confusing logic with epistemology. The whole of the first part of the Logic deals with the formation of concepts. The mental operation of judging, treated in the second part, concerns the joining together of concepts in affirmations and denials, that is to say logical propositions. The fourth part, dealing with the mental operation of disposition, has to do with the putting of ideas and judgments in due order.[79] For both the Logic and the Grammar, the 'operations of the mind' and the existence of mental concepts are basic.

The Port-Royal Logic should not be simply treated as a prolegomenon to the *Grammaire générale*, as is the case with Ramus' Logic and Grammar, but the two works should be taken as constituting, together with the *Nouvelle Méthode latine*, the complete corpus of Port-Royal grammatical doctrine.[80] Large parts of the Logic are incontestably Cartesian, which brings us to the controversial question of the extent to which the *GGR* itself can be viewed as a product of Cartesianism. Since however I have treated this topic at some length in my volume on the Latin tradition,[81] a few remarks must suffice.

---

[77] See W. S. Howell, *Logic and Rhetoric*, p. 347.

[78] *The Development of Logic*, p. 316.

[79] The four parts of the Port-Royal Logic are reminiscent of the Ramist–Baconian treatment of logic under four heads of which the first two are *invention* and *judgment* (Ramus' *disposition*). The resemblances are however superficial, the Port-Royal authors being in reaction against Ramism. For Bacon's system see *The Works of Francis Bacon*, ed. J. Spedding et al., III, 383–4, and cf. Rossi, *Francis Bacon*, p. 136, for a discussion of the relevant section of Bacon's *Of the Advancement of Learning*. Rossi notes (p. 158) that for Ramus (as indeed for Cicero and Quintilian) *judicium* and *dispositio* are one.

[80] See Chevalier, *Histoire de la syntaxe*, p. 490. As Chevalier says, the great originality of the Port-Royal Logic lies in its presenting logic as basically thought about language.

[81] Padley, *Grammatical Theory* (1976), pp. 222–40.

The controversy was sparked off in 1966 by the publication of Chomsky's *Cartesian Linguistics*, but he was not of course the first to ascribe Cartesian origins to the *GGR*. Here again, it was the influential work of Brunot that gave impetus to the opinion that, following on a short period during which usage-based grammars of the type associated with the name of Vaugelas reigned supreme, 'Cartesianism came into grammar.'[82] Chomsky himself however concedes that Descartes makes but 'scant reference' to language in his writings, and what he takes to be 'Cartesian' seems to be a certain way (including its nineteenth-century manifestations) of explaining language acquisition and creativity, rather than any specifically Cartesian linguistic theory. Others have seen the influence of Descartes as being on Port-Royal pedagogy rather than on grammatical theory, J. W. Adamson for instance regarding 'the whole bent of their educational practice' as determined by Cartesianism.[83] Those points of Cartesian doctrine that are of direct relevance for Port-Royal theory may however be briefly glanced at. As we have seen, the Port-Royal Logic holds the Scholastic doctrine that the mind is by its nature predisposed to arrive at the truth. Thomists had already defined one aspect of truth as being an *adaequatio rei et intellectus*, a conformity of things and the understanding. In the Renaissance period the idea of an affinity between the mind and nature was taken to extreme lengths in Telesian nature philosophy and neo-Platonic and kabbalistic doctrines. J. C. Scaliger had stated in 1540 that the mind mirrors nature – 'est quasi rerum speculum intellectus noster'. For the Cartesians, if it is thought to be reflecting clearly it can be assumed to be purveying the truth – with the proviso that it is not, as with Scaliger, acting through sense impressions, but is observing its own operations. Descartes concludes that, apart from the existence of God, the only things of which he can be certain (to the exclusion of the outside world) are his own mental concepts, some of which are clearer, and hence more likely to convey the truth than others. Basil Willey notes that this belief has far-reaching consequences: 'The feeling that whatever can be clearly and distinctly conceived is

[82] *Histoire de la langue française*, IV, 57. This view is repeated, in precisely the same terms, by Kukenheim, *Esquisse historique de la linguistique française*, p. 28: 'Avec cet ouvrage le cartésianisme fait son entrée en grammaire.'
[83] *Pioneers of Modern Education 1600–1700*, p. 260. Cf. Cadet, *Port-Royal Education*, pp. 301–31: 'The greatest merit of the Port-Royal Logic is to have introduced Cartesianism into teaching...to give logic...especially more practical utility.'

"true" means that the very structure of things is assumed to conform with the laws of the human mind.'[84] I would add that if the structure of things is in fact held to conform with the workings of the mind, linguistic theorists will be tempted, once having assumed this conformity (as does Scaliger), to confine their analyses to the operations of the mind and produce grammars of concepts in which the material component of the linguistic sign is largely ignored. Descartes' system does not in fact require such a conformity: 'the principal error and the commonest...consists in my judging that the ideas that are in me are similar or conformable to the things which are outside me'. Only by considering ideas as solely modes of his thought can he suppose that they would 'scarcely give me material for error'.[85] He is left only with the operations of the mind. In one respect Chomsky is right. Cartesianism results in a 'virtual identification of linguistic and mental processes'. Certain strands in Cartesianism are indeed not repugnant to the *GGR*'s view of language as a matter of concepts and mental operations. These notions are however already present in a long tradition of 'philosophical' grammar stretching back to the Middle Ages, and including the works of Scaliger and Sanctius. It is my belief that Lancelot has to a large extent simply continued this tradition, with a veneer of justificatory Cartesian terms supplied by Arnauld.

Chomsky seems to require, as justification of his own theory of language acquisition, that the 'ideas' in the mind should be innate, a view he takes to be shared by Descartes and guaranteed by the latter's anti-sensualism. A position requiring the existence of innate ideas is developed in Lord Herbert of Cherbury's *De Veritate* of 1624.[86] This transitional work, mingling Scholasticism with neo-Platonic, Stoic and Theosophical currents, was known to Descartes, whose doctrines it anticipates at several points. Herbert too sees truth as being attained when there is conformity between objects, and faculties already inherent in the mind. The truths of the intellect

[84] *The Seventeenth Century Background*, London, 1934, p. 87.
[85] *Meditations on the First Philosophy* (translated by E. S. Haldane and G. R. T. Ross) in *Great Books of the Western World*, xxxi, ed. R. M. Hutchins (Meditation iii, p. 83).
[86] No place of publication given. See also M. H. Carré, *De Veritate by Edward, Lord Herbert of Cherbury, Translated with an Introduction*, Bristol, 1937. On the question of the championship of innate ideas one should however note Carré's qualifying statement (p. 25) that though Herbert finally 'formulates a rationalism in which the operation of the senses almost recedes from view', his 'recognition of the complex conditions of knowledge saves him from denying any place to sense-perception in knowing'.

depend on the 'common notions' present in all men, and indeed it is the existence of these, and the assumption of their identity in all minds, that form the basis for universal grammar as the Port-Royal authors see it. Seventeenth-century thinkers as varied as Locke, Hobbes and Descartes all have in common a belief in the presence in the mind of concepts whose existence precedes that of the words found to express them. Where they differ is in whether or not they ascribe innateness to those concepts. The matter would not seem to be a vital one for universal grammar. Chomsky however, in holding that 'the central doctrine of Cartesian linguistics is that the general features of grammatical structure are common to all languages and reflect certain fundamental properties of the mind,'[87] requires these fundamental properties to be innate, in order to account for the creative aspect of language use, and the rapidity and efficiency of first-language acquisition by children.[88] No doubt enough ink has already been expended on this controversy. Suffice it to quote H. Aarsleff's dry remark when noting that no universal grammar ever postulates the existence of innate ideas as a basis for its abstract apparatus: 'To be a universal grammarian, it is enough to be a rationalist.'[89]

A fascinating subsidiary line of thought is opened up by the thesis of V. Salmon, among others, that the Port-Royalists were interested in Descartes' philosophy because they saw it as 'a revival of Augustinian thought and therefore an ally of their own kind of theology'.[90] If H. E. Brekle[91] is right in saying that Cartesianism was accepted at Port-Royal precisely in so far as it was found to be compatible with Augustinianism, and that hence Arnauld and Nicole

---

[87] *Cartesian Linguistics*, p. 59.

[88] *Ibid.*, p. 59: 'By attributing such principles to the mind, *as an innate property*, it becomes possible to account for the fact that the speaker of a language knows a great deal that he has not learned' (my italics).

[89] On the 'Cartesian linguistics' controversy see Aarsleff's article, 'The History of Linguistics and Professor Chomsky', pp. 570–85.

[90] Salmon, review of Chomsky's *Cartesian Linguistics*, quoting W. and M. Kneale, *The Development of Logic*, p. 316. G. Rodis-Lewis, 'Augustinisme et cartésianisme dans Port-Royal', *Descartes et le cartésianisme hollandais*, ed. E. Guilhan, Paris and Amsterdam, 1950, pp. 131–82, comes to the same conclusion, citing a letter from Mersenne holding that 'plus un homme sera savant dans la doctrine de Saint Augustin, et plus sera-t-il disposé à embrasser la philosophie de Descartes'. Cf. however Robinet's contention (*Le Langage à l'âge classique*, p. 79) that Arnauld and Pascal were prepared to admit Cartesian doctrine only in so far as it 'reprend et oriente, en fonction du XVIIe siècle, les dispositions immatérialistes de l'augustinisme'.

[91] 'The Seventeenth Century', p. 337, discussing J. Miel, 'Pascal, Port-Royal and Cartesian Linguistics', *Journal of the History of Ideas*, xxx (1969), pp. 261–71.

can be called Cartesians 'in only a limited sense', it follows that it is not a particularly fruitful enterprise to seek for an overwhelmingly Cartesian orientation in the *Grammaire générale*. A more likely influence on the semiotic sections of the grammar is St Augustine himself, whose theory of signs would presumably be known to the Port-Royal authors. It seems unlikely, to quote W. K. Percival, that Descartes' own statements on language represent a novel departure from the traditional position, or that his ideas 'influenced universal grammars in fundamental respects'.[92] J.-C. Chevalier's contention that the 'whole weight' of Descartes lies behind the Port-Royal system, leaving merely a 'not negligible' role to the grammatical tradition exemplified by Scaliger, Sanctius and Ramus, which is held to have contributed to the development of 'what is called Cartesianism',[93] seems to be untenable. I incline more to R. Lakoff's view[94] that the *GGR* has its sources in pre-Cartesian grammatical works, that Cartesian psychological and philosophical theories are 'not present to any usable or intelligible extent' in it, and that Descartes' role was limited to creating a favourable mental climate in which the linguistic ideas of a long-standing Latin tradition could be applied to the first universal grammar in the French vernacular. Though Chomsky regards the Cartesian origins of the *GGR* as a 'commonplace',[95] its sources are not in any statement by Descartes, but in a grammatical tradition which has roots in medieval practice, and spreads with growing force from 1540 onwards in the pages of the Latin grammarians Scaliger, Sanctius, Vossius, Campanella and Caramuel. This movement aims to apply reason to grammatical analysis, to apply it at the level of the underlying grammatical system rather than at the level of discourse, and to seek beneath the details of usage the reasoned framework of *rationes* and *causae*. The mistake in my view has lain in regarding the *Grammaire générale et raisonnée* as inaugurating this tradition, rather than simply forming part of it.

[92] See W. K. Percival's 'On the Non-Existence of Cartesian Linguistics', *Cartesian Studies*, ed. R. J. Butler, Oxford, 1972, pp. 137–45.

[93] *Histoire de la syntaxe*, p. 11. Whether the Port-Royal approach is Cartesian or not, Chevalier is not in favour of it: 'on doit toujours se défier de confondre langage et opération mentale' (*ibid.*, p. 180).

[94] Review of Brekle's edition of the *GGR*, in *Language*, XLV (1969), pp. 347, 355. Cf. also p. 363: 'it is a mistake to consider the *GGR* a work of "Cartesian linguistics". Linguistically, its theory is pre-Cartesian; that marriage [of various elements]…that has been termed Cartesian actually does not come into being…until the work of Cordemoy and Du Marsais.'

[95] *Cartesian Linguistics*, note 3.

If the Port-Royal *Logic*, then, must be read together with the *Grammar* as the embodiment of a certain theory of language, neither it nor Cartesianism in general must be supposed to represent the *source* of that theory. The fact that *Logic* and *Grammar* are complementary underlines however the extent to which the two 'arts' are increasingly becoming one. If for Port-Royal, logic is thought about language, grammar in turn is the representation of thought. In this reversal of the Ramist revolution, rhetoric too has its part to play. The third and equally complementary work in the Port-Royal trio of grammar, logic and rhetoric is Bernard Lamy's *Art de parler*,[96] which may be regarded as the Port-Royal Rhetoric. Just as the *GGR* proposes to 'do by the application of reason [*science*] what others do only by custom', so does the *Art de parler* claim, contrary to ordinary rhetorics, to 'reveal the true foundations of the art of speech'. The author, while conceding that usage is the 'master and supreme arbiter' of language, and (following the *GGR*) that an accepted and well-established usage must be followed even when it is contrary to reason, none the less sees a role for reason where the speaker has a choice of expressions. It is in fact by the exercise of this choice based on reason that languages rid themselves of impurities. Though reason can prescribe but a few laws, it is important that these laws should have a sure basis, and Lamy condemns those rhetorics that 'propose rules without first making known the principles' on which they are founded. Of absolutely primary importance for seventeenth- and eighteenth-century language theory is his assumption that before any utterance the speaker 'forms in his mind a picture of what he wants to say'. Discourse is 'a painting of our thoughts', in which language is the painter's brush and words are the colours. Thought thus precedes language, and the first concern of the speaker must be to put into a 'natural order' those things that he wishes to paint by means of words. It is at this point that rhetoric, grammar and logic meet, for though, significantly, it is logicians who must decide this natural order so as to 'mark differences in thought' and indicate 'what is going on in our minds', we also have need of 'words of different kinds'. Following the *GGR* again, Lamy supposes the diversity of

[96] Published anonymously in Paris, 1676. The title of the third edition (1688), with Lamy given as the author, is *La rhétorique, ou l'art de parler*. An English translation, *The Art of Speaking... by Messieurs du Port-Royal*, appeared in London in 1676. Michael, *English Grammatical Categories*, p. 167, notes that it is not known whether the attribution to Port-Royal was made in good faith.

words in human language to be a direct result of the diversity of mental operations.[97] It follows that the whole foundation of the 'art of speaking' consists of the parts of speech, and here again, as compared with Ramus' approach, we may note a blurring of the lines separating grammar from rhetoric. To Lamy's Rhetoric, a grammar of the parts of speech is an essential accompaniment.[98]

Port-Royal communication theory thus has its 'art of speech' or rhetoric, its 'art of thought' or logic, and its grammar. In the title of the *Grammaire générale et raisonnée* the three are united, for it proposes a treatment of the 'foundations of the art of speech', of the 'reasons underlying what is common to all languages', and of the chief differences between them.[99] Behind its treatment however there lies the authors' own *Nouvelle Méthode latine* and the syntactic doctrines of Sanctius, which allow them to incorporate a consideration of rhetorical devices into their grammar as a necessary part of linguistic theory. A major innovation is their introduction into French vernacular grammar of the doctrine of the linguistic sign, and this has been seen by some as the expression in linguistic terms of the Cartesian body/mind dichotomy. At the very outset the authors make plain that by speech they mean the indication of thought by signs specially invented for the purpose. These signs, as in present-day theory, have a double face, a (phonetic) form and a meaning, and it is to the latter component that the major section of the *GGR* is devoted. Forms signal mental processes, and the authors' statement of that fact constitutes the manifesto of their linguistic programme: 'a knowledge of what is going on in our minds is necessary in order to understand the foundations of grammar; and on that depends the diversity of the words that make up speech'.[100] As in Lamy's Rhetoric, the classification of the parts of speech reflects the 'operations of the mind'. There is at first sight nothing new in the

[97] *L'Art de parler*, pp. 4–7.

[98] Relevant here is M. Foucault's remark (*Les Mots et les choses*, Paris, 1966, p. 98) that 'la Grammaire suppose la nature rhétorique des langages' – 'La Rhétorique définit la spatialité de la représentation...la Grammaire définit pour chaque langue l'ordre qui répartit dans le temps cette spatialité'.

[99] C. Lancelot and A. Arnauld, *Grammaire générale et raisonnée, contenant les fondemens de l'art de parler...les raisons de ce qui est commun à toutes les langues, et des principales différences qui s'y recontrent; et plusieurs remarques nouvelles sur la Langue Françoise*, Paris, 1660. In quotations directly from the French I have followed modern accentuation practice, but otherwise the orthography is left unchanged. In the treatment that follows certain matters already discussed in my volume on the Latin tradition will inevitably be repeated. That tradition is of course highly relevant to vernacular theory. [100] *GGR*, p. 26.

authors' sign theory. They were presumably familiar with St
Augustine of Hippo's remarks on the subject, and they would also
know Scaliger's definition of the word as 'the mark of an idea in the
mind',[101] and even perhaps be aware of the medieval tradition
behind it.[102] Some scholars have credited them with reintroducing
the medieval doctrine, I. Michael for instance regarding them as once
again working towards the question that interested medieval
grammarians, namely the relation of the structure of language to the
structure of external reality.[103] It is however not the correspondence
between language and the real world that is the authors' concern,
but the isomorphism of linguistic structure and the structure of
thought. Medieval modistic thinkers saw signification as a process
involving *three* terms: the external object, the intermediary concept,
and the linguistic sign with its twin facets of meaning and form. The
modistic grammarians' 'modi essendi', the manner in which things
have their being in the universe, have only a seeming parallel in the
'objets de nos pensées' of the Port-Royal system. In the latter, the
mind simply observes its own operations. Nor should it be thought
that the Port-Royal preoccupation with signs is peculiar to rationalist
Cartesians. Locke's view of words as 'sensible Marks of Ideas',
standing 'in their primary and immediate Signification...for nothing,
but the Ideas in the Mind of him that uses them', is identical with
theirs.[104] His definition of words as 'names of Ideas in the Mind' is
indicative of a major change of stance since the early humanist
grammarians. For them, following Latin grammatical precedent,
nouns signified (i.e. were signs of) *things* in the real world.[105] By the
time of Colet's contribution to Lily's Latin grammar they have
become the *names* of things, indicating the beginnings of a move away
from the notion of signification towards mere nomenclature. Finally,

---

[101] 'Nota unius speciei, quae est in animo'.
[102] For a discussion of that tradition see Padley, *Grammatical Theory* (1976), pp. 234–5.
[103] *English Grammatical Categories*, p. 168. Similar opinions as to the reintroduction of medieval doctrine are expressed by Kukenheim (*Esquisse historique de la linguistique française*, pp. 16, 241) and Chevalier (*Histoire de la syntaxe*, pp. 484, 496).
[104] *An Essay Concerning Humane Understanding*, London, 1690, pp. 185, 228. W. and M. Kneale, *The Development of Logic*, p. 312, note that Locke's 'doctrine of ideas as signs, is very similar to Ockham's account of *intentiones*...Since Ockham's *Summa Totius Logicae* was reprinted at Oxford in 1675...it is difficult to believe that the similarity can be mere coincidence.' For Rossi, *Francis Bacon*, p. x, 'the typical seventeenth-century intellectual probings are a direct legacy of Occamist empiricism', of nominalism, and of doctrines which questioned the Thomist (and hence, I would add, the modistic) compromise.
[105] Cf. e.g. Melanchthon's 'nomen significat rem'.

with Locke and the Port-Royalists, they are *names* of *ideas*, items in a list of the contents of the mind. It is true that, as a convinced Sensualist, Locke adds that 'those Ideas are collected from the Things, which they are supposed to represent', but his position does not in practice differ materially from that of Port-Royal. Hobbes goes to the full extreme, holding that names, 'signs of our conceptions', are manifestly not 'signs of the things themselves'.[106] Sign theory is a commonplace of late-seventeenth-century speculation, and both the Sensualist and Rationalist versions of it have a common source in medieval Scholastic philosophy. The seventeenth century espouses however the nominalist variant of that philosophy, which was sceptical of any necessary connection between name and thing, and it is this very scepticism that lies at the root of modern science. The Port-Royal authors, in transferring the debate to French vernacular grammar, show a similar nominalism. Their view of the sign further involves the loss of the notion of the consignification of grammatical meanings implied in the medieval use of the term 'modus significandi', which their use of the term 'manière de signifier' only goes part of the way towards restoring. In these various respects they cannot be regarded as perpetuating medieval tradition, or at any rate the version of it that is present in the Latin 'philosophical' grammars of Scaliger and Campanella.

Two recent writers on the conception of the linguistic sign in the seventeenth century have both noticed a shift in the way the sign is envisaged. A. Robinet (*Le Langage à l'âge classique*, 1978) attributes the fact that it is no longer a sign of a thing, but a sign of thought, to the Port-Royal authors' Augustinianism.[107] For him, the originality of the *GGR* lies not in its sudden replacement of an empirically based grammar by a logically based 'general' grammar (this view is of course erroneous), but – and here the influence is that of Arnauld – in its operation of a change in the philosophy of the sign. According to

[106] *Elements of Philosophy: I. Concerning Body*, in *The English Works of Thomas Hobbes*, ed. W. Molesworth, London, 1839–40, I, 17. Hobbes feels obliged to add (*Leviathan*, part I, 'Of Man', in Molesworth, III, 1) that 'there is no conception in a man's mind, which hath not at first...been begotten upon the organs of sense'. Elsewhere however he allows the full consequences of his nominalism to stand: 'colligimus rationem nihil omnino de natura rerum, sed de earum appellationibus' (*Thomae Hobbes...Opera philosophica quae Latine scripsit*, ed. Molesworth, V, London, 1845, p. 258).

[107] *Le Langage à l'âge classique*, p. 15: for Augustine, 'le signe est signe de la pensée, non de la chose, signe de la chose-idée, non de la chose-corps'; p. 17: 'Le mot n'est plus l'indice de la chose: il est moniteur de vérité'; p. 19: 'Le mot est signe de la pensée.'

M. Foucault (*Les Mots et les choses*, 1966) this major change is brought
about by the weakening and disappearance of the link between signs
and resemblances. Renaissance sign theory implied the existence of
three separate elements: the *signifié*, the *signifiant*, and that element
which allowed the presupposition of a link between them. This third
element is the resemblance between the two: 'the sign was a mark
of denotation to the extent that it was "almost the same thing" as
that which it designated'.[108] Foucault too – though on different
grounds from those I have suggested above – sees the Port-Royal
doctrine of the sign as essentially the replacement of a three-part
system by a purely binary one.[109] This identity of sign and thought
has the result that for the Augustinianism in vogue at Port-Royal –
and this point is made by Robinet – the sign is no longer strictly
necessary for the exercise of pure thought. As the Logic, under the
influence of Arnauld's Augustinianism, points out, 'if the reflections
we make on our thoughts had never concerned anyone but ourselves,
it would have sufficed to consider them in themselves, without
clothing them in words or signs'.[110] For the Logic, if we do in fact
continue to join our thoughts to signs in the process of thinking, when
no act of communication is involved, it is only by force of habit. Pure
thought is autonomous, and the Logic is here providing the theoretic
bases for that 'virtual identification of linguistic and mental processes'
(Chomsky's term) that is the hall-mark of the *Grammaire générale*. The
way is free for it to become a grammar of concepts. If the link between
the sign and external reality is no longer necessary for the exercise
of thought, grammar can turn in on itself and concern itself only with
the processes of the mind and thought's due arrangement.[111] For
Foucault Cartesianism, having renounced the necessity of 'resemblance' as a condition of knowledge, can now turn to the analysis
of thought in terms of identities and differences, and it is this that
makes of the seventeenth century one of the two great turning-points
in the *episteme* of Western thought.[112] Since signs are now coextensive

[108] *Les Mots et les choses*, p. 77. On what the sign represented for 'l'âge classique', and in
particular for the Port-Royal Logic, see pp. 72–81.
[109] Foucault (*ibid.*, p. 81) suggests that if Saussure's definition of the sign as the union of
a concept and an image seems 'psychologiste', it is because 'en fait il redécouvrait là la
condition classique pour penser la nature binaire du signe'.
[110] See Robinet, *Le Langage à l'âge classique*, p. 21. Cf. his additional remark that 'Le cogito,
perdant son étole augustinienne, jette la chose et autrui hors du moi'.
[111] Cf. Robinet, *ibid.*, p. 25.
[112] *Les Mots et les choses*, pp. 13, 66. Cf. p. 78: 'Le rapport du signifiant au signifié se loge
maintenant dans un espace où nulle figure intermédiaire n'assure plus leur recontre.'

with thought, language can be treated simply as its linear expression, as its arrangement in an order that will render it comprehensible to the hearer.[113] The order is different for each language: the thought is the same.

The considerations that lie behind the Port-Royal authors' treatment of the age-old doctrine of the linguistic sign are made clear when, in close parallel to their Logic, they announce that 'all philosophers' are agreed on the existence of three operations of the mind: the formation of concepts, the use of the judgment, and the exercise of reason. These mental operations are essential to their system, for 'We cannot properly understand the various kinds of meaning that are enclosed in words,' i.e. cannot proceed to a classification of the parts of speech, 'unless we have first well understood what goes on in our thoughts'.[114] This emphasis on mental operations can obviously be referred back to such sources in Descartes as his awareness of 'thoughts which proceed solely from the faculty of thinking that is within me'.[115] It is not however specifically Cartesian, for Locke, rooted as he is in Bacon and sense-realism, notes that observation is of two kinds: that of 'external, sensible Objects', which he calls *sensation*; and that of the mind's own 'internal Operations', which he calls *reflection*.[116] For Port-Royal these mental operations function on two levels, on that of the formation of concepts, and on that of the making of judgments concerning them. As we have seen, the exercise of the judgment is regarded as the chief preoccupation of logic. In the Port-Royal Logic the term 'judgment' is identical with 'proposition', defined as consisting of a subject and a predicate, the action of our minds in linking the two being represented in speech by the verb *to be*. This logical, Aristotelian definition of the sentence, though common enough in logics, had not normally been used in grammar, authors

---

[113] Cf. *ibid.*, p. 97: 'C'est en ce sens stricte que le langage est *analyse* de la pensée: non pas simple découpage, mais instauration profonde de l'ordre dans l'espace...La Grammaire générale, c'est l'étude de l'ordre verbal dans son rapport à la simultanéité qu'elle a pour charge de représenter.' There is here a striking parallel with Martinet's definition of the function of syntax.   [114] *GGR*, p. 30.

[115] *Notes Directed Against a Certain Programme*, in *The Philosophical Works of Descartes*, translated by E. S. Haldane and G. R. T. Ross, Cambridge, 1967, I, 442.

[116] *Essay*, II, 37–8. Locke cannot bring himself entirely to divorce 'reflection' from his sense-based system. Its source, 'though it be not sense...yet it is very like it, and might properly enough be called internal Sense'. Equally with Port-Royal however, he allows for the mind's own 'internal operations'. As Aarsleff remarks ('The History of Linguistics and Professor Chomsky', p. 581), universal grammar can be done on a Lockean basis just as well as on a Cartesian one.

preferring to use variants of Dionysius Thrax's and Priscian's 'arrangement of words in grammatical agreement expressing complete sense'.[117] The Port-Royal authors now, free of Ramist constraints on the province of each separate 'art', transfer this definition to grammar:

> The judgment we make concerning things, as when I say *the earth is round*, is called a PROPOSITION; and thus every proposition necessarily includes two terms: one called *subject*, which is that about which we affirm something...the other called *attribute*, which is what we affirm...and in addition the link between these two terms, *is*.[118]

The theory of the grammatical sentence is thus identical with the theory of the logical proposition. As J.-C. Chevalier[119] points out, it is no longer the formal subject–verb relationship that determines the sentence, but the logical subject–predicate relationship, to which items of linguistic structure are required to correspond. The subject–predicate schema becomes the essential framework for every utterance,[120] the touchstone of syntactic analysis. Given its obvious importance however, this section remains curiously unintegrated into the rest of the grammar, apart from a few brief remarks regarding the verb, and relative constructions. The reference to 'the knowledge of what goes on in our minds' as necessary to an understanding of grammar, the short excursion into sign theory, and finally this brief discussion of the proposition, form self-contained wholes. It is almost as if Lancelot, having already composed his grammar, only then consulted Arnauld for logical and philosophical support to his statements, which he afterwards inserted into the text. That being said, there can be no doubt that the lead given by the Port-Royal authors turned grammatical practice away from the centuries-old word-based treatment of grammar, in which syntax and morphology were inextricably mingled, to a consideration of the sentence as a whole.

It is this view of the proposition as the linking together of two terms in a judgment made about them that forms the basis for the Port-Royal classification of the parts of speech. The two linked terms are the province of the first, concept-forming operation of the mind, while

[117] Priscian (Keil, *Grammatici Latini*, II, 53): 'Oratio est ordinatio dictionum congrua, sententiam perfectam demonstrans.'

[118] *GGR*, pp. 28–9.   [119] *Histoire de la syntaxe*, p. 500.

[120] Cf. Joly, 'La linguistique cartésienne', p. 183: 'Port-Royal ne sort pas du cadre de la proposition; tout le problème consiste à lier et délier nos idées dans cet espace de prédication...'

the linking process itself forms the second operation. In considering what takes place in the mind, a broad dichotomy is instituted contrasting the 'objects of our thoughts' and the 'form or manner of our thoughts', of which judgment is the chief manifestation. Since language and the operations of the mind are congruent,[121] the word-classes too indicate either the 'objects' or the 'manner' of thought. To the former class belong noun, article, pronoun, participle, preposition and adverb; to the latter verb, conjunction and interjection.[122] Here it is interesting to see verb and conjunction put on the same footing as performing a linking function, and the dichotomy is conceived in parallel terms to those presented in the Logic: 'We call *concevoir* the simple view we have of the things that present themselves to our minds...We call *juger* the action of our mind by which, joining together various ideas, it affirms...or denies.'[123] The cardinal point is that in their organization of the word-classes the authors are no longer basing themselves on the common seventeenth-century distinction between things and the modes of things, but are replacing it by one between concepts and the way in which the thought-process organizes those concepts.

The more usual seventeenth-century distinction is however present in the Logic, which sees concepts as presented to the mind in three ways: as things, as the manner of things, and as modified things. A thing is 'that which is conceived as subsisting by itself...Another name for it is substance.' This is orthodox doctrine drawn from Aristotle's ten predicaments, and a commonplace of Scholastic philosophy. The authors go on, in modistic and Scaligeran fashion, to apply this hylomorphism to language: those nouns (*terre, esprit, Dieu*) used to express things are called substances.[124] The Logic goes on to define 'the manner of a thing, or mode, or attribute or quality', as that which 'being conceived in the thing, and as not being able to subsist without it, determines it to exist in a certain way'. This

[121] Perhaps it is rash to speak of an *exact* congruence. Cf. Chevalier, *Histoire de la syntaxe*, p. 499: 'on ne saurait dire avec exactitude que logique et expression sont parallèles, mais bien plutôt que la langue est une forme muable...dont le système pourtant est tel qu'il permet...de renvoyer à une pensée claire et distincte'.

[122] For a penetrating criticism of the criteria underlying the Port-Royal dichotomy, see Donzé, *La Grammaire générale et raisonnée de Port-Royal*, pp. 62–5. B. Foucault, 'La Grammaire générale de Port-Royal', *Langages*, VII (1967), pp. 7–15, makes an interesting attempt to explain the system in terms of six semantic strata.

[123] *GGR*, pp. 27–8.

[124] One may note that *Dieu* and *esprit*, yet more than *terre*, are for the Cartesians entities of whose existence they can be sure.

too is straightforward Aristotelianism. In close parallel the *GGR* uses this substance/accident dichotomy in defining substantive and adjective: the former 'signify substances' while the latter 'signify accidents, and indicate the subject to which those accidents are appropriate'.[125] My point here is that this type of analysis, though eminently acceptable to Cartesian philosophy, had been made a thousand times by medieval and humanist grammarians. The authors of the *GGR* go on however to say that this 'first' origin of substantives and adjectives did not content those who established human language. Since substance in the real world subsists independently by itself, by a parallel argumentation on the linguistic level a substantive could be defined as being syntactically independent, as 'subsisting by itself in discourse', and the adjective as that which, by its 'manner of signifying', needs syntactic support. This is to substitute a syntactic criterion for the philosophical one, and it is interesting to note that modistic grammar exhibits precisely the same duality: its syntactic 'mode of that which stands by itself' and 'mode of that which is adjoined to another' are specifically stated to be drawn from the philosophical substance/accident criterion.[126] The Port-Royal authors have simply repeated the centuries-old modistic argument.[127] Capital here is their contention that in passing from one criterion to the other they are moving from *signification* to *manière de signifier*, from philosophical and lexical considerations to purely grammatical ones. It is tempting to regard the term *manière de signifier* as a direct transfer to the vernacular of medieval grammar's *modus significandi*, which implied the addition of a grammatical meaning to a lexical word. Here it is relevant that in applying the substance/accident criterion medieval grammar had difficulties with those words which, while signifying accidents, have the syntactic behaviour of substantives, and vice versa. The word *rationalis* for instance, held to signify substance because seen as identical in meaning with *homo*, none the less appeared in syntactic congruence with other substantives. Similar difficulties arose with *rex* and *philosophus*, behaving grammatically as substantives but originally

125 *GGR*, pp. 30–1.
126 See Thomas of Erfurt, *Grammatica speculativa*, cap. x.
127 Brekle ('The Seventeenth Century', p. 341) gives the Port-Royal authors the credit for 'transforming the ontology-based scholastic notions of "substantia" and "accidentia" into categories that are defined by intra-grammatical criteria'. But the medieval modistic grammarians had already done this, and the *GGR* is simply repeating their analysis!

adjectival in meaning. It is specifically in order to get round such difficulties that the Port-Royal authors introduce the device of the *manière de signifier*, which allows them to recognize certain terms (e.g. *roi* and *philosophe*), as grammatically substantives, 'even if [lexically] they signify accidents', and others, 'even those which [lexically] signify substances', as grammatically adjectives.[128] Thus far however, in their discussion of substantive and adjective, they have produced nothing that is not a commonplace of either medieval or humanist theory, or of both. It is true that philosophical parallels in Descartes can easily be found, as in the remark in the *Principia philosophiae* that 'When we conceive substance, we conceive only a thing that exists in such a way, that it only has need of itself to exist.' It is however insufficient to claim, as does G. Sahlin, that in establishing the substantive/adjective dichotomy the authors took as their primary inspiration 'the Cartesian notion of substance'.[129] The Port-Royalists' treatment simply follows medieval precedent, and an impressive amount of sixteenth- and seventeenth-century Latin practice. Apart from medieval examples, the definition of substantive and adjective in the philosophical terms of the signification of substance and accident appears in a humanist grammar as early as 1481, in the Spaniard Nebrija's *Introductiones Latinae*,[130] and is perpetuated by Melanchthon and Scaliger. The syntactic criterion (ability to stand alone in discourse) appears in Linacre, while the combined philosophical and syntactic definition is to be found in Campanella and in Vossius' *De arte grammatica* of 1635, which specifically invokes Aristotle's authority for it.

In a further attempt to decide exactly what it is that distinguishes substantive and adjective the authors have recourse to yet another medieval solution, but one that has a source in logic and is rarely found in previous grammars. To find a parallel, one has to turn to a few scattered indications in Nebrija, and in Scaliger and Campanella. This solution is based on the distinction between denotation and connotation, and here again it is the Port-Royal Logic that sets out

[128] *GGR*, p. 31. In his 'Semiotik und linguistische Semantik in Port-Royal', *Indogermanische Forschungen*, LXIX (1964), Brekle interpreted 'manière de signifier' in terms of a 'meaning = use' theory. In 'The Seventeenth Century' (p. 341, n. 126) he abandons this approach, treating 'manière de signifier' as equivalent to the medieval 'modus significandi'.
[129] *César Chesneau du Marsais*, p. 159.
[130] Published in Salamanca. I have consulted this work in later versions: *Ars nova grammatices* (Lyons, 1509) and *Grammatica Antonii Nebrissensis* (Saragossa, 1533).

the underlying theory: 'The nouns which signify things as modified, indicating in the first place and directly the thing though more confusedly; and indirectly the mode though more distinctly, are called adjectives *or connotatives*.'[131] The sources of this lie far back in Scholastic logic, in views such as William of Ockham's 'The connotative noun properly signifies one thing primarily and another secondarily, one thing directly and another indirectly... An example is this concept white... It signifies its subject directly, and whiteness indirectly.'[132] Though there is a more immediate grammatical source in Scaliger's idea that adjectives *denote* qualities or accidents but at the same time *connote* the substance of the noun they are constructed with,[133] this section of the *GGR* is no doubt supplied by the logician Arnauld. The statement that the adjective *rouge* clearly denotes redness, but confusedly (Scaliger says 'aliqua ratione') connotes whatever it is that *is* red, could however equally well have come from Scaliger. This analysis enables the authors to make certain semantic permutations. If connotation is subtracted from the adjective it becomes a substantive (*rouge rougeur*). If however it is added to the substantive, it turns it into an adjective (*homme humain*). When this adjective *humain* is in turn deprived of connotation, it again becomes a substantive (*humanité*).[134] In this type of analysis grammar is no longer the study of specifically *grammatical* meanings consignified by changes in the morphological form or the syntactic positions of words, but a matter of the addition or subtraction of logical concepts. It may well be however that the pains taken by Lancelot and Arnauld to distinguish substantive and adjective, for so long treated as sub-classes of a single part of speech, were ultimately decisive in bringing about their final separation.

The verb, as was noted above, belongs to those word-classes that

---

[131] *Logique* (1674 ed.), p. 55 (my italics).

[132] *Quodlibeta*, v, quaestio xxv. Ockham discusses 'termini connotativi' or concepts that are amenable to an analysis of the type *white = that which has whiteness*, or *Socrates is white* = the two propositions *Socrates is* and *whiteness inheres in Socrates*. On his approach see C. Prantl, *Geschichte der Logik im Abendlande*, Leipzig, 1867, iii, 386.

[133] *De causis linguae Latinae*, cap. xcvii.

[134] This somewhat involved theory of connotation leads (*GGR*, pp. 31–2) to the attribution of two significations to the adjective: 'the one distinct, which is that of the form [i.e. accident]; the other imprecise, which is that of the subject [i.e. the philosophical subject in which the accident inheres]'. The subject, though imprecisely connotated, is signified directly ('in recto'), while the form, though distinct, is signified indirectly ('in obliquo'). The adjective *blanc* accordingly connotes its subject (that which has whiteness) directly but imprecisely, whereas it signifies whiteness itself indirectly, but just as clearly as does the substantive *blancheur*.

signify 'the form and manner of our thoughts', and is thus, its function being to link subject and attribute in the logical proposition, given a role analogous to that of the conjunction.[135] Already in his *Nouvelle Méthode latine* Lancelot had noted that Scaliger regards all verbs as reducible to the verb *to be*, their 'root and foundation', and the fully developed Port-Royal theory requires, in medieval fashion, all verbs to be analysable into the verb *to be* (treated as a copula or link) and an attribute. It is interesting to note that – perhaps because it cannot be paralleled in the actual usage of the Ancients? – Sanctius nowhere suggests the 'resolution' *amat = est amans*. G. Clerico[136] remarks that this fact in itself is sufficient to cast doubt on a supposed continuity of thought from the medieval *modistae via Sanctius* to the *Grammaire générale*. But this does not disprove my thesis that modistic grammar and Scaliger, and indeed the preceding Latin grammatical tradition in general, are major elements in the evolution of Port-Royal thought. It is interesting here to note how the emphasis of later editions of the *NML* changed once Lancelot had consulted Arnauld. The earlier editions still have the common seventeenth-century definition of the verb in the terms of the signification of *actio* and *passio*, justified philosophically by the statement that any motion in the real world must involve one of these two. In later editions however and in the *GGR* all such divisions, together with Scaliger's modistic view of the verb as signifying *res fluentes*, are rejected on the grounds that the 'essential nature' of the verb is to indicate an affirmation. This ultimately Aristotelian basis as given in the *NML* is, including the use of the term 'verbs adjective', precisely that of the medieval Schoolmen: 'The verbs substantive are those which simply indicate an affirmation...The verbs adjective are those which in addition to the affirmation common to all verbs, contain yet another meaning peculiar to themselves; as *amo*, which is the same as *sum amans*.'[137] The example given must have been repeated in medieval grammar times without number. The *GGR* gives further philosophical credence to this definition by deducing that since affirmation is the principal 'manner of our thoughts', the verb must be 'a word whose chief use

[135] For a consideration of certain aspects of the classification of the verb by both the Greek grammarian Apollonius Dyscolus and the *GGR*, see J.-C. Chevalier, '*Grammaire générale* de Port-Royal et tradition grecque', *La Grammaire générale des modistes aux idéologues*, ed. A. Joly and J. Stéfanini, Lille, 1977, pp. 145–56.
[136] *Franciscus Sanctius*, pp. 28–9.
[137] This is the definition contained in e.g. the 1681 edition of the *NML*, p. 458.

is to signify affirmation'.[138] As is so often the case with the Port-Royal authors however, a commonplace of Latin grammatical theory, medieval (and therefore ultimately Aristotelian) in origin, is presented in a new guise. It would be tedious to list more than a handful of the precedents. In the post-medieval period, one may note the progressive application of such notions to Latin grammar in Scaliger's view of the verb as adding something to the meaning of the noun subject,[139] in his treatment of the copula as a 'mark of conjunction' joining the subject to one of its qualities,[140] and finally in Caramuel's definition of the verb substantive *to be* as a 'judicativa copula', a judgment-forming link, joining the logical subject to the logical predicate. Above all perhaps, Campanella's treatment of the copula as devoid of tense and linking 'ideas, not things' may be seen as a forerunner.[141] The view of the verb *to be* as a copula or link is not uncommon in the later part of the seventeenth century, and one may compare the Port-Royal treatment with that in Dalgarno's *Ars signorum* (1661) and Wilkins' *Essay* (1668), in which the 'verb adjective' receives a minor status as compared with that of the copula, Wilkins for instance treating the latter as a consignifying particle 'essential in every compleat sentence.' Certainly Lancelot's statement in the *NML* that the verb substantive merely indicates an affirmation closely resembles Dalgarno's expansion *amamus = nos sumus amantes = nos +* present tense *+ ita amantes*, where the copula, a 'sign of the act of the mind in judging', can be replaced by the mark of affirmation *ita*. Since Wilkins acknowledges Campanella and Caramuel as his predecessors, perhaps they can be regarded together with Scaliger as common sources of both the Empiricist–Sensualist (Royal Society) and the Rationalist (supposedly Cartesian) traditions in universal grammar. The emphasis on what Dalgarno calls the 'sign of the act of the mind in judging', and Campanella's view of the tenseless copula as joining 'ideas, not things', form an instructive parallel to the Port-Royal treatment of the verb as 'the link we make in our minds between the two terms

---

[138] *GGR*, p. 90.

[139] *De causis linguae Latinae*, cap. clxii.

[140] *Ibid.*, cap. xc. In *Caesar est clemens* the copula is a 'nota coniunctionis, qua clementia in Caesare praedicetur'. Cf. cap. cxii, where the verb in *Caesar est albus* is described as 'quasi nexum, et copulam...qua albedo jungeretur Caesari'.

[141] *Grammatica*, p. 50. The copula joins 'notiones, non res'. Cf. Hobbes' definition of the proposition as 'a speech consisting of two names copulated'.

of a proposition', and of the verb *to be* as the pristine signifier of affirmation 'without any difference of person or tense'.[142] Ultimately however the roots of all this are in medieval practice. Starting from the modistic grammarians' *amat = est amans*,[143] the Port-Royal authors add a logically orientated insistence on judgment and affirmation: 'We call judging the action of the mind by which, joining together various ideas, it affirms that one is the other, or denies that one is the other.'[144] If the attribute and the copula are both logically present in a single verb form, it is because – an important notion to which we shall return – 'men are naturally inclined to abbreviate their expressions'.[145]

By moving around the pieces on their conceptual draught-board the Port-Royal authors are now in a position to define participles and infinitives:

rubet (= *est rubens*)	= 'is red' (affirmation plus attribute, i.e. verb)
rubens	= 'red' (verb minus affirmation, i.e. adjective)
rubere	= 'redness' (adjective minus the connotation of whatever it is that is red, i.e. substantive)[146]

Having no affirming function, the participle belongs with those word-classes that signify 'the objects of our thoughts'. Conjunctions however resemble the copula in linking mental concepts, thus carrying out 'the very operation itself of our minds', and they include in their number the word *non* as an indication of 'the judgment we make that one thing is not another'. Here again, in giving the conjunction a purely grammatical, linking function the authors are heirs to a long tradition that begins with Dionysius Thrax.[147]

Part of the treatment of those word-classes that signify 'the objects of our thoughts' depends on the *GGR*'s seeming assumption of (to use modern terms which have become common currency) a 'deep' and a 'surface' structure to language. The adverb for instance, in a

---

[142] *GGR*, p. 96.
[143] Scaliger and Campanella both follow this medieval practice. Cf. Campanella, *Grammatica*, p. 102: 'Omnia verba resolvuntur in substantivum *sum*...idem ergo valet *ego curro*, quod *ego sum currens*'. Kukenheim, *Esquisse historique de la linguistique française*, p. 24, seemingly regards this procedure as an invention of the Port-Royal authors themselves.
[144] *Logique*, p. 27. [145] *GGR*, p. 91.
[146] *Ibid.*, p. 96. But in e.g. *Scio malum esse fugiendum*, the infinitive links two propositions, and hence has verbal function and retains affirmation (*ibid*, pp. 111–12). This analysis has universalist implications, for it allows the authors to equate the Latin example with the French *Je sais que le mal est à fuir*, which similarly contains two propositions.
[147] See Steinthal, *Geschichte der Sprachwissenschaft bei den Griechen und Römern*, II, 211.

similar way to the verb which cumulates in one word both affirmation and attribute, is seen as resulting from 'the desire men have to abbreviate discourse'. As I. Michael notes,[148] it had long been observed that the adverb (including, in the earlier part of the tradition, the interjection) could function as the equivalent of an expression made up of several words, or even as a sentence-equivalent. This approach gives the authors the opportunity to demonstrate a logical equivalence between Latin structures and vernacular ones, the 'langues vulgaires' being able to express the semantic content of adverbs equally well, and indeed 'more elegantly', by means of a prepositional phrase. Closely allied to this question is the *GGR*'s treatment of case-marked nouns as equivalent to structures consisting of noun preceded by 'particle' (i.e. preposition). It is noted that some languages indicate certain syntactic relationships by means of cases, while others use 'particles which take their place'. This has led I. Poldauf for example to credit the Port-Royal authors with being the first to recognize this identity of function, thus giving 'the first impulse to John Locke's concern with the various ways of expressing relations'.[149] Locke observes in his *Essay* that particles 'are made use of, to signifie the connexion that the Mind gives to Ideas, or Propositions, one with another', and adds that 'this part of grammar has been neglected'.[150] The *GGR* may well be his immediate source, but Poldauf's remark is yet another example of the tendency to regard the Port-Royal grammarians as brilliant innovators when they are in fact repeating information that would be already known to those of their readers well-read in Latin grammar. Linacre's *Rudimenta* of *c.* 1512, published in Paris in 1533, had preceded them in observing that prepositions in the vernaculars are 'articles or marks' of case.[151] Further, early grammarians of the vernaculars, including French, had themselves in their pedagogy treated certain 'articles' as *signa casuum* with the same function as the Latin cases, and Port-Royal doctrine is also anticipated, or at least paralleled, in John Wallis' treatment of prepositions in his *Grammatica linguae Anglicanae* (1653) as 'common affections' (i.e. accidents) of substantives. In his fifth edition of 1699, Wallis in fact accuses the Port-Royalists of imitating him, though their source could equally well be Campanella, who had

[148] *English Grammatical Categories*, pp. 73, 449.
[149] 'On the History of Some Problems of English Grammar', p. 159.
[150] *Essay*, p. 228.   [151] P. 39.

already noted in 1638 that 'articles' in the vernaculars perform precisely the same grammatical function as is performed in the classical languages by case. The point involved however is that, whatever its source in earlier work, the functional parallel drawn between cases and prepositions implies for the Port-Royal authors the assumption of a common underlying logical basis to all languages.

For a treatment of this underlying logical basis it is above all to the *Nouvelle Méthode latine*, with its admitted debt to Sanctius, that we must turn. Since the logical structure is most cogently manifested in the structure of the proposition, a study of the *NML*'s discussion of elliptical constructions is a necessary preliminary to consideration of the *Grammaire générale et raisonnée* itself. It is difficult not to agree with R. Lakoff that 'many of the half-enunciated ideas in the *GGR* are fully enunciated in the NML', and that 'the *GGR* is a puzzling document, since it gives so little justification for the concept that underlies it'. For Lakoff, only when the ideas in the *Grammaire* are 'supplemented with proofs' contained in the Latin work, of which it is a 'sort of abstract', do they become fully intelligible[152] – yet another illustration of the fact that vernacular grammatical theory can only be properly understood within a total context of which Latin practice forms a part. Particularly is this true of the Port-Royal authors, who could assume that their readers were familiar not only with the *Nouvelle Méthode*, but with a still living tradition of Latin grammar in general.[153] It is easy to see why modern commentators, coming to the *GGR* without a knowledge of this background, have assumed its analyses to be original to itself and to Cartesianism. Even more than Ramus' works were said to be however, the *GGR* is a formless bear-cub to whose licking into shape the *NML* must in large measure contribute. Not that there is any justificatory philosophical theory, Cartesian or otherwise, in the *NML*. It simply applies Sanctius' syntactic notions to the structure of Latin, in a more carefully organized fashion than the *GGR*, and these notions, so much admired by Lancelot, involve the belief that the 'figurative construction' of discourse, containing elements which are 'understood without being expressed', is an abbreviation of the 'essential

[152] Review of H. Brekle's edition of the *GGR*, pp. 347, 350. A long and persuasive analysis of the question is given in pp. 347–59.

[153] Donzé (*La Grammaire générale et raisonnée de Port-Royal*, p. 34) holds that the *GGR* 's'adresse visiblement à un lecteur... [qui a] une première connaissance des langues classiques'.

construction' of the underlying linguistic system. The syntactic
operations stemming from this belief are ultimately traceable to the
ancient, literary functions of grammar treated by the *grammatica
exegetica* of classical times, whose business was among other things to
explain obscure passages in poets and prose writers. This section of
grammar went into eclipse with the rise of dialectics in Paris in the
Middle Ages, and under the rule of Ramus was hived off into
rhetoric. The notion that certain supposedly missing elements in
discourse must be 'understood' is an ancient one, illustrated in
Quintilian's remark that 'aliud est latine, aliud grammatice loqui',
which is quoted approvingly by Sanctius and glossed by W. K.
Percival as 'elegance transcends grammaticality'.[154] Seen from the
point of view of rhetoric, the function of ellipse is to render sentences
stylistically more acceptable. It is this rhetorical tradition that stands
behind Linacre's (1524) division of construction into 'justa and
figurata', and Scioppius' (1628) 'syntaxis regularis' and 'irregu-
laris'. What is new, or rather a revival of medieval doctrine, in
Linacre's and Sanctius' treatment of ellipse is that they regard the
elliptic constructions as incomplete manifestations of a normal and
essential underlying logical structure. Linacre defines his 'constructio
justa' as that which correctly reproduces the 'sensus animi' or mental
structure of concepts preceding utterance, and elliptic structures as
involving the lack of elements 'necessary to the legitimate
construction',[155] a formula that is repeated in Sanctius' claim that
a 'theory of suppletion is absolutely necessary' to grammatical
description.[156] The orientation in the Port-Royal Logic is still
rhetorical, but it involves the idea that the 'ordinary' syntax is
somehow closer to the truth than the figurative one: 'the figurative
expressions signify, in addition to the principal matter, the movement
and passion of the speaker, thus imprinting the one and the other
in the mind, whereas the simple expression indicates only the naked
truth'.[157] The *GGR* echoes this, regarding the 'natural order' of
syntax as 'in conformity with the natural expression of our thoughts',
and referring the reader to the *Nouvelle Méthode*, where the question
has been 'amply treated'.[158] The latter work in fact makes a remark

[154] 'Deep and Surface Structure Concepts', p. 242.
[155] *De emendata structura*, ff. xxii[v] and xxiii[r].
[156] Sanctius repeats Linacre's definitions of the two types of structure virtually word for word (*Minerva*, f. 164[v]), and later adds 'doctrinam supplendi esse valde necessariam'.
[157] *Logique* (1674 ed.), p. 128.   [158] *GGR*, pp. 145, 147.

that is of primary importance for the Port-Royal attitude to the vernacular: 'The regular [construction] is that which follows the natural order, and approaches closely the manner of speaking in the vulgar languages.'[159] The notion of a 'natural order' is of course present in the works of classical writers on language such as Quintilian.[160] Increasingly in the seventeenth century however, the classical languages are seen as unnecessarily elaborate in contrast to the French vernacular, which simply stays close to Nature. With the requirement that language be amenable to reason, and the growing view of French as an apt instrument of reason, the natural order is transformed from a defect into a virtue.[161] Though the *GGR* and the *NML* have a common author, and both treat the concept of a 'natural order' in syntax, R. Ogle has suggested that the two works 'represent two quite distinct and to some extent incompatible approaches to the question of what principles govern the formation of the most basic or natural sentence structures'.[162] The Latin grammar he sees as following 'purely formal considerations', the *GGR* 'primarily principles of logic'.[163] However this may be, there is no doubt that the belief that the structure of French coincides with Nature's own reasonings is of great importance in the development of attitudes to the French language, culminating in the often repeated dictum that 'Ce qui n'est pas clair n'est pas français.' Of capital importance for the Port-Royal approach on a more general level is their rejection of Ramus' rigidly prescribed boundaries to the three arts of rhetoric, logic and grammar. This not only allows them to take account of the rhetorical 'figurative' constructions in a linguistic theory, but at one and the same time to make their expansion into 'ordinary and essential' constructions the main task of grammar, and to provide these procedures with a logical justification. Rhetoric and grammar now come together once again (though their relationship

---

[159] *NML* (1681 ed.), p. 355.
[160] See A. D. Scaglione, *The Classical Theory of Composition*, Chapel Hill, 1972, pp. 74ff.
[161] Cf. Chevalier, *Histoire de la syntaxe*, p. 484.
[162] 'Two Port-Royal Theories of Natural Order', p. 102.
[163] *Ibid.*, p. 110. Some of Ogle's examples of the supposedly more logically orientated approach pursued in the *GGR* (e.g. the classification of *roi*, *philosophe* and *soldat* as semantically adjectival) are just as much part of the inherited Latin tradition as the more 'formal' approach he finds in the *NML*, and do not represent a radical new departure. Beyond the indication of this more logical approach, Ogle has little to say, given the paucity of the authors' own remarks, on word order in the *GGR*. Beauzée, singled out as continuing the logical bias of the *GGR*, is (see Clerico, *Franciscus Sanctius*, p. 82) of all Sanctius' disciples the one who is closest to him in approach, and thus is in line with the acknowledged source of much in the *NML*.

has undergone a significant change), and one is reminded of the quiet little remark hidden away in the *NML* to the effect that 'eloquence is the fruit of grammar'.[164] For Ramus, in constrast, it was an optional embellishment added separately after grammar had been established.[165]

For J.-C. Chevalier the Port-Royal authors go further than Sanctius, whose lack of an explicit metalanguage resulted in an insufficient distinction between the logical and the rhetorical values of ellipse.[166] Against this however must be set W. K. Percival's opinion that there is no doubt that for Sanctius the non-figurative constructions are 'logically prior'.[167] The Port-Royalists' 'temptation', according to Chevalier, is to turn solely to logic for a solution. What they owe to Linacre and Sanctius and the medieval tradition behind them is however capital, and this debt is illustrated more clearly in the *NML* than in the *GGR*. Examples of the expansion of elliptical constructions in the *NML* could be multiplied,[168] the doctrine that every verb must have a subject expressed or understood leading for instance to expansions of the type *vivitur = vita vivitur*, already familiar to readers of Linacre's *De emendata structura*.[169] Lancelot's doctrine that impersonal verbs cumulate in one word 'an entire proposition' (*poenitet me = poenitentia poenitet me*) had equally been common currency since Priscian.

It is this concept of discourse as frequently the abbreviation of fuller, more logical structures – a cardinal one for universal grammarians[170] – that is carried over into the *GGR*. Its most celebrated example is the sentence *Dieu invisible a créé le monde visible*, which is held to contain the three separate judgments *Dieu est invisible*, *Dieu a créé le monde* and *Le monde est visible*, and is hence regarded as an abbreviation of the complete logical structure *Dieu qui est invisible a créé le monde qui est visible*.[171] Two important points are made here. The first is the attribution to the relative, in line with the authors' insistence on mental operations, of a linking function in which 'it is stripped of its pronominal use and retains only its other use of uniting

---

[164] *NML* (1681 ed.), p. 12.
[165] Cf. Ramus' dismissal of any stylistic discussion as a grammatical 'pars nulla'.
[166] *Histoire de la syntaxe*, p. 502.
[167] 'Deep and Surface Structure Concepts', p. 243, n. 23.
[168] See Padley, *Grammatical Theory* (1976), pp. 213–15.
[169] Cf. Linacre's *sedetur = sessio sedetur* and *pluit = pluvia pluit*.
[170] It may be noted that for Locke words are abbreviations of experience.
[171] *GGR*, pp. 68–9.

the proposition in which it stands to another one'.[172] In this way they introduce the theory of the subordinate clause, which can 'form part of the subject or attribute of another proposition, which may be called the principal one', and which is 'often in our mind without being expressed by words'.[173] In this discussion it becomes particularly obvious that the *GGR* presupposes in its readers a knowledge of the *NML*, which itself owes a debt to the preceding Latin tradition. The *NML* too regards the relative pronoun as 'a link to cause a subordinate proposition to become part of another which we may call the principal one'.[174] It further specifies however that it must always be seen as linking two separate case-forms of the noun it refers to, as in *BELLUM tantum, quo BELLO omnes premebantur*. It adds – and here is the relevance for Port-Royal syntactic theory – that 'usually the following case is suppressed, because it is sufficiently expressed by the relative itself...although it must always be understood'.[175] As an example of a proposition in which the second of the case-marked nouns is deleted it gives *Est pater quem amo*, which is an abbreviation of the full logical structure *Est PATER quem PATREM amo*. This in turn echoes earlier examples such as Sanctius' *Vidi HOMINEM qui HOMO disputabat* and *hoc NEGOTIUM, quod NEGOTIUM abs te rogo*. The theoretical apparatus also has a precedent in Campanella's 'Every relative makes a sentence double, and is like a nominal conjunction of sentences.'[176] In connection with this issue R. Lakoff makes two very pertinent points: (1) 'If one cannot assume that the antecedent is logically present...both in the main clause and in the relative clause, it will be impossible to establish the...claim, that the relative clause serves as a connection between a main and a subordinate proposition'; and (2) it is the demonstration in the *NML* that 'the noun which the relative replaces was always there in the simple construction', that validates the discussion in the *GGR*, where it is taken for granted that the reader is aware of the treatment in the Latin work.[177] A similar source in the Latin tradition must be ascribed to the Port-Royal explanation of *canis currens* as an abbreviation of *canis qui currit*. The abbreviated form is held to contain 'a relative in the sense', and the explicit or implicit status of the relative

[172] *Ibid.*, pp. 72–3.
[173] The authors themselves use the term 'proposition incidente' for these dependent clauses.
[174] *NML* (1681 ed.), p. 452.   [175] *Ibid.*, p. 358.
[176] *Grammatica*, p. 99. Cf. Salmon's review of Chomsky's *Cartesian Linguistics*, p. 178.
[177] Review of Brekle's edition of the *GGR*.

(it is normally explicit in this construction in French) depends on 'the genius of each language'.

Chomsky's question as to whether the Port-Royal grammarians can in some sense be seen as 'proto-transformationalists' thus resolves itself into the one of whether their models can be so regarded. Whatever conclusions are come to,[178] the fact remains that their immediate source is to be found not in any doctrine of Descartes, but in Sanctius' *Minerva* of 1587. And behind Sanctius there lies an impressive body of medieval and humanist precedent. Given that for the first time in a French vernacular grammar the vision is raised from the preceding word-for-word approach to embrace the proposition in its entirety, it is not surprising that J.-C. Chevalier regards the Port-Royal authors as the founders of modern syntax.[179] Their approach is however ultimately based on centuries of work in the Latin tradition. The modistic view of syntax as the joining together of concepts[180] and their claim that oral discourse and 'verbum mentis' (the syntax of the mind) do not always coincide; the medieval doctrine that the concept of 'being' underlies all verbs, leading to the analysis of the verb into the components affirmation and attribute; Sanctius' and Scaliger's notion of a *ratio* underlying discourse and their expression of it in terms of elliptical constructions; Vossius' application to grammar of the Aristotelian theory of predication;[181] Caramuel's view of the verb *to be* as a 'judicativa copula',[182] a judgment-forming link between the two parts of the logical proposition – all these are precedents without which the Port-Royal Grammar could never have been written.

What are however significant are the points at which the Port-Royal authors refuse to follow the Latin tradition. They are, it is true,

[178] Among those, besides Lakoff, who have discussed this question may be mentioned K. E. Zimmer (review of Chomsky's *Cartesian Linguistics*, in *International Journal of American Linguistics*, xxxiv (1968), pp. 290–303), and W. K. Percival ('On the Non-Existence of Cartesian Linguistics', pp. 137–45). Percival regards it as a mistake by Chomsky to equate 'his notion of deep structure with the set of basic propositions which, the Port-Royal grammarians claimed, underlie complex sentences'. Lakoff finds Chomsky's claims in the last resort dubious, but concedes that Lancelot and Arnauld were 'in some sense' generative grammarians because of their belief in an underlying logical level of language.

[179] *Histoire de la syntaxe*, p. 493.

[180] Cf. R. G. Godfrey, 'Late Medieval Linguistic Meta-Theory and Chomsky's Syntactic Structures', *Word*, xxi:2 (1965), p. 255: 'Construction [for Thomas of Erfurt] is a deliberate, overt act of the human mind in which meaning forms (*constructibilia*) are united in order to express a composite mental concept.'

[181] See Padley, *Grammatical Theory* (1976), pp. 122, 127.

[182] See *Grammatica audax*, p. 31.

aiming to produce a universally applicable grammar, but also one that does not patently fly in the face of the empirical facts of the French language. Though they follow the tradition in holding that transitive verbs used without an object normally have that object 'understood', they regard Linacre's expansion of *vivo* into *vivo vitam* as an artificial creation abstracted from an actually occurring form such as *vivo vitam beatam*. They similarly reject the expansion of *curro* into *curro cursum* or *curro currere*. Their argument is that just as the adjective *candidus* signifies 'whiteness' and additionally connotes an object in which that whiteness inheres, so *curro* signifies 'running' and additionally makes an affirmation. It follows that it is pleonastic to complete the verb by adding an infinitive or a noun, for if *curro* implied *currere*, so equally would *candidus* imply *candore*.[183] 'There is no foundation', says the *NML*, 'for saying that a word is understood when it has never been seen expressed, and cannot in fact *be* expressed without a seeming absurdity.'[184] Though they break this rule with their expansion of *Pierre aime* into *Pierre est aimant*, the rule is significant in suggesting that if they *do* have a concept of deep structure, it is limited to those expressions in which it coincides with an expanded surface structure that occurs in actual usage. Their approach to subaudition has then, in this refusal to produce expansions that have no counterpart in usage or are patently absurd, its empirical side, which raises the question of the extent to which in practice they are prepared to elevate the claims of reason above those of usage. Here it must constantly be borne in mind that the Port-Royalists have, in common with so many seventeenth-century grammarians, a strong pedagogical motivation. Pedagogy and grammatical theory are bound to influence each other, and even in the preceding century, so concerned in vernacular grammar with the empirical description of facts and the all-pervading Renaissance cult of correct usage, teachers were well aware of what seemed to them the conflicting claims of use and reason.[185] J.-C. Chevalier sees them as placed before a dilemma which they could not satisfactorily resolve: whether to confine themselves to the production of straight-forward manuals for pedagogical purposes, or to engage in the complicated analyses dictated by the prevailing morphological

---

[183] *GGR*, pp. 19–20.
[184] *NML* (1681 ed.), p. 487. Similarly *GGR*, p. 124.
[185] Cf. Chevalier, *Histoire de la syntaxe*, p. 387.

approach to syntax.[186] In a pedagogy based on memory and imitation however, the bias towards the inculcation of correct usage tends to be privileged. Much of the avoidance of theoretical apparatus may be put down to the common humanist reaction against Scholastic cerebration, and this could provide an at least partial explanation for the fact that no theoretically orientated grammars of the French vernacular appear in the hundred years between Ramus and Port-Royal. During the whole of that period grammars have an empirical bias, and are often the work of minor pedagogues, their approach culminating in the important seventeenth-century usage-based school whose best-known representative is Vaugelas. This state of affairs no doubt explains why scholars working solely on the French vernacular tradition have been prone to see the Port-Royal Grammar as a revolutionary new departure.

The use of the word *méthode* in so many seventeenth-century titles is a reflection not only of Descartes' preoccupation with method, but of a general obsession of seventeenth-century pedagogy. This obsession runs through earlier work: Scaliger, Ramus, Sanctius and Ratke are all in their separate ways in search of a method, in enterprises in which usage and reason are both pedagogically motivated. The Ramist promise of a short-cut to learning is very much in evidence in the book-titles of the period: the orthographical 'method' of Choiseul[187] (founder of a Parisian *Ecole de la Charité* attaching great importance to the teaching of the vernacular) promises to teach more in three months than would ordinarily be achieved in ten years. Always the accent is on efficiency. If Claude Fleury's *Traité du choix et de la méthode des études*[188] proposes that grammar be first studied in the vernacular, it is because of the immense saving of time he foresees. A brash Ramist effectiveness pervades these titles, and indeed the insistence on method is, via practical pedagogy, very much a product of Ramus' thought, of which Descartes on this point represents the culmination. H. Aarsleff[189] notes that all the great general grammars of the period arise in the context of this pedagogical problem, Sanctius for instance claiming to inculcate a good knowledge of Latin in the short space

---

[186] *Ibid.*, p. 76.
[187] *Nouvelle et ancienne orthographe françoise*, Paris, 1654.
[188] Paris, 1686.
[189] 'The History of Linguistics and Professor Chomsky', p. 574.

of eight months. Pedagogically, the search for the *rationes* and *causae* underlying language was justified by the claim that it would reduce the amount of rote learning that had to be done.[190] For a very long time however pedagogy was to remain based on the two great Renaissance principles of memory and imitation, and it was precisely this that encouraged the continuation of a word-based grammar consisting of paradigms that the pupil could learn by heart.[191]

Protestant schools were ahead in these matters, but though they were suppressed along with the Jansenist *Petites Ecoles* of Port-Royal, parallel progress was being made in Catholic schools by the Oratorians, who taught history and the catechism in French, together with the elements of the vernacular as a preparation for Latin studies. Port-Royal's *Petites Ecoles*,[192] in conscious opposition to the Jesuits, based their practice on the development of the reasoning powers rather than the memory. Though they had a practical bent consonant with the austere goals of Jansenism, they also gave a literary bias to education, and were unequalled in the success with which they taught the mother tongue. Their wider aim was, in Sainte-Beuve's graphic phrase,[193] to 'décrasser' the learned and instruct polite society. The text-books produced for these schools share the preoccupation of the times with method, as is shown by the titles of the various *Nouvelles Méthodes* for Latin, Greek, Italian and Spanish. They were also however attempting to put an end to the type of rhetorical delivery practised by those whose style had been formed by the study of dead languages. If, as Sainte-Beuve puts it,[194] the originality of Louis XIV's century lies in its having ceased to speak Latin in French, some at least of the thanks must go to Port-Royal. They also aimed to change a situation in which, to cite Sainte-Beuve yet again, pupils were expected to reach the unknown by way of the unintelligible. 'French must be learnt before Latin; and children must be so grounded in the everyday, common style of French...that the Latin they learn later will be unable to change and

---

[190] According to Aarsleff (*ibid.*, pp. 574–5) it is in this pedagogical light that the frequent occurrence of the word 'method' in book titles must be understood. Cf. Comenius' use of it in his *Linguarum methodus novissima*.

[191] Cf. Chevalier, *Histoire de la syntaxe*, p. 379. I am indebted to several of Chevalier's insights in this section.

[192] On these schools see Adamson, *Pioneers of Modern Education 1600–1700*, pp. 259–61; Cadet, *Port-Royal Education*.

[193] See *Sainte-Beuve Port-Royal*, ed. M. Leroy, Paris, 1953–5, which reproduces the third edition (1867) of Sainte-Beuve's *Port-Royal*. Book four of the second volume is devoted to the *Petites Ecoles*.   [194] *Ibid.*, II, 457.

corrupt the purity of their French.'[195] The various grammars are accordingly written in the vernacular. In contrast to the *GGR*, the *Nouvelles Méthodes* for Italian and Spanish[196] are practical teaching manuals, in which the material is kept to a minimum. They are virtually devoid of any overt grammatical theory, their interest for this study lying in the pedagogical orientation of their explanatory prefaces. This orientation is in some respects patently Ramist, enjoining that rules must at the earliest opportunity be accompanied by actual use of the language. This means that after a brief introduction to articles (important for 'declining' nouns), auxiliary verbs and the regular conjugations – the barest necessary framework – the pupil begins to read authors. In accordance with this, a mere three or four pages of the Italian grammar are given up to a 'general abstract of the whole of grammar, shorter and more methodical than can be found elsewhere'. As for the rest of grammar, 'it can be left to the teacher to point it out in actual usage'. Equal importance is attached however to the requirement that attention should be drawn to the 'general analogy' of languages, the phrase 'as in all languages' occurring regularly in both grammars. Above all, Lancelot points to the fact – so insisted upon, as we have seen, by Ratke – that these practical teaching manuals both follow the same plan. The overriding aim of these manuals is incontestably pedagogical, their purpose identical with that already enunciated by Ascham – that pupils should no longer be 'corrupted in judgment'[197] by the methods in common use.

J.-C. Chevalier's account of some of the more advanced of the new, contrasting pedagogical methods shows that they have important implications for attitudes to vernacular structure. Having listened to the presentation of a Latin text in French, pupils were then required to take the text and rewrite it in 'the natural order', which was of course the order of the mother tongue itself. Such methods needed to be complemented by well-set-out grammars and it is this that Chevalier believes, in an interesting theory, to lie behind the return, at a moment when stress was being laid as never before on usage-based grammars, to the doctrines of Scholasticism.[198] It is easy to demon-

[195] T. Guyot, *Billets que Cicéron a écrits*, Paris, 1668, preface.

[196] Both published in Paris in 1660, under Lancelot's pseudonym 'D.T.' or 'de Trigny'.

[197] Ascham, *Scholemaster*, p. 185.

[198] *Histoire de la syntaxe*, p. 390. As A. Joly points out in his edition of F. Thurot's introduction to Harris' *Hermes* (*Tableau des progrès*. pp. 17–18), this seemingly small revolution in pedagogical method has considerable epistemological consequences.

strate Scholastic influence on the 'philosophical' grammarians and on Port-Royal. What is not so easy is to show just *why* this influence returns so strongly in the seventeenth century, and Chevalier has here provided one possible answer. In this tension between the exigences of practical pedagogy and the need for some kind of explanatory theory, the question arises of the extent to which the *GGR* is a 'grammaire raisonnée', and the extent to which it resembles the Port-Royal grammars of other modern languages in the pedagogical drive to inculcate the empirically determined essentials. As we have seen, it is by no means ready to accept theoretically based expansions when they fly in the face of actual linguistic usage. It has been traditionally represented as a reaction against the usage-based grammars typified by Vaugelas' *Remarques sur la langue françoise* (1647), which is consciously based on 'le sens commun'.[199] Certainly the Port-Royalists engaged in vigorous polemics with supporters of the usage school, more particularly the Jesuit Bouhours.[200] Vaugelas' approach had confirmed the prevailing bias towards empirical observation, and his fame effectively meant that all philosophical speculation, any attempt to introduce explanatory theory, were banned from vernacular grammar for over a generation. Seen in this context, the *GGR* does represent a return to a theoretical approach, and at first sight its aims would seem to be identical with those of the Port-Royal Logic – the upholding of the claims of reason against those of authority. Again it is Ferdinand Brunot's *Histoire de la langue française*, with its Port-Royal chapter[201] entitled 'un nouveau maître, la raison', that is a major factor in inaugurating or perpetuating this view. And yet again L. Kukenheim's history of French linguistics follows his lead: with the arrival of the *GGR* 'the idea of reason tends to supplant that of usage, whose utility and practicability are put in doubt'.[202] A closer look at Brunot's chapter reveals however that he is far from supporting a view as extreme as that of Kukenheim. Though he speaks of 'the tyranny of usage' and sees the *GGR* as having unsettled people's faith in it, he finds the authors do not live up to the promise of their title-page. Instead of applying reason to purge the language of the 'caprices without reason or contrary to reason' of court usage, they in practice leave Vaugelas' rules

---

[199] Thus e.g. Chomsky, *Cartesian Linguistics*, p. 54.
[200] For an account of the Jansenists' quarrel with Bouhours see T. Rosset, 'Le P. Bouhours critique de la langue des écrivains jansénistes', *Annales de l'Université de Grenoble*, xx:1 (1908), pp. 55–125.   [201] Vol. IV, book 1, ch. 5.
[202] *Esquisse historique de la linguistique française*, p. 28.

untouched, applying Arnauld's philosophy 'to explain usage rather than correct it'.[203] In this connection he notes disapprovingly Scaliger's contention that 'it is the philosopher's business to place reason before human caprice'.[204] Brunot sees Arnauld, for him the real author of the *GGR*, as so 'penetrated with current doctrines' on correct usage that he leaves Vaugelas' prescriptions uncontested.[205] Vaugelas' sway, based on usage, at least allowed for change. For Brunot the philosophical method, which could have delivered the language from 'stupid tyrannies', in practice enslaved it yet more rigidly.[206] Kukenheim again follows him on this point, observing that it is the Port-Royalists' aim to explain usage rather than change it. More extreme than either, and typical of the established view, is M. Leroy's condemnation of the authors for 'sweeping away Vaugelas' observations based on good sense' and establishing the rule of reason for the next two centuries.[207]

A useful corrective to such extreme views is provided in an important article on Vaugelas and Port-Royal by W. K. Percival,[208] who treats the question of whether there is in fact a 'radical difference' in orientation between the two approaches. Aspects of Vaugelas' work itself, according to Percival, can hardly be labelled as pure descriptivism. The Port-Royal criticism of him turns on his complete omission of certain empirical facts, and on his prescribing of rules which fail to cover *all* the facts – in other words they accuse him of 'observational inadequacy'.[209] If we turn to the authors' theoretical stance on the matter, the Port-Royal Logic is quite clear that usage prescribed by authority must not be allowed unlimited freedom, reason being 'quite justified in not suffering the human sciences, which profess to base themselves only on reason, to be enslaved by authority *against* reason'. The *NML* takes a similar view, holding that 'in received matters nothing should be changed unnecessarily and without good reason'. It is true that these passages may be thought to refer solely to academic freedom and to pedagogical

[203] *Histoire de la langue française*, IV, 53–5, 58.
[204] *De causis linguae Latinae*, cap. lxiii.
[205] As an example Brunot cites the authors' retention of Vaugelas' dictum that *aimé(e)* is a 'gérondif' in *j'ai aimé la chasse*, but a passive participle in *la chasse qu'il a aimée*.
[206] H. Arens, *Sprachwissenschaft* (2nd ed.), Freiburg/Munich 1969, similarly sees the Port-Royal approach as a 'tyranny of reason'.
[207] *Les Grands Courants de la linguistique moderne* (2nd ed.), Brussels and Paris, 1971, p. 12.
[208] 'The Notion of Usage in Vaugelas and in the Port Royal Grammar', *History of Linguistic Thought and Contemporary Linguistics*, ed. H. Parret, Berlin and New York, 1976, pp. 374–82.
[209] *Ibid.*, p. 379.

method. Certainly they bear out Brunot's contention that the authors are unwilling to change received usage, and their position as stated in the *GGR* would seem to bear this out: though 'those ways of speaking that are authorized by general and uncontested usage must be regarded as good, even if they are contrary to the rules and analogy of the language', they must never 'be cited in order to put the rules in doubt and upset analogy'.[210] The reason behind this, as the authors make plain, is the common seventeenth-century view that unbridled usage will, if left to itself, deprive the language of sure and certain principles on which to base its rules. The *NML* however sees a place for usage within the system: 'just as the rules are the key to usage, so also usage confirms the rules'.[211] Percival sees little to distinguish this from Vaugelas' practice, regarding the parties as in full agreement as to the 'primacy of usage' and the 'desirability of revealing explanation'.

In the preface to the *NML* Lancelot informs the reader that he has 'a great aversion to all these finicky little details of grammar, of which Quintilian so well says that they dry up and enfeeble the mind'. This does not however prevent the authors of the *GGR* from taking up some quite detailed points of usage, such as the one covered by Vaugelas' rule that a relative pronoun cannot refer to an antecedent noun not accompanied by an article, a rule that excludes as ungrammatical structures like *Il a fait cela par avarice qui est capable de tout*. In the face of structures such as *une sorte de bois qui est fort dur*, which contradict Vaugelas' rule, they modify it to accommodate usage: '*qui* must not be placed after a common noun, if it is not determined by an article, or by something else which determines it no less than an article would'.[212] Various terms – *ce, quelque, plusieurs*, and words such as *sorte* and *espèce* – are held to have the same determining function as articles, thus permitting such utterances as *une sorte de fruit qui est meur en hyver*. The theoretical justification of this rule is that 'a common noun must be taken to be determined, when there is something which indicates that it is to be understood in its fullest extent'.[213] The function of the article is thus to determine the semantic extent ('étendue') of nouns, so much so that in e.g. *Il vit en Roy*, the particle *en* must be held to 'contain within itself' an article, the sentence being an abbreviation of *Il vit comme un Roy* or *en la manière*

[210] *GGR*, pp. 82–3.
[211] *NML* (1681 ed.), pp. 21, 467, 472.
[212] *GGR*, p. 77.
[213] *Ibid.*, pp. 77–8.

d'un Roy. A similar care is taken to establish the agreement or non-agreement of participles, taking as the point of departure Vaugelas' decree that those participial forms which govern nouns, as do verbs, are 'gerundives' rather than adjectives, and hence show no agreement. Basing himself on evidence like this, Percival concludes that the *GGR* is 'not a reaction against a previously held linguistic theory'. Arnauld and Lancelot, far from repudiating Vaugelas, 'transcended him completely and in the process incorporated many of his ideas'. Those sections of the *GGR* in which the authors, in spite of the disclaimer in the *NML* as to the 'petites pointilleries' of grammar, proceed to a discussion of the finer points of usage, would seem to furnish proof of this thesis.

Syntax is dismissed in the *GGR* in a scant seven pages, of which two-and-a-half treat of the 'figures of construction'. Yet again one is ineluctably drawn back to the argument that it is the Port-Royal Latin grammar that provides the best illustration of syntactic theory, the *GGR* being simply an accompanying, and rather sketchy, explanatory manual. But if the *NML*, the *GGR* and the Logic are treated as a single grammatico-logical work in three volumes, the result is a coherent body of doctrine and practice. J.-C. Chevalier contends that the *GGR* is 'only in appearance' a logician's grammar, being as far removed from a logically based grammar such as that of Ramus, as in our own century Chomsky's transformational-generative approach is from that of the Bloomfieldian distribution-alists. His thesis is that whereas earlier grammar analysed the *forms* of language and then sought their justification in logic, Port-Royal analyses the *logical content*, and then supposes linguistic structures to be isomorphic with it.[214] The all-important result of this is that the *GGR* reasons 'by wholes', passing from a syntax of words in contact, to one founded on entire propositions. With all this one can be wholeheartedly in agreement. Chevalier is bent however on demon-strating an unmistakably *original* Port-Royal contribution, and to this end he regards the authors' acknowledged debt to Sanctius as not of central importance, for they are no longer 'in the same line' as the philosophical grammarians.[215] For him the great divide in the history of grammar is clear. Before Port-Royal linguistic analysis

[214] *Histoire de la syntaxe,* pp. 495, 499, 538.
[215] *Ibid.,* p. 503. Chevalier says F. Brunot (*Histoire de la langue française,* IV, 55) erroneously sees Arnauld as having applied the philosophical method of Scaliger and Scioppius to French, 'comme si le mérite était d'avoir changé de grille, de code'.

takes place on the level of discourse. After Port-Royal it takes place on the level of linguistic content.[216] Certainly by the late seventeenth century grammar had reached a cross-roads. It had arrived at the point where grammarians had to decide whether to continue with the inherited approach, whose analysis confined itself to 'surface' structure, or to follow the path traced by Scaliger, Sanctius, Caramuel and Campanella, and transfer their attention decisively from 'verbum oris' to 'verbum mentis', from external discourse to the internal discourse of the mind. Chevalier rightly regards Ramus' formalism as having exhausted the possibilities of a method founded on the analysis of external discourse, but it is Port-Royal that he regards as having made the historic break-through. Intent as he is on seeing the application of Port-Royal methods to the *vernacular* as providing new insights, he confines his analyses to the *GGR* itself. As a corrective to this view one may cite R. Lakoff's contention that the *GGR* is 'not a primary linguistic work: by itself it is not intelligible, but is rather an abstract of a larger work [the *NML*], and contains few, if any, insights demonstrably its own'.[217] In refuting possibly exaggerated claims made for the *Grammaire générale et raisonnée* it is however not necessary to go as far as H. Arens[218] and attribute to it no more than the pedestrian motivation of providing an introduction to grammar for the pupils of the *Petites Ecoles* – though that was indeed its immediate purpose. But it is equally exaggerated to speak of the 'revolution' of Port-Royal insights when they can almost all be traced to sources in the preceding Latin tradition. Far from being originators, I believe, they brought to the attention of a wider public notions that had been current among Latin grammarians for

[216] *Ibid.*, pp. 490–1, 499: 'jusque-là...on raisonne au niveau du discours...à partir de Port-Royal, on raisonne au niveau du contenu'.

[217] Review of Brekle's edition of the *GGR*, p. 363. Since in his view the *NML* and the *GGR* 'contain widely differing conceptions of natural order', Ogle ('Two Port-Royal Theories of Natural Order', p. 102) does not accept Lakoff's claim that the latter 'derives its basic theoretical tenets' from the former. Ogle holds (p. 110) that the *GGR* 'far from being a mere abstract of the *NML*, constitutes a sharp break with the formalist tradition the latter represents'. But in the last resort both works are based on the Sanctian theory of elliptic constructions, itself highly logical in character, of which the *NML* simply gives an exemplification, but a much fuller one than that in the *GGR*. In my own view, the *GGR* is not so much as 'abstract' of the *NML* as a justificatory manual in the vernacular, with a superimposed logical apparatus provided by Arnauld. Clerico's thesis (*Franciscus Sanctius*, p. 75) that the *GGR* is not in a direct line of descent from the *NML*, having, in a situation in which 'l'environnement culturel est si changé que le type de grammaire s'en ressent', moved away from the Sanctian theory of double construction, is an attractive one, but does not in my view carry conviction.

[218] *Sprachwissenschaft*, p. 74.

a very long time. These notions consist of the belief that language and mental operations can be brought to coincide, and that its underlying 'reasons' and 'causes' are amenable to logical analysis. For long regarded as the Port-Royal contribution par excellence to linguistic theory, these assumptions are all pre-Cartesian, and demonstrably present in the work of certain of the Port-Royal authors' predecessors, both medieval and humanist. Any view of the *Grammaire générale et raisonnée* as being somehow *sui generis* is the result of an approach the present volume is designed to invalidate – namely the study of European grammatical theory from within the confines of one particular vernacular tradition.

The single overriding tenet of the grammarians considered in this section may be stated as the belief that language is the mirror of *thought*. For those to whom we now turn, in a major shift in epistemological premises, it becomes the mirror of *things*.

5. LANGUAGE THE MIRROR OF THINGS: FROM CAMPANELLA TO WILKINS

At the same time as a rationalist approach to universal grammar was being developed on the Continent, another approach was taking shape in Britain, rooted not so much in the application of reason to language as in the empiricism of the new science whose ideals were embodied in the Royal Society. In this context interest in general grammar is but one element in a wider cultural shift, in a movement towards a greater emphasis on *things* and on empirical verification. Despite the incontestable modernism of this, the renewed stress on the obtaining of knowledge through the senses has Aristotelian sources, and provides yet one more instance of the continued influence of Scholasticism. Despite the self-conscious anti-medievalism of seventeenth-century thought, many of its roots go back to Nominalism, which paved the way for the century's distrust of words and its fascination with nomenclature. Many of the Scholastic strands that influence seventeenth-century thought are present in the works of the Italian Tommaso Campanella, whose neo-Scholastic *Grammatica* provides the basis for important analyses in Bishop Wilkins' *Essay Towards a Real Character and a Philosophical Language* (1668). A further trend, whose *anti*-Scholastic bias is equally typical of the seventeenth century, is that represented by Baconian 'sense-realism', which rejects Aristotelianism but equally leads to a profound distrust of words. This last-named trait links up again with the utilitarianism of contemporary puritans, many of them Ramists, with their emphasis on a plain preaching style and their preference for the world of 'things'. Particularly among the new men of science, who in this join hands with the puritans and with pedagogical reformers such as Comenius, there is a desire to achieve contact with reality and use it to practical ends. It is this that lies behind the contemporary longing for a system of communication that would be free of the treacherous ambiguities of natural languages, and in which concepts (by definition the same in all men) would each have their single, unalterable sign. In order to achieve this, the universe had first to be cut up into its constituent parts, analysed and labelled, and it is here that the continuing Scholastic influence becomes paramount. The new scientists look for, and of course find, a classification of the universe that corresponds to the categories already established by Aristotle. 'Things', once established, have the old labels attached to them; or rather, perhaps, 'things' are found which will fit the labels. Here, the quest for an artificial language is just one manifestation of a general drive towards scientific classification, and M. Slaughter has been able to show that the taxonomies used in for instance botanical studies set the tone for the planners of artificial languages.[1] Further, though in England the devising of a 'real character' or alphabet for the exact notification of 'things' grows out of practical experiments with shorthand and sign systems for the deaf,[2] the desire for a language that will mirror the universe also has Scholastic echoes, going back to Scaliger and beyond him to the medieval 'speculative grammars'. Various sources from Scholasticism are brought together in Wilkins' *Essay*:

[Natural grammar] hath been treated but by few, which makes our learned Verulam [i.e. Bacon] put it among his *Desiderata*; I do not know any more that have purposely written of it, but Scotus[3] in his *Grammatica Speculativa*, and Caramuel in his *Grammatica Audax*, and Campanella in his *Grammatica Philosophica*...Besides which, something hath been occasionally spoken of it, by Scaliger in his book *de causis linguae latinae*.[4]

Bacon

Bacon's *Advancement of Learning* (1605) states grammar to be of two kinds: 'the one popular, which is for the speedy and perfect attaining

---

[1] *Universal Languages and Scientific Taxonomy in the Seventeenth Century*, Cambridge, 1982. On the general cultural background see also Padley, *Grammatical Theory* (1976), pp. 132–53, 184–91.

[2] On the connection between early systems of shorthand (or 'brachygraphy') and the artificial language movement see V. Salmon, *The Works of Francis Lodwick*, London, 1972, pp. 60–4, 247–54 and *passim*.

[3] Wilkins and his contemporaries ascribed to Duns Scotus the *Grammatica speculativa* (c.1310) that is now known to be the work of Thomas of Erfurt. Reprinted in Paris in 1605, it had appeared in Leyden in 1693 in Wadding's edition, and was no doubt well known to seventeenth-century scholars with an interest in linguistic theory.

[4] *An Essay Towards a Real Character and a Philosophical Language*, London, 1668, p. 297.

of languages...the other philosophical, examining the power and nature of words as they are the footsteps and prints of reason'.[5] The difference between rationalists and empiricists on these points is partly a matter of emphasis, the latter stressing the utilitarian value of an isomorphism between language and the universe. The opposition of *res* and *verba* is central to the empiricist argument, Bacon rejecting the type of ratiocination that 'did chiefly reign amongst the schoolmen ...their wits being shut up in the cells of a few authors (chiefly Aristotle their dictator)'.[6] In this matter of anti-Aristotelianism the parallels between Bacon and Ramus are instructive. Like Ramus, Bacon aimed to reorganize the whole of learning, shifting it from its centuries-old basis in Aristotle's *Organon* and reorientating it by means of his own 'new instrument' (*Novum organum*) towards an 'instauratio magna' or complete renovation of studies. Though Bacon regarded Ramus' method as producing 'dry and barren husks' rather than the 'kernels and grains of sciences',[7] his own methods are not exempt from an arid materialism[8] – a criticism that can be extended to Hobbes and to other linguistic philosophers of the age. In their desire to bring all learning under the sway of reason, Bacon and Descartes form part of the same intellectual tide. Central to Bacon's approach however is his declaration that 'to resolve nature into abstractions is less to our purpose than to dissect her into parts...Matter rather than forms should be the object of our attention.'[9] Here speaks the empiricist, the forerunner of the new science, who treats knowledge as experience and concerns himself above all with 'senses and particulars'. Though Baconianism and Cartesianism have a common origin in the climate of scepticism that is the legacy of the medieval Nominalists, there is a cardinal difference between them: while the intellect is for Descartes its own object of study, it is 'fastened by Bacon to the leading-strings of nature'.[10] It is the Baconian tendency in seventeenth-century thought

---

[5] *The Philosophical Works of Francis Bacon, Reprinted from the Texts...of Ellis and Spedding*, ed. J. M. Robertson, London, 1905, p. 122. In the Latin version, *De augmentis scientiarum* (1623), there is a further reference to 'grammatica literaria' and 'grammatica philosophica', the latter of which 'should diligently inquire, not the analogy of words with one another, but the analogy between words and things, or reason' (*ibid.*, p. 523).

[6] *Of the Advancement of Learning*, in *ibid.*, p. 54.

[7] *De augmentis scientiarum*, in R. L. Ellis, J. Spedding and D. D. Heath, *The Works of Francis Bacon*, London, 1887–92, I, 663. [8] Cf. Rossi, *Francis Bacon*, p. 172.

[9] *Novum organum* (1620), aphorism li, in *The Philosophical Works*, ed. J. M. Robertson, p. 267.

[10] K. Fischer, *Francis Bacon of Verulam: Realistic Philosophy and its Age*, translated from the German by J. Oxenford, London, 1857, p. 74.

that not only produces Locke and Hobbes, but is also responsible in part for the artificial-language projectors and their universalist schemes, rooted as they are in empiricism and 'sense-realism'.

Baconianism is very much part of the intellectual movement that produced the new science of the seventeenth century and its embodiment in the Royal Society,[11] of which Wilkins and others of the artificial-language planners were members. A new empiricism is taking shape, in which in Bacon's words deductive reasoning taking as its starting-point 'the most general axioms' is replaced by an inductive approach in which observation 'derives axioms from the senses and particulars, rising by a gradual and unbroken ascent, so that it arrives at the most general axioms last of all'.[12] This is according to Bacon 'the true way, but as yet untried', but it is a way that is to deal the final blow, among scientists at any rate, to Ramus' Aristotelian dogma of 'universaliter primum', the priority of the general. One consequence of Bacon's new paradigm is, according to P. Rossi,[13] that logic is transformed from a method of verbal definition to an instrument for controlling a situation. A paradox of seventeenth-century thought is that this would-be realistic approach based on the prior observation of facts is accompanied by a widespread Nominalism, a fascination with nomenclature. If we are to follow K. Fischer in holding that 'the whole philosophy of experience, together with Bacon, is nominalistic in its views',[14] then it would seem not unlikely that this is a medieval inheritance and, like so much of seventeenth-century thought, ultimately rooted in Scholasticism. The result is a split, which had been long in declaring itself, between revealed truth and empirical truth. For the seventeenth century, Truth is no longer one and indivisible: 'in this regard Bacon belongs with Duns Scotus and Occam. If you hold that individual "things" alone are real, and reject universals and abstractions as "names"... you have no alternative but to accept...[this] dichotomy of "truth", and to try...to keep the two kinds from contaminating each other.'[15]

---

[11] Cf. however Webster, *The Great Instauration*, pp. 494–5. While not denying the presence of a 'serious Baconian motivation' within the Royal Society, Webster thinks it dangerous to assume 'too great a uniformity of ethos' among its members. His monumental work is indispensable reading for an understanding of the contribution of the 'Puritan World View' to science and learning.   [12] *Novum organum*, aphorism xx, p. 261.

[13] *Francis Bacon*, p. 61.   [14] *Francis Bacon of Verulam*, p. 412.

[15] Willey, *The Seventeenth Century Background*, p. 27. Willey notes (pp. 14–15) that for the Scholastics 'there was little or no distinction between a "fact" and a theological or metaphysical "truth".'

The zeal with which Hobbes rejects universals and abstractions as mere 'names' is more than equalled by the industry the age devotes to labelling, to the providing of names for the 'senses and particulars' of the universe. Their quarrel with existing names is that they are not sufficiently precise, or have been misapplied by the unthinking mass of men, by the 'apprehension of the vulgar'.[16] The application of mathematics to natural phenomena had encouraged the idea that words ought to have the rigour of mathematical symbols, with a precise one-to-one correspondence between name and referent. It is here that some of Bacon's suggestions are relevant to the aims of the language-planners, particularly his idea that non-verbal symbols – 'whatsoever is capable of sufficient differences, and those perceptible by the sense' – might be used to express mental concepts. Here Bacon gives the first impulse to the language-planners' search for 'real characters', that is to say symbols not representing words but referring directly to things, or at any rate to men's concepts of them. With Bacon as with others it was a misunderstanding of the principles of Chinese writing that provided the inspiration for these 'Characters Real, which express neither letters nor words in gross, but Things or Notions'.[17] In the *Advancement of Learning* they represent concepts, are 'notes of cogitations', but in the later *De augmentis* have become 'notes of things', consonant with Bacon's theory that phenomena can be reduced to a limited number of elements or 'simple natures', each capable of being represented by a non-verbal symbol. The relevance for Wilkins' work is made yet plainer by Bacon's statement that these real characters should coincide in number with the 'radical words' of his ideal language. Bacon's task was to make the intellectual world coincide in extent with the newfound breadth of the material one, and to this end he opposed to Aristotle's theory of art as the imitation of nature his own theory of the 'congruity of natural and artificial phenomena'.[18] It follows that as an arbitrary human institution language too must exhibit this congruence, and the language-planners certainly proceed on that assumption, returning in this respect to

[16] Bacon, *Novum organum*, aphorism xliii, p. 264.
[17] Bacon, *Of the Advancement of Learning*, p. 121. V. Salmon, '"Philosophical" Grammar in John Wilkins's "Essay"', *Canadian Journal of Linguistics*, xx:2 (1975), p. 153, n. 10, observes that 'the erroneous idea that Chinese represented pure thought, without the interference of grammar, was very prevalent in the seventeenth century', being shared by Bacon, Wilkins and Campanella.
[18] Rossi, *Francis Bacon*, p. 145.

Scholasticism and Scaliger. The latter's theory forms a link between the Thomist doctrine of a natural conformity between language and phenomena, and the seventeenth-century demand for a language which, in the interests of scientific thought, should reflect the universe. Though it is for Scaliger the *understanding* that is the mirror of things – 'Est quasi rerum speculum intellectus noster' – his definition of the material part of the linguistic sign as, in the terms also used by Bacon, 'a note of those notions that are in the mind', shows that it is language itself, at one remove, that is ultimately the mirror of the universe.[19] Here it is indeed relevant that, among the other sources he cites, Wilkins has read Scaliger.

In the last resort however Bacon is unwilling to put complete faith in his wished-for congruence of 'real characters' and 'things and notions'. If the human mind is indeed a mirror, it is a 'false mirror, which distorts and discolours the nature of things by mingling its own nature with it'.[20] This conclusion, which again smacks of Nominalism, calls in question the whole raison d'être of the seventeenth-century empiricist's insistence on the need for a direct knowledge of *things*, for it throws doubt on the validity of the link between thing and concept. Bacon is very much aware of the 'profound kinds of fallacies' in the mind of man, including what he calls the 'idols of the market-place' (misconceptions deriving from language and society), the remedy against which is 'the formation of ideas and axioms by true induction and greater care in definition'. Only by this means, by the elimination of incorrect notions, can names be found to fit reality. Yet even definitions are finally bound to be inadequate to deal with the lack of congruence between phenomena and natural languages, for they themselves consist of words.[21] There are many reasons why so many of the best minds in the seventeenth century distrusted words.[22] Bacon cites 'the admiration of ancient authors, the hate of the schoolmen, the

[19] *De causis linguae Latinae*, caps. i, lxvi.

[20] *Novum organum*, aphorism xli, p. 264. Bacon thus constitutes a partial exception to Willey's claim (*The Seventeenth Century Background*, pp. 27–8) that 'little meaning could have been attached, in the seventeenth century...to the theory that the mind is in some sense constitutive of reality, even a "fact" being in part a thing made, an act of the mind'.

[21] *Ibid.*, aphorism lix, p. 269. Cf. *ibid.*, aphorism xliii (p. 264), where words 'throw all into confusion, and lead men away into numberless empty controversies and idle fancies'.

[22] The common dichotomy of 'words and things' originates according to A. C. Howell ('*Res et verba*: Words and Things', *ELH A Journal of English Literary History*, XIII (1946), p. 131) in a rhetorical distinction: 'the term *res*, meaning *subject-matter*, seems to have become confused with *res* meaning *things*...The origin of the use of this pair of words is, of course, classical; and it was from their study of classical rhetoric that seventeenth century critics learned it.'

exact study of languages, and the efficacy of preaching, [which] did bring in an affectionate study of eloquence and copie [i.e. super-abundance] of speech'. He concludes that 'it is almost necessary in all controversies and dispositions to imitate the wisdom of the Mathematicians'.[23] Such passages in Bacon embody both the language-planners' distrust of natural languages, rendered unreliable by misuse, and their desire for a mathematical rigour in which the relation between symbol and referent or concept would be un-equivocal, constant and instantly recognizable. But in early studies of the artificial-language movement the importance of Bacon was emphasized to the detriment of other possible sources.[24] More recently it has been objected that not only did Bacon not have in mind a 'philosophical language' of the type later produced by Wilkins and others but merely a 'universal character' or alphabet of symbols, but also (as I have indicated above) his distrust of words did not allow him to envisage the possibility of a reliable correspondence between word and referent.[25] The fact remains however that the language-planners themselves regarded him as providing the starting-point for their investigations.

Campanella and Caramuel

Bacon is not the only seventeenth-century author mentioned by Wilkins as having treated 'natural grammar'. He also cites Tommaso Campanella's *Grammatica* of 1638,[26] which sees grammar as the first of the five parts of 'rational philosophy', the others being logic, rhetoric, poetics and historiography. This work should rank with J. C. Scaliger's *De causis linguae Latinae* (1540), for they represent the two most ambitious attempts to return grammar to some kind of 'explanatory adequacy' based on the metalanguage of Scholastic

[23] *Of the Advancement of Learning*, pp. 54, 120.
[24] E.g. Funke, 'Zum Weltsprachenproblem in England im 17. Jahrhundert'; R. F. Jones, 'Science and Language in England of the Mid-Seventeenth Century', *Journal of English and Germanic Philology*, XXXI (1932) (reprinted in *The Seventeenth Century*, Stanford, 1951).
[25] See V. Salmon, 'Language-Planning in Seventeenth-Century England', *In Memory of J. R. Firth*, ed. C. E. Bazell, J. C. Catford, M. A. K. Halliday and K. H. Robins, London, 1966, p. 385. Salmon claims elsewhere ('"Philosophical" Grammar in John Wilkins's "Essay"', p. 134) that 'there is no doubt that Wilkins himself regarded Bacon as his major source of inspiration'.
[26] *Philosophiae rationalis partes quimque. Videlicet: grammatica, dialectica, rhetorica, poetica, historiographia. Pars prima: grammatica*, Paris, 1638. For a treatment of the grammar see Padley, *Grammatical Theory* (1976), pp. 160–78.

philosophy. Opinions as to the extent to which Scholasticism still held an attraction for the seventeenth-century mind are changing. In 1905 J. W. Adamson[27] could still claim that though early in the century it maintained a precarious hold in the Universities, 'with respect to the intellectual life and tendencies of the time as a whole, Scholasticism was a spent force'. In the last decade, on the contrary, V. H. H. Green asserts that there were throughout Europe 'signs of a neo-scholastic revival, both anti-Ramist and anti-Calvinist in direction', whose adherents 'paid a renewed attention to Aristotelianism and scholastic philosophy in general'.[28] He cautiously adds that it is 'not very easy to deduce from all this anything more than a certain conservatism of attitude' designed to support the *status quo*. There is no doubt however that a good deal of intellectual activity of a neo-Scholastic character was going on, and W. S. Howell's *Logic and Rhetoric in England, 1500–1700* lists quite a number of logics written, the most influential of them before 1620, to revive a Scholastic approach while at the same time maintaining certain Ramist features.[29] Campanella's work forms an important part of this Scholastic reaction, but can also be seen as constituting a link between it and Baconian empiricism. He was also, paradoxically, a devotee of the Italian nature-philosophy expounded by Bernardino Telesio (1509–88), which started as part of the neo-Platonic revival and ended up in 'a naturalistic view of the world completely opposed to scholasticism'[30] and in opposition to the Aristotelian approach to nature. Campanella's synthesis of this nature-philosophy, in which medieval and modern elements are mingled, with neo-Platonism and Thomism (like Aquinas he was a Dominican), make him a precursor not only, in some sense, of Bacon, but also of Descartes.[31] Since the English language-planner John Wilkins follows Campanella closely in sections of his work, he is manifestly the heir to at least the

[27] *Pioneers of Modern Education 1600–1700*, p. 2.

[28] *A History of Oxford University*, p. 60. On the position of logic in the universities at this period see J. A. Trentman, 'The Study of Logic and Language in England in the Early Seventeenth Century', *Historiographia Linguistica*, III:2 (1976), pp. 179–201. Trentman agrees (pp. 179–80) that 'What is most characteristic about all the thought of the period is that it generally represents an Aristotelian revival' leading to renewed interest in Scholastic philosophy, in spite of the fact that much of the English university curriculum still 'looks very much like the tail end of the standard medieval higher education'.

[29] E.g. Samuel Smith's *Aditus ad logicam* (1613), which Howell describes on p. 293 as presenting a conception of logic 'more like that of scholastics than of the Ramists'.

[30] K. Fischer, *Descartes and his School* (3rd ed.), translated by J. P. Gordy, London, 1887, p. 106.   [31] See *ibid.*, p. 113.

Scholastic elements in his doctrines, and furnishes important confirmation of the extent to which the seventeenth century is still
indebted to Scholastic philosophy. Campanella's 'philosophical
grammar' claims to investigate the apprehension by the intellect of
phenomena as they are found in *Nature*. Not – and here he ties in with
the Baconians and the English scientists of the Royal Society – Nature
as presented in the writings of Aristotle, but Nature as it really is.
The seventeenth-century approach to Nature was however still
inextricably entangled with all kinds of occultism: astrology, the
Kabbalah, alchemy, and various kinds of magic.[32] Some of these
views were dangerous to propagate, and it is hardly surprising that
Campanella's espousal of them resulted in the attentions of the Holy
Office and a long spell in prison. Though there are dissenting voices
in the seventeenth century for whom 'the use of Words is not to
explaine the Natures of Things, but to stand as signs in their stead',[33]
Campanella is not one of them. His insistence on taking Nature as
the starting-point is illustrated in his suggestion for a philosophical
language in which names are attributed 'ex rerum natura'. This is
a prerequisite to grammar, but not the task of the grammarian
himself. The order of procedure is first to obtain a knowledge of
things; then to give names to them; and finally to make use of the
explanatory role of the grammarian.[34] Holding the theory of an
original affinity between words and things, obscured after the
confusion of tongues,[35] Campanella shares with scholars such as
Wilkins a desire to restore this affinity in order to abolish ambiguity.[36]
Thus, following the methods of medieval modistic enquiry – of
'Scotus', as Campanella has it – and proceeding 'ex rei natura', the
pristine correspondence between language and nature will be
restored. Wilkins too starts out from an examination of Nature. But
scientists need taxonomies,[37] and for his classificatory system he

[32] G. Sortais, *La Philosophie moderne depuis Bacon jusqu'à Leibniz*, I, Paris, 1920, p. 87, sees
Campanella's nature doctrines as one among several attempts to 'élaborer prématurément de
vastes synthèses'. E. Boutroux (ed. of Leibniz' *Nouveaux Essais sur l'entendement humain*, Paris,
1886, p. 166, n. 4) sees them as linked with the Platonic theory of the world soul and with
pantheism.
[33] S. Parker, *A Free and Impartial Censure of the Platonick Philosophie*, Oxford, 1666. Parker takes
the view that 'Names are as unable to explaine abstracted Natures, as figures are to solve
Arithmetical Problems.' [34] *Philosophiae rationalis partes quinque*, I, 152.
[35] *Realis philosophiae epilogisticae partes quatuor*, Frankfurt-am-Main, 1623, p. 160.
[36] Cf. Salmon, *The Works of Francis Lodwick*, pp. 25, 78, 88.
[37] For the extent to which the new men of science depend on Aristotelian taxonomies see
Slaughter's *Universal Languages and Scientific Taxonomy in the Seventeenth Century*.

uncomplainingly dons once again, like Ramus before him and contrary to the tenets of nature-philosophy, the straitjacket of Aristotelianism.

The parallels with Locke and Descartes are striking, knowledge for Campanella having two sources: the experience of *external* facts, consisting of sense perceptions, and *internal* ones or reflection, the consideration of the certainty of one's own existence. The parallels with Locke's derivation of ideas from *sensation* and *reflection* ('the perception of the operations of our own minds within us'), and with Descartes' 'Cogito, ergo sum', are obvious.[38] Given his emphasis on sense-perception and on the wished-for congruence of language and natural phenomena, Campanella adopts an approach 'secundum rem' (i.e. semantically based) rather than 'secundum vocem' (based on the form of words), an approach which leads him to catalogue the qualities and relationships of *things* rather than those of formal linguistic units. Using as his metalanguage the categories of Scholastic philosophy, he arrives at the world-view reflected by them and believes it to be universally valid. Wilkins and his fellows, using the Aristotelian categories in their dissection of the universe, will do no less.[39] Just as the categories *essentia*, *existentia*, *actus* and *potentia* constituted for the Schoolmen attributes of the real world, so for Campanella they form the framework around which his grammar is constituted:

$$
\text{essence } (\textit{essentia})
\begin{cases}
\text{substance}
\begin{cases}
\text{prime matter} \\
\text{substantial form}
\end{cases} \\
\text{accidents}
\begin{cases}
\text{quantity, action,} \\
\text{quality, time,} \\
\text{space, relation}^{40}
\end{cases}
\end{cases}
$$

existence (*esse*)

Campanella's Platonism leads him to posit a science of being, hence the importance for him of the notion of *essentia* (a term which, in common with Scaliger, he prefers to Aristotle's *substantia*) in his grammatical system, which reposes on a dichotomy between *being* and *action*. It is such traits that demonstrate that his preoccupation

---

[38] Salmon, in her review of Chomsky's *Cartesian Linguistics*, gives facts and dates to prove that Campanella could not have been influenced by Descartes.

[39] W. S. Howell (*Logic and Rhetoric in England*, p. 19) defines Aristotle's predicaments as 'those words which name the possible scientific conceptions men may have as to the nature of reality'.

[40] This schematization of the Scholastic categories is taken from M. De Wulf, *Medieval Philosophy Illustrated from the System of Thomas Aquinas*, Cambridge, Mass., 1922, p. 78.

with *things* and with sense-perception, with the necessity for congruence between language and phenomena, have their source in Scholasticism rather than in Baconian empiricism. His method, bearing the rationalist imprint of the age, is still close to that of the medieval *grammaticae speculativae*. Rather than a new departure, his work is a restatement of grammar in the terms of Scholastic philosophy.

Apart from 'Scotus' and J.-C. Scaliger, the other author of a 'natural' grammar mentioned by Wilkins[41] is the Spanish bishop Juan Caramuel y Lobkowitz, whose *Praecursor logicus*, including what he calls a *Grammatica audax*, appeared in 1654.[42] Caramuel too claims to treat grammar 'philosophically', stating that to the best of his knowledge only 'Scotus',[43] Scaliger and Campanella have produced what he calls *grammaticae speculativae*. Speculative grammar he defines as that whose 'meditationes abstractissimae' provide laws applicable to all languages.[44] Again, his importance for a language-planner such as Wilkins lies in his contention that names should be imposed by philosophers, and in his citing of Chinese characters in the evident belief that in that language there is a one-to-one correspondence between words and things.[45] Incontestably, Wilkins' *Essay* has a debt to both this author and Campanella. As to the general lines of development of the artificial-language movement, to which it would be inappropriate to devote undue space in a survey such as this, the reader is referred to the various treatments listed in the bibliography.[46]

[41] Wilkins also cites the Dutch grammarian Vossius (*De arte grammatica*, 1635), whose work is less to our purpose here. Wilkins refers to it as the *Aristarchus*, by which title it was known from the 1662 edition onward.

[42] *Caramuelis praecursor logicus, complectens grammaticem audacem, cuius partes sunt tres, methodica, metrica, critica*, Frankfurt-am-Main, 1654. For an interesting discussion of some aspects of Wilkins' debt to Caramuel and Campanella, see Salmon's '"Philosophical" grammar in John Wilkins's "Essay"', pp. 147–52. See also on Caramuel K. Hubka, 'Caramuelova "Grammatica audax"', *Listy Filologické*, c (1977), pp. 16–29, and Padley, *Grammatical Theory* (1976), pp. 179–84.

[43] I.e. Thomas of Erfurt.   [44] *Grammatica audax*, p. 3.

[45] He quotes in support the Scholastic tag 'non sunt multiplicanda entia absque necessitate'.

[46] The following may be mentioned as indispensable reading: Funke, 'Zum Weltsprachenproblem in England im 17. Jahrhundert'; B. De Mott, 'The Sources and Development of John Wilkins' Philosophical Language', *Journal of English and Germanic Philology*, LVII (1958), pp. 1–13; O. Funke, 'On the Sources of John Wilkins' Philosophical Language (1668)', *English Studies*, XL (1959), pp. 208–14; Jones, 'Science and Language in England of the Mid-Seventeenth Century'; Salmon, 'Language-Planning in Seventeenth-Century England'; B. J. Shapiro, *John Wilkins 1614–1672*, Berkeley, 1969; Salmon, *The Works of Francis Lodwick*; Salmon, '"Philosophical" Grammar in John Wilkins's "Essay"'; J. Knowlson, *Universal Language Schemes in England and France 1600–1800*, Toronto, 1975; Slaughter, *Universal Languages and Scientific Taxonomy in the Seventeenth Century*. See also Padley, *Grammatical Theory* (1976), pp. 184–98.

Additional contributions to the artificial-language question were made, on a wider European stage, by Descartes and Hobbes, and more importantly by the internationally known pedagogical reformer Comenius. Descartes' contribution was slight, though no doubt fruitful in view of his influence and prestige. A letter of November 1629 from him to the indefatigable Mersenne suggests the institution of a language in which words would have an analogy to things, and there can be little doubt that his interest in mathematics played an important role in the orientation of thought on the matter. An indication of the extent to which mathematical models are in vogue, leading to a belief that natural languages can be replaced by the clarity of a system in which each phenomenon in the universe has its corresponding symbol unambiguously denoting its nature and properties, is provided by Hobbes. Bacon's proposed system of 'simple natures' each with its own quasi-mathematical symbol reaches its logical, and arid, conclusion in Hobbes' view of reasoning as 'nothing but reckoning, that is adding and subtracting'.[47] Language thus becomes the manipulation of signs which have a one-to-one correspondence with their referents, and in this respect Hobbes' view of logic as a 'computatio' is revealing.[48] It is an approach that will be repeated in Leibniz' *De arte combinatoria* (1666) with its notion of a 'calculus ratiocinator' recalling, as does much else in seventeenth-century linguistic thought, the work of the thirteenth-century Catalan scholar Ramón Lull, inventor of a system of grouped fundamental concepts that came to be known as the *Ars magna*.[49]

Comenius

Of much wider importance is the influence of the Moravian reformer Jan Amos Comenius (1592–1670),[50] in whom once again several strands of seventeenth-century thought converge. The primary motivation of much of the century's endeavours was pedagogical, and

[47] *Leviathan*, in *The English Works of Thomas Hobbes*, ed. W. Molesworth, London, 1839–40, III, 30.
[48] Hobbes' work on logic is entitled *Computatio sive logica*.
[49] For details on Lull and his influence on seventeenth-century thought see Salmon, *The Works of Francis Lodwick*, pp. 118–21, 140.
[50] As a proponent of practical methods in language teaching Comenius has an early predecessor in J. L. Vives, whose *De studii puerilis ratione* (Oxford, 1523) prescribes that language norms must be taken from living usage, and that the mother tongue must be used in the early stages of Latin teaching.

it is important to remember that for Comenius, the most important contemporary reformer of these matters, language was (as with Ratke) largely an educational question rather than a philosophical or scientific one. That Comenius was quite early in life influenced by Ratke is made probable by his frequentation of Bishop Lánecký, himself a disciple of Ratke, and by his production in 1615–16 of an elementary school grammar – the *Grammaticae facilioris praecepta*[51] – based on the Ratichian method. Another parallel with Ratke lies in the union, in Comenius, of a strong pedagogical motivation and religious, moralistic aims. With Comenius too, the mainspring of his action is provided by the Protestant Reform. Since he had been the pupil at Herborn of Johann Heinrich Alsted, he shares with Ratke the Ramist tendency towards encyclopedism.[52] This is particularly evident in the logical ordering of items in his *Didactica magna*, written between 1627 and 1632.[53] Alsted was himself a Ramist, and according to W. J. Ong the 'pure didactic' – a phenomenon virtually confined to Germany – of the *Didactica magna* is the 'direct heir' of the Ramist dialectic, representing, after the demise of Ramus' teaching as a separate and distinct movement, 'one of the myriad ways in which Ramism is perpetuated in disguise'.[54] Further Alsted based his teaching at least in part on the *Ars magna* of the thirteenth-century Catalan scholar Ramón Lull,[55] and though V. T. Miškovská is reluctant to see aspects of Comenius' work as in any way a continuation of this early tradition,[56] it incontestably forms part of the seventeenth century's general inheritance from Scholasticism. More importantly, in the *Didactica magna* Comenius himself – he was resident in England in the months immediately preceding the Civil War – makes a flattering reference to Campanella and Francis Bacon as 'glorious restorers of Philosophy', and though for instance J. W. Adamson sees no proof that he had much acquaintance with Bacon's

[51] Published in Prague in 1616, but no longer extant. Comenius mentions it in the foreword to his *Opera didactica omnia*, Amsterdam, 1657.

[52] On logical and rhetorical influences on Comenius, see K. Hubka, 'On Some Rhetoric-Logic Topoi in Comenius' Pansophia Christiana', *Listy Filologické*, CI (1978), pp. 94–105. Hubka thinks it essential to consider Comenius' methods in a Ramist context.

[53] In *Opera didactica omnia* (1657). The version completed in 1632 was in Czech. The work remained in oblivion until rescued by K. von Raumer, *Geschichte der Pädagogik*, Stuttgart, 1843–51.   [54] Ong, *Ramus*, p. 163.

[55] According to J. Kvačala, *Die pädagogische Reform des Comenius in Deutschland bis zum Ausgange des XVII. Jahrhunderts*, Berlin, 1904, II, 5.

[56] V. T. Miškovská, 'Komenský ve vývoji gramatikých teorií', *Studia Comeniana et historica*, XIII:6 (1976), p. 38.

writings, he finds enough internal evidence in Comenius' works to show that 'he was fully in sympathy with that New Philosophy of Natural Science, which later generations came to associate with Bacon more especially'. He concludes that in general treatment and indeed in specific details the *Didactica magna* is 'distinctly Baconian'.[57] Confirmation of this view, though it presupposes a close knowledge of Bacon's work that Adamson is reluctant to admit, is found in K. von Raumer's earlier statement that Comenius' chief inspiration came from Bacon's *Instauratio magna*, for which he professed a great admiration. Comenius' first impulse towards 'pedagogical realism' comes however, as von Raumer notes, from the Spaniard Luis Vives, and he would also seem to be indebted to Tommaso Campanella, who as we shall see is of importance for the grammatical components of universal language schemes in England.[58] Campanella was influenced by Bernardino Telesio's anti-Aristotelian nature-philosophy, being accused by the Inquisition of magical practices, and here he joins hands with that mystic strain that, via the Kabbalah and certain indications in Valentin Ickelsamer and the writings of Luther, is a recurrent trait in German attitudes to language. Comenius himself shows facets which, in spite of his supposed Baconianism, transcend rationality, as in his chiliastic beliefs and his adherence to the Rosicrucians. Throughout his life he turned to mystical experience; there are links in his work with the ideas of medieval mystics such as Meister Eckehart, and with Jacob Boehme,[59] the 'divinely-inspired Teutonick' referred to in John Webster's *Academiarum examen* of 1654. If for him the German language can by careful cultivation recover something of its former true nature, it is because it still bears traces of something divine hidden within it.

Though Comenius is much more than a pedagogical reformer, it is this aspect of his endeavours that has been emphasized, and indeed it provided him with a primary motivation, whose aim, in accordance with the principles of the Protestant Reform, was to use learning as a means of instilling morality and piety. It is no doubt these ends that are envisaged in his proposal that all children between the ages of six and twelve are to attend *scholae vernaculae* or schools for the inculcation of the mother tongue, an aim that had been central to

[57] *Pioneers of Modern Education 1600–1700*, pp. 48–9.
[58] K. von Raumer, *Geschichte der Pädagogik* (3rd ed.), Stuttgart, 1857, II, 66–7.
[59] See J. E. Sadler, *J. A. Comenius and the Concept of Universal Education*, London, 1966, p. 42.

the Ratichian reforms.[60] The pedagogical work of Comenius best known to his contemporaries is the *Janua linguarum* (1631)[61] in Latin and German, which in the same year came out in an English, French and Latin version under the title *Porta linguarum*.[62] Latin was of course still the language of international scholarship, and one of Comenius' major early preoccupations, leading ultimately to his interest in the artificial-language movement, was to establish Latin as the universal language, thus countering the evil results of the confusion of tongues at Babel, and ensuring mutual understanding and peace among the peoples of the world. The *Janua* accordingly corresponds to Comenius' first priority of simplifying the introduction to Latin and harmonizing it with practical needs of communication, and provides a vocabulary basis of several thousand words for the most familiar objects and ideas. These are set out in sentences, and the whole is arranged in conceptual classes by the encyclopedic methods Comenius had learnt from Alsted. Though Lull may, *pace* V. T. Miškovská, be regarded as the remote ancestor of such arrangements under conceptual headings, Comenius had a more immediate model close at hand, and indeed one which he freely acknowledges in his preface. He takes both his title and his method from a *Janua linguarum* published in Spain in 1611 by the Jesuits,[63] convincing proof if any were needed of the necessity, in writing a history of grammatical theory, of linking together what is going on in various European countries at the same time. This *Janua* is the work of a little nest of Irish Jesuits in Salamanca, notably William Bathe, and uses the method of placing bilingual (in this case Latin and Spanish) or multilingual texts in parallel with each other to facilitate learning. Though the method is here intended for the teaching of Latin to those with a prior knowledge of Spanish, the printer's note claims that the work can also be used for the teaching of any language whatever.[64] The first chapter says the aim of the work is to demonstrate a method for

[60] Geissler, *Comenius und die Sprache*, p. 84, though treating this as a 'new principle' introduced by Comenius, admits that it had already been stressed by Ratke.

[61] Published in Leszna, the work was translated into twelve European and several Asiatic languages.

[62] Published in London by the Frenchman J. A. Anchoran. I have also used Thomas Horn's translation (entitled *Janua linguarum*) (6th ed.), London, 1643.

[63] Published in Salamanca. This work, ascribed to William Bathe in the British Library catalogue, is the subject of S. F. O'Mahony's 'The Preface to William Bathe's Janua linguarum (1611)', *Historiographia linguistica*, VIII:1 (1981), pp. 131–64.

[64] This work is by no means the first example of an interest in vernacular pedagogy in Spain. Bernabé Busto's *Introductiones grammaticas* (Salamanca, 1533) notes that much of the difficulty in teaching Latin can be avoided by presenting the rules 'en romance castellano'.

learning all languages with certainty, ease and brevity, while a prefatory note by Luys de Valdivia S.J., a missionary to India, expects this method to spare others the great labour he has himself expended on learning Indian languages. As for the pedagogical claims of the work, a similar note by a professor at the University of Salamanca says the method when used by him bore more fruit in three months than the usual approach in three years. Allowing for the exaggerations of self-advertisement, it is evident that the authors had high hopes for their method, which was published in various combinations of languages during the rest of the century. One of the best-known of these adaptations was Scioppius' *Mercurius quadrilinguis* (Padua, 1637) with parallel sentences in Latin, Greek, Hebrew and Italian.[65] Of interest to us here is the use of a vernacular, already known to the student, in teaching Latin, or indeed 'any other' language, and it is worthy of note that not only Latin itself, but also Portuguese and Spanish, were soon being taught in this way.[66] Apart from the continuing obsession with method, brought to a position of primacy by Ramus, the growing interest in vocabulary could not but increase the evolution of grammar in the direction of lexicography. Bathe and his confrères wrote in fact at a time of intense interest in educational methodology, and it is their 'prooemium' or preface that now gives their work value.[67] Given the missionary activities of the Society of Jesus, second-language teaching had long been one of their major preoccupations, and the publication of the definitive version of the *Ratio atque institutio studiorum Societatis Jesu* in 1599 shows the extent to which they were ahead of other religious orders in these matters.[68] There was however a conflict between their desire to equip their missionaries with a knowledge of sometimes exotic vernaculars, and their actual pedagogical practice in teaching Latin, oral fluency in which remained one of their chief aims. As with others, emphasis here was on the imitation of classical authors – with the difference that the Jesuits if anything put even more stress than usual on the memorization of set passages of the language. In this respect, as S. F. O'Mahony has pointed out, Bathe is at variance with the

[65] The Basle edition of the same year substitutes German for Italian.
[66] See Conde de la Viñaza, *Biblioteca histórica de la filogía castellana*, Madrid, 1893, 1, 266. Amaro de Roboredo brought out a Portuguese *Porta de linguas* in Lisbon in 1623.
[67] O'Mahony's 'The Preface to William Bathe's *Janua linguarum* (1611)' gives a facsimile of this *prooemium*, together with the ten chapters in which pedagogical method is discussed.
[68] For details here I am indebted to O'Mahony, 'Preface'.

accepted wisdom of his Order, offering in Ramist fashion a quick and easy method for learning languages. His placing of sentences of the language already known and of that to be acquired on facing pages must have seemed in its day revolutionary, but it led to the belief that several languages could be acquired simultaneously in this way,[69] and also no doubt, since the same *meaning* was being expressed in each language, fostered the growth of universal grammar. By what Bathe calls the 'middle method', all precepts 'which are set out in grammars as rules can also be taught aptly in sentences, so that they impress themselves on the mind with greater facility... than could be achieved by grammatical rules alone... *especially in the case of modern languages which do not require a scientific knowledge of what appertains to grammatical method*'.[70] Since for Bathe each language consists of words, concordance, phrases (the particular modes of expression of each individual tongue) and elegance, it may well be their deficiency in the second of these that is the cause why the vernaculars – and it is a common enough belief at the period – can be learnt without grammar.

The popularity of Comenius' own *Janua*, added to that of the Jesuit work, carried these methods far and wide in the second half of the seventeenth century. As a pedagogical reformer however his fame far outstripped theirs, no doubt because of its impressive theoretical basis. His *Didactica magna* has been called the *Novum organum* of pedagogy,[71] and Comenius himself regarded it as of universal application. Its universality is ensured by its being based on nature itself, a requirement that recalls both Ramus and Vives' observation that practical education presupposes 'the silent contemplation of nature'. Vives was the earliest educationist to recommend nature-observation as a pedagogical method, holding like Ramus that whatever was in the arts was first found in Nature.[72] As the title-page of the *Didactica magna* puts it, 'Fundamental principles are elicited from the very nature of Things.' This thoroughly seventeenth-century emphasis on *things* determines Comenius' whole pedagogical standpoint: 'Men should be taught... not to know things out of

[69] See O'Mahony, 'Preface', pp. 133–4.

[70] *Janua linguarum*, cap. vi (p. 160 of O'Mahony's facsimile): 'idque maxime in linguis vulgaribus, in quibus non est necesse scientifice percipere quae ad methodum Grammaticalem pertinent'. I have used O'Mahony's translation, italicizing the final section.

[71] Adamson, *Pioneers of Modern Education 1600–1700*, p. 53.

[72] See Watson, *Luis Vives el gran Valenciano (1492–1540)*.

books, but from the sky, the earth, oaks and beeches: things
themselves, not merely observations about them from elsewhere.'[73]
To put an end to a system in which schools first teach a language
('artes sermocinatrices') and only secondarily go on to acquaint the
pupil with the world of things, Comenius introduces as a pedagogical
principle the parallelism of words and things. The child must be
familiar not only with names, but also with their referents. The
London edition of the *Vestibulum linguae Latinae* (1656) is accordingly
no mere grammar primer, but promises in its title to set out the basis
of both languages and things,[74] while the *Orbis sensualium pictus*
(English edition, 1659), a 'picture and nomenclature of all the chief
things that are in the world', clearly states Comenius' chief
programmatic principle: 'to exercise the senses well about the right
perceiving of the differences of things, will be to lay the grounds for
all wisdom'.[75] This charming little work, with its illustrations of
everything from the Trinity (in diagrammatic form) to grape-picking,
bottles at sea, and tennis, has been aptly called by J. E. Sadler[76] an
attempt at 'a true anatomy of the universe'. At once naïve and
workmanlike, it proceeds on the Aristotelian assumption that there
is 'nothing in the Understanding which was not before in the Sense',
and inserts itself into an English pedagogical movement represented
for instance by Mark Lewis' (*c.* 1670) *Essay to Facilitate the Education
of Youth, by bringing down the Rudiments of Grammar to the Sense of Seeing.*
It also, though but a minor part of Comenius' work, well illustrates
the contemporary preoccupation, present in the endeavours of the
Royal Society, with things and the labels to be attached to them.
Above all, it reinforces the belief of English puritanism that words
and things, language teaching and practical knowledge, must go
hand in hand. In this context, it is only natural that the English
framers of artificial languages will begin their work with a classification
of *things*, and will require their universal grammars to reflect the
things, actions and modes of the universe. For Comenius, the aim
of Latin teaching is no longer that of making accessible a great

[73] *Didactica magna*, XVIII, v, 28 (*Opera didactica omnia*, col. 192).
[74] *Vestibulum linguae Latinae rerum et linguarum fundamenta exhibens*, first published as *Januae
linguarum reseratae vestibulum*, Leszna, 1633.
[75] This is Charles Hoole's English/Latin edition, *John Amos Commenius's Visible World*. The
first edition (Nuremberg, 1658), in Latin and German, has the vernacular title *Die sichtbare
Welt, das ist, aller vornehmsten Welt-Dinge und Lebensverrichtungen, Vorbildung und Benahmung.*
[76] Facsimile edition of Hoole's text of 1659 (Oxford, 1968). There is also a Scolar Press
facsimile, Menston, 1970.

literature, but that of conveying knowledge about phenomena. As his *Linguarum methodus*, influenced by Vives, puts it, 'the true method teaches the pupil accurately to observe, form a conception of, and express things and words at one and the same time'.[77]

No understanding of Comenius can be complete that does not take into account the would-be universalism of his work, and it is here that his preoccupations join those of universal grammarians and the inventors of artificial languages for international use. His greatest work, universal in scope and addressing itself to primary problems of European culture, communication and society, sets as its goal nothing less than 'the improvement of human affairs'. This work, *De rerum humanarum emendatione consultatio catholica*, lay long forgotten in manuscript form, but has recently been printed.[78] It consists of seven parts:

I. 'Panegersia' or universal awakening, dealing with the re-lationship of men to things, to their fellows, and to God;
II. 'Panaugia', showing the way to the light of the spirit;
III. 'Pantaxia' or 'pansophia', the universal classification of all things in the universe;
IV. 'Pampaedia' or universal pedagogy, whose aim is to show man his proper place in the universe, and his correct relationship to all created things;
V. 'Panglottia' or universal language;
VI. 'Panorthosia', treating the possibility, using the afore-mentioned means, of improving learning, religion and politics, and inaugurating an era of peace;
VII. 'Pannuthesia', the admonition to all Christians to see that these reforms are duly carried out.

The kernel of this system is contained in parts III–V, containing as they do the anatomy of the universe, a pedagogy of general application, and Comenius' philosophy of language. All three are of direct relevance to the seventeenth-century world-view. Though it is clear that it is the 'Pansophia'[79] or universal encyclopedia that Comenius regarded as the great task of his life, it has to be seen in

[77] *Linguarum methodus novissima*, Leszna, 1648, ix, 4. The word *res* here has perhaps the more precise meaning of 'subject matter'.
[78] Its MS fragments were discovered in Halle in 1934, and published in Prague in 1966 (edited by J. Červenka and V. T. Miškovská).
[79] Cf. Comenius' *Schola pansophica. Hoc est, universalis sapientiae officina*, s. l., 1651.

context as part of the moral and philosophical base of his entire reform of society. In turn however it provides the intellectual foundation on which the whole of the *Consultatio* is built. It is deeply embedded in the culture of the times, representing in some respects an almost mystical theory with affinities with certain ideas of Jacob Boehme, and with the 'chain of being' doctrine presupposing an ontological correspondence between the order of the universe and the order of the mind. This latter idea is rooted in neo-Platonic theories according to which the divine powers are unfolded in the cosmos in a series of gradations, decreasing in perfection as they move from the divine source into the forms of the world of sense. Several threads in seventeenth-century thought come together here, for he who penetrates the secrets of nature penetrates also those of the Divine, hence the interest among German and other students of language in the Kabbalah, which claimed to have received those secrets in ancient times, and in Telesio's nature-philosophy. The 'Pansophia' in its turn, in a line of thought initiated by Lull, even if he is not Comenius' direct model, ranges phenomena in ordered gradations, in a 'ladder of being' which must have its counterpart in language.[80] The pansophic system provides a philosophical mirror of the world,[81] it is isomorphic with creation. It is thus, as in the conceptual systems of the language-planners, a link in the isomorphism of nature and language, and in this respect Comenius is perhaps the supreme illustration of the seventeenth century's duality of thought: its obsession with *nomenclature* and its predilection for *things*. The aim of the 'Pansophia' goes however far beyond the simple amassing of facts and the attaching of labels to them. Not only does it, in its search for the unity underlying all things, catalogue phenomena, but it also takes as its basis – hence its interest for universal grammar – the 'innate Norms of knowledge' common to all men and, in obvious similarity to Ratke, the Divine Revelation itself, 'for ever unveiling more mysteries'.[82] Over and above all this however, binding the system into a single pedagogical and philosophical whole, lies

[80] Leibniz' *De arte combinatoria* (1666), which proposes a kind of alphabet acting as a notation of simple ideas, which can be combined to form more complex notions, would seem (besides its debt to Hobbes) to owe something to Lull. It is reprinted in C. J. Gerhardt (ed.), *Die philosophischen Schriften von Gottfried Wilhelm Leibniz*, IV, Berlin, 1880, pp. 27–104.

[81] See V. T. Miškovská, 'Comenius (Komensky) on Lexical Symbolism in an Artificial Language', *Philosophy*, XXXVII (1962), pp. 238–44.

[82] See Sadler, *Comenius and the Concept of Universal Education*, p. 60.

Comenius' perception of a harmonious unity binding together all things. His universe is 'a manifestation of a single pervading law and therefore knowledge of it must go further than sense perception to the pure form of which it is an approximation'.[83]

Comenius' perception of this all-pervading and unifying harmony is reminiscent of Ratke's *Gleichförmigkeit* or 'harmony of faith, nature and languages', but it is made far more explicit, and its demonstration is the ultimate goal of the 'Pansophia'. Only when the harmony of the Whole has been grasped can one finally proceed to the description of individual parts of it. The penetration of these notions into the general culture of the times is illustrated by a passage in Richard Burthogge's *Organuum* of 1678: 'And seeing Truth is Harmony, and the Universe itself...is but one system; it follows that properly there is but one *Science* (which some call Pansophy) one Globe of knowledge, as there is of Things.' The use of the term 'Pansophy' and the presumed parallelism of the 'globe of knowledge' and the 'globe of things' point to a source in Comenius or at any rate in someone who knew of his system. The author adds – and it is an indication of the extent to which in some respects the tide is flowing against Ramus – 'the partition of Sciences, or rather the crumbling of them into so many, hath been a great impediment of Science'.[84] Comenius' idea of innate 'Norms of knowledge' perhaps inevitably leads to a notion similar to that of Ramus' 'natural logic' in the mind,[85] and here again Burthogge's statement, possibly following Comenius, that the harmony and system of natural reasoning 'is evident in the Natural Reasonings of Plain and Illiterate', also has repercussions for artificial-language schemes and universal grammar.

Whether or not Comenius' thought had much influence on their systems, it is incontestable that Commonwealth linguistic and educational reformers such as Samuel Hartlib looked to him for guidance. As for Comenius' own knowledge of what was going on in England at the time, his visit in 1641 had doubtless allowed him to become acquainted with contemporary projects, and V. T. Miškovská holds that he not only followed the preparatory stages of Wilkins' work with interest, but also knew and quoted that of

[83] *Ibid.*, p. 65.
[84] *Organum vetus et novum. Or, a Discourse of reason and truth. Wherein the natural logick common to mankinde is briefly and plainly described*, London, 1678.
[85] For Ramus, logic is an 'imago naturalis dialecticae'. Cf. *Aristotelicae animadversiones*, f. 3ᵛ: 'the art of dialectic should proceed from the imitation and observation of the natural dialectic'.

Dalgarno.[86] His own tentative schemes are in many ways simply an outgrowth of his 'Pansophia' and his theory of harmony. A universal language was essential as a vehicle for the pansophic reforms, as an 'Ariadne's thread to lead mankind out of the labyrinth',[87] but it was also, among other things, 'a regularity, like musical harmony, by which it establishes between things and concepts and between concepts and words a context in which it is possible to conceive things as they are and express them as they are conceived'.[88] Comenius' own scheme seemingly owes little to Bacon, for though he regards the latter's 'ingenious induction' as 'an open road by which to penetrate into the hidden things of Nature', it is inadequate in that it stops short at that mere empiricism and does not, like Comenius himself, look to the *rerum universitas* or all-embracing unity of things.[89] Further, as with Ratke, his linguistic universalism is but part of a wider cultural and religious context in which, for the first time since the Middle Ages, the Protestant Reform and its vernacular Bible make a unity of faith and culture, at any rate within Protestantism itself, a serious proposition. If Comenius thinks in terms of a universal language it is because the time is ripe for such an undertaking. His first ideas on the subject appear in a chapter, written in 1641–2, of his *Via lucis*, which was finally published in 1668,[90] the year of the appearance of Wilkins' *Essay*, and contains a reference to the newly formed Royal Society, 'Torch Bearers of this Enlightened Age now bringing real philosophy to a happy birth'. The work proposes the framing of a 'language absolutely new, absolutely easy, absolutely rational, in brief a Pansophic language', in which everything 'must be adapted to the exact and perfect representation of things'. In this language there would be a precise, one-to-one correspondence between names and referents, on lines similar to those adopted by the artificial-language planners. Of the more ambitious scheme that was subsequently drawn up only two manuscript fragments remain – the

[86] 'Comenius on Lexical Symbolism', p. 238.
[87] Comenius so describes it in a letter to his Amsterdam printer, Montanus (see Sadler, *Comenius and the Concept of Universal Education*, p. 149).
[88] 'Panglottia', III, 6 (cited, *ibid.*, pp. 150–1, by Sadler, whose translation I have retained unchanged).
[89] *Opera didactica omnia*, I, col. 432.
[90] Published in Amsterdam. In Padley, *Grammatical Theory* (1976) the year 1642 is erroneously given as the date of publication. It is of course the *composition* that partially dates from that year. See also E. T. Campagnac's translation, *The Way of Light by John Amos Comenius*, Liverpool, 1938.

'Panglottia' (fifth section of the *Consultatio*), and a treatise entitled 'Novae linguae harmonicae tentamen primum'. Both propose a lexicon of basic concepts from which other notions and their symbolization may be derived. The 'Panglottia', in this resembling some of the English schemes, sees the substantive as the basic term, while the 'Tentamen' gives priority to verbal concepts. What emerges as a general characteristic of Comenius' proposed system is an emphasis on labelling in which, in the effort to maintain the parallelism between words and things, each language is treated as a nomenclature. As Anchoran's edition of the *Porta linguarum* puts it, 'Hee hath laid the grounds and foundation of all learning, that hath thoroughly learned the nomenclature or surname of things.'[91] Though the promise of a third, grammatical part to the *Vestibulum linguae Latinae* is not kept, it makes clear that 'rightly to understand things' is a necessary preliminary to language study: 'The first part...shall teach you to understand the things themselves...This shall be called the *Nomenclature of things*.'[92] The drift of grammar towards nomenclature and lexicography does not of course begin with Comenius. It is already present for instance in Colet's definition of the noun, in his section of Lily's Latin grammar, as 'the name of a thing that may be seen, felt, heard or understand'.[93] What Comenius does is to justify this type of definition in the name of a pedagogical theory. Since it is entirely wrong, according to the *Didactica magna*, to begin a child's education with grammar, on the pedagogical grounds that the material must precede the formal, it follows that it is preliminary acquaintance with *things* and their names that determines the presuppositions on which grammar is based. Accordingly, in the simplified second reworking of the *Vestibulum* (1649), substantives depend on a prior knowledge of things, adjectives on 'modes of things', verbs on 'motions of things', adverbs on 'modes of actions', prepositions on 'circumstances of things and actions', etc. Since phenomena and their modes and actions are the same for all men, it follows that the basic grammatical system that is isomorphic with them will also be the same in essentials. Thus, in learning a new language – and here the influence of Ratke is apparent – the pupil only needs to have pointed out to him divergences from the basic

[91] *Porta linguarum* (1631), p. 1.
[92] *Vestibulum* [1656], foreword.
[93] *A Short Introduction of Grammar* (1557), p. 7.

grammar he already knows. This is doubtless in part the reasoning behind the Jesuit *Janua linguarum*, in which sentences from the unknown language are placed in parallel with sentences from the known one, and no doubt the system worked well as long as the languages in question all belonged to the Indo-European family. The *Vestibulum* provides however little more than the preliminary grounding in things and their modes and actions, and the labels to be attached to them, though it is easy to see the impetus all this gave to for instance the now long-familiar definition of the verb in purely lexical terms as a 'word of action'. Comenius' own exemplification of grammatical theory is slight, being limited to a few indications in the *Grammatica janualis* attached to the 1664 edition of his *Ars ornatoria*.[94] In this simple grammar, patently based on the parallelism with phenomena, the noun is a 'word denoting a thing', the adjective a 'word denoting some mode of a thing'. True to Comenius' belief that the same basic grammar will serve for all languages, it gives only the barest essentials.

Interesting as an appendix to the debate, initiated by Chomsky's *Cartesian Linguistics*, on whether innate ideas are necessary to a theory of universal grammar, is Comenius' theory of 'innate principles': 'all men have innate Principles of three kinds... In every man there are innate Norms of knowledge, which are *Common Notions*, and the Stimuli of Desire, which we name *Common Instincts*; and the organs for doing everything, which it may be permissible to call Common Faculties... Hitherto philosophers have spoken only of *Common Notions*.'[95] The 'innate norms of knowledge' or 'common notions' were in fact very much at the centre of discussion at the time.[96] The doctrine of 'principles or notions implanted in the mind' is present in Lord Herbert of Cherbury's *De veritate* (1624)[97] and in certain passages in Descartes.[98] The central importance of these 'common notions' for Comenius' 'pansophia' is obvious. It is precisely because

---

[94] *Ars ornatoria, sive grammatica elegans...cui insuper accessit grammatica eiusdem janualis*, London. The *Grammatica elegans* is a rhetoric, teaching 'eleganter loquendi ars'. The work also includes an *Eruditionis scholasticae atrium* or compendium of things, published separately at Nuremberg in 1655.

[95] *Via lucis*, p. 6 (my italics).

[96] For a discussion of the history of this matter see Padley, *Grammatical Theory* (1976), pp. 233–40.

[97] No place of publication given.

[98] *Principia philosophiae*, Amsterdam, 1644, p. xlix: 'veritas quaedam aeterna, quae in mente nostra sedem habet, vocaturque *communis notio*, sive axioma' (my italics).

men are 'necessarily united in these roots of Human General Intelligence' that he is able to envisage a 'single and comprehensive scheme of Human Omni-Science'. This is also true of the schemes advanced by the English language-planners, but though L. Formigari[99] holds that Comenius' pansophic language is probably the most direct source of Seth Ward's scheme, which she claims is embodied in Wilkins' *Essay*, the fact remains that the latter is based on narrower foundations than Comenius' 'pansophia'. Comenius' 'common faculties' would perhaps have offered a surer basis for Chomsky's thesis than the purely cognitive 'innate ideas' he takes from Descartes. For our present purposes Comenius has a double importance: while on the one hand he represents a powerful force in the movement to bring the vernaculars into the educational system, on the other he provides a link between this pedagogical motivation and, via schemes for artificial languages, the development of universal grammar. Above all, he is an important influence in the evolution of that type of universal grammar that bases itself on isomorphism with *things*, taking its universality from the mirroring of a real world common to all men.[100]

ii THE NEW EPISTEMOLOGY
Locke

John Wilkins' *Essay Towards a Real Character and a Philosophical Language* came out in 1668. At about the same time, in the early 1670s Locke began working on the project for his *Essay Concerning Humane Understanding*, which was published in 1689.[101] Just as Descartes and Augustinianism set the tone of late-seventeenth-century debate in France, so does Locke's *Essay* reflect the empirical, 'sensualist' intellectual background of English endeavours which centre around the newly formed Royal Society. The aim of this society was the promotion of knowledge, and in the same way as for instance the Ratichian general grammars produced in Germany have pedagogical goals, so do those written by the English language-planners have epistemological ones. Whereas the Cartesian intellectual climate in

[99] *Linguistica ed empirismo nel seicento inglese*, Bari, 1970, p. 135.
[100] On this aspect of Comenius' influence, and on the general evolution of the artificial language movement, Salmon's *The Works of Francis Lodwick* is invaluable.
[101] Though the title-page bears the date 1690, the *Essay* was in fact published before the end of the preceding year.

which the Port-Royal authors are working predisposes them to put
emphasis on the formation of the judgment, language is above all for
Locke – whose *Essay* is the epistemological manual of the Royal
Society – an instrument for the acquisition of knowledge. It cannot
be too strongly emphasized that whereas in the Middle Ages and the
Renaissance semantic enquiry based itself on logic and grammar,
Locke's *Essay* ushers in a 'new epistemological orientation of
semantics',[102] and has repercussions for the development of artificial-
language theories in seventeenth-century England, which are also
epistemological in character. Hence, though there are close resemblances at several points between universal grammars produced
within the rationalist tradition on the Continent and those stemming
from the English empirical tradition, the basic assumptions underlying
the two types show a difference of emphasis. Unlike Descartes, Locke
supposes that all knowledge enters the mind via the senses. In theory
at any rate he derives knowledge, in Baconian fashion, from
experience. His 'simple ideas' or concepts cannot be produced by the
mind itself, but 'must necessarily be the product of things operating
on the mind in a natural way and producing therein those perceptions,
which...they are ordained and adapted to'.[103] There are however
contradictions, as in the following statement that the Port-Royal
authors and the Cartesians would by no means have rejected: 'the
mind, in all its thoughts and reasonings, hath no other immediate
object but its own ideas, which it alone does or can contemplate'.[104]

[102] N. Kretzmann, 'The Main Thesis of Locke's Semantic Theory', *History of Linguistic
Thought and Contemporary Linguistics*, ed. H. Parret, Berlin and New York, 1976, p. 331.

[103] *Essay*, book IV, ch. iv, sect. 4. In quotations from Locke I have, for greater ease in reading,
removed capitalizations other than sentence-initial ones.

[104] *Ibid.*, IV, i, 1. See J. E. Ashworth, 'The Scholastic Background to Locke's Theory of
Language', *Progress in Linguistic Historiography*, ed. K. Koerner, Amsterdam, 1980, pp. 59–68,
for a discussion of the sources in seventeenth-century logic manuals of Locke's statement (*Essay*,
III, ii, 2) that 'Words in their primary or immediate signification, stand for nothing, but the
ideas in the mind of him that uses them.' Kretzmann ('The Main Thesis of Locke's Semantic
Theory', p. 332) calls Locke's presentation of this statement, implying that meaning depends
on private mental events, 'one of the classical blunders in semantic theory'. As Ashworth points
out however (p. 66), Locke's formula does not imply any intention 'to deny the obvious
corollary that we use words to signify things secondarily and mediately'. Kretzmann is careful
to establish not only (p. 347) that Locke himself did not maintain his thesis in all its details,
but also (p. 334) that he makes an exception for connectives and the copula, which he treats
as not 'names of ideas in the mind', but as being 'made use of to signify the *connexion* that
the mind gives to ideas, or to propositions, one with another'. Kretzmann concludes (p. 335)
that 'the only kind of word unmistakably referred to by Locke in his thesis that words signify
ideas is the "name"'. (See also, on Locke's treatment of connective particles, S. J. Schmidt,
Sprache und Denken als sprachphilosophisches Problem von Locke bis Wittgenstein, The Hague, 1968,
p. 16.)

In an attempt to reconcile these two viewpoints, Locke concludes that though all knowledge is ultimately founded in experience, observation may be employed in two ways – 'either about external, sensible objects; or about the internal operations of our minds, perceived and reflected on by our selves'[105] – by means of the two 'fountains of knowledge' sensation and reflection. These 'internal operations of our minds' would seem to be identical with Port-Royal's 'opérations de notre esprit' which do not originate from sense impressions, and there is here a contradiction which Locke needs some kind of *deus ex machina* to resolve.[106] Another stumbling-block is provided by words referring to abstractions, and Locke is forced to hold that in spite of the fact that they refer to 'actions and notions quite removed from sense', they are none the less 'taken from the operations of sensible things'.[107] Further, though Locke at first sight upholds the realist (Thomistic) thesis that our knowledge can be held to be reliable when there is a conformity between our ideas and phenomena (an assumption on which the whole of medieval modistic theory about language reposes), his position is in fact a Nominalist one, in which words do not refer to the 'real essences' of things, but to their 'nominal essences'. Here, as with Port-Royal, though men in practice 'suppose their words to stand also for the reality of things', the emphasis is on the link between word and concept: 'Words in their primary and immediate signification, stand for nothing, but the ideas in the mind of him that uses them.'[108] The link between word and idea is close – 'Between the nominal essence, and the name, there is so near a connexion, that the name of any sort of things cannot be attributed to any particular being, but what has this essence, whereby it answers that abstract idea, whereof that name is the sign'[109] – but it does not guarantee contact with reality. Hobbes too, whose *Leviathan* has been called 'the flowering of the past and the seed-box of the future',[110] is clear that 'seeing names are signs of our conceptions, it is manifest they are not signs of the things

---

[105] *Essay*, II, i, 1.
[106] Cf. Willey, *The Seventeenth Century Background*, p. 287: Locke 'never allowed himself, as Berkeley afterwards did, to accept the whole implication of his own statement that the mind has "no other immediate object but its own ideas"'.   [107] *Essay*, III, i, 5.
[108] *Ibid.*, II, ii, 2: 'Nor can any one apply them, as marks immediately to anything else, but the ideas that he himself hath: for this would be to make them signs of his own conception, and yet apply them to other ideas; which would be to make them signs, and not signs of his ideas at the same time; and so in effect, to have no signification at all.'
[109] *Ibid.*, III, iii, 16.
[110] M. Oakeshott, introduction to his edition of *Leviathan*, Oxford, 1946, p. liii.

themselves'.[111] He too is sceptical before the 'great deception of sense'[112] which does not convey reality. Words – 'marks... [by means of which] such *thoughts* may be recalled to our mind as are like those *thoughts* for which we took them'[113] – are for him as for Port-Royal signs of what is going on within the mind. Nominalism and the preoccupation with mental operations lead alike to the identification of mental and linguistic processes. Locke's system does not result, like Scaliger's Scholastic realist one, in the *mirroring* of reality, but in the setting up of an *arbitrary scheme* of reality.[114] Like Bacon before him, he too in the last resort weakens the bond between word and thing.[115] From their separate standpoints Locke and the Port-Royal authors attain the same result: the enclosing of language within its own autonomy.[116]

Lodwick

Leibniz wrote his *Nouveaux Essais sur l'endendement humain*, in refutation of Locke, in 1704, but since the work was not published until 1765 it had no real influence in the immediate post-seventeenth-century period.[117] In many ways however – he himself published in 1666 a *De arte combinatoria* or attempt at a universal alphabetic notation – his ideas were more consonant with those of the language-planners than Locke's. H. Aarsleff[118] sees him as seeking to rescue language from Locke's doctrine that words 'signify only Mens peculiar Ideas'. For him however, just as much as for the Port-Royal authors, language is 'le meilleur miroir de l'esprit humain'. The artificial-language projectors, in contrast to the scepticism of contemporary philosophers,

---

[111] *Elements of Philosophy: I. Concerning Body*, in *The English Works of Thomas Hobbes*, ed. W. Molesworth, London, 1839, I, 17.

[112] *Human Nature: Or the Fundamental Elements of Policy*, in *The English Works of Thomas Hobbes*, ed. W. Molesworth, London, 1840, IV, 8.

[113] *Elements of Philosophy*, in Molesworth, *ibid.*, I, 13.

[114] Cf. Formigari, *Linguistica ed empirismo*, p. 156: 'l'essenza nominale non constituisce un segno naturale della cosa, perché è una collezione di idee che non ha un modello in natura...Le essenze, pertanto, che esercitano la mediazione fra linguaggio e realtà, in quanto essenzi nominali, constituiscono uno schema arbitrario della realtà stessa.'

[115] Cf. Arens, *Sprachwissenschaft*, pp. 70–1: as a result of Locke's procedures 'der blosse Bereich des Wortes übrigbleibt: zugleich also eine Leugnung der Erkenntnismöglichkeit durch die Sprache und eine Verselbständigung ihres Bereiches'.

[116] Locke's *Some Thoughts Concerning Education* (London, 1693) owes little to his theories of language, covering already established points of progressive pedagogical doctrine.

[117] A modern edition is that of E. Boutroux, Paris, 1886.

[118] 'Leibniz on Locke on Language', p. 185.

are bent on making language once again, but in more precise fashion, the mirror of *things*. But since their classification of phenomena rests in large part on the Aristotelian categories, they too may be held to be imposing an 'arbitrary scheme' on the universe. It is, as K. Fischer remarks, this 'creeping away into the leading-strings of Aristotle' that signals the final victory of the Nominalist doctrine of knowledge.[119] These Aristotelian taxonomies have their counterpart in a proliferation of labels referring to concepts, for as with Comenius a necessary preliminary to linguistic analysis is the establishment of a nomenclature. Among those who, gravitating around the Royal Society, interested themselves in the artificial-language movement in England, two authors concern us particularly as having appended to their projects universal grammars with implications for the English vernacular. They are the Flemish immigrant Francis Lodwick[120] or Lodowyck, and John Wilkins, Warden of Wadham College Oxford and later Bishop of Chester. Since these works – more particularly that of Wilkins – are deeply dependent, as Wilkins' list of sources shows, on the tradition of Latin 'philosophical' grammar exemplified by the modistic grammarians and Campanella, they were treated in my first volume as examples of the continued strength of that tradition. They are also however of importance in the development of vernacular grammar, illustrating the different emphasis of the English universal grammar movement as compared with the French one initiated by Port-Royal, in providing a model for parts of the approach in A. Lane's *Key to the Art of Letters* (a vernacular grammar with universalist claims) at the end of the century, and in contributing to the cultural climate in which late-seventeenth-century vernacular grammarians were working.[121] Accordingly, they are also treated here. A third work, G. Dalgarno's *Ars signorum* (1661) is written in Latin and belongs more obviously to a continuing Latin tradition. Its genesis is however so closely intertwined with that of Wilkins' *Essay* (1668) that it is impossible to consider the latter without reference

---

[119] *Descartes and his School*, p. 69.

[120] For a full study of Lodwick's life and works see Salmon, *The Works of Francis Lodwick*. Also, for biographical details, E. J. Dobson, *English Pronunciation 1500–1700* (2nd ed.), Oxford, 1968, 1, 272–3.

[121] As D. Cram remarks ('George Dalgarno on "Ars signorum" and Wilkins' "Essay"', *Progress in Linguistic Historiography*, ed. K. Koerner, Amsterdam, 1980, p. 113), these philosophical language projects have 'for the modern linguist arguably as much relevance as what was going on in Port Royal at about the same time'.

to it.[122] The first two attempts at an artificial language, each including a sketch of a general grammar, are by Lodwick. They are *A Common Writing* (1647)[123] and *The Ground-Work...for the Framing of a New Perfect Language* (1652).[124] The first work presents a scheme of characters devised to be suitable for the writing of any language, while the second, basing itself on the current notion that language should reflect the order of nature, and names ought to indicate the essential properties of things, is an attempt at an artificial language. Both works include universal grammars, which though clumsy and inadequate are of interest in foreshadowing trends which will be more fully developed by Wilkins, and in containing features reminiscent of treatments in Campanella.

A distinction between nouns signifying *things* and verbs signifying *actions* had, as we have seen, been present in grammatical theory since Melanchthon's Latin grammar of 1525. This dichotomy was the common one in seventeenth-century grammar, which increasingly defines nouns as being the names of things, and the verb as indicating action or the undergoing of action. Lodwick's overall division of the word-classes in *A Common Writing* has a dichotomy of verbal 'radixes' (i.e. the basic lexemes that can be diversified grammatically by the addition of 'distinctionall markes') signifying action, and non-verbal ones not signifying action. In the *Ground-Work*, perhaps in an attempt to demonstrate some kind of congruence between grammar and natural phenomena, nouns are treated as 'names' and all other parts of speech are classified as signifying 'action' (verbs), 'quality' (adjectives) and 'help' (pronouns, adverbs, prepositions and conjunctions). The term 'help' simply indicates that the last four word-classes are grammatically dependent. In *A Common Writing*, in a treatment recalling Campanella, nouns as well as verbs can signify action, according to six semantically determined classes:

(1)   The actor. *Drinker*.
(2)   That wherein, or wherewith is acted. *Drink*.

[122] V. Salmon observes that 'The genesis of this work is so closely linked to that of the *Essay*...that it is impossible to know whether Dalgarno's grammatical theory is derived from Wilkins's, or vice versa.' For an examination of the relationship between the two works see her article 'The Evolution of Dalgarno's *Ars signorum*', *Studies in Language and Literature in Honour of Margaret Schlauch*, ed. I. Dobrzycka, M. Brahmer, S. Helsztynski and J. Krzyzanowski, Warsaw, 1966, pp. 335–71.

[123] No place of publication given. The preface attributes the authorship to 'F. L. W.', with the remark that 'this work commeth not from a Scholar, but from a mechanick'.

[124] Also published anonymously, with no indication of place of publication. There are facsimile reproductions of both this work and *A Common Writing* in Salmon's *The Works of Francis Lodwick*.

(3)   The inclination. *A drunkard.*
(4)   The abstract of the denominative adjective. *Drunkenness.*
(5)   The act. *The drinking.*
(6)   The place accustomary to the action. *A drink-house.*[125]

For so many centuries, grammarians seemed unable to proceed without subjecting the noun to a minute semantic classification that did not always correspond with grammatical function. Traditional Latin grammar was full of such complications, and Lodwick's system only differs in being largely based on the signification of 'action' and 'inclination' (Scholastic philosophy's *potentia*). Since however each of the semantic classes is to be provided with its own separate 'distinctionall marke' in the system of writing, it must be supposed that Lodwick regarded them as universally necessary, and needing expression in any language. That he is also preoccupied with the ideal form of natural languages is shown by his coining of such terms as *laughard* to fill supposed gaps in the structure of English. The persistence of Scholastic logic-chopping in the definitions of the common noun as signifying a thing 'only for the present, in relation to some action done or suffered', and the proper noun as that 'by which any thing is constantly denominated',[126] is at first sight curious. All these various features can however be traced back, either through Lodwick's own reading or via his contacts with other language-planners (in particular Wilkins), to Campanella. The attribution of the signification of action to nouns is for instance ultimately traceable to Campanella's Scholastically based dictum that every essence must have an act. As for the distinction between common and proper nouns, it recalls Wilkins' view that tense ought, 'according to the true Philosophy of Speech', to be a feature of substantives as well as of verbs, a view which in turn stems from indications in Campanella.[127] Though Lodwick's distinction would seem to be an aspectual rather than a temporal one, his source is clear enough. The point here is that though his treatment of *Peter*, *man* and *horse* as signifying permanent states and *murderer* as signifying a temporary one seems at first sight to reflect an arbitrary whim, it is in fact rooted in a widespread revival, among linguistic scholars, of categories taken from medieval philosophy. In Lodwick's approach *dog*, since it indicates permanency, is as much a 'proper' noun as *John*

---

[125] *A Common Writing*, pp. 8–9.
[126] *Ibid.*, pp. 7–8.
[127] Cf. Salmon, '"Philosophical" Grammar in John Wilkins's "Essay"', pp. 149–50.

or *Paul*. The question arises of how to distinguish these two types separately in the writing system, and Lodwick admits that in this matter 'lyeth all the difficulty which can be objected against this Art'. The division of adjectives into active and passive ('commonly called participles') is also, perhaps via an intermediate source, taken from Campanella:

$$\left.\begin{array}{l}\text{Active, as } a \text{ } loving\\ \text{Passive, as } a \text{ } beloved\\ \text{Denominative, as } a \text{ } lovely\end{array}\right\} man^{128}$$

The verb is similarly divided into semantically determined classes, based on the existence of Latin forms such as the inchoatives (e.g. *senesco*, 'I become old'), in order that the proposed artificial language may be capable of expressing 'certain augmentations' in meaning. There are accordingly verbs signifying a customary action (Latin *minitor*, 'I threaten'), a 'desire to the action' (Latin *esurio*, 'I desire to eat'), diminution (Latin *cantillo*, 'I sing low or little') etc.[129] Though J. Knowlson regards Lodwick as an important figure in seventeenth-century linguistics, 'comparable certainly with William Holder and John Wallis',[130] and V. Salmon has established his importance for the artificial-language movement in England, his contribution to specifically *grammatical* theory is slight and derivative. Apart from a heavy reliance on the structure of Latin in determining what categories to prescribe as necessarily present in all languages, his system of 'posed signs' indicative of case, corresponding to the signs *of*, *to* and *from* in English, is obviously indebted to Lily. Many of the features he regards as essential to his ideal language – formally invariable adjectives, verbs not marked for person or number, the distinguishing of nominative and accusative by position within the sentence – are quite patently taken from English. His interest for this study lies in fact in his use of English examples, and in his indications of what he takes to be the ideal structure of the vernacular.

[128] These parallels are also present in Wilkins' *Essay*, and will be treated when that more important work is considered below.
[129] *A Common Writing*, p. 2.
[130] *Universal Language Schemes in England and France 1600–1800*.

The sources of Wilkins' 'Essay'

The most important work produced by a language-planner is the celebrated *Essay Towards a Real Character and a Philosophical Language* (1668) by John Wilkins, Bishop of Chester.[131] Apart from the list given by Wilkins himself, various suggestions have been put forward as to its immediate sources. O. Funke regards Dalgarno as a primary influence, citing in support a statement in a letter from John Wallis to the first president of the Royal Society pointing out the importance for Wilkins of Dalgarno's work.[132] It is true that Dalgarno was closely involved with a number of scholars at Oxford including, beside Wilkins himself, Seth Ward the Professor of Astronomy, John Wallis and other future fellows of the Royal Society,[133] and as we have seen V. Salmon regards his work and Wilkins' as so closely intertwined in origin that it is difficult to determine who influenced whom.[134] It would be inappropriate to repeat in full here the discussion of Wilkins' sources in my volume on the Latin tradition,[135] but it may be pointed out that some recent scholarship, less ready than in the past to ascribe purely Baconian origins to the *Essay*, is also in doubt concerning Dalgarno's claims. Opinion is divided between those who like B. De Mott see the notion of an artificial language as 'in significant measure a contagion transmitted from abroad',[136] and those including B. Shapiro and V. Salmon who regard the English language-planning movement as largely *sui generis*. Outside influences suggested range from Cartesianism to an impulse, via Samuel Hartlib, from the educational reformers Cyprian Kinner and Jan Amos Comenius. In respect to the first of these influences V. Salmon notes, in spite of her overall conclusion that English language-planning took place very much within its own circumscribed world, the existence in Paris in the 1630s of a group of amateur scientists who discussed Descartes' proposal, formulated in a letter to Mersenne in 1629, for a universal language based on conceptual classification.

---

[131] As Bishop of Chester, Wilkins signed his name *John Cestri* [*ensis*], a fact which has not been understood by the author and collaborators of A. Jacob's *Genèse de la pensée linguistique*, Paris, 1973 (p. 47), who describe Wilkins as 'évêque de Cestri', and further compound their howler with a footnote explaining that 'Cestri' is a 'ville de Cilicie, sur la frontière de l'Isaurie'.

[132] 'On the Sources of John Wilkins' 'Philosophical Language (1668)', pp. 208–9.

[133] See Salmon, *The Works of Francis Lodwick*, pp. 19–20.

[134] See note 122 above.

[135] Padley, *Grammatical Theory* (1976), pp. 194–5, 198, 205, 208.

[136] 'The Sources and Development of John Wilkins' Philosophical Language', p. 11.

Their proceedings were published in 1636 and in an English version in 1664–5, and must according to Salmon have been known in England before 1640.[137] I. Michael goes so far as to say that in Wilkins' *Essay* 'the influence of Port-Royal is clearly apparent'.[138] Those who favour a largely foreign origin for the language-planning movement are also in general those who play down the Baconian influence posited by Funke. Although B. J. Shapiro regards Bacon as a 'persuasive symbol behind which support for scientific activity whatever its intellectual origins must be mustered', she makes the telling point that on the crucial question of epistemology Wilkins did not in fact follow him, and emphasizes the international nature of the seventeenth-century scientific community.[139] Within the Royal Society itself – and this coincides with C. Webster's opinion[140] – the facts 'seem to suggest a lesser role for Baconianism' than has been claimed.[141]   Bacon apart, the main candidates as influences on the English language-projectors are Comenius and his Silesian disciple Kinner, whose case is espoused by B. De Mott, basing himself on the papers of Samuel Hartlib. There are sound reasons, according to De Mott, for supposing that the ideas of Kinner and Comenius, put into circulation by Hartlib, had reached the English language-planners by 1650.[142] Certainly these ideas antedate those of Wilkins and Dalgarno by several years, and De Mott assumes that Wilkins must have modelled his 'basic plan' on them. Comenius' proposals were widely known, but his *Via lucis* (which appeared in England under the title *The Way of Light*), though written in 1641, did not appear in print until 1668,[143] the year in which Wilkins' own *Essay* appeared. In H. E. Brekle's opinion, De Mott's thesis that the basic plan of Wilkins' *Essay* originated with Comenius and Kinner, with some native contributions from Ward and Boyle, is convincing.[144] Other

---

[137] *The Works of Francis Lodwick*, pp. 24–5. Descartes (*Oeuvres philosophiques (1618–1637)*, ed. F. Alquié, Paris, 1963–, p. 231) calls for a universal language which, above all, 'aiderait au jugement, lui représentant si distinctement toutes choses, qu'il lui serait presque impossible de se tromper'.

[138] *English Grammatical Categories*, p. 26.

[139] *John Wilkins 1614–1672*, pp. 58–60, 205.

[140] *The Great Instauration*, pp. 494–5. See note 11 above.

[141] *John Wilkins 1614–1672*, pp. 204–5.

[142] 'The Sources and Development of John Wilkins' Philosophical Language', p. 8.

[143] See Miškovská, 'Komenský ve vývoji gramatikych teorií' (review of G. A. Padley, *Grammatical Theory in Western Europe 1500–1700*, Cambridge, 1976), *Studia Comeniana et historica*, XIII: 6 (1976).

[144] 'The Seventeenth Century', p. 305.

scholars, while giving greater to weight to indigenous influences other than Bacon, deny any important role to Comenius and Kinner. O. Funke, taking as his starting-point De Mott's article on Wilkins' sources, had already in 1959 dismissed any suggestion of a direct and decisive influence by Kinner.[145] As for Hartlib, the publicizer in England of Comenius' and Kinner's work, Shapiro notes that both his and Wilkins' efforts did not in the 1640s go beyond the promotion of a 'real character'. V. Salmon in particular has taken pains to reexamine the controversy surrounding Comenius' putative influence on Wilkins, and finds the language-planners 'strangely silent' on the subject of their supposed debt to the *Via lucis*. While there is no proof that the projectors knew this work, and 'external evidence hardly justifies the important role which has been assigned to Comenius in the development of language-planning in the seventeenth century', Salmon none the less wonders whether the fundamental change in orientation that took place after 1650 could have come about entirely without the *Via lucis*. Certainly, as she notes, the arrangement of lexical items in conceptual classes was no new thing in England, being a well-known pedagogical device used by grammarians of Latin.[146] Timothy Bright's *Characterie*, as J. Knowlson points out, employs conceptual classification and may, via John Willis' *Art of Stenographie*, have influenced the English language-planners,[147] and indeed a copy of this work was in the possession of Seth Ward, whom Wilkins acknowledges as a source of his classificatory system. Ward's influence is emphasized by Shapiro, Wilkins' plan being traced directly, on Wilkins' own admission, to the one described by Ward in the *Vindiciae academiarum* of 1654, of which they were joint authors. Ward's method in fact, with its matching of 'simple notions' to symbols, involved a conceptual classification, and Shapiro notes that the manifest similarities of Wilkins' and Dalgarno's approaches may be due to their being jointly dependent on earlier work by Ward. Shapiro holds however that Ward's contribution was but one among several indigenous ones, Wilkins' efforts being motivated by the collective concern of the Oxford group of scientists and their later corporate manifestation, the Royal Society.[148] This view of Wilkins' project as at least to some extent a cooperative and purely British venture is

---

[145] 'On the Sources of John Wilkins' Philosophical Language (1668)', p. 208.
[146] 'Language-Planning in Seventeenth-Century England', pp. 375, 378–81, 393–4.
[147] *Universal Language Schemes*, p. 20. See also Salmon, 'The Evolution of Dalgarno's "Ars signorum"', p. 355. [148] *John Wilkins 1614–1672*, pp. 213, 208.

supported by V. Salmon, who dismisses any notion of an influence from the Port-Royal grammarians with the remark that Wilkins had been at work on his project since at least 1657.[149]

Many of the scholars mentioned above have stressed the materialism of the English language-planning movement, its ties with the Nominalism of the preceding medieval centuries. There is, as J. Knowlson points out, yet another school of thought (represented by H. Aarsleff and P. Rossi, and certain pages of De Mott) which draws attention to links with the mysticism of Jacob Boehme and others. For Knowlson, both this view and the Nominalist thesis according to which the language-planners sought to reduce language to the aridity of mathematical equations are extremist. His own thesis is that though the idea of a set of symbols standing in a direct relationship with reality may have its roots in occultism, the language-planners transformed it into what it was for Comenius and Kircher – 'both an attempt to renew contact with divine harmony in the universe and a crucial effort to bring about a reconciliation between men'.[150] So, in the great sweep of European pedagogical and linguistic theory, we come back to Ratke. The disentangling of Wilkins' sources is a complicated matter, much of it relevant to the genesis and relationships of the artificial-language movement itself rather than to the history of grammatical theory. In the last analysis the *Essay* represents a convergence of currents of European medieval and Renaissance thought which had been developing and maturing for a very long time. For the specifically grammatical section of the *Essay* however there is a direct antecedent. Writing in 1975, at the time when my first volume was about to go to the press, V. Salmon notes that the sole aspect of the *Essay* that has not previously been treated in any detail is the one that shows its author to be 'the heir to a philosophico-grammatical tradition which was largely created in the Middle Ages, and survived in a few grammars which Wilkins used as sources'.[151] She also claims that, in the few works dealing with the history of grammar in the Renaissance and the seventeenth century, no one, apart from a brief note by Pagliaro,[152] had made other than short

[149] *The Works of Francis Lodwick*, p. 30.
[150] *Universal Language Schemes*, p. 15, citing P. Rossi, *Clavis universalis*, Milan and Naples, 1960, p. 213.
[151] '"Philosophical" Grammar in John Wilkins's "Essay"', pp. 131–2.
[152] A. Pagliaro, 'Sommario di linguistica arioeuropea', *Pubblicazoni della scuola di filologia classica presso la R. Università di Roma*, series 2, ii, fasc. 1, Rome, 1930.

references to Campanella. If this is so, my thesis 'Grammatical Theory in Western Europe 1500–1700'[153] must have been the first work on the history of linguistics to give an extended treatment of Campanella's grammar, and to show by detailed comparison how closely he is followed by Wilkins. When the resulting book[154] was about to be printed however, V. Salmon's article '"Philosophical" grammar in John Wilkins's "Essay"' (1975) appeared, and though we had obviously been working independently on the same subject, to her must go the honour of first having treated certain parallels between Wilkins and Campanella in print.

Dalgarno

As far as the grammatical section of Wilkins' *Essay* is concerned, there are two important sources: Dalgarno (because of the close collaboration that took place between him and Wilkins)[155] and Campanella. In the seventeenth century, European linguistic culture is still largely one and unfragmented, and grammars written in the vernacular cannot be considered *in vacuo* without reference to contemporary work in Latin.[156] Particularly is this so in the case of Wilkins' *Essay* (1668) and Dalgarno's *Ars signorum* published seven years previously. Dalgarno too stems from the empirical tradition initiated by Bacon, having originally set out to improve an existing system of 'brachigraphy' or shorthand.[157] He too however stands under the influence of Latin 'philosophical' and universal grammarians, and nowhere is this more striking than in the primacy he gives to logic, in his refusal to 'separate the inseparable' by divorcing grammar and logic[158] which, differing only as does the sign from that which is signified, are complementary facets of the same science.[159]

[153] Oxford University doctoral thesis, 1970.
[154] *Grammatical Theory in Western Europe 1500–1700: The Latin Tradition*, Cambridge, 1976.
[155] Cram ('George Dalgarno on "Ars signorum" and Wilkins' "Essay"', pp. 116–17) notes that contemporary opinion was convinced that Wilkins had 'reaped the harvest where Dalgarno had sown the seed', a censure of Wilkins that modern scholarship has by and large repeated. A hitherto unpublished treatise by Dalgarno, consulted by Cram, shows however that Dalgarno saw the basic principles of his own work and Wilkins' as diametrically opposed.
[156] In devoting five pages of his *English Grammatical Categories* to Dalgarno, Michael is obviously conscious of this fact.
[157] Salmon's 'The Evolution of Dalgarno's "Ars signorum"' gives a full treatment of the question of Dalgarno's indebtedness to an anonymous shorthand system.
[158] *Ars signorum*, London, 1661, p. 7.
[159] *Ibid.*, p. 18: 'omnino eorum [sc. signorum et signatorum] eadem debet esse scientia'. 'Grammatica non aliter differt ab his [i.e. metaphysica et logica] quam Signum a Signato'.

361

In warning the reader of his work not to treat the logical and grammatical sections as separate compartments of knowledge, Dalgarno is returning to the earlier conceptions of an age when logic, grammar and rhetoric together constituted a complete theory of communication.[160] Thanks to Ramus' insistence, in his search for criteria in delimiting the boundaries of each 'art', on their separation, these three sections of the trivium were by the mid-seventeenth century 'elaborately partitioned' (to borrow I. Michael's phrase), their practitioners 'no longer raising their eyes from the ground'.[161] Dalgarno however regards speech itself as 'a logical analysis of our conceptions', as a tool without which men would merely repeat standardized formulae after the manner of parrots ('more psitta-corum'). Like the other language-planners and universal gram-marians, he regards language as the expression of mental concepts, with however the added stipulation that only by using logic can the 'animi sensa' be communicated. His procedure as an analyst of language, or the creator of a synthetic one, must accordingly, given that names ought to be imposed 'by logical rules drawn from the nature of things themselves', be 'secundum Analogiam Logico-Grammaticam'.[162] Not surprisingly, one of the aims of the *Ars signorum* is to promote a more thorough knowledge of things, a 'penitiorem et interiorem rerum cognitionem'.[163] It follows that the proposed 'art of signs' must model itself on an 'art of things' – 'Ars signorum artem rerum sequatur' – the conceptual classification of the universe must have its corresponding symbolization. The *signa* are meant to reflect a system of classification of 'simple notions' into seventeen abstract classes, such as *ens*, *substantia* and *corpus*, subdivided in Aristotelian fashion into *species* and *differentiae*. The foundation of such classifications, much in vogue with the language-planners, is in fact Aristotle's ten predicaments, eked out with categories from Scholastic philosophy. This gives rise to a circularity in which scholars, claiming to catalogue the real world as a preliminary to its symbolization, take as their starting-point such Aristotelian categories as substance and accident, and then seek properties in phenomena to correspond to them. As M. Slaughter has shown in her *Universal Languages and Scientific Taxonomy in the Seventeenth Century* (1982), this

---

[160] Cf. W. S. Howell, *Logic and Rhetoric*, p. 4.
[161] *English Grammatical Categories*, p. 243.
[162] *Ars signorum*, p. 18. [163] *Ibid.*, p. 33.

procedure is not peculiar to the inventors of artificial languages, but is common to all the new supposedly empirical sciences, being particularly prevalent in botanical classification. As she remarks (p. 147), 'Although Dalgarno was not constructing a taxonomy for the same purposes as the botanists, what is interesting is that the degree of classification and the hierarchical structure of the classification is similar. Like the taxonomies created by the botanists, it reflects a combination of folk taxonomy with Aristotelian logical taxonomy.' By the application of systems of logical classification to the task of constructing an artificial language, Dalgarno hopes to bring 'a great deal of clearnesse to the acts of the understanding', to civilize barbarous nations, propagate the Gospel, and increase 'traffique and commerce'.[164] Optimism and puritan empiricism go hand in hand.

Wilkins

Universal grammar in England cannot be considered apart from the artificial-language movement, for their sources and motivations are closely related. This means that the 'natural' grammar contained in Wilkins' *Essay* cannot be regarded as an isolated phenomenon, unconnected to the much more voluminous work on a 'real character' and the assumptions underlying a 'philosophical language' in which it appears.[165] It is part of an empirical and rationalist undertaking reflecting a specific epistemology, including a thoroughgoing attempt at the classification of phenomena, and motivated at least in part by contemporary dissatisfaction with existing natural languages. The second of the *Essay*'s four parts, with its exhaustive conceptual classifications, its table of 'things and notions', forms the indispensable foundation for the whole, occupying as it does over half of the book. The reference to 'things' is important, for it denotes yet another shift in the attitude to the nature of the linguistic sign. As A. Robinet has perceived, certain 'strange characteristics' in the seventeenth century 'were bringing back the sign from garment for ideas to expression of *things*, from representation of the order of thought to representation

---

[164] Similarly, the 'avertissement' to P. Labbé's *Grammaire* (2nd ed.), Paris, 1663, sees his project for a universal language as 'l'instrument général pour établir le commerce et planter la Foi Chrétienne par toutes les nations de la terre'. Cave Beck's *The Universal Character* (London, 1657) sees an identical application for his own system.

[165] Wilkins' grammar has been treated in Padley, *Grammatical Theory* (1976), pp. 195–208. The present discussion will inevitably involve some repetition.

of *the structure of the world*'.[166] Wilkins is convinced that this philosophical classification, with aims similar to those of Comenius' *Pansophia*, represents 'a much better and readier course, for the entring and training up of men in the knowledge of things, than any other way of institution'. Again, as throughout seventeenth-century endeavours, the primary motive is a pedagogical one. In line with the hopes of scholars such as Comenius is also Wilkins' belief that his classification of concepts and the universal language based on it will 'contribute much to the clearing of some of our modern differences in religion, by unmasking wild errors, that shelter themselves under the disguise of affected phrases'. The 'real character' he elaborates will contribute to this, for it will 'not signifie words, but things and notions', and hence will be 'legible by any nation in their own tongue'. Taken both together, the 'real character' and the philosophical language will facilitate 'mutual commerce' among the nations, improve 'natural knowledge', and spread an understanding of religion. The utilitarian character of Wilkins' puritanism is obvious enough. As with Ratke, it is accompanied by a belief that natural knowledge and religious knowledge go together. Language is no longer here, as in A. Richardson's *Logicians School-Master* (1657), 'a garment to cloath our reason', but as in so many intellectual enterprises of the seventeenth century, the aim is to bring men closer to the world of things, and here there is yet another link with kabbalistic theory and widely held views as to Adam's direct communion with Nature. Adam 'came into the world a philosopher', declares Robert South in a sermon preached in St Paul's in 1662, 'he could view essences in themselves, and read forms without the comment of their respective properties...An Aristotle was but the rubbish of Adam.'[167] Similar references to the unique powers enjoyed by Adam could be multiplied, but they all have in common the assumption that these powers consisted in the knowledge of the *true names* of all created things, and that the elements of each name corresponded in some way to the characteristics of its referent. As A. Richardson puts it, 'Adam by seeing into the nature of every Creature, could see their names...So God called the day *jam* because of the jumbling noise that is made in it.'[168] The endless seventeenth-

[166] *Le Langage à l'âge classique*, foreword.
[167] *Sermons Preached on Several Occasions*, 1, Oxford, 1823.
[168] *The Logicians School-Master*, p. 13.

century speculations as to which language was the original one were accordingly not mere impractical theorizing, for whichever language it was, obviously held the key to the mysteries of the universe. The English planners of artificial languages were attempting to produce a language which, like that spoken by Adam, had a perfect correspondence to phenomena. As D. Katz remarks, once scholars had come to the conclusion that the language of Adam was Hebrew, they were ipso facto steered towards Jewish interpretations of language.[169] Wilkins himself makes this connection, stating on the one hand that according to the Jews 'the Holy spirit hath purposely involved in the words of the Scripture, every secret that belongs to any Art or Science, under such Cabalisms as these', and on the other that 'if a man were but expert in unfolding of them, it were easier for him to get as much knowledge as Adam had in his innocencie'.[170] As Katz observes, this particular influence of the Kabbalah, tying in with the view of Adam as holding the linguistic key to the innermost secrets of Nature, has hitherto been neglected in studies of seventeenth-century linguistic thought. In this context it has an obvious link with the German theories of language discussed above. Hebrew is however not the only candidate for the title of original language, and if John Webb thinks it ridiculous to maintain, with Goropius Becanus, that 'Adam spoke Dutch in Paradice,' he has another pretender in Chinese, that 'primitive Tongue, which was common to the whole World before the Flood'.[171] It was Chinese, which supposedly represented things directly by 'real characters' without the intermediary of words, that finally provided the model for the language projectors, and it is significant that it is also of importance for Campanella and Caramuel. But as J. Knowlson has well pointed out, since the 'real character' symbolizes things directly without the intermediary of words, providing a reflection of phenomena, the philosophical language is no longer simply a *means* to knowledge, but becomes knowledge itself. Hence the vast epistemological importance of Wilkins' project. This 'transition that took place in the middle years of the century...from a character which

[169] D. Katz, in the chapter 'Babel Reversed: The Search for a Universal Language and the Glorification of Hebrew' of his *Philo-Semitism and the Readmission of the Jews to England 1603–1655*, p. 71. See also, for a consideration of the Adamic language, the same author's 'The Language of Adam in Seventeenth-Century England'.
[170] *Mercury, or The Secret and Swift Messenger*, London, 1641, p. 101 (wrongly numbered 83).
[171] *An Historical Essay*, London, 1669, pp. 42–4.

merely *represented* things and notions by agreement, to one which *mirrored* the whole of human knowledge by the combinations of its elements'[172] involves the attribution of symbols to the various *properties* of a thing (thus defining it, in pursuit of Bacon's demand for closer definition), and the grouping of concepts according to genera, species and differences. The Aristotelian provenance of the criteria would be obvious to Wilkins' readers, though an influence from the medieval classifications of Ramón Lull should not be ruled out.[173] The search for a symbolism that will mirror phenomena exactly without recourse to the vocabulary of existing languages and constitute an immediate system of knowledge is not however Wilkins' only motivation. In common with others he has a profound dissatisfaction not only with Latin – the universal language of the times – but also with the imperfections and imprecise abundance of synonyms that characterize the vernacular.

If a proposed new universal language is to be intelligible to all men, it must have not only a 'character' suited to the notation of concepts, but also a universally valid system of grammar. Accordingly, in 'the framing of such a Natural Grammar, as might be suited to the Philosophy of Speech', Wilkins bases himself – and in this he does not differ from universal grammarians of supposedly 'Cartesian' provenance – on Aristotle's claim that 'the mental affections themselves, of which words are primarily signs, are the same for all mankind':[174]

As men do generally agree in the same Principle of Reason, so do they likewise agree in the same *Internal Notions* or *Apprehension of things*...So that, if men should generally consent upon the same way or manner of *Expression*, as they do in the same *Notion*, we should then be freed from that Curse in the confusion of Tongues, with all the unhappy consequences of it.[175]

Fundamental to the whole question of a 'philosophical language', this assumption is also essential to the framing of a universal grammar. Though much attention has been paid to Wilkins' 'real character and philosophical language', there has been little in the way of an attempt to place his 'natural grammar' in the context of

---

[172] Knowlson, *Universal Language Schemes*, pp. 8, 74.

[173] Cf. Salmon, '"Philosophical" Grammar in John Wilkins's "Essay"', p. 151. Salmon notes that Campanella quotes Lull as a source for his own lexical inventions of terms, lacking in Latin, that an ideal language would require.

[174] *De interpretatione*, 1, in Cooke, *Aristotle: the Organon*, p. 115.

[175] *An Essay Towards a Real Character and a Philosophical Language*, p. 20.

the general development of grammatical theory on a European scale. J. Knowlson, confining himself to 'universal language schemes', gives no account of Wilkins' grammar, and M. Slaughter's interest[176] is in the wide field of seventeenth-century scientific taxonomy. But it is more particularly in his grammar that Wilkins relies on a long-standing European tradition exemplified in the works of the medieval modistic grammarians and in Campanella and J. C. Scaliger. He makes no use, except in treating phonetics and orthography, of his vernacular predecessors, and patently regards himself, in spite of his list of those authors who have treated 'natural grammar' before him, as breaking new ground.

Having completed his 'enumeration and description of such things and notions, as are to be known, and to which names are to be assigned',[177] Wilkins is ready to approach the task of designing a grammar. As with the whole domain of science, a necessary preliminary is the cataloguing and conceptual classification of the world of things. It is again a leading principle, as with Ramus, that the grammarian must take Nature as his guide, and in this sense 'natural' grammar is for Wilkins an abstraction from the grammars of existing languages, his criticism of even the models he cites turning on the fact that they did not 'sufficiently abstract their rules according to Nature'.[178] Possibly relevant here, given Wilkins' insistence on this abstraction, is Caramuel's definition of philosophical grammar as proceeding by *abstractissimae notiones*,[179] the distilled essence of what is necessary to grammar. The division of grammar by Wilkins into 'natural and general' and 'instituted and particular' is not peculiar to him.[180] What does seem to be original to him is the idea that the former is abstracted from the latter by 'abstracting from those many unnecessary rules belong to instituted language'. Wilkins' view of the function of grammar may be thought to have affinities with certain approaches in Locke.[181] Reminiscent of the latter is Wilkins' reference to 'things and notions...of a more simple nature',

---

[176] *Universal Languages and Scientific Taxonomy in the Seventeenth Century.*
[177] *Essay*, p. 297.   [178] *Ibid.*, pp. 297–8.
[179] *Grammatica audax*, p. 3.
[180] It is found e.g. in Vossius' (*De arte grammatica*, 1635) division of grammar into 'naturalis' and 'artificialis', and corresponds to Campanella's 'grammatica philosophica' and 'grammatica civilis'.
[181] G. McColley claims ('John Wilkins – a precursor of Locke', *Philosophical Review*, XLVII (1938), p. 643) that Wilkins 'did much to preserve and foster the climate of ideas' within which Locke developed his own doctrines.

and to more complex notions that have to be expressed peri-phrastically. The comparison that immediately comes to mind is with Locke's statement that 'When the Understanding is once stored with these simple Ideas, it has the power to repeat, compare, and unite them...and so can make at Pleasure new complex Ideas.'[182] Wilkins' view of linguistic structure as analysable into these 'notions of a more simple nature', and of grammar as concerning itself with their combination into 'complex propositions and discourses'[183] has obvious affinities with the Port-Royal approach, but in view of his close dependence on him elsewhere, his source is much more likely to be Campanella.[184] Further, though both Wilkins and the Port-Royal authors are of course very much concerned with concepts, they set out from different epistemological bases. While Port-Royal in practice confines its analysis to the operations of the mind, Wilkins' grammar presupposes, in a return to the modistic authors' 'grammatica est de signis rerum', a preliminary analysis of natural phenomena. His approach depends in the first instance neither on intuitions about the mind's own operations nor on empirical observation of language, but on a system of philosophical categorizations isomorphic with the real world. The catch is however that, in a kind of circularity, these categorizations are taken ready-made from Aristotle, and things in the real world are required to conform with them. Even with Aristotle himself, it is by no means clear whether his ten predicaments are classifying 'symbols or what they symbolize, words or, in a very wide sense, things',[185] and Wilkins' forty conceptual classes, with thirty-four *genera* grouped according to the predicaments of substance and quality, action and relation, etc., with each *genus* subdivided into its *species*, were already thought by some not to be according to nature.[186]

This Aristotelian approach results in Wilkins' grammar[187] in the typical late-seventeenth-century view of the universe as consisting of

---

[182] *Essay Concerning Humane Understanding*, pp. 45–6.

[183] Wilkins' *Essay*, p. 297.

[184] The idea that each 'thing' in the universe should have its corresponding 'simple notion', expressible by a single word, is obviously an attractive one to universal grammarians. Salmon (*The Works of Francis Lodwick*, p. 108) traces it to N. De-Lawne's *The Elements of Logick* (1624), translated from the French of Pierre du Moulin. Cf. Seth Ward's statement (*Vindiciae academiarum*, Oxford, 1654) that words either signify simple notions or are 'resolvable' into them.

[185] W. and M. Kneale, *The Development of Logic*, pp. 25, 27, 29.

[186] e.g. Thomas Baker, *Reflections upon Learning*, pp. 17–18.

[187] The grammar occupies pp. 297–384 of the *Essay*.

things and actions, and the modes of those things and actions. Where, similarly to Lodwick, he differs widely from previous authors is in his allowing action to be signified by both nouns and verbs. Vossius (one of the grammarians mentioned by Wilkins) had already, in his *De arte grammatica* of 1635, pointed out that a noun such as *calefactio* signifies an action just as plainly as does a verb – a remark many a twentieth-century grammar book would have done well to heed. His way out of the dilemma (the noun signifies *actio, passio* or *ens*, the verb *agere, pati* or *esse*) is interesting, for it obviously implies the modistic view of nouns as signifying states of being, and the verb as signifying being actually in process. In this respect Vossius' approach represents yet another of those forlorn echoes of Scholasticism that are typical of the century. The emphasis is however no longer the modistic one on the consignification of *grammatical* meanings, but on purely *lexical* meanings. The whole trend of seventeenth-century grammar is towards nomenclature and lexicography, and in this Wilkins is no exception. His Aristotelian categorization of the universe leads him to treat grammar as a matter of semantic labelling. Once the notion of specifically *grammatical* function, as opposed to nomenclature, is lost sight of, Wilkins is free to apply the categories of Scholastic semantics to linguistic description. And here there seems little doubt that his source is Campanella, who regards action as one of the categories of 'essence', and hence of the noun. Wilkins' division of the word-classes into 'integrals' capable of semantic independence and 'particles' not thus capable is, as we have seen, nothing new in grammar, representing a not uncommon Aristotelian division. His definition of his integrals rests squarely however on Campanella's neo-Scholasticism:

By Integrals or Principal words, I mean such as signifie some entire thing or notion: whether the Ens or Thing it self, or the Essence of a thing, as Nouns Neuters, whether concrete or abstract; or the Doing or Suffering of a thing as Nouns Active or Passive; or the manner and affection of it, as Derived Adverbs.[188]

Here it is noteworthy – a matter to which we shall return – that the verb is no longer treated as a 'principal word'. The insistence that verbs consist logically of copula plus attribute leads, with both Wilkins and Port-Royal, to a significant change in its status. With Port-Royal it is given a special position as an indicator of the

[188] *Essay*, p. 298.

'operations of our minds', while with Wilkins it is virtually excluded altogether in favour of the copula. In Wilkins' case this major shift of emphasis leads in effect to a two-word-class system in sharp contrast to the tripartite one of the other major 'philosophical' grammarians Sanctius, Vossius and Campanella. It is in details such as this that the closeness of the connections between Wilkins' work and that of Dalgarno becomes apparent, for Dalgarno sets up only one primary word-class, the noun, of which the other classes or particles are nothing more than 'flexions' or 'cases', reflecting the importance given in his system to 'ens' or static being.[189] In adopting this scheme Wilkins joins the other grammarians of English who already, before 1700, produce what I. Michael calls 'modified systems' of the parts of speech,[190] though his classification is sharply differentiated from others in this minor status given to the verb. Apart from Dalgarno, an obvious source for this viewpoint is again Campanella, who regarded all verbs as derivatives of 'essence', and all acts as ultimately 'acts of an essence'. More important then than the role of the verb is that of the copula, which though classified as a particle (as with Port-Royal it is a connecting link) is 'essential in every compleat sentence'. The remaining particles, including the pronoun defined as a substitute for an integral, and the interjection as a substitute for a sentence or a 'complex part' thereof, are by contrast inessential. In a similar dichotomy, prepositions are seen as particles constructing word with word, and conjunctions and non-derivative adverbs as particles constructing sentence with sentence. Finally, certain particles are 'declarative of some accident', the article indicating an accident of an integral, mood an accident of the copula, and tense an accident of either. Here it should be remembered that the 'particles' tense and mood each have their corresponding distinctive mark in Wilkins' proposed writing system. His use of the term 'accident', which has formal implications, thus recalls Lodwick's 'distinctionall additions' employed as adjuncts to a system of 'radixes' or lexical significations common to all languages. Of importance here is Wilkins' realization that the methods by which the classical languages indicate the 'accidental difference' of words are 'not suited' to the vernacular, though he notes that many

---

[189] Cf. *Ars signorum*, p. 62.
[190] *English Grammatical Categories*. Michael lists Wilkins' as the twenty-seventh variety of such systems up to 1800.

grammarians proceed as if they were. Syntax in a universal grammar 'ought to be founded upon the Philosophy of speech and such *Natural* grounds, as do necessarily belong to Language', rather than in terms of case, 'which is not so essential and natural to Substantives, as to be provided for in the word it self, by varying the Terminations of it'. Case – and here there are evident similarities with the Port-Royal approach – is 'nothing else but that obliquity in the sence of a Substantive, which is caused and signified by some Preposition annexed to it'.[191]

Though 'accidental differences' will have to be provided for by formal notations in Wilkins' system of writing, the grammatical section of his work is overwhelmingly concerned with the establishment of those philosophically based categories that will need to be so distinguished in all languages. These categories are isomorphic with reality, in a treatment recalling Dalgarno's dictum that grammarians 'ought to impose names according to logical concepts and rules deduced from the nature of things themselves'.[192] Though the Port-Royal authors would in the last resort have agreed that concepts represent things, their system very much stays, in what Chomsky has called a 'virtual identification of linguistic and mental processes', within the sphere of the operations of the mind. Wilkins' system is overtly based on a correspondence with things themselves. Since the universe consists of essences, it follows that all the 'radical' words of a language ought to be substantives (Scaliger regarded them as significations of essence), and only because existing languages are defective, are substantial notions sometimes expressed by adjectives or by an 'aggregate of words'. Substantives signify the types of essence that are found in the real world, that is to say *things*, *actions* and the *undergoing of actions* (in Campanella's Scholastic system action is one aspect under which essence reveals itself), and *persons* functioning as the agents or recipients of actions. There is here a direct link with Campanella, whose substantives signify *essentiam puram*, *essentiam actionis* and *essentiam passionis*. Basing himself, via Campanella and Scholastic philosophy, on the categories of reality, Wilkins lists the following varieties of noun:

'substantives of the thing'	*calor*
'substantives of the action'	*calefactio*

[191] *Essay*, p. 352.   [192] *Ars signorum*, p. 18.

'substantives of the passion'	τὸ *calefieri*
'substantives of the person agent'	*calefactor*
'substantives of the person patient'	*calefactus*[193]

The last four of these are derived from the first and one wonders
whether, had these forms not already existed in Latin, it would have
occurred to Wilkins to set up the series. That it does not overtly rest
on formal criteria is shown however by the derivation of the
substantive of the action *illuminatio* from the substantive of the thing
lux. Wilkins' categories are seemingly semantic, Aristotelian ones with
which a large number of forms in Latin happen to coincide – which
raises the whole question of whether Aristotle did not himself find
his categories ready-made in the structure of Greek. If Latin lacks
a form coinciding with a particular meaning, Wilkins is happy to
supply a different one with the required meaning from elsewhere in
the language. Thus, despite the fact that there is no *formal* derivation
involved, he can derive the 'substantive of the action' *gubernatio* from
the 'substantive of the person' *magistratus*. He is equally ready, and
in this he resembles Campanella, to invent terms, as when he in turn
derives from *gubernatio* the corresponding 'substantives of the thing
active and passive' *gubernans res* and *gubernata res*. It must be
remembered however that he is not describing the structure of Latin,
but is deliberately looking for lexical meanings that will receive
formal embodiment in his system of 'real characters'. It is typical of
his age that he cannot do it without an appeal to Latin. In the
establishing of this taxonomy grammatical consignification goes
overboard however, Wilkins seeming to make no real *grammatical*
distinction between his basic substantives 'of a thing', his substantives
'capable of an action' (Campanella's sub-class – e.g. *amator* – of
nouns signifying 'essentiam cum virtute ad actum'), and the actives
and passives 'commonly called verbs' that can be formed from the
latter. These derivations do not rest on differences in form in observed
languages but on the philosophical argument, taken from Campanella,
that every essence must have its corresponding act.[194] It follows that
in the ideal language Wilkins and his fellow-workers are seeking,
every noun ought to have its corresponding verb.

These categories taken from the real world, or rather from

[193] *Essay*, p. 299.
[194] For Campanella every 'actus' is an 'actus essentiae'.

Aristotle's representation of it, are cross-cut by others taken perhaps from Caramuel, as in the division of substantives into concrete (signifying 'the *Ens* or thing it self') and abstract (signifying 'the essence of things').[195] The abstract substantives may, like the concrete ones, be neuter, active or passive: neuters denote the 'naked Essence of a thing' (*deity*), actives 'a proclivity to action') (*amorousness*), passives 'a capacity or fitness for receiving...an action' (*amiableness*).[196] The general view of abstract nouns as denoting 'a proclivity or capacity'[197] coincides with that of Campanella, and noteworthy here is the extent to which Wilkins employs Scholastic philosophy's notion of an inclination or *potentia* towards action. It is more particularly in the treatment of substantives and adjectives that the parallels between Wilkins and Campanella would seem to be more than fortuitous. I do not propose to repeat here the more detailed exposition given in my first volume,[198] but certain close resemblances in the classification of adjectives are worth recalling:

Wilkins	Campanella
Concrete *active* (*calefaciens*)	Participial noun signifying 'essentiam cum *actu* praesenti' (*amans*)
Abstract neuter representing 'a proclivity or capacity' (*caloritativus*)	Participial noun with '*potentiam* ad actum' (*amativus*)
Abstract active (*calefactivus*)	Noun signifying 'essentiam cum possibilitate *activa*' (*calefactivus*)
Abstract passive (*calefactibilis*)	Noun signifying 'essentiam cum possibilitate *passiva*' (*calefactibilis*)

These correspondences not only indicate the extent to which Wilkins has based himself on Campanella. They are also a reminder of how far, for all its seeming modernity, seventeenth-century thought is still

[195] In the pre-1700 grammars I have consulted, I have not found the terms 'concrete' and 'abstract' as descriptions of substantives elsewhere than in Wilkins and Caramuel, and in Cooper's (1685) imitation of Wilkins. John Danes' Latin grammars however (*A Light to Lilie*, 1637 and *Paralipomena*, 1638/9) treat substantives and adjectives as signifying respectively 'rem in concreto' and 'rem in abstracto'. Adjectives and abstract substantives are frequently placed on the same footing in the seventeenth century as indications of 'qualitas'.

[196] Wilkins' attribution of *ens* to the concrete noun and *essentia* to the abstract one runs counter to the modistic grammarians' view that all nouns signify 'per modum entis' by virtue of their possession of *essentia* (cf. Thomas of Erfurt, *Grammatica speculativa*, cap. viii). It also differs from Campanella's definition of all nouns as signifying 'essentiam cuiusque rei'.

[197] *Essay*, p. 299.

[198] Padley, *Grammatical Theory* (1976), pp. 202–4.

conditioned by the entities, essences, acts and potentialities of Scholastic philosophy.

It is perhaps in the treatment of the verb that Wilkins' grammar is most reminiscent of Port-Royal theory, but as we have seen, it was a long-standing practice of medieval logical and grammatical doctrine to regard the verb *to be* as the 'root and foundation' of all other verbs. It is so described by Scaliger,[199] and expansions of the type *legit = est legens* were not only a commonplace of medieval theory, but were not unknown to humanist grammarians.[200] Wilkins' immediate models would no doubt be Campanella, and Caramuel's definition of the verb *to be* as a 'judicativa copula' joining two nouns in a logical proposition. In short, his sources were those available to the Port-Royal grammarians. Thus, when he states that the verb 'ought to have no distinct place amongst Integrals in a Philosophical Grammar', being in reality the copula plus an adjective, he is saying nothing that is not present by implication in centuries of philosophically orientated grammatical theory. What he has done is to take the logical further step, basing himself on the sequence *amo = sum amans*, of also using past-participial and non-participial adjectives as the second component. If the transitive verb *caleficio* can be expanded into *sum calefaciens*, then obviously the intransitive *caleo* is equivalent to *sum calidus*, and the passive *calefio* to *sum calefactus*.[201] The Port-Royal authors similarly treat the intransitive verb *rubet* as an abbreviation of 'is red',[202] and it may be noted that Leibniz' proposed artificial language would treat verbs as the logical equivalent of *to be* plus adjective.[203] Wilkins regards the subject and predicate of a sentence 'as the Logicians do', that is to say as respectively what precedes and what follows the copula.[204] I. Michael notes[205] that Wilkins is the first to use the term 'subject' in an English grammatical work. The logical terms 'subject' and 'predicate' were imported into Latin grammar by Vossius,[206] and the term 'subject' by itself much earlier in Corradus' *De lingua Latina* (1575), but Sanctius is still in 1587 using

[199] Scaliger uses the expression 'fundamentum, sive radix omnium verborum'. Thus also Peter of Spain, *c.*1250 (see Mullally, *The Summulae Logicales of Peter of Spain*, p. xc).

[200] Despauterius for instance has this expansion.

[201] *Essay*, p. 303.

[202] *Grammaire générale et raisonnée*, p. 96: 'Ainsi *rubet* verbe, signifie *est rouge*, enfermant tout ensemble l'affirmation et l'attribut.'

[203] See L. Couturat, *La Logique de Leibniz d'après des documents inédits*, Paris, 1901, p. 70.

[204] *Essay*, p. 304.   [205] *English Grammatical Categories*, p. 484.

[206] E.g. in his *De arte grammatica* (1635).

the medieval grammatical terms 'suppositum' and 'appositum'. The most interesting of the contemporary developments – and of importance because Wilkins' doctrines and his form a single corpus – is Dalgarno's analysis of *amamus* into the four separate logical components subject pronoun, present tense, copula (devoid of tense), and present participle: *nos* + present tense + *sumus amantes*. Here the copula can be replaced by the sign of affirmation *ita* ('thus'), paralleling the Port-Royal view that 'the signification common to all verbs is that of affirmation'.[207] Though for Dalgarno the verb itself is a derivative of *ens* or being, the copula is not, but constitutes 'something distinct from the notion of being'.[208] It is a 'sign of the act of the mind in judging',[209] an independent statement of, and very close parallel to, the Port-Royal doctrine that the verb indicates a mental operation constituting 'un jugement de nostre âme'. Since tense is extrinsic to the judgment of the mind (and here the parallelism between Dalgarno and Wilkins is similarly close), the copula is for the former the 'essential and chiefest part of the proposition',[210] and for the latter 'essential and perpetual' and serving 'for the uniting of the Subject and Predicate'. These to my mind represent independent statements of the Port-Royal position, the identity of views being explained by the fact that both parties used the same sources.[211]

Except in being a subsection of a two-part instead of the usual three-part system of word-classes, Wilkins' 'less principal words, which may be said to consignifie serving to circumstantiate and modifie those Integral words, with which they are joyned',[212] do not differ as a class from other systems (e.g. that of Sanctius) containing consignifying 'particles'. Whereas however the usual systems are in practice a hold-all for adverb, preposition and conjunction, Wilkins classes not only the copula as a particle, but also mood and tense. This is no doubt because in his writing system separate diacritics have to be invented to cater for them. Particles are either *grammatical*, modifying the sense of an 'integral' by means of inflection and

---

[207] *Grammaire générale et raisonnée*. p. 115.

[208] *Ars signorum*, p. 62.

[209] *Ibid.*, p. 63. Cf. Caramuel's use of the term 'copula judicativa'.

[210] *Ibid.*, p. 64.

[211] It has been assumed by some that Wilkins took his ideas on these matters from the Port-Royal authors. Michael for instance (*English Grammatical Categories*, p. 250, n. 1) states that Wilkins has the expansion of *caleo* into *sum calidus* 'from the Port Royal grammar'.

[212] *Essay*, p. 304.

abbreviation, etc., or *transcendental*, varying the primary sense by means of 'tropes' and other devices. This bringing of rhetorical matters within the sway of the particles is also an innovation, indicating Wilkins' desire to render every facet of language use by means of his 'real characters'. A contrast is however made between 'more absolute' particles in syntactic use, such as prepositions, and the 'servile' particles mood and tense. Moods are primary (indicative and imperative) and secondary, the latter being used in 'modal propositions' whose action is considered 'in its causes from which it proceeds either contingently or necessarily'.[213] Contingent proposi- tions are those Englished by *can, could, may, might, will, would,* necessary ones those rendered by *must, ought, shall, should* – 'servile words' obviously in the tradition of Lily's 'signs'. Since substantives can as we have seen be active or passive, it is not surprising that Wilkins claims that they should also, 'according to the true Philosophy of Speech', be marked for tense. Here again, following Campanella,[214] he adds to the existing Latin present *amatio*, a perfect *amavitio* and future *amaturitio*. The paucity of the treatment of articles is perhaps indicative of the extent to which Latin rather than English gram- matical features are regarded by Wilkins as universally applicable. The function of prepositions is 'to joyn Integral with Integral on the same side of the Copula; signifying some respect of Cause, Place, Time, or other circumstance'.[215] The wording here recalls Campan- ella's view of the preposition as consignifying 'respectus et circunstantias',[216] but the attribution of a linking function is already present in Melanchthon's Latin grammar of 1525. Wilkins shows the typical late-seventeenth-century tendency to regard prepositions and adverbs as basically the same word-class, the 'difference between these two parts of speech being so nice, that 'tis hard in some cases to distinguish them'.[217]

Syntax receives scant attention in Wilkins' *Essay*. Interesting however is his treatment of interjections as sentence substitutes used to 'supply the room of some sentence or complex part of it',[218] an approach which according to I. Michael has no precedent in the

---

[213] *Ibid.*, p. 306.
[214] Cf. Salmon, '"Philosophical" Grammar in John Wilkins's "Essay"', pp. 149–50.
[215] *Essay*, p. 309.
[216] That Wilkins has a knowledge of Campanella's work is further shown by his citing of the latter's term *adnomen* for the preposition.
[217] *Essay*, p. 312.   [218] *Ibid.*, p. 308.

grammatical tradition. Michael notes Mark Lewis' reference[219] to the interjection as a 'contracted sentence', but feels that he does not write as if the idea is his own. His source may well be Wilkins' *Essay*, but Michael sees any source beyond this, apart from a possible vague origin in Port-Royal's 'desire men have to abbreviate discourse', as uncertain.[220] The idea was obviously in the air at the time, probably via Wilkins, for it is also present in W. Clare's similar reference in his *Via naturalis* (1688) to 'interjections (which are the brutal language) and are contracted sentences'.[221] I would again suggest that the immediate *theoretical* source of Wilkins' treatment is Campanella, whose interjection functions 'complexe per modum orationis, non per modum vocabuli', that is to say its syntactic province is not the word but the sentence. This approach of Campanella provides a striking parallel with Port-Royal's grouping of the interjection not with those word-classes that signify concepts, but with those that signify 'the form and manner of our thoughts' and hence have a function on the level of the proposition.[222] Wilkins has however an exact precedent in Vossius' 'dictio per se sententiam perficiens',[223] and since he lists Vossius among his few predecessors in 'natural grammar', one need look no further for his source. Its origins can however be traced far back in the Latin tradition, as witness Linacre's reference to Priscian's separation of the interjection from the adverb on the grounds that 'it seems to contain in itself the sense of the verb and to show the full meaning of the disposition of the mind, even if the verb is not added'.[224] Since the verb was regarded as the essential component of the sentence it is easy to see how, on this basis, the interjection came to be looked upon as a sentence substitute.

Though Wilkins' guiding principle is that 'in a Philosophical Language, every word ought in strictness to have but one proper sense and acception', he seems to feel the need to alleviate the aridity of a quasi-mathematical system in which each symbol stands in a rigid one-to-one correspondence with an unvarying concept. It would, he states, 'much promote copiousness and elegancy, if there might be any way so to change and vary the sense of any word, as may with all, leave it free from ambiguity'. It is for this purpose, as indeed for

[219] In his *Essay to Facilitate the Education of Youth*, c.1670, p. 17.
[220] *English Grammatical Categories*, p. 464.
[221] *Via naturalis...or, The Natural Way to Learn the Latin Tongue*, London, 1688.
[222] *Grammaire générale et raisonnée*, p. 30.
[223] *De arte grammatica* (1635).
[224] *De emendata structura* (1524), ff. 31^v–32^r.

the 'abbreviating of language' where necessary, that he introduces his 'transcendental particles' intended to symbolize tropes and other rhetorical figures. But though he tries to cater for such nuances, his grammar (or rather his universal system of notation for transcribing concepts) rests on two assumptions, the second unavowed: that the universe is isomorphic with the categories of Aristotelian philosophy; and that his ideal language will conform in structure to the model of Latin. Though Latin in some respects falls short of the ideal, he takes the categories he finds ready to hand in it, expresses them in philosophical terms taken in large part from Campanella's neo-Scholasticism, and assumes the resultant system to have universal validity. In view of this, B. Shapiro's description of Wilkins' work as a demonstration that seventeenth-century science in England 'was not committed, as is frequently asserted, exclusively to empiricism and experimentation'[225] takes on the appearance of an under-statement. If, as I think is sufficiently shown, Wilkins' major source in the grammatical section of his *Essay* is Campanella, and the latter in turn relies heavily on modistic sources and Scholastic philosophy, it follows that for all his apparent modernity elsewhere Wilkins, in common with much of seventeenth-century intellectual endeavour, is ultimately indebted to those same sources.

Lane and linguistic isomorphism with the universe

Wilkins' grammar both forms part of a larger enterprise aimed at the establishment of an artificial language for universal use by scholars, and is based on a Latin framework. It is however written in the vernacular, and has important implications for the succeeding development of English grammars.[226] Its assumption of isomorphism with the categories of reality could not but reinforce the seventeenth-century tendency to treat grammar in the semantic terms of the signification of *things* and *actions*. An example is found at the very end of the century in A. Lane's *Key to the Art of Letters*, which though superficially in the same line of thought as the Port-Royal Grammar, shows to a greater extent the influence of the British language-planners.

[225] *John Wilkins 1614–1672*, p. 57.
[226] On the contemporary reception of Wilkins' project in a wider context than that of grammar, and on a proposed scheme of revision after his death, see V. Salmon, 'John Wilkins' *Essay* (1668). Critics and continuators', *Historiographia Linguistica*, 1:2 (1974), pp. 147–63.

The pedagogical implications of Lane's work have already been treated above. But his *Rational and Speedy Method of Attaining to the Latin Tongue* (1695) has a wider interest than its customary claim to quicker results than 'several Years Drudgery in the common Road'. It also promises that 'most Logical Terms being in this Treatise explained, the Art of Reasoning may be perfectly learned without much further Trouble'. The first part of this work, containing 'such Precepts as are common to all Languages', is used with very little change as the model for the greater part of the same author's vernacular *Key to the Art of Letters* (1700). Though the mother tongue is to be used in instruction, Lane's aim is to impart not Latin grammar, but grammar as such, a hypostatic grammar, separate from any language to which it may be applied, and which 'polishes and perfects those noble Faculties of Reason and Speech, by which Men are distinguished from Brutes', prescribing those 'unalterable Rules of right Reason, which are the same in all Languages how different soever they be'.[227] To acquire these rules, the pupil must have a sure grasp of logical terminology, so if Lane uses terms hitherto more commonly met with in logics than in grammars, such as *subject*, *predicate* and *object*, it is because he is 'persuaded that Aristotle borrowed them first from Grammar'.[228] Aristotle's logic, indeed, is 'nothing else but Grammar'. This equation of grammar and logic recalls the Port-Royal authors, and whether or not Lane has undergone the influence of the *Grammaire générale et raisonnée*, his view on this particular point certainly coincides with theirs. A similar close parallel is provided by his statement that 'the Art of thinking and speaking are not two, but one Art'.[229] The difficulties he has with those words which are adjectives in lexical meaning but substantives in grammatical function are identical with those experienced by the Port-Royal authors and indeed by medieval grammarians. His solution depends on a long-established tradition of ellipsis, in which since *amicus* implies *vir* and *regia* implies *domus* they are regarded as 'real Adjectives, wherein some Substantive is suppress'd'.[230] But though the Port-Royal Grammar equally treats such expressions as elliptic, it is not necessarily Lane's source. Certainly he makes no attempt to apply their explanation in terms of denotation and connotation, nor to extend it to the similar problem of abstract nouns.

[227] *Key*, preface, pp. vii, x.   [228] *Ibid.*, p. xvii.
[229] *Ibid.*, p. xvii.   [230] *Method*, p. 100.

His treatment is on a simpler basis, whose terminology recalls Wilkins and his model Campanella: 'The same *Quality* is both a Substantive and an Adjective, in different forms; in the *Abstract* (or as it is conceiv'd without the Subject)[231] it is a Substantive; in the *Concrete* (or as it is joined with the Subject or Substantive) it is an Adjective.'[232] This is a somewhat curious employment of the term 'concrete', but the fact that Lane uses it at all would seem to indicate a source in Wilkins.[233] It is also tempting to ascribe Port-Royal origins to the treatment of adverbs of time and place as 'abbreviatures' of prepositional phrases with 'case' functions, *then* for example being seen as a contraction of the 'ablative' expression *at that time*. One should note however the similar treatment, in the Latin section of the *Method*, of the imperative as an 'abbreviature', where the expansion of *audi me* into *jubeo ut audias me* would seem to have a more immediate origin in identical analyses in Sanctius and Linacre. This 'abbreviature' is repeated in the *Key*, with the examples *go thou* and *I command that thou go*. These are logical analyses, and one facet of Lane's linguistic theory requires language to be identical with logic. Here it is of interest to note that R. Burthogge's *Organum vetus et novum* of 1678 makes a distinction between the 'artificial logick' of Aristotle and the 'natural logick of plain and illiterate men'. This latter type of logic is 'universal, a logick of the whole kinde; what in natural logick is reason to one man, is so to all; for all having the same faculties, and using them in the same method, must needs come to the same issue, and by the same principles arrive at the same conclusion'.[234] It is no doubt a 'natural logic' (also a Ramist tenet) of this type that underlies the Port-Royal approach, which rests on a correspondence between on the one hand language, and on the other hand concepts ('the objects of our thoughts') and mental operations ('the manner of our thoughts'). Such a logic has no need to take isomorphism with the real world as its starting-point.

Whereas the Port-Royal Grammar takes *concepts* as its basis, Lane's emphasis however is on *things*, on the direct reflection by language of the universe. If for him there are only four possible parts of speech (substantive, adjective, verb and particle), it is because the *universe* contains only things and actions, and their modes of operation. For

[231] 'Subject' is here a philosophical term, meaning that in which an accident inheres.
[232] *Key*, p. 62.
[233] Also indicative of a debt to Wilkins, and beyond him Campanella, are Lane's substantives 'of the actor or doer' and 'of the action', each with its appropriate ending added to the 'theam of the verb'. [234] p. 43.

the Port-Royal authors it is the *mind* and its operations that are reflected by language, and it is this that provides their justification for equating grammar and logic. Lane's approach is in the spirit of the British language-planners: 'I know there are but four kinds of Words, because there are but four kinds of Things to be signified by Words: for whatsoever is in the whole Universe, is either a Thing, or the Manner of a Thing; the Action of a Thing, or the Manner of an Action.'[235] This quadripartite word-class system, as I. Michael points out, was to become the distinctive feature of the self-consciously anti-Latinizing works of the eighteenth-century movement for grammatical reform.[236] It is in Lane's case patently based on a supposed one-to-one correspondence between words and things, involving the assumption that, in the tradition of Bishop Wilkins and his Royal Society colleagues, language is isomorphic with the universe. One trenchant result of this is that it allows Lane to contrast the adjective (an expression of the manner in which things subsist in the universe) with the substantive (signifying the thing itself), and this contrast allows him, and he is the first English grammarian after Lewis to do so, finally to give the adjective the status of a separate part of speech that had been imminent throughout the seventeenth century. For Lane and the language-planners, however, the isomorphism is assured by an application, not of Burthogge's 'natural' logic, but of Aristotelian logic, that is to say of a ready-made grill of criteria. The various entities in the universe are assumed to fall into the classification prescribed by Aristotle's categories, and it is these categories that language in turn is supposed to reflect.

It is however the firm belief of the grammarians considered in this section that, consonant with their desire to escape empty verbal formularies and regain contact with the real world, language does in fact mirror *things*. In a profound epistemological reversal, it is no longer taken to be a reflection of *thought*. Ultimately, since for Scaliger the intellect is 'as it were the mirror of things', he may be regarded, in spite of the all-pervading Nominalism of the seventeenth century, as a remote ancestor of the language-planners' approach.

[235] *Key*, p. 19; *Method*, p. 1.
[236] *English Grammatical Categories*, p. 271. See also p. 254, where Michael is of the opinion that Lane's fourfold system 'does not seem to have...any single source, though it is most immediately under the influence of the Port Royal grammar of 1660'. Further, p. 510: 'If a source has to be located for this classification it is almost certainly the Port Royal grammar, beyond which stands Wallis, and behind him Gill.' Lane's own philosophical bases for the classification do not however in my view necessarily imply a Port-Royal origin.

CONCLUSION

A. Joly and J. Stéfanini have pointed out the dangers for linguistic historiography of any approach that treats grammatical development as a succession of Copernican revolutions in which now Port-Royal, now Saussure are seen as presenting completely new departures in theory. The history of grammar is on the contrary made up of 'advances and retreats...of movements whose very profundity means they are not directly perceptible, and must be reconstituted by the historian'.[1] It is possible however to see, in the broad sweep of grammatical theory over a period of two centuries, a number of opposing forces at work. Stated in very general terms, the issues resolve themselves into the question of which shall have the upper hand: a formally based, 'structuralist' approach of the Ramist type, or a system in which the notion of a logically orientated underlying content is used to explain seeming anomalies in 'surface' structure. A more profound consequence of the Ramist revolution than its formalist approach is however its maintaining of the three basic 'arts' of communication, logic, rhetoric and grammar in separate compartments, with no possibility of cross-fertilization. A second great movement in the period under consideration consists of the attempt to bring these three back into harmony, and indeed to see logic and the rhetorical figure of ellipse as necessary components of a theory of linguistic description. Further, Ramus' importation of Aristotelianism into grammar-writing as a primary factor in decisions as to its plan and content paved the way for a widespread use of Aristotle's categories by the artificial-language planners in the later part of the seventeenth century. Ramism however proved to be a dead end in linguistic theory. What survived, particularly in Germany, were its spatial analogies and diagrammatic tendencies, above all its fondness for proliferating dichotomies. On the level of grammatical theory Ramus' methods involve a circularity which encloses the

[1] A. Joly and J. Stéfanini (eds.), *La grammaire générale des modistes aux idéologues*, Lille, 1977.

382

linguist within his own system. In Aristotle's own name, Aristotelian categories of thought are rejected as explanations of language structure. And since the emphasis is on morphological markers rather than on relational syntax, any real consideration of the proposition (and hence of the logical relationships implied in it) is absent. More germane to the present study is the fact that Ramus' system, conceived for the morphologically rich Latin language, is inappropriate to the description of the vernaculars. Inevitably, those who tried to apply his various procedures were obliged in practice to temper its rigidity by a 'mixed' approach.

More important than Ramus' linguistic theory, which was destined not to last, is the impact of his methodology, which in this respect provides the impetus for a seventeenth century in which the key word is perhaps 'method'. Basically, the Ramist revolution is a pedagogical one, at a time when in grammar-writing pedagogy and theory are inextricably mixed. More particularly, since Ramism is the basis of the Ratichian reforms, this pedagogical drive lies behind much of German grammatical practice. Using Ramus' methodological framework rather than his linguistic theory, they mingle it with quasi-mystical approaches to the German language that would have been anathema to Ramus himself. Here, the importance of the Lutheran reform in attitudes to the German language can hardly be over-estimated. The drive to take the Bible to the people via the vernacular means that pedagogy is the overriding consideration, a fact which finds expression in the all-embracing educational schemes of Ratke and Comenius. In English pedagogically orientated grammars of the period, the centre of interest (in a situation in which the dialectal problems are less acute than in Germany) is the slow emancipation of the vernacular from Latin. Wallis' and Cooper's interest in the syntactic relationships indicated by prepositions at once show increasing awareness of vernacular structure and (particularly in the case of Cooper's use of a semasiological and philosophical framework) prepare the way for theories of general grammar.

National themes, once implanted, have a way of working themselves out over the centuries, whether it be English empiricism, French rationalism, or German interest in the mystic and the occult. Though German general grammar is again pedagogical in orientation, it combines this element with theories of 'universal harmony' (Ratke) or of a 'Grundrichtigkeit' (Schottel) immanent in the German

Conclusion

language. Here there is a direct line of continuity in German thought about linguistic matters that stretches from the kabbalistic theories of Ickelsamer, via Luther and Schottel down to Wilhelm von Humboldt in the nineteenth century. German general grammar is in this respect idiosyncratic. Elsewhere in Europe two major trends may be observed, according as language is seen as the mirror of *thought* or the mirror of *things*. The first approach, after an absence of theoretically based vernacular works that extends over a century, is that of the Port-Royal Grammar, whose theories result in what Chomsky has called a 'virtual identification of linguistic and mental processes'. The second approach is that of English empiricism, of the artificial-language planners in the orbit of the Royal Society. It is here that the importance of the great Latin grammarians – Linacre, Scaliger, Sanctius, Campanella – is apparent. Norms in linguistic thought are not only matters of preferred usage, but also involve the choice of a theoretical model.

Accordingly, the present study aims to underline the importance of two things. First, vernacular grammars of the sixteenth and seventeenth centuries cannot be usefully considered apart from prior or parallel developments in grammars of Latin. Secondly, any study of the evolution of vernacular linguistic theory must be pan-European, or at least include consideration of the chief works written in the five major languages. Only by proceeding in this way can a relatively complete picture be obtained and distortions be avoided.

BIBLIOGRAPHY

Aarsleff, H. 'Leibniz on Locke on Language', *American Philosophical Quarterly*,
    1 (1964), pp. 165–88
  'The History of Linguistics and Professor Chomsky', *Language*, XLVI
    (1970), pp. 570–85
  '"Cartesian Linguistics": History or Fantasy?', *Language Sciences*, XVII
    (1971), pp. 1–12
Adamson, J. W. *Pioneers of Modern Education 1600–1700 (Contributions to the
    History of Education* III), Cambridge, 1905
Agricola, R. *De inventione dialectica*, Louvain, 1515 (composed *c.*1479)
Aickin, J. *The English Grammar: or, The English Tongue Reduced to Grammatical
    Rules*, London, 1693.
Albertus, L. *Teutsch Grammatick oder Sprachkunst*, Augsburg, 1573
Alsted, J. H. *Artium liberalium ac facultatum omnium systema mnemonicum de modo
    discendi...cum encyclopaediae, artis Lullianae et Cabbalisticae perfectissima
    explicatione*, Frankfurt-am-Main, *c.*1610
  Systema mnemonicum duplex, Frankfurt-am-Main, 1610
  Scientiarum omnium encyclopaedia septem tomis distincta, Herborn, 1630
Alston, R. C. *A Bibliography of the English Language from the Invention of Printing
    to the Year 1800*, Leeds and Bradford, 1965–: I. *English Grammars Written
    in English and English Grammars written in Latin by Native Speakers*, II.
    Polyglot Dictionaries and Grammars
Ames, J. *Typographical Antiquities*, London, 1749
  An augmented ed., London, 1785–90
Anon. *An Examen of the Way of Teaching the Latin Tongue to Little Children, by
    Use alone. Englished out of French*, London, 1669 (Scolar Press facsimile,
    Menston, 1969)
  Animadversions upon Lillie's Grammar, or Lilly Scanned, London, 1625
  *Priscianus nascens or A Key to the Grammar School. Serving much to the exposition
    of the Grammatical Rules of Lilly and the more easie and certain Translating
    of English into Latine*, London, 1660
Arens, H. *Sprachwissenschaft: der Gang ihrer Entwicklung von der Antike bis zur
    Gegenwart* (2nd ed.), Freiburg/Munich, 1969
Aristotle, *Aristotle's Posterior Analytics*, trans. E. S. Bouchier, Oxford, 1901
  De interpretatione, in *The Organon*, ed. H. P. Cooke, London and Cambridge,
    Mass., 1938
Arnauld, A. and Nicole, P., *La Logique ou l'art de penser: contenant...plusieurs
    observations nouvelles propres à former le jugement*, Paris, 1662

Bibliography

Ascham, R. *The Scholemaster Or plaine and perfite way of teachying children, to understand, write, and speake, the Latin tong*, London, 1570, in *Roger Ascham, English Works*, ed. W. A. Wright, Cambridge, 1904, reprinted 1970, pp. 171–302

Ashworth, J. E. 'The Scholastic Background to Locke's Theory of Language', *Progress in Linguistic Historiography*, ed. K. Koerner, Amsterdam, 1980, pp. 59–68

Aventinus (= Johann Turmair) *Grammatica omnium utilissima et brevissima mirabili ordine composita*, Munich, 1512.
Another ed., *Grammatica nova fundamentalis*, Hagenau, 1513

Bacon, F. *The Philosophical Works of Francis Bacon, Reprinted from the Texts and Translations...of Ellis and Spedding*, ed. J. M. Robertson, London, 1905
The Works of Francis Bacon, ed. R. L. Ellis, J. Spedding and D. D. Heath, London, 1887–92

Bacon, R. *Greek Grammar*, ed. E. Nolan and S. A. Hirsch, Cambridge, 1902

Baker, T. *Reflections upon Learning, wherein is shewn the Insufficiency thereof* (2nd ed.), London, 1700 (1st ed. Cambridge, 1699)

Barnard, H. *German Educational Reformers. Memoirs of Eminent Teachers and Educators in Germany; with Contributions to the History of Education from the Fourteenth to the Nineteenth Century*, New York, 1863 (an English version, with added chapters on Pestalozzi, of K. von Raumer's *Geschichte der Pädagogik* (3rd ed.), Stuttgart, 1857)

Bathe, W. *Janua linguarum, sive modus maxime accommodatus, quo patefit aditus ad omnes linguas intelligendas. Industria patrum Hibernorum Societatis Jesu, qui in collegio eiusdem nationis Salmanticae degunt, in lucem edita: et nunc ad linguam Latinam perdiscendam accommodata. In qua totius linguae vocabula, quae frequentiora, et fundamentalia sunt continentur: cum translatione Hispanica eiusdem tractatus*, Salamanca, 1611

Becherer, J. *Theses pro synopsi grammatica*, Erfurt, 1609
Synopsis grammaticae tam Germanicae quam Latinae et Graecae, Mülhausen, 1596

Beck, C. *The Universal Character, by which all the Nations in the World may understand one anothers Conceptions*, London, 1657

Bellin, J. *Syntaxis praepositionum Teutonicarum; oder Deutscher Forwoerter kunstmaessige Fuegung; nebenst forhergesaezter, notwaending erfoderter Abwandelung der Geschlaecht-Naen-Fuernaen-und Mittelwoerter*, Lübeck, 1660

Bembo, P. *Prose nelle quali si ragiona della volgar lingua*, Venice, 1525

Benoist, A. *De la Syntaxe française entre Palsgrave et Vaugelas*, Paris, 1877

Blekastad, M. *Comenius. Versuch eines Umrisses von Leben, Werk und Schicksal des Jan Amos Komensky*, Oslo and Prague, 1969

Bödiker, J. *Johann Bödikers Grundsäze der Teutschen Sprache mit dessen eigenen und Johann Leonhard Frischens vollständigen Anmerkungen. Durch neue zusäze vermehret von Johann Jacob Wippel*, Berlin, 1746 (the first ed. of Bödiker's *Grund-Sätze* was published in Cölln an der Spree in 1690)

Boehme, J. *De signatura rerum: das ist, Bezeichnung aller Dingen, wie das Innere vom Eusseren bezeichnet wird* [Amsterdam?], 1635

Bibliography

Signatura rerum, or the Signature of all things, shewing the Sign and Signification of the severall Forms and Shapes in the Creation, and what the beginning, ruin, and cure of everything is, translated by J. Ellistone, London, 1651

Bolgar, R. R. *The Classical Heritage and its Beneficiaries*, Cambridge, 1954

Brekle, H. E. 'Semiotik und linguistische Semantik in Port-Royal', *Indogermanische Forschungen*, LXIX (1964), pp. 103–21

Grammaire générale et raisonnée ou La Grammaire de Port-Royal, Edition critique, Tome I: Nouvelle impression en facsimilé de la troisième édition de 1676 (Grammatica Universalis I: Meisterwerke der Sprachwissenschaft), Stuttgart-Bad Cannstatt, 1966

'Die Bedeutung der *Grammaire générale et raisonnée* für die heutige Sprachwissenschaft', *Indogermanische Forschungen*, LXXII (1967), pp. 1–21

'The Seventeenth Century', *Current Trends in Linguistics*, XIII (1975), ed. T. A. Sebeok, The Hague and Paris, pp. 277–382

Breva-Claramonte, M. 'Sanctius' *Minerva* of 1562 and the Evolution of his Linguistic Theory', *Historiographia Linguistica*, II:1 (1975), pp. 44–66

'Sanctius's Antecedents: The Beginnings of Transformational Grammar', *Language Sciences*, XLIV (1977), pp. 10–18

'Sanctius's Antecedents (Part 2)', *Language Sciences*, XLV (1977), pp. 6–21

'Logical Structures in Sanctius' Linguistic Theory', *Progress in Linguistic Historiography*, ed. K. Koerner, Amsterdam, 1980, pp. 45–57

Sanctius' Theory of Language. A contribution to the History of Renaissance Linguistics (Amsterdam Studies in the Theory and History of Linguistic Science, ed. E. F. K. Koerner, Series 3, Studies in the History of Linguistics, XXVII), Amsterdam and Philadelphia, 1983

Bright, T. *Characterie, an Arte of shorte, swifte, and secrete writing by Character*, London, 1588

Brinsley, J. *Ludus literarius: or, The Grammar Schoole; Shewing how to Proceede from the First Entrance into Learning, to the Highest Perfection Required in the Grammar Schooles...onely according to our Common Grammar, and Ordinary Classical Authours*, London, 1612

The Posing of the Parts, or, A most Plaine and Easie Way of Examining the Accidence and Grammar, by Questions and Answers (2nd ed.), London, 1615

Brookbank, J. *A Breviate of our King's whole Latin Grammar, Vulgarly called, Lillies*, London, 1660

Brookes, W. 'General Observations Concerning the Art of Teaching', in British Library MS Sloane 1466

'Mr Brookes Method of Teaching Grammar', in British Library MS Sloane 1466

Brücker, J. *Teutsche Grammatic*, Frankfurt-am-Main, 1620

Brunot, F. *Histoire de la langue française des origines à nos jours*, Paris, 1966–

Bullokar, W. *Bref Grammar for English*, London, 1586. (The title page of the Bodleian Copy, Tanner 67, used here, is missing. The Christ Church Oxford copy is complete)

M. Plessow (ed.) *Neudruck von Bullokars...'Bref Grammar for English' 1586, und 'Pamphlet for Grammar' 1586 (Palaestra, LII*, Berlin, 1906, pp. cxliv–lii,

Bibliography

Bibliography

Bibliography

331–88). Follows the Bodleian copy, which is misbound, and hence treats the *Grammar* as two separate works

Buonmattei, B. *Delle Cagioni della lingua toscana* Venice, 1623, consulted in vol. IV of the anonymous *Degli Autori del ben parlare per secolari, e religiose opere diverse*, Venice, 1643

Della Lingua toscana, Florence, 1643 (described on title page as 3rd impression)

Burckhardt, J. *Die Kultur der Renaissance in Italien* (vol. III of *Gesammelte Werke*), Basle, 1955. (The text follows that of the 2nd ed. of 1869)

Burles, E. *Grammatica Burlesa or a New English Grammar Made Plain and Easie for Teacher and Scholar*, London, 1652

Bursill-Hall, G. L. *Speculative Grammars of the Middle Ages. The Doctrine of Partes Orationis of the Modistae*, The Hague and Paris, 1971

Burthogge, R. *Organum vetus et novum. Or, a Discourse of Reason and Truth. Wherein the Natural Logick common to Mankinde is briefly and plainly described*, London, 1678

Bush, D. *The Renaissance and English Humanism*, Toronto, 1939

Busto, B. *Introductiones grammaticas: breves & compendiosas: compuestas por el doctor Busto. Maestro de los pajes de su Majestad*, Salamanca, 1533

Butler, C. *Rhetoricae libri duo*, Oxford, second ed., 1600

The English Grammar, or the Institution of Letters, Syllables, and Words, in the English Tongue, Oxford, 1633

Cadet, F. *Port-Royal Education*, translated from the French (*L'Education à Port-Royal*, Paris, 1887) by A. D. Jones, London, 1898

Campanella, T. *Realis philosophiae epilogisticae partes quatuor*, Frankfurt-am-Main, 1623

Philosophiae rationalis partes quinque. Videlicet: grammatica, dialectica, rhetorica, poetica, historiographia. Pars prima: grammatica, Paris, 1638

Caramuel y Lobkowitz, J. *Praecursor logicus, complectens grammaticem audacem, cuius partes sunt tres, methodica, metrica, critica*, Frankfurt-am-Main, 1654

Carré, M. H. *De Veritate by Edward, Lord Herbert of Cherbury, Translated with an Introduction*, Bristol, 1937

Caspari, F. *Humanism and the Social Order in Tudor England*, Chicago, 1954

Castiglione, B. *Il Libro del Cortegiano*, Venice, 1528 (composed 1513–18)

Cave, T. *The Cornucopian Text. Problems of Writing in the French Renaissance*, Oxford, 1979

Chevalier, J.-C. *Histoire de la syntaxe: naissance de la notion de complément dans la grammaire française (1530–1750)*, Geneva, 1968

'*Grammaire générale* de Port-Royal et tradition grecque. La construction des parties du discours: classement et signification', *La Grammaire générale des modistes aux idéologues*, ed. A. Joly and F. Stéfanini, Lille, 1977, pp. 145–56

Choiseul *Nouvelle et Ancienne Orthographe françoise*, Paris, 1654

Chomsky, N. *Aspects of the Theory of Syntax*, Cambridge, Mass., 1965

Cartesian Linguistics: A Chapter in the History of Rationalist Thought, New York, 1966

Language and Mind, New York, 1968

Bibliography

Cicero M. *Tulli Ciceronis de oratore libri tres, a Philippo Melanchthone scholiis ac notulis quibusdam illustrati*, Paris, 1534

Clajus, J. *Grammatica Germanicae linguae, ex biblis Lutheri Germanicis et aliis eius libris collecta*, s. l., 1578

F. Weidling (ed.), *Die deutsche Grammatik des Johannes Clajus*, Strasbourg, 1894

Clare, W. *Via naturalis... or, the Natural Way to Learn the Latin Tongue*, London, 1688

Clerico, G. 'F. Sanctius: histoire d'une réhabilitation', *La Grammaire générale des modistes aux idéologues*, ed. A. Joly and J. Stéfanini, Lille, 1977, pp. 125–41

Franciscus Sanctius, Minerve ou les causes de la langue latine, Introduction, traduction et notes, Lille, 1982

Colet, J. *Ioannis Coleti theologi, olim decani divi Pauli, aeditio, una cum quibusdam G. Lilii grammatices rudimentis*, Antwerp, 1537

Comenius, J. A. *Janua linguarum reserata sive seminarium linguarum et scientiarum omnium. Hoc est, compendiosa Latinam (et quamlibet aliam) linguam una cum scientiarum artiumque fundamentis, perdiscendi methodus*, [Leszna], 1631

Porta linguarum trilinguis reserata et aperta, sive seminarium linguarum et scientiarum omnium / The Gate of Tongues Unlocked and Opened, or else a Seminarie or Seed-plot of all Tongues and Sciences, London, 1631

Januae linguarum reseratae vestibulum, quo primus ad Latinam linguam aditus tirunculis paratur, Leszna, 1633

Janua linguarum reserata: sive omnium scientiarum et linguarum seminarium. The Gate of Languages Unlocked: or a Seed-plot of all Arts and Tongues. Formerly translated by Tho. Horn: afterwards much corrected and amended by Joh. Robotham (6th ed.), London, 1643

Linguarum methodus novissima, fundamentis didacticis solide superstructa: Latinae linguae exempla realiter demonstrata, Leszna, 1648

Schola pansophica. Hoc est, universalis sapientiae officina, s. l., 1651

Eruditionis scholasticae atrium. Rerum et linguarum ornamenta exhibens, Nuremberg, 1655

Vestibulum linguae Latinae rerum et linguarum fundamenta exhibens...una cum dictionario vestibulari Latino-Anglico, London [1656]

Didactica magna, universale omnes omnia docendi artificium exhibens, in *Opera didactica omnia ab anno 1627 ad 1657 continuata*, Amsterdam, 1657

Opera didactica omnia ab anno 1627 ad 1657 continuata, Amsterdam, 1657

Orbis sensualium pictus. Hoc est omnium fundamentalium in mundo rerum, et in vita actionum, pictura et nomenclatura / Die sichtbare Welt, das ist, aller vornehmsten Welt-Dinge und Lebensverrichtungen, Vorbildung und Benahmung, Nuremberg, 1658

John Amos Commenii Orbis sensualium pictus. Hoc est omnium fundamentalium in mundo rerum, et in vita actionum, pictura et nomenclatura. John Amos Commenius's Visible World. Or, A Picture and Nomenclature of all the Chief Things that are in the World; and of Mens Employments Therein...By Charles Hoole, London, 1659 (Scolar Press facsimile, Menston, 1970)

Ars ornatoria, sive grammatica elegans, et eruditionis scholasticae atrium, rerum et linguarum ornamenta exhibens: cui insuper accessit grammatica eiusdem janualis, London, 1664

Via lucis, vestigata et vestiganda, hoc est rationalis disquisitio, quibus modis intellectualis animorum lux, sapientia, per omnes omnium hominum mentes et gentes...spargi possit, Amsterdam, 1668

The Way of Light by John Amos Comenius Translated into English, with Introduction, ed. E. T. Campagnac, Liverpool, 1938

J. Červenka and V. T. Miškovská (eds.) *De rerum humanarum emendatione consultatio catholica*, Prague, 1966

Cominius, G. H. *De restauratione linguae Latinae*, 1533, ed. C. Mattheeussen, Leipzig, 1978

Constantinescu, I. 'John Wallis (1616–1703): A Reappraisal of his Contribution to the Study of English', *Historiographia Linguistica*, 1:3 (1974), pp. 297–311

Cooper, C. *Grammatica linguae Anglicanae. Peregrinis eam addiscendi pernecessaria, nec non Anglis praecipue scholis, plurimum profutura*, London, 1685

J. D. Jones (ed.), *Coopers Grammatica Linguae Anglicanae* (1685) (*Neudrücke Frühneuenglischer Grammatiken herausgegeben von R. Brotanek*, v), Halle, 1911

The English Teacher, London, 1687 (reprinted by Bertil Sundby, *Lund Studies in English*, XXII, 1953)

Corradus, Q. M. *De lingua Latina*, Bologna, 1575

Correas, G. Conde de la Viñaza (ed.), *Arte grande de la lengua castellana compuesta en 1626 por el Maestro Gonzalo Correas*, Madrid, 1903

E. A. García (ed.), *Gonzalo Correas Arte de la Lengua Española Castellana edición prólogo* (= *Revista de Filología Española*, anejo LVI), Madrid, 1954

Trilingue de tres artes de las tres lenguas castellana, latina, i griega, todas en romanze, Salamanca, 1627

Couturat, L. *La Logique de Leibniz d'après des documents inédits*, Paris, 1901

Cram, D. F. 'George Dalgarno on "Ars signorum" and Wilkins' "Essay"', *Progress in Linguistic Historiography*, ed. K. Koerner, Amsterdam, 1980, pp. 113–21

Croce, B. *Estetica come scienza dell'espressione e linguistica generale*, Milan, 1902

Dalgarno, G. *Ars signorum, vulgo character universalis et lingua philosophica*, London, 1661

Danes, J. *A Light to Lilie. Being an Easie Method for the Better Teaching and Learning of the Grounds of the Latine Tongue*, London, 1637

Paralipomena orthographiae, etymologiae, prosodiae, London, 1638/9 (first title-page dated 1639, second 1638)

Daube, A. *Der Aufstieg der Muttersprache im deutschen Denken des 15. und 16. Jahrhunderts*, Frankfurt-am-Main, 1940

'Die Anfänge einer deutschen Sprachlehre im Zusammenhang deutscher Geistesgeschichte', *Zeitschrift für deutsche Bildung*, XVIII (1942), pp. 19–37

De Mott, B. 'The Sources and Development of John Wilkins' Philosophical Language', *Journal of English and Germanic Philology*, LVII (1958), pp. 1–13

Descartes, R. *Discours de la méthode pour bien conduire sa raison, et chercher la vérité dans les sciences*, Leyden, 1637

Bibliography

Principia philosophiae, Amsterdam, 1644

Notae in programma quoddam, Amsterdam, 1648

Meditations on the First Philosophy, translated by E. S. Haldane and G. R. T. Ross, in *Great Books of the Western World*, xxxi, ed. R. M. Hutchins, Chicago, 1952

Rules for the Direction of Mind translated by E. S. Haldane and G. R. T. Ross, in *Great Books of the Western World*, xxxi, ed. R. M. Hutchins, Chicago, 1952

Oeuvres philosophiques (1618–1637), ed. F. Alquié, Paris, 1963–

Notes Directed Against a Certain Programme, in *The Philosophical Works of Descartes*, translated by E. S. Haldane and G. T. Ross, Cambridge, 1967

Despauterius, J. *Rudimenta* (2nd ed.), Paris, 1527 (first ed., 1514)

Commentarii grammatici, Paris 1537/8 (dated 1537 on title-page, but date of printing given at end of vol. as 1538)

De Wulf, M. *Medieval Philosophy Illustrated from the System of Thomas Aquinas*, Cambridge, Mass., 1922

Digby, E. *De duplici methodo libri duo, unicam P. Rami methodum refutantes*, London, 1580

Dobson, E. J. *English Pronunciation 1500–1700*, (2nd ed.), Oxford, 1968

Donzé, R. *La Grammaire générale et raisonnée de Port-Royal: Contribution à l'histoire des idées grammaticales en France*, Berne, 1967

Droseé, J. *Grammaticae quadrilinguis partitiones*, Paris, 1544

Du Bellay, J. *La Deffence et illustration de la langue francoyse* (Paris, 1549), ed. H. Chamard, Paris, 1948

Dubois, J. (Jacobus Sylvius Ambianus), *In linguam Gallicam isagωge, una cum eiusdem Grammatica Latino-Gallica*, Paris, 1531

Duhamel, P. A. 'The Logic and Rhetoric of Peter Ramus', *Modern Philology*, xlvi (1949), pp. 163–71

Elyot, T. *The Boke named the Governour*, London, 1531. (There is a Scolar Press facsimile, Menston, 1970)

Erasmus, D. *Absolutissimus de octo orationis partium constructione libellus* (an emendation of Lily, with a preface by Colet), Strasbourg, 1515

Estienne, H. *Traité de la conformité du language françois avec le grec*, Geneva, 1565

Evelyn, J. 'The English Grammer', c.1650 (British Library Add. MS 15950, ff. 94–8)

Fage, R. *Compendium of the Art of Logick and Rhetorick in the English Tongue, Containing all that P. Ramus, Aristotle, and Others have Writ Thereon*, London, 1651

Faithfull, R. G. Review of P. A. Verburg, *Taal en Functionaliteit*, Wageningen, 1952, in *Archivum Linguisticum*, vii:2 (1955), pp. 144–50

Fechner, H. *Vier seltene Schriften des sechzehnten Jahrhunderts...mit einer bisher ungedruckten Abhandlung über Valentinus Ickelsamer von Dr. F. L. Karl Weigand*, Berlin, 1882

Finck, C. and Helwig, C. *Grammatica Latina* (2nd ed.), Giessen, 1615

Bibliography

Fischer, K. *Francis Bacon of Verulam: Realistic Philosophy and its Age*, translated from the German by J. Oxenford, London, 1857
Descartes and his School (3rd ed.), translated by J. P. Gordy, London, 1887
Fleury, C. *Traité du choix et de la méthode des études*, Paris, 1686
Formigari, L. *Linguistica ed empirismo nel seicento inglese*, Bari, 1970
Foucault, B. 'La grammaire générale de Port-Royal', *Langages*, VII (1967), pp. 7–15
Foucault, M. *Les Mots et les choses: une archéologie des sciences humaines*, Paris, 1966
Fouquelin (or Foclin), A. *La Rhetorique francoise d'Antoine Foclin de Chauny en Vermandois*, Paris, 1555
Fraunce, A. *The Lawiers Logike, exemplifying the Praecepts of Logike by the Practice of the Common Lawe*, London, 1588
Frischlin, N. *Quaestionum grammaticarum libri* IIX (? = VIII), Venice, 1584
Fromant, Abbé *Réflexions sur les fondemens de l'art de parler, pour servir d'éclaircissements et de supplément à la Grammaire générale et raisonnée*, Paris, 1756
Funke, O. 'Zum Weltsprachenproblem in England im 17. Jahrhundert', *Anglistische Forschungen*, LXIX (1929), pp. i–v, 1–163
'William Bullokars *Bref Grammar for English* (1586). Ein Beitrag zur Geschichte der frühneuenglischen Grammatik', *Anglia*, LXII (1938), pp. 116–37
'Ben Jonsons *English Grammar* (1640)', *Anglia*, LXIV (1940), pp. 117–34
'Die Frühzeit der englischen Grammatik. Die humanistisch-antike Sprachlehre und der national-sprachliche Gedanke im Spiegel der frühneuenglischen Grammatiker von *Bullokar* (1586) bis *Wallis* (1653). Die grammatische Systematik und die Klassifikation der Redeteile', *Schriften der literarischen Gesellschaft Bern*, IV (1941), pp. 1–91
'On the Sources of John Wilkins' Philosophical Language (1668)', *English Studies*, XL (1959), pp. 208–14
García, C. *Contribución a la historia de los conceptos gramaticales: la aportación del Brocense*, Madrid, 1960
Geissler, H. *Comenius und die Sprache* (*Pädagogische Forschungen, Veröffentlichungen des Comenius-Instituts*, x), Heidelberg, 1959
Giambullari, P. *De la Lingua che si parla e scrive in Firenze*, Florence, 1551
Gill, A. *Logonomia Anglica. Qua gentis sermo facilius addiscitur* (2nd ed.), London, 1621. (There is a Scolar Press, Menston, 1968, facsimile of this edition)
Gilson, E. *The Philosophy of St Thomas Aquinas. Authorised translation from the third revised edition of 'Le Thomisme' by Etienne Gilson... Translated by Edward Bullough*, Cambridge, 1924
Girbert, J. *Die Deutsche Grammatica oder Sprachkunst*, Muelhausen in Dueringen, 1653
Godfrey, R. G. 'Late Medieval Linguistic Meta-Theory and Chomsky's Syntactic Structures', *Word*, XXI:2 (1965), pp. 251–6
Granger, T. *Syntagma Grammaticum, Or an easie and methodicall explanation of Lillie's Grammar*, London, 1616

Bibliography

Syntagma logicum, or The Divine Logike, Serving Especially for the Use of Divines in the Practice of Preaching, London, 1620

Grantham, T. *The Brainbreakers-Breaker: or, The Apologie of Thomas Grantham, for his Method in Teaching*, London, 1644

Graves, F. P. *Petrus Ramus and the Educational Reformation of the Sixteenth Century*, New York, 1912

A History of Education during the Middle Ages and the Transition to Modern Times, New York, 1914

Grawer, Brendel, Walter and Wolf *Didactica oder Lehrkunst Wolfgangi Ratichii*, Magdeburg, 1614 (authors not named in title-page) (reproduced in P. Stötzner, *Ratichianische Schriften*, I, Leipzig, 1892)

Greaves, P. *Grammatica Anglicana, praecipue quatenus a Latina differt, ad unicam P. Rami methodum concinnata. In qua perspicue docetur quicquid ad huius linguae cognitionem requiritur. Authore P. G.*, Cambridge, 1594 (only known copy British Library 7479)

O. Funke (ed.), *Grammatica Anglicana von P. Gr. (1594) Nach dem Exemplar des Britischen Museums herausgegeben und mit einer Einleitung versehen (Wiener Beiträge zur englischen Philologie, LX)*, Vienna and Leipzig, 1938

Green, V. H. H. *A History of Oxford University*, London, 1974

Guarino Veronese [Regulae grammaticales] beginning '[P]artes grammaticae sunt quattuor. videlicet littera, syllaba, dictio et oratio', s. l., 1480? (British Library IA 30276. The authorship is ascribed by the British Library catalogue)

Gueintz, C. *Deutscher Sprachlehre Entwurf*, Köthen, 1641

Guyot, T. *Billets que Cicéron a écrits tant à ses amis communs qu'à Attique son ami particulier (Traduits par Le Bachelier)*, Paris, 1667

Haine, W. *Lillies Rules Construed*, London, 1642

Hankamer, P. *Die Sprache, ihr Begriff und ihre Deutung im sechzehnten und siebzehnten Jahrhundert. Ein Beitrag zur Frage der literaturhistorischen Gliederung des Zeitraums*, Bonn, 1927

Hartlib, S. 'The Progresse in Teaching', British Library MS Sloane 1466

Hayne, T. *Grammatices Latinae compendium*, London, 1640

Hearne, T. *The Works of Thomas Hearne*, London, 1810

Helwig, C. *Libri didactici grammaticae universalis, Latinae, Graecae, Hebraicae, Chaldicae/Sprachkünste: I. Allgemaine welche das jenige so allen Sprachen gemein ist in sich begreifft. II. Lateinische. III. Hebraische*, Giessen, 1619

Helwig, C. and Jung, J. *Kurtzer Bericht von der Didactica, oder Lehrkunst Wolfgangi Ratichii*, Frankfurt-am-Main, 1613

Herbert of Cherbury, Baron *De Veritate prout distinguitur a revelatione, a verisimili, a possibili, et a falso*, s. l., 1624

M. H. Carré (ed.), *De Veritate by Edward, Lord Herbert of Cherbury Translated with an Introduction*, Bristol, 1937

Herford, C. H. and Simpson, P., *Ben Jonson*, Oxford, 1925

Hewes, J. *A Perfect Survey of the English Tongue, Taken According to the Use and Analogie of the Latine*, London [1624]

Hexham, H. *A Copious English and Netherduytch Dictionarie...as also a*

393

compendious Grammar for the Instruction of the Learner, Rotterdam, 1660 (1st ed., 1648)

Hobbes, T. *Computatio sive logica*, contained in *Elementorum philosophiae, Sectio prima, De corpore, in Thomae Hobbes Malmesburiensis Opera philosophica quae Latine scripsit*, ed. W. Molesworth, I, London, 1839; v, London, 1845; *Elements of Philosophy: I. Concerning Body*, in The English Works of Thomas Hobbes, ed. W. Molesworth, I, London, 1839

Leviathan: I. of Man, in *The English Works of Thomas Hobbes*, ed. W. Molesworth, III, London, 1840

Leviathan or the Matter, Forme and Power of a Commonwealth Ecclesiastical and Civil, ed. M. Oakeshott, Oxford [1946] (1st ed., 1651)

Hoole, C. *The Latine Grammar Fitted for the Use of Schools/Grammatica Latina in usum scholarum adornata*, London, 1651

A New Discovery of the Old Art of Teaching Schoole, London, 1660

Horman, W. *Vulgaria*, London, 1519

Howell, A. C. '*Res et verba*: Words and Things', *ELH A Journal of English Literary History*, XIII (1946), pp. 131–42

Howell, J. *Epistolae Ho-Elianae ... Familiar Letters domestic and forren*, London, 1645

A New English Grammar Rendred into Spanish/Gramatica inglesa rendida en castellano, London, 1662

Howell, W. S. 'Ramus and English Rhetoric: 1574–1681', *Quarterly Journal of Speech*, XXXVII (1951), pp. 308–10

Logic and Rhetoric in England, 1500–1700, Princeton, 1956

Hubka, K. 'Caramuelova "Grammatica audax"', *Listy Filologické*, C (1977), pp. 16–29

'On some Rhetoric-Logic Topoi in Comenius' Pansophia Christiana', *Listy Filologické*, CI (1978), pp. 94–105

Humboldt, W. von *Über die Verschiedenheit des menschlichen Sprachbaues*, Berlin, 1836

Hume, A. *Prima elementa grammaticae in usum juventutis Scoticae*, Edinburgh, 1612

Grammatica nova in usum juventutis Scoticae ad methodum revocata, Edinburgh, 1612

Schola grammatica ad singula capita grammaticae ... accommodata (bound in same volume as preceding work)

Of the Orthographie and Congruitie of the Britan Tongue; A Treates, noe shorter then necessarie, for the Schooles [1617?], ed. H. B. Wheatley, Early English Text Society, v, London, 1865

Huth, G. 'Jacques Dubois Verfasser der ersten latein-französischen Grammatik (1531)', *Programm des Königl. Marienstifts-Gymasiums zu Stettin*, Stettin, 1899, pp. 3–21

Ickelsamer, V. *Ein Teütsche Grammatica*, Augsburg?, *c*.1534, reprinted in H. Fechner, *Vier seltene Schriften*, Berlin, 1882

Ising, E. *Wolfgang Ratkes Schriften zur deutschen Grammatik (1612–1630)*, Berlin, 1959 (= *Deutsche Akademie der Wissenschaften zu Berlin, Veröffentlichung der Sprachwissenschaftlichen Kommission*, III)

Bibliography

Jacob, A. *Genèse de la pensée linguistique*, Paris, 1973

Jellinek, M. H. 'Zur Geschichte der Verdeutschung der grammatischen Kunstwörter', *Zeitschrift für deutsche Wortforschung*, XIII (1911–12), p. 83
Geschichte der neuhochdeutschen Grammatik von den Anfängen bis auf Adelung, Heidelberg, 1913–14

Jespersen, O. *The Philosophy of Grammar*, New York, 1965 (1st ed., 1924)

Joly, A. *F. Thurot, Tableau des progrès de la science grammaticale* (*Discours préliminaire à 'Hermes'*), Bordeaux, 1970
'La linguistique cartésienne: une erreur mémorable', *La grammaire générale des modistes aux idéologues*, ed. A. Joly and F. Stéfanini, Lille, 1977, pp. 165–99
Review of G. A. Padley, *Grammatical Theory in Western Europe 1500–1700: The Latin Tradition*, Cambridge, 1976, in *Historiographia Linguistica*, IV:3 (1977), pp. 392–401

Joly, A. and Stéfanini, J. (eds.), *La Grammaire générale des modistes aux idéologues*, Lille, 1977

Jones, B. *Herm'aelogium: or, An Essay at the Rationality of the Art of Speaking. As a Supplement to Lillie's Grammer, Philosophically, Mythologically, & Emblematically*, London, 1659

Jones, R. F. 'Science and Language in England of the Mid-Seventeenth Century', *Journal of English and Germanic Philology*, XXXI (1932) (reprinted in *The Seventeenth Century*, Stanford, 1951, pp. 143–60)
'Science and Criticism in the Neo-Classical Age of English Literature', *Journal of the History of Ideas*, I (1940) (reprinted in *The Seventeenth Century*, Stanford, 1951, pp. 41–74)
The Seventeenth Century: Studies in the History of English Thought and Literature from Bacon to Pope, by Richard Foster Jones and Others Writing in His Honor, Stanford, 1951
The Triumph of the English Language. A Survey of Opinions Concerning the Vernacular from the Introduction of Printing to the Restoration, London, 1953

Jonson, B. *The English Grammar*, 1640, in *The Workes of Ben Jonson*, London, 1640–1, II, 31–84. (There is a Scolar Press facsimile, Menston, 1972)
The English Grammar, ed. A. V. Waite, New York, 1909
S. Gibson (ed.), *The English Grammar made by Ben Jonson for the Benefit of all Strangers Out of His Observations of the English Language Now Spoken and in Use*, Lanston Monotype Corporation facsimile, London, 1928

Kaltz, B. 'Christoph Helwig, ein vergessener Vertreter der allgemeinen Grammatik in Deutschland', *Historiographia Linguistica*, V:3 (1978), pp. 227–35

Katz, D. S. 'The Language of Adam in Seventeenth-Century England', *History and Imagination. Essays in Honour of H. R. Trevor-Roper*, ed. H. Lloyd-Jones, V. Pearl and B. Worden, London, 1981, pp. 132–45
Philo-Semitism and the Readmission of the Jews to England 1603–1655, Oxford, 1982

Keil, H. *Grammatici Latini*, Leipzig, 1857–74, I–IV (reprinted Hildesheim, 1961)

Kelly, L. G. *Twenty-five Centuries of Language Teaching*, Rowley, Mass., 1969

Bibliography

Kemp, J. A. *John Wallis's Grammar of the English Language with an introductory grammatico-physical Treatise on Speech (or on the formation of all speech sounds). A new edition with translation and commentary*, London, 1972

Kirkby, J. *A New English Grammar*, London, 1746

Kneale, W. and M. *The Development of Logic*, Oxford, 1962

Knowlson, J. *Universal Language Schemes in England and France 1600–1800*, Toronto and Buffalo, 1975

Koerner, E. F. K. *Towards a Historiography of Linguistics: Selected Essays (Amsterdam Studies in the Theory and History of Linguistic Science*, ed. E. F. K. Koerner, Series 3, xix), Amsterdam, 1978

(ed.) *Progress in Linguistic Historiography. Papers from the international conference on the history of the language sciences (Ottawa, 28–31 August 1978) (Amsterdam Studies in the Theory and History of Linguistic Science*, Series 3, xx), Amsterdam, 1980

Kohonen, V. 'On the Development of an Awareness of English Syntax in Early (1500–1660) Descriptions of Word Order by English Grammarians, Logicians and Rhetoricians', *Neuphilologische Mitteilungen* (1978), pp. 44–58

Krause, G. *Wolfgang Ratichius, oder Ratke im Lichte seiner und der Zeitgenossen Briefe, und als Didacticus in Cöthen und Magdeburg*, Leipzig, 1872

Kretzmann, N. 'The Main thesis of Locke's Semantic Theory', *History of Linguistic Thought and Contemporary Linguistics*, ed. H. Parret, Berlin and New York, 1976, pp. 331–47

Kromayer, J. *Deutsche Grammatica, zum neuen Methodo, der Jugend zum besten, zugerichtet*, Weimar, 1625 (1st ed. 1618)

Kukenheim, L. *Contributions à l'histoire de la grammaire italienne, espagnole et française à l'époque de la Renaissance*, Amsterdam, 1932 (reprinted Utrecht, 1974)

Contributions à l'histoire de la grammaire grecque, latine et hébraïque à l'époque de la Renaissance, Leyden, 1951

Esquisse historique de la linguistique française et de ses rapports avec la linguistique générale, Leyden, 1962

Kvačala, J. *Die Pädagogische Reform des Comenius in Deutschland bis zum Ausgange des XVII. Jahrhunderts*, ii (= *Monumenta Germaniae Paedagogica*, xxxii), Berlin, 1904

Labbé, P. *Grammaire de la langue universelle des missions et du commerce* (2nd ed.), Paris, undated. (A Latin edition appeared in Paris in 1663)

Lakoff, R. Review of C. Lancelot and A. Arnauld, *Grammaire générale et raisonnée*, ed. H. Brekle, Stuttgart-Bad Cannstatt, 1966, in *Language*, xlv (1969), pp. 343–64

Lambley, K. *The Teaching and Cultivation of the French Language during Tudor and Stuart Times*, Manchester, 1920

Lamy, B. *L'Art de parler*, Paris, 1676

The Art of Speaking: Written in French by Messieurs du Port Royal: in pursuance of a former Treatise, intituled, The Art of Thinking, London, 1676

Lancelot, C. *Nouvelle Méthode pour apprendre facilement et en peu de temps la langue latine*, Paris, 1644; 3rd ed., Paris, 1654; 5th ed., Paris, 1656; 8th ed. (with A. Arnauld and P. Nicole), Paris, 1681

(With A. Arnauld and P. Nicole) *Nouvelle Méthode pour apprendre facilement la langue grecque*, Paris, 1655: 2nd ed., Paris, 1656

(With A. Arnauld) *Grammaire générale et raisonnée, contenant les fondemens de l'art de parler...les raisons de ce qui est commun à toutes les langues, et les principales différences qui s'y recontrent; et plusieurs remarques nouvelles sur la langue françoise*, Paris, 1660

Nouvelle Méthode pour apprendre facilement et en peu de temps la langue espagnole, Paris, 1660

Nouvelle Méthode pour apprendre facilement et en peu de temps la langue italienne, Paris, 1660. These last two works were published under Lancelot's pseudonym 'D. T.' or 'de Trigny'

Land, S. K. *From Signs to Propositions: The Concept of Form in Eighteenth-Century Semantic Theory*, London, 1974

Lane, A. *A Rational and Speedy Method of Attaining to the Latin Tongue*, London, 1695

A Key to the Art of Letters: or, English a Learned Language, Full of Art, Elegancy and Variety, London, 1700

Lara, F. de *Diálogos de las cosas notables de Granada y lengua española*, Seville, 1603

Lattmann, J. *Ratichius und die Ratichianer*, Göttingen, 1898

Leech, J. *A Booke of Grammar Questions, for the helpe of yong Scholars, to further them in the understanding of the Accidence, and Lilies verses* (4th ed.), London, 1650

Lehnert, M. 'Die Grammatik des englischen Sprachmeisters John Wallis (1616–1703)', *Sprache und Kultur der germanischen und romanischen Völker: Anglistische Reihe*, XXI (1936), pp. i–ix, 1–156

Leibniz, G. W. von *De arte combinatoria* (1666), in C. J. Gerhardt (ed.), *Die philosophischen Schriften von Gottfried Wilhelm Leibniz*, IV, Berlin, 1880, pp. 27–104

Nouveaux essais sur l'entendement humain (*avant-propos et livre premier*), ed. E. Boutroux, Paris, 1886 (1704; first published 1765)

Leroy, M. *Les Grands Courants de la linguistique moderne*, Brussels and Paris (2nd ed.), 1971

Lewis, M. *An Apologie for a Grammar Printed about Twenty Years Since, by M. Lewis and Reprinted for the Use of a Private School at Tottenham High Cross*, in [*Institutio?*] *grammaticae puerilis; or the Rudiments of the Latin and Greek Tongues*, London?, 1671?

An Essay to Facilitate the Education of Youth, by bringing down the Rudiments of Grammar to the Sense of Seeing, in [*Institutio?*] *grammaticae puerilis; or the Rudiments of the Latin and Greek Tongues*, London?, 1671?

Plain, and short Rules for Pointing Periods, and Reading Sentences Grammatically, with the great Use of them, in [*Institutio?*] *grammaticae puerilis; or the Rudiments of the Latin and Greek Tongues*, London?, 1671?

Vestibulum technicum: or, An Artificial Vestibulum wherein the sense of Janua linguarum is contained, London, 1675

397

Bibliography

Lily, W. *A Shorte Introduction of Grammar*, London, 1549

    A Short Introduction of Grammar, London, 1557. (The 1549 edition I have used, which is unpaginated, is imperfect, beginning on what is p. 8 in the 1557 edition and ending on what is p. 116 in that edition. Otherwise, apart from Edward VI's foreword to the 1549 edition, the two are identical

Linacre, T. *Rudimenta grammatices Thomae Linacri ex Anglico sermone in Latinum versa, interprete Georgio Buchanano Scoto*, Paris, 1533 (1st ed., c.1512)

    De emendata structura Latini sermonis libri sex, London, 1524

Livet, C.-L. *La Grammaire française et les grammairiens du XVIe siècle*, Paris, 1859

Lobstein, P. *Petrus Ramus als Theologe*, Strasbourg, 1878

Locke, J. *An Essay Concerning Humane Understanding*, London, 1690 (Scolar Press edition, Menston, 1970)

    Some Thoughts Concerning Education, London, 1693

Lodwick, F. *A Common Writing: Whereby Two, Although not Understanding the One the Others Language...May Communicate Their Minds One to Another*, s. l., 1647

    The Ground-Work or Foundation Laid (or so intended) for the Framing of a New Perfect Language...By a Well-Willer to Learning, s. l., 1652

Loiseau, A. *Etude historique et philologique sur Jean Pillot et les doctrines grammaticales du XVIe siècle*, Paris, 1866

Lull, R. *R. Lull. ars magna, generalis et ultima*, ed. B. la Vinheta, Lyons, 1517

Luther, M. *An die Radherrn aller stedte deutsches lands: das sie Christliche Schulen auffrichten und hallten sollen*, Wittenberg, 1524

    Tischreden oder Colloquia Doct. Martin Luthers, ed. J. Aurifaber, Eisleben, 1566

McColley, G. 'John Wilkins – a precursor of Locke', *Philosophical Review*, XLVII (1938)

McIntosh, M. M. C. 'The Phonetic and Linguistic Theory of the Royal Society School, from Wallis to Cooper', unpublished Oxford University B. Litt. thesis, 1956

Madera, G. L. *Discurso de la certidumbre de las reliquias descubiertas en Granada desde el año 1588 hasta el de 1598*, Granada, 1611

Martinet, A. *Eléments de linguistique générale (Collection Armand Colin no. 349)*, Paris, 1960

Meigret, L. *Le Tretté de la grammere françoeze*, Paris, 1550

Melanchthon, P. *De rhetorica libri tres*, Wittenberg, 1519

    Grammatica Latina ab auctore nuper aucta et recognita, Paris, 1527 (1st ed., 1525)

    Syntaxis, recens nata et edita, Paris, 1528 (1st ed., 1526)

Menéndez y Pelayo, M. *Obras completas*, ed. E. Sánchez, XXXVIII, Reyes, 1947

Michael, I. *English Grammatical Categories and the Tradition to 1800*, Cambridge, 1970

Miège, G. *A New French Grammar; or, a New Method for Learning the French Tongue*, London, 1678

    The English Grammar, setting forth the Grounds of the English Tongue; and particularly its Genius in making Compounds and Derivatives...With a Prefatory

Bibliography

Discourse about the Original, and Excellency of the English Tongue...A Necessary Work in general for all Persons desirous to understand the Grounds and Genius of the English, and very proper to prepare Young Men for the Latine Tongue (2nd ed.), London, 1691 (1st ed., 1688)

Miel, J. 'Pascal, Port-Royal and Cartesian linguistics', *Journal of the History of Ideas*, xxx (1969), pp. 261–71

Migliorini, B. *The Italian Language*, abridged and recast by T. Gwynfor Griffith, London, 1966 (reprinted 1974; first published in Florence, 1960, under the title *Storia della lingua italiana*)

Miles, K. *The Strong Verb in Schottel's Ausführliche Arbeit von der teutschen Haubt Sprache*, Philadelphia, 1933

Miller, P. G. E. *The New England Mind: The Seventeenth Century*, New York, 1939

Milton, J. *Artis logicae plenior institutio ad P. Rami methodum concinnata*, London, 1672

Miškovská, V. T. 'Komenský ve vývoji gramatikych teorií' (review of G. A. Padley, *Grammatical Theory in Western Europe 1500–1700*, Cambridge, 1976), *Studia Comeniana et historica*, xiii:vi (1976)

'Comenius (Komensky) on Lexical Symbolism in an Artificial Language', *Philosophy*, xxxvii (1962), pp. 238–44

Morel, L. *De Johannis Wallisii Grammatica linguae Anglicanae et Tractatu de loquela*, Paris, 1895

Moulin, P. de *Eléments de logique*, Sedan, 1621 (trans. as *The Elements of Logic* by N. De-Lawne, London, 1624)

Mulcaster, R. *The First Part of the Elementarie which entreateth chefelie of the Right Writing of our English Tung*, London, 1582 (Scolar Press facsimile, Menston, 1970)

Mullally, J. P. *The Summulae Logicales of Peter of Spain* (*University of Notre Dame Publications in Mediaeval Studies*), Notre Dame, Indiana, 1945

Nancel, N. de *Petri Rami vita*, Paris, 1599 (printed in *Declinationum liber*, Paris, 1600)

Nebrija, A. de *Ars nova grammatices*, Lyons, 1509 (first published as *Introductiones Latinae*, Salamanca, 1481)

Another ed., *Grammatica Antonii Nebrissensis*, Saragossa, 1533

Gramatica de la lengua castellana, Salamanca, 1492, in E. Walberg (ed.), *Gramatica Castellana. Reproduction phototypique de l'édition princeps (1492)*, Halle, 1909

Neumarck, G. *Poetische Tafeln, oder Gründliche Anweisung zur Teutschen Verskunst*, Jena, 1667

Newton, J. *School Pastime for Young Children: or the rudiments of grammar, in an easie and delightful method, for the teaching of children to read English distinctly, and to write it truly*, London, 1669

Ockham, William of *Quotlibeta septem*, Strasbourg, 1491

Ogle, R. 'Two Port-Royal Theories of Natural Order', *Progress in Linguistic Historiography*, ed. K. Koerner, Amsterdam, 1980, pp. 102–12

Olearius, T. *Deutsche Sprachkunst...Sampt angehengten newen methodo, die Lateinische Sprache geschwinde und mit Lust zu lernen*, Halle, 1630

Bibliography

Ölinger, A. *Underricht der Hoch Teutschen Spraach : Grammatica seu institutio verae Germanicae linguae*, Strasbourg, 1574

O'Mahony, S. F. 'The Preface to William Bathe's *Janua linguarum* (1611)', *Historiographia Linguistica*, VIII:1 (1981), pp. 131–64

Ong, W. J. *Ramus and Talon Inventory. A short-title inventory of the published works of Peter Ramus (1515–1572) and of Omer Talon (ca. 1510–1562)*, Cambridge, Mass. 1958

   Ramus : Method, and the Decay of Dialogue. From the Art of Discourse to the Art of Reason. Cambridge, Mass., 1958

Padley, G. A. 'Grammatical Theory in Western Europe 1500–1700. A consideration of the theories of the Latin grammarians, and of their application by the vernacular grammarians of English and French', Oxford doctoral thesis, 1970, pp. 252–458

   Grammatical Theory in Western Europe 1500–1700: the Latin Tradition, Cambridge, 1976

   'L'importance de Thomas Linacre (env. 1460–1524) comme source dans l'évolution des théories grammaticales en Europe au XVIe et au XVIIe siècles', *Langues et Linguistique*, Université Laval, Quebec, VIII:2 (1982), pp. 17–56

   'La norme dans la tradition des grammairiens', *La norme linguistique*, ed. E. Bédard and J. Maurais, Quebec and Paris, 1983, pp. 69–104

Pagliaro, A. 'Sommario di linguistica arioeuropea', *Pubblicazioni della scuola di filologia classica presso la R. Università di Roma*, series 2, II, fasc. 1, Rome, 1930

Palsgrave, J. *Lesclarcissement de la langue francoyse* [London], 1530

Parker, S. *A Free and Impartial Censure of the Platonick Philosophie*, Oxford, 1666

Percival, W. K. 'On the non-existence of Cartesian linguistics', *Cartesian Studies*, ed. R. J. Butler, Oxford, 1972, pp. 137–45

   'The Grammatical Tradition and the Rise of the Vernaculars', *Current Trends in Linguistics*, ed. T. A. Sebeok, The Hague and Paris, XIII, 1975, pp. 231–75

   'Deep and Surface Structure Concepts in Renaissance and Medieval Syntactic Theory', *History of Linguistic Thought and Contemporary Linguistics*, ed. H. Parret, Berlin and New York, 1976, pp. 228–53

   'The Notion of Usage in Vaugelas and in the Port Royal Grammar', *History of Linguistic Thought and Contemporary Linguistics*, ed. H. Parret, Berlin and New York, 1976, pp. 374–82

Perotti, N. *Rudimenta grammatices*, Venice, 1473; composed *c*.1464.

   Grammatica...cum additionibus regularum; et metrice artis Guarini veronensis, Basle, 1500?

   Grammatica...cum additionibus regularum; et metrice artis Guarini veronensis, Venice, 1505

Peter of Spain *Summulae logicales* – see Mullally, J. P.

Phillips, E. *The Mysteries of Love and Eloquence; on the arts of wooing and complementing*, 1658

Poldauf, I. 'On the History of some Problems of English Grammar before 1800', *Prague Studies in English*, LV (1948), pp. 1–322

Bibliography

Polemann, J. *Novum lumen medicum; wherein the excellent and most necessary Doctrine of Helmont is fundamentally cleared*, London, 1662

Pölmann, I. *Neuer hoochdeutscher Donat, zum Grund gelegt der neuen hoochdeutschen Grammatik*, Berlin, 1671

Poole, J. *The English Accidence: or, A Short, Plaine, and Easie Way, for the more speedy attaining to the Latine tongue, by the help of the English*, London, 1646

Prantl, G. *Geschichte der Logik im Abendlande*, III and IV, Leipzig, 1867

Prasch, J. L. *Neue, kurtz-und-deutliche Sprachkunst*. Regensburg, 1687

Priscian *Prisciani institutiones grammatice*, Paris, 1517

Pudor, C. *Der Teutschen Sprache Grundrichtigkeit und Zierlichkeit*, Cölln an der Spree, 1672, reprinted in *Documenta Linguistica, Quellen zur Geschichte der deutschen Sprache des 15. bis 20. Jahrhunderts herausgegeben von Ludwig Erich Schmidt (Reihe V, Deutsche Grammatiken des 16. bis 18. Jahrhunderts herausgegeben von Monika Rössing-Hager)*, Hildesheim and New York, 1975

Quintilian *The Institutio oratoria of Marcus Fabius Quintilianus with an English Summary and Concordance*, ed. C. E. Little, Nashville, Tennessee, 1951

Ramus, P. (Pierre de la Ramée) *Aristotelicae animadversiones*, Paris, 1543

Dialecticae institutiones, Paris, 1543

Dialecticae partitiones, Paris, 1543

Dialectique de Pierre de la Ramee a Charles de Lorraine cardinal, son Mecene, Paris, 1555

Scholae grammaticae, Paris, 1559

P. Rami dialecticae libri duo, Audomari Talaei praelectionibus illustrati ad Carolum Lotharingum cardinalem, Paris, 1560

The Logike of the Moste Excellent Philosopher P. Ramus Martyr, Newly Translated...per M. Roll. Makylmenaeum Scotum, London, 1574. (There is a Scolar Press reprint, Leeds, 1966)

Rudimenta grammaticae Latinae, Frankfurt-am-Main, 1576 (1st ed., 1559)

Grammatica, Frankfurt-am-Main, 1576 (1st ed., 1559)

Scholae in liberales artes, Basle, 1578, 1589 (1st ed., 1559)

Scholarum grammaticarum libri XX (in *Scholae in liberales artes*, 1578 ed., Basle)

The Latine Grammar of P. Ramus, translated into English, London, 1585. (The Cambridge edition of the same year is virtually identical)

P. Rami Dialectica verdeutscht, ed. F. Beurhaus, Erfurt, 1587

Grammaire de P. de la Ramee...a la royne, mere du roy, Paris, 1572 (1st ed., *Gramere*, 1562, very rare; 1587 ed., *Grammaire de Pierre de la Ramée...revue et enrichie en plusieurs endroits*, Paris)

Grammatica Latino-Francica, a Petro Ramo Francice scripta, Latina vero facta... per Pantaleontem Thevenium, Frankfurt-am-Main, 1583

Raney, G. W. 'The Accidence and Syntax in J. Wallis's *Grammatica linguae Anglicanae*: A translation and commentary on its alleged relationship to the 1660 Port-Royal *Grammaire générale et raisonnée*', unpublished Ph.D. thesis, University of Michigan

Ratke (Ratichius), W. 'Memorial' (1612), in E. Ising, *Wolfgang Ratkes Schriften*, Berlin, 1959, 1, 101–4

'Sprachkunst' (1615), in E. Ising, *Wolfgang Ratkes Schriften*, Berlin, 1959, II, 9–22

'Wortschickungslehr' (c.1630), in E. Ising, *Wolfgang Ratkes Schriften*, Berlin, 1959, II, 97–268

'Wortbedeutungslehr' (after 1630), in E. Ising, *Wolfgang Ratkes Schriften*, Berlin, 1959, II, 271–318

'Anlaitung in der Lehrkunst W. Ratichii' (1614/15), in P. Stötzner, *Ratichianische Schriften* II (*Neudrucke pädagogischer Schriften herausgegeben von Albert Richter* XII), Leipzig, 1893

'Artickel auf welchen fürnehmlich die Ratichianische Lehrkunst beruhet' (1614/15), in P. Stötzner, *Ratichianische Schriften* II (*Neudrucke, pädagogischer Schriften herausgegeben von Albert Richter* XII), Leipzig, 1893

'In methodum linguarum generalis introductio' (1615), in P. Stötzner, *Ratichianische Schriften* II (*Neudrucke pädagogischer Schriften herausgegeben von Albert Richter* XII), Leipzig, 1893

Allgemeine Anleitung in die Didacticam, Köthen, 1617 (Evenius' pirated edition *Desiderata methodus nova Ratichiana, linguae compendiose et artificiose discendi* published in Halle, 1615)

Grammatica universalis pro didactica Ratichii/Allgemeine Sprachlehr nach der Lehrart Ratichii, Köthen, 1619

Compendium grammaticae Latinae ad didacticam, Köthen, 1620

'Schuldieneramstslehr', Landesbibliothek Gotha, MS. Cod. B28, 1631–2

Raumer, K. von *Geschichte der Pädagogik vom Wiederaufblühen klassischer Studien bis auf unsere Zeit* (3rd ed.), Stuttgart, 1857

Raumer, R. von 'Der Unterricht im Deutschen', in K. von Raumer, *Geschichte der Pädagogik* (3rd ed.), Stuttgart, 1857, part iii, 130–296

Reeve, E. *The Rules of the Latine Grammar, construed*, London, 1657

Reuchlin, J. *Cnapnion vel de verbo mirifico*, Basle, 1494

De arte cabalistica libri tres, Hagenau, 1517

Rhenius, J. *Methodus institutionis quadruplex*, Leipzig, 1617

Richardson, A. *The Logicians School-Master or, a Comment upon Ramus Logick, Whereunto are added, His prelections on Ramus his Grammer*, London, 1657

Rioux, G. *L'Oeuvre pédagogique de Wolfgangus Ratichius (1571–1635)*, Paris, 1963

Ritter, S. *Grammatica Germanica nova*, Marburg, 1616

Robinet, A. *Le Langage à l'âge classique*, Paris, 1978

Robins, R. H. *Ancient and Mediaeval Grammatical Theory in Europe*, London, 1951

A Short History of Linguistics (2nd ed.), London, 1979

Roboredo, A. de, *Porta de linguas*, Lisbon, 1623

Rodis-Lewis, G. 'Augustinisme et cartésianisme dans Port-Royal', *Descartes et le cartésianisme hollandais*, ed. E. Guilhan, Paris and Amsterdam, 1950, pp. 131–82

Roos, H. 'Sprachdenken im Mittelalter', *Classica et Mediaevalia*, IX (1947), pp. 200–15

Rosset, T. 'Le P. Bouhours critique de la langue des écrivains jansénistes', *Annales de l'Université de Grenoble* XX:1 (1908), pp. 55–125

Bibliography

Rossi, P. *Clavis universalis. Arti mnemoniche e logica combinatoria da Lullo a Leibniz*, Milan and Naples, 1960

Francis Bacon: From Magic to Science, translated from the Italian (*Francesco Bacone: dalla magia alla scienza*, Bari, 1957) by S. Rabinovitch, London, 1968

Ruscelli, G. *De' Commentarii della lingua italiana libri VII. Ne'quali...si tratta tutto quello, che alla vera e perfetta notitia di detta lingua s'appartiene*, Venice, 1581

Sadler, J. E. *J. A. Comenius and the Concept of Universal Education*, London, 1966

Sahlin, G. *César Chesneau du Marsais et son rôle dans l'évolution de la grammaire générale*, Paris [1928]

Sainte-Beuve, C. A. *Port-Royal*, in *Sainte-Beuve Port-Royal. Texte présenté et annoté par Maxime Leroy* (vols. XCIII, XCIX and CVII of *Bibliothèque de la Pléiade*), Paris, 1953–5. (Leroy reproduces Sainte-Beuve's third edition of 1867)

Salmon, V. 'A Pioneer of the Direct Method in the Erasmian Circle', *Latomus*, XIX (1960), pp. 567–77

'James Shirley and Some Problems of Seventeenth-Century Grammar', *Archiv für das Studium der neueren Sprachen und Literaturen*, CXCVII:4 (1961), reprinted in *The Study of Language in Seventeenth-Century England* (*Amsterdam Studies in the Theory and History of Linguistic Science*, ed. E. F. K. Koerner, Series 3, XVII), Amsterdam, 1979, pp. 87–96

'Joseph Webbe: Some Seventeenth-Century Views on Language-Teaching and the Nature of Meaning', *Bibliothèque d'Humanisme et Renaissance*, XXIII (1961), reprinted in *The Study of Language in Seventeenth-Century England* (*Amsterdam Studies in the Theory and History of Linguistic Science*, ed. E. F. K. Koerner, Series 3, XVII), Amsterdam, 1979, pp. 15–31

'Problems of Language-Teaching; A Discussion among Hartlib's Friends', *Modern Language Review*, LIX (1964), reprinted in *The Study of Language in Seventeenth-Century England* (*Amsterdam Studies in the Theory and History of Linguistic Science*, ed. E. F. K. Koerner, Series 3, XVII), Amsterdam, 1979, pp. 3–14

'Language-Planning in Seventeenth-Century England, its context and aims', *In Memory of J. R. Firth*, ed. C. E. Bazell, J. C. Catford, M. A. K. Halliday and R. H. Robins, London, 1966, reprinted in *The Study of Language in Seventeenth-Century England* (*Amsterdam Studies in the Theory and History of Linguistic Science*, ed. E. F. K. Koerner, Series 3, XVII), Amsterdam, 1979, pp. 129–56

'The Evolution of Dalgarno's "Ars signorum" (1661)', *Studies in Language and Literature in Honour of Margaret Schlauch*, ed. I. Dobrzycka, M. Brahmer, S. Helsztynski and J. Krzyzanowski, Warsaw, 1966, reprinted in *The Study of Language in Seventeenth-Century England* (*Amsterdam Studies in the Theory and History of Linguistic Science*, ed. E. F. K. Koerner, Series 3, XVII), Amsterdam, 1979, pp. 157–75

Review of N. Chomsky, *Cartesian Linguistics*, New York, 1966, in *Journal of Linguistics*, v (1969), pp. 165–87, reprinted in V. Salmon, *The Study of Language in Seventeenth-Century England*, pp. 63–85, under the title 'Pre-Cartesian Linguistics'

The Works of Francis Lodwick. A Study of his writings in the context of the seventeenth century, London, 1972.

'John Wilkins' "Essay" (1668): Critics and continuators', *Historiographia Linguistica*, 1:2 (1974), reprinted in *The Study of Language in Seventeenth-Century England* (*Amsterdam Studies in the Theory and History of Linguistic Science*, ed. E. F. K. Koerner, Series 3, xvii), Amsterdam, 1979, pp. 191–206

'John Brinsley, Seventeenth-Century Pioneer in Applied Linguistics', *Historiographia Linguistica*, ii:2 (1975), reprinted in *The Study of Language in Seventeenth-Century England* (*Amsterdam Studies in the Theory and History of Linguistic Science*, ed. E. F. K. Koerner, Series 3, xvii), Amsterdam, 1979, pp. 33–46

'"Philosophical" grammar in John Wilkins's "Essay"'', *Canadian Journal of Linguistics*, xx:2 (1975), reprinted in *The Study of Language in Seventeenth-Century England* (*Amsterdam Studies in the Theory and History of Linguistic Science*, ed. E. F. K. Koerner, Series 3, xvii), Amsterdam, 1979, pp. 97–126

'Wh- and yes-no questions: Charles Butler's *Grammar* (1633) and the history of a linguistic concept', *Language Form and Linguistic Variation. Papers dedicated to Angus McIntosh*, ed. J. Anderson, Amsterdam, 1982, pp. 401–26

Salviati, L. (principal compiler) *Vocabulario degli Accademici della Crusca*, Venice, 1612

Sánchez Barrado, M. *La elipsis según el Brocense*, Segovia, 1919

Sanctius, F. *Minerva: seu de causis linguae Latinae*, Salamanca, 1587

Sandys, J. E. *A History of Classical Scholarship*, Cambridge, 1908

Saussure, F. de *Cours de linguistique générale*, Paris, 1964

Scaglione, A. D. *The Classical Theory of Composition*, Chapel Hill, 1972

Scaliger, J. C. *De causis linguae Latinae libri tredecim*, Lyons, 1540

Scheurweghs, G. 'Problems of English Grammar: The Grammatica Anglicana of Paul Greaves (1594)', *English Studies*, LX (1959), pp. 135–6

Schmidt, S. J. *Sprache und Denken als sprachphilosophisches Problem von Locke bis Wittgenstein*, The Hague, 1968

Scholem, G. *On the Kabbalah and its Symbolism*, New York, 1969

Schöpf, H. *Institutiones in linguam Germanicam, sive Allemannicam*, Mainz, 1625

Schottel, J. G. *Der Teutschen Sprach Einleitung zu richtiger Gewisheit und grundmessigen Vermügen der Teutschen Haubtsprache samt beygefügten Erklärungen*, Lübeck, 1643

Teutsche Sprachkunst darinn die allerwortreichste prächtigste reinlichste volkommene uhralte Haubstsprache der Teutschen aus ihren Gründen erhoben dero Eigenschafften und Kunststücke völliglich entdeckt und also in eine richtige Form der Kunst zum ersten Mahle gebracht worden, Brunswick, 1641

Ausführliche Arbeit von der Teutschen Haubt Sprache, worin enthalten Gemelter dieser Haubt Sprache Uhrankunft, Uhraltertum, Reinlichkeit, Eigenschaft, Vermögen, Unvergleichlichkeit, Brunswick, 1663

Scioppius, G. (K. Schoppe) *Grammatica philosophica,* Amsterdam, 1659 (1st ed., 1628)

Mercurius quadrilinguis, Padua, 1637

Seiler, K. *Das pädagogische System Wolfgang Ratkes nach den handschriftlichen Quellen im Zusammenhang der europäischen Geistesgeschichte dargestellt,* Erlangen, 1931

Shapiro, B. J. *John Wilkins 1614–1672: An Intellectual Biography,* Berkeley, 1969

Shirley, J. *Via ad Latinam linguam complanata / The Way Made Plain to the Latine Tongue,* London, 1649

Grammatica Anglo-Latina / An English and Latine Grammar, London, 1651

The Rudiments of Grammar, London, 1656

Manuductio: or, A Leading of Children by the Hand Through the Principles of Grammar (2nd ed.), London, 1660

Slaughter, M. *Universal Languages and Scientific Taxonomy in the Seventeenth Century,* Cambridge, 1982

Smith, S. *Aditus ad logicam,* Oxford, 1613

Sonderegger, S. 'Nachwort', appendix to K. Stieler, *Der Teutschen Sprache Stammbaum,* ed. M. Bircher and F. Kemp (facsimile), Munich, 1968

Sortais, G. *La Philosophie moderne depuis Bacon jusqu'à Leibniz,* I, Paris, 1920

South, R. *Sermons Preached on Several Occasions,* I, Oxford, 1823

Spencer, T. *Logicke Unfolded: or, The Body of Logicke in Englishe Made Plaine to the Meanest Capacity,* London, 1656

Spingarn, J. E. *A History of Literary Criticism in the Renaissance. With special reference to the influence of Italy in the formation and development of modern classicism,* New York, 1899

Stanbridge, J. *Vulgaria,* in B. White (ed.), *The Vulgaria of John Stanbridge and the Vulgaria of Robert Whittinton* (Early English Text Society, original series, 187), London, 1932

Stéfanini, J. 'Jules César Scaliger et son De causis linguae Latinae', *History of Linguistic Thought and Contemporary Linguistics,* ed. H. Parret, Berlin and New York, 1976, pp. 317–30

Steinthal, H. *Geschichte der Sprachwissenschaft bei den Griechen und Römern mit besonderer Rücksicht auf die Logik* (2nd ed.), Berlin, 1891

Stengel, E. *Chronologisches Verzeichnis französischer Grammatiken vom Ende des 14. bis zum Ausgange des 18. Jahrhunderts,* Oppeln, 1890

Stieler, K. *Der Teutschen Sprache Stammbaum und Fortwachs oder Teutscher Sprachschatz, worinnen alle und jede teutsche Wurzeln oder Stammwörter... nebst ihrer Ankunft, abgeleiteten, duppelungen, und vornemsten Redearten... gesamlet von dem Spaten,* Nuremberg, 1691. (The facsimile ed. in the series *Deutsche Barock-Literatur,* ed. M. Bircher and F. Kemp, Munich, 1968, is used here)

Kurze Lehrschrift von der Hochteutschen Sprachkunst / Brevis grammaticae imperialis linguae delineatio, pp. 1–243 of *Der Teutschen Sprache Stammbaum und Fortwachs*, Nuremberg, 1691

Stockwood, J. *A plaine and easie Laying open of the Meaning and Understanding of the Rules of Construction in the English Accidence*, London, 1590

The Treatise of the Figures...in the Latin Grammar...for the help of the weaker sort in the Grammar Schools, London, 1609

Stötzner, P. *Ratichianische Schriften* (*Neudrucke pädagogischer Schriften herausgegeben von Albert Richter*, IX), I, Leipzig, 1892; II, Leipzig, 1893

Sulpizio, G. *Grammatica*, Nuremberg, 1482 (1st ed., 1475)

Syms, C. *An Introduction to, or the Art of Teaching, the Latine Speach* [Dublin, 1634]

Talon, O. *Audomari Talaei Veromandui Institutiones oratoriae*, Paris, 1545

Dialecticae commentarii tres authore Audomaro Talaeo editi, Paris, 1546. (Although ascribed to Omer Talon, this work is almost certainly by Ramus)

A. Talaei Rhetorica, P. Rami praelectionibus illustrata, Paris, 1567

Tell, J. *Les Grammairiens français depuis l'origine de la grammaire en France jusqu'aux dernières oeuvres connues*, Paris, 1874

Temple, W. (pseudonym F. Mildapet) *Admonitio de unica P. Rami methodo. From Francis Mildapet of Navarre to Everard Digby of England, an Admonition that the Single Method of Peter Ramus be Retained and the Rest Rejected*, London, 1580

Thomas of Erfurt *Grammatica speculativa. An edition with translation and commentary*, ed. G. L. Bursill-Hall, London, 1972

Thurot, C. *Extraits de divers manuscrits latins pour servir à l'histoire des doctrines grammaticales au moyen âge*, Paris, 1869

Tomkis, T. 'De analogia Anglicani sermonis liber grammaticus', 1612 (British Library MS 12 Reg. F. xviii, ff. 1–15)

Trabalza, C. *Storia della grammatica italiana*, Bologna, 1963

Trentman, J. A. 'The Study of Logic and Language in England in the early Seventeenth Century', *Historiographia Linguistica*, III:2 (1976), pp. 179–201

Trissino, G. G. *Dubbii grammaticali*, Vicenza, 1529

Troike, C. R. 'Lest the Wheel be too oft Re-invented: Towards a reassessment of the intellectual history of Linguistics', in M. A. Jazayery, E. C. Polomé and W. Winter, *Linguistic and Literary Studies in Honour of Archibald A. Hill*, Lisse, 1976

Valla, L. *De linguae Latinae elegantia*, Venice, 1471. (This is the date of first printing. The work was composed *c.*1440)

Varchi, B. *L'Ercolano dialogo di Benedetto Varchi dove si ragiona delle lingue e in particolare della Toscana e Fiorentina*, ed. P. dal Rio, Florence, 1846 (1st ed., 1570)

Vaugelas, C. Favre de *Remarques sur la langue françoise, utiles à ceux qui veulent bien parler et bien écrire*, Paris, 1647

Verburg, P. A. *Taal en Functionaliteit: een historisch-critische studie over de*

Bibliography

opvattingen aangaarde de functies der taal vanaf de prae-humanistische philologie van Orleans tot de rationalistische linguistiek van Bopp, Wageningen, 1952

Viñaza, Conde de la (= C. Muñoz y Manzano) *Biblioteca historica de la filología castellana*, Madrid, 1893

'Dos libros inéditos de Maestro Gonzalo Correas: notas bibliográfico-críticas', *Homenaje á Menéndez y Pelayo en el año vigésimo de su profesorado. Estudios de erudición española con un prólogo de Juan Valera*, Madrid, 1899, pp. 601–14

Vives, J. L. *De studii puerilis ratione*, Oxford, 1523

De tradendis disciplinis (1531), in *Libri XII de disciplinis. Hi de corruptis artibus...illi de tradendis disciplinis*, Leyden?, 1612

Vogt, G. *Wolfgang Ratichius, der Vorgänger des Amos Comenius (Die Klassiker der Pädagogik* XVII), Langensalza, 1894

Vorlat, E. *English Grammatical Theory 1586–1737*, Louvain, 1975

Vossius, G. J. *De arte grammatica libri septem*, Amsterdam, 1635

Waddington, C. *Ramus: sa vie, ses écrits, et ses opinions*, Paris, 1855

Walker, O. *Of Education, Especially of Young Gentlemen*, Oxford, 1673

Wallis, J. *Grammatica linguae Anglicanae. Cui praefigitur, De loquela sive sonorum formatione, tractatus grammatico-physicus*, Oxford, 1653

Ward, S. *Vindiciae academiarum containing, Some briefe Animadversions upon Mr Websters Book, stiled The Examination of Academies*, Oxford, 1654

Watson, F. *The English Grammar Schools to 1660: their Curriculum and Practice*, Cambridge, 1908

Luis Vives el gran Valenciano (1492–1540) (Hispanic Notes and Monographs IV), Oxford, 1922

Webb, J. *An Historical Essay, endeavouring a probability that the Language of the Empire of China is the Primitive Language*, London, 1669

Webbe, J. *An Appeale to Truth, in the Controversie betweene Art, and Use; about the most expedient Course in Languages*, London, 1622

A Petition to the High Court of Parliament, in the behalf of auncient and authentique authors, London, 1623

Lessons and Exercises out of Cicero ad Atticum, London, 1627

'Methodi in docendo', British Library MS Sloane 1466

'Propositions concerning Teaching of Languages', British Library MS Sloane 1466

Webster, C. *The Great Instauration. Science, Medicine and Reform 1626–1660*, London, 1975

Webster, J. *Academiarum examen*, London, 1654

Weiss, R. *Humanism in England during the Fifteenth Century*, Oxford, 1941

Wharton, J. *The English-Grammar...More especially profitable for Scholars, immediately before their entrance into the Rudiments of the Latine-tongue*, London, 1654

White, J. *The English Verb; a grammatical essay in the didactive form*, London, 1761

Whittinton, R. *Vulgaria*, in B. White (ed.), *The Vulgaria of John Stanbridge*

407

and the Vulgaria of Robert Whittinton (Early English Text Society, original series, 187), London, 1932

Wilkins, J. *Mercury, or The Secret and Swift Messenger: Shewing, How a Man may with Privacy and Speed communicate his Thoughts to a Friend at any Distance*, London, 1641

An Essay Towards a Real Character and Philosophical Language, London, 1668

Willey, B. *The Seventeenth Century Background: Studies in the Thought of the Age in Relation to Poetry and Religion*, London, 1934

Willis, J. *The Art of Stenographie*, 1602

Wilson, T. *The Arte of Rhetorique, for the use of all suche as are studious of eloquence, sette forthe in English* [London], 1533

The Rule of Reason, conteinyng the Arte of Logique, set forth in Englishe [London], 1551

Woodward, H. *A Light to Grammar*, London?, 1641

Woodward, W. H. *Studies in Education during the Age of the Renaissance 1400–1600* (*Contributions to the History of Education*, II), Cambridge, 1906

Zimmer, K. E. Review of N. Chomsky, *Cartesian Linguistics*, New York, 1966, in *International Journal of American Linguistics*, XXXIV (1968), pp. 290–303

INDEX

Index

Index

Rossi, P., 296n., 328, 360
Royal Society, 5, 191, 193–4, 214, 268, 325, 328, 333, 342, 346, 349–50, 353, 357–9, 381, 384
Ruscelli, G., 252–4, 276

Sadler, J. E., 175, 342
Sainte-Beuve, C. A., 317
Sahlin, G., 303
Salamanca University, 46, 340
Salviati, Lionardo, 121, 256
Salmon, V., 57, 156, 161n., 213n., 329n., 349n., 354n., 356–61, 368n.
Sanctius, Franciscus, 5, 14, 24, 34, 43, 45–6, 51, 73, 85, 115, 128, 135n., 140, 165, 199, 220, 223, 233–4, 237–9, 242, 246n., 257, 269–84, 286, 291, 293, 305, 309–10, 312, 314, 316, 374–5, 380, 384
Sandys, J. E., 10
Saussure, F. de, 238, 243n.
Scaliger, Julius Caesar, 2, 5, 14, 23n., 24, 45, 48, 50, 73, 85, 110–11, 113, 116, 129, 131, 175, 204, 206, 212, 220, 223, 227, 233–4, 238, 242–4, 246, 248–58, 260–70, 276, 280, 290–1, 293, 297, 301, 303–7, 314, 316, 320, 323, 326, 330–1, 334–5, 352, 367, 371, 374, 381, 384
Scholasticism, 10, 12–15, 17–18, 21, 43, 107–9, 196, 198–9, 207, 214, 219–21, 234–5, 242, 258, 290, 301, 316, 318–19, 325–6, 328, 330–5, 337, 352, 355, 362, 369, 371, 374, 378
Schöpf, Heinrich, 98n.
Schottel, Justus Georg, 86, 88–9, 95, 112, 121–2, 124, 130–1, 138, 141–5, 221, 224–32, 238, 250, 383; *Ausführliche Arbeit*, 85, 126–7, 137–9, 224, 226–32, 255; *Teutsche Sprachkunst*, 85, 224–31
Scioppius (Schoppe), Kaspar, 256, 310, 340
Seiler, K., 100, 106n., 108–9, 116
Seneca, 227
'sense' as a linguistic criterion, 184–7
Sensualism, 119, 174–7, 181, 215, 258–9, 288, 297, 306, 325, 328, 334, 342, 349–52
Shapiro, B., 357–9, 378
Shirley, J., 157, 161–2
sign theory, 242–3, 246, 252–3, 258–9, 295–9, 350–1, 361–4
Slaughter, M., 326, 362–3, 367
South, Robert, 364
St Andrews, 53–4
Stéfanini, J., 242n., 382
Stieler, Kaspar, 96, 121, 137–42, 144–5, 225
Stötzner, P., 102
Sturm, Johann, 13, 18, 93

'subject' as a term of grammar, 186, 188, 213n., 374, 379
suppositum, 43, 188, 213n., 375
Syms, Christofer, 161

Talon, Omer, 15–16
Telesio, Bernardino, 290, 332, 338, 344
Temple, William, 54, 56
Theodore Gaza, 40, 77
Thomas Aquinas, 106
Thomas of Erfurt, 219, 234n., 235, 261, 271n., 302n., 314n., 326n., 373n.
Thrax, Dionysius, 9, 26, 184, 300, 307
Tolomei, Claudio, 276
Tomkis, Thomas, 66n., 172n., 200n.
topical logic, 13, 20
Trabalza, C., 251, 256–7
Trentman, J. A., 332n.
Trinity College Dublin, 57
Trissino, Gian Giorgio, 251–2, 276
Turmair, Johann, *see* Aventinus

usage, 4, 23, 26–7, 30, 42, 44, 59, 85–6, 94–6, 118, 121–4, 139–40, 145, 194, 214, 226–9, 232, 249, 251, 256, 278–9, 284, 290, 315–16, 318–22

Valdivia, L. de, 340
Valla, Lorenzo, 3, 11, 23, 237–8
Varchi, Benedetto, 252
Varro, M. Terentius, 26, 30, 34, 36, 63, 72, 140, 160–1, 199
Vaugelas, Claude Favre de, 4, 44, 194, 214, 290, 316, 319–22
Vautrouiller, Thomas, 54
verbum mentis/oris, 219, 234
Verburg, P. A., 24n.
Vergil, 124, 227
Vives, Juan Luis, 11, 18, 146, 336n., 338, 341, 343
Vorlat, E., 72n., 73n., 208
Vossius, Gerard Johannes, 160, 166, 169n., 185, 199, 208, 230, 293, 303, 314, 335n., 367n., 369–70, 374, 377
Vulgaria, 151

Waddington, C., 21n., 28
Wadham College Oxford, 353
Walker, Obadiah, 147
Wallis, John, 158, 183, 185, 187, 190–6, 199–205, 210–14, 308, 356–7, 381n., 383
Ward, Seth, 193, 349, 357–9
Webb, John, 365
Webbe, Joseph, 70, 154–6, 161, 175
Webster, C., 328n., 358
Webster, John, 87, 89, 155, 338

413